In the late 19th century, huge building projects ripped holes in the capital. When photographs were commissioned to chart this technological progress, a close partnership sprang up between engineer and photographer. This transformed the photographer from artist to skilled technician, methodically recording the metamorphosis of the site. These candid photographs (c. 1890) convey a celebration of modernity and an absolute confidence in a new world.

Photographers at the end of the 19th century took a special interest in the capital's heritage. Their patrons, principally institutions, preferred the pictures not to include people. As a result, the photographs were long shots, accentuating the documentary quality of these topographical views. At the same time, the tradition of photographing people, usually in humble occupations, grouped Parisians into socioprofessional categories. Atget, Paul Géniaux, Louis Vert and Lansiaux, among others, patiently recorded an unusual Paris in the throes of change.
(Below, *Tourists in St-Germain, Floods* by Lansiaux, 1920.)

After the austere, horror-filled years of World War Two, France began to rebuild. Humanitarian values and a desire to work together were the keynotes of this new society. Illustrated magazines played their part in the country's rebirth by publishing photographs of simple, evocative moments which showed a love of life. In the leading journals of the day, photographers like Boubat (*Quai du Louvre et l'Institut*, 1952, below), Doisneau, Ronis and Izis published sensitive, highly subjective pictures which were, quite naturally, dubbed humanist photography. On their solitary walks, they re-created a personal record of a bygone Parisian society.

EVERYMAN GUIDES
PUBLISHED BY DAVID CAMPBELL PUBLISHERS LTD, LONDON

PARIS – ISBN 1-85715-611-0

© 1995 David Campbell Publishers Ltd
© 1995 Editions Nouveaux-Loisirs, a subsidiary of Gallimard, Paris

First published December 1995
This edition September 1998

NUMEROUS SPECIALISTS AND ACADEMICS HAVE
CONTRIBUTED TO THIS GUIDE.
EDITOR: Clotilde Lefebvre
ADVISORS: Danièle Chadych , M. A. Corcuff,
Jean-Pierre Le Dantec, Alfred Fierro, Marc
Gaillard, Jean-Claude Garreta, Brigitte Gournay,
Bertrand Lemoine, Jean-Marc Léri , Guilhem
Lesaffre, Michel Le Moël, Marguerite Pennec
GALLIMARD AUTHORS
Marie-Hélène Albertini-Viennot, Laurence de
Bélizal, Liesel Couvreur Schiffer, Gilles Février,
Corinne Hewlett, Catherine Ianco, Béatrice Jaulin
Anne-Josyane Magniant, Sybille d'Oiron, Nina
Paronian, Édouard de Pazzis, Christine Puget,
Nicolas Ragonneau, Michel Spagnol

AUTHORS: G. Adam, J.-P. Adam, M.-C. Adès,
M. Amandry, I.Bachelard, S. Baratte, C. Barbillon,
M.-N. Baudoin Matuszeck, G. Bauer, A. Bavelier,
B. Blache, F. Bellec, V. Berecz, L. Bergeron,
M. Bernus-Taylor, D. Blaizot, Mme Bordaz,
N Botta-kouznetzoff, M. Bouchard, G. Boulinier,
J.-M. Bruson, T. Burogard, T. Burollet,
D. Cailleaux, M.F. Callas, M. Carlier, T. Carneiro,
A. Caubet, A.-M. Châtelet, G. Cheyssial,
M. Courant-Vidal, Mme Causse Fouqueray,
M.-V. Clin, N. Daliès, M. Deming, M. Dunoyer de
Segonzac, D. Ferriot, Alfred Fierro, M. de Fleury,
D. Freignac, J. Fritsch, N. Gasc, C. Genet-
Bondeville, G. Genty, L. Gervereau, P. Georgel,
S. Gohel, P.-M. Grineval, S. Grossiord, L. Guyard,
R. Herbaut, C. Horel, A. Jacob, M. Jaoul,
M. Kuraszewski, G. Lacambre, S. Lecombre,
J.-M. Leniaud, J.-M. Léri, C. Levisse-Touzé,
S. de Lisle, A. Lefébure, M.-C. Le Floch,
C. Madoni, H. Marraud, M. Maucuer, J. Mayer,
J.-H. Martin, C. Merle-Portalès, K. Michel-Haciski,
B. Mons, J.-P. Midant, J. Mouliérac, I. Neto,
A. Nardin, C. Nossoc, A. Okada, I. Ottaviani,
A. Panchont, F. Pascaud, A. Pasquier, J.-D. Pariset,
P.-P. Perraud, A Perrot, J.-M. Peyronnet, P. Pinon,
D. Petermüller, M. Polonovski, V. Pomarède,

B. Quette, C. de Quiqueran Beaujeu, T. du Regard,
B. Rondot, V. Roudot, C. Savary, N. Sainte-Fare-
Garnot, D. Soutat, H. Seckel, M Werner Szanbien,
J. Treuttel, G. Viatte, F. Viatte, V. Vignon,
P. de Vogüe, V. Wiesinger
PICTURE RESEARCH:
Coordination: Nathalie Beaud, Marie-Amélie Beri,
Carine Lepied, Nils Warolin, assisted by Annie-
Claire Auliard and Mélanie Tissandier
LAYOUT: Michèle Bisgambiglia, Olivier Brunot,
François Chentrier, Béatrice Desrousseaux, Carole
Gaborit, Alain Gouessant, Roberta Maranzano,
Philippe Marchand, Riccardo Tremori, Isabelle
Roller
ILLUSTRATIONS
NATURE: F. Bony, J. Chevallier, F. Desbordes,
B. Duhem, C. Felloni, J.-M. Kacédan, J. Wilkinson,
C. Lachaud, P. Robin
ARCHITECTURE:
Coordination: François Brosse, P. Biard, P. Candé,
D. Grant, J.-M. Guillou, J.-B. Héron, O. Hubert,
P. de Hugo, J.-F. Lecomte, P. Lhez, J.-F. Peneau,
J.-P. Pocabare, C. Quiec, C. Rivière, J.-S. Roveri,
A. Soro
ITINERARIES: A. Brandière, F. Moireau
PRACTICAL INFORMATION: M. Pommier
MAPS: Atelier de Bayonne (F. Callède,
D. Duplantier, R. Etcheberry, F. Liéval;
colouring: M. Gros, L. Dousset, G. Mersch)
COMPUTER GRAPHICS: P. Alexandre, E. Calamy,
C. Chemineau, P. Coulbois, Klik Développement,
Latitude, A. Leray
PHOTOGRAPHERS: X. Richer, P. Delance,
L. de Selva, F. Buxin, E. Valentin

Special thanks to: the RATP, the Musées de la Ville
de Paris and the Direction des affaires culturelles de
la Ville de Paris, whose support has made this guide
reality; in particular, thanks to Jean-Jacques
Aillagon, directeur des affaires culturelles de la Ville
de Paris, Bernard Schotter, sous-directeur du
Patrimoine de la Ville de Paris and Sophie
Durrleman, chef du Bureau des Musées, direction
des affaires culturelles de la Ville de Paris.

TRANSLATED BY
WENDY ALLATSON, MICHAEL CUNNINGHAM, SUSAN MACKERVOY AND SUE ROSE.
EDITED AND TYPESET BY BOOK CREATION SERVICES, LONDON.
PRINTED IN ITALY BY EDITORIALE LLOYD

EVERYMAN GUIDES
Gloucester Mansions, 140a Shaftesbury Avenue
London WC2H 8DH

PARIS

EVERYMAN GUIDES

Contents

Contents

HOW TO USE THIS GUIDE

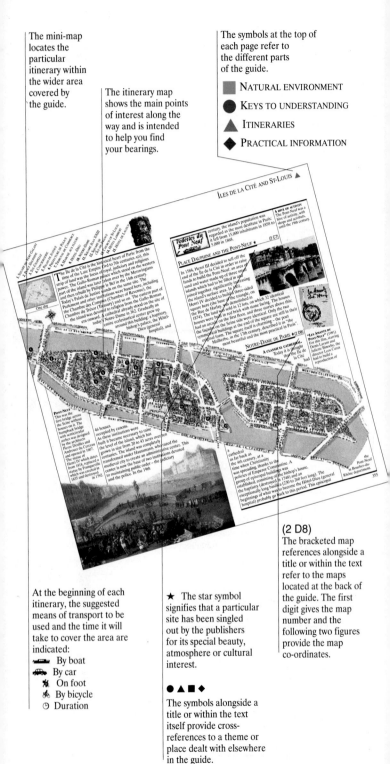

The mini-map locates the particular itinerary within the wider area covered by the guide.

The itinerary map shows the main points of interest along the way and is intended to help you find your bearings.

The symbols at the top of each page refer to the different parts of the guide.

■ NATURAL ENVIRONMENT

● KEYS TO UNDERSTANDING

▲ ITINERARIES

◆ PRACTICAL INFORMATION

At the beginning of each itinerary, the suggested means of transport to be used and the time it will take to cover the area are indicated:

🚢 By boat
🚗 By car
🚶 On foot
🚲 By bicycle
🕐 Duration

★ The star symbol signifies that a particular site has been singled out by the publishers for its special beauty, atmosphere or cultural interest.

● ▲ ■ ◆

The symbols alongside a title or within the text itself provide cross-references to a theme or place dealt with elsewhere in the guide.

(2 D8)
The bracketed map references alongside a title or within the text refer to the maps located at the back of the guide. The first digit gives the map number and the following two figures provide the map co-ordinates.

History

-5000	-3000	Bronze Age	-500	The Parisii settle in the Cité.	0	Lutetia spreads along the Left Bank.	200	280 Walls are erected around the Cité.	400

Hunter-fishermen inhabit the banks of the Seine near Bercy.	Bronze weapons and implements from the second millennium.	52 Battle of Lutetia.	14–37 Parisii boatmen's pillar is raised to the glory of Jupiter.	250 Saint Denis is martyred.	451 Invasion by the Huns.

PREHISTORY

THE PALEOLITHIC PERIOD TO ROMANIZATION

Prehistoric man, whose chief occupation was hunting and gathering food, occupied the Paris Basin from around 700,000 BC: in fact, evidence of Paleolithic settlement has been excavated in Paris itself. In the Neolithic period, around 5000 BC, Danubian tribes who farmed and lived in villages of wooden or cob houses had settled in what is now the Île de France region. The population boom of the middle Neolithic period caused territorial disputes, forcing the population to take refuge behind palisades, embankments and

ditches. Traces of this so-called ribbon pottery culture have been found on the sites of the Jardin du Carrousel, the Place du Châtelet and the Porte de Vitry. In September 1991 building work at Bercy uncovered an arch dating from the Cerny period (4500–4200 BC), three oak dugout canoes from the mid-Neolithic period (4200–3400 BC) and an array of

implements and pottery proving that a permanent settlement existed there. Megaliths dating from the final Neolithic period (3400–1800 BC) have been discovered near Châtelet, behind the Hôtel de Ville, near St-Merri and in the Rue St-Dominique. In the Bronze Age (1800–750 BC) the Seine became a key trade route for English tin bound for the Mediterranean

and Central Europe. The Celts settled on the banks of the river during the late Iron Age (475–52 BC), and around 250–225 BC the Gallic tribe of the Parisii settled along the Seine between its confluences with the Marne and the Oise. At that time Lutetia was confined to the Île de la Cité and served as a refuge in times of war and as a ford for crossing the river. Gold coins dating from around 100 BC bear witness to the Parisii's thriving economic activity.

ANTIQUITY AND THE EARLY MIDDLE AGES

In 58 BC Julius Caesar began his conquest of Gaul. The battle of Lutetia in 52 BC and the surrender of

Vercingetorix and the Gallic chief Camulogenes assured Rome's victory. Lutetia was rebuilt in stone with a grid of paved streets ● 56 after the model of Italian cities. The Roman governor settled in the Île de la Cité, and the town spread along the Left

Bank, down the slopes of Mount Ste-Geneviève, on top of which stood the forum. The neglected Right Bank had only a temple to Mercury, erected on the hill at Montmartre.

The city covered some 124 acres at this point and had about five thousand inhabitants.

THE GRAND INVASIONS

Three centuries of Roman peace ended in AD 275 with the first of a series of raids by tribes of the outer Rhine. Lutetia was pillaged and the inhabitants fled back to the Cité, which was hastily fortified. This fortification was given the name of Paris toward the end

of the 3rd century. Christianity, which according to tradition appeared around 250 with Saint Denis the first bishop, triumphed in the 5th century with Saint Geneviève, the city's patroness. Her faith helped her to turn back Attila's hordes in 451, who were

defeated by the Roman general Actius in what is now known as the Champagne area. In 486 the Franks, a Germanic tribe who were native to the Rhine estuary and commanded by Clovis, seized the city, which served sporadically as their

capital. Their Carolingian successors abandoned it for the valley of the Meuse and Aix-la-Chapelle. The Normans looted the area around the Cité but were unable to seize the island despite a lengthy siege in 885–6.

511–558	987	1190–1210
Notre-Dame is constructed.	Huguès Capet is crowned king.	The Philippe-Auguste wall is built.
600	**800** **1000**	**1100**	**1200** **1300**

| 508 | 756 | 885 | 1163 | 1215 | 1257–74 |
| Clovis makes Paris his capital. | Pippin the Short is crowned in the Abbey of St-Denis. | Normans lay siege to the Cité. The Parisians resist. | Notre-Dame is reconstructed. | Foundation of the University of Paris. | The Sorbonne is founded by Robert de Sorbon. |

THE MIDDLE AGES

PARIS, CAPITAL OF FRANCE

With the coronation of Huguès Capet in 987, Paris became the kingdom's capital. Having considered Orléans, the kings settled for good in the Palais de la Cité under the reign of Louis VI the Fat (1108–37). In 1141 an undeveloped area on the site of what is now the Hôtel de Ville was granted in perpetuity by Louis VII to the bourgeoisie for their trading operations. Between 1310 and 1830 executions were carried out on this square. Philippe-Auguste (1180–1223) founded Les Halles, had the streets paved, and surrounded the city with a fortified wall. In 1215 the Pope founded the University of Paris

● 22. Colleges sprang up in the late 12th century and thrived in the 13th century.

Louis IX's chaplain, Robert de Sorbon, founded one of the most famous of these colleges, the Sorbonne, in 1257: this was to be the home of the Faculty of Theology in the 15th century. Under the reigns of Louis IX (1226–70) and Philippe the Fair ● 23 (1285–1314) Paris became the most densely populated city in Europe, with over 200,000 inhabitants in 1328.

ÉTIENNE MARCEL (1315–58). Provost of the merchants of Paris, Étienne Marcel came from a family of wealthy drapers and was the leader of the Third Estate in the States-General of 1355 and 1356. Protesting poor royal administration, he encouraged the estates to call for the foundation of a regency council and for institutional reform. For a year he commanded the capital. On February 22, 1358, the conflict culminated in the murder of two of the Dauphin's key counselors. Supporters of the Dauphin assassinated Étienne Marcel on July 31.

MUNICIPAL GOVERNMENT IS BORN

The boatmen's guild held the monopoly on river trade upstream and downstream of Paris. Based in the Place de Grève, the municipal government of the Parloir aux Bourgeois was formed to regulate this traffic administratively and legally. In the records kept, the first

provosts of the merchants and aldermen appear in 1263.

ROYAL AUTHORITY CHALLENGED

Despite the ever-increasing burden of taxes, relations between the monarchy and the bourgeoisie remained excellent until the outbreak of war between France and England, which ended in disaster at Crécy (1346). The Great Plague of 1348 decimated the population, and the defeat of John the Good by the English created a terrible crisis. When the dauphin, Charles, brought together the estates in a bid to raise more money to continue the war, he crossed swords with the provost of the merchants, Étienne Marcel.

PARISIAN CRISES

Devastated by war, the Île de France was rocked by a peasant uprising in May 1358. The assassination of Étienne Marcel on July 31 restored civil peace and royal authority in Paris. Once on the throne, Charles V built the Bastille, as well as a city wall on the Right Bank around the newly built quarters. In March 1382 taxation triggered the Maillotin revolt. In retaliation, municipal autonomy was revoked. The King's madness and his uncles' struggle for power enabled Parisians to regain control of their institutions. The butchers' faction, led first by Simon Caboche, then by the executioner Capeluche, unleashed a reign of terror on the city in 1413 and 1418. After the Duke of Burgundy was murdered, his supporters allied themselves with the English, who entered Paris. Henry VI of England assumed the crown of France on the death of Charles VI. His son, Charles VII, took refuge in Bourges until 1436. After eighty years of stormy dealings with the capital, the monarchy withdrew to the Loire. Paris became a city peopled by citizens of independent means and civil servants.

1364–80			1528	1606
City wall built by			The new Louvre is	Place des Vosges
Charles V.			constructed.	is built.

| 1300 | 1350 | 1400 | 1500 | 1550 | 1600 |

1348	1358	1418	1420	1528	1572	1610
Widespread	Étienne Marcel	Plague	The English	François I takes	St Bartholomew's	Assassination
epidemic of the	stirs up Paris	epidemic.	occupy Paris.	up residence in	Day massacre.	of Henri IV.
Great Plague.	against Charles V.			Paris.	

FROM THE RENAISSANCE TO THE ENLIGHTENMENT

RELIGION AND HUMANISM

The religious crisis which set Catholics against Protestants was started in 1517 by Luther's protests against the decadence of the Church and culminated in the St Bartholomew's Day massacre in 1572 ● 24. The crisis had forced the monarchy in 1528 to take up residence once again in its capital, which in turn boosted town-planning activity in Paris. François I entrusted the Italian architect Pietro da Cortona with the task of transforming the fortress of the Louvre ▲ 324 into a Renaissance palace. He also reformed the education system. At the request of the Hellenist Guillaume Budé, he founded the Collège de France to counteract the inflexibility of the University ● 22, which was hostile to Italian humanism. The city joined forces with the Holy League against the King and was besieged twice, in 1589 and 1590, and yielded to Henri IV only after he had abjured Protestantism in 1594.

Guillaume Budé.

THE GLOOMY 17TH CENTURY

During the 17th century French sovereigns worked hard to improve the appearance of Paris. The Place des Vosges was constructed in the reign of Henri IV,

the Île St-Louis started to take shape in 1614, and the Marais spread under Louis XIII. Louis XIV had the old rampart walls of Paris knocked down and replaced with wide boulevards, started the fashion for public gardens, and oversaw the widespread installation of street lighting. In the reign of Louis XV, Gabriel designed the Place Royale, which was to become the Place de la Concorde. But the capital was rocked by political disturbances. In 1635 France's entry into the Thirty Years' War caused epidemics and shortages in Paris and eventually landed the Parisians in a civil war, the Fronde, which lasted from 1648 to 1652. In 1666, traumatized by the events of his childhood, Louis XIV abandoned Paris for Versailles, where he had a palace built. He undertook increasingly dangerous campaigns, which sparked dreadful revolts in the capital in 1692 and 1709. The monarchy's desertion of the city caused discontent among Parisians. Undermined by the disputes between Jesuits and Jansenists, religious faith came under open attack in the 18th century salons, where the ideas of the philosophers were discussed. Even the commoners were opposed to the power of an absolute and remote monarch. The construction of tollhouses around the city increased hostilities.

THE FRONDE
The parliament of Paris, opposed to the government's financial measures, attempted to restrict royal power. The arrest of the leaders triggered protest among the populace, who barracaded the streets. Various princes joined the "frondeurs", including Condé. While marching on Paris, he clashed with Turenne's troops. Deserted by the bourgeoisie, he was forced to flee. From that time onward the heads of state steered clear of the capital.

The Prince of Condé.
(Below) The Holy League marching to the Place de Grève.

1633	1763	1786
Creation of the Jardin des Plantes.	Inauguration of the Place Louis XV.	Construction of the toll-houses.

1700	**1750**	**1770**	**1780**	**1790**

1648	1715	1751–72	1774	1789	July 14	January 21, 1793
The Fronde.	Death of Louis XIV.	Publication of the *Encyclopédie*.	Louis XVI restores the former parliament of Paris.	Convocation of the States General at Versailles.	Taking of the Bastille.	Execution of Louis XVI.

THE REVOLUTION

Even on the eve of the Revolution, Paris continued to grow. The thoroughfare connecting the Louvre with the Tuileries was finally completed, and an ordinance of 1783 prescribed a minimum width of 30 feet for new streets ● *52*. From the Chaussée d'Antin to the Faubourg St-Martin there was an unbroken vista of new buildings under construction. However, in 1789 this expansion was brought to an abrupt halt. The bankruptcy of state finances led to the collapse of the monarchy. Haunted by the specter of food shortages, unrest swept through the Faubourg St-Antoine and Faubourg St-Marcel. The nobility and the clergy refused to attend the States General with the Third Estate, who set themselves up as a National Assembly. The announcement of the dismissal of Finance Minister Necker was the last straw. On July 14 the

Bastille was stormed. Louis XVI returned to the capital. For five years revolutionary Paris, with the Jacobin *sans-culottes* at the helm and dominated by the imposing figure of Robespierre, forced the rest of the nation to toe the line. The populace invaded the Tuileries on August 10, 1792, and overthrew the monarchy. The moderate Girondins were ousted on June 2, 1793, and from September 1793 to July 1794, the *sans-culottes* instituted the official Reign of Terror. In March and April 1794, the Hébertists and the Dantonists were eliminated. Then came the about-turn. With the Thermidorian reaction, the

Robespierrists were marched to the scaffold in July 1794, to the delight of a population pushed too far by the Terror. Famine riots in the French revolutionary months of Germinal and Prairial (March and May 1795) and the abortive Royalist insurrection in Vendémiaire (October 1795) marked the death throes of the capital.

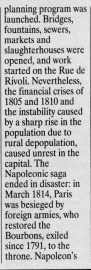

THE CONSULATE AND THE EMPIRE

Victorious in battle, Napoleon had himself elected First Consul, then crowned himself Emperor in 1804 and stripped Paris of all municipal power, for fear of a repeat of the excesses of the Revolution. Foreign visitors saw imperial Paris as a thriving city. The Vendôme column, a symbol of Napoleonic glory decorated with a bas-relief retracing the feats of the Grande Armée, was inaugurated on August 15, 1810. At the instigation of the prefect Frochot, an ambitious town-planning program was launched. Bridges, fountains, sewers, markets and slaughterhouses were opened, and work started on the Rue de Rivoli. Nevertheless, the financial crises of 1805 and 1810 and the instability caused by a sharp rise in the population due to rural depopulation, caused unrest in the capital. The Napoleonic saga ended in disaster: in March 1814, Paris was besieged by foreign armies, who restored the Bourbons, exiled since 1791, to the throne. Napoleon's return to the Tuileries a year later during the Hundred Days was merely incidental; Waterloo forced the Emperor to abdicate once again.

1800	1820	1840	1860	1880	1900

1853 Haussmann starts work.

1860 Division into twenty arrondissements.

1875 Paris Opera House is completed.

1889 Completion of the Eiffel Tower.

1804 Bonaparte is crowned Emperor in Notre-Dame.

July 27–9, 1830 *Les Trois Glorieuses*, the three-day revolution.

December 2, 1851 Coup d'état by Napoleon Bonaparte.

1870–1 Paris besieged by the Germans.

1871 Paris Commune.

1894–9 Dreyfus affair.

THE 19TH CENTURY

REVOLUTIONS IN PARIS

Paris was modernized during the Restoration: markets and canals improved the city's access to supplies. Bridges, sidewalks, gas lighting and buses made it easier for its inhabitants to get around. The capital acquired a stock exchange, the Palais de la Bourse ▲ 353, which opened for business in 1825. Parisians wasted no time in opposing an outmoded moral code and political regime. The July Revolution, *Les Trois Glorieuses*, forced Charles X to abdicate. The younger branch of the Orléans family succeeded the Bourbons to the French throne with Louis-Philippe. The July Monarchy represented a golden age for the bourgeoisie. Arcades and showy monuments like the obelisk in the Place de la Concorde and the Arc de Triomphe ▲ 316 were all the rage: many artists and writers reaped the benefits of this growing affluence. In 1832 a cholera epidemic swept Paris, hitting the poverty-stricken quarters in the center and southeast particularly hard. Fearing another foreign invasion, prime minister Thiers surrounded Paris with a wall on the site of what is now the ring road circling Paris. In 1847 an economic crisis broke out: Louis-Philippe showed little patience with the rules of parliamentary monarchy, and as a result of his behavior a new revolution overthrew the regime and set up the Second Republic in February 1848. This abortive working-class and socialist revolution, which was suppressed in June 1848, threw the bourgeoisie into the arms of Napoleon's nephew. The future Napoleon III had himself elected Emperor one year after his coup d'état of December 2, 1851.

HAUSSMANN'S PARIS

In 1853 Napoleon III appointed Haussmann ● 72 prefect of the Seine. He demolished entire districts, built avenues and boulevards, and created parks and gardens. Europeans who had come for the various universal exhibitions ● 30 were dazzled by the street lighting. The improvement of the sewer system and the supply of running water to all buildings went hand in hand with the growth of a city which attracted thousands of immigrants every year. Paris, which had topped a million inhabitants in 1846, now had 700,000 more. On January 1, 1860, the inner suburbs were annexed to the capital in order to rationalize town planning, which increased the number of arrondissements from twelve to twenty. But the Franco-German war was to topple the regime on September 4, 1870. While the Emperor was a prisoner of the Prussians, an interim government was set up in Paris, several days before the enemy surrounded the city. The siege,

capitulation and loss of Alsace-Lorraine infuriated the populace, sparking off the bloody revolt of the Commune ● 28.

THE BELLE ÉPOQUE

Under the Third Republic the city continued to expand, but it was not until the end of the century, during the Belle Époque, that the capital regained the dynamism it had known under Haussmann. The Exhibition of 1889 ● 30 ushered in this new era. The regime withstood the unrest caused by the Boulanger affair (1889) and the Dreyfus affair (1894). Paris, along with Vienna, was a cultural center of Europe. As Haussmann's work was being completed, Art Nouveau was demolishing the prefect's concepts. The construction of the Metro ● 40 was finally started in 1900.

THE JULY REVOLUTION
Charles X wanted nothing to do with a parliamentary monarchy, and his authoritarianism provoked violent opposition. Between July 27 and 29, 1830, the Days of the Barricades, there were some bloody clashes. The royal troops under the command of Marshal Marmont were defeated by the rebels.

1921	1925	1969	1977		1997
Fortifications of Paris demolished.	Exhibition of Decorative Arts.	Creation of the RER.	Inauguration of Beaubourg.		Inauguration of the Grand Louvre
1920	1940	1960	1980	1990	2000

| 1914 | June 14, 1940 | August 1944 | March 25, 1977 | 1986–8 | 1989 |
| Assassination of Jaurès. Outbreak of World War One. | Germans occupy Paris. | Liberation of Paris. | Paris elects a mayor. | First Cohabitation. | Bicentenary of the Revolution. |

MODERN TIMES

In the early years of the 20th century, the population of Paris increased by 25 percent, but war arrested this trend. Paris peaked at just under three million inhabitants in 1921. Construction ground almost completely to a halt between 1919 and 1939. After this, the inner suburbs absorbed the new arrivals, and Paris suffered urban sprawl. Parisian industry relocated there, taking advantage of lower costs and an abundant supply of labor. The formation of a *ceinture rouge*, a ring of left-wing suburbs around Paris, gradually pointed up the divide between the capital and its suburbs. The capital still fascinated the world, with the bohemian lifestyle of painters of the School of Paris, mainly led by foreigners who had settled in Montparnasse ▲ 272.

Despite the Roaring Twenties, the international prestige enjoyed by the City of Light during the Belle Époque had become tarnished: the Exhibitions of 1925 and 1931 were pale reflections of those in 1889 and 1900.

THE MEGALOPOLIS

After the Nazi occupation ● 32, which deeply affected the city, Paris and its suburbs resumed their growth. The housing shortage was worsened by the demolitions. The bistros reaped the benefits of widespread overcrowding, which favored the growing popularity of literary cafés like the Flore and the Deux-Magots. The St-Germain-des-Prés of Boris Vian and nightclubs sprang up partly as a result of the recession and the general need to forget. The terrible winter of 1954 saw the appearance of Abbot Pierre and led to the launch of an extensive building program. This activity was speeded up when a new political group came to power in 1958. The outer suburbs outstripped the inner suburbs in 1962, while the city's population dropped to some two million inhabitants. Paris began to revamp its older quarters – especially the Marais, helped by the 1962 Malraux Law – in an attempt to justify its image as the showcase of France. Large-scale public works carried out under the Fifth Republic created a modern transport system for a city and suburbs of around ten million people. In 1969, the first RER line was opened.

The suburbs were now just a stone's throw from the capital, and five new towns were built around Paris. The city, now largely populated by the middle and upper classes, became more gentrified. Although the regime was rocked by the student revolts of 1968 ● 34, the fear of a new Commune had vanished. The Pompidou years were marked by the realization of large-scale public works projects planned by De Gaulle: les Halles, Beaubourg, Rungis, la Défense and the Montparnasse Tower. Treating any controversy with contempt, the new

leaders drastically altered the face of the capital. The period of economic expansion in France (1945–75) came to an end with the oil crisis. France under Valéry Giscard d'Estaing became more conservative. Paris rehabilitated, protected and developed its open spaces and private facilities. In 1976 the city was granted municipal status similar to that of other cities in France, and the following year it elected its first mayor in modern times. One of Pompidou's most eccentric projects, running the A10 freeway through Paris, was abandoned. During his first term

of office, François Mitterrand had to deal with a housing crisis, worsened by the Quillot Law, which placed various restrictions on landlords. A change in policy led to a boom in the construction of housing and offices beginning in 1988, coupled with an ambitious planning and development program for Paris and the Île de France. Whole districts, especially in the east of Paris, were remodeled. At the same time, owing to Mitterand's major building projects, Paris acquired a dazzling array of public buildings, including the Opéra Bastille, the Grande Arche de la Défense, the Grand Louvre and the Bibliothèque Nationale. A recent project is the Stade de France stadium in St-Denis, which was opened in 1998 for the soccer World Cup.

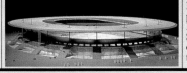

THE UNIVERSITY IN THE MIDDLE AGES

Descended from the chapter school of Notre-Dame cathedral, the University of Paris took shape during the 17th century. The restrictions imposed by the chancellor of Notre-Dame, who supervised the teaching and awarded the diplomas, very soon prompted some teachers to put themselves beyond the reach of his authority, taking up residence on the Left Bank, where the Abbey of Ste-Geneviève allowed them to teach. One of the first to cross the Seine was Abelard, who was persecuted in the Cité.

THE BIRTH

A studious but unruly throng of students and teachers took over the hitherto deserted slopes of Ste-Geneviève. Before the colleges were built, classes were held in stables or barns. Fond of brawling and carousing, the students provoked hostility and fear. Following a brawl in a tavern which claimed the lives of five people in 1200, Philippe-Auguste decided that the students would come under the exclusive jurisdiction of the Church and not that of the state. In 1215 the University was given its statutes by Robert de Courson, the papal legate. A compromise drawn up in 1238 by Pope Gregory IX outlined a division of powers: teachers in the faculties of Theology and Canonic Law would receive their degrees from the chancellor of Notre-Dame, while the chancellor of Ste-Geneviève would award arts degrees. The vice-chancellor, who represented the University after 1211, was merely the head of the Faculty of Arts, elected by the bursars from the four nations.

THE NATIONS

These were clubs, guilds and brotherhoods at one and the same time. The nation of France was divided into five clans, corresponding to Paris and the archdioceses of Sens, Reims, Tours and Bourges. The other nations were those of Picardy, Normandy, and England along with Belgium, Germany and Scandinavia.

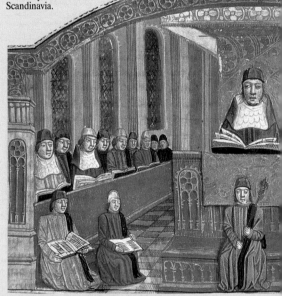

GREAT DISPUTES

The University interfered in all the major political and religious disputes of the Middle Ages. Not satisfied with fighting heretical ideas and trying to find a way of resolving the Great Schism, it also tried to impose its will on royal authority during John the Good's captivity and Étienne Marcel's rebellion.

STUDIES

These began around the age of fourteen at the Faculty of Arts and included the *trivium* (grammar, rhetoric and dialectics) and the *quadrivium* (mathematics, geometry, music and astronomy). After six years students sat for their baccalauréat, then a master's degree, which enabled them to teach. Bachelors of arts could then study canonic law or medicine and obtain a doctorate. A doctorate from the Faculty of Theology, the crowning glory of the university required some further fifteen years of study.

THE SORBONNE

Colleges, which sprang up around 1250, were originally hotels or boarding houses lodging people from the provinces or abroad who had come to study in Paris. In the 14th century tutors living on site gave the boarders extra tuition. There were, in the following century, some sixty colleges housing nearly seven hundred students. The most famous was founded in 1257 by Robert de Sorbon and became the seat of the Sorbonne's Faculty of Theology in the 15th century. The major religious orders, especially the Dominicans, Franciscans and Cistercians, had their own colleges for monks who came to study theology.

Seal of the University of Paris.

THE MARTINETS

Martinets catered for their own needs, studied under form-masters, and threw in their lot with a professor only for examinations. Having no means of support, they lived by their wits, often engaging in criminal activities. Their scandalous lifestyles painted a shady picture of the student world, evoked by the life of poet François Villon.

23

● ST BARTHOLOMEW'S DAY

Catherine de' Medici.

The French Reformed Church, founded in Paris in 1559, remained a minority in the face of widespread Catholicism: its only power base was south of the Loire. The massacre of Protestants at Wassy in March 1562, perpetrated by the Duc de Guise's men, triggered the first of the eight Wars of Religion which were to ravage the country until 1598. The atrocities reached their climax with the St Bartholomew's Day massacre on August 24, 1572, in Paris. Peace was restored when Henri IV abjured Calvinism in 1593 and granted freedom of worship to the Protestants with the Edict of Nantes in 1598.

THE PROTESTANTS IN PARIS

The bulk of the Reformation's urban contingent was supplied by petty magistrates, well-educated craftsmen, furriers, drapers, silversmiths and booksellers. In high society the noblest lineages – Bourbon, Condé, Bouillon, Turenne and La Rochefoucauld – rallied to Calvinism. The illiterate and superstitious lower classes, surrounded by their priests and mendicant sermonizing monks, developed a hatred of the Huguenots, whose wealth they coveted.

THE BACKGROUND TO THE TRAGEDY

Henri II's widow, Catherine de' Medici, wielded power in the name of her son, Charles IX. Despised as much by the Protestants as by the Catholics, she vacillated between the two camps. Unable to overcome the Calvinists by force of arms, she negotiated with them out of fear of King Philippe II of Spain, whose lands surrounded France. The marriage of her daughter Marguerite to Henri de Bourbon, King of Navarre, was meant to seal the reconciliation between French citizens of both denominations.

THE MAIN PLAYERS

On July 9 or 10, the King of Navarre, his cousin Condé, Admiral de Coligny and La Rochefoucauld entered Paris with a thousand Gascon gentlemen. The infuriated Catholic Parisians welcomed the De Guise family, who had arrived from Lorraine. The latter took up residence in their mansion and their retinue in the inns around the Louvre.

Coligny persuaded the weak Charles IX to come to the aid of the Protestants in the Netherlands, who had revolted against the King of Spain. The Queen Mother threatened to leave for Florence if her son complied and at the same time decided to get rid of Coligny, who had become too influential.

THE BLOODY WEDDING

On August 18 the King of Navarre married Marguerite de Valois. On the morning of August 22, Coligny was shot twice but was saved by Ambroise Paré. On the following evening Catherine de' Medici confessed to her son that she had bribed the would-be assassin Maurevert and resumed her blackmail: she would go back to Florence if the King refused to annihilate the Huguenots. Charles IX resigned himself to the task. The provost of the merchants was ordered to close the city gates and put the militia on alert.

THE MASSACRE

The signal for the slaughter was given at around three or four in the morning by the bell of St-Germain-l'Auxerrois. The Duc de Guise and his men killed Admiral de Coligny first. The King of Navarre's most loyal companions had their throats slit while in bed at the Louvre. The massacre lasted until August 29 and claimed between fifteen hundred and two thousand lives, wiping out the cream of the Protestant nobility. Only Henri de Bourbon was spared and kept prisoner. The capital's Calvinist bourgeoisie was also severely hit, and Protestantism was practically eradicated in Paris. The St Bartholomew's Day massacre was to be the root cause of a further twenty years of civil war in France.

The French Revolution began at the Bastille, the symbol of absolute monarchy: the constitutional monarchy was overthrown in the Palais des Tuileries and wiped out in the Place de la Concorde, where Louis XVI was beheaded. A few paces from where the Terror had begun, it ended with the massacre of the final victims in the Place de la Nation. After a bitter four-year struggle along this east–west axis, Paris gained local power for itself in place of the absolutism of Versailles.

A POLITICAL MAP
Paris inherited a political geography from the Revolution. The Faubourg St-Antoine became the stronghold of a democratic artisan community. The old working-class quarters on the Right Bank acquired a new importance in Parisian political life: the mouthpieces of power – the Assembly and the Jacobin and Feuillant clubs – were set up around the château between what are now Rue St-Honoré and Rue de Rivoli. The Champs-de-Mars, a symbol of national unity at the Festival of Federation in 1790, was the scene of some of the clashes which heralded civil war in July 1791.

THE TOLLHOUSES BURNT
From the point of view of the city, if not the nation, a highly symbolic event took place in the summer of 1789: the barely completed tollhouses, which embellished Paris' new customs barrier, were burnt down. As a result, some of Claude Nicolas Ledoux's work was lost to the country's architectural heritage.

> **"OVER PARIS, WHICH HAS NO BREAD, RISES THE HARD WHEAT OF PIKES. WITH ITS CORNFLOWERS OF STEEL, ITS POPPIES OF BLOOD, HERE IS THE HARVEST OF PROTRACTED ANGER."**
>
> MAX-POL FOUCHET

THE TERROR

The whole population was affected by the Terror: 115 priests were killed including 2 bishops and 1 archbishop; more than 2,800 people were guillotined in the Place de la Concorde. Picpus cemetery is full of graves belonging to the nobility as well as to working-class people.

THE CHANGING FACE OF PARIS

During the Terror, a great deal of property changed hands due to the institutional and social upheaval. Goods belonging to the Church, the city and the aristocracy were sold. The finest mansions and convents fell into the hands of architects, lawyers, notaries, bankers, tradesmen and manufacturers or became the property of the state. Part of the prestigious Faubourg St-Germain was transformed into a ministerial quarter, while the Elysée Palace started its glorious career in the Faubourg St-Honoré. Speculators were busy demolishing many great structures including the convent buildings belonging to the Abbey of St-Germain-des-Prés. The result was a great loss to the Roman-Gothic architectural heritage of Paris.

● THE COMMUNE

The Commune marked one of the most serious crises in the history of Paris: even during the June days of 1848 and the St Bartholomew's Day massacre, blood had never flowed so freely. The Franco-Prussian war was at the root of this bloodbath. After the defeat of Sedan and the fall of the Empire, the enemy arrived at the walls of Paris and besieged the recently fortified capital. This widened the rift between the patriotic Parisians and the government, which, forced to surrender in early 1871, fell back to Bordeaux. When the government returned to Versailles, it convoked the National Assembly and forced Paris to capitulate, triggering the hostilities.

WAR ABROAD

The events of the spring of 1871 were preceded by the siege of Paris by the Prussians, the final military and political episode in the war waged during the summer of 1870. The enemy bombarded the city with twelve thousand shells between January 5 and 27, 1871. These shells fell mainly on the Left Bank, hitting 1,400 houses, the Museum, the greenhouse in the Jardin des Plantes, the Necker Hospital, the Institut des Jeunes Aveugles and many other buildings. Outside Paris the Prussians destroyed Château de St-Cloud (October 23, 1870) and the Château de Meudon (January 31, 1871) just after the armistice had been signed.

THE COMMUNE

The Parisian working-class movement was infuriated by the siege and the government's capitulation, as well as the political hijacking of patriotic fervor. This resulted in a confrontation between Paris and Versailles which was the seat of the legal government under the leadership of Thiers on March 18, 1871. Two armies clashed: the regular troops and the Federalists of the National Guard. The latter imbued Montmartre with its revolutionary spirit by preventing the men of Versailles from taking away the guns belonging by right to Parisians, which had been stored on a piece of wasteland on top of the hill. Ironically, ten years later the monumental staircase leading to the basilica of the Sacré-Coeur was built on the same site.

WAR IN THE CITY

It was no mean task to regain Paris; despite Haussmann's thoroughfares, the dense and virtually impenetrable city hindered the deployment of an army. This problem was compounded by the fact that the streets were bristling with barricades.

THE BLOODY WEEK
(MAY 21–7, 1871)

The Federalists' Wall in the Père Lachaise cemetery ▲ *412* witnessed the death of only a small number of the Commune's 20,000 victims (according to some estimates, the figure was as high as 35,000 deaths), but the massacre took its toll on the surrounding quarter. The street battles here were bitter, earning residents of Belleville the epithet of "barbarians". The Bloody Week badly scarred the city. Falling back gradually toward the east of Paris, the Communards resorted to arson and whole streets were destroyed. The Tuileries Palace was torched, later razed in 1882 and replaced by gardens. The Cour des Comptes on the banks of the Seine remained in ruins until 1898. The Louvre itself only barely escaped damage.

Five universal exhibitions were held in Paris during the 19th century but only one in the 20th century, in 1937. The difficulties of recovering from the devastation of World War One partly account for the decline in the number of exhibitions. These temporary exhibitions were first and foremost a showcase for the industrial skills of the participating nations and the great strides made in the domain of technical progress, which they helped to popularize. France was particularly fond of these events, which provided ample opportunity to show off its artistic and scientific creativity, as well as its high-quality production, geared to luxury items. Paris had inherited a rich architectural heritage, making it an ideal setting for international exhibitions.

1855 AND 1867
The innovative nature of the exhibitions during the Second Empire rivaled that of Crystal Palace in London in 1851. They ushered in the era of great halls with metal frames, and vast glass roofs, like that of the breathtaking Palais de l'Industrie. The exhibitions also encouraged huge influxes of tourists (eleven million visitors atttended in 1867) and helped to give the hotel industry a boost. The first Parisian luxury hotels date from this period.

The exhibitions of 1878 and 1889

These two exhibitions were organized in praise of the Third Republic. The exhibition in 1878 helped blot out the bad memories of 1871, while that of 1889 coincided with the centenary of the Revolution. They formed a strong link between the Left and Right banks near the 7th and 8th arrondissements and these areas became the most elegant parts of Paris.

The Trocadero, the palace built on a hill at Chaillot, and the Eiffel Tower were also the fruits of these exhibitions. The plan for the Eiffel Tower was the object of much public derision but once erected it became the most popular monument in Paris. The École Militaire,

which until then had been tucked away on the outer edges of the working-class district of Grenelle, now became part of the capital.

The exhibition of 1937

This strange event provided a forum for the shaky prestige of the democratic states of the world, while the two showiest pavilions confronting each other on the banks of the Seine were those of the Soviet Union and the Third Reich. All that remains of this exhibition is the memory of social unrest which nearly jeopardized the completion of construction work and the new Palais de Chaillot, a building with Mussolinian echoes.

The Universal Exhibition of 1900

The Grand Palais replaced the Palais de l'Industrie, facing the Petit Palais on a new triumphal avenue linking the Élysée Palace to the Hôtel des Invalides via the Alexandre III bridge, which had been built for the occasion. For the first time the monuments of a universal exhibition were built to last. The two palaces and the bridge were the showpieces of a new architectural style which combined conventional stonework and decorative motifs with the innovative use of metalwork. This triumphant industrial architecture blended in perfectly with the state buildings of the Left Bank, which were built by Louis XIV and Louis XV.

OCCUPIED PARIS, LIBERATED PARIS

From June 14, 1940, to August 25, 1944, the German army had military command over the occupied zone. When the French government departed on June 10, 1940, Paris was proclaimed an open city and was spared Allied bombing raids. Its liberation, however, gave rise to violent street fighting.

OCCUPIED PARIS
Imagine a city without buses or taxis and with few gas-fueled vehicles; instead there were some diesel vehicles, bicycles, tandem bicycles with passenger trailers for hire, and horse-driven vehicles. The Metro, closed from 11am to 3pm and at weekends, ran until 11pm; this famous "last Metro" enabled people to get home before curfew.

The army's presence could not be ignored; all signs were in German, and red flags flew from the tops of public buildings guarded by armed sentries. The commander-in-chief of the Luftwaffe was based at the Palais du Luxembourg, the governor of Paris at the Hôtel Meurice, and the government of occupied France at the Majestic. The occupiers could also be found in black-market restaurants and luxury nightclubs such as the Shéhérazade and the Suzy Solidor.

SHADOWY AREAS
Grim memories abound at 74, avenue Foch and 9, rue des Saussaies, where the Gestapo officiated; the prisons of the Cherche-Midi (54, boulevard Raspail) and Mont-Valérien (4,500 were shot between 1941 and 1944); the Vélodrome d'Hiver, where Jews were rounded up in July 1942; not to mention the prisons in the suburbs: Drancy, Fresnes and Romainville. Occupied Paris also worked for Germany: the tunnel of St-Cloud housed a submarine torpedo factory employing as many as five thousand prisoners.

RESISTANCE PARIS
Colonel Fabien dared to commit the first public act of resistance on August 21, 1941, by killing a German officer at the Metro station that now bears his name. A convent on the Rue de la Glacière housed the representative of the Intelligence Service. Thirty-seven young Resistance fighters were executed in front of the waterfall in the Bois de Boulogne.

PARIS UNDER THREAT

The forty-five bridges crossing the Seine between Le Pecq and Choisy were not destroyed, unlike those farther down river. Consequently, Paris became a strategic thoroughfare, playing a key role in the German defense of northern and eastern France. Hitler gave Governor von Choltitz strict orders to defend every inch of Paris and to reduce the city to ashes in case of a withdrawal following defeat. So the bridges, state buildings, supply routes, railways and stations were all mined. The systematic destruction of any quarter which attempted rebellion was also ordered.

LIBERATED PARIS

The Liberation left its mark along the entire length of the Left Bank. On August 24 and 25, 1944, Leclerc's Second Armored Division and assorted American forces entered Paris via the Porte d'Orléans, the Porte de Vanves and the Porte de Sèvres. The bells of Notre-Dame pealed out a welcome for the vanguard, while General de Gaulle's epic march down the Champs-Élysées blotted out the memory of the Wehrmacht march in 1940. There was fighting all over Paris. There are plaques on many of the capital's buildings reminding people of the dark hours that the city lived through.

PARIS IN REVOLT

The uprising of Paris began on the 1,518th day of the occupation, on August 19, 1944. The various branches of the Resistance seized the police headquarters and, from the Catacombs, called for barricades to be erected. More than two hundred were raised in three days. The fighting was particularly fierce along the south–north thoroughfares, especially boulevards St-Michel and St-Germain, the junction of which was called the "crossroads of death", as well as the Place de la République and the Rue La Fayette. The Grand Palais was partially destroyed. A representative of the Gaullist Resistance took up his post without difficulty in the Hôtel Matignon, which Pierre Laval had just deserted.

● MAY 1968

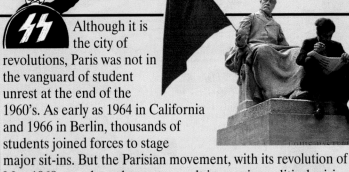

Although it is the city of revolutions, Paris was not in the vanguard of student unrest at the end of the 1960's. As early as 1964 in California and 1966 in Berlin, thousands of students joined forces to stage major sit-ins. But the Parisian movement, with its revolution of May 1968, was the only one to result in a major political crisis on a national scale, almost succeeding in overthrowing the government.

NANTERRE: BIRTH OF A MOVEMENT

The university academic year of 1967–8 was extremely turbulent, disrupted by general protest meetings, demonstrations and clashes with the police. A class strike ended the year at Nanterre, a new campus in the suburbs built cheek-by-jowl with the poor quarters, and whose name, like that of Berkeley, was to become famous. The protest movement got underway on March 22, 1968, when forty-two students invaded the university's administrative offices.

THE LATIN QUARTER

When Nanterre closed on May 2, the Sorbonne took over. On May 3 demonstrators in the courtyard were expelled by the military. From then on there were daily violent clashes on the Left Bank between university and high school students and the French riot police, the CRS. On May 7 the French student union, the UNEF, organized a huge march from the Latin Quarter to the Arc de Triomphe.

THE DAY OF MAY 10

The unrest took on another dimension during the night of May 10–11, when barricades were erected in the Latin Quarter, sparking a violent counter attack by the police. The students then changed their tactics and occupied a number of buildings. The Sorbonne, Censier and the Odéon Theater became hotbeds of student unrest. Today the only reminders of this turbulent period are the old posters and graffiti scrawled across the walls of the Sorbonne.

RENAULT

Amid total confusion, links were forged between the student movement and the trade-union movement; Billancourt, Flins and Cléon became the centers of a social unrest which threatened to spread to every sector of French society. The old stadium of Charléty, near the recently rebuilt residence halls, was the site of a major political demonstration on May 27, which called for the formation of a transitional government.

RESTORING ORDER

In response to this chaos, there was a major demonstration down the Champs-Élysées on May 30 in support of General de Gaulle. The value of such a symbolic gesture, reminiscent of his march in 1944, was not lost on the country, and he was seen as the figure most able to restore order. However, the situation remained unstable for several weeks.

PARISIAN SCENES

Despite the three million cars that drive through Paris every day, the city remains the domain of pedestrians, whose lot was greatly improved at the end of the last century when sidewalks were laid across the city and public health became a concern. Nowadays, police officers and street cleaners have replaced the many peddlers who used to work the city's streets before the war. But the Parisian street retains much of its picturesque charm, and the open-air markets still echo with the cries of days gone by.

THE PEDESTRIANS OF PARIS

Under the Ancien Régime, only the more important citizens were allowed to walk on the sides of the street. Others were left to share the central part of the road with the waste water. In 1780 the first sidewalks were laid, but they did not become common until the Second Empire.

THE CLEAN PREFECT

In 1884 Eugène Poubelle (above), prefect of the Seine, made it obligatory for Parisians to use trash cans (to which he gave his name). Two years later, he introduced a sewer system. Despite the hostility of those who saw it as an infringement on their liberty, health became a public matter toward the end of that century. From then on, the streets which formed the nervous system of Haussmann's city were to be used by all and sundry.

POLICE OFFICERS

Emergency help, community policing and traffic control are the main responsibilities of the police, who ensure the safety of the Republic's most important institutions, based in the capital. It is administered by a central organization at police headquarters – *la préfecture de police*.

Photographed in 1904, one of the largest markets in Paris is still still held two mornings a week on the Boulevard de Belleville.

Every year traffic officers or members of the Paris security forces issue eight million parking tickets to motorists.

The glowing colors of the market in the Rue Mouffetard at the heart of the Latin Quarter.

Parisian garbage collectors now preach the virtues of recycling and "keeping Paris clean", a slogan found on every street corner.

THE CRIES OF PARIS

"Buy my tender artichokes!" If you want to hear the "cries of Paris", simply go to one of the city's fifty or so food markets, which spread out along the sidewalks and central islands in the streets. But only a few of the many peddlers who used to walk the streets of Paris before the war have survived. From time to time, you will still hear the ringing cries of the glazier and the knife grinder, as well as the refrain of the street musician who sings for coins thrown down from your window.

A woman selling roasted chestnuts (below).

THE CONCIERGE

The concierge is a colorful character in Parisian life, inherited from the 19th century, when every rented property had its own caretaker's room. These caretakers have gradually been replaced by the electronic keypad.

La place de la Concorde vue de l'hôtel de la Marine

● PARISIAN STREET LIFE

Carnivals disappeared from the streets of Paris in 1914. Students are among the few to continue the tradition.

Women from the suburbs marching on Versailles to clamor for bread, the Communards erecting barricades against the king's men from Versailles, the endless Front Populaire marches, the paving stones of May 1968 – at regular intervals throughout its history, Paris has been engulfed in strife, and angry crowds have rampaged through its streets. Although the capital does not spawn a revolution every day, it nevertheless continues to live up to its reputation: 1,500 protest demonstrations are held every year, an average of four a day.

POLITICAL ROUTES

After half a century, marches and demonstrations have split the city into two distinct political worlds. From 1934 on, the main Bastille–Nation and Bastille–République roads became left-wing demonstration routes; the political parties and unions which brought the Front Populaire to power once again commandeered the symbolic power of the revolutionary suburbs. On the other side of the political spectrum, Liberation transformed the Champs-Élysées into a Gaullist route. On May 30, 1968, one million people gathered there to demand an end to the *chienlit* (student protests).

ROUGH CUT

Weighing between 2 and 4 pounds, the Parisian *pavé*, a roughly cut granite paving stone, can be thrown as far as 65 feet. A favorite weapons of rioters, it was also their creed: "Sous les pavés la plage" (meaning "Beneath harsh reality lies a brighter tomorrow") declared the student protesters of May 1968.

DEMO INSTRUCTIONS

Any demonstration on a public road comes under the jurisdiction of the police, which prescribes a minimum of 3½ square yards per person if a crowd is to be able to move in complete safety.

BARRICADES

"Dreadful masterpieces of civil war" in Victor Hugo's words, the barricades were a characteristic feature of the revolutions of 1830 and 1848 and the

Commune (left, Place de la Concorde, 1871). One of the sayings of the Liberation was: "Everyone to the barricades!" Dozens were erected in the Latin Quarter in May 1968.

Concerts in the streets and dancing until the small hours of the morning: this is how Parisians have celebrated Midsummer's Eve since the summer music festival was created in 1981. On the evening of July 14 dances are held everywhere. Among the most popular are those held in fire stations and the one in the Place de la Bastille (left).

FIELD OF HONOR

In 1804, Napoleon I organized a spectacular party along the Champs-Élysées ▲ *312* to celebrate his marriage to Marie-Louise. The Champs-Élysées acquired its patriotic and official status with the victory parade on July 14, 1919. This was reinforced when the ashes of the Unknown Soldier were moved to the Arc de Triomphe in 1921.

39

Packed like sardines in the Metro during the rush hour, Parisians dream of a different way of life. "Métro, boulot, dodo" ("metro, work, sleep") – a saying inherited from the 1970's – mocks the commuter's life style. But this underground kingdom created in 1900 by the engineer Fulgence Bienvenüe (left), after forty years of procrastination and conflict between the city and the state, has its finer moments: when a talented musician livens up your journey, when a station becomes a museum, or when a train crosses the Seine at sunset on the elevated section of the Metro.

PARIS VERSUS THE SUBURBS
Paris did not want a Metro system which served the suburbs and insisted that it run exclusively within the city boundaries, taking care that it traveled on the right, in the opposite direction of the trains, to prevent a future link-up.

HERITAGE
Guimard designed eighty-four Art Nouveau entrance signs (top, facing page) as well as advertisement panels composed of white earthenware tiles with carved borders.

PARALLEL LINES
Rather than negotiating with private landowners, the city excavated state-owned land. Hence, most lines followed the path of existing roads instead of plotting new routes ▲ 281.

SAINT GEORGES

SUBTERRANEAN CULTURE
Launched in 1967 by André Malraux, who transformed the Louvre Metro station into a museum, the policy for themed stations has endured. The Assemblée Nationale station (left).

PROFESSIONAL, AUTOMATON OR IDLER?
Passengers on the Metro fall into three categories: the first makes his daily journey as quickly and efficiently as possible, the second travels like an automaton, and the third wanders along, stopping to look at the slightest distraction.

REFUGE
The Metro has always been a refuge for some of the 25,000 homeless in Paris. They tell their life stories or sell magazines devoted to the issues of homelessness (below) in the Metro cars. They are all at one time or another pulled in by the "Blues" from the welfare service for homeless people or by SAMU, the ambulance and emergency service of the city of Paris, for medical treatment and checkups.

THE SONG OF THE METRO
Accordions, violins, tom-toms and guitars – the Metro echoes with all the rhythms of the world. After banishing amateur musicians from its subways for many years, RATP is now granting them licences and sites.

A handful of prestigious cafés have assured the fame of this most Parisian of institutions. The first of these, the Procope, buzzed with the rivalry between its illustrious customers, the philosophers of the Enlightenment. But just as legendary are the local bistros with their canvas canopies and their tables which spill out over the sidewalks at the break of dawn. Cafés are ideal for meeting people and doing business, and there are no fewer than one for every two hundred citizens.

FROM THE PROCOPE . . .
(13, rue de l'Ancienne Comédie, 75006) In 1686 a Sicilian, Francesco Procopio, opened a coffee shop in Paris. He decorated it lavishly – mirrors, chandeliers, gilt fittings – and attracted members of polite society who until then had hardly ever visited taverns. They regarded this new drink from the East, *Kahve,* as a tonic for the brain.

. . . TO THE LOCAL BISTRO
In the 19th century the luxurious cafés on the grand boulevards and the small bars in the working-class quarters, as pilloried by Zola in *L'Assommoir,* existed cheek-by-jowl. At the turn of the century the two types of establishments merged to give birth to the modern café.

CAFÉ DES DEUX MAGOTS

CAFÉ GLOSSARY

Petit noir (espresso): 2 ounces of strong coffee, made by forcing steam through the ground beans.

Noisette: espresso with a dash of milk.
Petit crème, grand crème: coffee with milk, either *bien blanc* (very light) or *bien noir* (dark).
Ballon: 6 ounces of red or white wine served in a round wine glass.
Demi: 9 ounces of draft beer originally served in pint glasses.

DE CARBOU! N'IA . . .

"Coal for sale!" was the call in patois of people from the Auvergne, who came to Paris in the 19th century to sell wine and coal. Gradually the coal merchants (*bougnats*) turned to barkeeping and they dominate the profession to this day. *Mastroquet* was the name formerly given to wine merchants. The word, from which *troquet* (meaning bar) is derived, comes from *demi-stroc*, which was a measure of wine.

"ZINC"

The *zinc*, or bar-counter, whose elongated shape often dictates that of the room, is the focal point of any café. It first appeared in the 19th-century *assommoirs* (cheap bars), as it enabled a greater number of customers to be served. At that time it was made of an alloy of tin and zinc, from which it derived its name: some fine examples still exist.

SALON ON THE STREET

With its glass façade tempting you to take some time out, the Parisian café functions as a salon on the street. Right from the start, this nonpartisan, democratic meeting place provided intellectuals with a perfect forum for debate and inspiration. Diderot and D'Alembert probably

launched the *Encyclopédie* at the Procope. Molière and Voltaire, who lived nearby, were regular customers. Camille Desmoulins incited the people to revolt from the Café de Foy in the Palais-Royal. The surrealists, followed by Sartre and De Beauvoir, transformed certain cafés in St-Germain-des-Prés into literary meccas.

THE WAITER

The traditional costume worn by a café waiter, or *rondin*, is black trousers, white shirt, bow tie and a waistcoat with many pockets for dividing up the loose change. A white apron encircles his waist, calling to mind a log of wood, or *rondin*. Every year a waiters' contest is organized in Paris.

43

Every twenty years or so, Paris invents new locations for entertainment, places where you can eat and drink while watching a show. The Revolution had its *cafés-chantants* (cafés with performing artists), the July Monarchy its musical societies and glee clubs, the Belle Époque its *café-concerts* (cafés with live music) and their working-class equivalent in music halls, the 20th century its music-hall revues and its cabarets. In the 1970's *café-théâtre* (cafés with live theater) took over, encouraging a new generation of actors and authors. Today, there is a revival of *cafés-chantants*, small bistros with performances by musicians and raconteurs in a friendly, informal location.

CAFÉS-CONCERTS

Derived from the simple cafés which welcomed appearances by artistes, the *cafés-concerts* became an institution under the Second Empire. From 1870, establishments, designed to stage shows (Folies-Bergère, Ba Ta Clan, Moulin-Rouge), developed similarities with music-hall.

THE RETURN OF CAFÉS-CHANTANTS

Music and song are making a decisive comeback in Parisian cafés. Often tiny, these cafés have strange and evocative names – Le Baron Rouge (the Red Baron), L'Ogre de Barbarie (the Barbaric Ogre), L'Oreille Cassée (the Split Ear), La Patate Bleue (the Blue Potato), La Liberté. Eclectic in style, they are also responsible for reviving the tradition of accordion music and French ballad.

PARISIAN REVUE

The revue consisted of various performances by scantily-clad women on a raised stage. The revue was at its height during the the inter-war period with its stars Mistinguett and Josephine Baker.

Grand Succès de la Revue du Moulin Rouge

VALSE CHALOUPÉE
"The Apach's Dance"

Créée et réglée par M. MAX DEARLY
Dansée par MISTINGUETT' et MAX DEARLY
dans "LA REVUE DU MOULIN"

sur des motifs
DE
J. OFFENBACH

Nº 1. Piano seul .... Prix: 6ᶠ
Nº 2. Piano et Violon 6ᶠ
Nº 3. Mandoline et Piano .. 6ᶠ

Paris, CHOUDENS. Éditeur
30, Boulevard des Capucines, 30

U.S.A Copyright by Choudens, 1908.

ARTISTIC CABARETS

Heir to the glee clubs of the July Monarchy – working-class choirs singing songs by anti-establishment poets in the backrooms of small bars – the artistic cabaret was born in Montmartre at the end of the last century. Aristide Bruant and Yvette Guilbert invented the political and satirical song at the Mirliton and at the Divan Japonais. The impertinent and provocative spirit of cabaret was kept alive in the 1920's at the Boeuf sur le Toit, then after the war in St-Germain-des-Prés.

CAFÉ-THÉÂTRE

In the 1960's a generation of young authors and actors in search of unconventional places to perform directed their attention to cafés. A new genre and a new term was born – *café-théâtre*. Le Royal in Montparnasse, La Vieille Grille in the Latin Quarter and Le Fanal in Les Halles were among the trail-blazers. *Café-théâtre*, a melting pot of new talent which was responsible for the discovery of artists such as Coluche and Gérard Depardieu, is still going strong and favors witty and satirical material.

SCHOOL FOR ARTISTES

Cafés-chantants, cabarets and *café-théâtres*, where artistes perform to demanding audiences at close proximity, have always played a role in fostering new talent. Georges Brassens and Léo Ferré (left) made their debuts in cabarets during the 1950's.

Between Avenue Foch and Faubourg-St-Antoine, between the Étoile and the Bastille, two very different worlds are juxtaposed. The spotless rows of houses in the west provide a contrast with the motley collections of buildings in the east. However, the boundary between bourgeois Paris and working-class Paris, the residential west and the industrial east, is not quite so clear-cut. The phenomenon of fashionable quarters, which had become the exclusive property of the élite in the 19th century, is now on the wane. Paris, emptied of a working class which has moved out to the suburbs, and populated mainly by white-collar workers and professionals, is now only a small part of Greater Paris.

The victorious bourgeoisie of the 19th century, symbolized by the portrait of François Bertin (Ingres, 1832). Around 1900, gangs of hooligans ▲ *410* (below), who held sway in Belleville, embodied the insolent humor of working-class Paris.

THE FASHIONABLE QUARTERS
Paris was split in two during the 19th century with Haussmann's remodeling of the capital and the proliferation of buildings entirely devoted to the bourgeoisie. In the west were the stylish quarters, which annexed the suburb of Neuilly, making it part of the exclusive bourgeois domain. In the east were the working-class quarters, with their narrow streets and workshops.

THE PIANO NOBILE

Until the beginning of the 19th century, the different social classes lived in the same areas, and often under the same roof. But fortunes dwindled the higher you climbed (above). The *piano nobile*, with its high ceilings and lavishly decorated windows, was on the second or third floor.

NAP VERSUS RAP

Two types of Parisian youth. *Nap* refers to the epicenter of the stylish west, the quarters of Neuilly, Auteuil and Passy.

HOW THE EAST WAS WON

In the early 1980's many artists and professionals moved to the old workshops in eastern Paris. Restoration and large-scale public works – Bercy, Bastille, Tolbiac – have created some prestigious buildings in this area. The former divide between east and west is eroding.

● LEFT BANK, RIGHT BANK

"The wind of intellect does not blow across the Pont du Carrousel", stated the writer Roger Martin du Gard before World War Two.

6ᵉ Arrᵗ
PLACE SAINT-GERMAIN DES-PRÉS

RIVE DROITE ITINERAIRE CONSEILLE ➤ The Seine crisscrosses Paris and symbolically divides the city into two worlds. The Right Bank is the world of business, luxury and commerce, while the Left Bank represents the world of culture, education and the professions. This dichotomy, which dates back to the 12th century, reached its peak in the 1930's and 1940's, when St-Germain-des-Prés aspired to the title of cultural center of the world.

THE LATIN-SPEAKING BANK
The cultural calling of the 5th, 6th and 7th arrondissements, on the Left Bank, began to take shape in the 12th century with the foundation of the University. The Latin Quarter ▲ 246 was so called because the majority of its inhabitants spoke Latin. Although most of the universities and

important schools have moved out of the area, it has not lost its reputation, albeit purely symbolic today, of being the quarter of the intellectual élite. There are still some prestigious institutions here, such as the Louis-le-Grand and the Henri IV *lycées* and the École Normale Supérieure or "Normale Sup", a teacher-training college.

"LE VENTRE DE PARIS"
Among the first business activities to gain a foothold on the Right Bank were the markets on the site of what was to be the central covered market, or *ventre* (belly) *de Paris*. Haussmann's town-planning program was mainly on the Right Bank.

THE BUSINESS QUARTER
Dedicated to business, the Right Bank is the site of banks, insurance companies, head offices, prestigious hotels and department stores.

THE LITERARY REPUBLIC
Because of its schools and universities, the Left Bank acted as a magnet for publishing-related trades. As early as the Middle Ages illuminators took up residence in the Latin Quarter. This area still has the highest concentration of publishing houses and bookstores in Paris, and it is considered *de rigueur* for a writer to live on the Left Bank. Place St-Germain-des-Prés is the epicenter of this

literary republic, where even the cafés (Lipp, Flore and Deux Magots) award literary prizes.

ARCHITECTURE

Because it was founded on a limestone basin, Paris has largely been built out of stone. Until the 18th century, the materials for its monuments came from quarries in the city's basements, and excavations accounted for nearly 10 percent of the capital's surface. Later on these materials were quarried from neighboring regions, particularly the Oise. Besides freestone, many of these quarries supplied rough-hewn limestone and gypsum, or plaster, which were the basic components used in everyday architecture. Brick, which was given pride of place in the town-planning programs of Henri IV and Louis XIII, made a comeback at the end of the 19th century. Zinc (used for roofs), glass and iron (often combined), and concrete were the three great innovations of the last century.

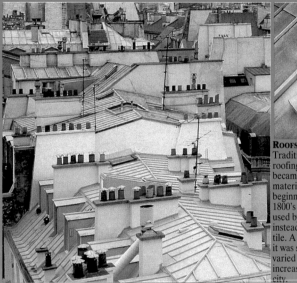

ROOFS
Traditionally used for roofing details, zinc became a full roofing material at the beginning of the 1800's and was widely used by Haussmann instead of slate and tile. A soft material, it was suitable for the varied roof work in an increasingly built-up city.

BRICK
Regarded for many years as a filling material, brick was used in addition to stone at the end of the 19th century, playing its part in the revival of modern ornamental style. During the interwar period Parisian brick reached its apogee; it was used for many public buildings, such as the Institute of Art and Archeology, almost to the exclusion of all other materials.

STONE. Freestone was widely used in buildings designed by Haussmann. From the 1930's onward, stone was used in the form of a facing attached by clamps or cement. The modern Parisian building was created by the architect Roux-Spitz, who pioneered this technique. Today there is an ongoing debate between supporters of stone and champions of glass.

PLASTER

Until the 19th century stone was reserved for public buildings and mansions for the wealthy, while creators of more ordinary housing opted for a plaster façade over a wooden structure filled with brick, rough-hewn limestone and rubble. Plaster façades were often decorated with moldings, cornices or fluting, which were meant to imitate the appearance of stone. These composite buildings were said to be built of "Paris stone".

IRON AND GLASS

From the Eiffel Tower to Beaubourg, there has always been a whiff of revolt in the use of iron. Appearing in the late 1800's, it was soon used in conjunction with glass. The use of glass has recently been revived in the form of cemented glass walls.

555,000 GOLD LEAVES This is the number of gold leaves which were used to regild the dome of Les Invalides. Often statues and railings were also gilded.

The first town-planning regulations were implemented in Paris as early as the Middle Ages. These have been modified and supplemented over the centuries in response to the vagaries of land apportionment, changing trends in housing, and large-scale town-planning projects. They governed land use, the height of buildings in relation to the road width, and the design of façades. Occasionally they determined the way buildings were decorated and the materials used in their construction. The uniformity of the urban landscape of Paris is due to their strict application.

The narrow plots of land and the cantilevered buildings of the Middle Ages.

Alignment and widening of the streets in the 17th century.

THE FIRST SIDEWALKS

Sidewalks first appeared at the end of the 18th century. They transformed the Parisian landscape, since their arrival led to the disappearance of the central gutter, which ran down the center of the road like an open sewer, in favor of cambered roads. Rambuteau, prefect of the Seine between 1833 and 1848, built the first wide avenues with side gutters, prefiguring Haussmann's system for the city.

First thoroughfares by Rambuteau.

HAUSSMANNIZATION

The 1859 regulations set extremely stringent building standards. The design and materials of façades were often prescribed, as was the size of buildings: they had to be between 49 to 82 feet long and measure 66 feet to the cornice, on top of which a further 16½ feet was allowed for the attic. This gave the new boulevards a square profile, their width being equal to the height of the buildings at the cornice.

1859: Haussmann's standards.

1902: Buildings were higher and their decoration more lavish.

20 ft.

72 ft.

Façade: 1

STREETS IN THE MIDDLE AGES
Plots of land were long and narrow (16½ by 98 feet), a legacy from the agricultural system. Cantilevered wooden structures jutted out over the streets, which had no sidewalks and at best had been provided with a central gutter for drainage (opposite page, top).

SPLENDORS OF THE BELLE ÉPOQUE
The 1902 regulations softened the severity of Haussmann's designs: bow windows were allowed to hang out over the street, buildings could be 115 feet wide and 72 feet high up to the cornice, and a further 20 feet was allowed for the story set back from the street. Attics and façades boasted a wealth of ornamentation, which was to disappear in the 1930's.

HEALTH AND EMBELLISHMENT
As early as the Middle Ages the city made recommendations regarding fire prevention, sewage disposal and street lighting, without a great deal of success. In 1607 the monarchy required that buildings be aligned along the street. At the end of the 17th century cantilevered structures projecting out over the road were prohibited, and the use of fire-resistant plaster as a revetment for façades, as well as the use of brick and stone for the first rented houses, became requirements.

1967: Irregularly spaced, high-rise buildings and sidewalks.

Height of building = width of road.

1967: A BREAK WITH THE PAST
The 1967 regulations genuinely altered the Parisian landscape. Buildings could now soar as high as 121 feet, but they had to be set back from the road so as not to block the light. This change, which favored the erection of high-rise buildings, broke up the continuity of the streets.

CONTEMPORARY SYNTHESIS
In 1977 new regulations insisted that buildings must once again be aligned along the street and be a height in proportion with the width of the road. These regulations also preserved rulings made in the previous decade concerning light; consequently, inner courtyards had to be generously proportioned. On the other hand, façades were still of a considerable length. These regulations produced a series of Haussmann pastiches which soon gave way to a great architectural eclecticism, providing a showcase for every trend imaginable.

72 ft.

1977: The well-spaced, eclectic city.

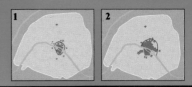

Paris remained within its 14th-century city walls for many years despite its steady growth in population (2). The demolition of this wall by Louis XIV, and the later inclusion of extensive tracts of open land within the customs barrier of the Farmers General Wall (4), did nothing to encourage expansion, as the inhabitants preferred to congregate near the center of the city, with its thriving business activities. In the early decades of the 19th

THE PHILIPPE-AUGUSTE WALL (1213) (1). Over 3 miles long, this wall encompassed an equal area on either side of the Seine: the river was blocked by chains near the Pont des Arts in the west, and Pont Marie and Pont de la Tournelle in the east. The wall was never demolished, and some parts of it still survive, mainly in the Marais.

THE CHARLES V RAMPART WALL (1383) (2). This wall enlarged the area on the Right Bank encompassed by the Philippe-Auguste wall. It followed the present route of the Pont Royal, Porte St-Denis, Porte St-Martin and Bassin de l'Arsenal. Around 1635, Louis XIII enlarged it toward the northwest (3). It marked the boundaries of the area of the Right Bank that was not marshland; beyond that stretched an old channel of the Seine.

THE NEW COURSE (1705) (3). Since France's borders were now defended, Louis XIV demolished the fortifications built by Charles V and Louis XIII on the Right Bank, replacing them with a wide promenade. The main gates, like those of St-Denis and St-Martin, were adorned with triumphal arches. This wide boulevard became the center of Parisian life in the mid-19th century.

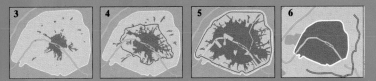

century, a rapid growth in population, the first affordable public transport systems, and the commitment of the authorities to ease traffic around the center reversed this trend. By the time the Thiers fortifications (5) were demolished, around 1920, the city wall had not been used for defensive purposes for many years. The famous *fortifs* had become popular places to take a stroll, and a huge shanty town stretched over the area, which was unsuitable for development.

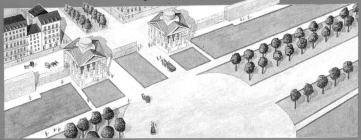

THE FARMERS GENERAL WALL (1787) (4). Built in order to collect taxes on goods bound for the capital, the wall had no defensive function. Forming a ring over 328 feet wide, it followed a north–south route corresponding to the present Nation–Étoile Metro line. Sixty tollhouses, designed by the architect Ledoux of which four have survived were posted along the wall.

THE THIERS FORTIFICATIONS (1844) (5). Stretching 24 miles these fortifications form the longest city wall in the world. Replaced in the interwar period, they formed a 984-foot-wide barrier unsuitable for development. Sixteen isolated forts, such as Mount Valérien, stood several miles outside the fortifications.

THE PÉRIPHÉRIQUE (1973) (6). This ring road is 22 miles long, of which 4 miles are underground. Acting as a modern city wall, it can be crossed only in certain places. Unlike the uniform façades constructed along the boulevards, the landscape bordering the *périf* is as disordered as it is disparate. The *périphérique* marks the administrative limits of the capital.

Lutetia in the Gallo-Roman period.

In 52 BC, Caesar's general Labenius seized Lutetia, the city of the Parisii. Like other cities in Gaul, its architecture and layout were to be completely remodeled along Roman lines. The rustic Gallic houses were replaced by houses lining a grid of streets. A new town, supplied with water from an aqueduct, sprang up on Mount Ste-Geneviève, on the Left Bank of the river, where the main public monuments stood. Around the end of the 3rd century, the threat of barbarian invasion forced the inhabitants to fortify the island and convert the Forum into a fortress. The city had been renamed Paris and became the capital of the Frank kingdom under Clovis; it was to stagnate until the Capetians came to power in the 10th century.

PLAN OF LUTETIA

Shortly after the conquest, town planners imposed a typically Roman plan encompassing the Île de la Cité and Mount Ste-Geneviève; this was where the forum, three thermal baths, a theater and an amphitheater were built. The *cardo*, or north–south road, was laid and supplemented by a grid of secondary roads. The *cardo* continued toward Senlis and Orléans. The cemeteries were situated outside the town along the main roads.

BOATMEN'S PILLAR

Erected on the Île de la Cité in the early part of the 1st century, this public monument was dedicated to the emperor Tiberius and to Jupiter by the boatmen's guild. The combined images of Gallic and Roman gods bear witness to the early assimilation of indigenous divinities into the Roman pantheon.

THERMAL HEATING
Furnaces in the basement sent hot air into a cavity called the *hypocaust* beneath the *caldarium* and the *tepidarium*. Ceramic pipes, or *tabuli*, carried the warm air inside the partitions, heating floors, pools and walls.

CONSOLES
The vaulting of the *frigidarium* rests on the prows of merchant ships, the seal of the boatmen's guild.

MASONRY
The mortar masonry, alternating rubble and brick, was concealed by painted plaster.

FORUM
This building was a religious, political and commercial complex, the nerve center of any Roman city. Lutetia's Forum stretched over 590 feet on what is now the Rue Soufflot, from the Boulevard St-Michel to the Rue St-Jacques. Here, as everywhere, it formed a self-contained area closed to urban traffic.

THE HEART OF THE CITY
Within the Forum stood a great temple and a civic and judicial basilica running eastward along the *cardo*. The central area was surrounded by porticos housing shops, which doubled as a shelter and a meeting place. These shops opened onto the streets surrounding the Forum.

A VAST COMPLEX
Apart from the main buildings, the thermal-baths complex included a vast open space used as an outdoor gymnasium. This complex, along with Lutetia's two other thermal baths, reveals the great emphasis placed on physical fitness in Lutetia, like everywhere else in the Roman empire. The thermal baths played a key part in the Romanization of the city.

CLUNY THERMAL BATHS
These thermal baths in the north are Lutetia's finest monument. The immense vaulted *frigidarium* (cold room) can still be seen, as can the remains of the *caldarium* and the *tepidarium*, as well as one of two gymnasiums (bottom left), formerly covered. Its water came from the Wissous aqueduct.

MEDIEVAL PARIS:
THE URBAN INFRASTRUCTURE

The city which Clovis made the center of his kingdom in 508 still bo
the marks of its Gallo-Roman heritage, with its ramparts, network
public roads, thermal baths and arenas. The Île de la Cité was the
site of the kings' palace, while the episcopal complex which was to
give birth to Notre-Dame cathedral sprawled along the eastern
tip. Geographic and economic factors as much as
religious and intellectual considerations contributed
to the growth of Paris from the 6th century
through the Middle Ages, first on the Left
Bank, then the Right Bank. A series of
city walls marked the spread of Paris
and its suburbs.

Paris in 1380.

**PARIS AT THE DEATH
OF CHARLES V**
With 1,082 acres
inside the city walls
and a population of
100,000, Paris was the
largest city in France.

GEOGRAPHIC FACTORS

The waters
of the Marne,
the Oise, the
Yonne, the
Loing and the Seine
converge in the Paris
Basin, which was
originally easily
accessible. The
Bièvre and the Sèvre
also flowed into the
Seine in Paris. The
river, whose course
was more convoluted
at that time, and the
marais (marsh),
which gave its name
to the oldest quarter
on the Right Bank,
used to form a double
defense. This role was
assumed by the city
walls when the marsh
was drained and the
city spread along
the banks. The
Seine became the
main artery of
transport for
foodstuffs and
merchandise.

ECONOMIC FACTORS

From the Île de la Cité, businesses and shops sprawled along the existing roads around the bridges and gates, although growth was more dynamic on the Right Bank than the Left. Trading activity increased along the riverbank between St-Gervais and St-Merry, where it was easy to land. The butchers' guild, followed by many others, took up residence near the Châtelet, and the first markets were built in 1183.

RELIGIOUS FACTORS

Between the palace and the episcopal complex, a dense web of homes and businesses sprang up in the Île de la Cité, encircling the churches, hospices and monasteries. On the banks of the Seine around the fortified monasteries founded in the 6th century, various rural market towns appeared: St-Germain-des-Prés and Ste-Geneviève on the Left Bank, and St-Martin-des-Champs on the Right Bank.

INTELLECTUAL FACTORS

The first important intellectual development in Paris took place on the Île de la Cité and the Left Bank, where eminent lecturers such as Pierre Abelard attracted up to 10,000 students. The colleges founded to accommodate them were to become reputable schools.

THE NETWORK OF PUBLIC ROADS

The Île de la Cité was linked to the riverbanks by four bridges. The quays formed the city's first promenades.

Gothic architecture, whose main innovations were the systematic use of ribbed vaults and pointed arches, was first used for royal residences in and around the Île-de-France in the early 12th century, taking the place of Romanesque architecture. There are several periods of Gothic architecture: early Gothic, from 1125 to 1290; classical Gothic, up to 1250; Rayonnant Gothic, up to 1380; and Flamboyant Gothic up to the beginning of the 16th century.

ST-MARTIN-DES-CHAMPS

Both the multifoil plan and the carving of this church, built around 1130, are still Romanesque in inspiration. However, Gothic innovations can be seen in the spatial layout (double ambulatory, open radiating chapels and large central chapel), as well as in the vaults of the choir supported by buttresses and in the ribbed vaults.

ST-GERMAIN-DES-PRÉS

This church, with its radiating chapels and flying buttresses dating from the middle of the 12th century reveals an architectural innovation in its treatment of the choir. This formula was to be widely adopted and developed by Gothic architecture.

NOTRE-DAME

When the upper windows of the choir were enlarged, flying buttresses rising 49 feet were added and chapels were built between them. The combination of stone and metal in Rayonnant-style Gothic architecture meant that windows could be larger, as can be seen in the south rose window of Notre-Dame (1258–70).

CAPITALS

The slender capitals of Ste-Chapelle, with their floral decoration and colors set off by gold, share the monument's mystic symbolism.

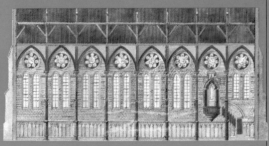

BASTILLE
Used first for defense, then as a state prison, the Bastille is an example of military art from the Gothic period: the firepower was concentrated in the base and on the flat roof.

REFECTORY OF ST-MARTIN-DES-CHAMPS
This building, whose dimensions (39 by 138 feet) make it unique, is a testimony to the consummate technical mastery of the classical Gothic architects, in this case Pierre de Montreuil. The two naves with their ribbed vaults, the slender columns which separate them, and the quality of the decoration are its crowning glories.

LOUVRE
The pillar in the *salle basse* of the royal château is an example of the intense stylistic development which took place during the classical period of Gothic architecture.

TOUR DE JEAN-SANS-PEUR
A rare example of Parisian feudal architecture, this early-15th-century tower still has its spiral staircase, which is crowned with a vault boasting some remarkable floral decoration.

STE-CHAPELLE
The spire of Ste-Chapelle dates from 1853. Its restoration, like that of the rest of the building, ranks among the most successful projects of the 19th century. Resting on a delicate cast-iron frame, the present spire is modeled on the one by the carpenter Robert Fouchier, who at the end of the 14th century erected a flawless gem of Rayonnant-style Gothic architecture.

TOUR ST-JACQUES
The archivolts (moldings around the arches), pinnacles and gables make this a masterpiece of Flamboyant-style Gothic architecture.

Royal squares – spaces created as settings for statues of sovereigns – are among the Ancien Régime's most enduring urban initiatives. The five in Paris bear witness to the dynastic continuity of the Bourbons from Henri IV to Louis XV, in spite of the fact that they do not adhere to a fixed model. Open-plan to a greater or lesser degree, their architecture as well as the symbolism of the décor and statuary evolved in line with the monarchy's changing political requirements.

THE WARRIOR KING
At night, four lamps in the Place des Victoires are used to illuminate this statue of Louis XIV surrounded by captives.

PLACE DAUPHINE
Henri IV set about changing the face of Paris by creating a coherent urban ensemble on the tip

of the Île de la Cité linked to the Pont-Neuf. This bridge, which was devoid of houses, at last made it possible for the city to open out onto the river. The ensemble of buildings did not assume its true significance until the addition of the statue of the king.

PLACE DE LA CONCORDE
The former Place-Louis-XV completed the Right Bank's triumphal perspective: buildings were constructed on one side only, thereby respecting continuity. The two palaces by Gabriel (right), which form the monumental decoration of the square, were inspired by the colonnade at the Louvre. The positioning of the equestrian statue of Louis XV at the intersection of the two main axes is in accordance with the traditional 17th-century scheme.

TO THE WEST
Initially on the outskirts of the city, Place de la Concorde paved the way for Paris to be extended westward.

PLACE DES VOSGES

Except for the two large pavilions which indicate the entrances, the brick and stone houses boast a uniformity accentuated by the closed nature of this urban cloister (above).

The individual houses can be distinguished only by looking at the division of the roofs.

PLACE DES VICTOIRES. This perfect circle (above), designed as a setting for the statue of Louis XIV, was one of the major sites dedicated to royalty.

LOUIS XV
Bouchardon revived the tradition of the equestrian statue by glorifying the virtues of the peacemaking king.

The concept of the town as a well-ordered organism took hold under Louis XIV. The fact that the kingdom was now defended at its borders made Paris an open city surrounded by wide boulevards, while triumphal gates, like those of St-Denis and St-Martin, replaced the old city gates. The Academy of Architecture, founded in 1671, created an appreciation for an increasingly austere style of architecture, which could be seen in the simplicity of the decoration, the moderate proportions and the constant preoccupation with symmetry. French-style classicism had arrived.

INVALIDES
The epitome of classical architecture, the Invalides' uncompromising symmetry drew its inspiration from the Escorial near Madrid.

OBSERVATORY
The first national observatory dates from 1667. Its façades are oriented toward the cardinal points of the compass and boast a precision which reflects that of the exact sciences, emphasized by the horizontal balustrade. The structure was built of top-quality stone laid with meticulous care. This building, which is reminiscent of a civil-engineering structure or a fortification, prefigures the rationalist architecture of the 18th century.

HÔTEL DES INVALIDES
In 1670, Louis XIV decided to erect a hospital for his soldiers. The building displays a long, austere façade, simply adorned by dormer windows shaped like trophies; at either end groups of statues serve as pediments. This severity acts as a foil for the central frontispiece, a genuine triumphal arch erected to the glory of the king. Long, sober buildings, gallery-covered arcades and enclosed square courts are evocative of a barracks or a convent.

FAÇADE OF ST-ROCH
This faithfully reflects the classical design of Jesuit style: a high bay with a pediment between two low bays, all punctuated by columns.

ST-LOUIS-DES-INVALIDES
Like St Peter's in Rome, the church of the Invalides incorporates both an elongated plan and a cruciform plan. The austere Soldiers' Church, with three naves and based on an elongated plan, opens into the sumptuous Royal Chapel, which is designed on a cruciform plan and is crowned by two superposed domes, a system which allowed the fresco of the lower dome to be illuminated indirectly.

CHURCH OF ST-ROCH
Begun in 1653 by Lemercier, the church (above) is, at 410 feet long, one of the largest in Paris. Its dimensions and the quality of its decoration also make it one of the finest examples of classical architecture.

Although its façade combines baroque and classical elements, its interior is medieval: a barrel-vaulted nave with lunettes, aisles with chapels, a deep choir and a transept with almost nonexistent arms. The two chapels beyond the choir, extended later by the Calvary chapel, create a sequence of theatrical effects which are highly baroque in flavor. This unusual plan was never repeated.

BERNINI COLONNADE
In 1664 Bernini submitted a highly baroque plan for the colonnade of the Louvre. His plan was rejected after work was started, but the combination of a rusticated first floor and two stories joined by an order of colossal proportion was to be a source of inspiration for many architects.

COLONNADE OF THE LOUVRE
In 1667 Louis XIV accepted the plan by Charles Perrault for the Louvre's east façade, oriented toward the city. Although its high base reflects Italian tradition, the scale of its colonnade is baroque and the severity of its straight lines is classical.

PARISIAN MANSIONS

At the end of the Middle Ages, the city's mansions, or *hôtels*, were built around an inner courtyard used by one family alone. In the 16th century this plan was codified: a main building in which every room overlooked both the courtyard and the garden, two wings forming a U-shape housing the outbuildings and a gallery, and an enclosed courtyard on the street side. Having made its first appearance in the Marais, the mansion spread to the faubourgs St-Germain and St-Honoré in the 17th century. It remained U-shaped in plan, but the layout of the rooms became more complicated. By the end of the 18th century, the wings had disappeared completely.

HÔTEL CARNAVALET

The only surviving 16th-century mansion in Paris, this has been greatly modified. With it, the plan of the mansion became truly urban: the modest building overlooking the street housed the kitchens and stables, while the main residence was sheltered at the back of the courtyard.

HÔTEL DE CLUNY

The mansion owned by the abbots of Cluny (above), whose construction was started in 1480, is a very early example of a typical Parisian mansion. Its main building is sandwiched between courtyard and garden, its left wing has a superposed portico and gallery, and its boundary wall overlooks the street. It is entered by an external turret staircase, a distinguishing feature of wealthy residences.

HÔTEL MATIGNON

The interior layout of the rooms in the double main buildings was improved in the 18th century, as seen in this mansion from 1720. The symmetry of two suites of rooms divided by a longitudinal wall was replaced by a more irregular layout. The two façades overlooking the courtyard and the garden are not aligned, a feature handed down from the early 17th century.

The recessed gateway allows carriages to maneuver more easily.

FRONT ELEVATION
Two large pavilions framing a small, flat-roofed entrance indicate the grandeur of this stone-built mansion.

HÔTEL DE SULLY

Impeccably restored, the Hôtel de Sully (below) is the epitome of the grand Parisian early-17th-century mansion. It faithfully reproduces the U-shaped plan of the previous century: it has a single main building, each room overlooks both garden and courtyard; and the central stairwell is crossed to get from one to the other. The lavish ornamentation of its façades is in keeping with Renaissance style. The mansion still has an orangery at the back of its gardens.

GALLERY OF THE HÔTEL LA VRILLIÈRE

The gallery (above), a room designed as a showcase for a mansion's splendor, was used for receptions. The heavy Rococo décor of this room dates from 1718.

ROOFS

Until the 17th century, mansions had steeply pitched Gothic roofs with high stone dormer windows. They then adopted curb or mansard roofs, with discrete wooden dormer windows, occasionally concealed by a balustrade. These roofs were much better suited to the double main buildings.

Tall, steeply pitched, medieval-style roofs.

Classical mansard roofs.

WINGS

Wings of the same height as the main building were characteristic of the early 17th century.

HÔTEL BIRON

Constructed in 1727, this mansion (right) typifies the move toward a greater sophistication in design with its isolated main building and borrowings from contemporary châteaux.

The architects of the Enlightenment did their utmost to contribute to social progress. Every type of building was remodeled so that its layout and character reflected its function. This craving for modernity was most clearly seen in public architecture, which enabled architects to reinterpret classical models using simplified forms and new techniques. By appealing both to the senses and to reason, this architecture applied a certain logic to the urban landscape.

ODÉON

The vogue for theatergoing in the second half of the 18th century transformed the urban auditorium (left). It was promoted to the rank of a public monument, reviving classical traditions. The Nouvelle-Comédie (1782) was a recognizable, autonomous block whose façade was graced with a portico but no pediment. The interior layout reflected an emphasis on audience comfort.

THE NATION'S FIRST TEMPLE

The basilica of Ste-Geneviève by Soufflot (1755–90), a meditation on the foundations of architecture, ushered in the neoclassical era.

AN ELOQUENT URBAN ART

The plan for a monumental theater presupposed an expressive urban setting. The Nouvelle-Comédie fitted into a new residential district, creating an unexpected rapport between a public building and its surroundings. It governed the way this quarter was divided up, with five radiating streets (above) leading to an amphitheatrical square which functioned as a curtain-raiser to the theater; these streets were lined with elegant uniform buildings. This was the first district in Paris to have English-style sidewalks.

BETWEEN CHÂTEAU AND MANSION

The desire for privacy, along with a courtly life style of conversation, music and amateur theatricals, accounted for the construction of small houses, or follies, around Paris and in its new quarters. In 1770, Ledoux erected a pavilion for a kept dancer, Mademoiselle Guimard. He made it a temple to Terpsichore, giving free reign to his fondness for visual contrasts.

THE VILLETTE BARRIER

Around the customs barrier erected on the eve of the Revolution, Claude Nicolas Ledoux built some fifty tollhouses, which were treated as monuments. Each one is different, although they were characterized by simple geometrical forms and by their free interpretation of ancient orders.

THE PERFECT CHURCH

Soufflot set out to reform church architecture by drawing up an extremely controversial plan based on a cruciform, which was both rational and poetic. The structure was to be kept very simple by bracing it with a metal framework within the masonry and supporting it with flying buttresses. In this way, the lightness of Gothic building was united with classical harmony, the complexity of the vaulting echoing the beauty of the weight-bearing columns. The dome was made up of three cup-shaped structures.

ÉCOLE DE CHIRURGIE

This building, constructed in 1775, proved that classical art could give a new lease on life to public architecture. An open colonnade includes a doorway in the guise of a triumphal arch opening onto a temple façade; the classical theater and a demi-cupola inspired by the Panthéon merge in the lecture hall.

The Arc de Triomphe.

The population of Paris doubled during this time, and the disparity between the wealthy western part of the city and the poverty-stricken central and eastern districts became even more pronounced. The authorities planned some new thoroughfares to clean up the city and improve access to certain areas in the capital.

The Restoration was marked by the dividing up of quarters in the west of the city and the building of churches.

Arc de Triomphe
This was based on a classical model like many public buildings of the time.

St-Vincent-de-Paul
Located in the heart of a new quarter, this church was built on the basilical plan, which was common at that time.

Assemblée Nationale
The façade which decorates the front of the Assemblée Nationale (below) dates from 1806, while the building itself was the product of modifications made to the Palais Bourbon in 1795. Its Corinthian colonnade echoes that of the Madeleine, on the other side of the Place de la Concorde. It disguises the fact that the building is not in line with the bridge.

Rue de Rivoli
Initially designed to stretch as far as the Palais Royal, this urban promenade (below) overlooking the terrace of the Tuileries, was extended eastward after 1848. The homogenous façade gives the street its monumental nature, prefiguring Haussmann's grand thoroughfares.

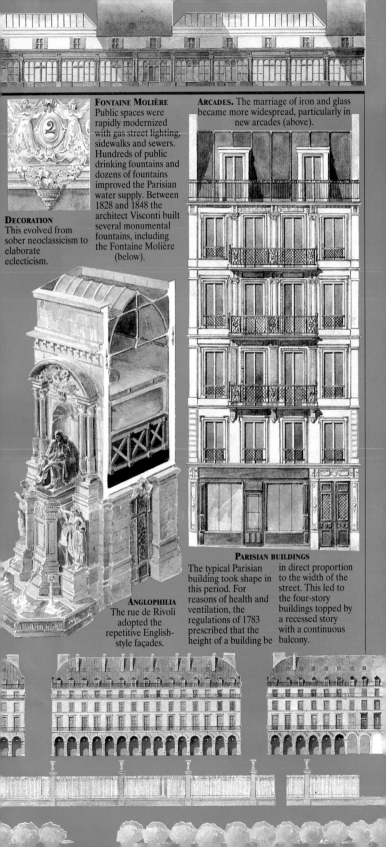

FONTAINE MOLIÈRE
Public spaces were rapidly modernized with gas street lighting, sidewalks and sewers. Hundreds of public drinking fountains and dozens of fountains improved the Parisian water supply. Between 1828 and 1848 the architect Visconti built several monumental fountains, including the Fontaine Molière (below).

DECORATION
This evolved from sober neoclassicism to elaborate eclecticism.

ARCADES. The marriage of iron and glass became more widespread, particularly in new arcades (above).

ANGLOPHILIA
The rue de Rivoli adopted the repetitive English-style façades.

PARISIAN BUILDINGS
The typical Parisian building took shape in this period. For reasons of health and ventilation, the regulations of 1783 prescribed that the height of a building be in direct proportion to the width of the street. This led to the four-story buildings topped by a recessed story with a continuous balcony.

The grand public works of Paris were the work of Georges-Eugène Haussmann, prefect of the Seine from 1853 to 1870. Besides providing buildings with a fresh water supply, extending the sewer system, creating gardens, squares and public buildings (churches, town halls, theaters, hospitals and barracks), he was also responsible for laying new roads. He envisioned a network of thoroughfares crossing Paris from one side to the other, which would move the congested center farther to the northwest. These wide roads cut across the city in an attempt to ease traffic and thereby make the city a healthier place to live, as well as to improve the appearance of the urban landscape. Some roads were even designed to combat possible civil unrest.

HAUSSMANN'S GREAT THOROUGHFARES

The Second Empire's program of road building presupposed specific financing, compulsory purchases and demolitions. However, the scheme swallowed up huge amounts of money and caused Haussmann's downfall before that of the regime. Although demolitions were carefully thought out in line with skillfully devised plans and confined to what was strictly necessary, they drove out many landlords and tenants. Only the landlords were ever compensated. The plan did not spare monuments from the Middle Ages, particularly in the Île de la Cité, whose dense infrastructure was largely destroyed.

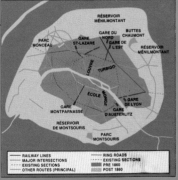

PLACE DE L'OPÉRA

Before the competition of 1860 for the construction of the Opéra, Haussmann's architects designed the square and the surrounding streets and determined the size of the buildings and the disposition of the façades. The Avenue de l'Opéra remains one of the best examples of Haussmann's straight, uniform roads, in spite of the fact that Garnier, the architect, stopped the avenue from being planted with trees.

RÉSERVOIR MÉNILMONTANT

PARC MONCEAU

GARE ST-LAZARE

GARE DU NORD

BUTTES CHAUMONT

GARE DE L'EST

RÉSERVOIR MÉNILMONTANT

LOUVRE

TURBIGO

ÉCOLE

GARE MONTPARNASSE

GARE DE LYON

GARE D'AUSTERLITZ

RÉSERVOIR DE MONTSOURIS

PARC MONTSOURIS

RAILWAY LINES	RING ROADS
MAJOR INTERSECTIONS	EXISTING SECTIONS
EXISTING SECTIONS	PRE 1860
OTHER ROUTES (PRINCIPAL)	POST 1860

THOROUGHFARE ESTHETICS

Thoroughfares in the Second Empire were characterized by straight lines. The lie of the land rmitting, their axes had to coincide with impressive vistas. This concept was applied to roads from the mid-1800's onward. The Boulevard Henri-IV provides a visual link between the July Column in the Place de la Bastille and the dome of the Panthéon.

Haussmann did not devise a program for architecture in the way that he did for the layout of the city. Although the growing problem of working-class housing concerned Napoleon III, who financed the construction of several housing projects, it left Haussmann cold. However, construction became necessary as a result of the thoroughfares: houses had to be reconstructed, and the new quarters of Paris did not have any public buildings. Haussmann preferred to use humble practitioners like Gabriel Davioud because they were easier to manipulate.

THE URBAN LANDSCAPE

Davioud designed some meticulously ordered buildings for the Place St-Michel and a fountain to match the scale of these buildings. The square sets off the corner of the Rue Danton and the Boulevard St-Michel, drawing attention away from the lack of alignment between the boulevard and the bridge, which ran counter to Second Empire tastes.

CIVIC BUILDINGS

Like monuments, civic buildings can mark the focal points of the city's structure. This is the case with the town hall in the 11th arrondissement at the corner of the Boulevard Voltaire and Avenue Parmentier (above). The building was inspired by 18th-century French style.

Eclecticism was the order of the day, and the choice of style depended on the nature of the building: neo-Byzantine, Romanesque or Gothic for churches, neo-Renaissance or classical for civic buildings. The building program for the town halls became vitally important in 1860, when the districts around Paris were annexed.

A DISCRETE MONUMENTALITY

Although Haussmann accepted that buildings should display a certain monumentality, he also believed that monuments should blend in with their urban surroundings. The two theaters by Davioud flanking the Place du Châtelet are still the most striking example of this discretion. Despite the classically monumental façades, their architecture reflects the scale of the neighboring buildings, and only the volume essential for the auditorium makes it stand out. The façades overlooking the Seine observe the rhythm and alignment of the buildings on the quayside.

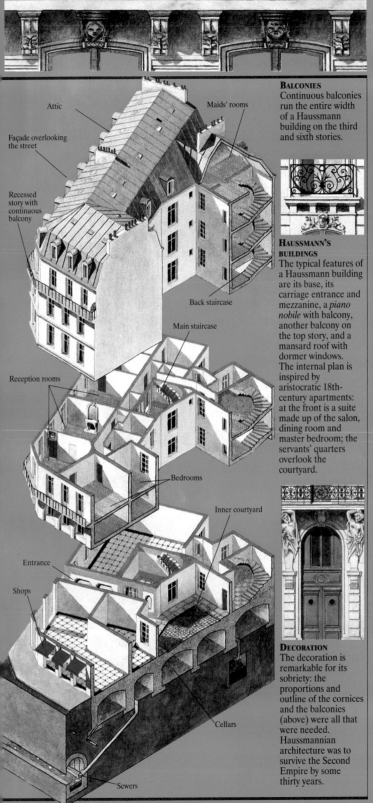

Attic

Façade overlooking the street

Recessed story with continuous balcony

Reception rooms

Entrance

Shops

Maids' rooms

Back staircase

Main staircase

Bedrooms

Inner courtyard

Cellars

Sewers

BALCONIES
Continuous balconies run the entire width of a Haussmann building on the third and sixth stories.

HAUSSMANN'S BUILDINGS
The typical features of a Haussmann building are its base, its carriage entrance and mezzanine, a *piano nobile* with balcony, another balcony on the top story, and a mansard roof with dormer windows. The internal plan is inspired by aristocratic 18th-century apartments: at the front is a suite made up of the salon, dining room and master bedroom; the servants' quarters overlook the courtyard.

DECORATION
The decoration is remarkable for its sobriety: the proportions and outline of the cornices and the balconies (above) were all that were needed. Haussmannian architecture was to survive the Second Empire by some thirty years.

75

Iron architecture, of which Paris has an abundance, proved to be one of the successes of the 19th century. Linked to the growth of industrial society, it bears witness to a symbiosis peculiar to this period between technical progress and a liking for decoration. The extent of its triumph is revealed by the debates about its esthetic appeal and modernity.

IRON AND CAST IRON

Until 1880 iron structures were supported by columns made of cast iron, a material which lent itself to ornamentation, as can be seen by the capital above.

PONT ALEXANDRE-III

Built in 1900, this was the first bridge to cross the Seine in a single span which had an almost horizontal road.

GARE DU NORD

The great station halls, like the Gare du Nord, built in 1863 (above), are among the first examples of the marriage of iron and glass, which was to be repeated in a variety of ways for countless glass roofs.

STRUCTURE AND DÉCOR

The Alexandre III bridge was inspired by the technique used for stone bridges. This made it possible to build the road lower than usual, in order not to mar the perspective between the Invalides and the Grand Palais. The vault of fifteen arches is composed of cast-steel components called *voussoirs*, which are assembled with bolts. The elaborate decoration, typical of the end of the century, is the work of several sculptors.

It has been added to the arch without distorting its purity of line, reflecting the 19th-century spirit of synthesis between ornamentation and structure.

RIVETS

The rivets used in assembly were hot-welded.

GREENHOUSES: GLASS SETTINGS
The first entirely glazed roofs were designed for greenhouses. The roof at Auteuil for the overhead section of the Metro, designed by the architect Formigé, shows how "transparent" metal can become when combined with glass.

LES HALLES
A much-imitated model, the central market, by Baltard and Callet, succeeded for the first time in combining metal, brick and glass. Les Halles was completed in 1874 and demolished in 1971.

GLASS ROOFS
The strength of iron made it possible to reduce the thickness of the uprights and let in more light. The double dome in the Galeries Lafayette exploits this.

EIFFEL TOWER
The star attraction of the Universal Exhibition of 1889, the tower ▲ 296 is a skillful framework composed of a lattice of girders which reaches a height of 984 feet.

A RATIONALIST STYLE OF ARCHITECTURE
Iron architecture is the work of both engineers and architects who sought to find a language suitable for a new material: often concealed behind more worthy stone, iron eventually made its esthetic appeal felt.

ASSEMBLY
Small posts bonded by braces support the pavement.

ORNAMENTATION
Decoration had no structural role and kept to the building's lines of force.

At the beginning of the 20th century, architectural design was characterized by the construction of lavishly decorated buildings. This new style, so dear to Guimard, was altered under the influence of theories of hygienics, and low-cost housing was developed. Sauvage with his stepped buildings and Le Corbusier with his Cité du Refuge (Salvation Army Hostel) built versions of their own social ideal. Mallet-Stevens designed a new street as if it were an avant-garde stage set, while monumental architecture reigned victorious on the Chaillot hill up until the eve of World War Two.

CAST-IRON ORNAMENTS
Anchors shaped like seahorses and railings with cheerful masks adorned the Castel Béranger. Designed and cast to the specifications of the architect, they revealed his desire to control every detail of a building, which was regarded as a work of art.

CERAMICS
Ceramic decorations were much in demand by builders at the turn of the century. The

CASTEL BÉRANGER
The Castel Béranger reveals a chaotic interplay of volumes, a mix of materials and the desire by Guimard to pay attention to each detail within this luxury apartment building, in which every apartment was different. These features, characteristic of Parisian Art Nouveau as inspired by Viollet-le-Duc, were realized around 1900.

Perret brothers used this type of decoration in 1904 on a building in the 16th arrondissement when they dropped stoneware lozenges in concrete to form plantlike motifs.

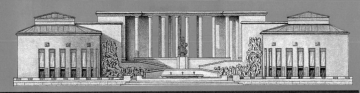

Tokyo Palace

With its colonnade on either side of a central axis and its terraces populated by hieratic sculptures, the Museum of Modern Art, built in 1937, reflects the international academic trend of the times.

Stepped buildings

The receding steps of the buildings by Henri Sauvage made the streets lighter while allowing light into all the apartments. With the low-cost housing of the Rue des Amiraux, built ten years after the block on the Rue Vavin, modern architecture had arrived on the low-cost housing market.

Layout

A rational internal layout and terraces were designed to create a new way of living.

Public amenities

Hollowing out the center of this enormous block, Sauvage installed a swimming pool for relaxation, sport and hygiene, reflecting the social aspirations of the time.

Avant-garde colors

Polychromy was the only form of decoration tolerated by the modernists, who despised bourgeois taste and excessive ornamentation: the architect became a self-styled colorist. The entrance to the Cité de Refuge, at 12, rue Cantagrel, a monumental portico built in 1933 by Le Corbusier, is treated like an exhibition pavilion. The façade of the main building was remodeled after World War Two.

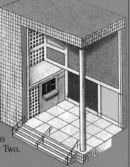

Rue Mallet-Stevens

In this uniform street by Mallet-Stevens, who ignored the burning issue of housing for the masses, there are five mansions and a caretaker's house. Inaugurated in 1927, this was to represent a manifesto for the modern city. However, despite the interplay of recessed stories, the overlapping of cubic and cylindrical volumes, and the flat roofs so admired today, these prototypes were used only by the architect, his friends and his patrons, and did not make it into general use.

Since the Renaissance, the banks of the Seine have had various urban monuments and groups of buildings erected on them. Today they are the site of projects and new districts which have extended the city center. The quarters of Bercy and Seine Rive Gauche – home of the Ministry of Finance and the Bibliothèque de France – bear witness to the attention now being paid to this part of the city center. The desire to provide the capital with public buildings which reflect its international standing, as well as the wish to revitalize architectural design in France, can be clearly seen in the remodeling of existing sites such as the Louvre.

ORSAY: A MUSEUM IN A TRAIN STATION
The conversion of the Gare d'Orsay (left) into a museum, with a central nave measuring 459 feet long and 115 feet high, was designed in conflict rather than in stylistic accord with the 19th-century building: beneath the chasing of the arches of the vault is a massive monumental aisle, as well as galleries with solid walls and a balcony.

The new quarter of Bercy (below).

BENEATH THE LOUVRE
In 1979 underground development was first used for Les Halles; it is now being applied to the heart of the city, where the infrastructure is extremely dense. The 15 acres created under the Louvre (below) eased traffic problems and provided modern machinery vital to a major museum.

BERCY
The quarter of Bercy is an example of new-style Parisian town planning, with its perfectly straight continuation of existing streets. The park, the housing which borders it on one side, the Palais Omnisports, the hotel and business complex and the proposed Maison du Cinéma have created a new center, an initiative typical of the late 1980's. The eclectic architectural styles echo the diversity of the buildings.

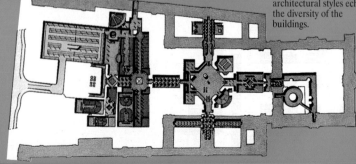

BERCY PARK HOUSING

Each U-shaped block overlooking the park surrounds a smaller building. The entire development is the product of an original approach: the uniformity of the buildings, designed by several architects, is guaranteed by the balconies which link them together, along with a set of common building regulations.

INSTITUT DU MONDE ARABE

The IMA building (below) combines the exterior and strict alignment of Haussmann's city with contemporary glass and a metal façade. The inner courtyard opening onto a narrow passage, the south façade with its Arabic shapes, the spiral library in the prow and the highly contemporary interplay of transparent effects provide endless references while successfully integrating the building into the historic heart of the city.

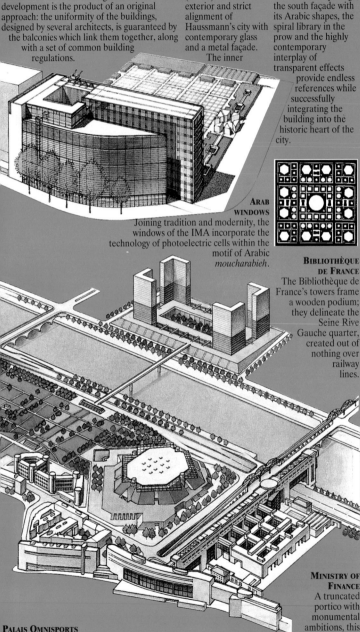

ARAB WINDOWS

Joining tradition and modernity, the windows of the IMA incorporate the technology of photoelectric cells within the motif of Arabic *moucharabieh*.

BIBLIOTHÈQUE DE FRANCE

The Bibliothèque de France's towers frame a wooden podium; they delineate the Seine Rive Gauche quarter, created out of nothing over railway lines.

MINISTRY OF FINANCE

A truncated portico with monumental ambitions, this building is heir to the megastructures of the 1970's, which often never made it off the drawing board. It enjoys a unique position in the Parisian landscape.

PALAIS OMNISPORTS

The Palais Omnisports is an unusual sight, blending in with the park owing to the turf which covers its sloping façades. This flattened pyramid, which provides a forum for sporting events and large concerts, is a showcase for numerous architectural feats.

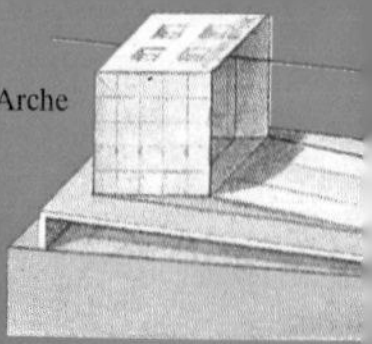

Grande Arche

La Défense demonstrates how the ideas of the modern movement have been applied to the city: isolated high-rise buildings on either side of an esplanade, and traffic relegated to the outskirts or below the immense pedestrian podium. Although La Défense has been criticized for its scale, it is a fine realization of modernity. It has broken away from the traditional cityscape yet respects the vista from the west of Paris, which governs the central open space and the position of the buildings and of the Grande Arche.

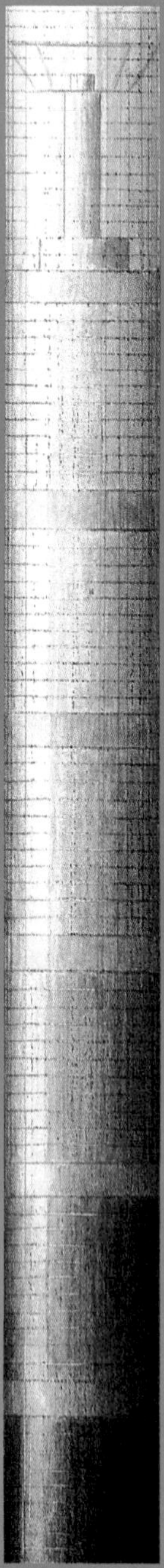

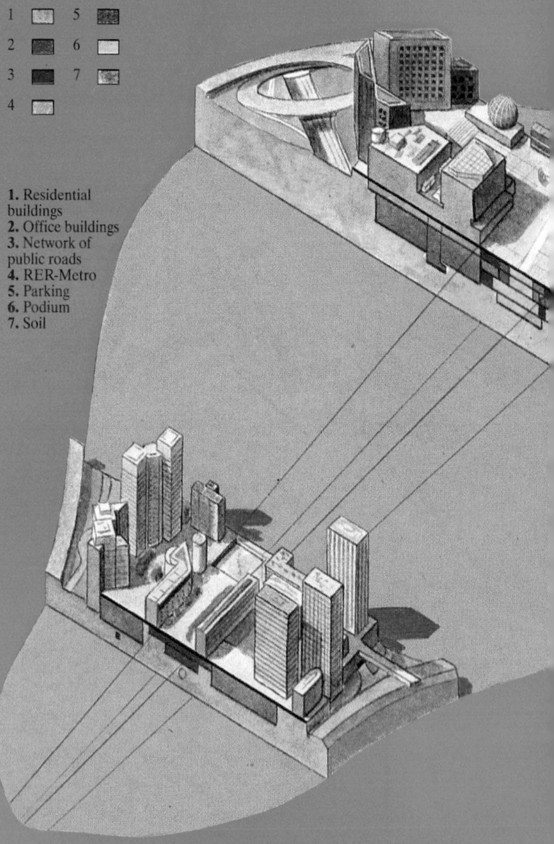

1
2
3
4
5
6
7

1. Residential buildings
2. Office buildings
3. Network of public roads
4. RER-Metro
5. Parking
6. Podium
7. Soil

LA TOUR SANS FIN
With a proposed height of 1,312 feet and a diameter of only 131 feet, giving a ratio of 1 : 10 instead of the customary 1 : 5, the "Tower of Infinity" project, the final progeny of the planners of La Défense, will now never be realized.

A TWO-TIERED CITY
La Défense resembles a ship whose water line would be marked by its podium: above, pedestrians and towers; below, layer upon layer of galleries. Trains, RER and Métro are found in the bed-rock: above these are the network of roads, then the station entrance halls, parking and various facilities.

Arc de triomphe   Arc du Carrousel

AN ARCH OUT OF LINE
From the Carrousel, the perspective of the great axis passes under the Arc de Triomphe, then over a slope to terminate at the Grande Arche. The arch is slightly out of line with the axis, and this reveals its depth and volume. The construction suspended between its walls scales down the building's proportions for pedestrians at its threshold seeing it up close.

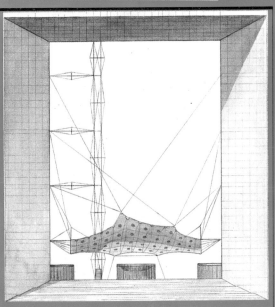

A GIANT CUBE
This almost perfect colossal cube, which measures about 361 feet high, wide and deep, could easily accommodate Notre-Dame cathedral, which rises to 305 feet.

THE GRANDE ARCHE
The Arche is supported by twelve piers, each 98 feet tall (right), integrated into a transport network where it was impossible to dig foundations. These piers carry the cube, whose upper and lower platforms and walls are held together by enormous frames. Prestressed concrete, which is commonly used in large civil engineering projects was used for the first time in this building.

CNIT
The Centre National des Industries et Techniques (CNIT), built in 1958, was La Défense's first building. It is a remarkable design owing to its concrete vault, at 781 feet one of the largest in the world. The three sections of this vault are composed of a double shell of thin concrete and rest on three abutment piers linked to each other by steel rods buried underground.

Davioud made a lasting impact on the Parisian landscape by furnishing Haussmann's boulevards and avenues with many utilitarian and decorative structures. These pieces of street furniture, supplemented from the early 1970's onward by small public conveniences in line with new requirements, still punctuate and emphasize the capital's boulevards.

FAITHFUL REPRODUCTIONS
These circular iron gratings were designed to surround the trees that were planted in rows during the Second Empire. The ones manufactured today are exact replicas.

LAMPS
These 19th-century lamps are still in use.

MORRIS COLUMNS
These columns, an early version of the hoardings which used to advertise forthcoming attractions, are topped by onion domes in the exotic style favored by the Second Empire. The current version can accommodate public toilets or telephones.

LIGHTING
With the advent of gas lighting, iron street lamps, often ornamented with plantlike motifs, made their appearance on the Parisian scene.

Double bench.

NEW FURNITURE
Bus shelters, portable toilets, public telephones and bulletin boards (below) satisfy new needs while respecting the rows of trees.

FONTAINE WALLACE
This iron drinking fountain is an archetypal example of street furniture of the 19th century. It reflected the hygienic concerns of the period.

PARIS
AS SEEN BY PAINTERS

FESTIVE PARIS

Paris provided the setting for many festivities connected with the presence of its kings, as well as for the celebrations of its populace. One of the most lavish royal celebrations was organized in 1615 on the occasion of the marriage of Louis XIII to Anne of Austria. A *carrousel* (parade) lasting three whole days took place against the backdrop of celebrations for the newly inaugurated Place Royale (now Place des Vosges). This ANONYMOUS ARTIST condensed the three days into one composition **(1)**, which serves to highlight the contrast between the attractive confusion of the entrances and the regularity of the façades. The most popular working-class festival under the Ancien Régime was the carnival. By the beginning of this century it had become a much quieter affair, amounting to a procession of floats on the third Thursday of Lent. LUIGI LOIR (1845–1916), whose prolific output was devoted almost exclusively to Paris, took the carnival as a subject for several canvases. In his *Mi-Carême à Paris* **(2)**, Loir widened the rue de Rivoli out of all proportion, making its severity, rendered in muted shades, a perfect foil for the dazzling colors of the floats. Another festival, the Universal Exhibition of 1878 ● *30*, provided France with the opportunity to show off its new-found prosperity. The streets of Paris were

decked with thousands of flags on the day of its opening, the result of a unanimous surge of patriotism. CLAUDE MONET (1840–1926) was moved by this spectacular sight. His *Rue Montorgeuil* (1878) **(4)** conveys

the shimmering effect of the moving colors and also recreates the lively confusion of movement in the street. Since July 14 was created a public holiday in 1880, this spectacle can be staged every year. RAOUL DUFY's (1877–1953) *Rue*

pavoisée **(3)** is still impressionistic in mood, but the broad strokes and the innovative use of color mark a distinct shift toward Fauvism.

86

Raoul Dufy

> "NOTHING IS MORE BEAUTIFUL THAN THE WAY THE GREAT HILL LOOKS WHEN THE SUN SHINES ON ITS SOIL OF RED OCHER, VEINED WITH GYPSUM AND CLAY...WOUND ABOUT BY RAVINES AND FOOTPATHS." GÉRARD DE NERVAL

As Canaletto did with Venice, JEAN-BAPTISTE RAGUENET (1715–93) specialized in painting the sights of Paris. With painstaking objectivity and charm, he preserved images of the city in the 18th century for future generations. One of his most meticulous paintings, *Joute des Mariniers* (4), brings to mind the water festivals which regularly took place on the Seine under the Ancien Régime and depicts the houses which crowded along the top of the Pont Notre-Dame at that time. In fact, all the bridges of Paris except the Pont-Neuf were covered with buildings which were eventually demolished by royal edict in 1786. The widespread demolitions in the reign of Napoleon III elicited a great deal of nostalgia. Many painters who loved the old medieval city strove to preserve a picture of the condemned sites for generations to come, in the same way that the photographer Atget did later on. PAUL SCHAAN, L. MEYER and ALBERT PIERSON were among these artists. Their output, although neglected, is full of charm. Schaan, with his *Bièvre au bief de la rue de Valence* (1) preserved the memory of the river which flowed through the 13th and 5th arrondissements to pour into the Seine at what is now the Gare Austerlitz. Meyer has handed down an extremely evocative view of the *Maquis de Montmartre* (2). This legendary spot, which inspired so many artists, covered the north slope of the hill. The vast area of open land was gradually covered with precarious shacks, forming an extensive shantytown which disappeared when the Avenue Junot was built. Pierson, with his *Passage des singes* (3), depicting the view of the thoroughfare between the Rue Vieille-du-Temple and the Rue des Guillemites, conjures up the intricate and complex network of courtyards and passageways which used to weave through the heart of Paris.

1	2	3
4		

Claude Monet

The metamorphosis of Paris under the Second Empire gave fresh impetus to the genre of the urban landscape: the pursuit of the picturesque was abandoned for a celebration of modernity. The most representative painter of this new type of urban landscape was CAMILLE PISSARRO (1830–1903). *L'Avenue de l'Opéra* (1897) **(2)** is typical of a whole series of bird's-eye views of the city's main thoroughfares. JEAN BÉRAUD (1849–1936), in his many *Vues du boulevard* **(3)**, shared a similar goal, but he was also fond of painting crowd scenes with a meticulous attention to detail, which gave his work a documentary quality. The Gare St-Lazare inspired MONET (1840–1926) on many occasions. In the painting *La Gare St-Lazare* (1877) **(1)**, which now hangs in the Musée d'Orsay, the immense iron-and-glass nave forms a rigid framework encompassing the thick scrolls of bluish steam belching out of the locomotive against a background of golden light. In *Toits sous la neige* **(4)**, GUSTAVE CAILLEBOTTE (1848–94) takes his search for the surprising to the extreme: his view of the capital's rooftops assumes an almost abstract quality, which gives it a singular charm.

1		
2	3	4

THE EIFFEL TOWER

The Eiffel Tower, that quintessential symbol of both modern Paris and the most daring of innovations in what was basically industrial architecture, found an admirer in ROBERT DELAUNAY (1885–1941) **(1)**. Seeing it as the steel muse of a new world which he observed, contemplated and adored from every angle, he adopted it as a favorite subject from 1909 until the end of his career. At first treated in a disjointed manner in the spirit of Cubism, the tower later became an excuse for juxtaposing rich colors which composed the painting unaided. This is the case with the canvas in the Musée d'Art Moderne **(2)**, dated 1923, in which Delaunay manages to highlight the tower's dizzy slenderness from below through a simple combination of vibrant colors. Although the Eiffel Tower had not been such a constant source of inspiration for anyone before Delaunay, many earlier painters had nevertheless taken it as a model. The most important of these is probably PAUL-LOUIS DELANCE, a little-known artist who painted an extremely attractive canvas dated January 1889 **(3)**.

"SHEPHERDESS O EIFFEL TOWER
YOUR FLOCK OF BRIDGES
ARE BLEATING THIS MORNING."
GUILLAUME APOLLINAIRE

This painting depicts the progress of the work several months before the World Exhibition opened in 1889. Shrouding the metal structure in smoke from the building site, he successfully transforms the tower into a kind of allegory for industrial activity. Several years later LOUIS-WELDEN HAWKINS (1849–1910), an Englishman who became a naturalized French citizen, gave the tower a supporting role in a strange composition (4): with its height and width chopped out of the picture, the tower is used as a foil for one of the former Trocadero's ornamental statues. After Delaunay's compositions, one of the most intense visions of the Eiffel Tower is probably that of NICOLAS DE STAËL (1914–55). After years of pure abstraction, the artist returned to a type of representation with this picture (5) in 1954. Despite the extremely simplified outlines, the monument remains perfectly recognizable.

93

From the 17th
century onward,
the banks of the
Seine have been a
frequently depicted
Parisian motif.
Certain painters,
such as JOHAN
BARTHOLD JONGKIND
(1819–91), were
more receptive to its
charms than others.
Born and trained in
Holland, he took
pains to depict the
many different faces
of the Seine during
his long stays in Paris.
His *View of Notre-
Dame* **(3)**, dating
from 1864, bears the
stamp of his meeting
with Monet, as can
be seen by the
innovative treatment
of the play of light on
moving water.
ALBERT MARQUET
(1875–1947)
restricted his views of
the Seine to a small
number of vantage
points, repeated
endlessly,
corresponding to
what he could see
from the windows of
his successive studios.
His *Vue de Notre-
Dame sous la neige*
(1) and *Vue du Pont-
Neuf, effet de*

brouillard **(2)** date
from after the Fauvist
period, which ended
in 1907. The dazzling
hues of his early
views of Paris were
replaced by a subtle
chromatic quality,
which he
subsequently favored.
Between 1899 and

1909, HENRI MATISSE
(1869–1954)
occupied a studio
near Marquet's and
also painted many
views of the Seine
during this period.
His *Notre-Dame, en
fin d'après-midi*
(1902) **(4)** is vivid
proof of this.

1		
2	4	
3		

PAUL SIGNAC (1863–1935), the theorist of Divisionism, applied his method to a great variety of subjects, including the sights of Paris. In *La Seine à Grenelle*, Signac strayed from the rules which he himself devised and broadened his stroke to such an extent that the canvas looks like a mosaic.

PARIS AS SEEN BY WRITERS

PARISIANS

IMPRESSIONS OF PARIS

The most celebrated English biography is a group portrait in which one extraordinary man paints the picture of a dozen more. At the center of a brilliant circle, James Boswell (1740-95) captures the powerful, troubled and witty figure of Samuel Johnson (1709-84), who, in the year 1775 went to travel through France, and spent some time in Paris.

❝OCT. 10. Tuesday. We saw the *Ecole Militaire*, in which one hundred and fifty young boys are educated for the army. They have arms of different sizes, according to the age; – flints of wood. The building is very large, but nothing fine except the council-room. The French have large squares in the windows; – they make good iron palisades. Their meals are gross. **❞**

❝We passed through *Place de Vendôme*, a fine square, about as big as Hanover-square. – Inhabited by the high families. – Lewis XIV. on horse-back in the middle.**❞**

❝OCT. 12. Thursday. We went to the Gobelins. – Tapestry makes a good picture: – imitates flesh exactly. – One piece with a gold ground; – the birds not exactly coloured. – Thence we went to the King's Cabinet; – very neat, not, perhaps, perfect. – Gold ore. – Candles of the candle-tree. – Seeds. – Woods. Thence to Gagnier's house, where I saw rooms nine, furnished with a profusion of wealth and elegance which I never had seen before. – Vases. – Pictures. – The dragon china. – The lustre said to be of crystal, and to have cost 3,500l. – The whole furniture said to have cost 125,000l. – Damask hangings covered with pictures. – Porphyry. – This house struck me.**❞**

❝OCT. 17. Tuesday. The sight of palaces, and other great buildings, leaves no very distinct images, unless to those who talk of them. As I entered, my wife was in my mind: she would have been pleased. Having now nobody to please, I am little pleased.**❞**

❝OCT. 19. Thursday. At Court, we saw the apartments; – the King's bed-chamber and council-chamber extremely splendid. – Persons of all ranks in the external rooms through which the family passes; – servants and masters. – Brunet with us the second time.
The introductor came to us; – civil to me. – Presenting. – I had scruples. – Not necessary. – We went and saw the King and Queen at dinner. – We saw the other ladies at dinner. – Madame Elizabeth, with the Princess of Guimené. – At night we went to a comedy. I neither saw nor heard. Drunken women. – Mrs Th. preferred one to the other.**❞**

❝OCT 20. Friday. We saw the Queen mount in the forest. – Brown habit; rode aside: one lady rode aside. – The Queen's horse light grey; – martingale. – She galloped. – We then went to the apartment, and admired them. – Then wandered through the palace. In the passages, stalls and shops. – Painting in Fresco by a great master, worn out. – We saw the King's horses and dogs. – The dogs almost all English. – Degenerate. The horses not much commended. – The stables cool; the kennel filthy... The king fed himself with his left hand as we.**❞**

❝Oct 28. Saturday. Hotel – a guinea a day. – Coach, three guineas a week. – Valet de place, three l. a day. – *Avantcoureur*, a guinea a week. – Ordinary dinner, six l. a head. – Our ordinary seems to be about five guineas a day. – Our extraordinary expences, as diversions, gratuities, clothes, I cannot reckon. – Our travelling is ten guineas a day.**❞**

JAMES BOSWELL, *THE LIFE OF SAMUEL JOHNSON*,
EVERYMAN'S LIBRARY, LONDON,
ALFRED A. KNOPF, INC. NEW YORK, 1992

THE BELLS

François Rabelais (c. 1494–c. 1553) was well known for his satirical tales of the two giants Gargantua and Pantagruel.

*How Gargantua payed his welcome to the Parisians, and how
he took away the great Bells of our Ladies Church.*

❝Some few dayes after that they had refresh't themselves, he went to see the city, and was beheld of every body there with great admiration; for the People of *Paris* are so sottish, so badot, so foolish and fond by nature, that a juglr, a carrier of indulgences, a sumpter-horse, or mule with cymbals, or tinkling bells, a blinde fidler in the middle of a crosse lane, shall draw a greater confluence of people together, then an Evangelical Preacher: and they prest so hard upon him, that he was constrained to rest himself upon the towers of our Ladies Church; at which place, seeing so many about him, he said with a loud voice, I beleeve that these buzzards wil have me to pay them here my welcom hither, and my *Proficiat*: it is but good reason, I will now give them their wine, but it shall be only in sport; Then smiling, he untied his faire *Braguette*, and drawing out his *mentul* into the open aire, he so bitterly all-to-bepist them, that he drowned two hundred and sixty thousand, foure hundred and eighteen, besides the women and little children: some neverthelesse of the company escaped this piss-flood by meer speed of foot, who when they were at the higher end of the University, sweating, coughing, spitting, and out of breath, they began to swear and curse, some in good hot earnest, and others in jest, *Carimari, Carimara: Golynoly, Golynolo*: by me sweet Sanctesse, we are wash't in sport, a sport truly to laugh at, in *French Par ris*, for which that city hath been ever since called Paris, whose name formerly was *Leucotia*, (as *Strabo* testifieth, *lib. quarto*) from the Greek word λενκστηζ, whitenesse, because of the white thighs of the Ladies of that place. And forasamuch as at this imposition of a new name, all the people that were there, swore every one by the Sancts of his parish, the *Parisians*, which are patch'd up of all nations, and all pieces of

99

countreyes, are by nature both good *Jurers*, and good *Jurists*, and somewhat overweening; whereupon *Joanninus de Barrauco libro de copiositate reverentiarum*, thinks that they are called *Parisians*, from the *Greek* word παρρησια, which signifies boldnesse and liberty in speech. This done, he considered the great bells, which were in the said tours, and made them sound very harmoniously, which whilest he was doing, it came into his minde, that they would serve very well for *tingling Tantans*, and *ringing Campanels*, to hang about his mares neck, when she should be sent back to his father, (as he intended to do) loaded with *Brie* cheese, and fresh herring; and indeed he forthwith carried them to his lodging. In the mean while there came a master begar of the Fryers of S. *Anthonie*, to demand in his canting way the usual benevolence of some hoggish stuffe, who, that he might be heard afar off, and to make the bacon, he was in quest of, shake in the very chimneys, made account to filch them away privily. Neverthelesse, he left them behinde very honestly, not for that they were too hot, but that they were somewhat too heavy for his carriage. This was not he of *Bourg*, for he was too good a friend of mine. All the city was risen up in sedition, they being (as you know) upon any slight occasion, so ready to uproars and insurrections, that forreign nations wonder at the patience of the Kings of *France*, who do not by good justice restrain them from such tumultuous courses, seeing the manifold incoveniences which thence arise from day to day. Would to God I knew the shop, wherein are forged these divisions, and factious combinations, that I might bring them to light in the confraternities of my parish. Beleeve for a truth, that the place wherein the people gathered together, were thus sulfured, hopurymated, moiled and bepist, was called *Nesle*, where then was, (but now is no more) the Oracle of *Leucotia*: There was the case proposed, and the inconvenience shewed of the transporting of the bells: After they had well *ergoted pro* and *con*, they concluded in *Baralipton*, that they should send the oldest and most sufficient of the facultie unto *Gargantua*, to signifie unto him the great and horrible prejudice they sustain by the want of those bells; and notwithstanding the good reasons given in by some of the University, why this charge was fitter for an Oratour then a Sophister, there was chosen for this purpose our Master *Janotus de Bragmardo*. **99**

FRANÇOIS RABELAIS, *GARGANTUA AND PANTAGRUEL*,
TRANS. SIR THOMAS URQUHART AND PIERRE LE MOTTEUX,
PUB. EVERYMAN'S LIBRARY, LONDON, 1994

NOTRE-DAME

Victor Hugo (1802–85) was a novelist, poet and dramatist, as well as a politician with changing affiliations. One of his best-known works "Notre-Dame de Paris" (translated into English as "The Hunchback of Notre Dame") tells the story of a wild romance against the medieval setting of the old cathedral.

❝That façade, as we now see it, has lost three important accessories: in the first place, the flight of eleven steps, which raised it above the level of the ground; in the next, the lower range of statues which filled the niches of the three porches, and the upper range of twenty-eight more ancient sovereigns of France which adorned the gallery of the first story, commencing with Childebert and ending with Philip Augustus, holding in his hand 'the imperial globe.'

Time, raising by a slow and irresistible progress the level of the city, occasioned the removal of the steps; but if this rising tide of the pavement of Paris has swallowed up, one after another, those eleven steps which added to the majestic height of the edifice, Time has given to the church more perhaps than it has taken away; for it is Time that has imparted to the façade that sombre hue of antiquity which makes the old age of buildings the period of their greatest beauty.

But who has thrown down the two ranges of statues? – who has left the niches empty? – who has inserted that new and bastard pointed arch in the middle of the beautiful central porch? – who has dared to set up that tasteless and heavy door of wood, carved in the style of Louis XV, beside the arabesques of Biscornette? – The men, the architects, the artists, of our days.❞

VICTOR HUGO, *THE HUNCHBACK OF NOTRE-DAME*,
PUB. RICHARD BENTLEY, EDINBURGH, 1838

HISTORY

COURT OF THE SUN KING

Louis, Duc de Saint-Simon (1675–1755), has depicted better than anyone else the reign of Louis XIV. The definitive text of his "Mémoires" was written between 1739 and 1750. He came from a grand family and from his birth was destined to the highest responsibilities in the kingdom. Louis XIV and Marie-Thérèse held him at his baptism, an early friend was the Duc de Chartres, the king's nephew and later Regent. His father was a favorite of Louis XIII, and a cousin of the Montmorency and the Condé families. On his mother's side, he was a cousin of Mme de Montespan. A politician and a diplomat, he was obsessed with history. For him the character of great men was what determined history, hence his care to note every detail of the court and the life of his contemporaries.

❝The Chevalier de Bouillon, who since the death of the Comte d'Auvergne's son had begun to call himself the Prince d'Auvergne, asked the Regent to allow public balls at the Opéra three times a week, with payment on entry, masked or unmasked, the boxes making a convenient refuge for those who wished to watch without joining the dance. It was thought that public balls, supervised as the Opéra always is during performances, would be safe from scandal, and might discourage people from attending shady little dance-halls scattered over Paris, where scandals so often originate. The Opéra balls were duly inaugurated, with huge crowds and all the desired effect. The proposer was at once given a pension of six thousand livres, and a wonderful new machine was invented that swiftly and easily covered the orchestra pit, bringing the stage and the auditorium to the same level, and perfectly flat. What was most unfortunate was that M. le Duc d'Orléans had only to walk a step to go there after his suppers, and very frequently showed himself in a most unseemly condition. The Duc de Noailles, ever anxious to pay his court, appeared at the first one of all, so drunk that there was no filthiness he did not commit.**"**

"Tessé waited an entire day at Beaumont lest the Czar should arrive early. He at length appeared on Friday, 7 May, at noon precisely. Tessé made his bow at the coach door, had the honour of dining with him afterwards, and that same afternoon escorted him to Paris. When they arrived, however, the Czar chose to enter the city in one of the Marshal's coaches, but not in his company, preferring to drive with three members of his own staff. Thus Tessé followed in a second coach. They alighted at the Louvre at nine in the evening. The Czar inspected every room of the Queen-mother's suite, but thought them too luxurious and too brightly lit. He at once stepped back into his coach and went to the Hôtel de Lesdiguières, where he decided to lodge. There also he thought the rooms much too grand; and he had his camp-bed set up in one of the closets. The Maréchal de Tessé, whose duty it was to do the honours of his house and table and accompany him everywhere, also had rooms in the Hôtel de Lesdiguières. He had his work cut out in trying to stay with the Czar, and was sometimes reduced to chasing after him. Verton, one of the King's stewards, had charge of the service, and of the tables for the retinue, numbering altogether forty persons, twelve or fifteen of whom were of sufficient importance either by birth or function to eat at the Czar's table. Verton had his wits about him, and figured large in certain circles. He was a great one for good eating and gambling high. He ordered the household so efficiently and showed so much tact and goodwill that the Czar became remarkably friendly with him, and so did the suite.**"**

HISTORICAL MEMOIRS OF THE DUC DE SAINT-SIMON,
VOL. III: 1715–23, ED. AND TRANS. LUCY NORTON,
PUB. HAMISH HAMILTON, LONDON, 1972

AFTER THE WAR

Alice B. Toklas (1877–1967) was the friend, secretary and companion of Gertrude Stein (1874–1946), and moved with her to Paris where Stein lived in the Rue de Fleurus, and developed a literary salon. The autobiography quoted below is Stein's own memoir, which she published using Toklas' name.

"It was a changed Paris. Everything was changed, and everybody was cheerful.

During our absence Eve had died and Picasso was now living in a little home in Montrouge. We went out to see him. He had a marvellous rose pink silk counterpane on his bed. Where did that come from Pablo, asked Gertrude Stein. Ah ça, said Picasso with much satisfaction, that is a lady. It was a well-known chilean society woman who had given it to him. It was a marvel. He was very cheerful. He was constantly coming to the house, bringing Paquerette a girl who was very nice or Irène a very lovely woman who came from the mountains and wanted to be free. He brought Erik Satie and the Princesse de Polignac and Blaise Cendrars.

It was a great pleasure to know Erik Satie. He was from Normandy and very fond of it. Marie Laurencin comes from Normandy, so also does Braque. Once when after the war Satie and Marie Laurencin were at the house for lunch they were delightully enthusiastic about each other as being normans. Erik Satie liked food and wine and knew a lot about both. We had at that time some very good eau de vie that the husband of Mildred Aldrich's servant had given us and Erik Satie, drinking his glass slowly and with appreciation, told stories of the country in his youth.

Only once in the half dozen times that Erik Satie was at the house did he talk about music. He said that it had always been his opinion and he was glad that it was being recognised that modern french music owed nothing to modern Germany. That after Debussy had led the way french musicians had either followed him or found their own french way. . . .

It was a changed Paris. Guillaume Apollinaire was dead. We saw a tremendous number of people but none of them as far as I can remember that we had ever known before. Paris was crowded. As Clive Bell remarked, they say that an awful lot of people were killed in the war but it seems to me that an extraordinary large number of grown men and women have suddenly been born.

As I say we were restless and we were economical and all day and all evening we were seeing people and at last there was the defile, the procession under the Arc de Triomphe, of the allies.

The members of the American Fund for French Wounded were to have seats on the benches that were put up the length of the Champs Elysées but quite rightly the people of Paris objected as these seats would make it impossible for them to see the parade and so Clémenceau promptly had them taken down. Luckily for us Jessie Whitehead's room in her hotel looked right over the Arc de Triomphe and she asked us to come to it to see the parade. We accepted gladly. It was a wonderful day.

We got up at sunrise, as later it would have been impossible for them to cross Paris in a car. This was one of the last trips Auntie made. By this time the red cross was painted off it but it was still a truck. . . .

Auntie then was making practically her last trip. We left her near the river and walked up to the hotel. Everybody was on the streets, men, women, children, soldiers, priests, nuns, we saw two nuns being helped into a tree from which they would be able to see. And we were admirably placed and we saw perfectly.

We saw it all, we saw first the few wounded from the Invalides in their wheeling chairs wheeling themselves. It is an old french custom that a military procession should always be preceded by the veterans from the Invalides. They all marched past through the Arc de Triomphe. Gertrude Stein remembered that when as a child she used to swing on the chains that were around the Arc de Triomphe her governess had told her that no one must walk underneath since the german armies had marched under it after 1870. And now everybody except the germans were passing through.

All the nations marched differently, some slowly, some quickly, the french carry their flags the best of all, Pershing and his officer carrying the flag behind him were perhaps the most perfectly spaced. It was this scene that Gertrude Stein described in the movie she wrote about this time that I have published in Operas and Plays in the Plain Edition.

However it all finally came to an end. We wandered up and we wandered down the Champs Elysées and the war was over and the piles of captured canon that had made two pyramids were being taken away and peace was upon us. **99**

The Autobiography of Alice B. Toklas,
pub. John Lane, The Bodley Head,
London, 1935

Daily life

Local customs

"Birds of America" by Mary McCarthy (1912–89) is a novel in which the protagonist is a young American boy living in Paris and Rome, and complaining about the tourist industry in both cities.

66The French, like the Italians, only buy what they need for one day. I had a shock, though, yesterday, when I went to do my marketing at the Marché Buci – that big outdoor market, near the Odéon. At one stall, I asked for a carrot, and the *type* refused to sell me one. He said I had to buy a kilo. Like you, dearest Ma, I started to argue. I wanted to know why. How it would damage him to sell me one carrot or one apple or one pear. I explained that I didn't have an icebox and that I was just one person. '*Ça ne me regarde pas,*' he growled. Finally we compromised on a pound. That's quite a lot of carrots for a single man. While he was weighing them, I got into conversation with an Italian, who had been watching me and smiling – very nice, about the *babbo*'s age, an intellectual. He said that in Italy not only would they sell you one carrot but divide it in four. According to him, this only proved that Italy is a poor country, while France is a rich country. I said the Italians had more heart than the French even if they gyp you sometimes. The French *grudge* gypping you, Mother. Maybe, I said, people in poor countries had more heart than people in rich countries. After all, Poverty used to be represented as a virtue. I hadn't noticed any statues of Poverty on French churches.**99**

66That reminds me. Did you know that you're supposed to tip the usher in a French movie house? I didn't know and got hissed at by the woman the other day when I went to see an Antonioni flick. All the students in the vicinity stopped necking and turned to ogle me as I stumbled into my seat. I gather I was being called a '*sale américain*', but if she knew I was an American, she might have enlightened me about the local customs. It must happen all the time with foreigners. But I suppose that's what makes her mad. Usually when I'm in some place like a stand-up coffee bar. I watch what the other customers do and follow their example, but in a movie house you're literally in the dark. This little incident wrecked the film for me. I hardly saw Monica Vitti because of the rage I was in.

The picture was half over before I finally grasped what I'd done that was so horrible. Then it was too late to rectify it – at least without getting stared at some more. Besides, I couldn't see how much the other customers were giving. In case you want to know, it's a franc on the Champs-Elysées and fifty centimes in the little places. The clerk at my hotel told me.**"**

MARY McCARTHY, *BIRDS OF AMERICA*,
PUB. WEIDENFELD AND NICOLSON,
LONDON, 1971

VISITING GERTRUDE STEIN

In "A Moveable Feast", Hemingway (1899–1961) writes with hindsight in the late 1950's about the ex-patriate literary set who lived in Paris in the 1920's. These included Ezra Pound, Ford Maddox Ford and Gertrude Stein.

"If I walked down by different streets to the Jardin du Luxembourg in the afternoon I could walk through the gardens and then go to the Musée du Luxembourg where the great paintings were that have now mostly been transferred to the Louvre and the Jeu de Paume. I went there nearly every day for the Cézannes and to see the Manets and the Monets and the other Impressionists that I had first come to know about in the Art Institute at Chicago. I was learning something from the painting of Cézanne that made writing simple true sentences far from enough to make the stories have the dimensions that I was trying to put in them. I was learning very much from him but I was not articulate enough to explain it to anyone. Besides, it was a secret. But if the light was gone in the Luxembourg I would walk up through the gardens and stop in at the studio apartment where Gertrude Stein lived at 27 rue de Fleurus.

My wife and I had called on Miss Stein, and she and the friend who lived with her had been very cordial and friendly and we had loved the big studio with the great paintings. It was like one of the best rooms in the finest museum except there was a big fireplace and it was warm and comfortable and they gave you good things to eat and tea and natural distilled liqueurs made from purple plums, yellow plums or wild raspberries. These were fragrant, colourless alcohols served from cut-glass carafes in small glasses and whether they were *quetsche, mirabelle* or framboise they all tasted like the fruits they came from, converted into a controlled fire on your tongue that warmed you and loosened it.

Miss Stein was very big but not tall and was heavily built like a peasant woman. She had beautiful eyes and a strong German-Jewish face that also could have been *friulano* and she reminded me of a northern Italian peasant woman with her clothes, her mobile face and her

lovely thick, alive, immigrant hair which she wore put up in the same way she had probably worn it in college. She talked all the time and at first it was about people and places. **99**

ERNEST HEMINGWAY, *A MOVEABLE FEAST*, PUB. JONATHAN CAPE, LONDON, 1964

RETURNING TO THE CITY

In the letter below, Gustave Flaubert (1821–80) writes to his friend from adolescence, Alfred Le Poittevin, on April 2, 1845. Flaubert studied law in Paris, from 1841–5.

66I enjoyed seeing Paris again; I looked at the boulevards, the rue de Rivoli, the sidewalks, as though I were back among them after being away a hundred years; and I don't know why, but I felt happy in the midst of all that noise and all that human flood. (But I have no one with me, alas! The moment you and I part, we set foot in some strange land where people do not speak our language nor we theirs.) No sooner was I off the train than I put on my city shoes, boarded a bus, and began my visits. The stairs of the Mint left me breathless, because there are a hundred of them and also because I remembered the evenings, gone never to return, when I used to climb them on my way to dinner. I greeted Mme and Mlle Darcet, who were in mourning; I sat down, talked for half an hour, and then decamped.

Everywhere I went I walked in my own past, pushing through it as though striding knee-deep against the current of a flowing, murmuring river. I went to the Champs-Elysées, to see the two women with whom I used to spend entire afternoons (which I probably wouldn't do now, I've become such a lout). The invalid was still half-lying in an armchair. She greeted me with the same smile and the same voice. The furniture was still the same, and the rug no more worn. In exquisite affinity, one of those rare harmonies that can be perceived only by the artist, a street-organ began to play under the windows, just as it used to when I would be reading them *Hernani* or *René*.**"**

GUSTAVE FLAUBERT, *THE LETTERS OF GUSTAVE FLAUBERT 1830–1857*,
ED. AND TRANS. FRANCIS STEEGMULLER, PUB. FABER AND FABER, LONDON, 1981
AND HARVARD UNIVERSITY PRESS, HARVARD, 1979

JAMES JOYCE AT DINNER

Sylvia Beach published the first edition of Joyce's Ulysses in 1922 at her bookshop Librairie Shakespeare. She was a friend and patron of many of the ex-patriate literary set and wrote about them in the memoir "Shakespeare and Company".

"In Paris, Joyce and his family dined out every evening. His particular restaurant – this was in the early 'twenties – was the one opposite the Gare Montparnasse, Les Trianons. The proprietor and the entire personnel were devoted to Joyce. They were at the door of his taxi before he alighted and they escorted him to a table reserved for him at the back, where he could be more or less unmolested by people who came to stare at him as he dined, or brought copies of his works to be autographed.

The head-waiter would read to him the items on the bill of fare so that he would be spared the trouble of getting out several pairs of glasses and perhaps a magnifying glass. Joyce pretended to take an interest in fine dishes, but food meant nothing to him, unless it was something to do with his work. He urged his family and the friends who might be dining with him to choose the best food on the menu. He liked to have them eat a hearty meal and persuaded them to try such and such a wine. He himself ate scarcely anything, and was satisfied with the most ordinary white wine just as long as there was plenty of it. As he never drank a drop all day long, he was pretty thirsty by dinnertime. The waiter kept his glass filled. Joyce would have sat there with his family and friends and his white wine till all hours if at a certain moment Nora hadn't decided it was time to go. He ended by obeying her – it was according to an understanding between them, one of the many understandings between this couple who understood each other so well.

Wherever Joyce went, he was received like royalty, such was his personal charm, his consideration for others. When he started on his way downstairs to the men's room, several waiters came hurrying to escort him. His blindness drew people to him a great deal.

Joyce's tips were famous; the waiters, the boy who fetched him a taxi, all those who served him, must have retired with a fortune. I never grudged tips, but, knowing the circumstances, it seemed to me that Joyce overtipped.**"**

SYLVIA BEACH, *SHAKESPEARE AND COMPANY*,
PUB. FABER AND FABER, LONDON, 1960

PARIS 1787–90

Arthur Young (1741–1820) was an agricultural theorist who displayed acute powers of politicial and social observation in his writings.

1787

"OCT 25TH. This great city appears to be in many respects the most ineligible and inconvenient for the residence of a person of small fortune of any that I have seen; and vastly inferior to London. The streets are very narrow, and many of them crowded, nine-tenths dirty, and all without foot pavements. Walking, which in London is so pleasant and so clean, that ladies do it every day, is here a toil and a fatigue to a man, and an impossibility to a well-dressed woman. The coaches are numerous, and, what are much worse, there are an

infinity of horse cabriolets, which are driven by young men of fashion and their imitators, alike fools, with such rapidity as to be real nuisances, and render the streets exceedingly dangerous, without an incessant caution."

" . . . in other respects I take it to be a most eligible residence for such as prefer a great city. The society for a man of letters, or [for one] who has any scientific pursuit, cannot be exceeded. The intercourse between such men and the great, which, if it is not upon an equal footing, ought never to exist at all, is respectable. Persons of the highest rank pay an attention to science and literature, and emulate the character they confer. I should pity the man who expected, without other advantages of a very different nature, to be well received in a brilliant circle at London, because he was a fellow of the Royal Society. But this would not be the case with a member of the Academy of Sciences at Paris; he is sure of a good reception everywhere. Perhaps this contrasts depends in a great measure on the difference of the governments of the two countries. Politics are too much attended to in England to allow a due respect to be paid to anything else; and should the French establish a freer government, academicians will not be held in such estimation, when rivalled in the public esteem by the orators who hold forth liberty and property in a free parliament."

1789

"JUNE 9TH. The business going forward at present in the pamphlet shops in Paris is incredible. I went to the Palais-Royal to see what new things were published, and to procure a catalogue of all. Every hour produces something new. Thirteen came out to-day, sixteen yesterday, and ninety-two last week. We think sometimes that Debrett's or Stockdale's shops at London are crowded, but they are mere deserts compared to Desein's [Desennes], and some others here, in which one can scarcely squeeze from the door to the counter. The price of printing two years ago was from 27 *livres* to 30 *livres* per sheet, but now it is from 60 *livres* to 80 *livres*. This spirit of reading political tracts, they say, spreads into the provinces, so that all the presses of France are equally employed. Nineteen-twentieths of these productions are in favour of liberty, and commonly violent against the clergy and nobility."

❝It is easy to conceive the spirit that must thus be raised among the people. But the coffee-houses in the Palais-Royal present yet more singular and astonishing spectacles; they are not only crowded within, but other expectant crowds are at the doors and windows, listening *à gorge déployée* to certain orators, who from chairs or tables harangue each his little audience. The eagerness with which they are heard, and the thunder of applause they receive for every sentiment of more than common hardiness or violence against the present government, cannot easily be imagined.❞

❝JUNE 26TH. Every hour that passes seems to give the people fresh spirit: the meetings at the Palais-Royal are more numerous, more violent, and more assured; and in the assembly of electors, at Paris, for sending a deputation to the National Assembly, the language that was talked, by all ranks of people, was nothing less than a revolution in the government, and the establishment of a free constitution. What they mean by a free constitution is easily understood – *a republic*; for the doctrine of the times runs everyday more and more to that point; yet they profess, that the kingdom ought to be a monarchy too; or, at least, that there ought to be a king. In the streets one is stunned by the hawkers of seditious pamphlets, and descriptions of pretended events, that all tend to keep the people equally ignorant and alarmed. The supineness and even stupidity of the Court is without example; the moment demands the greatest decision, and yesterday, while it was actually a question whether he should be a doge of Venice, or a king of France, the King went a hunting!❞

1790

JAN. 4TH. After breakfast, walk in the gardens of the Tuileries, where there is the most extraordinary sight that either French or English eyes could ever behold at Paris. The King, walking with six grenadiers of the *milice bourgeoise*, with an officer or two of his household, and a page. The doors of the gardens are kept shut in respect to him, in order to exclude everybody but deputies, or those who have admission-tickets. When he entered the palace, the doors of the gardens were thrown open for all without distinction, though the Queen was still walking with a lady of her court. She also was attented so closely by the *gardes bourgeoises*, that she could not speak, but in a low voice, without being heard by them. A mob followed her, talking very loud, and paying no other apparent respect than that of taking off their hats wherever she passed, which was indeed more than I expected. Her Majesty does not appear to be in health; she seems to be much affected, and shows it in her face; but the King is as plump as ease can render him. By his orders, there is a little garden railed off for the Dauphin to amuse himself in, and a small room is built in it to retire to in case of rain; here he was at work with his little hoe and rake, but not without a guard of two grenadiers. He is a very pretty good-natured-looking boy, of five or six years old, with an agreeable countenance; wherever he goes, all hats are taken off to him, which I was glad to observe. All the family being kept thus close prisoners (for such they are in effect) affords, at first view, a shocking spectacle; and is really so, if the act were not absolutely necessary to effect the revolution; this I conceive to be impossible; but if it were necessary, no one can blame the people for taking every measure possible to secure that liberty they had seized in the violence of a revolution.❞

ARTHUR YOUNG, *TRAVELS IN FRANCE
DURING THE YEARS 1787, 1788, 1789*,
ED. CONSTANTIA MAXWELL,
PUB. CAMBRIDGE UNIVERSITY PRESS, 1950

WALKING AT NIGHT

In "Nightwood", Djuna Barnes describes a nightmare world (chiefly based on Paris and New York), in which the characters are troubled and desperate.

❝Close to the church of *St. Sulpice*, around the corner in the *rue Servandoni*, lived a doctor. His small slouching figure was a feature of the *Place*. To the proprietor of the *Café de la Mairie du VIe* he was almost a son. This relatively small square, through which tram lines ran in several directions, bounded on the one side by the church and on the other by the court, was the doctor's 'city'. What he would not find here to answer to his needs, could be found in the narrow streets that ran into it. Here he had been seen ordering details for funerals in the parlour with its black broadcloth curtains and mounted pictures of hearses; buying holy pictures and *petits Jésus* in the boutique displaying vestments and flowering candles. . . .

He walked, pathetic and alone, among the pasteboard booths of the *Foire St. Germain* when for a time its imitation castles squatted in the square. He was seen coming at a smart pace down the left side of the church to go into Mass; bathing in the holy water stoup as if he were its single and beholden bird, pushing aside weary French maids and local tradespeople with the impatience of a soul in physical stress.

Sometimes, late at night, before turning into the *Café de la Mairie du VIe*, he would be observed staring up at the huge towers of the church which rose into the sky, unlovely but reassuring, running a thick warm finger around his throat, where, in spite of its customs, his hair surprised him, lifting along his back and creeping up over his collar. Standing small and insubordinate, he would watch the basins of the fountain loosing their skirts of water in a ragged and flowing hem, sometimes crying to a man's departing shadow: 'Aren't you the beauty!'❞

DJUNA BARNES, *NIGHTWOOD*,
PUB. FABER AND FABER,
LONDON, 1936

WALKING BY DAY

Henry James (1843–1916) describes his early years in "A Small Boy and Others". Here he describes walking in Paris with his elder brother, William James, later a philosopher and psychologist.

❝That autumn renewed, I make out, our long and beguiled walks, my own with W. J. in especial; at the same time that I have somehow the sense of the whole more broken appeal on the part of Paris, the scanter confidence and ease it inspired in us, the perhaps more numerous and composite, but obscurer and more baffled imitations. Not indeed – for all my brother's later vision of an accepted flatness in it – that there was not some joy and some grasp; why else were we forever (as I seem to conceive we were) measuring the great space that separated us from the gallery of the Luxembourg, every step of which, either way we took it, fed us with some interesting, some admirable image, kept us in relation to something nobly intended? That particular walk was not prescribed us, yet we appear to have hugged it, across the Champs-Elysées to the river, and so over the nearest bridge and the quays of the left bank to the Rue de Seine, as if it somehow held the secret of our future; to the extent even of my more or less sneaking off on occasion to take it by myself, to taste of it with a due undiverted intensity and the throb as of the finest, which *could* only mean the most Parisian, adventure. The further quays, with their innumerable old bookshops and print-shops, the long cases of each of these commodities, exposed on the parapets in especial, must have come to know us almost as well as we knew them; with plot thickening and emotion deepening steadily, however, as we mounted the long, black Rue de Seine – *such* a stretch of perspective, *such* an intensity of tone as it offered in those days; where every low-browed vitrine waylaid us and we moved in a world of which the dark message, expressed in we couldn't have said what sinister way too, might have been 'Art, art, art, don't you see? Learn, little gaping pilgrims, what *that* is!' Oh we learned, that is we tried to, as hard as ever we could, and were fairly well at it, I always felt, even by the time we had passed up into that comparatively short but wider and finer vista of the Rue de Tournon, which in those days more abruptly crowned the more compressed approach and served in a manner as a great outer vestibule to the Palace. Style, dimly described, looked down there, as with conscious encouragement, from the high grey-headed, clear-faced, straight-standing old houses – very much as if wishing to say 'Yes, small staring jeune homme, we are dignity and memory and measure, we are conscience and proportion and taste, not to mention strong sense too: for all of which good things take us – you won't find one of them when you find (as you're going soon to begin to at such a rate) vulgarity.' This, I admit, was an abundance of remark to such young ears; but it did all, I maintain, tremble in the air, with the sense that the Rue de Tournon, cobbled and a little grass-grown, might more or less have figured some fine old street *de province*: I cherished in short its very name and think I really hadn't to wait to prefer the then, the unmenaced, the inviolate Café Foyot of the left hand corner, the much-loved and so haunted Café Foyot of the old Paris, to its – well, to its roaring successor.❞

HENRY JAMES, *AUTOBIOGRAPHY VOL. I, A SMALL BOY AND OTHERS*,
PUB. CHARLES SCRIBNER, NEW YORK, 1913

ATMOSPHERE

TASTE

Evelyn Waugh (1903-66) had some typically caustic criticisms of the French reputation for good taste.

❝ There is nothing essentially modish in the atmosphere of Paris, any more than there is anything specifically medical in the atmosphere of Harley Street. In almost all matters except the business of dress-making, Parisian taste is notably lower and less progressive than Berlin or Vienna or even London. The French, through the defects rather than the qualities of their taste, are saved from the peculiarly English horrors of folk dancing, arts and crafts, and the collection of cottage antiquities, only to fall victim, one false thing driving out another, to the worst sort of sham modernity. If the choice is inevitable beween pewter-*cum*-warming-pan-*cum*-timbered-gables and the glass of M. Lalique, it is surely better to be imposed upon by a past which one has not seen than by a present of which one is one oneself a part ? **99**

EVELYN WAUGH, *LABELS: A MEDITERRANEAN JOURNAL*, PUB. DUCKWORTH, LONDON, 1930

LE BISTRO

George Orwell (1903-50) worked in a series of low-paid jobs in Paris and enjoyed the social life.

66 We had some jolly evenings, on Saturdays, in the little *bistro* at the foot of the Hôtel des Trois Moineaux.

The brick-floored room, fifteen feet square, was packed with twenty people, and the air dim with smoke. The noise was deafening, for everyone was either talking at the top of his voice or singing. Sometimes it was just a confused din of voices; sometimes everyone would burst out together in the same song – the 'Marseillaise', or the 'Internationale', or 'Madelon', or 'Les Fraises et les Framboises'. Azaya, a great clumping peasant girl who worked fourteen hours a day in a glass factory sang a song about, '*Il a perdu ses pantalons, tout en dans*ant *le Charleston*'. Her friend Marinette, a thin, dark Corsican girl of obstinate virtue, tied her knees together and danced the *danse du ventre*. The old Rougiers wandered in and out, cadging drinks and trying to tell a long, involved story about someone who had once cheated them over a bedstead. T., cadaverous and silent, sat in his corner quietly boozing. Charlie, drunk, half danced, half staggered to and fro with a glass of sham absinthe balanced in one fat hand, pinching the women's breasts and declaiming poetry. People played darts and diced for drinks. Manuel, a Spaniard, dragged the girls to the bar and shook the dice-box against their bellies, for luck. Madame F. stood at the bar rapidly pouring *chopines* of wine through the pewter funnel, with a wet dishcloth always handy, because every man in the room tried to make love to her. Two children, bastards of big Louis the bricklayer, sat in a corner sharing a glass of syrop. Every one was very happy, overwhelmingly certain that the world was a good place and we a notable set of people. **99**

GEORGE ORWELL, *DOWN AND OUT IN PARIS AND LONDON*, PUB. PENGUIN BOOKS, LONDON, 1940

PARISIAN THEMES

Paris chic: explore the world of fashion and couture ▲ 115–32.

Museums: discover the great museums and the artists' studios ▲ 133–72.

A city for gourmets: from famous restaurants to family-run eateries ▲ 173–90.

Nature: discover the parks of Paris and their unexpected wildlife ▲ 191–212.

Along the Seine: the bridges, quays and the most beautiful avenue in Paris ▲ 215–31.

The world capital of elegance, Paris has some remarkably fashionable quarters where only the most luxurious goods are for sale. The history of these places is easy to trace, since it has mirrored the successive ups and downs of the aristocracy and the bourgeoisie. After settling close to the Chaussée d'Antin in the 18th century, high society moved off toward the Tuileries and the Palais-Royal in the following century. Under the Second Empire, it embraced Étoile and the

Champs-Élysées, districts which remained at the very heart of this vibrant city until the 1960's. On the celebrated avenue, it was always considered "de rigueur" to be elegantly dressed. These days, fashionable residences and the leading shops and boutiques have parted company: shops are now concentrated in the "golden triangle" formed by the Avenue Montaigne, Avenue George V (home to the best dress designers) and Rue François Iᵉʳ. Fashionable *Parisiennes* now have their clothes designed by Givenchy on Avenue George V, buy a pin at Van Cleef & Arpels in Place Vendôme and pick up a scarf at Hermès on Rue du Faubourg St-Honoré.

♦ 524

The proclamation of the Second Empire signaled the demi of the small, exclusive dressmaker. The rise of haute coutu was dominated by two Paris-based English tailors, Redfern and Worth, and a Frenchman called Doucet. They imposed their own ideas and used fashionable embroiderers, feather dressers and pleaters. They also worked hard to ensure that their creations' renown established Paris's reputation for impeccable taste. Their illustrious successors have included Jean Patou, Robert Piguet, Elsa Schiaparelli and Cristóbal Balenciaga.

THE ELEGANCE OF DOUCET

Jacques Doucet inherited a lingerie shop at 21, rue de la Paix, and in 1875 turned it into a fashion house. He had an unmatched reputation for expensive gowns, designing clothes for the actresses Sarah Bernhardt and Réjane.

EUGÉNIE'S CONTRIBUTION

The Empress Eugénie was able to support luxury industries thanks to the pomp of the court. She was also responsible for launching an unusually ostentatious fashion that demanded large amounts of fabric.

A CITY OF COUTURIERS

Since the 19th century Paris has boasted of an abundance of talented couturiers and milliners: some are commemorated in pavement inscriptions. There are dedications at the corner of the Avenue

Montaigne and the Rue-François I to the following: Jeanne Paquin, a dressmaker from the Rue de la Paix who designed the high-waisted "Directoire" look; Madeleine Vionnet, a designer famous for her bias-cut crepes who opened her own house in 1912; and the Callot sisters. A creation by Lucien Lelong (left).

1950'S STYLE
Essential fashion
accessories of the
1950's included fans,
gloves, parasols and
highly acclaimed
Parisian hats.

eanne Lanvin
uture, Mode, Fourrures, Lingerie
22, Faubourg Saint. Honoré, Paris.

**JEANNE LANVIN, OR
MOTHERLY LOVE**
Paul Iribe's design for the
company's future logo in
1927 symbolized Lanvin's
love for her daughter, her
main source of inspiration.

**PAUL POIRET, SULTAN
AND REVOLUTIONARY**
Pupil of Worth and
Doucet, Paul Poiret,
here caricatured by
Rip, influenced the
world of fashion from
1909 until the interwar
years. He shocked
society with his
extraordinary Eastern-
influenced shimmering
gowns with matching
turbans, which were
designed to be worn
without
corsets.

WORTH, THE INVENTOR OF HAUTE COUTURE

Charles Frederick
Worth moved from
London to Paris in
1845, at the age of
twenty, and worked in
a draper's shop

until he was able to
open his own shop at
7, rue de la Paix, in
1858. Specializing in
well-cut clothes, he
lightened the female
silhouette and
instituted the seasonal
rhythms of fashion by
preparing his
collections in advance.
One of his
innovations was
to use live
models for
fashion shows.

Parisian women are acknowledged paragons of elegance and charm the world over: indeed, it is said that couturiers always have Parisian women in their mind's eye when dreaming up new creations. They are also admired for their natural chic, wit and smart appearance. Her image has changed, however, from the turn-of-the-century *cocotte*, a woman of easy virtue kept by rich lovers, who launched fashions and spent a fortune shopping, to the assiduous, businesslike *Parisienne* of today.

Liane de Pougy, a celebrated Parisian courtesan.

IN BLACK AND WHITE

Parisian women have long been objects of admiration and jealousy, and have inspired many writers. Henri Becque (1837–99) entitled one of his plays *La Parisienne*; Colette described her impressions of a provincial woman who comes to Paris in *Claudine à Paris*; and in 1950, Jacques Laurent launched a literary review called *La Parisienne*.

WORLDLY WOMEN

The reign of the *cocottes* began under the Second Empire: at that time they had little difficulty in eclipsing society ladies. Women in French high society were not only cultured but curious and loquacious; they took their revenge in the early years of the 20th century by opening literary *salons*. The most celebrated *salons* included those of the Countess Anna de Noailles (above), a noted storyteller and poet; the Duchess of La Rochefoucauld, who received the writer Paul Valéry in the Place des États-Unis; and the Comtesse de Fels, who wrote on her invitations: "A little tea, a little conversation."

A SILHOUETTE IN TOWN

This was how the couturier Olivier Lapidus described modern Parisian women, as represented by the actress Sabine Azéma, photographed here by Robert Doisneau.

THE INIMITABLE PARISIENNE

A character in Léon Gozlan's *Parisian Mistresses* says of the typical *Parisienne*: "She is a composite of grace and sensitivity; an inexhaustible source of seduction . . . the kind of woman you dream about when you're sixteen, and the only one you remember when you're sixty." Not all Parisian women are members of high society, but the one sketched here by Gruau is celebrated for her innate confidence in her appearance.

FREEDOM AND ELEGANCE

The *tailleur Bar*, created by Christian Dior after the end of World War Two, symbolized a return to opulent, affluent living standards after the privations of the German Occupation. However, the great sophistication of the New Look, which was quickly adopted by the majority of Parisian women, deterred others, who were afraid of losing their physical and social freedom.

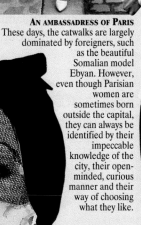

AN AMBASSADRESS OF PARIS

These days, the catwalks are largely dominated by foreigners, such as the beautiful Somalian model Ebyan. However, even though Parisian women are sometimes born outside the capital, they can always be identified by their impeccable knowledge of the city, their open-minded, curious manner and their way of choosing what they like.

Yves Saint Laurent

According to the sociologist Jean Baudrillard, "Couturiers are the modern world's last adventurers: they cultivate the gratuitous act." A virtual laboratory for French fashion and taste, haute couture brings together people with astonishing creative talent. The designers themselves are endowed with exceptional ability and work for a clientele of no more than two thousand women all over the world. A fashion house can describe itself as haute couture only if it meets certain criteria relating to fittings and presentations of collections in January and July; since 1994, these have taken place at the Carrousel du Louvre.

◆ 524

MODERN ELEGANCE FROM CHANEL
29–31, rue Cambon 75008.
"Fashions pass away; style lives on." This was the byword of Gabrielle (Coco) Chanel, who is remembered for her comfortable yet chic women's clothes between the two wars. Her fashion house in the Rue Cambon was best known for its cardigans, black dresses decorated with costume jewelry, camellias and straw hats as well as the famous "little suit". Since taking over the firm in 1983, Karl Lagerfeld has continued to steer the same course, occasionally adding touches of irreverent humor.

YVES SAINT LAURENT'S IMPECCABLE CHIC
5, avenue Marceau 75008.
After working as an assistant to Dior, Saint Laurent presented his first collection in 1962 in the house once inhabited by the painter Forain in the Rue Spontini. His innovations included putting women in dinner jackets: he also sought inspiration from foreign cultures and from art. He created the image of a woman who was sophisticated and elegant in any setting.

CHANEL

MYTHS AND RITES
The presentation of collections takes up a great deal of media space these days. The public revels in the life styles of famous models and loves to see the couturier emerging at the end of a fashion show.

CHRISTIAN DIOR: ETERNAL FEMININITY

30, avenue Montaigne 75008

Once established in the Avenue Montaigne, Dior turned fashion upside down with the New Look. This marked a return to opulence and included flowing gowns made of luxurious materials and hemlines a good eight inches longer. Today Dior's modernist, classical rigor has been sustained by Gianfranco Ferré.

GIVENCHY: UNPARALLELED DISTINCTION

3–5, avenue George-V 75008

Hubert de Givenchy, who was known as the gentleman of haute couture, discovered his vocation on a visit to the Pavilion of Elegance at the 1937 Universal Exhibition. He opened his own house in 1952. Givenchy specialized in elaborate evening dresses and was noted for pure, sculpted lines.

CHRISTIAN LACROIX: LUXURY AND IMAGINATION

26, avenue Montaigne 75008

Lacroix, a native of Arles, devoted his first collection, in 1987, to Provence. He drew on Provençal folklore for his summery colors and rich fabrics embroidered in 18th-century styles. He gives the female form an outline that is often extravagant but always seductive.

OLIVIER LAPIDUS: A NEW TALENT

35, rue François-Ier 75008

When Olivier inherited the house of Lapidus from his father, Ted, in 1989, he was very much the newcomer to the high-fashion scene. Lapidus is a tireless seeker of new materials and in his efforts to please refined, modern women employs the finest talents in the fashion business, including Lyons silk merchants, embroiderers and lacemakers.

510

The 1960's focus on youth encouraged a new wave of creative designers. Of these, Daniel Hechter, Cacherel, Emmanuelle Khanh and Dorothée Bis defended the idea that fashion was no longer the preserve of the couturiers. Courrèges designed geometrically styled clothes made of synthetic materials, Paco Rabanne produced gowns made of aluminum, and Pierre Cardin developed his ready-to-wear line. These currents gave rise to an avant-garde which flourished during the 1980's in the Place des Victoires.

AGNÈS B. – THE SPIRIT OF "ANTI-FASHION"

The work of Agnès B. evokes a relaxed, urban lifestyle. As far back as 1979 she invented the cotton cardigan with metal poppers, available in a wide range of colors. This summed up perfectly the philosophy of a designer who loved to create simple clothes that you mix and match as you like, suitable for wearing day or night, in any combination and in any social situation.

ALAÏA, A DESIGNER WHO GLORIFIES WOMEN

7, rue de Moussy 75004
The gowns designed by Azzedine Alaïa, a proud Parisian originally from Tunisia, are meant for elegant women who are confident of their seductive powers. Alaïa ostentatiously underlines the female form and reveals parts of the body by the skillful use of soft fabrics.

He designed these low-cut shoes for the woman who is sensual and also has a sense of humor.

MUGLER: STRUCTURED ELEGANCE

49, av. Montaigne 75008
These designs were inspired by the ballerinas with whom Thierry Mugler worked when he trained as a dancer. He produces a sublime version of the female form and is well known for his spectacular shows.

CASTELBAJAC: WIT AND COLOR

6, pl. St-Sulpice 75006
Jean-Charles de Castelbajac is instantly recognizable for his motifs in primary colors and his use of unusual materials. An example was the "fur" coat he made out of Teddy Bear material.

SONIA RYKIEL AND "DÉMODE"

175, bd. St-Germain 75006
Rykiel's creations are intended to be worn exactly as the wearer wishes. Their sober hues and simple forms adorned with accessories are a rich combination of humor and sophistication.

JEAN-PAUL GAULTIER: ICONOCLAST

30, rue du Faubourg St-Antoine 75012
"Everything is beautiful if you think it is beautiful" says the man whose designs have revolutionized fashion. Gaultier has no taboos and easily moves from punk to frock coats.

MONTANA: SPIRIT OF THE 1980's

131, rue St-Denis 75001
Claude Montana has said he wants to design clothes that people will enjoy rediscovering. He achieves a rigorous, futuristic style with his use of leather and shoulder pads.

123

▲ FASHION ACCESSORIES

SIDONIE LARIZZI: QUEEN OF HIGH HEELS
Larizzi works for the very best couturiers. The fine line of her shoes, made of such expensive materials as lizard and ostrich skin, or unusual materials like cork or straw, and the way in which the material is cut along the instep has made the reputation of this designer.

◆ 525 Dictionaries define accessory as something that is "extra", "additional" or "an adjunct"; the word comes from the Latin *accedere* which means to add. Objects of adornment, fashion accessories may be divided into two categories: those that are worn, like hats, and those that are carried, like handbags. The ways in which these objects are now used reflects how customs have changed: at one time a fan was a must for every society woman, and no lady would be seen without a hat.

CHRISTIAN LOUBOUTIN'S SHOES
19, rue J.-J. Rousseau
75001
The extremely expensive and elegant shoes of this Parisian designer have been popular with fashionable women ever since he opened his boutique in the Galerie Vérot-Dodat. Louboutin selects from a wide variety of materials, including calfskin and eel skin, and is keen on fish-scale designs and a wide range of colors. His shoes with wooden heels decorated in gold leaf are minor masterpieces.

ELVIS POMPILIO AND HIS FUNNY HATS
62, rue des Sts-Pères
75006
This Italian designer first went to Brussels and now has a shop in the middle of St-Germain-des-Prés. He reminds one a little of the Mad Hatter in *Alice in Wonderland:* his strange kitsch yet chic hats sometimes consist of objects he has picked up in the flea market.

GEORGES GASPAR: UMBRELLAS, CANES AND PARASOLS
Georges Gaspar is the undisputed leader in the field of umbrellas: he supplies the most famous shops, boutiques, theater costume departments and department stores the world over. Gaspar came to Paris from Hungary in 1931 and started up his small company six years later. His daughter continues the tradition, making elegant and beautifully detailed objects.

PHILIPPE MODEL, THE MASTER OF THE FASHION ACCESSORY

33, place du Marché St-Honoré 75001

Model revolutionized hat design, taking it out of its rather conventional rut and introducing materials as diverse as straw and plastic. A lover of bright colors he combined them to stunning effect. He extended his repertoire to bags, gloves and shoes, thus giving fashionable women the option of color-coordinating their accessories.

MARIE MERCIÉ: A HEADY IMAGINATION

56, rue Tiquetonne 75001

Mercié knows how hats ought to be worn. The themes running through her shows range from Viennese cakes and Zulu to Cubism.

GÉRARD TRÉMOLET: THE SPIRIT OF PARIS

Trémolet works for the house of Lesage and allies 18th-century frivolities to a bubbly, very contemporary sense of humor. His magnificent embroidery is unrivaled, and the motifs of his accessories are often inspired by the capital itself.

♦ 523

Like the regal luxury ocean liners of the past or vast temples of consumption, the big department stores of Paris – almost all one hundred years old – are visited by many tourists each year. These stores sprang up under the Second Empire. They introduced modern sales techniques and, by encouraging customers to browse without obligation, they made luxury living accessible to all. Les Magasins du Louvre and La Belle Jardinière have gone, but surviving stores have hardly changed and now include prestigious designer labels among their offerings.

A CITY WITHIN A CITY

The luxurious world through which the customer moves gives no hint of the frenetic beehive atmosphere that reigns in the rest of the building. This cross-section (above) of Le Printemps, between Rue du Havre and Rue Caumartin, dates from 1889 and reveals some of the store's mysteries as well as its complex structure. Storage space, next to the machinery for lighting and heating, is in the basement, in order to facilitate daily deliveries. Offices are now on alternate floors; they used to be just underneath what were once the bedrooms and dining rooms used by resident staff.

PROFIT AND PHILANTHROPY

Entrepreneurs like Aristide Boucicault (1810–77), the founder of Le Bon Marché, also took an interest in his employees' personal development and social well-being.

CHRISTMAS WINDOWS

The windows of the *grands magasins* are famous the world over. The imaginatively thought-out scenes are designed to promote the sale of toys – and to cause crowds to gather on the sidewalks.

> "APART FROM THE MURMUR OF THE BREEZE, ALL THAT REMAINED WAS THE SENSE OF AN ENORMOUS PARIS – ONE SO ENORMOUS THAT IT WOULD ALWAYS HAVE ENOUGH TO PROVIDE FOR SHOPPERS." ÉMILE ZOLA

LE BON MARCHÉ
22, rue de Sèvres 75007
This store opened on the Left Bank in 1852 and was the first of its type. It inspired Émile Zola's novel *Au bonheur des dames*.

The cupola of Le Printemps, which was built in 1923, is a fine example of Art Nouveau. It is 64 feet wide and 52½ feet high. The cupola was torn down during World War Two.

THE BEST USE OF ADVERTISING
Big department stores in Paris devote much of their advertising budgets to publicity, including brochures, shopping bags and calendars.

SYMBOLIC AND FUNCTIONAL ARCHITECTURE
These colossal cathedrals of commerce were built to inspire respect and to tempt customers to spend money. They were the work of such architects as Gustave Eiffel, who designed Le Bon Marché, and Paul Sédille, who was responsible for Le Printemps. The interiors have been redone many times and the current directors are commissioning well-known artists to give their establishments a younger look. This stairway in Le Bon Marché is the work of Andrée Putman.

◆ 525

The quick fortunes that were made during the Second Empire did muc' for the prosperity of jewelers who h forsaken the Palais-Royal for the Rue de la Pai and the Place Vendôme: Mellerio (one of whos creations is shown below, right) was the oldest these firms. The excesses of the Belle Époque gave the jewelers' skills a new boost, and fresh impetus was provided by the development of diamond mining in South Africa. The Place Vendôme has been the center of the jewelers' trade ever since.

TRADITION AND INNOVATION
The house of Cartier dates from 1847. This family firm was involved in the early days of baguette-cut stones and jewels set in platinum.

A BESTIARY BY CARTIER
23, place Vendôme 75001
These parrots made of diamonds are an example of the animal themes which Cartier loved. Other examples include a marvelous panther (1914) set on a bracelet watch and a pink flamingo brooch, both commissioned by the Duchess of Windsor.

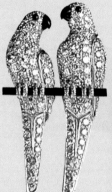

MAUBOUSSIN:
A MASTER OF COLOR
20, place Vendôme 7500
The house of Mauboussi was established in 1827. It is best known for its combinations of colored stones and carved moth of-pearl. This pearl colla includes a 130-carat eme

Chaumet's modern designs have the same peerless quality as these jewels designed especially for the Empress Marie-Louise.

CHAUMET, THE IMPERIAL JEWELER

12, place Vendôme 75001
A collection of diadems belonging to Nitot, founder of the house of Chaumet, is kept in the Hôtel Saint-James, which has also housed the shop since 1907. Nitot achieved prominence when Napoleon I made him responsible for the decorations for his coronation.

Frédéric Boucheron (1830–1902), the founder of a dynasty of jewelers.

BOUCHERON: A PASSION FOR PRECIOUS STONES

20, place Vendôme 75001
A gold medal at the Universal Exhibition of 1867 turned Boucheron into the favorite jewelry house of Paris' cosmopolitan high society. It has occupied premises in the Place Vendôme since 1893 and is credited with bringing rock crystal back into fashion.

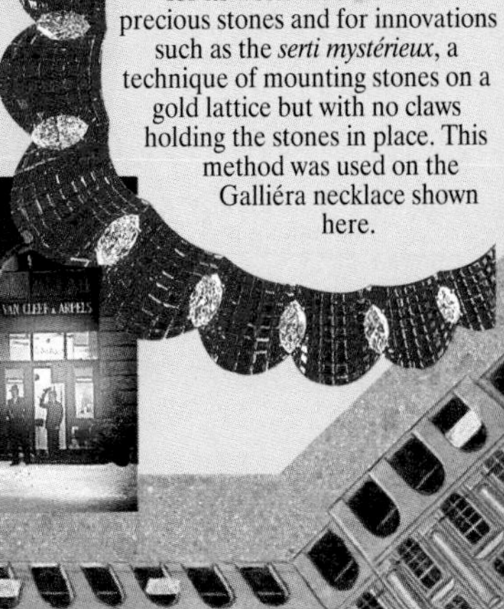

THE CREATIVE GENIUS OF VAN CLEEF & ARPELS

22, place Vendôme 75001
This jeweler, which has been no. 22 since 1906, is well known for its worldwide search for precious stones and for innovations such as the *serti mystérieux*, a technique of mounting stones on a gold lattice but with no claws holding the stones in place. This method was used on the Galliéra necklace shown here.

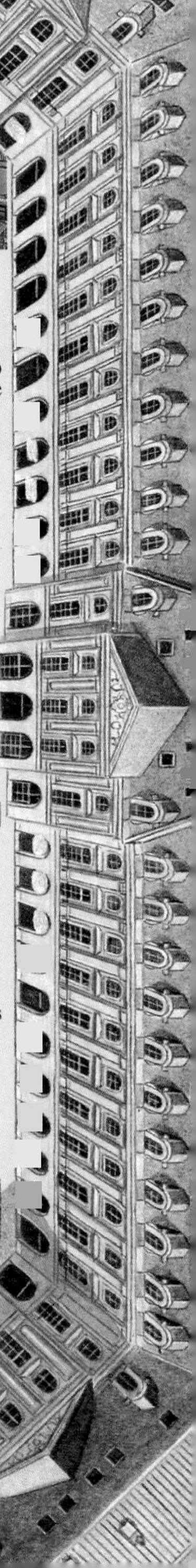

Producers of luxury goods have promoted an image of sumptuous living that has given France, and Paris in particular, a worldwide reputation. They are the guardians of old traditions based on unique skills. These artists' talents combine creativity with exceptional technical skills requiring years of study. Their interests are served by the Colbert Committee, which was set up by the perfumer Jean-Jacques Guerlain in 1954 to promote these artists and protect them from fraudulent imitations.

♦ 526

LALIQUE FANTASIES
11, rue Royale 75008
The founder of the company René Lalique was a jeweler until 1911, when he turned to the design of perfume bottles, which are now collectors' items. Lalique's inimitable style – he often took his inspiration from nature – is based on a combination of transparent and glazed glass which gives his work a mysterious, almost unreal appearance. This modern statue (below) is a good example. The purity of crystal is sometimes enhanced by the use of bright colors.

CHRISTOFLE:
TABLE SETTINGS
9, rue Royale, 75008
This coffee pot, which won a prize at the 1880 Concours Général des Arts en Métal, is the work of the designer Carrier-Belleuse. It shows Christofle's abiding interest in the

decorative arts since the firm's foundation in 1833. He was also a notable designer of deluxe table decoration. At one time he supplied steamships: clients today include major restaurants.

BACCARAT: A MASTER OF CRYSTAL WORK
30, rue de Paradis 75010

The Baccarat museum in the Rue de Paradis contains items that date from 1823: Baccarat's most important works, they are exhibited against a background of mirrors and wood. The collection also includes superb candelabra commissioned by Czar Nicholas II, paperweights, and vases (above) from the early part of the century.

HERMÈS AND THE EQUESTRIAN STYLE
24, rue du Faubourg St-Honoré 75008

This square of silk, one of Hermès' most notable products, is a reminder of the former saddlery which opened in the Faubourg St-Honoré in 1879. The Hermès style, which is both sporty and elegant, is celebrated for its high-quality leather and ingenious designs.

LOUIS VUITTON: A PASSION FOR TRAVEL
54, avenue Montaigne 75008

This trunkmaker settled in Paris in 1854. One of his many innovations was a single key that would open every piece of a customer's luggage. Baggage marked with his initials is recognized the world over. The company today is also a patron of the arts: it funded the restoration of the Opéra's museum-library in 1989. It also publishes works written by great authors containing references to travel.

THE POSSI LAMP
The style is inspired by plant motifs and by Daum's love of naturalism.

DAUM: AN ARTISTIC GLASSMAKER
32, rue de Paradis 75010

His small workshop specializing in hand-made glass was first opened in Nancy in 1874: Daum soon acquired a reputation for his exceptional skill at such techniques as *verre martelé* (its surface like hammered pewter) and the making of *pâte de verre*. The refractive index in these crystal pieces is comparable to that found in diamonds.

♦ 526

As the poet Charles Baudelaire (1821–67) wrote in *Correspondences*, "fragrances, colors and sounds correspond". Perfume bottles from the turn of the century have become collectors' items since François Coty commissioned designs from Lalique and Baccarat. Many fine artists have been employed on promotional work as perfumes have become flagships for the fashion houses which have made them so well known (an illustration by Gruau for Dior, above).

THE GUERLAIN TRADITION

The house of Guerlain has occupied these premises at 2, place Vendôme since 1828. The firm's most celebrated products are *Jicky*, *L'Heure Bleue*, *Shalimar* and *Mitsouko*.

THE LEGENDARY CHANEL NO. 5

When Mlle Chanel said "luxury has its smells", she was undoubtedly thinking of this jasmine perfume which she created in 1921. *Chanel No. 5* has a timeless quality: it is the most widely sold perfume in the world.

EAU DE PARFUM N°5 CHANEL PARIS

THE FRAGRANCE OF DREAMS

Perfumes became fashionable during the 19th century, when it was customary to sprinkle them lightly on handkerchiefs and fans. During the Second Empire women wore Guerlain's *Bouquet de l'Impératrice*.

DIOR: THE CUTTING EDGE OF CHIC

Miss Dior, launched in 1947: the hound's-tooth bottle was also part of the New Look.

HERMÈS: LEATHER AND SCENTS

Bottles of *Calèche* and *Amazone* are sheathed in leather, a reminder of the horseriding that made Hermès famous.

In the last twenty years, virtually all of Paris' museums – from Beaubourg and the Louvre to the Picasso Museum and the Musée d'Orsay – have undergone major renovation. And the city has not cut corners when it comes to quality or quantity. Parisians and tourists alike now have almost a hundred museums at their disposal, ranging from what is perhaps the smallest museum in the world (Erik Satie's *Placard*) to the largest (the

Louvre). Often very original, these museums – whose collections include the anatomical wax figures in the Hôpital St-Louis or the entire works of individual artists such as Rodin and Gustave Moreau – reveal an astonishing variety of art and its techniques through the ages. Despite the many changes in their two hundred years of existence, the city's museums remain faithful to their original objectives: to bring paintings and sculpture together and keep them in good condition, and to exhibit works cleverly so as to instill knowledge, taste and esthetic pleasure for the many viewers.

See pages ◆ 476–81 for opening times.

MUSÉE D'ART MODERNE DE LA VILLE DE PARIS

11, av. du Président Wilson 75016 (1 B4)

Collections that predate the museum
The outbreak of World War Two prevented the installation of the museum's modern art collections in the Palais de Tokyo ▲ *303* – they remained in the Petit Palais. The Museum of Modern Art of the City of Paris did not open until 1961, but even before then its lasting prosperity had already been guaranteed by donors, collectors, artists and dealers (such as Ambroise Vollard). In 1937 the City of Paris acquired a number of major works, including Fernand Léger's *The Discs*.

Décor
The superb panels by Delaunay, Gleizes and Villon were made in 1938 for the Sculpture Room in the Tuileries, but presented to the Museum of Modern Art instead. They illustrate the revival that French abstract art enjoyed in the 1930's. The Matisse Room houses two huge triptychs: *The Unfinished Dance* and *The Dance in Paris*. They are two of the three versions of *The Dance*, which Dr Barnes commissioned from Matisse in 1930 for his foundation in Merion, near Philadelphia. The Dufy Room contains *The Spirit of Electricity*, which Dufy produced for the Pavilion of Electricity at the 1937 Universal Exhibition.

Main currents of the 20th century
Fauvism was dominated by Matisse, Derain, Vlaminck, Braque and Dufy, while Cubism was mainly represented by Picasso and Braque. During the interwar period, Dadaism made an impact through the work of Picabia, as did Surrealism through Ernst and De Chirico. The Paris School brought together foreign painters and sculptors already living in Paris, including Soutine, Modigliani and Zadkine. A room in the museum is devoted to color and the works of Bonnard, Vuillard, Dufy and Matisse. In 1931 the Abstraction-Creation Group brought together the European avant-garde of nonfigurative art. The main trends in postwar art include the lyric abstraction of the 1950's, France's new realists of the 1960's and *arte povera* in Italy. The 1970's were shared by Support-Surface, BMPT groups and "daily mythologies". The objective of the museum's contemporary art department (ARC) is to bring young talent and innovative research to the public's attention.

WOMAN WITH FAN
(1919, Modigliani) This portrait of Lunia Czechowska is notable for its references to hieratic traditions and simplicity of design.

THE CARDIFF TEAM
(1912–13, Robert Delaunay) In this work the artist puts into practice his research into the action of light on moving color. Solidly constructed planes give the painting a very architectural structure.

THE DISCS
*(1918, Fernand Léger) This seminal work from the artist's
mechanical period illustrates Léger's fascination with modern life
and with the world of "implacable and beautiful machines".*

between various
techniques, such
as carpentry,
cabinetmaking,
faïence decorated
with high-
temperature
colors and low-
temperature
enamels, soft and
hard porcelain,
glassware, enamel
work, bronzes, gold
work, jewelry and
tapestry. Certain
techniques are also
presented by
category, including
drawing, glassware,
wallpaper and toys.

A style evolves
The period rooms
have been restored
with decoration
and objects in the
same style. The
late-18th-century
Barriol Room and
Jeanne Lanvin's
apartment were
both created by
Armand Rateau.

Other museums
In addition to the
Musée des Arts
Décoratifs, the
UCAD manages
two other museums
within the Palais
du Louvre: the
Musée de la Mode
et du Textile,
established in
1982 by culture
minister Jack
Lang, and the
Musée de la
Publicité, a poster
museum, which
moved there
from the rue
de Paradis.

A phased reopening
The Musée des
Arts Décoratifs
is undergoing a
reorganization,
and at present
only the Middle
Ages and
Renaissance
rooms are open
to the public.

**MUSÉE DES ARTS
DÉCORATIFS**
107, rue de Rivoli
75001 (1 J5)

**Art and business
working in tandem**
The Union Centrale
des Beaux-Arts
Appliqués à l'
Industrie was set up
in 1864 after the
Universal Exposition
and later became the
Union Centrale des
Arts Décoratifs
(UCAD). Founded
to promote a revival
in the creation of
fine arts, it achieved
this by bringing
together artists and
business people and
enabling them to
create "beauty in
functional things". It
opened a library and
a museum with
collections
illustrating French
domestic decoration.
In 1905 the museum
and the library (now

housed in the
pavilion in the
Marsan Wing of the
Louvre) benefited
from new bequests,
gifts and purchases
of antique pieces
(works by Jules
Maciet, Raymond
Koechlin, Émile
Peyre and David
David-Weill) and
also began to buy
contemporary works
of importance.

**Understanding
techniques**
The museum's
collections, which
span the Middle
Ages to the present
day, are exhibited by
period and by
theme. Some of the
galleries contain
objects that date
from a particular
period; this enables
the visitor to draw
comparisons

SLOPING DESK
*(Mme de
Pompadour, at
Bellevue). This
18th-century piece
illustrates the
influence of
contemporary
enthusiasm for the
Far East.*

See pages ◆ 476–81 for opening times.

*Astrolabe (1567) by
G. Arsenius.*

MUSEÉ DES ARTS
ET MÉTIERS
292, rue St-Martin
75003 (2 F3)

From the historic . . .
The Conservatory of
Arts and Crafts,
which was created by
the Convention in
1794, has been
described as a
collection of
machines, models,
tools, drawings,
descriptions and
books connected
with arts and crafts
of all kinds. It is
housed in the former
Abbey of St-Martin-
des-Champs ▲ 382.
**. . . to the
picturesque**
The collections
include over eighty
thousand objects,
some in splendid
reconstructions of
the laboratories of
the chemist
Lavoisier (1743–94)
and of the physicists
Charles and
the Abbé Nollet. All
important inventions
since the 16th
century are
exhibited here, from
Cugnot's artillery
transporter (1770) to
Clément Ader's
airplane (1897).
Whole sections are
devoted to weights
and measures,
electric batteries and
models of steam
engines, which trace
the origins of these
innovations and
technological
advances. The
museum is currently
being refurbished
and will reopen at
the end of 1999.

MUSÉE DES ARTS
ET TRADITIONS
POPULAIRES
6, avenue du
Mahatma-
Gandhi 75016
(8 E2)

French ethnography
Since 1968 this
museum has been
divided into three
parts. The Gallery of
Culture contains
scenes from
traditional rural life
(reconstructions of
craft workshops,
domestic interiors,
ceramics, carved
wood, copper and
tin) as well as
exhibitions (colored
prints and
costumes). In the
Scientific Gallery
objects are carefully
categorized into
various groupings
including
agricultural
implements, tools
and everyday
objects, while the
Gallery of
Temporary
Exhibitions shows
new acquisitions.

MUSÉE DE
L'ASSISTANCE
PUBLIQUE
47, quai de la
Tournelle 75005
(2 E9)

A unique story
The Hôtel de
Miramion became
the Central
Pharmacy for
Hospitals in 1812,
and has housed this
museum of public
welfare since it
opened in 1934. The
collections provide
an account of the
history of charity,
public assistance and

BLACKSMITH'S SIGN
*This wrought-iron
sign is decorated with
bouquets made of
iron showing scenes
from the artist's
apprenticeship and
his work at the forge.
At the top is the
figure of Saint Eligius
the patron saint of
metalworkers.*

**BOURDELLE IN HIS WORKSHOP WITH
"HERACLES THE ARCHER" (C. 1910)**
*Once free of the influence of Rodin, Bourdelle
showed a rare talent for composition, a brilliant
use of space and a powerful
demonstration of tension.*

Parisian hospitals from the 12th century onward.
Origins of the modern hospital
The museum's collections were first put together at the end of the 19th century, and additions have been made subsequently. Seven hundred years of charitable activity are recounted in illuminated manuscripts, religious paintings, portraits of great believers and men of action

ABANDONED CHILDREN
From the end of the 17th century, these receptacles (left) were installed in front of hospitals and foundlings' hospices, as places to deposit unwanted children.

(Saint Vincent de Paul, for example), and engravings and plans of Paris' oldest hospitals and hospices (Hôtel-Dieu, St-Louis Hospital and the Hospice des Enfants Trouvés – foundling hospital). The role played by medicine in 19th-century hospitals highlights stages in the development of the modern hospital.

MUSÉE BOURDELLE
18, rue Antoine-Bourdelle 75015 (6 G1)

An artist's studio...
The sculptor Antoine Bourdelle moved here in 1885, when the street was called Impasse du Maine. He lived here until his death in 1929. His widow and daughter later gave the land and part of his collection to the City of Paris.
... becomes a museum
The museum opened on July 4, 1949, and contains over five hundred carved works, pastels, paintings, and fresco cartoons, as well as the artist's private collection.

137

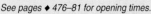

MUSÉE CARNAVALET
23 and 29, rue de
Sévigné, 75003 (2 G6)

**Museum of the
history of Paris**
Work was started on
the Hôtel Carnavalet
in 1548: it was
completed by the
City of Paris in 1866
to accommodate its
historical collections.
In 1989 the
revolutionary
collections of the
19th and 20th
centuries were put
on display at 29, rue
de Sévigné; the
Hôtel Le Peletier de
St-Fargeau, a
townhouse
completed around
1690.
Hôtel Carnavalet
▲ *390* This house

contains
archeological
remains and models
dating from
prehistory, the
Bronze and Iron
ages, the Gallo-
Roman town of
Lutetia, and Paris in
the Merovingian and
Carolingian eras.
The Middle Ages are
represented by
sculptures and by
stained glass from
buildings no longer
standing. Four
rooms on the first
floor recount the
history of Paris
during the
Renaissance and the
Wars of Religion.
Rooms on the
second floor trace
the life of Mme de
Sévigné, who lived in

the Hôtel
Carnavalet. The
remaining rooms
describe Paris
during the Ancien
Régime. The
decoration recalls
bourgeois and
aristocratic life in
the 17th and

18th centuries. The
museum also
contains a few
objects belonging to
Voltaire and
Rousseau.
**Hôtel Le Peletier de
St-Fargeau** ▲ *390*
The third floor
houses portraits,
objets d'art and

furniture which
recall the events that
shook Paris between
1789 and 1794. The
city in the 19th and
20th centuries is
illustrated by
portraits (*Madame*

Récamier by
Baron Gérard) and a
superb collection of
views that trace its
transformation in
the second half of
the 19th century. No
less remarkable is
the collection of

Opposite, top: Porcelain from Sèvres.
Opposite, bottom: Country picnic set in vermeil, belonging to Napoleon I. Below: "Plantation of the Tree of Freedom" by Jean-Jacques Champin, 1848.

brought back from his trip to Asia. He bequeathed to the City of Paris his home and his collections of Chinese and Japanese bronzes and Chinese ceramics. The museum was opened in 1898. Since then, the building has been refurbished on several occasions. The Chinese collections from the end of the Sung

A house built by Mansart
The City of Paris bought this townhouse and later handed it over to the Hunting and Nature Foundation, set up by François Sommer and his wife. They established a museum here and opened a private club for "defenders of nature".

Hunting weapons
The Museum of Hunting and Nature traces the history of

African Room, Musée de la Chasse.

terracotta caricatures by Jean-Pierre Dantan. The museum also boasts some marvelous rooms, including the shop of the jeweler Fouquet (1900) by Alphonse Mucha and the ballroom of the Hôtel de Wendel, decorated by José María Sert in 1924.

MUSÉE CERNUSCHI
7, avenue Vélasquez 75008 (9 E8)

Ancient Chinese art . . .
The financier Henri Cernuschi (1826–96) commissioned the architect Bouwens to build this townhouse in 1873 on the edge of Monceau Park. It was here that Cernuschi displayed the objects he had

STONE STELE
This stele is, surmounted by entwined dragons. It was carved during the Northern Ch'i Dynasty 550–570 and bears an inscription from the year 560.

Dynasty (13th century) have expanded significantly: they include Neolithic ceramics, ancient bronze and jade objects, and a remarkable group of funerary statuettes.

. . . and contemporary Chinese paintings
Thanks to a gift from Dr Kuo Yu-Shou in 1953, the museum now boasts a number of paintings, including works by Zhang Daqian (1899–1983), Fu Baoshi (1905–65) and Qi Baishi (1863–1957).

MUSÉE DE LA CHASSE ET DE LA NATURE
Hôtel Guénégaud 60, rue des Archives 75003 (2 F5) ▲ 387

firearms from matchlock harquebuses to more sophisticated weapons. The collection also includes hunting knives, swords, spears and crossbows.

Zoomorphic art
This art form reached its apogée in the 18th century with the work of Chardin, Oudry (*The Hound Bitch and Her Young*) and Desportes (portraits of Louis XIV's dogs). Important 19th-century artists in this field included Carle Vernet, Camille Corot and Alfred de Dreux.

African, Asian and American rooms
The stuffed animals are interspersed with trophies, weapons and objets d'art.

MUSÉE DE CLUNY
6, place Paul-Painlevé
75005 (2 C9)

From Gallo-Roman Antiquity to the Middle Ages
The Cluny Museum was formed in 1843 with the bringing together of Alexandre du Sommerard's collection of medieval and Renaissance objets d'art and the celebrated Gallo-Roman baths, containing a number of sculptures from Antiquity and the Middle Ages. There is now a museum specially devoted to Renaissance works at the Château d'Écouen and the Cluny Museum has established itself as the National Museum of Medieval Art and Culture.

Beautiful works of gold and enamel
Objects made of gold include 7th-century crowns from Gurrazar, Spain, and an early-11th-century altar from Basel. There are also objects of silver and copper. Some of them are enameled

LADY WITH UNICORN
To illustrate the theme of the vanity of the world (the pleasures of the five senses must yield to the asceticism of the spirit), the artist has combined the decorative and abstract spirit of a traditional mille-fleurs background with a newfound attachment to all the details of the real world.

(from workshops in Limousin) or adorned with precious stones. During the Middle Ages they constituted the treasuries of rich abbeys and princes.

Religious and profane tapestry
A 15th-century profane tapestry in six parts entitled *Lady with Unicorn* is housed in a specially built rotunda. The five senses are represented in five of the brightly colored, well-balanced pieces. The sixth, titled *My Sole Desire* (above), shows jewels placed in a chest: this symbolizes the renunciation of worldly goods.

MUSÉE COGNACQ-JAY
Hôtel Donon
8, rue Elzévir
75003 (2 G6)

Businessman, philanthropist and collector
Like the English art collector and philanthropist Sir Richard Wallace, the founder of the Samaritaine department store, Ernest Cognacq, was a great admirer of the Age of Enlightenment. Together with his wife, Marie-Louise Jay, he collected over a thousand paintings, drawings, sculptures, pieces of furniture, tapestries and objets d'art and bequeathed them to the City of Paris in

NYMPHS RESTING ON THEIR RETURN FROM THE HUNT (1745, attributed to François Boucher). Boucher was Louis XV's favorite painter, a master of courtly and rococo works. Boucher's world was sensual and gracious, and consisted of undulating forms, light, bright colors and flesh tones that recall mother-of-pearl.

RECLINING LEOPARD *(Kändler, 18th century). Johann Joachim Kändler was the director of the factory at Meissen, which jealously guarded the secret of making kaolin-based hard porcelain.*

1928. This collection, originally housed in the Boulevard des Capucines, is now in the Hôtel Donon.

The 18th century: a high point in French art
Court life is splendidly captured by Oeben's "mechanical" table and Jean-Marc Nattier's *Portrait of Marie Leczinska*. The museum also paints an intimate vision of a century that had a passion for refined spaces. All four floors contain work by the various guilds: these emphasize the important roles played by women and children, and a developing taste for the exotic. There is also a fine collection of snuffboxes.

MUSÉE DE LA CURIOSITÉ ET DE LA MAGIE
11, rue Saint-Paul 75004 (2 G8)
Magic has a museum all to itself in the Marais quarter. It is located in a maze of subterranean vaults that once served as a lodging house for travelers who arrived at night, in the era when the Marais was on the outskirts of Paris. In later years, the place was the scene of the

Marquis de Sade's salacious activities. Since 1993, various curiosities have been brought together here – magic amusement machines, colorful posters from the 19th century, automatons, fake objects – and classic tricks with evocative names – the Indian Trunk, the Hindu Basket, the Devil's Mirror – all tracing the long history of the world of illusionism.

MUSÉE GRÉVIN
10, bd. Montmartre 75009 (2 B2)
Waxworks
In 1881 the Parisian journalist Arthur Meyer opened a

A historical scene from the Musée Grévin: Mozart at the harpsichord, aged 7.

waxworks, with three-dimensional representations of prominent people of the day. He entrusted the task of designing the figures to Alfred Grévin. The museum now exhibits the most important figures in the arts, politics and sports. A variety of events are held in a second-floor theater (1900): the Palais des Mirages is well known for its magnificent sound-and-light shows.

Musée Grévin at the Forum des Halles
Niveau-1, Grand Balcon
1, rue Pierre-Lescot 75001
A waxwork Victor Hugo presents Belle Époque Paris.

FAKES
Evidence, in wood or metal, of the sheer ingenuity of conjurers. In the background is a reproduction of The Conjurer *by Jérome (Hieronymous) Bosch.*

See pages ◆ 476–81 for opening times.

MUSÉE GUIMET
6, place d'Iéna
75016 (1 A4)

Asian art and religions
The National Museum of Asian Art, otherwise known as the Guimet Museum, was based on a collection which Émile Guimet

BUDDHA SHIELDED BY THE NAGA MUCILINDA
(12th century) Khmer art in the style of the Bayon Temple.

(1836–1918) brought back from a trip to the Far East for a study of world religions. On his return to France, Guimet founded the Museum of the History of Religions in Lyons; then, in 1885, he gave his collections to the French state so that a similar museum could be established in Paris. The Guimet Museum was opened in 1889. It received sculptures from the Trocadéro Indo-Chinese museum, and in 1945 Asian works hitherto stored in the Louvre were also transferred here. The collection continued to expand with gifts, bequests and purchases, and

with objects given to the museum by French archeologists in India, Afghanistan, central Asia, Indochina and the Far East. The first floor contains art from Southeast Asia (Cambodia, Vietnam, Thailand, Indonesia, Laos and Burma) and Tibetan Buddhist art; the second houses art from India, Gandhara, Afghanistan (the Begram Treasure) and ancient China (the Rousset Collection); and the third is devoted to art from central Asia (discovered by Paul Pelliot), Japan and Korea, and Chinese ceramics (the Calmann and Grandidier Collections). The galleries of the Buddhist pantheon of Japan and China at 19, avenue d'Iéna, contain Émile Guimet's earliest finds in the Far East: they trace the history of religions, in which the museum's founder had a

particular interest. Renovations scheduled to end in in 1998 will improve the displays.

MUSÉE GUSTAVE-MOREAU
14, rue La Rochefoucauld
75009 (10 A9)

Symbolic mythology
As a young man Gustave Moreau (1826–98) was trained in the studio of the Academician François Picot. However, he was

more drawn to the Romantics and soon came under the influence of Théodore Chassériau. Later, on his trips to Italy, he discovered the genius of the ancient masters. Moreau's art was refined and sensual, and he eventually fell under the spell of medieval miniatures and enamel work. Through his allegorical and mythological subjects, he sought a spiritual vision of the world articulated by new means of expression.

THE APPARITION
After 1871, Gustave Moreau executed a series of variations on the theme of Salome and the beheading of John the Baptist.

SHIVA NATARAJA
(Southern India, 11th-century bronze)
The god Shiva performs a cosmic dance within a circle of flames. The dance at once destroys worlds and recreates and maintains them in existence.

MUSÉUM D'HISTOIRE NATURELLE
Jardin des Plantes
57, rue Cuvier
75005 (2 F10)

The Royal Medicinal Herb Garden opened in 1635 and was renamed the National Museum of Natural History in 1793. Its objectives – the preservation and expansion of collections, basic and applied research, and the teaching and diffusion of knowledge – have not changed since that time.

Gallery of Comparative Anatomy and Paleontology
This gallery provides a magnificent survey of the world of vertebrates. The Gallery of Paleontology, on the second floor, has a fine collection of fossils of invertebrates and extinct vertebrates, which trace the development of animal life on this planet. One room is devoted entirely to paleontology in the Paris Basin.

Grand Gallery
This glass-roofed building covers 10,700 square feet and was built at the end of the 1800's by Jules André. It contains a wide range of species and tells the story of man's role in the evolution of life. Animals selected from the collections – they were restored before being spectacularly exhibited – contribute to this graphic presentation. Another feature of the museum is the Gallery of Birds, which traces the history of ornithology.

Gallery of Paleobotany and Mineralogy
This gallery tells the story of plants since their first appearance on

Grand Gallery

Earth, using plant fossils, illustrations of the major groups in the plant world and dioramas.

The Gallery of Mineralogy contains over 500,000 items, ranging from giant crystals to meteorites.

Educational aims
The Gustave Moreau Museum is a rare example of a museum created by the artist for his work and preserved in its original state. After Moreau died in 1898, his sole heir, Henri Rupp, respected the artist's wishes regarding the displaying of his pictures. A series of pivoting panels enables visitors to see the thousands of drawings, watercolors and paintings; these cover the walls up as far as the ceiling and have served as models for subsequent generations.

Skull of Tautavel Man (c. 450,000 BC) and Krishna (India, painted micro-syenite) below.

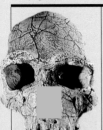

MUSÉE DE L'HOMME
Palais de Chaillot
Place du Trocadéro
75016 (8 J8)

Prehistory, ethnology and anthropology

The Trocadéro Museum of Ethnography changed its name to the Museum of Mankind in 1937; for the Universal Exhibition of Arts and Technology it occupied premises in the Passy wing of the Palais de Chaillot. The aim of the Musée de

l'Homme is to bring together everything about mankind – the origins, evolution and diversity of human culture. When it opened, some of the exhibits came from the cabinets of curiosities that French kings had owned since the 16th century. It received a wide range of ethnological collections, the fruits of archeological digs and human skeletons from the old ethnography museum. These were supplemented with items that were lent or donated by travelers and collectors, or provided by scientific missions throughout the world. The history of man and related issues are addressed using almost 35,000 skulls and several hundred full skeletons in the Laboratory of Biological Anthropology, and by more than 500,000 items in the Laboratory of Prehistory.

New additions

The Gallery of the Night of Time was opened in 1990; it traces the long evolution from the first primates to modern man and describes the slow progression of knowledge. The "All Parents, All Different" room, which was opened in 1992, underlines the enormous physical and biological diversity that marks the six billion people in the world who nonetheless all have a common and recent origin. The American Galleries were renovated in 1992; they take the visitor on a trip through the Americas from Alaska to Tierra del Fuego, and highlight the history of Native Americans from prehistory to the present day.

The Institut du Monde Arabe ▲ IV–V takes its key elements from arab architecture.

MUSÉE DE L'INSTITUT DU MONDE ARABE
1, rue des Fossés-St-Bernard
75005 (2 F9)

Art and civilization

The Museum of the Institute of the Arab World opened in 1987. It recounts the history of Arab and Islamic art and civilization from the origins of Islam to modern times. The collections are still growing and they are flexible and adapt easily to the building. The satin-like finish of the anodized aluminum provides a sober setting for the illuminations, ceramics, textiles and inlaid metals that have come from this refined urban civilization.

Comprehensive collections

A visit to the museum starts with a presentation of the

pre-Islamic era. This is followed by a few ancient pages on the critical role of the source of all Islamic law for Muslims: the Koran. Outstanding successes in scientific and technical skills, a field in which Spain played an active role, encouraged a heightened awareness of the arts. This was especially true of ceramics, which are well represented here. From the 10th century onward, the Muslim world has been characterized by unity and variety; and a dual approach, at once chronological and geographical, invites one to discover the links between forms, motifs and techniques in both time and space. The collections have been enlarged by long-term loans from Arab countries: following the first made by Syria and Tunisia, the museum was described as "the museum of all Arab museums". The Museum of the Institute of the Arab World also boasts a marvelous collection of contemporary Arab art, including paintings, sculptures, graphic art, tapestry and ceramics.

MUSÉES DES INVALIDES
Hôtel des Invalides 75007 (1 F7)

Musée d'Armée
This museum, founded in 1905, grew out of two others: the Artillery Museum, which opened in 1797, and the Army Historical Museum, which opened in 1897. Today's museum is the largest in France devoted to the army. It traces the history of armies from medieval times to today, and the 300,000 items on display include fine examples of arms and armor, small artillery models, and historical memorabilia and uniforms from the Ancien Régime to World War Two.

Musée d'Histoire Contemporaine
This museum was founded in 1914 and transferred to the Invalides in 1973. The exhibits are of considerable political, social and cultural significance. The 1.5 million items (dating from 1870 to the present day), include paintings, posters, political cartoons and photographs, and focus on the major events in the history of France and other countries.

Musée de l'Ordre de la Libération
This museum was able to open thanks to gifts made by the Companions of the order of the Liberation, an Order created by General de Gaulle in Brazzaville in 1940. The North Gallery deals with Free France, the South Gallery covers the Resistance, and the second floor is devoted to deportation.

Musée des Plans-Reliefs
These models of fortresses were made between 1668 and 1875 and were used for

CHARLES IX'S ARMOR
(France, 1564–74, carved gilt iron)

strategic purposes. The collection was originally on display in the Grande Galerie of the Louvre.

HEAD OF DROPSICAL MAN
(Attributed to Hans Holbein the Elder; pen and brown-wash drawing, green tempera, highlights in white and green gouache)

See pages ◆ 476–81 for opening times.

MUSÉE DU LOUVRE – GRAPHIC ARTS
Palais du Louvre
75001 (1 A5)

Royal origins
The initial collection consisted of the King's Cabinet, which has been in the Louvre since it opened and was expanded through the addition of Louis XIV's purchases and by items produced by the king's favorite painters. By 1730 there were 8,593 items, and this number was increased through the acquisition of a thousand drawings sold by Pierre-Jean Mariette in 1775. The collection continued to expand with the incorporation of items seized during the Revolution,

INTERIOR
(Edgar Degas, oil on paper) This tantalizing, thought-provoking sketch recalls the backgrounds to be found in some of Degas' portraits of the 1860's.

purchases, bequests, gifts and donations. In 1989, the Louvre acquired two studies of Leonardo's *Draperies* from the collection of the Countess of Béhague.

Everything on paper
The Graphic Arts department has about 126,000 items on paper, covering a period from the 14th to the early 20th century, and exclusively representing Western art. The formats and techniques are varied, and the works are often kept in albums or notebooks. There are pastels, gouaches and large sketches in addition to more traditional drawings and watercolors. The 19th-century pastels were transferred to the Musée d'Orsay in 1986. There is also a collection of miniatures in ivory and enamel, which the museum acquired thanks to the Doisteau (1919) and David-Weill (1947) bequests. The opening of the Richelieu Wing in 1993 enabled the museum to devote a small section to the graphic art of northern Europe. The Graphic Arts department also has a collection of 16,000 copperplates originally used for royal commissions.

HEAD OF MAN WEARING A TURBAN
(Salvator Rosa, black stone, pastel, highlights in white and red chalk on beige paper) This idealized and detailed study of a head probably dates from Rosa's second stay in Rome, from 1649 to 1660.

MUSÉE DU LOUVRE – PAINTING

From royal collections to a museum

The private collections that once belonged to the kings of France now constitute the basis of the paintings hanging in the Louvre. These have been joined by works seized during the Revolution, commissions given to artists during the Restoration and the Second Empire, generous donations made by collectors at the end of the 19th and start of the 20th centuries, and purchases.

Paintings presented by school

French painting is exhibited in rooms on the third floor of the Richelieu Wing. This section also includes primitives, the Fontainebleau School, and 16th-century works, as well as paintings of the 17th, 18th and 19th century, which are on display in rooms encircling the Cour Carrée. The Salles Rouges of the Denon Wing (Daru, Denon and Mollien) house the large paintings of the neoclassical and Romantic periods. Another tour starting in the Richelieu Wing is devoted to Flemish and Dutch painting. The Louvre has a number of primitives and works by contemporaries of Van Eyck, and important works by Rembrandt,

VIRGIN AND CHILD WITH SAINT ANNE
(c. 1500, Leonardo da Vinci). This work, which influenced many artists including the young Raphael, was brought to France by Leonardo when he was summoned there by François I. It became part of the royal collections on Leonardo's death.

Vermeer and Rubens. These include a magnificent cycle commissioned by Marie de' Medici for the glorification of royalty, which brings the tour to a close. A third tour is planned for 1997, passing through the Salon Carré, the Grande Galerie and adjacent rooms of the Denon Wing. It will focus on Italian painting from Giotto to Guardi, incorporating Caravaggio and Titian. The Spanish School, which includes works by El Greco, Murillo, Zurbarán and Velázquez, will be on display in the rooms beyond the Italian School. A selection of 18th- and 19th-century works of the German and English Schools is on display in the Denon Wing (room 76) but awaits a permanent home.

147

SPHINX HEAD OF KING DJEDEDFRE
(c. 2570 BC, quartzite)
This was found in a ditch alongside the king's pyramid near Giza. It is the head of a sphinx with the features of the king.

MUSÉE DU LOUVRE – EGYPT
The days of the archeologists
On May 15, 1826, the Egyptologist Jean-François Champollion was appointed director of the Charles X Museum. When Henry Salt, the British consul in Alexandria, put up for sale the 4,000 objects that he had brought back from Egypt, Champollion acquired them for the Louvre. Between 1850 and 1854, Auguste Mariette took part in archeological excavations of the sacred bulls at the Serapeum in Saqqara and sent 6,000 objects back to the Louvre. The French Institute of Oriental Archeology in Cairo, which was founded in 1880, provided many pieces from sites where it was taking part in digs.

A 4,000 year-old civilization
The first-floor rooms provide a picture of daily life through numerous objects connected with fishing, animal rearing, agriculture, hunting, writing, craft work, dwellings, dress, music and games. The Avenue of Sphinxes leads to the temple and into a world belonging to the gods: here, the crypt opens out onto an area devoted to the dead and to funerary rites. The worship of animals is illustrated by objects from the Serapeum. The rooms on the second floor take the visitor on a historic tour which starts with the wealth that characterized the final centuries of prehistory; included are decorated vases and votive objects, such as the *Palette de la Chasse*. The first two dynasties witnessed the early days of writing and the foundation of royalty (*Stele of the Serpent-King*). The Old Empire is represented by statuary and reliefs that came from the pyramids and tombs (including the *Crouching Scribe*), while the Middle Empire reunited Egypt after 200 years of turbulence; this is illustrated by the statues of Senroswet III. The successes that crowned the New Empire fill five rooms (18th Dynasty, Amarna and Ramesside). The last thousand years were those of

THE DIVINE CONSORT KAROMAMA
(870–825 BC; bronze inlaid with gold, silver and electrum) Jean-François Champollion fell in love with this statuette of the Princess of Thebes, the "mystical spouse" of the god Amun.

dynasties less famous and highly productive: an example is the *Triad of Osorkon*. After Cleopatra died, Egypt fell under Roman control and, as the rooms surrounding the Visconti Courtyard show, converted to Christianity.

MUSÉE DU LOUVRE – THE ORIENT

Nonstop excavations
The Department of Oriental Antiquities has about 90,000 pieces which came from French digs in the Middle East carried out under Paul-Émile Botta ▲ 150, Ernest Renan (Phoenicia, 1862) and Ernest de Sarzec (Tello, 1877), the man who rescued the Sumerians from oblivion. Marcel Dieulafoy's

IBEX GOBLET
(Iran, 4th millennium, terracotta)
Painted vases from the tombs at Susa are notable for their highly skilled use of very stylized but figurative forms.

HEAD OF GUDEA
(Tello, c. 2130 BC, diorite)
The prince is wearing royal headgear consisting of a hat made of woolly curls. His face is unusually broad.

PYX OF AL-MUGHIRA
(Cordoba, 968, ivory)
The detailed decoration has been sculpted, then carved again.

discovery of traces of the Persian Empire in Susa in 1884 was followed up by Jacques de Morgan (1897) and Roland de Mecquenem. In the 20th century, the Abbé de Génouillac was succeeded by André Parrot (Tello, Larsa and Mari, 1923) and Claude Schaeffer (Ougarit, 1929). Other major collections acquired by the Louvre include the finds made by Louis De Clercq in Syria at the beginning of the 20th century and given to the Museum by Henri de Boisgelin in 1967.

The ancient Orient: Mesopotamia, Iran and the Levant
The department acquired extra space in the Richelieu Wing in 1993. Since work on the Cour Carrée (Sully) was completed in 1997, the department is now in the process of putting together a finished and comprehensive display. The rooms are divided into three geographic areas – Mesopotamia, Iran and the Levant; they are then organized chronologically. The Richelieu Wing contains treasures from Mesopotamia, Sumer, Babylon and Assur, which are grouped around the Khorsabad Court ▲ 150. The Iran tour commences in the Richelieu Wing and continues in the north wing of the Cour Carrée with decorations from

---

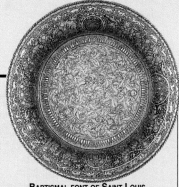

BAPTISMAL FONT OF SAINT LOUIS
(13th–14th century, Syria or Egypt)
This large receptacle is an outstanding example of Mameluke art and bears the signature of Muhammad ibn Zayn. It forms part of the French royal collections and in the 18th century became known (incorrectly) as the Baptismal font of Saint Louis, a misnomer which has survived. The decoration consists of large inlaid pieces of silver gilt.

Darius' palace in Susa (1997). The Levant, whose origins are fixed at the end of the second millennium, is located in the rooms adjoining Sully West: the continuation of the north wing of the Cour Carrée houses monuments from Palmyra, Cyprus and Phoenicia (1st millennium), together with a collection of anthropoid sarcophagi.

The Islamic world
The royal collections contained luxurious objects for many years, but an Islamic section was set up only in 1890. The

metal and ivory objects, ceramics, wainscoting, carpets, textiles, miniatures and drawings are exhibited in thirteen rooms on the mezzanine floor of Richelieu Wing. The first nine rooms are vaulted and have been specially adapted to house objects from the ancient and medieval periods. The remaining rooms are more modern in design and are situated under the Khorsabad Court. There are over a thousand objects, from an area extending from Spain to India, omitting North Africa ▲ 158.

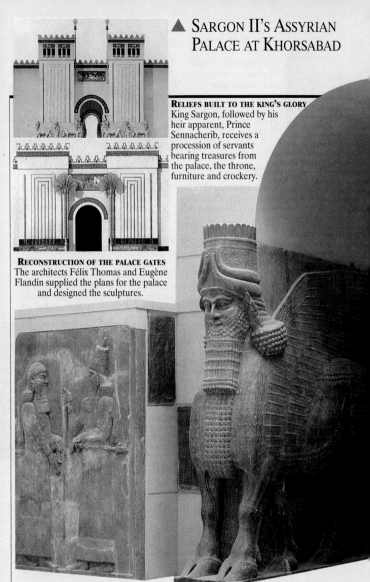

Reliefs built to the king's glory
King Sargon, followed by his heir apparent, Prince Sennacherib, receives a procession of servants bearing treasures from the palace, the throne, furniture and crockery.

Reconstruction of the palace gates
The architects Félix Thomas and Eugène Flandin supplied the plans for the palace and designed the sculptures.

Androcephalous bulls standing between the Cour Carrée and the Richelieu Wing.

In 1843 the French consul in Mosul, Paul-Émile Botta, made important Assyrian finds in the course of his research on the Khorsabad site. His copies of cuneiform writings led to the deciphering of ancient Mesopotamian writing, and the large reliefs which he sent back to the Louvre were put on display in the world's first Assyrian museum (1847). This museum, which became the Napoleon III Museum in 1857, existed until 1991. The opening of the Richelieu Wing in 1993 made it possible to reorganize the Assyrian collections and to refurbish the Khorsabad Court, which strongly evokes the monumental entrance to Sargon II's palace.

MONUMENTAL STONE DECORATION
The carved frieze which protected the base of brickwork walls is interrupted by doors bored into the wall. They are framed by mythological figures 14½ to 16 feet high, including winged bulls with men's heads.

THE EXCAVATIONS
The photographer Gabriel Tranchand was a friend of the Assyriologist Victor Place and successor to Botta. In 1853–4 he took photographs at the Khorsabad site showing the stages of the excavations.

ENTRANCE TO THE THRONE ROOM
Its monumental decoration, on the east wall of the courtyard, is evoked by a bull turning its head (the original is in Chicago); it is next to the hero, who is strangling a lion (pseudo-Gilgamesh), whose strength is a measurement of the king's power.

See pages ◆ 476–81 for opening times.

MUSÉE DU LOUVRE – GREEK, ETRUSCAN AND ROMAN ANTIQUITIES

A museum of antiquities

This museum was founded in 1792 and officially opened in 1800. At the time, it mainly housed sculptures from royal collections, but it was rapidly enlarged through the addition of goods seized from émigrés and numerous important works brought back by victorious French armies. More conventional acquisitions included the prestigious Borghese collection in 1808. After 1815, the number of sculptures was increased by the addition of the Parthenon Metope (1818) and part of the Albani collection. The *Venus de Milo*, a gift from the Marquis of Rivière to Louis XVIII, came to the Louvre in 1821; shortly afterward, the Greek state presented the marbles from Zeus' temple in Olympia.

Three civilizations

With the acquisition of the Tochon collection in 1818 and the arrival of the Durand collection in 1825, the Louvre at last had a strong display of Greek and Etruscan vases, and almost 2,000 bronzes. The *Winged Victory at Samothrace* was acquired under the Second Empire, together with the huge collection of the Marquès de Campana. This, at that time the most important collection in the world, consisted of around 12,000 objects, including hundreds of marbles, over 1,500 terracotta pieces, and 3,500 vases. The late 19th century saw the arrival of smaller objects, such as statuettes from Tanagra and Myrina, larger statues from Ancient Greece, and a superb treasury of Roman silverware discovered in a villa at Boscoreale, near Pompeii. More recently, the Louvre acquired new collections, including finds from Elaious in Thrace, a marvelous series of mosaics excavated at Antioch, and bronzes and jewelry from the De Clercq-Boisgelin donation.

KORE OF SAMOS
(Sámos, 570 BC, marble)
This representation of Persephone is typical of early Greek sculpture and is dedicated by Chéramyés to the goddess Hera.

TOMB OF PHILIPPE POT
(15th century) This monumental tomb, an outstanding piece of medieval funerary art, was found at Cîteaux.

SARCOPHAGUS OF A MARRIED COUPLE
(Cervetere, late 6th century BC; painted terracotta) This sarcophagus was the work of an artist from Cervetere and is one of the most characteristic works of Etruscan civilization.

MUSÉE DU LOUVRE – SCULPTURE

French sculpture

Since 1993, French sculpture has been displayed on the first floor of the Richelieu Wing, occupying some 30 rooms encircling the two main courtyards: one is devoted to statues, groups and vases from Marly (Cour Marly); the other contains outdoor sculptures from the 17th, 18th and 19th centuries (Cour Puget). The chronological tour takes the visitor from the oldest pre-Roman and Roman sculptures to neoclassicism and Romanticism, and includes major works, ranging from Jean Goujon's *Nymphs* to Pierre Puget's *Milo of Croton* to Pigalle's *Mercury*.

Foreign sculpture

Italian sculpture from the late Middle Ages and early Renaissance is particularly well represented. Northern Europe, particularly Germany, boasts a treasury of late-medieval wooden sculptures with polychrome decoration. Spanish sculpture, which is often felt by the French to be characterized by excessive realism, is poorly represented.

The rooms in the Denon Wing which were given over to sculpture in 1994 are very different. A respect for spaces and interior decoration, and the need for disparate works to be displayed together, meant that Napoleon III's former stables have been used for the presentation of pre-16th-century Italian and northern European pieces. The stables' brick and stone vaults have been refurbished, and the windows give onto the Cour Lefuel. The Mollien Gallery (Michelangelo Gallery) on the floor above contains an outstanding collection of Italian sculptures from Michelangelo to Canova, including the *Gate of Cremona*. One of the aims of this new layout is to highlight the department's three most famous sculptures: Michelangelo's two *Slaves* and Canova's *Psyche Revived by the Kiss of Eros.*

COUR MARLY
The huge glass roof ▲ 327 allows large quantities of natural light to enter this courtyard. The architect Michel Macary has made use of the symmetry of the two groups carved by Coustou and Coysevox.

LOUISE BRONGNIART
(1777, Jean-Antoine Houdon, terracotta) This artist executed a large number of children's portraits notable for their supple contours and lively expressions. Houdon earned a great deal of money producing busts of famous people, including Diderot, Benjamin Franklin, George Washington, the Comte de Buffon and Jean-Jacques Rousseau.

The Grand Salon in Napoleon III's apartments ▲ 325.

tables adorned with gold and porcelain from the royal factory at Sèvres.

MUSÉE DU LOUVRE – OBJETS D'ART

Royal objets d'art

The department has inherited a number of royal collections, including bronzes and precious stones belonging to Louis XIV and the Crown Jewels, as well as part of the treasure from the St-Denis Abbey: this included the regalia used in the coronations of French kings and vases collected by the French monk Suger in the 12th century. The decoration of paintings and gilt stucco in the Apollo Gallery was undertaken by Charles Lebrun in 1661; it was completed by Eugène Delacroix around 1850 with his *Triumph of Apollo*, which is in the center of the ceiling. There are also precious stones and some valuable snuffboxes.

Medieval and Renaissance collections

Chronological and geographical considerations have led to these collections being located on the second floor of the Richelieu Wing. The most remarkable works are pieces made by goldsmiths (final years of the Valois), glassmakers, enamelers (workshops in Limousin), artists working in ivory and bronze, and tapestry makers.

17th and 18th centuries

This period is represented to the north of the Cour Carrée by a large collection of furniture, tapestries and objects whose diversity and quality reflect the huge advances made by French civilization at that time. An example of this refinement can be seen in

CHARLES IX'S SHIELD *(embossed gold-plated iron and enamel) This ceremonial shield was made by Pierre Redon in Paris in 1572. It is symbolic of the luxurious life style and refinement enjoyed by the court of the Valois in its declining years.*

SUGER'S EAGLE *(Rome, Imperial era, porphyry, St-Denis before 1147, mounting in nielloed silver gilt). Suger, the Abbot of St-Denis Abbey and a counselor to Louis VI and Louis VII, turned this into a liturgical vase by placing it on a mounting in the form of an eagle's head.*

The first half of the 19th century

These collections have now been divided up: to the north of the Cour Marly are the most beautiful Empire pieces, particularly the furnishings of Mme Récamier's drawing room and bedchamber (1798). To the east of the Cour Carrée are decorative arts of the Restoration and the July Monarchy, together with innovations shown at the Expositions of Industrial Products. The chronological tour ends in the rooms that were decorated during the reign of Napoleon III and which served as reception rooms for the minister of finances from 1871 until 1989.

Portuguese sea compass, 1744.

LA DAUPHINE
(29-oar galley, 1736–92). Contemporary model (scale 1:24).

ships of the royal fleets is told in the Navy Museum's Grand Gallery. The story starts with the *Couronne* (1637), the first large vessel built in France, and includes the magnificent series of *Ports of France* painted by Joseph Vernet (1754–65). It concludes with models of the most up-to-date commercial craft and submarines to be launched in France's shipyards.

MUSÉE DE LA MARINE
Palais de Chaillot
Place du Trocadéro
75016 (8 J8)

A long tradition
In 1748 the inspector general of the navy, Louis-Henri Duhamel du Monceau, brought together a remarkable collection of model ships and naval machines. The objective was to give instruction to apprentice shipbuilders for whom a school had just been started in Paris. When Charles X opened a public museum in 1827, the Dauphin Museum's collections were enlarged by the addition of paintings from Versailles and the Louvre, ornaments from ships in the navy's various dockyards and artillery pieces.

A reminder of France's great maritime past
The entire history of the construction and strategic use of the

MUSÉE MARMOTTAN
2, rue Louis-Boilly
75016 (8 E9)

Where Impressionism is worshipped
The Marmottan Museum was originally a hunting lodge and then a private townhouse. It was converted by Paul Marmottan into a Napoleonic museum with an unusual collection of furniture, bronzes, sculptures and paintings. It now houses most of the Impressionists including Sisley, Pissarro, Renoir, Caillebotte, Guillaumin and Jongkind. It has over a hundred paintings by Monet.
The Wildenstein donation
Daniel Wildenstein presented the museum with his father's marvelous collection of illuminations in 1980. This comprised 228 miniatures from antiphonaries, missals and books of hours from various European countries.

DÉSIRÉE CLARY
(Baron Gérard, 1770–1837) Désirée Clary, Joseph Bonaparte's sister-in-law, married Marshal Bernadotte, who became King of Sweden in 1818.

See pages ◆ 476–81 for opening times.

A gold franc minted during the reign of Jean le Bon (1360)

MUSÉE DE LA MONNAIE

11, quai de Conti
75006 (2 B7)

The Museum of the Paris Mint is situated in the old room once used for striking coins. Its collections of 2,000 coins, 450 medals, tokens, sculptures, machines and tools, official documents, paintings, engravings and stained-glass windows are now housed in a more modern setting. The museum is unable to put its entire collection on

educational nature of the museum's presentation: this includes glass casings which enable visitors to see both sides of the coins and medals.

MUSÉE NATIONAL D'ART MODERNE

Centre Pompidou
6, rue Beaubourg
75004 (2 E5)

Fauvism and Cubism (Braque, Picasso and Léger). A second series of exhibits illustrates the developments made by abstract art (Kandinsky and Brancusi), Dadaism, and Suprematism (Malevitch), while the interwar period is represented by the Surrealists (Calder, Miró and Ernst), Rouault and Chagall. A visit to the National Museum of Modern Art concludes with European and American artistic developments of the

and works by Réquichot, Dado and Fahlström: these lead into Dubuffet's Winter Garden. The rooms containing contemporary art are regularly changed and there is a permanent facility for viewing videos both of the collections and of new design and architectural collections. These include significant examples of the principal artistic movements since the 1960's, such as Pop Art, New Realism, Conceptual Art, *Arte Povera*, Minimalism, Support-Surface and Free Figuration.
New works on show
The collection of the Musée National d'Art Moderne – Centre de Création Industrielle now consists of about 34,000 works. It is distantly related to the Royal Museum

THE SHEPHERD OF THE CLOUDS

*(1953, Jean Arp)
Arp followed his early figurative, Cubist work with abstract creations in which he explored the element of chance.*

LOUIS XIV AS A CHILD WITH JEAN VARIN

*(1654, attributed to François Lemaire)
The engraver Jean Varin initiated the young Louis XIV in the art of old coins.*

display and has therefore opted to concentrate on key moments in French history from antiquity to the present day. This is achieved through coins and medals which commemorate acts of daily life as well as great historical events. The architecture of the former coin-press room suggests a basilica. It also underlines the

Modern art
Every six months, the exhibition on the fifth floor of the historic collections from 1905 to the 1960's is changed: the items are arranged by artists and movements. This floor was refurbished in 1985 by the architect Gae Aulenti. The terraces, with sculptures by Laurens and Miró, lead on to Matisse,

1950's and 1960's: the sections devoted to Giacometti, Dubuffet, Balthus, Pollock and Newman are outstanding.
Contemporary art from the 1960's to the present day
Access to the fourth floor, which houses the contemporary collections, is along the southern terrace. The escalator deposits the visitor outside a number of rooms devoted to pieces from the Daniel Cordier donation,

NUDE WITH ORANGES
(1953, Matisse, India ink, gouache, cut and pasted paper) The museum has almost 150 works of Henri Matisse. It has been seeking to establish the artist's linear development by acquiring a series of key paintings, including "Greta Prozor" (1916), "French Window at Collioure" (1914) and the original sketches for "Jazz" (1943–6). This policy has now been implemented following a donation which the artist's son Pierre made to the museum on his death.

of Luxembourg, which opened in 1818 to cater to the needs of living artists, but the collection owes its revival in 1947 to Jean Cassou, the museum's first director. The presentation of the works is radically changed every six months and includes theme- or monograph-based exhibitions, which provide an excellent opportunity to view new acquisitions. Major structural changes to the building are planned for 1997, during which time the museum will occupy premises on the fourth, fifth and sixth floors.

NEW YORK CITY I
(1942, Mondrian; oil on canvas)
"New York City I" was painted during Mondrian's stay in that city. It makes a clean break with the black structure of his Parisian period and substitutes a range of primary colors which alone organize the rhythm and space of his paintings. This is one of the major pieces in a collection which also includes abstract works by Theo van Doesburg, Arp, Pevsner, Malevitch and Moholy-Nagy.

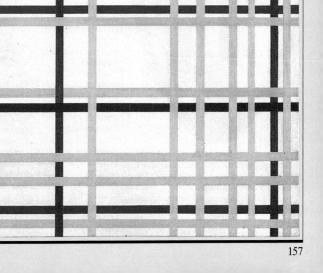

See pages ◆ 476–81 for opening times.

MUSÉE NATIONAL DES ARTS D'AFRIQUE ET D'OCÉANIE
293, avenue Daumesnil 75012 (4 H4)

A 1930's setting
This building was constructed from plans by Jaussely and Laprade for the Colonial Exhibition of 1931. It has retained some of the 1930's decoration, including a bas-relief by Janniot on the façade, frescos by Ducos de La Haille and interior furnishings by Ruhlmann and Printz. The museum was the only building of any size to survive the Colonial Exhibition, and from 1935 onward, it housed the Musée des Colonies (Colonial Museum). The building was taken over by the Ministry of Cultural Affairs in 1960, and André Malraux turned it into the National Museum of African and Oceanic Arts.

Black Africa and North Africa
A collection of Cameroon art bequeathed by Pierre Harter in 1991 is on display on the first floor; the second floor contains collections from West Africa which include highly stylized, geometrical forms of art from the savanna. It also displays work from central Africa – royal tapestries from Benin, beautiful 16th- to 19th-century bronze and ivory objects from Benin and Nigeria, and a wide range of geometrical, naturalistic and expressionistic sculptures from Nigeria, Cameroon, Gabon, Congo, Zaire and Angola. Collections from North Africa on the third floor are a reminder of Morocco, Algeria and Tunisia's links with the Orient and with Europe.

Oceania
The Australia Room on the first floor houses an impressive range of Aboriginal paintings on tree bark, acrylics on tiles and a number of traditional objects. Melanesia is characterized by a demonstration of the wide variety of uses to which materials are put (ritual and architectural objects).

Aquarium
The fish are exhibited by region and physiological characteristics.

STATUE OF THE GOD RAO
This wood statue from Mangareva Island, in the Gambier Archipelago survived the missionaries of the 19th century. It is remarkable for its thin body and smooth face, and the position of the arms. It was brought to Europe in 1836 by Fathers of the Picputian Society.

BIRD MASK
This mask of wood and brass was made by the Yaouré of the Ivory Coast. Carvings from the borderlands of Liberia, Upper Guinea and the Ivory Coast are usually masks of human faces. They comprise a variety of images, in a range of materials and decorations and are remarkable for their fine, simple lines.

"Rabâb" lute, created by an unknown lutemaker in Afghanistan

MUSÉE DE LA MUSIQUE

Cité de la Musique, 221, avenue Jean-Jaurès 75019 (11 D5)

Origins

The original Music Museum was founded in 1864 under the control of the Paris Music Conservatory, after their purchase of 300 instruments from the composer Louis Clapisson. Other prestigious acquisitions followed: in 1887, a Java gamelan thought to be one of the oldest in existence; in 1934, the rare instrument collection of Paul Cesbron; and in 1980, the Chambure collection, from the museum's director between 1961 and 1973.

A new museum

The idea of a new museum was born in the 1960's, and in 1979 the decision was taken to site it at La Villette, where plans already existed for the creation of a Cité de la Musique. Designed by Christian de Portzamparc, the Cité today houses two concert halls, information centres and a bookstore, as well as the new Musée de la Musique, which opened in 1997.

A unique collection

The museum displays in the region of 900 instruments from a total national collection of more than 4,500, grouped into nine major points in the history of music and the manufacture of instruments between the end of the 17th century and the present day. Each of the nine spaces is centred around one musical work, played by an ensemble and illustrated by a model of the setting in which it was composed. Thus the visitor moves from a room in the Mantoue Palace, where Monteverdi's *Orfeo* was created, to the Champs-Élysées theatre where the premiere of Igor Stravinsky's *The Rite of Spring* created a furore.

Early 17th-century Venetian arched lute.

MUSÉE NISSIM DE CAMONDO

63, rue de Monceau 75008 (9 F8)

The Hôtel de Camondo

Between 1911 and 1914, Moïse de Camondo, a wealthy banking heir with a strong enthusiasm for the decorative arts of the 18th century, chose a site at the edge of

The Blue Room at the Musée Nissim de Camondo

Monceau Park to build a mansion to house his large collection of objets d'art, consisting of furniture, paintings, carpets, tapestries, porcelain and gold plate. Following the death of his only son, Nissim de Camondo, in World War One, the count bequeathed the house and its collection to the Union Centrale des Arts Décoratifs (UCAD). The museum opened to the public in 1936.

Exceptional objets d'art

The collection created by Moïse de Camondo is devoted almost exclusively to the decorative arts of the second half of the 18th century. A few works represent the earlier Louis XIV period. One such is the carpet in the Grand Salon, which was commissioned from the house of Savonnerie for the Grande Galerie in the Louvre. From the neoclassical period, the collection shows the assembled works of the cabinet-makers to the king and court. These include curtained, balustrated pieces of furniture and a hollowed chiffonier table, both created by Jean-Henri Riesener, and a folding desk by Jean-François Leleu. A pair of vases covered in petrified wood, from the collection of Marie Antoinette, illustrates the refined nature of her Versailles apartments, of which Moïse de Camondo was so fond. Tableware holds a special place in this collection. Among the most spectacular of all the pieces are the large Sèvres porcelain dinner service decorated with a bird motif and known as the "Buffon", and the Orloff silverware commissioned by Catherine the Great.

▲ MUSÉE D'ORSAY

See pages ◆ 476–81 for opening times.

M 'O

M for Musée, O for Orsay: an attractive logo for one of the most successful gambles that the worlds of architecture and museums have known in the last ten years. The Gare d'Orsay was scheduled to be torn down in 1970 but survived by the skin of its teeth and became a landmarked building in 1978. The vast dimensions of this early 20th-century building have helped the new project and are ideally suited for a museum. The main hall is now bordered by a series of terraces and stepped landings, where the exhibits are housed. The whole building benefits from an abundance of natural light.

FROM PALACE TO RAILWAY STATION

In the middle of the 19th century, two buildings occupied the site of what is now the Musée d'Orsay: the barracks of a cavalry regiment and the offices of the Revenue Court and the Council of State. The fires of the Paris Commune (1870–1) left them in ruins. The Orléans Railway Company bought the land in 1897 with a view to constructing the Gare d'Orsay for trains serving Nantes, Bordeaux and Toulouse. The building was scheduled to be ready for the Universal Exhibition of 1900, and construction was completed in only two years.

QUAI D'ORSAY
The quai d'Orsay was built by Charles Boucher d'Orsay, Provost of the Merchants Paris in 1708. It was use for storing wood until 1810.

STEEL ARCHES AND PLASTER CAISSONS

The ceiling illustrates the close working relationship between the construction workers and the architects. It is characterized by a highly skilled system of roof timbers with

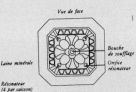

no tie beams and monumental ornamentation consisting of large caissons of molded plaster bound with vegetable fibers.

VICTOR LALOUX

(1850–1937)
Laloux was the young architect who won the competition to design the Gare d'Orsay. He added a hotel that faced the Rue de Bellechasse.

FROM RAILWAY STATION TO MUSEUM

The long-distance railway network came to a standstill in 1939, and the station – an immense hall with an arched vault 128 feet high and, running alongside it, a narrower hall topped by a series of seven cupolas – was then used for various purposes, including as an auction house and a theater.

ONE OF MANY PLANS

When it was decided to put the station to a new use in 1935, Raymond Lopez proposed transforming the building into an enormous sports complex containing a sailing basin that could be covered over by a removable floor and used for other activities. The outside walls were to be completely reworked in a strikingly modern style.

THE BIRTH OF MODERN PAINTING
(*Le Déjeuner sur l'herbe*, Manet, 1863)
This painting's theme suggested new ways of treating space and volumes, heralding the birth of 20th-century art.

SCULPTURE AND REALISM
(*The Dance*, Carpeaux, 1869)
This contrasts with the carved groups decorating the Paris Opéra.

THE BEGINNINGS OF EXPRESSIONISM
(*The Church at Auvers-sur-Oise*, Van Gogh, 1890) This striking picture (left) is notable for the irregular lines and thick layers of color: they appear to give each other strength. It established Van Gogh as the precursor of European Expressionism.

SCULPTU NATURALISM
(*Girl Dancer, a* Degas, 1880, b Degas was crit the academic traditions th were still la sculpture. a ruthless observer a opposed t forms of idealiza

IMPRESSIONISM
(*Rouen Cathedral: Blue and Gold Harmony, Bright Sunlight*, Monet, 1893)
As part of a study of the variations of light, Monet executed a series of paintings of the same subject at different times of the day (below, left).

IMPRESSIONNISTS

PONT-AVEN SCHOOL   NEOIMI

CÉZANNE

FAUVISM   NATURALISM

ART NOUVEAU   SYMBOLISM

CINEMA

DECORATIVE ARTS

ARCHITECTURE   PAINTING (P

BO

TEMPORARY EXHIBITION

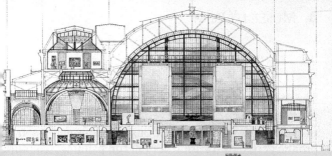

THE ARCHITECTS
The wide-ranging renovation was
carried out by two architectural
teams: ACT (Renaud Bardon,
Pierre Colboc and Jean-Paul
Philippon) and a team led by
Gae Aulenti.

IMAGINATION: A MORE POTENT FORCE THAN CAUTION

It was highly appropriate that a place where journeys had once started should be turned into a haven of preservation and contemplation. In order to respect the structure of the original building, Laloux's cast-iron pillars and beams, together with his stucco decoration, were preserved, restored and then removed. The stone elements and steel geometry of the new structures exude colossal strength, and provide a contrast with the ornate style of the original interior.

E ENTRANCE
e façade that overlooks
e de Bellechasse is
re peaceful than the
dy quay that faces
th and was therefore
sen for the main
rance.

A WARM WELCOME
The canopy, the old entrance hall and the café provide visitors with a warm welcome.

The quality materials used in the refurbishment work include an ocher-colored hard limestone from Buxy for the floors and certain moldings.

The collections in the Musée d'Orsay specialize in art of the late 19th and early 20th centuries. The museum seeks to capture the full diversity of this unusually dense and prolific period by focusing not only on painting, sculpture, and decorative and graphic arts but also on other visual arts such as architecture, town planning, movies, posters, the press and illustrated books. The abundant exhibits are displayed on three main floors, and a tour of the museum is chronological.

SCULPTURE AND CARICATURE
(*Ratapoil*, Honoré Daumier, c. 1850, bronze) Daumier was sculptor and painter but above all he was caricaturist who took delight in poking fun the politics and customs of his time.

PHOTOGRAPHY AT THE MUSÉE D'ORSAY: 1839–1918
Portrait of Charles Baudelaire by Nadar.

THE PRE-EMINENCE OF COLOR
(*Arearea*, Gauguin, 1892) Simplified forms, spaces lacking depth of field and flat colors were later taken up by the Pont-Aven School and then by the Nabis.

EARLY CUBISM
(*The Bridge at Maincy*, Cézanne, c. 1879) Cézanne broke with Impressionism at an early stage, opting for vigorous representation and classical composition; he also brought naturalism to simple geometric forms. His brush strokes, which were almost rectangular and very regular, became increasingly independent of what he was painting and varied only according to the direction in which it was inclined.

POINTILLISM
Woman with Umbrella, Signac, 1893)
The two theoretical principles of pointillism were the division of tone and the simultaneous contrast of colors.

Vase with festooned neck (Gallé, 1880–84)

NABIS

SCULPTURE (PRE-1870)

THEATER

BETWEEN EXPRESSIONISM AND SYMBOLISM
(*Mature Age*, Claudel, 1894–1903, bronze)

THE NABIS: PROPHETS OF A NEW ART FORM
(*The Box*, Bonnard, 1908) Pierre Bonnard's fellow students at the Académie Julian and the École des Beaux-Arts included Vuillard and Maurice Denis; they all drew inspiration from Gauguin. They were no less influenced by Japanese prints, and here Bonnard combines the flat colors, the simplification, and the almost nonexistent depth of field of Japanese prints with a freedom of composition and a most unusual composition.

▲ THE MUSEUMS OF PARIS
ORANGERIE – PETIT PALAIS

See pages ♦ 476–81 for opening times.

MUSÉE DE L'ORANGERIE
Place de la Concorde, Terrasse des Tuileries 75001 (1 H4)

From the gallery to the museum
The Orangerie Museum in the Tuileries was built in a former Second Empire orangery on the south terrace of the Tuileries. It has housed Monet's *Waterlilies* since 1927, and between 1929 and 1978 it also contained a prestigious contemporary gallery. When the Jean Walter–Paul Guillaume Collection was presented to the state on condition that it remain on permanent exhibition, much of the interior of the building was refurbished. Since then, the museum has been dedicated to the presentation of just two collections, the *Waterlilies* and the Walter–Guillaume Collection: they are very different but nonetheless share subtle affinities. It is hoped that imminent restoration work (particularly on the presentation of the *Waterlilies*) will further enhance these collections, and that an extension will encourage a renewed interest in temporary exhibitions.

The "Waterlilies"
This remarkable work, which takes up the two *Waterlilies* Rooms, was the culmination of Monet's own work and, through him, of Impressionism itself. It also represents several important threads in 20th-century art, extending from Kandinsky to Pollock, to which Monet contributed both chronologically and stylistically. The eight large compositions were inspired by the pond in the famous garden which he created on his land at Giverny. They cover the walls of two elliptical rooms: the layout projects a single, continuous sweep of painting incorporating the constant renewal of plant life and an unending flow of light, water and time.

The Jean Walter–Paul Guillaume Collection
This collection reflects the personalities and tastes of its two creators. One of these was the man who bought the paintings, Paul Guillaume, a champion of modern art in Paris between 1914 and 1934. The other was the second wife of the architect Jean Walter, Juliette (also known as Domenica), who made small alterations to the collection and bought the major works of Cézanne. Altogether there are 144 paintings, dating from the 1870's to the 1930's, grouped by artist with various rooms devoted to

"WATERLILIES" *(Claude Monet, room 2)*
This floating, seemingly limitless space is engulfed by an effusion of color and the artist's fluid, animated style. In this painting, in which the Impressionist revolution reaches its apogee, the viewer is invited to plunge headlong into a contemplative reverie, far removed from any neat description, nourished by an intense feeling for nature.

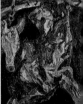

"OX AND CALF'S HEAD *(Chaim Soutine, 1925). Soutine examined his subject in series of variations they illustrate at once his weakness for perfection and his profoundly unhappy life.*

artists the couple was particularly fond of: Cézanne, Renoir, Rousseau, Soutine, Modigliani, Matisse, Derain and Picasso. A "return to the classical order", a movement that gained support after World War One, resulted in three major works:

Matisse's *Three Sisters*, Picasso's *Grande Baigneuse* and Derain's *Harlequin and Pierrot*.

MUSÉE DU PETIT PALAIS

Avenue Winston-Churchill 75008 (1 F4)

A treasury of ancient art

The building was constructed by Charles Girault ▲ *312* for the Universal Exhibition of 1900: it houses a collection of ancient art based on two major donations. The first was a unique collection bequeathed by the brothers Eugène and Auguste Dutuit

"**COURBET WITH BLACK DOG**" (Gustave Courbet, 1842). The contrast between the dark silhouettes of the painter and black dog and the whites and ochers of the rock provides a fine illustration of Courbet's sense of composition and command of color.

in 1902. This consisted of works of art of classical antiquity and medieval objects (not currently on show due to lack of space), priceless pieces from the French and Italian Renaissance (in particular terracotta objects from St-Porchaire), majolica figures, enamels from Limousin, glass objects, timepieces and the celebrated room of Flemish and Dutch paintings. In 1930 the Tuck Collection was added, largely made up of paintings, sculptures, tapestries and 18th-century objets d'art, and also including porcelain from China, Sèvres and Meissen, English snuffboxes and some magnificent Louis XV and Louis XIV furniture.

An overview of 19th-century art

This feature of the collections is the result of judicious commissions and purchases made by the City of Paris in the 20th century. One of the highlights was the acquisition of Jules Dalou's workshop; other major donations have included works by Courbet, Carpeaux, Carriès and Cézanne. This section boasts neoclassical paintings and sculpture, examples of troubadour art, and paintings from the Romantic, Realist,

Impressionist, post-Impressionist, Symbolist and Nabis schools. It also contains a large number of naturalist and allegorical sculptures and a collection of splendid objets d'art dating from the 1900's including ceramic stoneware pieces by Jean Carriès, glassware by Gallé and jewelry by Fouquet. The Petit Palais Museum presents some outstanding temporary exhibitions.

MODEL OF A MONUMENT PLANNED FOR THE PLACE DE LA RÉPUBLIQUE (Jules Dalou, 1879). This work, eventually made in bronze, was commissioned by the City of Paris for the Place de la Nation; it was unveiled in 1899. The group is evidence of the artist's lyrical inspiration, his free sense of design and his powerful treatment of the figures.

See pages ◆ 476–81 for opening times.

"PORTRAIT OF JACQUELINE WITH CROSSED HANDS"
(Vallauris, 1954) Jacqueline Roque was Picasso's haunting, ever-present model for almost twenty years: he married her in 1961. Here, he represents her as hieratic and compact, a true modern sphinx.

MUSÉE PICASSO
Hôtel Salé, 5, rue de Thorigny 75003
(2 G6)

The Picasso collection
Picasso liked to describe himself as "the world's leading collector of Picassos"; indeed, in his workshops and homes he kept a considerable proportion of his 80 years of artistic output. When he died in 1973 his heavy death duties were paid through the donation of some of his works. The selection, made in 1979, eventually formed the basis of a museum unique in the world for the number and range of his works. They included 203 paintings, 158 sculptures, 29 paintings in relief, 88 ceramic pieces, 15 *papiers collés*, almost 1,500 drawings, some 30 sketchbooks and over 1,600 prints.

They cover all periods of Picasso's working life. The collection of sculptures includes virtually all of his small Cubist constructions, the unique series of sand-coated reliefs from the summer of 1930, and the large carvings of heads that he did at Le Boisgeloup in the early 1930's. The sketchbooks, which include preparatory drawings for the *Demoiselles d'Avignon*, throw light both on the creative direction that Picasso was taking and on the genesis of some of his works. A second donation was added after his wife Jacqueline died in 1986. This complemented the collection which was lacking certain items (for example, *Portrait of Jacqueline with Crossed Hands*) and contributed another 24 magnificent sketchbooks, 2 sculptures, about 40 drawings and a number of prints and ceramics. In addition to these works by Picasso himself were items from his private collection, including works by Cézanne, Matisse, Rousseau, Derain, Braque and Miró and some pieces of primitive art.

The paintings find a home
An hôtel in the

"WOMAN'S HEAD"
(Le Boisgeloup, plaster original, 1931).

"STILL LIFE WITH CANE CHAIR"
(1912). This was the first time that Picasso used a real object (the oilcloth imitating the cane seating of a chair) in one of his paintings.

Marais, which had been empty, was chosen in 1976 to house the works that made up the first donation. Built between 1656 and 1659 for Pierre Aubert de Fontenoy, who had made a fortune collecting salt taxes, the house had been unusually expensive to build and came to be known as the Hôtel Salé ▲ 389 (salé, or "salty", means exorbitant prices). The most elaborate part of the original interior décor was a monumental staircase adorned with an abundance of carved wood made by the Marsy brothers and Martin Desjardins. The landmarked parts of the building were restored when the architect Roland Simounet carried out his refurbishments, and these have revealed its initial grandeur. The lamp and candelabra over the main stairway, the chandeliers in the hallway and second-floor drawing rooms, and the furniture in the other rooms were specially created for the museum by Diego Giacometti. The intermingled paintings, sculptures, drawings and engravings provide eloquent illustration of the varied technical approaches adopted by Picasso during his lifetime.

MUSÉE RODIN
Hôtel de Biron, 77, rue de Varenne 75007 (1 G7)

A rococo house
Auguste Rodin (1840–1917) moved into the Hôtel de Biron ▲ 268 in 1908 on the advice of his secretary, Rainer Maria Rilke. At the time, the building was divided into a number of artists' workshops. This splendid example of rococo architecture was built by Jean Aubert between

THE CATHEDRAL (stone, 1931). The two representations of the same hand face one another in such a way as to suggest a ribbed vault symbolizing the work's original title, the "Arche d'Alliance".

1729 and 1730, and was acquired by the state in 1911. Rodin handed his works over to the Hôtel de Biron in 1916; the drawings and sculptures, his private collection, the archives and the old photographs and works from the Villa des Brillants at Meudon formed the basis of the museum's collection when it opened in 1919.

Rodin, a sculptor of genius
Rodin was an independent spirit when it came to inspiration and its figurative application, but he nonetheless stood at the crossroads of a number of artistic movements: Romanticism, with its accent on pathos; Art Nouveau, with its fluidity and meandering curves; and Naturalism, with its concern for anatomical accuracy. Rodin's freedom of style can be seen in all the materials he used: the museum contains sculptures in marble, bronze and terracotta. There are works from his youth; representations of couples, groups, torsos and portraits; works by Camille Claudel, and studies of important monuments. There is also a selection of seven thousand drawings, and paintings by Carrières, Monet, Van Gogh (*Père Tanguy*) and Zuolaga from Rodin's private collection. The 8-acre garden, whose south-facing parterre has recently been renovated, contains monumental bronzes, including the *Gates of Hell*, the *Burghers of Calais* and *Balzac* as well as some antique pieces.

Gold medallion (1665).

THE ASSAS FOLLY
In 1928, Ossip Zadkine went to live in the Rue d'Assas, a curious rural oasis where he worked until his death in 1967.

MUSÉE ZADKINE
100 *bis*, rue d'Assas
75006 (5 A1)

From Primitivism to Abstraction
The sculptures in the garden and the

for monuments to poets (1938) were forerunners of his postwar Baroque output. An outstanding example is the model for his most famous

sculpture, *Destroyed City* (1951). Only when Zadkine was approaching the end of his career did the human form finally disappear from his work. This period was filled with projects for sculptures designed to contrast sharply with the austere styles of the 1960's: see *Floral Forms* (1967), below.

CABINET DES MÉDAILLES
Bibliothèque Nationale, 58, rue de Richelieu 75002 (2 B3)

AMASIS VASE
This Attic amphora (550–530 BC) decorated with black figures is signed by the potter Amasis. On one side it shows Athena and Poseidon; on the other, Dionysus entertains two maenads. On the handles is a representation of hoplites fighting.

five rooms illustrate each stage of Zadkine's work. Until the mid-1920's, Zadkine worked mainly in wood and stone in a style reminiscent of Brancusi and Modigliani; he did not produce his first Cubist works, such as *Woman with a Fan*, until 1923. During the 1930's, Zadkine pursued themes from Greco-Latin antiquity as revised and corrected by Cubism (*The Maenads*). His four projects

Coins, medals and antiques
This department of the Bibliothèque Nationale (National Library), known as the Cabinet des Médailles, was initially based on the manuscripts, gold plate, carved stones and old coins which the kings of France collected from the Middle Ages

Statue designed to go with the monument to Vincent Van Gogh at Auvers-sur-Oise, 1956.

onward. Until the 19th century, old coins were known as *médailles* (medals). The museum itself, which has occupied these premises since 1917, contains over 500,000 coins and medals and 15,000 nonmonetary objects. It was renovated in 1981: four of the rooms house the most prestigious objects (including the throne of Dagobert and a treasury of Gallo-Roman silver-plate found at Berthouville, northern France) and a choice selection of coins and medals. Two more rooms on the mezzanine are given over to minting techniques and a history of coins.

172

"Unquestionably where the best food in
the whole world is to be found."
This was how Grimod de
La Reynière, the doyen of food
writers, described Paris in 1803.
Almost two hundred years later, Paris is
still the gastronomic capital of France (some might say the
world). The history of good eating is closely
linked to the supply of wonderful
ingredients. The best produce
(including meat, cheese, fish and wine)
found its way to the capital during the
18th century, by road or by river. In 1791,
the abolition of the corporations which
had previously exercized a monopoly
over the selling of food led to the formation in
Paris of a completely new institution – the
restaurant. Before then, Parisians had gone to
sellers of prepared food (*traiteurs*) and roasted
meat (*rôtisseurs*) when they wanted to eat out. The
Revolution gave its blessing to this development by
forcing the chefs of the disgraced nobility to open
up their kitchens. Finally, Paris has a virtual
monopoly on all writing about food and
good living: the city now boasts an entire
generation of critics who have moved
from the table where they eat to the
one where they write.

MAXIM'

The first Paris restaurant was opened in 1785 by Boulanger in the Rue des Poulis. The sign read *"Venite ad me omnes qui stomacho laboratis et ego vos restaurabo"* (Come all who are hungry and I will restore you). Over the years cooking has gradually acquired the status of an art form, both perfectible and transmissable. In the early years of the 20th century, Auguste Escoffier defined the precepts of modern cuisine to which all the great chefs of today still adhere: that the chefs' cooking should attract gourmets from all over the world, and that the décor and history of the restaurants should make the meal into an experience of unique pleasure.

♦ 497

ALAIN SENDERENS
Senderens is one of the great artists of modern French cuisine. The wood paneling at the Lucas-Carton ♦ 497 (9, pl. de la Madeleine 75008) provides a superb setting for his talents. Senderens is famous for several creations including "La Cuisine Retrouvée de Marcel Proust", a dish which combines literature and gastronomy.

LA TOUR D'ARGENT
15–17, quai de la Tournelle 75005
This establishment, which has been an inn since the 16th century, is named for its stone tower which sparkles in the sunlight ♦ 500. Henri IV was often lured here by the heron pâté. The restaurant, on a promontory in the Seine, with endless bay windows in the upstairs dining room to take in the views of Notre-Dame and the Île de la Cité, is presided over by Claude Terrail.

RESTAURANT STAFF
The movements of staff, from the humblest waiter to the maître d'hôtel are strictly choreographed. Even their uniforms are designed for esthetic appeal.

> # "THE GOURMET IS ABOVE ALL A DINER WHO KNOWS WHAT TO EAT, AND WHO DOES NOT CHOOSE THE WRONG COMBINATIONS OF TASTES, AROMAS, WINES OR SPICES."
>
> LÉON-PAUL FARGUE

MICHELIN GUIDE
Founded in 1900 and originally aimed at motorists, this is one of the most highly regarded restaurant guides. It is feared by chefs, who attach great importance to the guide's system of awarding stars.

NOUVELLE CUISINE
The emergence of nouvelle cuisine in 1968 had a profound impact on cooking. The prime mover was the chef Michel Guérard: although nouvelle cuisine initially eschewed rich sauces, many of them now contain dairy products. The success of nouvelle cuisine – based on its remarkable ability to bring out the flavors of the very best ingredients – was assured when it was given a formal definition by the food writers Christian Millau and Henri Gault.

THE SOMMELIER
Philippe Faure-Brac, the top wine waiter of 1992, will certainly go along with the view that there is no such thing as a restaurant that serves good food with poor quality wine. The sommelier is the person who advises on, and oversees the serving of wines in serious restaurants. Down in the wine cellar his word is law.

A KEY FIGURE
Antonin Carême (1783–1833) came from a modest background but became a legend in the history of modern gastronomy. He was a great lover of the arts, particularly architecture, and after training with the pastry chef Bailly, set about producing dishes of extraordinary complexity. In 1815 he was in charge of the kitchens of the Prince Regent and later entered the service of the Czar Alexander of Russia. He spent the last few years of his life writing books on gastronomy.

CLIMBING THE GASTRONOMIC HEIGHTS
A meal of the highest class – 410 feet above the streets of Paris – awaits patrons of the Jules Verne ◆ 500 (Eiffel Tower, second floor 75007), a restaurant completed in 1983. Slavik's metal decoration is even more imaginative than the writings of Jules Verne himself and presents diners with a unique view of Paris.

◆ *501*

France is bordered by three seas and an ocean, so it is hardly surprising that fish and seafood occupy an important place in French cuisine. Paris excels when it comes to fish because it is so conveniently close to the coasts of Brittany and Normandy. Fresh produce is essential to a restaurant's reputation: the quality of the meal absolutely depends on it. Fish-farming techniques have also made it possible for fresh fish and seafood to be supplied all year round. The days when oysters were available only in winter are long gone.

BOUILLABAISSE

This Provençal specialty was originally a fish ragout that fishermen made from what was left over from their catches. Bouillabaisse is ideally made with small pieces of fish such as scorpion fish, whiting and John Dory; these are allowed to simmer in a stock containing tomatoes, onions, garlic, fennel and bay leaves. In fact, it is made with whatever fish is available on that day, which is why there is no definitive recipe.

LE DÔME ◆ *503*
108, bd. du Montparnasse 75014
The bustle of the Boulevard Montparnasse owes much to its restaurants especially, since 1923, Le Dôme. The menu boasts some of the best bouillabaisse in Paris, and the décor includes photos of artists looking down over the diners.

JACQUES LE DIVELLEC ◆ *501*
107, rue de l'Université 75007
The most chic fish restaurant in Paris is named after this self-styled "ambassador of the sea", who left La Rochelle in 1983 and started a business near Les Invalides. He made a magnificent lobster press in collaboration with the silversmith Christofle.

ROI DES COQUILLAGES

QUENELLES OF PIKE

This is one of the great dishes of Lyon. The quenelles are made with a purée of fillets of pike and fresh cream, and the velvety texture is provided by the white sauce which is mixed in with crayfish paste. The dish is ideally accompanied by a mild white wine.

SOLE MEUNIÈRE

This dish is as magnificent as it is simple. The fillets of sole are seasoned and rolled in flour before being sautéed in butter. Lemon juice, parsley, salt and pepper bring a spicy tang to the golden flesh, and finally a knob of butter is added.

LA MÉDITERRANÉE ◆ *501*
2, pl. de l'Odéon 75006
This restaurant, which was built in the Place de l'Odéon in 1930, became famous for its murals. It was painted blue and received artists and writers of the Latin Quarter, like Picasso, Balthus and Cocteau, one of whose drawings, dated 1960, decorates the menu. Patrons of this establishment have included Charlie Chaplin and Orson Welles.

FISH AND WINE

White wine is usually drunk with fish and other seafood. Vineyards close to the sea, such as Bordeaux, Loire and Côtes-de-Provence, produce wines which go extremely well with seafood recipes, while Chablis and Riesling are ideal with oysters and shrimp. More inland wines like Burgundy, Jura and Côtes-du-Rhône are perfect partners for freshwater fish like trout, perch and pike.

Brasseries occupy dominant positions on the city's main thoroughfares and at innumerable crossroads, and are ♦ 504 therefore of great importance to Paris' culinary landscape. The origins of the brasserie go back to the German annexation of Alsace-Lorraine in 1870, when the inhabitants of Alsace fled the oppressive régime and introduced this sort of eating establishment to Paris. The brasserie's unchanging décor – mirrors, glass, benches covered in moleskin and immaculate tablecloths – was ideally suited to a diet of sauerkraut and beer. The volume of conversation rises perceptibly at mealtimes and when Parisians drop by in the evening before or after a show, and then stay on long into the night.

BEER DRINKING IN BRASSERIES

Since the 16th century, the word brasserie has denoted a place that sells beer (*brasser* means to brew). In the 19th century it was a kind of bar that served not only drinks (mainly beer) but also food. Frédéric Bofinger, the owner of a brasserie in the Rue de la Bastille, was the first person to sell

BOFINGER ♦ 503

5–7, rue de la Bastille 75004
Bofinger opened in 1864 and was designated a protected landmark in 1982. It is one of the oldest brasseries in Paris. Its present décor is the work of the architect Legay and the decorator Mitgen: the magnificent cupola is by Neret and Royer.

SAUERKRAUT

Sauerkraut from Alsace is made by leaving shredded cabbage to ferment in salt for three weeks; it is served with sausages, potatoes, and other meats as *choucroute garnie*. In some restaurants, sauerkraut is accompanied by seafood.

bière à la pompe, or draft beer: this new, light-colored beverage was a huge success. Beer is drunk less these days with food, but it is still part of the atmosphere of the brasserie.

LIPP ◆ 504
151, bd. St-Germain 75006
A celebrated habitué of Lipp was the poet Léon-Paul Fargue (1876–1947), a customer well known for always being the last to arrive for dinner. His father

and uncle had created the faience panels. He suffered a stroke here while dining with Picasso and remained paralyzed for the rest of his life.

FLO ◆ 504
7, cour des Petites-Écuries 75010
In 1914 this brasserie, then called "Hans", was damaged by anti-German demonstrators. It later took the name Flo, a diminutive form of the name of its new owner, Robert Floderer.

ALSATIAN WINES
Alsace is best known for white wines, either dry or fruity. It has three AOC (Appellation d'Origine Contrôlée) wines: Vin d'Alsace, Alsace Grand Cru and Crémant d'Alsace. Wines made with Sylvaner, Riesling and Gewürztraminer grapes are an ideal accompaniment for sauerkraut.

CONFIT
Brasseries often have various rustic dishes on their menus: these include confit, a dish that uses up the leftover fat of ducks or geese, which are very popular birds in southwest France. The meat is first salted and left in an earthenware pot for 24 hours. Then it is gently cooked in fat until it is very tender.

179

Restaurants specializing in regional cuisine and home-style cooking

◆ 501

give the most accurate impression of French cooking generally and of what French people themselves ◆ today. These establishments are often family-run businesses with recipes and knowhow brought from the provinces. Regional restaurant specialties are like holiday postcards sent from Proven Burgundy or the southwest. Restaurants that go in for home-style cooking are more intimate and less fancy, but their simple and classical recipes are no less mouth-watering. Parisians particularly enjoy this type of food at lunch, typically opting for snails or chick and french fries before going back to work.

POT-AU-FEU
Alexandre Dumas claimed to have discovered this rustic dish; it comes from Lyons but is now eaten all over France. It takes 48 hours to prepare a good *pot au feu* and to bring out all the flavors. Place the vegetables (celery, carrots, turnips, leeks and cabbage) and meat (beef and marrow bones) in a pot of hot water in order to produce a good stock, then add a *bouquet garni*. The broth is eaten with croutons, and the meat and vegetables with various condiments.

CHARTIER ◆ 502
7, rue du Faubourg-Montmartre 75009
Chartier is still a cheap eatery (*bouillon*) and has the same sign that it had when it was opened by its founders, Camille

and Édouard Chartier, in 1895. A revolving door leads into the enormous dining room. The staff are dressed in long white aprons, vests and bowties, and the décor is pre-1940's. All of these curious and unexpected details give customers the impression they are in a time warp.

THE BLACKBOARD
In the dining room is a blackboard that has the menu and the *plat du jour* written in chalk. This typically Parisian device is now widespread.

BOEUF BOURGUIGNON
The meat is marinated in red Burgundy, and this wine is also the dish's ideal accompaniment. This rich, rustic meal is made with the rump cut into small pieces. Brown the meat in bacon fat with onions, add more wine and the marinade, and bring to a boil. Simmer for three hours with baby onions, garlic and a *bouquet garni*.

LESCURE ◆ 502
7, rue de Mondovi 75001
Lescure is situated near the Place de la Concorde and is one of the most pleasant – and least expensive – restaurants in this business quarter. It is a family concern and both rustic and classical dishes have been served in this warm, welcoming setting since 1919.

SNAILS
Francis Ponge, a poet noted for his championing of *escargots* (snails), makes no references to how they should be cooked. Only two kinds of snail are of any interest to the gourmet, he says: the Burgundy snail, which is well known in eastern France, and the *petit-gris*, from

Restaurant PHARAMOND
24, Rue de la Grande-Truandene - LES HALLES

Unusual for Les Halles district, the elaborate décor has remained intact. *Tripes à la mode de Caen* is allowed to simmer for 15 hours. It is always served here on individual plate-warmers, as it has been since the establishment moved to its present location in 1879.

PHARAMOND ◆ 500
24, rue de la Grande Truanderie 75001
Normandy cuisine is represented in Paris by Pharamond.

Gascony and Provence. Snails are traditionally prepared with garlic butter and *fines herbes*, but different regions have many other ways of cooking them. In Burgundy, snails may be cooked in Chablis before they are placed back in their shells, which have been filled with butter; in this recipe, the mantle (the liver and other organs, and the most nutritious part) is not removed.

CASSOULET
Cassoulet (a stew made with lamb, pork, goose and white beans) is the great specialty of southwest France and, according to the chef Prosper Montagné, "the god of Provençal cooking". The name comes from *cassole*, the terracotta dish in which the recipe is cooked.

A tour of Paris' restaurants is something like a trip around the world. The innumerable foreign communities in Paris are well represented by their respective cuisines, and their restaurants make great efforts to serve food in appropriate settings. The many North African, Chinese, Japanese and Italian restaurants present excellent food at very good prices and are very popular. More off the beaten track are Russian, Caribbean, Portuguese and South American restaurants, providing lots of surprises for the more adventurous palate.

◆ 502

NORTH AFRICA
One of the great traditional specialties of North Africa is *tagine*, which takes its name from the round earthenware dish with a cone-shaped lid of the same name. This stew of spiced lamb, veal or chicken with vegetables, dried fruits and nuts varies from region to region.

JAPAN
The greatest triumph of Japanese cooking is sushi: a small packet of rice sprinkled with rice vinegar, and a thin slice of raw fish is laid on top, then the whole thing is wrapped in a seaweed leaf.

SOUTHEAST ASIA
The most popular Vietnamese specialty in Paris is *cha gio*, a kind of spring roll filled with noodles, wrapped in mint and lettuce leaves, and sprinkled with *nuoc nam* (fish sauce).

SOUTH AMERICA
Of all the South American cuisines in Paris, the best known is Brazilian. The national Brazilian specialty is *feijoada*, a dish once cooked by slaves. The basic ingredients are black beans and pork, but like all such national dishes, *feijoada* can be cooked in many different ways.

PORTUGAL

Portuguese cuisine is difficult to find in Paris, although there are some excellent Portuguese restaurants. Fresh and salt cod figure among the specialties: salt cod is often cooked *en brandade* (pounded with garlic, oil and cream).

SPAIN

Paella is not the archetypal Spanish dish it is sometimes made out to be: it is a typical dish from Valencia and is based on rice with meat or fish. The name comes from the two-handled pan in which it is cooked.

ITALY

Italy has been the world's leading producer of wine for many years. Heady, powerful Chianti classico from Tuscany is the best known but Orvieto classico goes very well with fish and seafood.

RUSSIA

Russian restaurants always serve *borscht*. This soup of green cabbage, beets and various other vegetables was a great favorite of Simone de Beauvoir.

NEAR EAST

Lebanese restaurants offer genuine tabbouleh. Semolina is widely used in France but a different kind is found in this dish. It is prepared with chopped parsley, mint, tomatoes, onions and cracked wheat, then served on a bed of lettuce or cabbage.

CENTRAL EUROPE

This area is well represented by Ashkenazic Jewish restaurants, famous for *zakuski*, assorted hors d'oeuvres from Russia, and for stuffed carp. These restaurants use kosher products.

183

MOUTON-ROTHSCHILD
1926

French wine is celebrated throughout the world. The cultivation of grapevines in the South of France, and viticulture in other regions dates from the beginning of recorded history. The capital no longer keeps the majority of vines for itself, but the marketing of wine is closely linked to developments that have taken place in Paris. Events like the excitement surrounding the arrival each year of Beaujolais nouveau bring bistros and wine bars to life and give the whole city a holiday air. *Cavistes* will take every opportunity to remind one and all that wine drinking symbolizes the French art of living.

♦ 505

CAVISTES

Cavistes specialize in the selling of wine by the bottle. There are quite a number of independent *cavistes* in Paris, but most of them belong to chains like Nicolas and the Repaire de Bacchus.

Some *cavistes* organize general tastings for their customers; other tastings are based on a particular vineyard in order to stimulate interest in unknown grapes.

BLANC-CASSIS
The most popular aperitif in France is kir, a mixture of cassis and dry white wine, originally Bourgogne Aligoté. It was popularized by Canon Kir (1876–1968), a noted Resistance fighter and mayor of Dijon from 1945 to 1968.

CITY VINES
The last grapevines still growing in the capital owe their survival to the endeavors of a few hard-working Parisians. The Clos Montmartre, a vineyard dating back to the earliest years of our era, became operational again in 1935. The grapes are fermented in the cellars of the mayor's office, and 450 bottles of rosé are produced there annually. The Clos des Morillons, in the Georges-Brassens Park (15th arrondissement), has been producing grapes for red wine since 1982.

BERCY
Wines and brandies have been sold in Bercy since the 17th century, but the area's special interest in wine dates from 1790, when the autonomous commune escaped the capital city's toll. The market grew during the 19th century, when transport companies and merchants opened up offices there. Even 20 years ago, 20 percent of all wine drunk in France passed through Bercy.

RHÔNE VALLEY

Rhône Valley vineyards are situated on both sides of the Rhone. The wines have the powerful, individual characteristics of either the northern (Côte-Rôtie) or southern (Châteauneuf-du-Pape and Gigondas) slopes.

JUST A GLASS

Wine lovers flock to bars like the Vignes du Panthéon (4, rue des Fossés St-Jacques 75005), where wine can be drunk by the glass. The intimate atmosphere of these establishments enables the real wine buff to indulge his or her passion – and talk nonstop about the color of a Chablis or the bouquet of a St-Émilion. These bars sometimes serve rustic dishes that go well with the wines.

BORDEAUX

This, the biggest wine-producing area in France, is governed by three kinds of *appellation: générale, régionale* and *communale*. The smaller the locality specified, the better the wine. Tannin-rich Bordeaux wines offer an extremely wide range of full-bodied reds (Médoc and St-Émilion), dry and sweet whites (Graves and Sauternes), as well as a few rosés.

BURGUNDY

This area extends from the northwest (Chablis) to the south (Beaujolais). In the middle are the great Côte-d'Or wines, such as Vosne-Romanée and Puligny-Montrachet, for which Burgundy is best known.

JURA

This small wine-making area – the main town is Arbois – produces a variety of wines, ranging from reds and rosés to sparkling whites. However, it is best known for its nutty-tasting white wines like the exceptional Château-Chalon, a yellow wine made from Savagnin grape: it is left to age for six years in sealed wooden barrels and can last for decades.

LOIRE

Between Nevers and Nantes, the Loire is surrounded by numerous vineyards that produce delightfully fresh wines such as Muscadet and Vouvray (dry and sparkling whites) and Saumur-Champigny and Anjou (reds).

CHAMPAGNE

Champagne, the most famous wine in the world, is perfect for celebrations. It is made from two red grapes, Pinot Noir and Pinot Meunier. Blanc de blanc is made with white Chardonnay grapes. Different amounts of sugar are needed to produce brut, sec and demi-sec Champagne.

France has a proud rural tradition and boasts over four hundred varieties of cheese made from cows', goats' and sheep's milk. Accordingly, an enormous selection of cheeses is available in Paris. As the writer Colette succinctly put it "Paris has every sweet, sharp, aperitif and extra-mature cheese from home and abroad – and consumes every bit." There is just as much variety in the different types of French breads, the best known of all being the *baguette*.

♦ 528

BREAD VARIETIES
1. Walnut bread
2. Organic whole-wheat bread
3. Rye bread with raisins
4. Decorated loaf
5. Boule de campagne
6. Flûte Gana
7. Baguette

STAPLE DIET AND SACRED RITUAL

There is documentary evidence of bread being eaten in Egypt as long ago as 2500 BC. Indeed, it has been the staple of most civilizations because of its nutritious value and the fact that it keeps for long periods. It also plays a part in the Christian (the body of Christ in the Eucharist) and Jewish (bread is blessed before being eaten at table) liturgies.

BAGUETTE

French bread arouses so much anxiety that the state has tried to protect master bakers from the predations of big businesses which produce frozen baguettes. Under a decree passed in 1993 only bread kneaded and baked at the point of sale may now be referred to as *pain maison* (homemade bread).

TO GO WITH EVERY DISH

Bread is a foodstuff in its own right and needs to be chosen carefully to accompany certain dishes. It contributes to the overall balance of a meal: rye bread, for instance, is ideal with oysters and sour dough bread is best with foie gras while lemon bread goes best with fish.

CHEESE EXPERT
Expert cheese makers supervise the entire maturing process and check on how the cheeses are developing. In 1909 a Breton cheese maker by the name of Henri Androuët opened a shop selling cheese he had matured on the premises. In 1934 he launched a cheese cuisine restaurant – the first of its type – which was very popular with Sacha Guitry and Maria Callas.

ROQUEFORT (D)
Blue cheeses made from sheep's or cow's milk are marked by blue veins. These are caused by a type of fungus known as *penicillium* which forms during the maturing process, and gives Roquefort from Aveyron its veined appearance.

ÉPOISSES (C)
This cheese is strong-smelling and fully flavored. The maturing process takes two to four months: at the end of this the cheese is soaked in water and Marc de Bourgogne. Other cheeses with washed rinds are flavored with cider or beer according to the region.

CAMEMBERT (A)
This Normandy cheese is made with milk either straight from the cow or pasteurized and is soft and sweet. A good Camembert is left in the maturing room for an average of three to six weeks.

CANTAL (E)
This Auvergne cheese was first referred to by Pliny the Elder. It is so-called pressed cheese and is the oldest of all the French varieties. It is eaten fresh or after maturing for three months.

BRIE (B)
Originally from Île-de-France, Brie was once voted "king of cheeses" by a jury of European ambassadors being entertained by Talleyrand. This creamy cheese matures quickly: it tastes mildly of hazelnuts.

GOAT'S CHEESE
There are numerous types of small goat's cheese: they may be fresh, dry, hard or smoked, according to the length of the maturing process. The flavor matures as the cheese ages and farmhouse cheeses develop a blue mold. The best-known is Crottin de Chavignol.

BEST OF FRIENDS
The respective tastes of wine and cheese complement each other and result in the most delicate of harmonies. However, there are no hard-and-fast rules about which wine goes with which cheese, as the qualities of each vary from year to year. On the whole it is advisable to pair wines and cheeses from the same region.

The delights of restaurants are frequently concealed behind grand façades, but pastries, confectionery, ice creams and other wicked temptations flaunt themselves shamelessly in the windows of Parisian shops. Confectioners combine practical and esthetic skills to produce imaginative and mouth-watering delicacies. This tradition dates back to the end of the 19th century, when afternoon tea (or a short break from shopping) was the perfect excuse for a minor indulgence in a smart tea shop.

◆ 528

A BEVERAGE OF THE GODS
Chocolate is made from the beans of the cacao tree. The origin of chocolate as a cold drink dates back to pre-Colombian times, when it formed part of Aztec and Maya mythology: the god Quetzalcoatl is said to have gone mad after drinking it. His people viewed cocoa beans as valuable products and even used them as currency.

A DRAMATIC SUCCESS
The *opéra*, an almond pastry consisting of layers of coffee and chocolate, is a recent creation. Because its rectangular shape suggests a stage, Andrée Gavillon, the director of the Maison Dalloyau ◆ 528 (99–101 rue du Faubourg St-Honoré 75001), chose the name as a tribute to the corps de ballet of the Paris Opera.

EATING CHOCOLATE
Chocolate was consumed only as a drink until 19th-century confectioners succeeded in making cacao paste into chocolate sweets. Cocoa beans are roasted and crushed, then mixed with sugar and lecithin: after the mixture hardens it is compressed.

Americain auec Sa Choco latiere et Son Gobelet

Jean Béraud, 1889

PARIS-BREST

At the end of the 19th century, a pastrychef in the Paris suburbs conceived the idea of a pastry in the shape of a bicycle wheel while watching competitors in the famous Paris-Brest cycle race. That is how this most Parisian of cakes – choux-pastry filled with almond cream – came to be made.

"MILLEFEUILLE"

Antonin Carême layered *crème pâtissière* with puff pastry to produce *millefeuille*. In medieval times similar pastries had been well known in the East, and the recipe was brought back by Crusaders.

BERTHILLON ◆ 528

31, rue St-Louis-en-l'Île 75004
Raymond Berthillon's tiny ice cream parlor on the Île St-Louis has been hugely popular ever since it opened in 1954. It offers a range of 72 flavors, including 8 kinds of chocolate ice cream, as well as blueberry and fig sorbets.

OLD-FASHIONED ICE CREAM

Ice cream was in existence long before the invention of the refrigerator. The development of a cooling mixture – combination of crushed ice and salt – allowed ice cream to be kept at around 42 °F.

LENÔTRE

Gaston Lenôtre, from Normandy, is one of today's great pastry chefs. His success with pastries, confectionery and ice cream has enabled him to build a gastronomic empire: he has opened a large number of shops and has even set up his own cooking school.

BÊTISES DE CAMBRAI

Legend has it that these candies of boiled sugar owe their name to an error (*bêtise* means blunder) made by the son of a confectioner called Afchain in Cambrai (northern France) while measuring ingredients. The *Bêtises de Cambrai* are a mixture of boiled sugar, mint and caramelized sugar.

FLOWER CANDIES

Violettes de Toulouse are among the most unusual and elegant sweets to be found anywhere in France. The petals, and sometimes entire flowers, of violets are coated in crystallized sugar to preserve their subtle perfume.

Bêtises de Cambrai
AUX VRAIES
AFCHAIN
TRADITION MENTHE

◆ 529

Spices were used in the Middle Ages to help preserve fruit and meat. Pepper, nutmeg and saffron were most commonly used, and their commercial importance prompted some of the great explorations of the Renaissance. Today spices are minor ingredients whose flavors are nonetheless considered essential. The modern "spice route" through Paris takes in large and small shops (*épicerie* is now the general term used to mean grocery store) where bottles and jars sit waiting for an opportunity to send forth their exotic perfumes.

CHUTNEY
This sweet and sour Indian condiment is made by cooking fresh fruit and vegetables in vinegar with sugar and spices.

BALSAMIC VINEGAR
This originated in Modena in Italy. Its unique flavor comes from the must (unfermented juice) of white Trebbiano grapes. Aging in casks of various woods and sizes gives the vinegar its distinctive color and flavor.

HÉDIARD ◆ 529
21, pl. de la Madeleine 75008

In 1854 Ferdinand Hédiard opened an *épicerie* in Place de la Madeleine which specialized in imported produce. He realized that he could make money out of rare, exotic products and had papaya, guava, mango and loquat shipped to France. He is remembered for selling the writer Alexandre Dumas one of the first pineapples.

FAUCHON ◆ 529
26–30, pl. de la Madeleine 75008

From a modest family in Calvados, August Fauchon (1856–1938) moved to Paris to sell fruits and vegetables in the vicinity of the Madeleine. He was soon the owner of a number of shops, one of which, in the Place de la Madeleine, he turned into an *épicerie de luxe*: since the 1930's it has sold rare and unusual products.

GINGER
Different forms of this root are used in seasoning a large number of Eastern dishes. Candied ginger is also delicious as a confectionery.

CURRY
This mixture of spices (including pepper and turmeric) is used in the meat, fish and vegetable dishes that form part of traditional Indian cuisine.

JAMS
The last course in medieval banquets consisted of fruit preserves: these jams were made from fruit and numerous spices caramelized in sugar.

COMESTIBLES · CAVES · D

FAUCH

Paris is often described as a stony, rocky city with few green spaces, yet it has almost four hundred parks, gardens and squares, as well as Vincennes and the Bois de Boulogne. What can the city do about such misconceptions? The following chapter is a brief survey of Paris' gardens, explaining how nature has followed orderly principles down through the centuries. Much of Paris' flora and fauna are shy and little known. When you walk past a basement window, do you realize that there may be a rare form of fern growing there? Did you know how much the stock dove loves the steel girders of the Eiffel Tower? Or that small birds of prey – kestrels mostly – breed in the towers of Notre-Dame? Or that American crayfish swim in the waters of the St-Martin canal? Or that the underground reservoirs under the Opéra are like fish tanks – and full of magnificent barbels? The natural history of Paris abounds in such fascinating detail.

THE ROOFTOPS OF PARIS

STARLING
The starling is well adapted to cities. In the spring, it exchanges its plumage scattered with white spots for a dark, iridescent version.

Summer

Winter

Parisians and visitors alike are generally unaware of the wealth of bird life in the city. Birds live, eat and reproduce at roof level, far from the bustling streets; they share television antennas, chimney stacks and the skies while the pedestrians below completely ignore them. There are many species to look for apart from sparrows and pigeons: some of these, such as swifts and swallows, are migratory birds that travel thousands of miles between Paris and Africa every year.

House martin

Swift

KESTREL
Kestrels rule their territory from perches on high above the streets. The kestrels of Paris not only go hunting in the city but also make regular forays into Vincennes and the Bois de Boulogne. Their favorite prey are sparrows and small rodents. There are about thirty pairs of kestrels in the city. When they are here, these small falcons normally take up their positions on ancient monuments or office blocks: such buildings presumably remind them of the cliffs where they spend most of their time.

Male

Male

BLACK REDSTART
The black redstart occupies the rooftops from March to October or November. It likes to adopt a commanding position when singing or lying in wait for insects.

STOCK DOVE
This, one of the scarcest of the species to be found in Paris, makes its home in holes in walls or on disused chimney stacks. It can be recognized by its dark eye and blue-gray plumage.

ROCK PIGEON
The semi-domestic rock pigeon has its ferocious detractors as well as its faithful supporters. Measures have been taken to limit its numbers.

AERIAL HUNTERS
Swifts and house martins are perpetually on the lookout for flying insects, which they eat to the exclusion of anything else. They come to the capital only for a few months in the summer.

Magpie

PETITE CEINTURE RAILWAY

Even in the largest city in France there are still special areas
where nature has been left to its own devices and has partly
taken control of its own destiny. These forgotten corners –
abandoned gardens and other tranquil spots not generally
accessible to the public – are a secret paradise for the city's
nature-lovers. Over the years parts of the Petite Ceinture
railway have been overrun by flora and fauna: only a stone's
throw from the noise and bustle of the city, insects buzz, lizards
bask in the sun, and sparrows peacefully chirrup the afternoon
away.

CELANDINE
Its orange-yellow
juice is said to cure
warts.

TRAVELER'S JOY
This plant's feathery
fruit grows throughout
the winter.

COMMON ELDER
The elder's juicy berries
are eaten by a wide
variety of birds.

WHITE BRYONY
This climber bears
fruit until the autumn

Red admiral

Some butterflies are able to survive city life.

Azures

BUDDLEIA
The flowery clusters of this shrub, which originally came from China, are very popular with butterflies.

STONE MARTEN
With its superb climbing skills, the stone marten moves around the city with ease. It inhabits both the upper sections and basements of buildings. The relatively few stone martens in Paris have a preference for areas well endowed with green spaces.

WINTER WREN
Despite its size, this wren sings with impressive volume.

CHIFFCHAFF
This warbler returns to wooded parts of the city each spring.

ROBIN
The robin builds its nest on the ground in well-hidden areas among thick vegetation.

BLACKCAP
The fluted song of the male blackcap is particularly melodious.

HOUSE MOUSE
This mouse lives only in buildings – or underground – where it can find food, shelter and warmth.

HEDGEHOG
Hedgehogs live in some parks (Buttes-Chaumont and Montsouris) and in abandoned sections of the Petite Ceinture railway.

WALL LIZARD
This lizard is seen less and less in Paris these days. The drop in numbers is largely attributable to cats.

■ UNUSUAL MICRO-HABITATS

A gillyflower on its balcony.

The visitor who takes enough time – and knows where to look – will soon realize that Paris is teeming with nooks and crannies where flowers, insects and spiders lead a quiet but tenacious existence. An urban world in miniature awaits the assiduous enthusiast in the cracks in concrete and asphalt and the spaces between paving stones.

These "secret" plants need only a little moisture and mineral nutrients.

Young ailanthus

The tiny flowers of the ivy-leaved toadflax are best seen close up.

WOOD LOUSE
This small crustacean loves moisture but loathes light.

BEHIND BARS
Cavities sealed by iron grills sometimes provide shelter for plants and small invertebrates.

Meadow grass

Greater plaintain

Chickw

WILD CAMOMILE
This plant grows from April to October.

DANDELION
Dandelions are smaller in cities.

BETWEEN PAVING STONES
Where paving stones still exist, the gaps between them sometimes provide the settings for embryonic botanical gardens – as long as they are not disturbed by passing pedestrians.

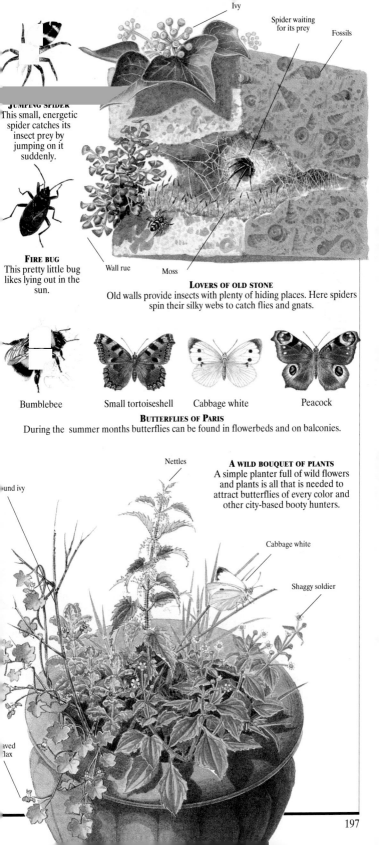

Ivy

Spider waiting for its prey

Fossils

JUMPING SPIDER
This small, energetic spider catches its insect prey by jumping on it suddenly.

FIRE BUG
This pretty little bug likes lying out in the sun.

Wall rue

Moss

LOVERS OF OLD STONE
Old walls provide insects with plenty of hiding places. Here spiders spin their silky webs to catch flies and gnats.

Bumblebee

Small tortoiseshell

Cabbage white

Peacock

BUTTERFLIES OF PARIS
During the summer months butterflies can be found in flowerbeds and on balconies.

Nettles

A WILD BOUQUET OF PLANTS
A simple planter full of wild flowers and plants is all that is needed to attract butterflies of every color and other city-based booty hunters.

und ivy

Cabbage white

Shaggy soldier

aved
lax

197

■ PARKS AND GARDENS

The parks and gardens of Paris are
welcome havens of green for numerous species of birds. The
selection presented here consists of resident species that can be
seen all year round. Some of them are very common and can be
seen anywhere, while others are either rarer or else lead more
discreet lives, demanding keen powers of observation from those
who want to see them. Each spring the capital's parks resound to
their cooing, warbling and trilling.

Male

Male

**LESSER SPOTTED
WOODPECKER**
This woodpecker,
hardly bigger than a
sparrow, is seen
mostly in the winter.

**SHORT-TOED
TREECREEPER**
These often avoid
detection because of
their bark-colored
plumage.

GREENFINCH
In spring, the male
indulges in elaborate
nuptial display
flights.

**HEDGE ACCENTOR
(DUNNOCK)**
This unassuming little
bird spends much of its
time shuffling jerkily
along on the ground.

Linden leaf

Norway maple leaf

Sweet chestnut leaf

The trees most often planted in the parks of Paris have to be capable of resisting disease and atmospheric pollution, and require frequent pruning.

MAGPIE
At the end of the winter, this bird builds its nest of twigs at the top of a chestnut tree or plane tree.

JAY
It is difficult to spot the jay among the foliage despite its harsh, raucous calls.

WOOD PIGEON
This pigeon may be identified by the white marks on its neck and its white wing-bars.

CHAFFINCH
When the chaffinch is looking for seeds, it travels along the ground in jerky leaps.

GREAT TIT
The great tit likes the nesting boxes to be found in Paris parks.

BLUE TIT
This bird is able to hang upside down on a branch when catching insects.

FIRECREST
This, the smallest of all European birds, visits the parks in winter.

The aim of the great classical gardens of Paris was to glorify the royal and princely palaces for posterity. These gardens created vast perspectives and by incorporating plants into geometrical shapes, they embodied the 17th-century desire for reason to triumph over nature.

TUILERIES AND JARDINS DU CARROUSEL (1 HI–J45)

Le Nôtre's garden
In the 16th century ▲ 332 Catherine de' Medici built a palace on the site of a former tile factory; attached to the site was an enclosed garden. André Le Nôtre turned it into a French-style

André Le Nôtre (1613–1700) studied architecture and painting before succeeding his grandfather, and then his father, as head gardener at the Tuileries.

garden in 1666. To establish the palace's domination over its natural environment – there was countryside to

the west and the river to the south – Le Nôtre erected two large terraces, forming a broad alley that extended the line of the palace some way beyond the garden boundaries. This followed the route of the future Champs-Élysées and traced the first section of the Grand Axis ▲ 308, the perspective that would one day run from the Louvre all the way to the Grande Arche of La Défense. The garden is divided into two parts. Next to the palace there is a wide-open expanse adorned by parterres with box-edged beds, including those in the shape of arabesques. There is also a wooded area, which becomes increasingly dense

Wall rue is a rare fern that grows in cracks in the old walls of the Tuileries.

and mysterious as it extends westward.
A prototype for a public park
The Tuileries were one of the first

gardens in Europe to open to the public. Long a favorite with visitors and Parisians alike, in the 18th century they became the model for public gardens throughout France and Europe. At the time it boasted cafés, kiosks, seats for rent and stone benches: it was also a place where all classes of society could come for relaxation. Until the end of the 19th century, successive

The Tuileries and Carrousel gardens contain about a hundred 17th-to-20th-century sculptures, including some by Aristide Maillol

"The Tuileries" (1876, Claude Monet).

governments organized festivals here, illuminating the park with fireworks.

The new Tuileries

Work on the Tuileries and Carrousel gardens, which had lain in poor condition for some years, was recently completed. The aim was to reincorporate the gardens into the extended Louvre Palace and the Grand Axis vista, while reviving the site's historical associations.

The Carrousel Garden

This 19th-century garden was created after the Tuileries

The parterres and private gardens of the Grand Carré (above) are to be restored to their original 19th-century layout. During the Restoration they were laid out beside the palace and reserved for the royal family. Napoleon III had the gardens enlarged.

Palace was destroyed by fire; the triumphal arch, the focal point of a sunburst pattern of hedges, is the gateway to the Tuileries. It can be described as the "green room" of the Louvre, adorned with its Maillol sculptures and topiarised trees and hedges. It opens out onto a terrace-belvedere: this was constructed over the underground path, on the exact site of the palace's former terrace. Adorned with a central stairway, the terrace descends to the Tuileries, where Le Nôtre's designs – both

the more manicured parterres of the Grand Carré and the wild thickets of the Grand Couvert – are unchanged: the latter have now been restored to their former wildness. Some five hundred trees are to be planted around the gardens by the year 2000.

The elaborate gardens were designed to be seen from the upper floors of the palace. In the late 19th century, they were replaced by lawns bordered with flower beds.

LE JARDIN DU PALAIS-ROYAL (2 AB4)

Virtually nothing remains of the original design for the garden which was built close to the Palais-Royal in the early 1600's. The garden was bigger than it is today: it consisted of parterres with box hedging and was decorated with pools and statues, while to the north it opened onto a small wood where Louis XIV went fox hunting as a child. The construction of nearby galleries and streets in the 18th century reduced the size of the grounds and shortened the perspective. Then it was turned into an English-style garden, before acquiring the layout we know today. The garden of the Palais-Royal covers an area of eight acres; it is shaded by four double rows of lime trees trimmed *en marquise*. The central pool with its fountain is flanked by two expanses of grass bordered by single-color flowerbeds decorated with 19th-century statues. In the years leading up to the Revolution and during the Directoire, this charming yet peaceful garden was one of the liveliest spots in all of Paris ▲ *338*: today, the peace of the Palais-Royal Garden is disturbed only by the screeching of swifts as they arrive from Africa in April.

"The Shepherd and the Goat" (1830), a marble statue by Paul Lemoyne in the Palais-Royal Garden.

LE JARDIN DU LUXEMBOURG (2 A9)

The garden which Marie de' Medici had built for her palace is laid out around a central parterre dominated by terraces. Two thousand elm trees arranged in a square once framed a view that ended abruptly at the Carthusian monastery. The monks refused to give up any of their land, and as a result the southern extension was not completed until the end of the 18th century – after the monastery had been torn down during the Revolution. The garden was restored during the First Empire by Chalgrin, who widened and lengthened the central vista and built an English-style garden to the southwest. The balustrades overhanging the central parterre and pool date from the same period. The construction of nearby streets and avenues during the Second Empire reduced the area covered by the garden, but its general appearance was not changed.

The Latin Quarter Garden
This princely park, where the painter Watteau paid clandestine visits to seek inspiration, was opened to the public in 1778. Since then, it has been a haunt for students and local residents, but,

The apiary in the Luxembourg Garden is home to some twenty colonies of bees (about twenty million individuals). Practical and theoretical courses are organized by the Société Centrale d'Apiculture.

The 17th-century de' Medici fountain in the Luxembourg Garden was built in the style of an Italian grotto and decorated with sculptures by Ottin (1866).

unlike other parks, it has rarely been used for grand festivities. The 19th century saw the introduction of a bandstand, a merry-go-round by Garnier and numerous shelters: a number of small areas designed for relaxation and entertainment have been added more recently.

Statues

About eighty statues, among them the renowned *Queens and Famous Women of France* series, are distributed around the garden: they are the work of several 19th-century artists, including Cain, Frémiet, Bourdelle and Marqueste. There are three fountains: the

Medici fountain (above), whose pediment bears the queen's coat of arms; the second is the Regard fountain (1869), and a fountain commemorating Eugène Delacroix, decorated with a bronze statue by Jules Dalou (1890).

Flora

The flower beds, which are replanted three times a year, are a riot of gillyflowers, salvias and dahlias; in summer they are joined by orange, date and pomegranate trees, and oleanders. The palace is surrounded on all sides by extensive wooded areas planted with white chestnut trees. The English Garden is cut off by a line of laurel, aucuba and privet hedges and boasts a huge variety of plants. There is

also an orchard – the remains of the Carthusian nursery – which contains two thousand varieties of apple and pear trees trained as espaliers.

The Observatory Gardens

These were laid out in 1867 but were recently renamed the Robert Cavelier

Between May and October plants are taken from the Luxembourg Orangerie and replanted in the central flowerbeds.

de La Salle and Marco Polo gardens: they form the final section of the perspective conceived by Chalgrin. The Observatory Gardens contain the superb Four-Corners-of-the-World fountain, a collective work completed in 1874 after plans by Davioud. The statues of four women supporting the globe, symbolizing the four corners of the world ▲ 272, are by Jean-Baptiste Carpeaux (1827–75).

Botanical gardens date from the Renaissance and were first used for educational purposes during the reign of Louis XIV. They have also been used for experiments on, and the conservation of, exotic specimens brought back from foreign expeditions.

Each century has made a contribution to the Jardin des Plantes. The numerous species of flora are meticulously labeled.

LE JARDIN DES PLANTES (5 FG1)

Louis XIII built the Royal Medicinal Herb Garden in 1633 for the use of medical students. In 1640, it became the first garden in Paris to open to the public. Under the supervision of Buffon (1739–88) the Botanical Gardens were enlarged and became a center of scientific learning. Scholars of the day included the three Jussieu brothers, who were botanists, and the naturalist Daubenton. In 1793 the National Convention awarded the garden the title of National Museum of Natural History; the museum's galleries were built during the 19th and 20th centuries ▲ *142*.

Botanical and horticultural collections

The collections of dahlias, cannas and geraniums are found in the French parterres, which extend from the Grande Galerie de l'Évolution to the railings by the entrance. There is also a rose garden and a section containing four hundred varieties of iris. The Ecological Park is set out in the English manner and boasts a fine collection of trees and shrubs growing wild; the Botany School identifies grasses and edible and medicinal plants. The rockery in the Alpine Garden is covered with two thousand species of alpine plants classified by region; it also has a curious microclimate which enables the temperature to vary by up to 46°F in different areas.

This 66-foot cedar of Lebanon, planted by

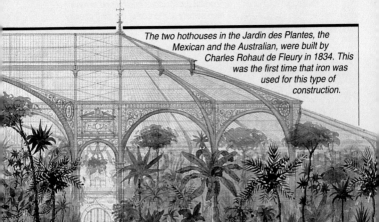

The two hothouses in the Jardin des Plantes, the Mexican and the Australian, were built by Charles Rohaut de Fleury in 1834. This was the first time that iron was used for this type of construction.

The maze

This was built around 1640 on an artificial mound, at the top of which is a bronze summer house, the oldest metal building in Paris. The column at the bottom stands over the tomb of Daubenton.

The menagerie

Added to the Jardin des Plantes during the Revolution, after the Royal Menagerie had been confiscated, the menagerie stands in an area laid out in the English style and incudes a vivarium containing snakes and crocodiles.

LE JARDIN DES SERRES D'AUTEUIL

This was laid out in 1898 by Jean-Camille Formigé on the site of Louis XV's former nurseries and included greenhouses. It is Paris' official orchard and is the supplier of indoor plants to the Hôtel de Ville and some of the mayors' offices. The Serres d'Auteuil Garden is also a botanical garden with well-labeled plants and trees. The most remarkable feature of the garden is the series of greenhouses which form the great hothouse: this is 325 feet long and has a central dome 53 feet high. It contains a palmarium and an abundance of tropical flora.

Bernard de Jussieu in 1734, is one of the oldest trees in Paris.

LE PARC FLORAL DE VINCENNES (4 GH7)

The floral park was opened in 1969 as a site for horticultural exhibitions. It covers 76 acres landscaped by Daniel Collin and abounds in valleys, artificial lakes and rivers. Groves of beech and cedar trees have been planted, which complement small clumps of Corsican pine and oaks. The style of the pavilions and patios, the design of the ponds and the fine statuary (works by Calder, Stahly and others) anchor the park in the esthetic traditions of the 1970's. Particularly striking is the Dahlia Garden, which winds its way through the pine forest like a long, multicolored river.

With a nod in the direction of pictorial art, the Valley of Flowers contains the flora that appear in Impressionist landscapes, including sunflowers, corn, sweet peas, hollyhocks and bindweed. The Pavillon des Papillons (Butterfly pavilion) of l'Île-de-France has

collections of wood lice, cockroaches, slugs and silkworms as well as butterflies.

The Chartres Folly, later Monceau Park, embodied the frivolous and refined behavior of high society at the end of the 18th century.

The picturesque garden (or *jardin anglo-chinois*) was very fashionable during the second half of the 18th century; it was the opposite of the French classical garden in every way. Here we are in a land of illusion dotted with curious and exotic ruins and buildings.

LE PARC MONCEAU (9 E8)

The Chartres Folly
Louis XVI's brother, the Duke of Chartres, had a folly built near the hamlet of Monceau in 1787: it was one of the first gardens in the *anglo-chinois*

The Naumachia in Monceau Park is in the form of a pond surrounded by a colonnade.

style. The architect Carmontelle – a dramatist, organizer of festivities and avant-garde landscape gardener – designed the park as an open-air Pandora's box of curiosities and as a location for festivities. The rivers, small woods, rockery and grottos which he built were set off by a number of extravagant constructions, of which only the Egyptian Tomb and the Naumachia have

Monceau Park contains one of the tallest trees in Paris: this Oriental plane is 200 years old and has a circumference of 23 feet.

survived. The park was enlarged in 1793 to include a rotunda by Claude Nicolas Ledoux ● 69,

the designer of the tollhouses of the Farmers-General Wall.
Haussmann's "renovations"
The park suffered as a result of Haussmann's apportionment of the Monceau Plain. Half of the land (20 acres) was sold to the Pereire brothers, who built streets and private houses; then the park was encircled

The tomb of the King of Hearts is on an island in Bagatelle Park.

by railings with monumental gates. It was later renovated by Alphand ▲ *208*, who introduced rare species of plants and complemented the old buildings with an Italianate bridge and a grotto with stalactites.

Flora and fauna
The park contains several specimens of trees planted in the 19th century and a number of rare species, including a fruit-bearing fig tree and the extraordinary *Davidia* (handkerchief tree). The bird life is exceptionally abundant and varied: there have even been sightings of the spotted fly-catcher, a rare visitor to Paris.

BAGATELLE (8 D3)

The Artois Folly In 1775, Louis XV's brother, the Count of Artois, had Bagatelle's castle and park built in only two months, in response to a challenge by Marie-Antoinette. Thomas Blaikie designed the park in the *anglo-chinois* style, introducing waterfalls, grottos, a pagoda and a lovers' pavilion. The grounds were further extended in the 19th century with an orangery and stables. A subsequent owner, Sir Richard Wallace, added two hunting lodges and the Trianon.

The property was bought by the City of Paris in 1904 and has since been used for horticultural shows. The park provides a remarkable cross-section of garden design spanning three centuries.

The English Garden, with its much-admired undergrowth, ponds and shaded grassy areas, also contains theme gardens, including an iris garden, a French-style parterre and an extraordinary rose garden built in 1904 by J.C.N. Forestier, the warden of parks and gardens and friend of Monet.

Of the many "lovers' pavilions" built in the Bois de Boulogne during the 19th century, Château Bagatelle (above) is the only one to have survived.

Bagatelle Park boasts a profusion of plants that grow all year round, but June is the best time to visit.

Landscape gardens, inspired by English parks, came into being during the Second Empire. Their irregular shapes gave the impression of a natural, varied landscape. Created as a pocket of greenery in the heart of a busy city, these hidden gardens offered private, winding paths for quiet walks.

LE PARC DES BUTTES-CHAUMONT

(11 B8)
As part of his drive to make Paris a healthier place in which to live, Napoleon III conceived an ambitious plan for green open spaces, and in seventeen years, no fewer than 4,950 acres of woods, parks, gardens and squares were laid out and 600,000 trees planted. Jean-Charles Alphand (1817–91) was in charge of

Two bridges lead across the ravines to the Temple of Sybil, on a cliff 292 feet high.

implementing the policy, assisted by the gardener Barillet-Deschamps, the architect Davioud and the engineer Belgrand. Behind the decision to build the Buttes-Chaumont Park in 1863 lay a desire to rehabilitate the surrounding slum area by creating one final park in the northeast.

An example of a landscape park
Alphand used dynamite charges to give new forms to the Buttes-Chaumont; the results included a lake, a number of waterfalls and rivers, embankments and large plantations.

The lake in Montsouris Park is the only place in Paris where the moorhen regularly nests.

When the park was opened in 1867 it was a typical Haussmann design: paths plunging deep into the undergrowth, clambering up rocks, and then opening out onto higher land and winding their way through the countryside. All of this formed part of an idealized picture of nature adorned by features of much picturesque charm, including a temple and a grotto with stalactites.

Flora

The park contains several remarkable trees including an example of *Gymnocladus canadensis* and two *Gingko biloba*.

Haussmann's parks are noted for their artifice: they abound in false rocks, false grottos and false woods.

LE PARC MONTSOURIS (5 AB8)

Montsouris Park was designed to be a copy of Buttes-Chaumont to the south. It was laid out by Alphand between 1867 and 1878 over the site of old quarries that had been turned

Montsouris Park contains about ten sculptures realized between 1880 and 1960.

into catacombs in the late 18th century. As with the Buttes-Chaumont Park, Alphand was obliged to conceal the railway lines, and he produced a landscape dotted with valleys. He also dug an artificial lake, built waterfalls and grottos, and laid out grassy areas and thickets to produce alternating blocked and unrestricted views. The highest point was once occupied by the Palais du Bardo: this building, which burned down in 1991, was a

reproduction of the Bey of Tunis' summer residence, a typically Moorish design built for the Universal Exhibition of 1867. The park also contains a meteorological station, constructed in 1947 next to the south bearing of the old Paris Meridian; this once stood in an observatory designed by Vaudoyer in 1806.

Birds

The southern extremity of the old Petite Ceinture railway track is carpeted with pines and abundant herbaceous vegetation. The area attracts numerous species of rare birds.

These include the crested and coal tit, the wren, the serin and the spotted fly-catcher.

Modern landscape artists like their parks to be fully integrated into local life and history. Forms are generally classical, but more modern ideas, including expanses of grass, are common. These areas of greenery are surrounded by theme gardens designed for public use.

PARC DE LA VILLETTE (11 D4)

This park was built in 1987 on the site of the old Halles: it is crossed by L'Ourcq canal and its 86 acres make it the largest green space in Paris. It was designed by Bernard Tschumi as a prototype of a 21st-century "garden

geometric pattern around the park. There is also an architectural promenade that gives visitors a cinematic experience of space; this leads to the theme gardens. With the exception of the Bamboo Garden (left), these are somewhat disappointing: the themes include plant life and water, imagination, play, fog, islands, children's fears and dragons.

city" and links two important cultural centers, the Cité des Sciences to the north and the Cité de la Musique and the Grande Halle to the south. La Villette Park is open day and night and is noted for its walks, entertainments, shows and displays of modern art: it is extremely popular. The most striking visual elements are twenty-one red follies arranged in a

The crested lark is particularly fond of the wide open spaces of La Villette.

PARC DE BELLEVILLE (3 B2)

Belleville Park was built on the side of a hill on a site covering 11 acres. Several aspects of the park are linked to local history ▲ 408. Examples include: a vine and numerous open-air cafés which call to

mind the wine-growing that was once a feature of these slopes; artificial grottos which recall the old gypsum quarries;

and waterfalls and pools which are reminders of the water that still flows underground. The wide-ranging selection of plants and trees are laid out in both traditional and modern styles.

Belleville Park is situated on some of the highest ground in Paris: there is a magnificent view from a belvedere at the summit.

PARC DE BERCY (4 B4)

This park, built on a site where bonded warehouses once stood, was designed as a garden of remembrance. Landmarks recall the area's history, including a paved track, warehouses, the ruins of Château

Bercy and about a hundred trees. Bercy Park was built on a classical model with broad expanses of grass, parterres and a terrace which, as in the Tuileries, runs down to the Seine. In a style evoking picturesque gardens, the parterres have four buildings dedicated to the seasons. The recent creation of a romantic garden around a canal, ending in a little island, completes the picture.

White garden

Glasshouse

Small glasshouse

Moving g

LE PARC ANDRÉ-CITROËN (7 G6)

Since 1993 this park has marked the center of a new district constructed over the site of the old motor car factory. The White Garden to the east underlines the closeness of the city, whereas the denser, more shaded Black Garden has the reverse effect. The main area, which runs down to the quays lining the Seine, is extremely classical and encircles a broad expanse of grass. There is an esplanade at the end of the perspective,

The two large greenhouses in the Parc André-Citroën, designed by Patrick Berger: one is an orangery, while the other houses southern Mediterranean flora.

Black garden

André-Citroën Park on the Left Bank was built by a team of architects and landscape artists. Its view of the Seine complements those from Champ-de-Mars and the Esplanade des Invalides.

...morphosis ...arden

Rock garden

which is also marked by two enormous greenhouses framing a peristyle adorned with 120 water jets. The ubiquitous theme of water is also taken up in the grassy section with its waterfalls and large canal. To the east is a line of six gardens each dedicated to one of the senses and, by virtue of its color, associated with a type of metal. Along the riverbank,

vegetation grows freely in this untended garden, a huge, unspoilt area dotted with wild flowers and *Graminaceae*.

The fallow land is also rich in flora.

The profusion of flowers and the wild nature of this garden attract numerous insects.

The Bois de Boulogne and the Bois de Vincennes are all that remain of an enormous forest that encircled Lutetia in the 1st century. The configuration of these two "green lungs" situated at the gates to Paris dates from the Second Empire.

LE BOIS DE BOULOGNE (Map 8)

A few pairs of green woodpeckers can still be found in the Bois de Boulogne: they spend a lot of time on the ground searching for anthills.

Thousands of Parisians flock to the Bois de Boulogne every weekend. Its 2,100 acres extend from Boulogne to Neuilly and contain wooded areas, lakes, footpaths, bridle paths, cycle tracks, sports facilities and restaurants. Contained within it are numerous gardens, including the Bagatelle ▲ 207, Pré-Catelan, Shakespeare and Serres d'Auteuil ▲ 205 gardens.

A royal park and lovers' rendezvous The Bois de Boulogne is now separated from the

Rouvray Forest, which stood to the northwest of Paris in medieval times. It became a royal park in the 13th century and acquired the name "Boulogne" after Philip the Fair had a small church built there in 1301 to commemorate a pilgrimage to Boulogne-sur-Mer. The forest was opened to the public by Louis XVI in the 18th century and gained a reputation as a place for loose living: following the example of the kings of France – Francis I had turned the Château de Madrid into a

lovers' rendezvous – the nobility built the châteaux of La Muette, Neuilly, La Folie St-James and Bagatelle.

A fashionable promenade in the Belle Époque Napoleon III renovated the area as soon as he came to power: it had been badly damaged during the Revolution and Allied occupation of 1814–15. The Bois de Boulogne was linked to Paris by the Allée de l'Impératrice (now Avenue Foch), and

it was then fundamentally redesigned by Alphand ▲ 208, who between 1852 and 1858 built 60 miles of paths, constructed lakes and rivers, and planted 400,000 trees. The addition of a children's amusement area, the Jardin de l'Acclimatation (1860), and the Pré-Catelan Garden (1855), followed by the Longchamp and Auteuil racecourses (1857 and 1873, respectively), made the Bois de

The Moulin de Longchamp (above) stands among the ruins of Longchamp Abbey in the Bois de Boulogne. The abbey, founded in 1256, was destroyed during the Revolution.

Boulogne one of the most fashionable promenades of the Belle Époque.

Flora and fauna Three kinds of oak account for over half the trees in the Bois de Boulogne: the *chêne rouvre* (which gave its name to Rouvray Forest), the pedunculate oak and the durmast oak. The area provides natural habitats for squirrels, bats and hedgehogs, as well as dozens of species of birds, including jays, tawny owls and

carrion crows. The Bois de Boulogne also contains a bird sanctuary.

Bank voles are normally reddish in color, but many in the Bois de Boulogne are black. This phenomenon often occurs among animals living close to or in the middle of big cities.

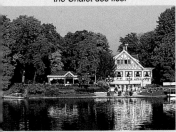

Lac Supérieur and Lac Inférieur are at different levels and are linked by a waterfall: the lower lake contains two islands. Below: the Chalet des Îles.

The common heron is sometimes seen near the lakes in the Bois de Vincennes.

LE BOIS DE VINCENNES (Map 4)

This forest was a royal hunting ground from the 12th century until it was turned into a public park during the reign of Louis XV. There was an unhappy period in the early years of the 19th century, when part of the land was cleared for military purposes.

The rock in Vincennes Zoo is entirely artificial and was recently restored.

In fact, it narrowly avoided being used for army maneuvers, but was dubbed "Canonville" just the same. Encouraged by the success of the Bois de Boulogne, Napoleon III and the planner Haussmann decided to lay out a park of comparable dimensions to the east in 1857. Alphand and his assistants built the relief topography (Gravelle Knoll) and three lakes (Minimes, St-Mandé and Gravelle); Lake Daumesnil was added later. The forest's 2,460 acres were then reforested and crisscrossed with new pathways, and the whole area was filled with expanses of greenery, hillocks, grottos, and restaurants and other buildings. The

forest acquired a hippodrome in 1863, the Imperial Farm in 1859, and in 1867 the School of Horticulture was established with its arboretum of 850 labeled species. Other attractions were added later: they included a zoo (1934), the Floral Park (1969) ▲ 205, and the Georges-Ville Farm (1989), designed with the specific purpose of introducing children to aspects of agriculture.

Vincennes Zoo
This replaced the Zoological Garden, which had been temporarily laid out for the Colonial Exhibition of 1931.

It contains 550 mammals, including endangered species such as the giant panda, rare species of seal and tapir, and 700 birds.

Flora and fauna
The Bois de Vincennes has

130,000 trees: mainly oaks and some fifteen other species, principally beech and maple. The most common animal is the *Crocidura russula*, a species of shrew that preys on grasshoppers. Tench, roach, carp, pike, and a range of insects and frogs

and toads can be found in the lakes, which also attract numerous aquatic birds, including the common heron and the black-headed gull.

ALONG THE SEINE ▲

In the days when the Seine used to supply Paris with most of its needs – travelers, coal, fruit, wood, meat and even fish reached the capital by river. Until the 17th century, large numbers of people lived at the foot of the quays within close range of the often stagnant, polluted low waters of the Seine (the river banks had not at that stage been built up). Parisians bathed in it, persuaded their horses to drink from it, and washed and worked in it, while mills churned up the river bed making flour, washing clothes and sharpening swords. Today the Seine is calm and quiescent as it winds its way through the city. It is regulated by a number of locks upstream and by the Suresnes dam downstream. Dramatic flooding and exceptionally low tides are things of the past. It is true that Paris is still the country's leading river port, and that barges loaded with grain, sand and gravel continue to ply the Seine, but factories have now been removed from the river banks. In some cases the banks have given way to freeways, but more frequently to walkways. Paris is therefore one of the few capital cities in the world that may be visited by river. The quays have now been handed back to pedestrians: they are adjacent to most of the city's most famous monuments and continue to be popular with strolling Parisians and tourists alike.

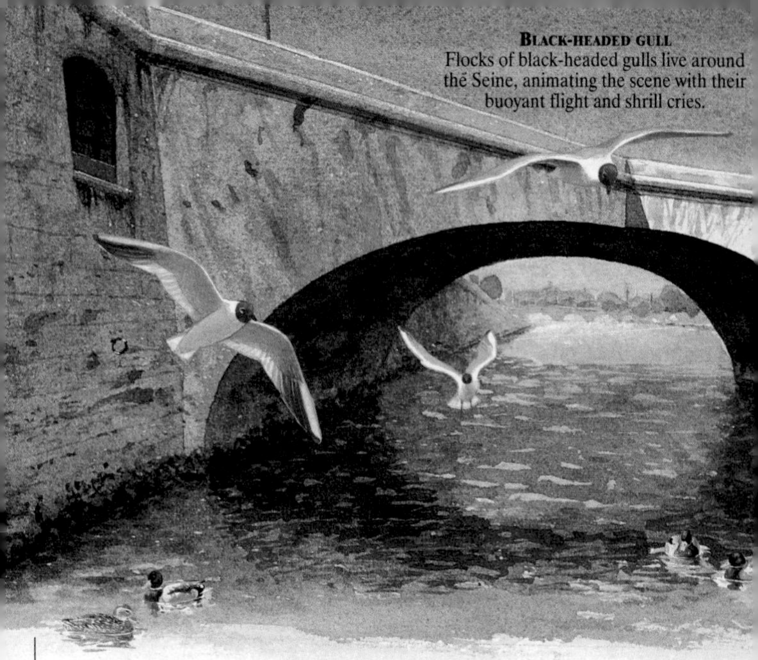

Thanks to progress in techniques of water treatment, the Seine is now less polluted than it has been for many years. The present cloudy appearance of the water is due simply to suspended mineral particles. As a result of this significant improvement in water quality, aquatic plants have been reintroduced, and over twenty species of fish have returned, even in the stretch of the river which runs through the city center. There is also the winter parade of gulls with their circling flight, giving the city an unexpected seaside atmosphere.

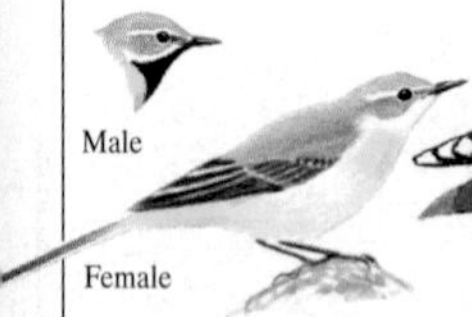

Male

Female

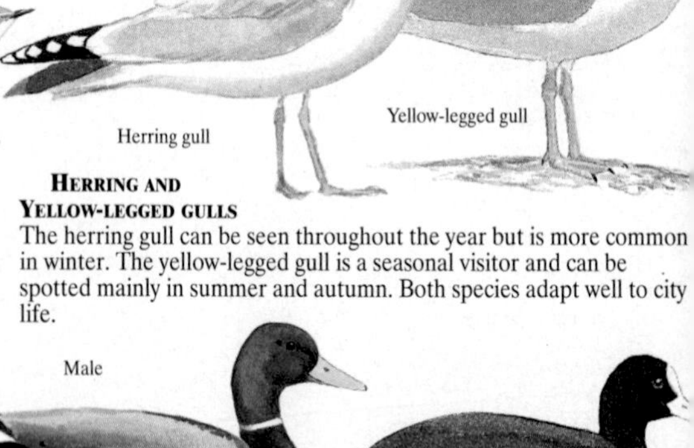

Yellow-legged gull

Herring gull

GRAY WAGTAIL
The wagtail scurries along the quays, pecking away as it runs.

HERRING AND YELLOW-LEGGED GULLS
The herring gull can be seen throughout the year but is more common in winter. The yellow-legged gull is a seasonal visitor and can be spotted mainly in summer and autumn. Both species adapt well to city life.

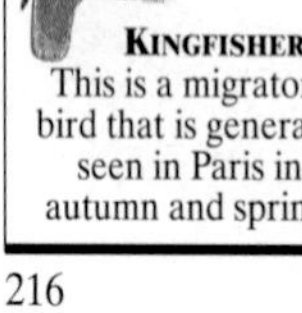

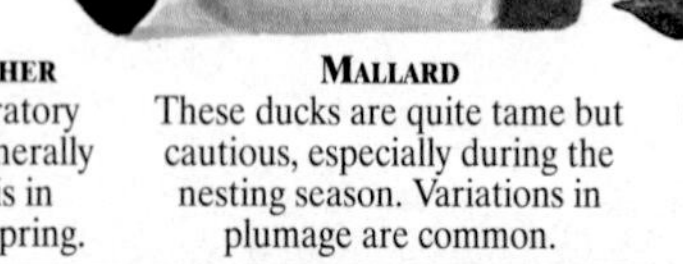

Male

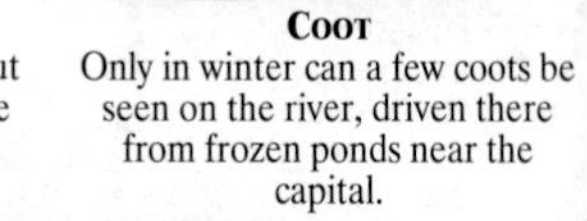

KINGFISHER
This is a migratory bird that is generally seen in Paris in autumn and spring.

MALLARD
These ducks are quite tame but cautious, especially during the nesting season. Variations in plumage are common.

COOT
Only in winter can a few coots be seen on the river, driven there from frozen ponds near the capital.

216

Two centuries ago the Seine was used as a trading route, a washing and watering place for animals; it also had high levels of organic pollution.

DACE
This fish can tolerate poor-quality water better than many other species.

GUDGEON
Gudgeons are very gregarious fish, swimming along the riverbed in shoals.

ON THE RIVERBANKS
The riverside supports plants well suited to the conditions, both above and below water-level. Plants which thrive in damp conditions grow in the tiniest crevices.

The pretty spikes of purple loosestrife can be seen from May to August.

Mosses and algae flourish close to outflows.

Young, hardy wall rocket manages to survive in cracks.

PIKE
This powerful, well-armed predator feeds on other fish, crayfish and ducklings.

BREAM
With their flat, curved bodies adult bream stay in deep water during the day.

ROACH
Shoals of roach thread through the underwater vegetation.

Curled pondweed

The introduced aquatic vegetation attracts the fish.

Water milfoil

217

The calm, meandering River Seine has never been used as a defensive barrier. Long ago the islands and the Left and Right banks joined forces to form the city of Paris, largely ignoring the water running between them. However, following the construction of the Pont-Neuf and Place Dauphine under Henri IV, the city began to come to terms with this river that flowed through its heart and to integrate it into city life. The resulting quays have now been named a World Heritage Site by UNESCO.

LIBERTY MADE TO MEASURE
This statue is a miniature of the American Statue of Liberty, presented to the United States by France in 1886 to commemorate the centenary of the Declaration of Independence. *Liberty Enlightening the World* and her tiny replica are the works of Auguste Bartholdi.

1. STATUE OF LIBERTY
2. MAISON DE RADIO FRANCE
9. TROCADÉRO PALACE

—— FOOTPATH

AV. DU PDT KENNEDY

PONT DE GRENELLE

QUAI DE GRENELLE

QUAI DE GRENEL

CANAL PLUS AND JARDIN CITROEN ☞

CANAL PLUS HEADQUARTERS
This building was designed by the New York architect Richard Meier. It is notable for its aluminum façade, glass walls and acoustic isolation techniques. It houses the TV company Canal Plus.

CITROËN GARDEN
▲ 211
One of the city's newest gardens, it is set out in 34 acres of land

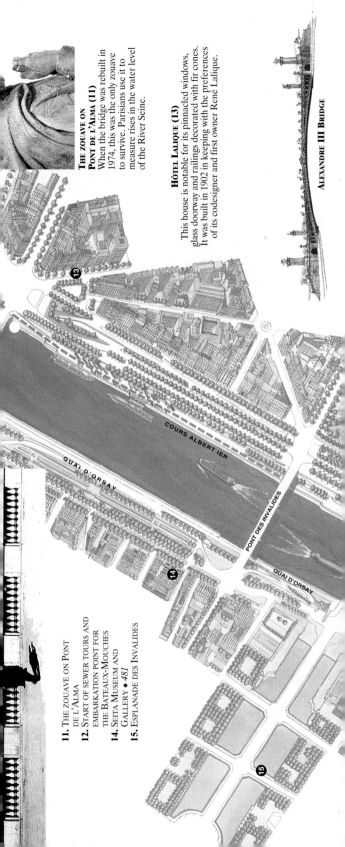

THE ZOUAVE ON
PONT DE L'ALMA (11)

When the bridge was rebuilt in 1974, this was the only zouave to survive. Parisians use it to measure rises in the water level of the River Seine.

HÔTEL LALIQUE (13)

This house is notable for its pinnacled windows, glass doorway and railings decorated with fir cones. It was built in 1902 in keeping with the preferences of its codesigner and first owner René Lalique.

ALEXANDRE III BRIDGE

COURS ALBERT IER

QUAI D'ORSAY

PONT DES INVALIDES

QUAI D'ORSAY

11. THE ZOUAVE ON PONT DE L'ALMA
12. START OF SEWER TOURS AND EMBARKATION POINT FOR THE BATEAUX-MOUCHES
14. SEITA MUSEUM AND GALLERY ◆ 481
15. ESPLANADE DES INVALIDES

ALEXANDRE III BRIDGE

By establishing an alliance with Russia in 1893, France broke free from the diplomatic isolation that Germany had orchestrated for the previous twenty years.

This newly built bridge was named after Czar Alexander III to mark the alliance.

The candelabra are copies of lamps on Trinity Bridge in St Petersburg, and the decoration includes lions made of stone, statues glistening with gold and keystones adorned with nymphs of the Seine and the Neva.

STATUE OF ALBERT I (17)

Albert I of Belgium remained in his invaded country throughout World War One and, with help from France, he never surrendered. This statue, built in 1938, commemorates Franco-Belgian friendship.

ART NOUVEAU

BIR-HAKEIM BRIDGE

THE TOWPATH
Before the invention of steam- and gas-driven engines, boats traveling along the River Seine upstream were towed by men or horses. The towpath upstream of Paris was on the Right Bank, and trees, ports and building works were not allowed to obstruct it.

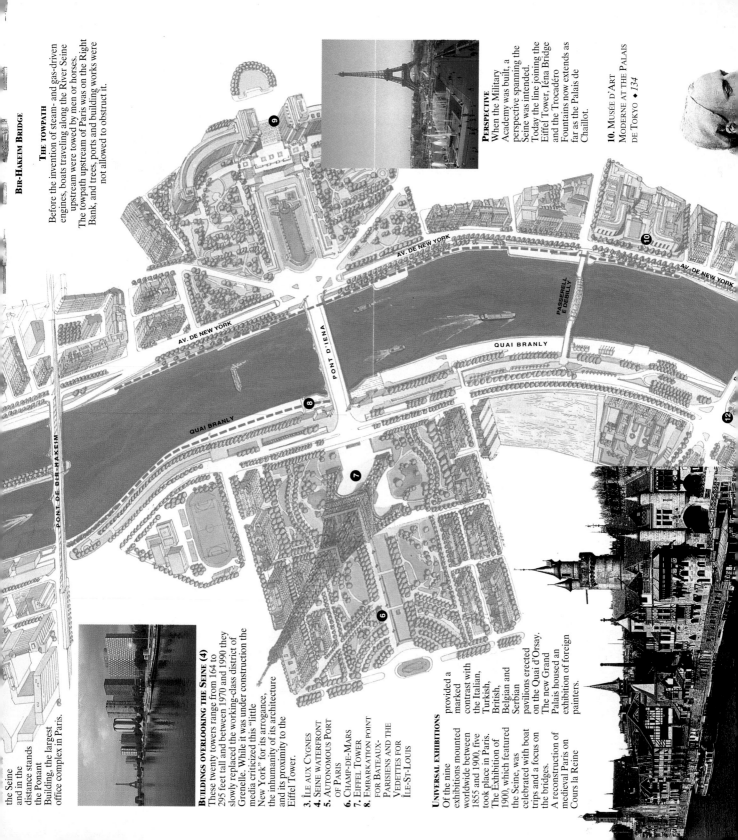

PERSPECTIVE
When the Military Academy was built, a perspective spanning the Seine was intended. Today the line joining the Eiffel Tower, Iéna Bridge and the Trocadéro Fountains now extends as far as the Palais de Chaillot.

10. MUSÉE D'ART MODERNE AT THE PALAIS DE TOKYO ◆ 134

the Seine and in the distance stands the Ponant Building, the largest office complex in Paris.

BUILDINGS OVERLOOKING THE SEINE (4)
These twenty towers range from 164 to 295 feet tall and between 1970 and 1990 they slowly replaced the working-class district of Grenelle. While it was under construction the media criticized this "little New York" for its arrogance, the inhumanity of its architecture and its proximity to the Eiffel Tower.

3. ÎLE AUX CYGNES
4. SEINE WATERFRONT
5. AUTONOMOUS PORT OF PARIS
6. CHAMP-DE-MARS
7. EIFFEL TOWER
8. EMBARKATION POINT FOR BATEAUX-PARISIENS AND THE VEDETTES FOR ÎLE-ST-LOUIS

UNIVERSAL EXHIBITIONS
Of the nine exhibitions mounted worldwide between 1855 and 1900, five took place in Paris. The Exhibition of 1900, which featured the Seine, was celebrated with boat trips and a focus on the bridges. A reconstruction of medieval Paris on Cours la Reine provided a marked contrast with the Italian, Turkish, British, Belgian and Serbian pavilions erected on the Quai d'Orsay. The new Grand Palais housed an exhibition of foreign painters.

QUAI BRANLY

AV. DE NEW YORK

AV. DE NEW YORK

PONT D'IENA

PONT DE BIR-HAKEIM

QUAI BRANLY

PASSERELLE DEBILLY

AV. DE NEW YORK

THE TUILERIES BY THE RIVERSIDE

The Tuileries Garden was commissioned by Catherine de' Medici in 1564 and was the first large park to be built on the banks of the Seine. Marie de' Medici later introduced the Florentine fashion for horse-driven carriage rides. The river was not lined with trees until the time of Napoleon III.

16. GRAND PALAIS
17. STATUE OF ALBERT I
18. PETIT PALAIS (▲ 169)
20. PLACE DE LA CONCORDE (▲ 316)
21. MUSÉE DE L'ORANGERIE (▲ 168)
23. JARDIN DES TUILERIES (▲ 200)
27. MUSÉE DU LOUVRE (▲ 146)

SECRET LIGHTING

Raymond Subes started work on the lamps for the Pont du Carrousel just as war broke out. When he returned from the front, he secretly acquired materials; the lights, which were completed in 1941, are telescopic.

ST-NICOLAS PORT

A large port grew up during the 17th and 18th centuries close to the Louvre (**27**); it supplied the court with corn, hay, wood, vegetables and meat. The Seine brought a large amount of merchandise into Paris, most of it from

France date from 1905 and are typical of the period.

FROM THE MADELEINE TO THE NATIONAL ASSEMBLY

From the Pont de la Concorde, the façade of the National Assembly is clearly a copy of the Madeleine. Pont de la Concorde is the only bridge in Paris with freestone arches.

19. NATIONAL ASSEMBLY
22. ART NOUVEAU BUILDINGS OF THE QUAI ANATOLE-FRANCE
24. MUSÉE DE LA LÉGION D'HONNEUR (◆ 479)
25. MUSÉE D'ORSAY (▲ 160)
26. CAISSE DE DÉPÔTS ET CONSIGNATIONS
28. ÉCOLE DES BEAUX-ARTS

DELIGNY SWIMMING POOL

Floating pools were fashionable from the 18th century onward: there was one close to the Tuileries and others beneath Pont-Neuf and near the Tournelle Bridge. The Deligny swimming pool, built near the National Assembly, sank in 1993.

THE INSTITUT DE FRANCE AND THE LOUVRE IN THE 18TH CENTURY

Map labels: QUAI DU LOUVRE, QUAI DES TUILERIES, QUAI DES TUILERIES, QUAI DES TUILERIES, PONT DE LA CONCORDE, PASSERELLE SOLFERINO, PONT ROYAL, PONT DU CARROUSEL, QUAI ANATOLE FRANCE, QUAI ANATOLE FRANCE, QUAI VOLTAIRE, QUAI MALAQUAIS

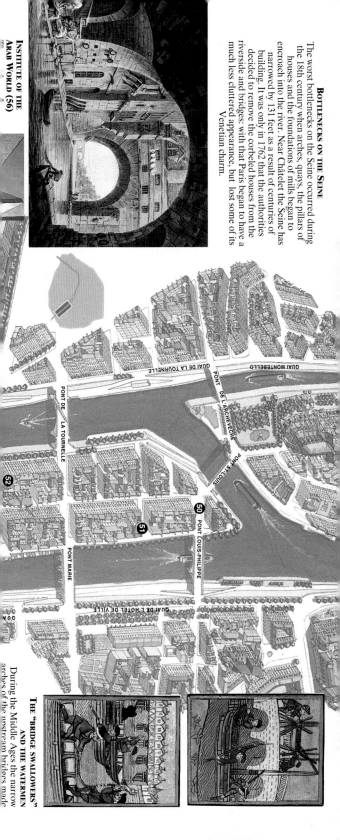

BOTTLENECKS ON THE SEINE

The worst bottlenecks on the Seine occurred during the 18th century when arches, quays, the pillars of houses and the foundations of mills began to encroach into the river. Near Châtelet the Seine has narrowed by 131 feet as a result of centuries of building. It was only in 1762 that the authorities decided to remove the corbeled houses from the riverside and bridges; with that Paris began to have a much less cluttered appearance, but lost some of its Venetian charm.

PONT DE LA TOURNELLE

QUAI DE LA TOURNELLE

QUAI MONTEBELLO

PONT DE L'ARCHEVÊCHÉ

PONT ST-LOUIS

PONT LOUIS-PHILIPPE

PONT MARIE

QUAI DE L'HOTEL DE VILLE

52

50

51

THE "BRIDGE SWALLOWERS"
AND THE WATERMEN

During the Middle Ages the narrow
arches of the upstream bridges made

occupations were probably
carried out in tandem.

NOTRE-DAME FROM THE TOURNELLE BRIDGE

WATER TOURNAMENTS
The *nautes* (Parisian
boatmen) organized
tournaments on
public holidays: the
events included races,
the uprooting of
targets and throwing
competitors into the
water. Tournaments
are still organized in
May on the Bassin de
la Villette.

sorla used new isolation techniques in the construction of this building, including photo-electric cells in windows to filter light.

"bridge swallowers" were authorized to do this work. Boats could be hauled against the tide with the help of rings that can still be seen under the bridges.

WATER AND GAS SUPPLY
The Louis-Philippe and Bercy bridges are decorated with bull's-eye windows that mark the water and gas lines on them.

LOUVIERS ISLAND
A branch of the Seine once flowed over what is now Boulevard Morland. The island was used for storing wood: firewood was stacked out in the open to dry, while timber unloaded onto the Quai de la Rapée was for the use of woodworkers in nearby Faubourg St-Antoine.

CHARLES DE GAULLE BRIDGE (64)
Shaped like an aircraft wing and laid out with broad sidewalks and dedicated cycle lanes, the new Charles de Gaulle Bridge, opened in 1997, is the thirty-seventh bridge in Paris. It spans the Seine between the Gare de Lyon and the Gare d'Austerlitz.

50. ÎLE ST-LOUIS
51. HÔTEL DE JASSAUD
52. CHURCH OF ST-LOUIS-EN-L'ÎLE
53. PORTICO OF THE FORMER HÔTEL DE

59. ARSENAL
60. PRÉFECTURE OF PARIS
61. BOULEVARD MORLAND
64. PONT CHARLES-DE-

ESTINS

JARDIN DES PLANTES
In the 1500's the Jardin des Plantes was a simple garden of medicinal herbs. Louis XIII and Louis XV converted it into an enormous park specializing in botanical research.

56. INSTITUT DU MONDE ARABE
57. UNIVERSITÉ DE JUSSIEU
62. JARDIN DES PLANTES
63. GARE D'AUSTERLITZ

THE LONG-FORGOTTEN BIÈVRE
During the reign of François I the foul-smelling business of this waterway became an open-air sewer. It is now

PONT SULLY
BD HENRI IV
QUAI HENRI IV
QUAI SAINT BERNARD
PONT D'AUSTERLITZ
PONT CHARLES-DE-GAULLE
QUAI D'AUSTERLITZ

BARGES
These craft were used from the 17th century onward to provide cheap passenger transport and were enormously popular until they were replaced by the railway.

THE KING'S ORANGES
Mandarins, Louis XIV's favorite fruit, were sold on this bridge during the 17th century.

BIRDCATCHERS
From 1600 onward canaries, warblers, quails, goldfinches, linnets, chaffinches, larks, starlings and blackbirds were sold between the Pont-Neuf and the Pont au Change. Bird catching has been forbidden between May and August.

CONCIERGERIE ▲ 366
SAINTE GENEVIÈVE
This woman's once dissuaded the Huns from attacking Lutetia: she became the patron saint of Paris. This statue made in 1928 by Paul Landowski has her facing east.

34. CHURCH OF ST-GERMAIN-L'AUXERROIS
35. SAMARITAINE DEPARTMENT STORE
38. THÉÂTRE DU CHATELET
39. PALM FOUNTAIN
40. THÉÂTRE DE LA VILLE
41. ST-JACQUES TOWER
47. HÔTEL DE VILLE
DEVICE FOR

THE PONT-NEUF WRAPPED BY CHRISTO (1985).

payment restricted its use to pedestrians.

29. COUR CARRÉE
30. INSTITUT DE FRANCE
31. MUSÉE DE LA MONNAIE (▲ 156)
32. ÎLE DE LA CITÉ
33. EMBARKATION POINT FOR THE VEDETTES DU PONT-NEUF
36. CONCIERGERIE
37. STE-CHAPELLE AND PALAIS DE JUSTICE
42. PRÉFECTURE OF POLICE
43. MAGISTRATES COURT
44. STATUE OF CHARLEMAGNE
45. NOTRE-DAME
46. HÔTEL DES URSINS
48. DEPORTATION MEMORIAL
49. DEVICE FOR MEASURING THE SEINE'S LEVEL

No!
This poster was part of a campaign mounted by Paris-lovers in 1973 against a project to build a freeway on the Left Bank. The plan was withdrawn on the death of President Pompidou in 1974.

NON À L'AUTOROUTE RIVE GAUCHE

FLOATING WASH HOUSES AND FISHING BOATS
Washerwomen used to wash clothes in the Seine and dry them in the open air on their boats on the quayside. The current that ran past the Île de la Cité was slow and, to avoid epidemics, the washerwomen were sometimes banned from using this stretch of water. The

Map labels:
QUAI DE LA MÉGISSERIE
Q. DE GESVRES
QUAI DE L'HÔTEL-DE-VILLE
PONT NEUF
Q. DE L'HORLOGE
QUAI DE
PONT AU CHANGE
PONT NOTRE-DAME
LA CORSE
PONT D'ARCOLE
PONT LOUIS-PHILIPPE
QUAI DE CONTI
BD DU PALAIS
RUE DE LA CITÉ
RUE D'ARCOLE
PONT ST-LOUIS
QUAI DES ORFÈVRES
QUAI DES GRANDS-AUGUSTINS
Q. DU-MARCHÉ-NEUF
PONT ST-MICHEL
PETIT PONT
PONT AU DOUBLE
PORT DE MONTEBELLO
PONT DE L'ARCHEVÊCHÉ
QUAI ST-MICHEL
QUAI DE MONTEBELLO

MINISTRY OF FINANCE (66)
Paul Chemetov and Huidobro Borja designed this building as a combination of gate to the city and bridge half immersed in the Seine. The Ministry of Finance moved here from the Louvre in 1989.

THE APPLE PORT
Until World War One the fruit market was based at the port of Grève and mainly sold apples. The boats were turned into shops by having tarpaulins drawn over them: in winter the fruit was left out in the open.

THE HALLES AT BERCY
Napoleon III's enormous Halles at Bercy supplied Paris with produce between 1860 and 1970. A few of the original buildings are preserved in Bercy Park.

PEE

66

PONT DE BERCY

QUAI DE BERCY

67

C. BLANC

PARLOIR DE BERCY

The project to build the monumental "Très Grande Bibliothèque" was announced by President Mitterrand on July 14, 1988, but the design has evolved greatly over the intervening years. Renamed the Bibliothèque de France in 1994, it opened to the public in 1996. Its four towers stand upriver from Gare d'Austerlitz and overlook the Left Bank of the Seine.

A TURBULENT HISTORY

President Mitterrand announced the decision to build a "very large library" (Très Grande Bibliothèque) of an entirely new type on July 14, 1988 – a construction project of great ambition. The library was to cover all fields of knowledge, be accessible to all, use the most modern data transmission technology, be available for consultation over long distances, and establish links with the other great libraries of Europe. One effect has been to highlight the plight of the present Bibliothèque Nationale ▲ 341; it is sent over fifty thousand books and other items of printed material every year, and its 75 miles of shelves are reaching saturation point. The Bibliothèque de France will hold between ten and twelve million books, including the old books currently held in Rue de Richelieu.

FOUR OPEN BOOKS

The design by architect Dominique Perrault consists of four open-book-shaped towers framing a ground-level garden: the height of the towers has been reduced from 328 ft to 262 ft and there is access to the garden from the outside along flights of steps. The towers contain offices and book storage areas: the first floor and garden level are surrounded by storage areas and divided into open-access reading rooms and facilities for researchers. The two floors are divided into four sections: philosophy, history and human sciences; political, legal and economic science; science and technology; and literature and art.

COLLECTIVE CATALOGUE
This combines the computer networks of the eighty-four main libraries in France.

PRESERVING THE BOOKS
The glass towers have air conditioning, storage spaces made of reinforced concrete and covered with brass and copper, and wooden isolation shutters, in order to protect the books kept there.

PARIS:
QUARTERS AND MONUMENTS

1. JARDINS DU LUXEMBOURG   2. SENATE   3. THÉÂTRE DE L'ODÉON   4. RÉFECTOIRE DES CORDELIERS

⊙ Half a day

WHERE CREATIVITY KNOWS NO BOUNDS
The spirit of St-Germain-des-Prés is embodied in detective stories such as the *Série noire* and magazines like *Les Temps Modernes*. Other examples include *Exercices de*

Style by Raymond Queneau, which Yves Robert made into a film entitled *La Rose rouge*, starring a team of athletic songsters, the Jacques Brothers (above); and Alfred Jarry's *Ubu Roi* and Jean-Paul Sartre's *No Exit* at the Théâtre du Vieux-Colombier.

The legendary rectangle of St-Germain-des-Prés is a round-the-clock melting pot of elderly residents, innumerable tourists, businesses that are constantly opening and closing down, street entertainers and the traditional hubbub of students and people visiting publishing houses. The most popular meeting places are the famous cafés and brasseries which date from the district's glory days (Lipp, Le Flore, Les Deux-Magots and La Rhumerie) and newer ones at the Odéon crossroads and Place St-André-des-Arts.

THE GRANDE ÉPOQUE

As early as the 1920's, St-Germain-des-Prés was a focal point for students, writers and artists living on the Left Bank. The war put a stop to this for a while, but writers and artists were soon lured back by the warmth of local cafés which had not been requisitioned: Jean-Paul Sartre and Simone de Beauvoir were only two of the many intellectuals who patronized Le Flore. The Liberation resulted in an explosion of intellectual fervor, and it was here that Existentialism found its natural breeding ground. This period not only had its high priests, like Sartre and Albert Camus, but also boasted temples in the form of wine bars such as Le Tabou and Le Lorientais. These echoed to new jazz rhythms – the clarinets of Sidney Bechet and Claude Luter and the trumpet of Boris Vian (left), an engineer, talented writer and organizer of local St-Germain activities. The period found its faithful in young people who were promptly carried away by their newfound freedom. The district also became immensely fashionable, and the American press was largely responsible for making St-Germain-des-Prés the "world meeting place for the intellectual and artistic élite".

TODAY. St-Germain is no longer the little village it was back in the 1950's, and reality has surpassed the legends: with its maze of winding, crisscrossing streets, its art galleries, its antique and book shops and its luxury boutiques, St-Germain is still a pleasure to live in and to visit. There are also wonderful strolls along the quays and in the Luxembourg Gardens.

ORIGINALLY AN ABBEY

HALF LEGEND, HALF HISTORY. When the son of Clovis, Childebert I, returned from the Iberian peninsula in 542, he brought back the tunic of Saint Vincent and rich booty, including a golden Toledan cross, probably the work of Salomon. Saint Germanus, then Bishop of Paris, advised the Merovingian king to construct a holy place to house these precious relics, and the Basilica of Ste-Croix and St-Vincent was built in 557; a monastery was added shortly afterward. The name St-Germain became established around the 9th century. Saint Germanus himself granted the abbey independence from episcopal jurisdiction. When he died in 576, large numbers of pilgrims gathered around his tomb, expecting a miracle. He was initially buried in the small St-Symphorien Chapel, close to the clock-tower porch: however, in 756 his remains were transferred to the basilica itself in the course of a religious ceremony that took place in the presence of Pippin the Short (715–68) and his son Charlemagne (747–814), then aged twelve. The basilica was used as a burial place for the Frankish kings until Dagobert.

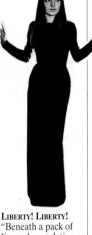

LIBERTY! LIBERTY!
"Beneath a pack of lies and speculation there lay a sliver of reality. The anxiety of those searching for themselves with a crazy desire for meeting up, for friendship, for sharing and exchanging; the cruel laugh of youth and the learning about our newfound liberty. We derive pleasure from every iota of meaning we can squeeze out of the word liberty."
Juliette Gréco
Jujube

235

● 16

● 54

"I HAVE STARTED TO BUILD A CHURCH . . ."
These were the words of Childebert I (c. 495–559), quoted in a document dated December 6, 558. The church he was referring to was built on the advice of the Bishop of Paris, the future Saint Germanus; it was initially dedicated to Saint Vincent, a deacon martyred in Zaragoza in 304.

The abbey underwent further decoration and was given immense tracts of land. It attracted much envy, and the building was frequently pillaged by Barbarian invaders ● 16.

THE ABBEY'S RENAISSANCE. A new basilica was built over the original Merovingian foundations in 990. A small town emerged and grew steadily. The abbey was situated beyond the confines of the royal walls (*enceintes*) ● 54 and was therefore obliged to develop its own system of defense.

After roads were built during the 14th century, the appearance of the town did not alter for another three hundred years.

SPIRITUAL RENEWAL AND INTELLECTUAL ASCENDANCY. After the Wars of Religion, a reform movement took hold of the Catholic Church, and in 1631 the abbey adopted the Rule of the Benedictines of Saint Maurus. By 1647, the Monastery of St-Germain-des-Prés had become the order's mother house, and it was soon one of Europe's leading intellectual centers, under such scholars as Dom Mabillon (1632–1717), the monastery's historian Dom Bouillart (1632–1707) and Dom Montfaucon (1655–1741).

A MIX OF LEGEND AND HISTORY
The monastery was commonly known as St-Germain-le-Doré on account of the magnificence of the basilica, with its precious marbles, ocher outer walls, mosaic pavement and gilt-bronze ceiling that glistened in the sun.

The church's capitals are varied in style and reflect the talent of immensely skilled artists.

THE REVOLUTION. After religious orders were abolished, on February 13, 1790, the monks were dispersed or, in many cases, executed. Their library, which was confiscated, contained about fifty thousand volumes and seven thousand manuscripts, including Pascal's *Pensées*; the Bibliothèque Nationale has around a thousand manuscripts which were saved from the fire of 1794. This splendid building was destroyed during the Revolution, and much of what remained was pulled down during construction work on the Rue de l'Abbaye in 1800. All that remains are the church and Abbot's Palace, and they survive only thanks to an energetic campaign that was led by Victor Hugo.

THE ABBOT'S CHURCH ● 60 (1 J8

The Church of St-Germain-des-Prés, which was reconsecrated in 1803, is notable for the abundant restoration work carried out between 1819 and the present day.

EXTERIOR ★. The Romanesque DOORWAY was badly damaged during the Revolution and is now covered over by a 17th-century porch. Only the side façades of the CLOCK-TOWER PORCH (990–1014), with bays adorned with Moorish arches, have preserved their original appearance. The flying buttresses of the chevet were among the first to be designed in a new architectural style.

INTERIOR. (Brochure available inside the entrance.) The NAVE dates from the 11th century, and the original framework, still visible, was vaulted in the 17th century. The CHOIR was rebuilt around 1145 on the model of the St-Denis Basilica ▲ 432 and Sens Cathedral; it was consecrated in 1163 by Pope Alexander III. Of great interest are a 15th-century *Virgin and Child*, which comes from Notre-Dame; a splendid CRUCIFIX next to the left-hand pillar in the nave; and some 13th-century stained-glass windows in the Ste-Geneviève Chapel (the work of Pierre de Montreuil ▲ 362), originally in the Virgin Chapel.

ST-SYMPHORIEN CHAPEL ★ (On the right, before the railing at the entrance to the church). This was built on the site of Saint Germanus' first burial place. Archeological excavations in the 1970's revealed both the Merovingian foundations and, on the intrados of the arch on the south wall, a FRAGMENT OF A MURAL PAINTING dating from the 13th century.

PALAIS ABBATIAL ★ (3 *bis*, rue de l'Abbaye). The bosses and pediments give the architecture of the Abbot's Palace (1586–1699) a strong classical sense of restraint. The palace prefigures much of the Place Royale ▲ 396.

PLACE DE FÜRSTENBERG ★
This square is in the former courtyard of the Abbot's Palace. A pillar surmounted by a flame ornament on the corner of the Rue de Fürstenberg is a remnant of the monastery's northern entrance. The Delacroix Museum ◆ 478 at no. 6 occupies what remains of the outhouses belonging to the Abbot's Palace.

PLACE
SAINT
SULPICE

"There is a lot to see in Place St-Sulpice, like the Mayor's Office, a financial institution, a police station, three cafés (one of which sells

tobacco), a cinema, a church with work by Le Vau, Gittard, Oppenord, Servandoni and Chalgrin (and dedicated to Clotaire II's chaplain who was Bishop of Bourges from 624 to 644 and whose feast day is January 17), a publishing house, an undertaker's, a travel agency, a bus stop, a tailor, a hotel, a fountain decorated by statues of the four great Christian orators (Bossuet, Fénelon, Fléchier and Massillon), a newspaper stall, a man selling devotional articles, a car park, a beauty clinic and many more things besides.**"**

Georges Pérec
*Attempt to Coax
Everything out of
Some Place in Paris*

CHURCH OF ST-SULPICE   (1 J9)

Reconstruction work on this 13th-century building commenced during the 1600's but it took 135 years, and each stage was marked by developments in architectural style. **Exterior.** In 1733 this Jesuit-style church was given an extraordinarily austere monumental façade: first Doric and then Ionic pillars were added later. The façade, which was never completed, was designed by Jean-Nicolas Servandoni (1695–1766), a painter, architect, decorator and noted rococo artist. The unfinished south tower was built by Maclaurin in 1749 and the north tower by Chalgrin in 1777–8.

Interior ★. The proportions of this church are stunning. The ground plan is similar to that found in Gothic churches. The plinths under the two fonts for holy water in the form of giant shellfish were carved by Jean-Baptiste Pigalle. The choir is adorned with statues by Edme Bouchardon (1698–1762) ▲ 268. Other fine rococo pieces include the tomb of the *curé* Languet de Gergy by Michel-Ange Slodtz and the wainscoting in the sacristy. The Virgin Chapel was built by Servandoni and restored by Charles de Wailly ▲ 240, who also designed the pulpit in 1788 (above, left). François Lemoyne ▲ 264 painted the frescos on the cupola, Pigalle carved the *Virgin and Child*, and Van Loo did the paintings on either side of the altar. The Holy Angels' Chapel, decorated with three frescos by Delacroix ◆ 478 between 1853 and 1863, is also of interest. The organ by F.A. Cliquot (1781) was restored by Aristide Cavaillé-Coll in the 19th century: it has a beautiful Louis XVI organ case designed by Chalgrin. Among the virtuoso organists who have played here are Charles-Marie Widor and Marcel Dupré. Many people still come to listen to this fine instrument every Sunday.

THE SENATE ★ (2 A9)

On the Left Bank of the Seine is the Luxembourg Palace (the seat of the Senate) and its garden which harmoniously combines architecture and modernity, history and the art of garden design.

MARIE DE' MEDICI'S PALACE. Widow of Henry IV, this Florentine queen chose faubourg St-Germain-des-Prés in her search for a garden to add to her residence. Her architect, Salomon de Brosse, an artist greatly influenced by Androuet du Cerceau and the Renaissance, synthesized French tradition and Florentine ideas taken from the Pitti Palace. The palace, built 1612 to 1622, follows the classical ground plan of a French château.

INTERIOR DECORATION. During her regency for her son, Louis XIII, Marie added sumptuous decorations to her second-floor apartments in the southwest of the palace. The painted ceiling panels and the wainscoting are elaborately decorated in gold and azure, and are adorned with arabesques that provided settings for series of paintings. A cycle of twenty-four canvases representing the life of Marie de' Medici (above: *Marie de' Medici as Bellona*) was painted for the west gallery by Rubens. It now hangs in the Louvre. After her final break with her son the king and exile in 1630, the palace passed to her second son, Gaston d'Orléans, after whom it was named. In 1778, Louis XVI gave it to his brother, the future Louis XVIII.

A NATIONAL PALACE. When the palace was taken over by the state in 1792, all of its art collections were removed. The Constitution of the year III declared the palace to be the seat of the Directoire and thereby gave it a new lease on life. Chalgrin refurbished it by building a neoclassical peristyle in the main hall and adding a main staircase, conference room and museum. In 1814 the Restoration turned it into the Chamber of Peers, but

following alterations by Henri de Gisors in 1834, the palace took on the appearance of a national assembly. Gisors enlarged it on the side facing the garden by building a new, identical façade and doubled the number of pavilions. He also designed the conference chamber (above), the Throne Gallery, the library and several salons.

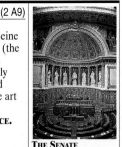

THE SENATE
The Senate is the direct successor to the Chamber of Peers and the Republican Senate, its functions having varied according to the political regime that happens to be in power. Under the Constitution of the Fifth Republic, the Senate and the National Assembly make up the French Parliament and vote on laws and control government activities; Senators themselves may propose and amend laws. In 1750 it became the first public museum in France and still has rooms managed by a museum built in 1886 and used for temporary exhibitions.

A house sign outside 18, rue des Canettes: it gave its name to one of the streets leading into Place St-Sulpice.

ODÉON SUCCESSES

Beaumarchais' *Marriage of Figaro* was staged here in 1784. The Odéon was also where Sarah Bernhardt made her début before going on to play the queen in Hugo's *Ruy Blas* in 1872. George Sand's *Marquis of Villemer* was another triumph, in 1864. Between 1906 and 1914, André Antoine mounted 364 plays; between 1959 and 1971, Jean-Louis Barrault produced Claudel, Ionesco, Beckett, Genet and Duras.

RUE DE L'ODÉON

In 1922 Sylvia Beach, owner of the bookstore Librairie Shakespeare at 12, rue de l'Odéon, took on the might of the British censors and published James Joyce's great prose epic *Ulysses*.

THÉÂTRE DE L'ODÉON (2 B9) ● 68 ◆ 511

Peyre and Wailly's plan to build a theater on the grounds of the Hôtel de Condé was one of the last examples of large-scale building carried out during the Ancien Régime (1778–81). It resolved the constraints imposed by traffic (roads converging and thereby facilitating the comings and goings of carriages) and responded to the new esthetic imperatives of adorning the city with styles inspired by ancient designs. The Théâtre de l'Odéon opened on April 9, 1782 with a performance given by the *Comédiens du Roi* (king's actors). Decorations to the square added shortly afterward respected the theater's overall architectural design. The theater was twice destroyed by fire, and an identical model was built in 1819, although on this occasion the two side arches flanked by pavilions (above) were omitted. The Odéon was further damaged when it was occupied by student protesters in May 1968 ● 34, but it is now making a new name for itself as the Odéon-Théâtre de l'Europe.

INTERIOR. The ceiling was decorated by André Masson in 1965. The small Salle Roger-Blin was added in 1967, allowing the introduction of experimental theater.

RUE DE L'ÉCOLE-DE-MÉDECINE (2 B8 and 9

Rue des Cordeliers follows the route of an old Gallo-Roman road. It was renamed Rue de l'École-de-Médecine during the Revolution, when the schools of Surgery (at no. 5) and Medicine (in Rue de la Bûcherie) were brought together in a single neoclassical building (1775) at no. 12.

REFECTORY OF THE CORDELIER MONASTERY ★ (no. 15). This was started in the 14th century and completed in the 16th. It consists of fourteen bays supported by fine buttresses which may be seen on the side walls. The refectory was on the first floor and the novices' sleeping quarters were on the second. The west façade has preserved its original two doors. The

argely wooden interior has been badly
damaged, although the original beams
and posts are on view during special
occasions.

SCHOOL OF MEDICINE AND SURGERY
(no. 12). The school was constructed over
the cloister of the Cordelier Monastery
and was opened in 1775. It was built by
Jacques Gondoin, an architect adept at
the architecture of antiquity ● 68.
Danton (1759–94) founded the Club des
Cordeliers in 1790 in what was left of the
monastery: this club played a key role during the Revolution,
particularly in the fall of the monarchy. Marat (1743–93),
famous for his vehement attacks on those in power, was
murdered by Charlotte Corday in his house in the nearby Rue
Antoine-Dubois; he was buried in the monastery garden. The

THE DEATH OF MARAT
Charlotte Corday
(1768–93) held Marat
responsible for the
fall of her Girondin
friends and for the
Reign of Terror. She
asked to see him, and
on July 13, 1793,
Marat received her in
his bath and she
stabbed him to death.
She was executed
shortly afterward.

School of Medicine was
enlarged (toward Boulevard
St-Germain and on either
side) in the late 19th
century by Paul Ginain and
is now part of the Université
René-Descartes-Paris-V. It
has preserved its old library
and today houses the Museum of the History of Medicine
▲ 479.

ST-ANDRÉ-DES-ARTS QUARTER ★   (2 BC8)

A stroll along these narrow streets lined with houses mostly
dating from the 17th and 18th centuries is recommended.
Much of their charm – balconies decorated with wrought iron,
keystones and medallions – is above eye level.
PLACE AND RUE ST-ANDRÉ-DES-ARTS. The square (below) was
built when Rue Danton was laid out over the site of both the
Collège d'Autun and the former Church of St-André-des-Arts
(1211–15), which was destroyed in the early 19th century. Rue
St-André-des-Arts once led up to the St-Germain Abbey; it is
now a bustling modern street.

Cour du Commerce-
St-André is a small
courtyard which leads
into Cour de Rohan,
a stunningly beautiful
spot.

(1761–1839)
This noted
archeologist had the
innovative idea of
bringing together a
collection of medieval
sculptures in the
Museum of French
Monuments. Most of
the sculpture came
from churches taken
over by the state
during the
Revolution. The
museum was one of
Paris' main tourist
attractions until it was
closed down in 1816.

ÉCOLE DES BEAUX-ARTS ★   (2 A6 and 7)

This School of Fine Art is housed in three buildings: the
remains of the Petit-Augustin Monastery (since 1806), built by
Marguerite de Valois in the early 17th century; the 17th-to-
18th-century Hôtel de Chimay; and a striking building added
by François Debret and Félix Duban in the 19th century.
MONASTERY OF THE PETITS-AUGUSTINS (14, rue Bonaparte).
Against the gable over the entrance to the church (1617) is
the central avant-corps from the façade of the Château
d'Anet (Eure-et-Loir), a fine work executed by
Philibert Delorme between 1547 and 1555.
The church contains a museum of Renaissance
moldings, and under the oldest dome in Paris
(1608) the Louanges Chapel houses a
collection of Michelangelo replicas. Here in1795
the archeologist Alexandre Lenoir founded the
Museum of French Monuments (left) ▲ 158.

INSTITUT DE FRANCE ★   (2 B7

The Institut de France, which was founded by
the Directory in 1795 to replace the learned
societies suppressed in 1793 by the Convention,

brings together five academies that have elected 325 members. Since 1805 it has housed the Collège des Quatre-Nations, itself founded thanks to a bequest by Cardinal Mazarin (1612–61). The institute was constructed on a general plan by Le Vau, who located it on the banks of the Seine, in view of the royal apartments in the Louvre. The institute's magnificent architecture extends from the chapel, the celebrated cupola of academic assemblies to the two quarter-circle wings ending in two square pavilions. The East Pavilion houses the MAZARIN LIBRARY, the first public library in France; its superb wainscoting is all that survives from the religious and civic libraries that existed before the Revolution.

ROLE OF THE INSTITUTE. The institute now devotes itself to the patronage and encouragement of letters, arts and science. Thanks to a very substantial cultural heritage, mainly consisting of the Jacquemart-André Museum, and the châteaux of Chantilly and Langeais, the institute embodies a unique French tradition through the prizes it awards annually, the initiatives that it sponsors and through its learned publications and meetings.

HÔTEL DE LA MONNAIE (2 B8)
▲ 156

The reasoning behind this design for the Mint by Jacques-Denis Antoine (1733–1801) was the impossibility of building a factory to manufacture coins and medals in a palace that truly matched the nation's opulence. Industrial and monumental architecture were closely related and were in keeping with

the new neoclassical style of the period. The Administration of Coins and Medals comes under the Ministry of Finance. It issues French currency and is responsible for manufacturing all legal tender. The Mint is one of the few metal works in the center of Paris, and its coin press rooms also turn out collection coins, official decorations and jewels.

THE FIVE ACADEMIES
The most famous is the French Academy, founded by Richelieu in 1635. The others are the Academy of Inscriptions and Letters (1663), the Academy of Sciences (1666) and the Academy of Fine Arts – which combined the academies of Painting and Sculpture (1648) and Architecture (1671) in 1816 – were founded by Colbert. The Academy of Moral and Political Sciences was established in 1795.

▲ SECONDHAND-BOOK SELLERS

The Seine flows through the middle of the longest library in the world. The secondhand-book stalls extend for 2½ miles, from the Musée d'Orsay to Pont de Sully, selling everything from masterpieces to minor works of little value. Rain or shine, these booksellers, known as the "peasants of Paris", cling to their sections of the parapet as if their lives depended on it. They are very much a part of the spirit of Paris.

Booksellers have given inspiration to many painters: (above) *Booksellers on Quai de la Mégisserie* (1900), by Galien-Laloue. They also have their eulogists: one was the writer Anatole France, an indefatigable friend of those men "so battered by the air, the rain, the frost, the fog and the sunshine that they end up looking like old statues in cathedrals".

The first booksellers worked along Quai Voltaire on the Left Bank and on Quai de la Mégisserie on the Right Bank. The more recent arriva have their stalls on the Quai des Célestins.

The City of Paris has granted 245 bookseller concessions: they are renewable each year and give the bookseller use of 27 feet of parapet. Moreover, so as not to disturb the view of passersby, the stall may not be more than 3½ ft high with the canopy open. Stalls sell a wide range of goods, from tourist postcards to first editions of Baudelaire's *Les Fleurs du Mal*.

The booksellers are always getting into trouble with the authorities. When André Malraux was Minister of Culture (1959–69), he banned them from ever using the quays alongside the Louvre.

"BOUQUINVILLE"
The road to fortune – from the purgatory of Quai Voltaire, Quai St-Bernard and Quai des Célestins to the paradise of "Bouquinville" (literally "book city", a number of shops around Place St-Michel) – can take generations.

A LONG-ESTABLISHED TRADE
The history of Paris' secondhand-book sellers goes back some four hundred years: it takes in hawkers peddling "subversive" books and playing hide-and-seek with the police on the Pont-Neuf to their modern successors working their parapets along the quays. The word used to describe secondhand-book sellers (*bouquinistes*) dates from the 18th century and is derived from *bouc* (foul odor); it refers to the musty smell of leather and paper that emanated from their stalls or from the Dutch word *boekin* (small book). Their work was not legalized until 1859.

▲ LATIN QUARTER

1. CHURCH OF ST-SÉVERIN
2. CHURCH OF ST-JULIEN-LE-PAUVRE
3. MUSÉE CLUNY
4. THE SORBONNE
5. COLLÈGE DE FRANCE
6. CHURCH OF ST-ÉTIENNE-DU-MONT
7. THE PANTHÉON
8. VAL-DE-GRÂCE
9. PORT-ROYAL
10. CHURCH OF ST-MÉDARD
11. THE ARENA
12. THE MOSQUE
13. JARDIN DES PLANTES
14. INSTITUT DU MONDE A

Two days

The Latin Quarter is somehow immutable yet still changing. Although it has not lost any of its soul or high spirits, it is also no longer what it once was. The fountain in Place St-Michel (2 C8) has become the meeting place for young people from all over the world – and also for individuals on the margins of society for whom Latin is not exactly the *lingua franca*. Today the Boul'Mich (Boulevard St-Michel) has been taken over by secondhand-clothes dealers and hamburger stalls, the RER drops off legions of suburban dwellers every morning, la Mouffe (Rue Mouffetard) and Rue St-Séveri have been colonized by Oriental restaurants and pizza parlors, the former École Polytechnique (2 D10) in Rue Descartes has emigrated to the suburbs, and the Sorbonne (2 C now occupies only part of what ha become a fragmented university.

ST-VICTOR ABBEY
(2 EF10)
The famous scholar Guillaume de Champeaux (c. 1070–1121) taught here from 1108. It was on his advice that King Louis VI (1080–1137) built an abbey here in 1113. The abbey acquired an enviable reputation but was torn down in 1811.

PRAYER AND STUDY

As the name suggests, the Latin Quarter has been marked by two traditions: religious and university life.

RELIGIOUS FOUNDATIONS. The foundation on the hilltop of a sanctuary, which later became Ste-Geneviève Abbey, is attributed to King Clovis (c. 456–511). In 1113 Louis IV founded St-Victor Abbey in the vicinity of Place Jussieu (2 EF10). Many religious communities subsequently settled around these two abbeys, which attracted large numbers of people, for whom parish churches were also built. The piety that marked the time of Louis XIV's reign accentuated the religious atmosphere of the place. Anne of Austria sought to revive the tradition of the early royal foundations and had the magnificent Val-de-Grâce monastery ▲ 258 constructed, older buildings extravagantly redecorated or partly rebuilt (including the nave and choir of the Church of St-Nicolas-du-Chardonnet) and new churches erected; these included the Church of St-Jacques-du-Haut-Pas, whose Jansenist austerity recalls the nearby Port-Royal Convent ▲ 257.

UNIVERSITY AND COLLEGES. The hilltop gained its intellectual standing with the arrival of dissident masters like Abelard during the 12th century, who brought with them their own retinues of scholars. This movement culminated in the establishment of the university statutes ● 22 and in the opening of colleges. Teaching at the University of Paris was of a higher standard than at Bologna and Oxford, but it was also rooted in scholasticism and soon yielded to the renewed assaults of humanism. In the 16th century François I founded the Collège de France ▲ 253 and the Jesuits opened the prestigious Clermont College; during the 17th century, science was served by the establishment of the Jardin des Plantes ▲ 204 and the Observatory ▲ 259. This concentration of learning continued with the foundation of the École Normale Supérieure and the École Polytechnique during the Revolution, the establishment of the two largest *lycées* in Paris (Louis-le-Grand, formerly Clermont College, and Henri IV, on the site of the Ste-Geneviève Abbey) under the Empire, and the revival of the Sorbonne ▲ 251 during the Third Republic.

ST-MICHEL FOUNTAIN
The view of Boulevard du Palais was interrupted by a twist in Boulevard St-Michel. To resolve this problem, Haussmann ● 74 had St-Michel Fountain built in order to provide a focus. Gabriel Davioud (1823–81), who was charged with the project, took

inspiration from the Trevi Fountain in Rome and the Marie de' Medici Fountain in the Luxembourg Gardens. Beneath an embossed triumphal arch, the fountain's main decorative element, stands a bronze statue of Saint Michael slaying the dragon by François-Joseph Duret (1804–65). Davioud's Second Empire pastiche consists of the fountain itself, an abundance of decorative motifs and carvings (including the raised representations of the cardinal virtues – Prudence, Justice, Strength and Temperance) and a rich variety of colors.

247

ST-SÉVERIN (2 CD8)

The old cobbled streets of the St-Séverin Quarter are very popular with tourists. The first jazz club, Le Caveau de la Huchette, in Rue de la Huchette, has remained faithful to this kind of music, and the plays of Ionesco continue to be performed at the Petit Théâtre de la Huchette, as they have since 1957. Rue St-Séverin is another bustling street: on the other side of Rue St-Jacques, it turns into picturesque Rue Galande and leads into the Maubert district, also known as la Maube. The area between the Musée de la Police and the Musée de l'Assistance Publique ▲ *136*, ♦ *476* is a delightful place for a stroll. Above left, a charming little square on the corner of Rue de la Bûcherie and Rue des Grands-Degrés.

CHURCH OF ST-SÉVERIN ★ (1, rue des Prêtres-St-Séverin). The main attraction of this parish church, rebuilt in 1495, is the ingenious construction of its processional corridor: it contains an extraordinary PALM GROVE, which makes St-Séverin one of Paris' best examples of Flamboyant Gothic style. There is some confusion over the dedication to Saint Séverin the Solitary (he had an oratory on this site around a Merovingian necropolis) and another dedication to one Saint Severinus, the Abbot of St-Maurice-d'Agaune of Switzerland, who was a friend of King Clovis.

EXTERIOR. This church boasts many excellent examples of Flamboyant style; the clock tower (1250) contains the oldest bell in Paris (1412).

INTERIOR. The choir was restored in the Italianesque style of the 17th century; it contains what is probably the oldest triforium in Paris. The twenty rib vaults of the apse spring from the middle of the processional path around an EXTRAORDINARY

SHAKESPEARE AND CO.
(2 D8, 37, rue de la Bûcherie)
This unusual English-language
bookstore sells books both old and
new: it is run by the grandson of
Walt Whitman.

WREATHED PILLAR (right) and then separate before falling
back on the supporting pillars with a grace only the greatest
artists can execute. Also of interest are two paintings: *Saint
Luke Writing the Gospel* (against the wall of the clock tower),
from the French School of the 17th century, and a *Crucifixion*
(opposite) painted on wood by Jan Bruegel (1568–1625). The
stained-glass windows in the first three bays have been restored,
but they are the only surviving work of 14th-century glass
painting. The decoration in the upper part of the nave and apse
are excellent examples of 15th- and 16th-century art. The
Church of St-Séverin is also well known for its concerts: its
18th-century organ is considered to be one
of the finest in Paris.

ST-JULIEN-LE-PAUVRE. The tiny Church of
St-Julien-le-Pauvre stands in the Square
Viviani. Dante is said to have prayed here,
and the square boasts the oldest tree in
Paris, a false acacia planted in 1620
(below). The Cluniac monks from
Longpont Abbey, northwest of Paris, had
the 6th-century basilica rebuilt in 1165 over
the foundations and on the plan of the original church: they
enclosed it within a priory. The University ● *22* frequently
used the premises, but following the contested election of a
rector in 1564 students sacked the church, and the priory's
decline was further accelerated. It was finally razed in the
17th century: the nave and the south aisle were separated
from two bays and the Gothic façade was replaced. The
church was used for storing salt during the Revolution; since
1889, it has been run by the Catholic sect of Melchites.

EXTERIOR. The buttresses supporting the apsidioles and the
apse are typical of 12th-century architecture. The absence of
flying buttresses is justified by the church's small dimensions.

INTERIOR. The capitals of the columns to the south are
decorated with four harpies, "heads of
women hatched in the nests of eagles",
according to Huysmans. The
iconostasis (a screen
separating the nave from
the sanctuary in
Byzantine churches)
conceals the full
glory of the Gothic
design: since 1900 it has
been decorated with a
supplication by
a Damascan
artist.

Jazz ambience at the
Caveau de la
Huchette.

**THE FALSE ACACIA
IN THE SQUARE
VIVIANI** (2 D8)
This false acacia
(*robinier*) takes its
name from J. Robin,
who brought back
some acacia seeds
from America in 1661
and sowed them in his
garden. Many acacias
were later
transplanted, but this
one is probably the
doyen of all the
acacias in
Paris.

ROMAN BATHS AND THE HÔTEL DE CLUNY ★

(2 C9) 6, place Paul-Painlevé. This Paris house of the monks of Cluny-en-Bourgogne is a rare example of late-medieval civil architecture and a magnificent illustration of Flamboyant Gothic style. It was built between 1485 and 1498 over the former Gallo-Roman baths ● 56. The medieval house and the Roman remains are now a museum ▲ 140.

THE TOWNHOUSE. The ground plan of this house, set between the courtyard and the garden and consisting of a main building with two wings at right angles, prefigured the design of Parisian townhouses (*hôtels*) ● 66. It was a kind of château within a town, and despite the military associations of the crenelated wall, central tower and covered way, it was notable for furnishings appropriate to a lavishly decorated country house devoted to leisure and comfortable living.

HYGIENE AND RELAXATION AT THE HÔTEL DE CLUNY. The 2nd-century baths to the north were constructed on the northern foothills of Mount Ste-Geneviève and on the edge of the marshes. The northern baths, the eastern baths (near the Collège de France) and the southern baths (beneath the Rue Gay-Lussac) constitute the three Gallo-Roman baths that have been discovered on the Left Bank. To the north, toward the Boulevard St-Germain, there are two symmetrical rooms (*palestrae*) linked by a corridor: these were used for exercising before bathing. The large *frigidarium*, which is encircled by oblong courtyards, is the best preserved room of the baths. It is over 46 feet high, and the

THE WELL-CONSTRUCTED ROMAN BATHS
The walls of the Roman Baths consist of regular layers of rubble alternating with rows of bricks, which were probably covered with plaster in ancient times. The baths are in remarkably good condition – the vaults and mortar of the *frigidarium* have survived despite the weight of the hanging garden built in the Middle Ages.

THE HÔTEL DE CLUNY AND A NEW DECORATIVE STYLE
The Flamboyant, exuberant décor of curves and countercurves was challenged by a play of rectilinear forms that anticipated classicism. The top of

the accoladed arches in the West Gallery is an example of this challenge: note the vertical impact of the mullioned windows and the horizontal presentation of the lintels, which contrast with the parallel lines of the balustrade of the covered way.

roof with its three barrel vaults is supported by consoles in the form of ship's bows – a reference to the Paris boatmen. The *tepidarium* to the east was a warm room divided into individual bathing chambers: it was used after the *frigidarium* and before the *caldarium*, a hot room offering saunas, steam baths and massage.

THE SORBONNE (2 C9)

(47, rue des Écoles). The Sorbonne today represents three great historical periods, which mirror the history of the nation.

THE MIDDLE AGES. This first period coincided with the expansion of the university during the 13th and 14th centuries ● *22* . The Collège de Sorbon (founded by Robert de Sorbon in 1257) became the Faculty of Theology, acquired an outstanding reputation, and had as many as ten thousand students. The first printing press in Paris was installed there, in 1470. The Sorbonne then shut itself off from the new ideas of the Renaissance and allowed Spain to organize the Counter Reformation. As a result the Faculty of Theology declined and was overtaken by the humanist teaching of the Jesuits and the future Collège de France.

THE MONARCHY. This period was associated with Cardinal Richelieu, who was in charge of the Collège de Sorbon from 1622 and decided that it should be rebuilt. The only surviving building, designed by Jacques Lemercier (1585–1654), is the chapel, with its opposed façades: one is a side of the main courtyard, while the other faces onto the Place de la Sorbonne.

THE SORBONNE:
THESIS AND CEREMONY
The solemnity of the Turgot Amphitheater and the Louis-Liard Room is very popular with students doing the oral section of their doctorate examinations. This exam comes at a critical stage in a student's career, marking both the end of many years of study and the presentation of the thesis; it is also supposed to catapult the student into higher education. The whole ritual is littered with fine compliments and harsh criticisms. It is like an academic joust, punctuated by calls of "honorable" or "very honorable", and the "congratulations of the jury" are – or are not – added. The oral presentation of a thesis makes a marked impression on those present, but it is invariably a very special moment in the life of any Sorbonne student. The miniature (above) shows a classroom in the Sorbonne during the 16th century.

The courtyard of the Old Sorbonne, by Lansyer.

The university was closed down during the Revolution. The Emperor reopened it in 1806 as a lay institution based outside the Latin Quarter. At the behest of the Duke of Richelieu, the newly restored Ancienne Maison de Sorbonne was incorporated into the Académie de Paris in 1821. It became highly thought of in intellectual circles under such renowned thinkers as Guizot and Michelet, but during the Second Empire its reputation once again fell due to its concentration on academic teaching.

REPUBLICANISM. The Third Republic gave the Sorbonne a new look and a new reputation. One of the consequences of the Siege of Paris by the Germans in 1870 ● *20* was that the founders of a lay, scientific republic had to reorganize the higher-education system. The New Sorbonne (1883–1901) was constructed after a plan by Henri-Paul Nénot (1853–1934): the college became a complex

machine responding to late-19th-century ideas with science laboratories, an observatory with a telescope (the Tower of Astronomy in the Rue St-Jacques), a library, classrooms and amphitheaters designed by official artists. All of these facilities gradually fell into disrepair. Immediately after the events of May 1968, the reforms of Edgar Faure finally brought the prestigious institutions together, forming the Académie de France and the Universities of Paris–III (New Sorbonne) and Paris–IV (Paris-Sorbonne).

SEATS OF LEARNING. The statues of Louis Pasteur (1822–95) and Victor Hugo (1802–85) symbolize the two buildings that line either side of the main courtyard. To the south, toward Rue Cujas, is the former Faculty of Sciences, dominated by the towers of Physics and Astronomy. The Faculty of Letters is to the north; inside the entrance on Rue des Écoles there is a double monumental staircase that leads up to a Pompeian peristyle and onto a large amphitheater (above: a door) and reception rooms.

CHAPEL OF STE-URSULE-DE-LA-SORBONNE (1635–42). The site of this early church built by Robert de Sorbon is marked by a double stipple in white on the floor of the courtyard.

ROBERT DE SORBON

The entrances, one to the north (in the ancient style and preceded by a peristyle) and one to the south (in the Jesuit style), and the church's two axes (which are approximately the same length) represent the building's double function: part college chapel, part funerary chapel to house Richelieu's tomb. The mausoleum was designed by François Girardon in 1694 after plans by Le Brun ▲ *438*: in accordance with custom, a cardinal's hat is suspended above the tomb. The cupola (opposite) over the crossing was decorated by Philippe de Champaigne (1602–74).

THE COLLÈGE DE FRANCE (2 D9)

(11, place Marcelin-Berthelot). The college was founded by François I in 1530 at the suggestion of the great humanist Guillaume Budé. In the 17th century it was renamed the Collège Royal de France, and it acquired its present name during the Revolution. At the time of the Renaissance the College was intended to provide the kind of modern education that the university had rejected. **"DOCET OMNIA" – IT TEACHES EVERYTHING.** Although continuing to increase the number of its professorships, the Collège de France has always been an unorthodox part of the French university system, since it does not award degrees and is under no obligation to recruit academics as teachers. This enabled the poet Paul Valéry to be elected there and allows Pierre Boulez to teach there today. During the 19th century, when Napoleon III abolished the chairs held by Jules Michelet, Edgar Quinet, Adam Mickiewicz and Ernest Renan, the college had its moments of glory as part of the intellectual opposition. Later, Marcelin Berthelot, Claude Bernard and then Frédéric Joliot-Curie built up the science department, and Henri Bergson's classes were exceptionally popular. Courses run by François Jacob, Claude Lévi-Strauss, Raymond Aron and Michel Foucault have further diversified the college's teaching. **THE BUILDINGS.** The Collège de France did not have its own premises until the 17th century. The sober, solemn buildings, reconstructed between 1774 and 1780 by Chalgrin, encircle the main courtyard. Those buildings designed by Letarouilly (1831–42) extend to the west in the direction of the Rue St-Jacques; they are similar in style to Chalgrin's but are more heavily decorated, and are organized around two courtyards (Guillaume-Budé and Letarouilly) separated by a portico with arcades and Pompeian decorations (above). The designer Wilmotte has been entrusted with the interior decoration currently taking place.

RICHELIEU'S TOMB
Richelieu's mausoleum, by François Girardon (1628–1715), is the finest example of French funerary sculpture from the 17th century. Girardon conceived this kind of tomb in the form of an altar. He was strongly influenced by Hellenistic statuary, and for his groups of people he also found inspiration in the pictorial representations of Poussin: the drape of the cloths, too, is in the style of the great painter. Richelieu's tomb escaped being destroyed during the Revolution thanks to Alexandre Lenoir, who removed it to the Museum of French Monuments ▲ *242*.

THE PATRON SAINT OF PARIS
Genovefa (c. 422–502) performed many miracles during her life, saving Paris from invasion more than once. King Clovis, his wife Clotilde and the entre population held Genovefa in the very highest esteem. Well into the 18th century, whenever calamities befell the city, her assistance continued to be sought .

STE-GENEVIÈVE ABBEY

The summit of what the Gallic historian Camille Jullian has called the "sacred hill of pagan Lutetia" is crowned by the CLOVIS TOWER (Lycée Henri-IV, 2 D10, 23, rue de Clovis), the CHURCH OF ST-ÉTIENNE-DU-MONT and the PANTHÉON. They are reminders of Ste-Geneviève Abbey, which together with the Abbey of St-Germain-des-Prés ▲ 234 has long played a critical part in the spiritual, intellectual and economic life of the Left Bank.

ST-ÉTIENNE-DU-MONT ★   (2 D10)

(1, place Ste-Geneviève). This church not only synthesizes Gothic style and new trends in Renaissance decorative art, it also contains elements of architectural confusion which give it great charm. It is a remarkably interesting church for several reasons: the shrine devoted to Saint Geneviève, the patron saint of Paris; the magnificently carved ROOD SCREEN – the only one in the city (opposite); and a fine series of 16th- and 17th-century stained-glass windows.

EXTERIOR. The unusual appearance of the façade is partly due to the imbalance brought about by the destruction of the former abbey church that once adjoined it (below): the two façades were architecturally symmetrical. The earliest parish church was dedicated to Saint Étienne in the 13th century and abutted the northern side of the Ste-Geneviève Abbey: it was rebuilt between 1492 and 1586. Part of the church's unique appeal lies in the exceptionally beautiful doorway in the main façade, completed around 1626. There are three pediments superimposed one behind the other, and each is marked by a distinct geometrical form: one is triangular, one is arched, and one, like the pediment of the early church, is gabled.

INTERIOR. The ground plan is Gothic, and the transept does not disturb the continuity of the chapels. The dominant style is Flamboyant, despite the addition of Renaissance decorative elements such as a semicircular arch instead of a Gothic arch in the nave. The vault with intersecting ribs in the choir is decorated with a range of different PENDANT KEYSTONES; the most extraordinary keystone, at the crossing, is 18 feet long and falls back on a network of star-shaped ribs.

STAINED-GLASS WINDOWS. The fourth chapel of the right-hand aisle contains a *Parable of the Wedding Guests* (1568) in painted glass, in the style of an enamel. It is the work of Nicolas Pinaigrier who was responsible for the stained glass in the nave's upper windows (1587–8) and who also worked in the windows in the Charnier Cloister .

> "NOTHING IN MY EARLY CHILDHOOD MADE SUCH AN IMPRESSION ON ME AS SEEING THE PANTHÉON BETWEEN ME AND THE SUN . . . THAT MOMENT IS STILL WITH ME AND CONTINUES TO ILLUMINATE MY INNER SELF."
>
> JULES MICHELET

THE ROOD SCREEN AT ST-ÉTIENNE-DU-MONT

A rood screen is a kind of tribune consisting of a transverse gallery that runs between the nave and the choir: the Epistles are read from here. The rood screen at St-Étienne-du-Mont (1525–35) escaped the widespread destruction that marred the 18th century. The architecture is Gothic – a basket-handle arch and three arcades surmounted with ribs – but the decoration, based on designs by Philippe Delorme, is directly influenced by the Italian Renaissance. The side doors date from the 17th century.

PAINTINGS. The ex-votos to Saint Geneviève are the work of two famous portrait artists. The first, by Nicolas de Largillère (1696), commemorates August 10, 1696, when the shrine was carried in a procession praying for deliverance from the drought then gripping the country; it was a gift of the Provost of Merchants. The second, by François de Troy (1726), begs Saint Geneviève to halt the heavy rains that were ruining the crops; this was a gift from the aldermen of Paris.

PLACE DU PANTHÉON   (2 CD10)

This square was designed by Germain Soufflot (1709–80) as a natural exit from the church into the street and opened up the view after it was extended as far as the Luxembourg Gardens. Place du Panthéon has two classical buildings with curvilinear façades: on the north side there is the mayor's office of the 5th arrondissement (1844) by Hittorff, and on the south, at the corner of the Rue Cujas, is the Faculty of Law; partly built by Soufflot, this was completed in 1822 and has frequently been restored.

BIBLIOTHÈQUE STE-GENEVIÈVE. This building was erected in 1844 by Henri Labrouste (1801–75). The only major library in Paris to survive the Revolution, it contains about three million volumes originating from the library of the former abbey. It is both a public and a university library. The interior décor is in sharp contrast to the severity of the façade: the colors and pictorial representations show the influence of the paintings and ancient monuments which Labrouste studied during his stay in Rome.

BIBLIOTHÈQUE STE-GENEVIÈVE

In constructing this neoclassical building, Labrouste used new 19th-century materials such as iron and cast iron. They were resistant, non-combustible and inexpensive, and they enabled the artist to marry architectural lightness (making use of natural light) with new forms of plasticity (applying rich decoration). This was the first time that a steel framework ● 77 was used on a public building, and the library served as a model for many subsequent designs.

Panthéon to watch the experiment (above) in 1851. The huge pendulum is now kept in the Conservatoire National des Arts et Métiers ▲ 136.

THE PANTHÉON (2 CD10

The Panthéon owes its existence to Louis XV's vow to rebuild the old Church of Ste-Geneviève: the king wished to give thanks for being cured of a serious illness during the Siege of Metz, in 1744.

THE NEW CHURCH. The design was entrusted to Jacques-Germain Soufflot, who sought to combine "the lightness of Gothic architecture and the magnificence of Greek architecture". The need to strengthen the basement impeded early progress, but work moved ahead thereafter until Soufflot's death in 1780. The project was taken over by Jean-Baptiste Rondelet (1743–1829), who embarked on a plan influenced by the Pantheon in Rome, building a church in the form of a Greek cross surmounted by an ovoid dome and preceded by a monumental portico.

"A GRATEFUL FATHERLAND THANKS ITS GREAT MEN." In 1791, the Assembly decided to turn the church into a burial place for great men. The first to be chosen were Mirabeau, Voltaire, Rousseau and Marat, although Mirabeau and Marat were soon removed. After all the religious trappings had been taken out, Quatremère de Quincy (1782–1857) was given

the task of making the building into a visible Elyseum", so he walled up the forty-two windows to accentuate the sepulchral effect. Throughout the 19th century the Panthéon swung between civic and religious functions: it was reconsecrated by Napoleon in 1806 but became the Panthéon in 1831 under Louis-Philippe. The pediment was decorated by David d'Angers (1788–1856). It was converted once more into a church under Napoleon III in 1852, but when Victor Hugo's body was brought here at the end of his grand state funeral (above) in 1885, the Panthéon was once and for all established as the site for Republican rituals.

INTERIOR. The Panthéon is 360 feet wide and 272 feet high. Each of the naves is lined with aisles delimited by a hundred Corinthian columns, and the walling-up of the windows – traces of which can be seen from the outside – has provided space for the production of a vast mural. There is also a *Life of Saint Geneviève* by Puvis de Chavannes, the greatest fresco artist of the 19th century, and the center of the cupola is decorated with a fresco by Antoine-Jean Gros (1771–1835) entitled *The Apotheosis of Saint Geneviève*.

THE CRYPT. This contains the tombs of Voltaire and Rousseau; from the latter emerges a hand carrying a torch – a curious symbol of posthumous influence. The Galerie des Couronnes houses the tombs of, among others, Victor Hugo, Émile Zola, the chemist Marcelin Berthelot (with his wife), Marie Curie, Victor Schoelcher (the anti-slavery campaigner), the socialist Jean Jaurès, the lawyer René Cassin (1987) and the politician Jean Monnet (1988). During the bicentenary celebrations commemorating the Revolution, the ashes of the Abbé Grégoire, the mathematician Gaspard Monge and the philosopher-mathematician Condorcet were transferred to the Panthéon.

FROM DE GAULLE TO MITTERRAND. Two recent important ceremonies have taken place in the Panthéon. One was the transferring of Resistance hero Jean Moulin's ashes, with a speech delivered by André Malraux in the presence of General de Gaulle, in 1964. The other was on May 21, 1980, when François Mitterrand marked his first term as president by laying a rose on the tombs of Jean Jaurès, Victor Schoelcher and Jean Moulin. And on November 23, 1996, André Malraux himself found his last resting-place within the Panthéon.

JACQUES-GERMAIN SOUFFLOT (1713–80) Soufflot was Controller of the King's Buildings in the final years of the Ancien Régime; he was also a representative figure in the artistic avant-garde of the Enlightenment. He achieved a unique synthesis of French classicism (which he

inherited), Greek design (which he had studied in the temples of southern Italy) and Gothic art. Several great national institutions were designed by him like the Gobelins and the Louvre, but the Panthéon is his greatest achievement.

THE VAL-DE-GRÂCE (5 B23

The Val-de-Grâce Monastery, founded in 1621 by Louis XIII's wife, Anne of Austria, is in the center of the Faubourg St-Jacques, a district noted for its many religious buildings. The Val-de-Grâce is an imposing example of 17th-century ecclesiastical architecture. It is also well preserved, thanks to the military hospital which has occupied the premises since the Revolution. Henrietta of France, wife of Charles I and daughter of Henri IV, is buried here, as are the hearts of twenty-six members of the French royal family including the son, grandson and great grandson of Louis XIV.

A CHURCH DEDICATED TO THE NATIVITY
(1, place Alphonse-Laveran). Anne of

BETWEEN BAROQUE AND CLASSICISM
The design of the canopy in Val-de-Grâce was influenced by the Bernini baldacchino in St Peter's in Rome, and the decoration of the cupola owes much to Lanfranco's fresco in the Church of Sant'Andrea della Valle in the same city. It earned the artist the sobriquet of "Mignard the Roman". However, the Italian atmosphere is tempered by the importance given to sculpture over

painting, particularly in the decoration of the vault and arcades of the nave. The carving is the work of Michel Anguier, and Philippe de Buyster was responsible for most of the decoration on the canopy, the capitals, the columns of the façade and the genies on the dome.

Austria vowed to build a magnificent temple in God's name if he sent her a son. The wish was granted twenty-three years later, when she gave birth to the future Louis XIV, but she was not able to discharge her obligation until she became regent in 1643. François Mansart (1598–1666) ▲ 291 was given the task of drawing up the plans, and the foundation stone was laid by the seven-year-old Louis XIV on April 1, 1645. The work, supervised first by Jacques Lemercier ▲ 249 and then by Pierre Le Muet, was completed by Gabriel Le Duc around 1669: all of the architectural interventions kept faith with Mansart's original plans.

A BAROQUE DOME. Gabriel Le Duc's dome is 62 feet in diameter and 135 feet high, with similarities between his design and the dome of St Peter's in Rome. There are also echoes of the Sorbonne ▲ 250 in the first floor (articulated with bays surmounted

The well-preserved Port-Royal cloister has a serenity entirely suited to religious retreats.

by semicircular and triangular pediments), the four lanterns, the cupola with two lines of dormer windows, and also in the campanile adorned with openwork design, encircled by a railing and ending in a globe supporting a cross.

INTERIOR. Val-de-Grâce has been variously adapted to its triple functions of parish church (nave), royal chapel (Chapel of St Anne) and abbey chapel (Chapel of St-Louis). However, the overall architecture has continued to be influenced by the Gesù Church in Rome, demonstrated by its central nave, wide side chapels, uniform transept, a crossing dominated by a cupola resting on pendentives, and a façade of superimposed orders. The interior contains some fine examples of the Italianate influence found in French religious art of the 17th century. The overall décor was given over to sculpture dominated by a form of classicism that challenged the lyricism of the Italian Baroque. On either side of the entrance are two paintings (an *Ascension* and a *Pentecost*), from the school of Philippe de Champaigne, who had decorated the apartments of the Queen's Pavilion.

FORMER ABBEY OF PORT-ROYAL (5 B3)

(123–5, boulevard de Port-Royal). The former Abbey of Port-Royal de Paris was transferred from the Jansenist Port-Royal-des-Champs by Mother Angélique Arnauld in 1626; what little remains is now part of the Baudelocque Maternity Home, where Chaptal founded a school for midwives in 1802. The cloister and the church are reminders that this abbey was once occupied by the Port-Royal hermits, who devoted their lives to caring for the sick. When Jansenism was banned by Louis XIV in 1664, the nuns refused to sign the censure of Jansenism and were expelled: their "maison des champs" was torn down in 1709.

A FORMER ABBEY CHURCH. (Open on Sundays). This church, which was built by Antoine Lepautre in 1646, consists of a single nave and a bay with side chapels. The crossing of the uniform transept is covered by a cupola resting on pendentives, and the overall decoration, including the wainscoting, is marked by characteristic Jansenist rigor.

A MIRACULOUS CURE
The daughter of the painter Philippe de Champaigne (1602–74) was a nun at Port-Royal. After she was cured of an illness, her father presented the convent with the celebrated *Ex-voto of 1662* showing the Mother Abbess praying at the young woman's bedside – the shaft of light refers to the miracle. This major work by Champaigne is notable for its simplicity and restraint.

THE OBSERVATORY
● *68* (5 A3)
61, avenue de l'Observatoire.
The Observatory was constructed between 1668 and 1672 by Claude Perrault; it is still one of the world's

leading research centers in the field of astronomy. It stands on the Paris meridian line, which was used until Greenwich was adopted in 1884. There are 135 bronze medallions on the line of the Parisian meridian, which pay tribute to the astronomer Dominique Arago (1786–1853); they are the work of the Dutch artist Jan Dibbets.

259

THE AMPHITHEATER
The sloping ground made it possible to place the two tiers of thirty-five steps on the natural inclination of the land. Only the front six steps have been restored. The seating higher up and close to the exterior walls lies on a construction similar to that used in the amphitheater at Nîmes: these walls contain semicircular bays separated by engaged columns and supporting a cornice.

RUE MOUFFETARD

Despite the road building that convulsed life on the hill during the 19th century, part of the township of St-Médard, a district formed around the tomb of the saint (who died in 545), was somehow preserved. The medieval route, which is popularly known as "La Mouffe" (Rue Mouffetard), tumbles down the hill from Place de la Contrescarpe to the Church of St-Médard, where a small permanent market is encircled by a line of stores and restaurants.

PLACE DE LA CONTRESCARPE (5 D1). This square (which is actually a circle) was built in 1852 and is one of the most colorful in all of Paris. At this point in the counterscarp (the outer wall of a ditch built for fortification purposes) stood the Bordelles Gate, later known as St-Marcel Gate, which was demolished in 1683. It formed part of the Philippe-Auguste Wall ● *54*, and a fragment of the rampart may still be seen at 3, rue Clovis. This entrance to the city was famous for its inns.

CHURCH OF ST-MÉDARD (5 D2) 141, rue Mouffetard. The façade, nave and clock tower were rebuilt in the 15th century, while the choir and the chapels date from the 16th and 17th centuries. Louis-François Petit-Radel built the Virgin Chapel in 1784 and recarved the columns in the choir in the Doric manner to blend with the ancient styles then in fashion: the porch was redone at the same time. The first chapel in the choir on the left contains a painting of *Saint Joseph Walking with the Child Jesus* (1636), attributed to Francisco de Zurbarán (1598–1664).

LUTETIAN ARENA   (5 E1)

(49, rue Monge). These remains dating from the Gallo-Roman period (1st–2nd centuries) were discovered when the Rue Monge was under construction in 1869 and were later restored by Louis-Joseph Capitant. The arena held fifteen

Place de la Contrescarpe
A plaque on a 19th-century house at no. 1 recalls that a tavern, the Pomme de Pin (fir cone), once stood in the square, probably opposite. A fir cone was widely used by wine merchants as a sign: it alluded to the resin that was used to seal the casks. The most famous of these taverns was one on the Île de la Cité praised by Rabelais and patronized by many literary figures, including Villon, Ronsard, Boileau, Racine, La Fontaine and Molière.

thousand people; its richly decorated stage was used mainly for dramatic representations and games, including fights between men and animals. The oval arena measures 170½ feet by 151 feet, and it is serviced by two broad side entrances.

THE MOSQUE OF PARIS (5 E1)

(1, place du Puits-de-l'Ermite). This was the first Muslim place of worship in Paris; it was built between 1922 and 1926 in recognition of the suffering that North African Muslims had undergone during World War One. Constructed by Charles Heubès, Robert Fournez and Maurice Mantout after plans by Maurice Tranchant de Lunel, the mosque is in the Moorish style and is influenced by the mosque at Fez. Local craftsmen, many of them Moroccan, were involved in applying the extremely elaborate decoration to the ornate doors, carved ceilings, mosaics and ceramics. The mosque is organized around courtyards and gardens, and consists of three groups of buildings encircled by a wall. Each is devoted to a particular activity: religious in the mosque surmounted by its square minaret; cultural at the Institute of Muslim Studies and in the main courtyard; and social around the Turkish baths, near the stores and café next to the exterior wall.

The 85-feet tall minaret and one of the interior courtyards of the Paris Mosque (above).

FAUBOURG ST-GERMAIN

1. CHURCH OF ST-THOMAS AQUINAS
2. MUSÉE D'ORSAY
3. HÔTEL DE SALM
4. ASSEMBLÉE NATIONALE
5. MIN. DES AFFAIRES ÉTRANGÈRES
6. BASILIQUE STE-CLOTHILDE

⏱ One day

Faubourg St-Germain now plays host to numerous ministries and embassies. Most of the district was built in the

THE PRÉ-AUX-CLERCS
This large field bordered by the Seine was once a favorite haunt of students (clercs) in the Latin Quarter.

It extended from the Monastery of St-Germain-des-Prés to the Champ-de-Mars. A ditch divided it, separating on one side the Petit-Pré-aux-Clercs (below), which ran from the Abbey to Rue Bonaparte, from the remainder of the park which was known as the Grand-Pré-aux-Clercs.

18th century and was, above all, a creation of the aristocracy; situated on the road that led to Versailles and two steps from the Louvre and Tuileries following the construction of the Pont Royal in 1685 – St-Germain became a fashionable district, overtaking the Marais ▲ 384, which had become crowded and unfashionable. St-Germain had also been attracting prominent families and princes of the royal line since the end of Louis XV's reign. The decades between the death of the old king and the Revolution were notable for the emergence of a new life style and refined tastes which spread through all the European courts, leaving an indelible mark on architecture,

7. Hôtel Matignon
8. Fountain of the Four Seasons
9. Musée Rodin
10. Jardin de Babylone
11. Chapel of the Miraculous Medal
12. Sém. des Missions-Étrangères
13. Bon Marché

interior design, furniture and objets d'art. Examples in architecture included the three hundred or so private townhouses (*hôtels*) built mostly during the 18th century, at the time of Voltaire and Rousseau, about a hundred of which survive today.

AROUND THE CARRÉ RIVE-GAUCHE ★

The rectangle known as the Carré Rive-Gauche is bounded by the Quai Voltaire, Rue du Bac, Rue des Sts-Pères and Rue de l'Université: it is remarkable for its unique mile-long stretch of 120 antique shops and art galleries which, since the 18th century, have perpetuated the Faubourg's passion for rare objects and works of art.

QUAI VOLTAIRE (1 l6). This quay was always very popular with artists: photographs below show the quay as it was at the beginning of this century and now it is today. The house at no. 9 was the home of Vivant Denon (1747–1825), an art lover, talented writer, engraver and diplomat who was also administrator of the Louvre during the Empire. The painters Ingres, Delacroix and Corot all

had studios here. Charles Baudelaire wrote *Les Fleurs du Mal* and Richard Wagner completed *Die Meistersinger* in the old house at no. 19. The quay was originally called Quai Malaquais, then Quai des Théatins after the Italian *teatini* who founded a convent there: one of the entrances can still be seen at 26, rue de Lille. It was renamed the Quai Voltaire in 1791, the year that the great philosopher died in the HÔTEL DE VILLETTE on the corner of the Rue de Beaune.

RUE DE L'UNIVERSITÉ (1 l1 to 6). The 18th-century building at no. 13, once known as the Hôtel Feydeau de Brou, was altered and enlarged in 1975 to accommodate the École Nationale d'Administration (ENA), a university institution for senior civil servants; most of the classes are now taught in Strasbourg. The long-established *Revue des Deux-Mondes*, which was founded in 1829 and made its reputation publishing the great names of 19th-century literature, now has premises at no. 15 in the 17th-century HÔTEL D'ALIGRE. The parliamentarian Tallemant des Réaux (1619–92) lived at no. 17 in the HÔTEL BOCHART DE SARON, a house built in 1639 and redecorated in 1770 by Jean-Baptiste Bochart de Saron. The Sieur des Réaux took a keen interest in the sciences and astronomy. He carried out some of the first experiments in the smelting of platinum and published historical works on his private printing press. The house now belongs to Éditions Gallimard.

29, QUAI VOLTAIRE (1 l6) During 1830 the beautiful Marie d'Agoult (1805–76), a writer and the companion of Franz Liszt, received guests here at the former Hôtel de Mailly-Nesle (1632). The ceiling (detail, above) was painted by Jean Bérain the Elder (1639–1711).

FAMILY RESIDENCES
A private townhouse – with the owner's coat of arms on the pediment – had reception rooms as well as private apartments with smaller rooms in which the furniture, often miniaturized, had been designed with new kinds of uses in mind. This was the era of boudoirs, "cabinets de curiosités" and secret rooms. It was also an age characterized by a hunger for novelty and intimacy. This weakness for beauty spelled ruin for many. When a house had to be sold, it usually acquired the name of its new owner.

ÉCOLE NATIONALE D'ADMINISTRATION (1 I7)13, rue de l'Université.
The ENA was set up at the time of the Liberation to provide prospective senior civil servants with an appropriately democratic system of education and training. It recruits its students by competitive examination. Graduates go on to work for the Quai d'Orsay (Foreign Office), the Tax Inspectorate, the Finance Office and the Council of State.

SERGE GAINSBOURG The front of Serge Gainsbourg's house (5 *bis*, rue de Verneuil) is covered with graffiti extolling the memory of the celebrated singer, writer and composer, who died in 1991.

RUE DES STS-PÈRES (1 I6). The chocolate shop DEBEAUVE ET GALLAIS, established in 1811 at no. 30, is notable for its beautiful façade by the First Empire architects Percier and Fontaine.

RUE DU BAC (1 I6). This old road was extended by a ferry (*bac*) which crossed over to the Right Bank of the Seine. The ferry was used in the 16th century to transport the stones required to construct the Tuileries Palace ▲ *200*. It was here that shops first sold articles at fixed prices and for cash in the 19th century. The former HÔTEL JACQUES-SAMUEL BERNARD (1740) at no. 46 has preserved its door with brackets surmounted by masks. The vast collection of animals and insects on sale at Deyrolle, the amazing taxidermist next door (opposite, bottom right) are a reminder of the popularity of such curiosities in the 18th century.

CHURCH OF ST-THOMAS AQUINAS (1 I7) Place St-Thomas d'Aquin. This church was originally the chapel of Dominican novitiates; the rest of the convent buildings are now occupied by the French Army. It was constructed in 1683 after plans by Pierre Bullet, and the Jesuit-style façade was built in 1770 by his brother Claude. The building extends behind the high altar by what was originally the choir; the ceiling was decorated in 1724 with a *Transfiguration* by François Lemoyne (1688–1737).

AROUND THE MUSÉE D'ORSAY ★   (1 HI6) ▲ *160*

The outrage aroused by the tearing down of Les Halles in 1971, and the sudden interest in French 19th-century architecture, saved the Gare d'Orsay, which had been under threat of demolition since 1961, from its fate and turned it into a museum. The railway station was built in 1898–1900 on the site of the old Cours des Comptes, set on fire in 1871 during the Commune like the former Hôtel de Belle-Isle (56, rue de Lille) on whose site is now the Caisse des Dépôts et Consignations whose entrance is graced by a Dubuffet sculpture.

HÔTEL DE SALM (1 H5)

64, rue de Lille. This house, which was built between 1782 and 1788 by Pierre Rousseau for Prince Frederic III of Salm Kyrbourg, boasts two contrasting faces: the monumental façade on the Rue de Lille has a double open colonnade with an Ionic order; the other façade, which overlooks the Seine, is more reminiscent of a country house (above: cross-section). Napoleon presented this house to the Chancellery of the Legion of Honor. It was later enlarged in order to provide premises for their museum ♦ 479. The interior was destroyed by fire during the Commune, but it was later rebuilt in the spirit of official 19th-century art (above, left).

HÔTEL DE BEAUHARNAIS AND HÔTEL DE SEIGNELAY (1 H5)

78 & 80, rue de Lille; German Embassy and Ministère du Commerce et de L'Artisanat. Germain Boffrand began work on these two adjoining houses in 1715. The Hôtel de Beauharnais was sold to J.B. Colbert de Torcy, nephew of the minister, and passed into the hands of Prince Eugène de Beauharnais, the stepson of Napoléon, who added Pompeian decoration fitting with imperial style (above: the bathroom and the Four Seasons drawing room). The prince sold the house to the Prussian Legation in 1817. The smaller Hôtel de Seignelay has a fine rococo drawing room on the garden side.

MAISON DES DAMES DE LA POSTE (1 I6)

41, rue de Lille. This house was built in 1907 for employees training to work for the Post Office. It provided accommodation for staff from the provinces, widows and spinsters. The Art Deco interior is unaltered, and the building is now used as a restaurant (Le Télégraphe).

HÔTEL POZZO DI BORGO, OR MAISONS, OR SOYÉCOURT (1 H6)

51, rue de l'Université. This house, built by Lassurance in 1707, contains a rococo drawing room by the celebrated Antwerp designer Jacob Verberckt (1704–71). The HÔTEL DE POULPRY, now a residence for École Polytechnique students, was built nearby in the same year at 12, rue de Poitiers. The decoration on one of the ceilings is attributed to Watteau.

THE ASSEMBLÉE NATIONALE (1 G5)

(126, rue de l'Université). The Palais-Bourbon has been the seat of the French government since 1798. Like the Hôtel de Lassay (no. 128), owned by the National Assembly since 1843, and the President's official residence, the palace's origins are aristocratic. It was built in

ÉDITIONS GALLIMARD (1 I7) 5, rue Sébastien-Bottin. The publishing house of Gallimard was founded in 1911, two years after the appearance of the journal *Nouvelle Revue Française*, founded by André Gide and his friends. The firm has since been sustained by a family dynasty:

Gaston (1882–1975) published a number of writers of importance, and his son Claude (1914–91) consolidated the family empire by publishing the Folio Collection and founding his own distribution company, Sodis. Today the company is run by Antoine Gallimard, the founder's grandson.

ALTERATIONS TO THE PALAIS-BOURBON
The semicircular Council Chamber and the loggia were constructed by J.P. Gisors and E.C. Leconte under the Directoire. In 1806 Bernard Poyet erected the ancient-style façade overlooking the river, facing the Madeleine Church. This wall conceals the absence of any axial

connection between the palace and the Pont de la Concorde. The sculptures of Sully, L'Hospital, Colbert and d'Aguesseau have survived, but the pediment erected to the glory of the Emperor was replaced during the July Monarchy by one in honor of Jean-Pierre Cortot. After 1828, Jean-Baptiste de Joly enlarged the chamber and built a new portico, with a pediment on the side of the courtyard.

1726 by Lassurance, Aubert and Gabriel for Louise-Françoise the legitimized daughter of Louis XIV and Mme de Montespan, widow of the Duke of Bourbon. The house next door was intended for the Marquis de Lassay, the lover of the Duchess of Bourbon. Nothing remains of the former building except the courtyard and the main façade, which has a colonnade and monumental porch facing the Rue de l'Université. Although a story was added in the 1840's, the Hôtel de Lassay has substantially preserved its original appearance. The Place du Palais-Bourbon and its Louis XVI houses form a jewel-box-like setting.

ALLEGORY ON THE PICTURE RAIL. Changes in government meant that certain styles of interior decoration went out of favor. Delacroix, whom Thiers imposed against the supporters of neoclassicism in 1833, added allegories to the decoration of the king's drawing room and the library: these were preserved by the Empire and the Republic.

MINISTÈRE DES AFFAIRES ÉTRANGÈRES
(1 F5) 130, rue de l'Université and 37, quai d'Orsay). The Ministry of Foreign Affairs was constructed in 1845 by J. Lacornée and was the first building in the district to be designed as a ministry.

"BUT I DON'T DARE SPEAK OF PARIS, WHERE I
HAVE LIVED FOR MORE THAN TWENTY YEARS.
TO KNOW IT IS THE WORK OF A LIFETIME."

STENDHAL

RUE ST-DOMINIQUE   (1 C TO H 6)

This former cattle trail takes its name from the Dominicans
who settled here in 1632. Rue St-Dominique (below, right)
was inhabited by many prominent families, and in the 18th
century it boasted a large number of townhouses. Many of
these disappeared when a third of the road was lost to the
newly constructed Boulevard St-Germain.

HÔTELS DE BRIENNE (1 G6) 14–16, Ministry of Defense.
These two houses were built in 1724 and 1728 by
F. Debias-Aubry and by President Duret, a gentleman who
had a hand in most property deals in the Faubourg
St-Germain. They had many owners, including Louis XVI's
treasury minister, M.-A. Loménie de Brienne, Lucien
Bonaparte and Napoleon's mother. After the buildings were
acquired by the state in 1817, they were extended on many
occasions along the Boulevard St-Germain. General de
Gaulle established his headquarters here on August 25, 1944.
The nearby Square Samuel-Rousseau contains the
Ste-Clothilde Basilica, which was constructed between 1846
and 1856 in the neo-Gothic style of the time by Gau and
Ballu.

HÔTEL DE ROQUELAURE ★
(1 H6) 246, boulevard
St-Germain, formerly 62, rue
St-Dominique. This house
was built by Lassurance in
1724 and later refurbished by
Leroux. Grotesque masks
ornament a superb Regency
façade, and the interior
contains some fine 18th-
century decoration, including
a magnificent rococo drawing
room.

RUE DE GRENELLE

There are many townhouses with large gardens between here
and the Boulevard des Invalides.

HÔTEL DE ROTHELIN-CHAROLAIS (1 G7) 101, Ministry of
Enterprises and Economic Development. This house was
built in 1704 by Lassurance, a supremely gifted architect who
had been influenced by Mansart. It was enlarged on the
orders of the Princess of Charolais in 1736, and the interior
was refurbished during the 19th century.

HÔTEL DE VILLARS (1 G7) 116, Mayor's Office of the 7th
arrondissement. This house, built in 1644, has been frequently
redecorated. There is a
beautiful Restoration drawing
room that was decorated by A.
Vauchelet in 1834.

HÔTEL DE ROCHECHOUART ★
(1 G7) 110, Ministry of
Education. M. Cherpitel built
this house in 1776 in Louis XVI
style. The Corinthian drawing
room has preserved its original
décor.

Rococo

Rococo style
represented a radical
departure from the
rigid principles of
classicism, with its
passion for frenzied
lines and
asymmetrical forms.
It takes its name
(*rocaille*) from the
rock-like materials
used in grottos and
fountains. One of its
many characteristics
is an enthusiasm for
shell ornament. The
style began to emerge
in France around
1725 and found its
most extreme
expression
in Germany.

In architecture, the
style's originality was
revealed through the
soundness of the
proportions allied to
ornamental sculpture;
the use of white Île-
de-France stone did
much to emphasize
the harmony.
However, the true
innovation of rococo
in interior decoration
is seen in furniture,
ornaments, vases,
mirrors, bronzes and
gold pieces, tapestries
and carpets – in a
word, everything that
enlivens a house.

FOUNTAIN OF THE FOUR SEASONS (1 H7)
57–59, rue de Grenelle. Constrained by space,
Edme Bouchardon produced a semicircular
construction with the main body at the
front flanked by two wing sections. The
design anticipated by several years a return
to ancient styles.

HÔTEL DE NOIRMOUTIER ★ (1 F6)
138, residence of the Prefect of the
Île-de-France region. Built by Jean
Courtonne, this is one of the most
elegant and beautifully balanced houses
in the district. The dining room has
attractive boiserie representing
La Fontaine's *Fables*.

HÔTEL DU CHÂTELET ★ (1 F6)
127, Ministry of Labor. This house was
built between 1772 and 1774 by Cherpitel
for the Duc du Châtelet, whose mother,
the Marquise du Châtelet, was a friend
of Voltaire. It is a magnificent example of
the neoclassical style that dominated the
final years of the century; features
include the severe Doric order
surrounding the main courtyard
and the monumental façade,
with its four massive columns.
The horizontal lines of the entablature and the attic story
make a powerful contrast with these columns, and are further
accentuated by balustrades that run along buildings that stand
on either side of the courtyard, which have not been raised.
The dining room and the drawing room give onto the garden;
the original wood paneling has been preserved.

RUE DE VARENNE

Of the many spacious gardens in this area, only the garden of
the Hôtel Matignon has preserved its original dimensions.
HÔTEL DE BOISGELIN (I H7 and 8) 47, Italian Embassy. This
townhouse (below), built around 1787 by Cartaud, was
enlarged and restored during the 19th and 20th centuries.
French and Italian 18th-century décor has been introduced
and adapted to the new setting.
HÔTEL DE GALLIFFET (1 H7) Italian Cultural Institute. This
house was built by F.E. Legrand, with the sculptor J.B.
Boiston, for Simon de Galliffet in 1784, a time of renewed
emphasis on ancient forms of art. The monumental façade
overlooking the courtyard, which had originally faced the Rue
du Bac, has Ionic columns
on two stories; the first-floor
reception rooms are
articulated by Ionic columns
with trompe l'oeil fluting
and have only recently been
decorated.
**HÔTEL DE BIRON, MUSÉE
RODIN ★ ▲** *170* (1 F6) no.
77. This residence was built
for the financier Peyrenc de
Moras in 1728 by Aubert
and Gabriel, the architects
of the Palais-Bourbon.
Typically, the layout consists
of a house standing between
a courtyard and a garden.
The house takes its name

SCIENCES-PO
(1 I8) 27, rue St-
Guillaume. In 1945
the Institut d'Études
Politiques, better
known as "Sciences-
Po", replaced the
École Libre des
Sciences Politiques, a
private institution set
up two years after the
Siege of Paris (1870)
by a group of liberals

under Émile Goutmy
(1835–1906) to
educate senior
officials. The school,
which subtly adapted
to the spirit of
republicanism, uses
teaching methods
which draw on the
German seminar
system and the British
tutorial system. It is
also a major research
institution and is now
the country's leading
training ground for
high flyers in both the
private and the public
sectors.

rom the Maréchal de Biron, who owned he house from 1753 to 1788. It was later ccupied by the religious order of the Dames du Sacré-Coeur, who removed he interior decoration; some of it was estored when the Rodin Museum was pened on the first floor. (Below: 'Ombre, c. 1880, bronze statue y Rodin.)

ΗÔTEL MATIGNON ★ (1 G7) no. 57, esidence of the Prime Minister. This townhouse is one of the 10st beautiful in the whole district. Like the Élysée Palace nd the Place Beauvau, it has come to symbolize the pinnacle f state power. It was built by Jean Courtonne in 1722; Jean Лazin continued to work on it for the Prince de Tingry, who old it to Jacques de Goyon, Sire de Matignon. As was ustomary in those days, the façade follows the semicircular ne of the courtyard – this configuration made it easier for arriages to come and go. Jean Courtonne was responsible for he construction of the façades, with their elaborate and bundant ornamentation, the layout, and the interior lecoration of both the large oval vestibule (by the ourtyard) and the octagonal drawing room, by the garden). The first-floor Golden drawing room, with lecorations by Mazin, has reserved much of its original lécor. In 1725 the Duc de Лatignon had a small Louis XV pavilion built at the ar end of the park, near the Rue de Babylone: this was he Petit Trianon (above ight). Opposite the Hôtel Matignon above), at no. 56, s the HÔTEL GOUFFIER DE CHOIX, endowed vith a remarkably peautiful rococo loor.

notable for their severe and monumental design, with a return to order and straight lines: examples include the hôtels de Salm, du Châtelet, de Rochechouart and de Galliffet. Similar trends were to be found in interior decoration and furniture, with straight lines replacing curves and arcs.

BABYLON GARDEN ★ (1 G9)
33, rue de Babylone.
This garden was once
the orchard of the
Convent of the
Daughters of Charity.

FOREIGN MISSIONS HOUSES (1 G8)
118–20, rue du Bac.
These houses, built
around 1713 to be
rented, look out over
the Square des
Missions-Étrangères
and a bust of
Chateaubriand: the
writer spent his last
years in this area.
The two main doors

are decorated with
medallions carved by
L. Dupin, and the
stone sculptures on
the tympana are the
work of J.B. Turreau,
known as "Toro".

Right: the Hôtel de
Galliffet, where in
1797 Mme de Staël
met Bonaparte for
the first time.

SÈVRES-BABYLONE ★

LE SÉMINAIRE DES MISSIONS-ÉTRANGÈRES (1 H8) 128, rue du Bac.
This institution has been operating in
the district almost without a break for
more than three hundred years. The
seminary used to train priests as missionaries: in 1658, French
vicars apostolic were appointed to Cochin China and Tonkin
(now North and South Vietnam), more than two hundred
years before France began to colonize these areas. The chapel
(1689) at nos. 124–8 has a façade with two rectangular levels
superimposed, as did other churches in the early years of the
following century. Behind this is the seminary's main building
which dates from 1732.

CHAPEL OF THE MIRACULOUS MEDAL (1 H8) 136, rue du Bac.
"Strike a medal in the image of this one, and everyone who
carries it will receive grace." These were the words of the
Virgin Mary on an occasion in 1830 when she is said to have
appeared to a young
novice at the Convent of
the Filles-de-la-Charité-
de-St-Vincent-de-Paul.
The nun in question,
Catherine Labouré, died
in 1876 and was
canonized in 1947. The
chapel is noted for its
devotion to the Virgin
and is the destination of
pilgrims who come
between November 27
and December 8, the
anniversary of the Virgin's
appearances.

BON MARCHÉ ▲ *126* (1 H8 and 9) 140, rue du Bac. The Bon
Marché started off as a small shop selling novelties on the
corner of the Rue du Bac and the Rue de Sèvres. Under
Aristide Boucicaut it grew rapidly, and by 1868 it employed
four hundred people. The demolition of the Hospice des
Petits-Ménages enabled the shop to expand even further
between 1869 and 1882. One of Boucicaut's objectives was to
complement his commercial success with a paternalistic social
attitude: this was described by Émile Zola in his *Au bonheur
des dames*.

LAENNEC HOSPITAL (1 H9) 42, rue de Sèvres. The
construction of this former Hospice for Incurables signaled
the expansion of Faubourg St-Germain; it was founded by
Cardinal de la Rochefoucauld in 1634 and was turned into a
hospital in 1878. The chapel, which was built by Gamard at
the same time, still has its original façade and spire.

CHAPEL OF PRIESTS OF THE CONGREGATION OF THE MISSION
(1 H9) 95, rue de
Sèvres. The
Congregation of
the Mission, an
order founded by
Saint Vincent de
Paul, had this
chapel built in
1826. The interior
décor (right) has
not been changed,
and the embalmed
body of Saint
Vincent de Paul is
kept above the
high altar.

🕐 One day

FOUR-CORNERS-OF-THE-WORLD FOUNTAIN
Av. de l'Observatoire.
This Davioud
fountain is decorated
by Carpeaux and
Frémiet ▲ *203*.

The atmosphere and myths surrounding the Bohemian district of Montparnasse have gone forever – supplanted by the urban growth that the area has embraced. However, for all the changes, the aura of old Montparnasse lingers on.

HISTORY. Montparnasse formed part of the fortifications built by Henri II (1519–59), but it was given its name – Mount Parnassus – by students in 1687. It is not known whether the hill was natural or simply a mound of rubbish and builder's rubble that was dumped when the Boulevard du Montparnasse was built. This fine thoroughfare designed during the reign of Louis XIV (1638–1715), was not completed until 1761. By the end of the 18th century it had become an elegant promenade with four rows of trees and lined with magnificent houses and gardens, overlooked by convents in the Rue Notre-Dame-des-Champs, which ran parallel to the boulevard.

THE BEGINNINGS OF MONTPARNASSE

This "admirable and deserted" spot, as Montparnasse was described in the early days, inspired a number of

Le Dome *LA ROTONDE*

entrepreneurs to open dance halls and open-air cafés (*Bal Bullier*, below, opposite).

EARLY EVENTS. During this early period the GRANDE CHAUMIÈRE opened which proved an exceptionally popular café until 1853, when it was supplanted by La Closerie des Lilas. The latter name was adopted some thirty years later by the establishment that bears it to this day, while that of La Grande Chaumière was transferred to a street and to an art school. From 1814 onward there was a popular spot for dancing on the corner of the Boulevard du Montparnasse and the Boulevard d'Enfer (Raspail): it later became the CARREFOUR VAVIN, a focal point of international art. It is still dominated by RODIN'S *BALZAC*, a powerful figure which many feel speaks for all art and literature.

EARLY CELEBRITIES. Prominent figures of the day were attracted by the hushed, almost rural charm of the streets of Montparnasse. In November 1826, Victor Hugo (1802–85) rented a house in the Rue Notre-Dame-des-Champs. Meanwhile, living in exile in the marvelous 18th-century Hôtel du Silène, the beautiful Milanese Princess Belgioioso (1808–71) received young writers and members of Italian Risorgimento high society who had taken refuge in Paris; she later sold her mansion to the celebrated Collège Stanislas. Another local resident was the critic Sainte-Beuve (1804–69), who settled at no. 16 in 1850 – it was, he said, "my final nest for my declining years". In the late 19th century, nothing could be more peaceful than this district of establishment painters and artists. The Rue Notre-Dame-des-Champs could boast the workshop of Gérome (1824–1904) and the house of Bouguereau (1825–1905); Bartholdi (1834–1904) had already moved into a house-cum-workshop on the corner of the Rue d'Assas and the Rue Vavin. James Whistler (1834–1903) was resident in the Rue d'Assas and the Dutchman Johan Jongkind (1819–91) ● *94* lived in a building in the Boulevard du Montparnasse that would later house Le Jockey, a famous jazz club.

URBAN DEVELOPMENT. Houses and other residential property began to spring up along the boulevard and adjoining streets. The Midi Cemetery ▲ *287*, later renamed the Montparnasse, had been built in 1824: now enlarged, it extended the length of the Boulevard Edgar-Quinet. The charming STATE RAILWAY STATION in the Place de Rennes was opened at about the same time as the new Church of Notre-Dame-des-Champs.

"BALZAC" BY RODIN
The plaster roughcast of this sculpture was commissioned by the Société des Gens de Lettres and was shown at their 1898 *salon*. It caused such a scandal (for representing the great writer in his dressing gown) that it was not exhibited publicly until 1939.

PLACE DENFERT-ROCHEREAU
As the two symmetrical pavilions by Claude Nicolas Ledoux ● *68* demonstrate, the old Place d'Enfer was cut into the Farmers General Wall in 1784. The square was named after Colonel Denfert-Rochereau, who had so heroically defended the town of Belfort in 1878. A replica of a lion carved by Bartholdi in the wall of the Belfort citadel stands in the center of the square. It looks down over a busy crossroads. There is also an entrance to the Catacombs nearby.

Paris owes much to what lies beneath its streets– the stone used to
its famous buildings and the water that
travels through miles of pipes before
gushing up through the fountains.

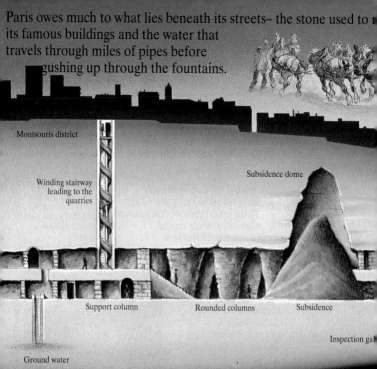

Montsouris district

Winding stairway
leading to the
quarries

Subsidence dome

Support column

Rounded columns

Subsidence

Inspection ga

Ground water

THE PARIS QUARRIES

Paris was built with gypsum and limestone extracted from below ground level. The Left Bank alone has 186 miles of underground tunnels that are not accessible to the public.

- Gypsum
- Coarse limestone

The Right Bank was quarried mainly for gypsum; these deposits have now been exhausted. Some quarries in the suburbs (below) are still open to visitors.

Undercutting

Cutting with a blade

Driving wedges into the stone

Removing block on rollers

INSPECTING THE QUARRIES

Intensive mining caused subsidence, and the quarries also encouraged the trading of a wide range of goods. To put a stop to this, a team of inspectors was set up in 1777 under the Sieur Guillaumot. He and his successor,

Héricart de Thury, were responsible for some public works of great beauty, including this inspection gallery with a semicircular arch entrance with raised keystones.

POMP
CLOI
CHAR

The first inspectors
on the right-hand sid
structures; these ena
and catacomb enthus
around. In the last
tunnels have been i
kind of sig

Institut de France

Siphon underneath the Pont de l'Alma

THE CITY'S NERVOUS SYSTEM

The sewers also accommodate other elements of the city's nervous system. Facilities such as running water (drinking and nondrinking), telephone cables, the pneumatic-express letter system (there are still two such lines in Paris) and the cables that operate traffic lights all run through the sewer pipes.

Main sewer

Branch sewer   Runoff sewer

THE NETWORK

This consists of over 1,300 miles of sewer mains which collect water from 18,000 drains from the city's gutters, and liquid waste through 63,000 connections installed under buildings.

SAGEP

A new addition to the sewer system is the Climespace distribution network; this is currently under construction.

THE SEWERS OF PARIS

The architect Bruneseau built the first modern sewers in Paris in the early 19th century. After the cholera epidemic of 1832, the authorities decided to go further, and within ten years the capital possessed 62 miles of pipes. In 1853 Haussmann and his right-hand man, the engineer Eugène Belgrand, started work on a more wide-ranging scheme. The broad-based nature of today's sewer system owes much to the genius of these two great men.

The main pipes take much of the sewage that Paris produces to the purification plant at Achères, 12 miles northwest of the capital.

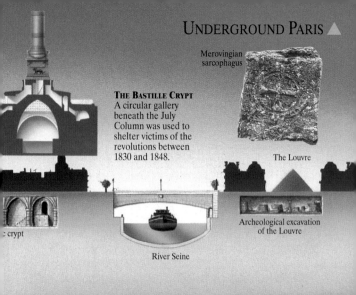

Merovingian sarcophagus

THE BASTILLE CRYPT
A circular gallery beneath the July Column was used to shelter victims of the revolutions between 1830 and 1848.

The Louvre

⌐ crypt

Archeological excavation of the Louvre

River Seine

CRYPTS AND CAVES

BERNARDINE CELLAR
Underneath the refectory of the former Bernardine Monastery in the Rue de Poissy, now used as an official building, there is a 14th-century Gothic cellar. This enormous room is banked up as high as the capitals of the 32 columns supporting the ceiling.

ST-SULPICE CRYPT
The Church of St-Sulpice ▲ 238 was built on the site of an older church in the domain of the Abbey of St-Germain-des-Prés. Organized tours use a staircase behind the sacristy to descend into the largest crypt in all of Paris. It contains a former cemetery, the foundations of the primitive church and the well that once stood in the square.

CRYPT OF ST DENIS
This chapel in Rue Pierre-Nicole is said to have been where Saint Denis made his first retreat.

ROMANESQUE REMAINS
The Church of Notre-Dame-des-Champs was constructed on this site in 1033 and enclosed all the existing buildings. It was taken over by the Carmelites in 1604 but was destroyed during the Revolution; only the primitive crypt remains. The nuns built a smaller convent in 1802 and restored the chapel but finally departed for good in 1902.

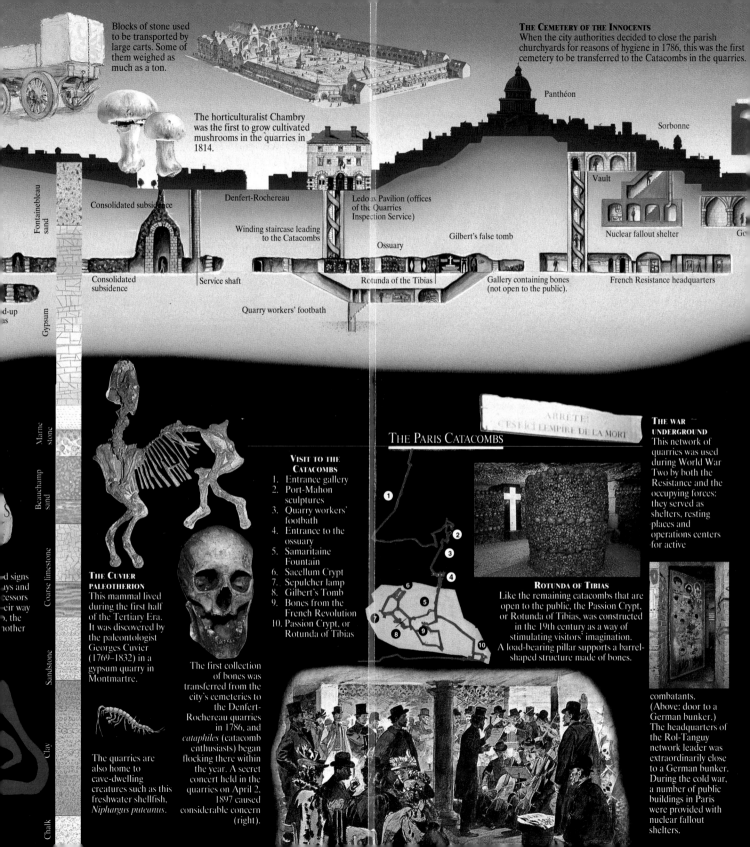

Blocks of stone used to be transported by large carts. Some of them weighed as much as a ton.

The horticulturalist Chambry was the first to grow cultivated mushrooms in the quarries in 1814.

THE CEMETERY OF THE INNOCENTS
When the city authorities decided to close the parish churchyards for reasons of hygiene in 1786, this was the first cemetery to be transferred to the Catacombs in the quarries.

Panthéon

Sorbonne

Vault

Nuclear fallout shelter

Consolidated subsidence

Denfert-Rochereau

Ledoux Pavilion (offices of the Quarries Inspection Service)

Winding staircase leading to the Catacombs

Gilbert's false tomb

Ossuary

Consolidated subsidence

Service shaft

Rotunda of the Tibias

Gallery containing bones (not open to the public).

French Resistance headquarters

Quarry workers' footbath

Fontainebleau sand

Gypsum

Marne stone

Beauchamp sand

Coarse limestone

Sandstone

Clay

Chalk

THE CUVIER PALEOTHERION
This mammal lived during the first half of the Tertiary Era. It was discovered by the paleontologist Georges Cuvier (1769–1832) in a gypsum quarry in Montmartre.

The quarries are also home to cave-dwelling creatures such as this freshwater shellfish, *Niphargus puteanus*.

The first collection of bones was transferred from the city's cemeteries to the Denfert-Rochereau quarries in 1786, and *cataphiles* (catacomb enthusiasts) began flocking there within the year. A secret concert held in the quarries on April 2, 1897 caused considerable concern (right).

VISIT TO THE CATACOMBS
1. Entrance gallery
2. Port-Mahon sculptures
3. Quarry workers' footbath
4. Entrance to the ossuary
5. Samaritaine Fountain
6. Sacellum Crypt
7. Sepulcher lamp
8. Gilbert's Tomb
9. Bones from the French Revolution
10. Passion Crypt, or Rotunda of Tibias

ARRÊTE! C'EST ICI L'EMPIRE DE LA MORT

THE PARIS CATACOMBS

THE WAR UNDERGROUND
This network of quarries was used during World War Two by both the Resistance and the occupying forces: they served as shelters, resting places and operations centers for active

ROTUNDA OF TIBIAS
Like the remaining catacombs that are open to the public, the Passion Crypt, or Rotunda of Tibias, was constructed in the 19th century as a way of stimulating visitors' imagination. A load-bearing pillar supports a barrel-shaped structure made of bones.

combatants. (Above: door to a German bunker.) The headquarters of the Rol-Tanguy network leader was extraordinarily close to a German bunker. During the cold war, a number of public buildings in Paris were provided with nuclear fallout shelters.

The five hundred workers who maintain the underground network can inspect every foot of gallery: they can gain access through one of 26,000 inspection holes distributed all over the capital.

THE LANTERNE INSPECTION POINT This inspection point is located in Place des Fêtes in the district of Belleville. It provides access to the beginning of the Belleville Aqueduct.

The fountain in Square Louvois by Visconti.

The fountain in Place de la Concorde ▲ 310 built by Hittorff.

The fountain in Square Louvois by Visconti.

The hill of Montmartre a Sacré-Coeur

Inspection port

Water main   Reservoir   Aqueduct

Access stairway

Longitudinal section of a sewer

Run-off sewer   Branch sewer

Main sewer

Well

St-Martin Canal

PARIS WATER

The earliest waterworks system was built by the Romans. By the Middle Ages, however, the city had no clean-water system at all: the ground water had become seriously contaminated and was polluting the wells. Philippe-Auguste inaugurated the city's first public fountain using spring water in 1184. Henri IV and Marie de' Medici constructed a water system that was based largely on the Roman network, but it was Haussmann who introduced the modern system.

DRINKING WATER
In 1852, Belgrand commenced work on diverting the springs which now supply half the city with its drinking water. The remaining inhabitants rely on water pumped from the Seine and Marne, which is filtered before distribution.

WATER CARRIERS
Until the end of the 19th century, many Parisians used the services of a water carrier to bring water to their homes.

MONTSOURIS RESERVOIR
This was built by Belgrand to take water from the River Dhuis. Constructed on two levels, it has a capacity of 3.25 million cubic feet and supplies some of eastern Paris with water.

View of the lower level of the Montsouris reservoir.

INTRUDERS The sewer system is infested with brown rats, and workers have to be vaccinated against leptospirosis. The inspection points are also swarming with cockroaches.

CLEARING OUT Top: a sluice boat clearing out a sewer main.
Bottom: clearing out a siphon sewer with a cleaning ball.

THE PUMP AT LA SAMARITAINE This hydraulic machine was built on piles abutting the Pont-Neuf during the reign of Henri IV. It supplied the Louvre and the Tuileries with water from the Seine.

Victor Hugo set part of *Les Misérables* in the Paris sewers.

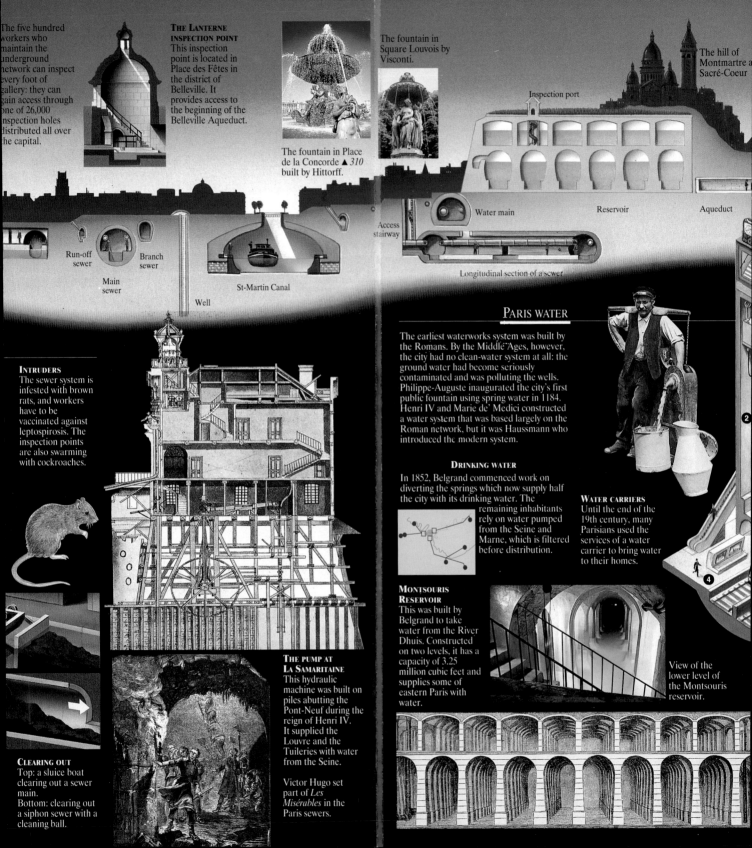

ICI AU CROISEME
DU BOULEVARD SÉBASTOP
ET DE LA RUE DE RIVOL
LE CHEMIN DE FER MÉTROPOLI
SSE AU DESSU

THE MÉTRO CRICKET
This insect thrives in the warm environment of the tunnels.

TRANSPORT AND COMMUNICATIONS

A large number of pipes, mains and cables run along the shallow substratum under Paris: they are part of the telephone, gas, electricity, steam, water and sewer systems. Road tunnels and the Métro are built below them, and the RER and express rail links use the deepest tunnels.

1. Underground route for cars
2. RER elevator
3. Upper level of RER station
4. RER station
5. Météor Project
6. Eole Project
7. Métro station
8. Urban heating system
9. Water main
10. Cable
11. Gas main
12. Telephone cables
13. Vault
14. Parking lot

THE CURTAIN RISES

At the beginning of this century, the scene was set for Montparnasse to become the CAPITAL OF CUBISM: the quarter was full of young artists from abroad who were later to constitute the Paris School. This Montparnasse, in Léon-Paul Fargue's description, "had neither walls nor doors. . . . The first lamp which shed light on the district – a district which has since become famous the world over – was the old 'bearded lamp' HENRI ROUSSEAU, also known as 'Le Douanier', who lived in the Avenue du Maine around 1895." (Above: *The Snake Charmer*, 1907.)

MODIGLIANI, KING OF MONTPARNASSE. An extraordinary set of newcomers moved into the area from central Europe and even from across the Atlantic. AMEDEO MODIGLIANI, a handsome Italian born in 1884 into an impoverished Jewish merchant family, came to Paris in 1906 and set up house in Montmartre. His health was not good and he

LA CLOSERIE DES LILAS ◆ *506* (5 A2) Every Tuesday evening from 1890 onward, the poet Paul Fort presided over a gathering of young writers in this establishment, formerly an open-air dance hall. In 1925 the survivors of this learned assembly organized a banquet in honor of the symbolist poet Saint-Pol-Roux (1861–1940). This event celebrating the author of *La Dame à la Faulx* ended in an indescribable fracas instigated by the Surrealists, who considered Saint-Pol-Roux to be one of their own.

returned to Italy to spend a few months with his family. He returned to Paris in 1910, this time settling in Montparnasse. Here he created the works which made him famous – so famous that his name was to be forever linked with the history of this quarter.

LA ROTONDE (6 I2). This little bistro became a meeting place for several artists who had settled in Montparnasse. As a young man, the Swiss writer Blaise Cendrars (1887–1961) spent hours at the slot machines by the bar (at this stage he still had both his arms). In its back room, where the mirrors were completely covered with "one hundred thousand declarations of love", Modigliani and his inseparable companion, Soutine (1894–1943), accompanied by a young Japanese painter called Fujita (1886–1968) (opposite), used to rub shoulders with Russian exiles. Trotsky had a regular table here and Lenin is said to have visited La Rotonde.

LE DÔME (6 I1). On the other side of the street is the huge, sunny terrace of Le Dôme. This café became a meeting place for German artists, especially members of the Munich School, who had come to Paris from the banks of the Spree.

LA CLOSERIE DES LILAS (5 A2). Paul Fort (1872–1960), elected the "prince of poets" in 1912, used to hold court here every Tuesday evening from 1890 onward. Francis Carno dedicated a long chapter to the famous Tuesdays at La Closerie in his *Memoirs of Another Life*. The café with its charming Art Deco interior is still a meeting place for today's literary set .

A NEW STYLE. Buildings in the MODERN STYLE were put up all along the boulevards Montparnasse and Raspail (completed in 1906), as well as in the neighboring streets. The house built by the architect Henri Sauvage (6 I1) is one of the most interesting of these creations (right). Building sites sprang up everywhere, and the country-style houses of the 19th century made way for blocks of studios – some can still be seen today – which artists could rent at very low rates. Yet it is to a sculptor, Alfred Boucher, that we owe the existence of La Ruche ▲ 288, a curious and unusual building put up in 1902: it took in young artists arriving in Paris, whatever their origins, nationality or artistic tendencies. Between 1902 and 1939, La Ruche housed many artists – from Léger to Soutine, from Chagall to Lipchitz, from Zadkine ▲ 172 to Kisling – who were to become the stars of the Paris School and make fortunes thanks to the astuteness of their dealers.

AMEDEO MODIGLIANI (1884–1920)
The Italian painter, draftsman and sculptor did not live to see the triumph of his works. Worn out by illness, alcohol and drugs, he literally let himself die on January 24, 1920, in the Hôpital de la Charité. His young mistress, Jeanne Hébuterne, committed suicide two days later. This tragic story was recounted in *Montparnasse 19*, a film by Jacques Becker, in which Gérard Philipe gave a stunning portrayal of the painter. (Left: *Woman's Head*, 1912).

"A SPORTY, TIERED HOUSE"
This is how architect Henri Sauvage (1873–1932) ● 79 described the building at 26, rue Vavin, which he built in 1912. Sauvage's house is covered with ceramic

tiles; its tiers, with their terrace gardens, allow more air and light into the interior. It was the forerunner of a new type of architectural design, heralding the post-war international style.

RUE SCHOELCHER
(6 J3) This door
belongs to the
building (no. 5)
created by Bigot in
1911. Picasso lived at
no. 5 *bis*, where he
kept a studio (below)
until 1917.

1914: THE END OF AN ERA

While La Ruche was a refuge for
impoverished artists in the first
decade of the 20th century, the
center of Montparnasse was home
to wealthier artists, like
Van Dongen, who held a lavish
party in his studio in the Rue
Denfert-Rochereau on May 24,
1914. Picasso had also moved into
the neighborhood, renting a luxurious
apartment in the Rue Schoelcher which
dazzled all his friends. On July 14, 1914, a
grand ball with Chinese lanterns was held at
the Carrefour Vavin, bringing together artists
and locals from all over Montparnasse.
These riotous celebrations were to be the swan song
of an era which was to end two weeks later when war was
declared, on August 2, 1914. This was the end of the golden
age of Montparnasse.

ACT TWO: THE CRAZY YEARS

After World War One, Montparnasse became
both a mecca for artists from all over the world
and a fashionable place attracting anyone who
desired to see and be seen. Thus the quarter
gained in celebrity but lost much of its former
charm.

TRANSFORMATION OF THE OLD CAFÉS. The
Carrefour Vavin became one of the focal points of
post-World War One Parisian life. LA ROTONDE
was enlarged, renovated and given a grill room
and a restaurant on the second story, where a jazz
orchestra played for diners. Père Libron's old
zinc-covered bar had changed from a modest
bistro into a luxury establishment where the
bourgeoisie came to dine in the vain hope of
spotting famous local artists. LE DÔME also underwent a
transformation: it took over the neighboring establishment,
where it opened a café-bar decorated in red leather with
nickel-plated Art Deco chairs and its terrace grew to vast
dimensions. Customers could see Fujita with his beautiful new
wife Yuki surrounded by the old celebrities of the area, like

**KIKI OF
MONTPARNASSE**
After World War
One, nightclubs
sprang up all over
Montparnasse. One
of these was Le
Jockey, founded by
an American and
initially located on
the corner of the Rue
Campagne-Première.
Le Jockey had a main
room and a bar with
very distinctive décor:
it was here that Kiki,
the undisputed queen
of Montparnasse,
held court, regaling
customers with her
bawdy songs. Kisling,
Man Ray and many
other artists painted
portraits of her.

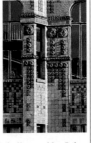

Kisling, who lived nearby in the Rue Joseph-Bara. Americans of the "lost generation" used to meet at LE SELECT, the first bar in Paris to stay open all night. On December 20, 1927, a bitterly cold night, a new and luxurious establishment with a domed roof called LA COUPOLE opened on the same street.

FESTIVE EXTRAVAGANCE. Parisians had decided to put the tribulations of war behind them. The terraces of the large cafés were overrun with extravagantly dressed crowds of all ages. Well-known artists were treated like royalty. Parties and dances were held for any and every occasion, or even for no occasion at all – like the famous BAL NÈGRE in the newly fashionable Rue Blomet, where the entire population of Montparnasse gathered to celebrate Ubu, the eponymous character in Alfred Jarry's play *Ubu Roi*. Jarry's famous satirical vision of life premiered in 1896 and was the first literary work of the "Absurd" movement.

THE SEVENTH ART. Two movie theaters vied for the avant-garde audiences of the 1930's. One of these was LE VAVIN, in the Rue Jules-Chaplain, which specialized in Soviet and Judeo-Polish movies –Waszynsky's extraordinary *Dybbuk* (1937) was screened here. The other was RASPAIL 216 where Parisians were able to see Bette Davis in her first important role in *Of Human Bondage* (1934) directed by John Cromwell, adapted from a novel by Somerset Maugham.

RUE DE LA GAÎTÉ (6 H23). This aptly named street offered the liveliest spectacle at this time – a variety of delights with a mixture of restaurants, accordionists and bistros. The old THÉÂTRE MONTPARNASSE of Seveste and La Rochelle had been renovated, cleaned and modernized, and once again became a center of dramatic activity, delighting a whole generation with the skills of the gifted magician Gaston Baty. BOBINO, the home of the popular song, witnessed performances by the leading performers of this genre. Celebrities who have performed here include Maurice Chevalier, Edith Piaf and Juliette Gréco.

LA COUPOLE (6 I1)
The immense dining room was supported by twenty-four pillars decorated by local artists. In the basement was a dance hall in red and black lacquer decorated with large mirrors: two orchestras played here. One of the most popular places in Paris was the bar at La Coupole, which opened onto the boulevard. Derain and Fujita were regular customers here and would generously buy rounds for all the drinkers on the tables around them at the end of the evening.

CROSSING THE RIVER
The architect Arfvidson designed the building known as Atelier 17 at 31, rue Campagne-Première

(6 J3); it had four stories of studios framed by arches decorated with stoneware. At one time or another Miró, Calder, Giacometti, Max Ernst and Kandinsky all worked here; however, many other artists, including Van Dongen and Picasso, had left the area to settle on the Right Bank.

The German occupation dealt a fatal blow to Montparnasse. The artists, many of them of Jewish origin, gradually left for safer places. The Germans took hold of Montparnasse in the first months of the occupation, requisitioning the large cafés for their personal use. For four years the terraces were "a sea of green", as a contemporary put it.

RUE DE LA GAÎTÉ
The Rue de la Gaîté no longer lived up to its name once it had lost Bobino, the famous home of the popular song, and many of its old bistros.

276, BOULEVARD RASPAIL (6 J4)
This turn-of-the-century building (above) is decorated on the theme of the couple: young love is portrayed on the left; in the middle is the arrival of the child; and old age is shown on the right.

TOUR MONTPARNASSE
Montparnasse Tower stands on the huge square in front of the new railway station, which serves Brittany with the high-speed TGV Atlantique. The tower has 58 stories of steel and smoked glass. It was widely criticized when it was first built in the mid-1940's, but has since become a familiar feature of the Paris landscape. From the top is a spectacular view of the city ◆ 482.

LIBERATION. On August 19, 1944, General Leclerc's 2nd Armored Division made a triumphal entry into Paris through the Avenue d'Orléans and the Boulevard du Montparnasse. The general set up his staff headquarters in the station on Place de Rennes, and it was here, on August 25, 1944, that General von Choltitz signed the treaty of surrender on behalf of the German occupying forces. Montparnasse did come alive again, but things were never the same: the area had been superseded by St-Germain-des-Prés ▲ 234, where new trends had been set in the cafés which had escaped German control.

DECLINE. Vavin, La Rotonde, Le Dôme and La Coupole held onto their traditions, but times had changed, and Montparnasse was a shadow of its former self. The only streets to retain their character were the old ones between the Boulevard du Montparnasse and the Luxembourg Gardens, with their charming buildings from the 1890's:

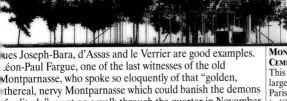

ues Joseph-Bara, d'Assas and le Verrier are good examples.
Léon-Paul Fargue, one of the last witnesses of the old
Montparnasse, who spoke so eloquently of that "golden,
ethereal, nervy Montparnasse which could banish the demons
of solitude", went on a walk through the quarter in November
1947 – his last walk as a "pedestrian of Paris" through streets
he knew so well, heading for Montparnasse Cemetery down
the avenue which Louis XIV had dreamed of.

THE MODERN AGE

The old bohemian haunts have gradually been replaced or
surrounded by contemporary buildings. The process started
with the new station (6 G2) and the MAINE-MONTPARNASSE
CENTER in which it is set, with its American-style
Montparnasse Tower. Although the project had been
proposed by Raoul Dautry as long ago as 1934, it began only
in 1969 and continued on into the 1980's, with the
redevelopment of the Guilleminot-Vercingétorix area on the
other side of the Place de Catalogne (6 G3). The Place de
Catalogne itself has a fountain designed by Shamaï Haber;
it is bordered by two apartment blocks designed by
Maurice Novarina in 1988, which follow the curve of the
square, matching Ricardo Bofill's Échelles du Baroque
building from 1983. Novarina's buildings are located on
either side of a central alley: LES COLONNES is elliptical,
while L'AMPHITHÉÂTRE is in the shape of a classical theater.
The design of the façades is in keeping
with the urban landscape and
the inner green area, which surrounds
a church.

NOTRE-DAME-DU-TRAVAIL. (6 G4) 35, rue
Guilleminot. This church, Our Lady of
Labor, was built especially for workers in
1899, following a popular subscription. Its
striking metallic framework gives it the
look of a factory, which is very apt. It is

decorated with superb Art Deco friezes and contemporary
works of art.

FONDATION CARTIER (6 G3) 261, boulevard Raspail.
In 1994 the jeweler Cartier set up this institute devoted to
contemporary art on the Left Bank, picking up on
Montparnasse's long artistic tradition. The architect Jean
Nouvel ▲ 218 was commissioned to design the building. As
Nouvel explained, "The style is one of lightness, using glass
and finely woven steel to blur the tangible limits of the
building and to dispel the impression of a solid volume in
hazy evanescence. A style which allows the quarter to enjoy a
beautiful garden which has long been hidden from view".
The institute is located on the site of the former American
Cultural Center, which was itself built on a place where the
writer Chateaubriand lived between 1826 and 1838. In his
Memoirs from Beyond the Grave, the writer records having
"planted twenty-three Solomon cedars" in the
garden; appropriately, one of these cedars now
stands by the entrance to the institute.

**MONTPARNASSE
CEMETERY** (6 IJ3)
This is the second
largest cemetery in
Paris. It was founded
in 1824 and has
become the
traditional burial
place of artists and
literary figures. The
Rue Émile-Richard,
built in 1890, divided
the cemetery's 48
acres into a small and
a large cemetery. The
poet Charles
Baudelaire, buried in
the sixth division, is
without a doubt the
star of the cemetery.
The sculptor José de
Charmoy created an
unusual memorial for
him (below) and for
Sainte-Beuve's tomb
in the seventh
division. Zadkine,
Tristan Tzara, Zao
Wou-ki, and Brancusi
are all buried here.

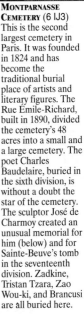

ES LA

▲ La Ruche: a city of artists

La Ruche (The Beehive), the home of Expressionism, stands as a symbol of Montparnasse bohemianism. It was built thanks to the great generosity of "Père Boucher", sculptor and philanthropist, and housed some of the great names of the Paris School. Its studios were saved from decay and destruction by the Seydoux Foundation in the 1970's. Hidden away among the greenery of a peaceful garden, it still receives artists from all over the world.

ALFRED BOUCHER

He reached the height of his fame at the end of the 19th century. Having made a fortune from his flattering busts of society figures and sculptures of fleshy nymphs, he put part of it in the service of young, impecunious artists. Boucher bought a piece of land near the horsemeat slaughterhouses of Vaugirard for next to nothing and had La Ruche built there.

THE BEEHIVE IN DECLINE

La Ruche went into decline between the two world wars: by the beginning of the 1960's it had deteriorated into a decaying, unattractive ruin. It was saved due to the efforts of artists like Simone Dat and the financial assistance of René Seydoux. The studios have been designated a historic monument.

Lipchitz and his wife (below) by Modigliani (right). *Sailor with Guitar*, sculpture by Lipchitz. Sketch of *La Ruche* by Fernand Léger (opposite).

LEGENDS OF LA RUCHE

Some of Père Boucher's "bees", like Chagall and Léger, were good workers while others, like Soutine, were incurable troublemakers. In the midst of this artistic melting pot, Modigliani and his mistress, Jeanne Hébuterne, played out the drama of their brief, tragic lives.

A MEDICI VILLA FOR THE POOR

The artists of La Ruche lived in poverty. Many came from Eastern Europe – Lipchitz, Zadkine, Chagall, Brancusi and Soutine – drawn toward this artistic crucible by Montparnasse's bohemian ambiance and cheap rents. Some French artists also stayed here, including Fernand Léger, drawing in their wake the poets and writers Apollinaire, Max Jacob, André Salmon and Blaise Cendrars.

THE ROTONDE DES VINS

Boucher took many ideas from the Universal Exhibition of 1900 – in particular, the Rotonde des Vins. This polygonal building in the shape of a beehive was divided into twenty-four tiny studios. They were nicknamed "slices of brie" because of their wedge shape.

TODAY'S BEEHIVE

The studios at 91, quai de la Gare, in the former refrigerated warehouses of Bercy, are today's successors to the bohemian artists' city. Since 1981 they have housed a colorful set of sculptors and musicians.

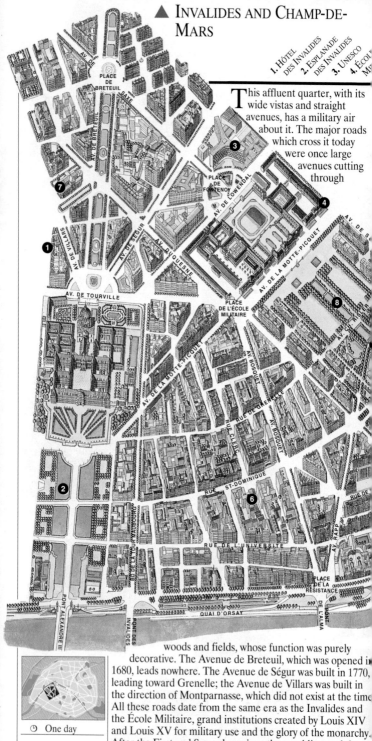

This affluent quarter, with its wide vistas and straight avenues, has a military air about it. The major roads which cross it today were once large avenues cutting through

⊙ One day

woods and fields, whose function was purely decorative. The Avenue de Breteuil, which was opened i 1680, leads nowhere. The Avenue de Ségur was built in 1770, leading toward Grenelle; the Avenue de Villars was built in the direction of Montparnasse, which did not exist at the time All these roads date from the same era as the Invalides and the École Militaire, grand institutions created by Louis XIV and Louis XV for military use and the glory of the monarchy. After the First and Second empires, the republics used the Invalides for displays of patriotism and dedicated the Champ-de-Mars, today one of Paris's largest parks, to the great exhibitions of the industrial era. The Eiffel Tower stands as a record of these grand events. At the crossroads of today's Ru

**THE INVALIDES
AT NIGHTFALL**
The long boulevard,
named after the
famous Hôtel des
Invalides, is lit up by
beacons.

Clerc and Rue St-Dominique was a village
built on land which was previously used
for truck farming. This village, Gros-
Caillou, expanded rapidly when the Hôtel
des Invalides was built and was swamped
by urban expansion at the end of the 19th
century. The laundresses of this village
were famous at the time: a "rugged band
of women armed with paddles", as
Michelet described them.

LES INVALIDES (1 EF7)

Louis XIV built the Hôtel des Invalides, the largest
architectural project of his reign after Versailles, for his
wounded soldiers who previously had no option but to live by
stealing if they refused to join the abbeys, which were obliged
to take them in.

CONSTRUCTION. Libéral Bruant, who had just completed
the Hôpital de la Salpêtrière, built the eastern half of
the building on the Grenelle plain between 1671
and 1674. The first group of veterans moved in
immediately. Before the western section was
completed, Louis replaced Bruant with
Jules Hardouin-Mansart, who built
the double church of the Invalides.
The Soldiers' Church, for the
pensioners' use, was opened
in 1677, while the Domed
Church, reserved for
the king and his
entourage, was opened in
1706. At this stage they were
not separated by a glass wall,
as they are now.

THE SOLDIERS' CHURCH. The
church is entered through a gallery
on the second story of the main court.
Its austere barrel vault is 230 feet long,
without a transept and very bright. The
custom of hanging captured enemy
flags from the ceiling goes back to the Empire.

**PARMENTIER'S
LABORATORY**
A number of
scientists also lived at
the Invalides. It was

from here that
Antoine Augustin
Parmentier
introduced the potato
to the French by
writing his famous
report on the dietary
merits of this tuber.
He came up against
stubborn opposition
from the "gray nuns"
assigned to look after
invalid veterans, who
saw Parmentier as a
threat to their control
of medical matters.
They put up a tough
fight and thought they
had won when
Parmentier lost his
laboratory in 1773.
Nonetheless, he did
not give up and
converted the
flowerbeds of the
Invalides gardens into
vegetable patches.

The opening of the
Invalides Church by
Louis XIV, painted by
Pierre Denis Martin
the Younger.

NAPOLEON'S VISIT TO THE INVALIDES
Just like the kings who preceded him, Napoleon was eager to present himself as an attentive and paternal benefactor to the veterans.

TONS OF 24-CARAT GOLD
More than 27,830 pounds of gold (555,000 gold leaves) were used on the dome, where up to ten master goldsmiths worked in 1989. From this viewpoint, the long roof of the Soldiers' Church can be seen flanked by two courtyards, then the main court, which has further buildings and side courts on either side. The infirmaries are on the right-hand side, out of view. Straight ahead is the Esplanade des Invalides, extending the main lines of the building into the distance.

The flags hung there all date from after March 17, 1814: on this date the allies entered Paris, and Marshal Sérurier, the Governor of the Invalides, ordered the destruction of all trophies. Marshals of the French army are buried in the crypts, which are not open to the public. On July 14, 1789, the crowd which later stormed the Bastille came here first; with the veterans' assistance they took some twenty-three thousand rifles and twenty-four cannons from the cellars.

THE DÔME. The young Jules Hardouin found the design for this building among the papers of his great-uncle François Mansart; the plan was originally conceived for a mausoleum of the Bourbons at St-Denis but had never been carried out. The complex, centralized design of the building allowed for optimal light, which gave prominence to Charles de la Fosse's paintings in the dome. Mansart's nephew was able to perfect the building's internal arrangement, following the classical model of a Greek cross set in a square, with a central dome and circular chapels at each of the corners. All parts of the church can be seen from the central rotonda, which can itself be admired from each of the chapels. After December 15, 1840, when Napoleon's ashes were brought back to Paris, the dome became the mausoleum of the Bonapartes. It took more than twenty-one years to adapt Mansart's church to its imperial function. The crypt, which was completed in 1861, is twenty feet deep, with an opening of forty-nine feet in diameter: it holds the Emperor's tomb, made in Finnish red porphyry, following a design by Louis-Joachim Visconti.

AROUND THE MAIN COURT. Projections and pediments do little to relieve the classical severity of this court, which is bordered by cloisters on the first floor, like those typically found in convents or hospitals. There are two stories of arcades above this. Richly decorated refectories were located on either side of the court. Administrative offices were housed in the 640-foot-long central building facing the Esplanade.

A RESOLUTELY MODERN INSTITUTION. The pensioners lived in the ancillary buildings. Ordinary soldiers slept five or six to a room, and officers' rooms had one or two beds. This set new standards for the time, as did the facilities for invalid pensioners, who had

individual rooms in the infirmary. Ten years of military service was the requirement for admittance to the Invalides, and prayers and mass were compulsory. Misdemeanors were punished with a seat at the "water drinkers' table" in the center of the refectory; however, anyone "found sleeping with a man or woman" was displayed on the "wooden horse", a large rack suspended by ropes. The building was designed to accommodate between fifteen hundred to two thousand veterans but had three thousand in 1710. It functioned as a small town.

WORKSHOPS. The pensioners could devote themselves to work. There were flourishing workshops for tapestry and ceramics, calligraphy and illumination: the Versailles *Antiphonary* and Louis XIV's *Book of Hours* were produced at the Invalides. Courses in anatomy and chemistry were also held here and the institution's surgeons were highly regarded. The Abbé Jean-Antoine Nollet's experiments with electricity inflamed the public's imagination in the mid-18th century, and this cure was used on paralyzed soldiers at the Invalides.

DECLINE. After the return of Napoleon's ashes, the mausoleum began to take precedence over the soldiers' home, which was the scene of a brief uprising in 1848. By this stage the number of pensioners had declined significantly: there were now only eighty or so. Today cannons no longer fire at the Invalides to announce great events, but it still has a very modern surgical hospital, and its buildings house the museums of the Army, of Relief Maps and Plans, and of the Liberation ▲ 145.

THE FAÇADE
The central pavilion with the entrance to the Invalides is rounded in shape. The pavilion is decorated with a carved pediment depicting the Sun King.

THE DÔME PAINTINGS
These were produced between 1702 and 1706 by several artists who worked for the glory of God and the monarchy: Charles de La Fosse painted the calotte (above) and Jouvenet the inner cupola. Coypel was brought in to paint the roof of the shrine, and Bon Boullogne decorated the corner chapels.

A COMPLEX ARRANGEMENT
Mansart's dome has two internal cupolas. The first ends at the second row of windows on the drum of the dome; the second forms a calotte, or cap, over the first. This double structure maximizes the lighting of the ceiling paintings. The device is perfect: from ground level the viewer is unaware of the complex construction. This ingenious arrangement was later used by Soufflot for the Panthéon ▲ 257.

VIEW OF THE 1889 EXHIBITION

The Exhibition spread beyond the Champ-de-Mars, encompassing the Trocadéro, the Champs-Élysées, the banks of the Seine and the Esplanade des Invalides. The Galerie des Machines was built alongside the Military Academy: like the Eiffel Tower, it was highly controversial. It was later used for bicycle races.

A total of 182 countries are represented at Unesco.

RACETRACK FROM 1833 TO 1860

The Jockey Club, created under the July Monarchy, converted the Champ-de-Mars into a racetrack facing the Military Academy, as shown in this painting (below). The prevailing fashion for all things English ensured that the venture was a success. However, after 1854 the Society for the Promotion and Improvement of Horse racing moved to Longchamp, which had a better track.

LE CHAMP-DE-MARS (1 BC7 and 8)

In 1751, Louis XV decreed the establishment of a military academy, to be built on the Grenelle plain: his aim was to secure the allegiance of France's impoverished nobility by guaranteeing its younger members a military education. The vast area stretching to the Seine was given the name Champ-de-Mars and dedicated to military exercises. Great national celebrations were held on the Champ-de-Mars during the Revolution: the Festival of the Federation on July 14, 1790, during which Louis XVI pledged allegiance to the constitution (a year later, in the same place, La Fayette ordered soldiers to shoot into the crowd, which was calling for the king's deposition), and the Festival of the Supreme Being on June 8, 1794, presided over by Robespierre. Napoleon came to the Champ-de-Mars on December 3, 1804, just after he had been made Emperor, to present imperial standards to the officers who had gathered to pledge their loyalty.

THE UNIVERSAL EXHIBITIONS. The tradition of great exhibitions on the Champ-de-Mars began under the Second Empire ● *30*. After exhibitions in 1867 and 1878, the Exhibition of 1889, on the centenary of the Revolution, was the most brilliant of all. Twenty-six million visitors came to see the Eiffel Tower, which had been built as the main attraction on the Champ-de-Mars. Another attraction was the GALERIE DES MACHINES, built by the architect Dutert and the engineer Contamin, which stood until 1909: its framework, in a single unit measuring 1,400 by 360 feet, heralded an architectural style which was to develop on an even grander scale with the advent of concrete. ELECTRICITY made a triumphant entrance at the Exhibition of 1900: the Champ-de-Mars was illuminated by a Palace of Electricity designed by the architect Hénart. The Great Wheel built on the corner of the Avenue Suffren and the Avenue de La Motte-Picquet towered over the area until 1937.

EXPOSITION UNIVERSELLE PARIS 1867

REDEVELOPMENT OF THE CHAMP-DE-MARS. In order to dispose of buildings left over from exhibitions and to raise funds, the City of Paris sold off plots of land around the perimeter of the Champ-de-Mars, which is now built up. Joseph Bouvard, Director of Promenades and Plantings, converted the central area into a garden of around 60 acres, which has become one of the most popular parks in the capital.

A patch of green: the Champ-de-Mars viewed from above.

THE ÉCOLE MILITAIRE (1 D8). The design of the building was entrusted to Jacques-Ange Gabriel, who also designed the Place Louis-XV (now Place de la Concorde). Construction work continued up to the eve of the Revolution. The long neoclassical façade overlooking the Champ-de-Mars is reproduced on the other side, which is not open to the public. The quadrangular dome can be seen from both sides. The wings, dating from the Second Empire, bear the inscriptions CAVALERIE and ARTILLERIE. The academy took in military cadets between 1777 and 1787 – among them Bonaparte. Today Gabriel's building houses the Institute of Advanced Studies for National Defense, as well as the Military Academy for Advanced Studies.

ART NOUVEAU FAÇADES
Jules Lavirotte designed this stunning façade at 29, avenue Rapp, in 1901 (1 C6). Curved lines form the basis of the ornamentation.

UNESCO (1 D9) 7, place de Fontenoy. The Y-shaped main building houses the general secretariat of Unesco. The building, which opened in 1958, was the work of Breuer (US), Nervi (Italy) and Zehrfuss (France). Works of art by Matta, Appel, Picasso and others decorate this major international institution.

The Eiffel Tower: this 1,000 feet of metal has come to symbolize Paris throughout the world. The tower was chosen among 107 projects as the centerpiece of the Universal Exhibition of 1889. Gustave Eiffel and his team of 50 engineers and 132 laborers took less than two years to achieve this technical feat, joining together 18,000 iron sections with 2.5 million rivets. The tower was originally designed to stand for twenty years but was saved for scientific purposes. Highly controversial and sneered at by artists from the very beginning, this paragon of metal architecture has attracted over 120 million visitors.

FAST WORK

The foundations were started on January 28, 1887, and took five months to complete. The four pillars were joined together by March 1888. The tower grew at a rate of 30 feet per month from the second story (190 feet high) to the third (370 feet high). After this, it grew more rapidly, rising to nearly 100 feet per month as it neared the summit. The sections arrived in preassembled 16-foot-long pieces.

GUSTAVE EIFFEL
(1832–1923)
Eiffel was a designer of
metal frameworks and an
unconventional engineer. His
creations included the viaducts
of Garabit (central France) and
Porto (Portugal), Pest Station
(Hungary) and the framework of the
Statue of Liberty.

NEW LIGHTING
Sodium lamps were installed in 1985,
casting a yellow-orange light from inside
the tower.

1949

Pe-tonnerre

Antenne 819 lignes

Girouette
Anémomètre   Baromètre
Abri mixte   Hygromètre
Thermomètre

Antenne 441 lignes

Antenne Police

Antre
Sapeurs

2 Phares
4 Balises   Paros-
                                             PARI

G. PÉRICAUD
CONSTRUCTEUR
83,63 Voltaire
PARIS (11)

T.S.F.

SCIENTIFIC USES

The Eiffel Tower was intended only as a temporary construction. Eiffel incorporated laboratories for meteorology, aerodynamics and instrument calibration, in order to demonstrate the tower's scientific utility. The tower later became a telegraph station (1898), a radio station (1921) and a television station (1959).

A SUCCESS WITH THE PUBLIC

The Eiffel Tower was opened on March 31, 1889. Gustave Eiffel climbed the 1,710 steps to place the French flag at the top. For six months the tower had twelve thousand visitors a day. After this, the number of visitors trailed off, until 1963. During those sixty years the tower had captured the hearts of new generations of poets and painters ● 92.

THE ICARUS OF PARIS

February 4, 1912, a tailor from ongjumeau named Reichelt w himself from the first level he tower strapped into a large terproof canvas: he flew . . . n crashed to the ground, 190 feet below.

▲ THE 16TH ARRONDISSEMENT
PASSY-CHAILLOT

The 16th arrondissement came into being in 1860 ● *21*, when three very rural villages were amalgamated. This soon became one of the capital's most elegant quarters. It is now an architectural goldmine, offering a unique overview of Art Nouveau and Art Deco styles, alongside charming little hamlets, a remnant of the area's rural past.

🕐 One day

> "In my spare time I would wander through the surrounding streets, which were named after painters: Scheffer, La Tour, David."
>
> Alfonso Reyes

PASSY   (8 CJ 5 to 10)

At first a simple hamlet, Passy was raised to the status of *seigneurie* (a lord's domain) in the 15th century. The presence of the court at the royal Château de la Muette and the development of thermal springs in the 18th century attracted wealthy Parisians to these vine-covered slopes. Under the Revolution the village, with only half a dozen streets, became an independent commune or parish. In 1825 Passy was divided into lots, creating the Élysée-Charles X quarter around Place Victor-Hugo: this was the first stage of urbanization.

RANELAGH GARDENS (8 F9 and 10). This green triangle frequented by children and joggers is all that remains of La Muette estate: it is bordered by quiet, opulent streets. It was from one of these streets, Allée Pilâtre-de-Rozier, that the first hot-air balloon flight took place in 1783. The Ancien Régime danced at the famous Ranelagh ball which was held in the gardens up to the Second Empire. Modern apartment blocks have largely replaced the Belle Époque houses around the gardens: only three of these remain, one of them the MUSÉE MARMOTTAN ▲ *155*.

BOULEVARD BEAUSÉJOUR (8 F10). The boulevard crosses what used to be a rural area, where Mme Récamier, Chateaubriand and Rossini stayed. Villa Beauséjour, at no. 7, has a surprise for passersby: three chocolate-colored *isbas* (log huts), remnants of the Universal Exhibition of 1867.

RUE DE PASSY (8 GI10). Formerly the main street of the village, this is still the area's liveliest

Balzac's house ◆ *477* overlooks the Hôtel de Lamballe, now the Turkish Embassy, where Maupassant died. Below, the Château de la Muette, which no longer exists.

road. It follows the same winding course as before, but fashionable shops have replaced the old stalls. The building where Louis XV kept his collection of scientific instruments is now occupied by Frank & Fils store: a sign of the times. The small Place de Passy, where the old town hall used to be, has kept something of its former rustic charm.

CIMETIÈRE DE PASSY (8 I8). (2, rue du-Commandant-Schloesing). Debussy, Manet and the poetess Renée Vivien are buried in this small, shady cemetery, the highlight of the quarter. Other tombs worthy of note include that of stage designer Ruhlmann and the Moorish tomb of Marie Baskirtseff, a painter and poetess who died in her prime, acquiring posthumous fame through her diary.

CHAILLOT (8 J8)

THE INSPIRED HILL. Up to the Revolution Chaillot was the preserve of two religious orders. The monastery of the Minims, more often known as the Bonshommes, was directly next to that of the Visitandines which was destroyed in 1794 when the Grenelle powder magazine exploded. The hill was leveled during building works undertaken by Napoleon I and Napoleon III and Davioud built a Moorish palace on it for the Universal Exhibition in 1878. The palace was rebuilt in its present form in 1937 when the organizers of the

RANELAGH MOVIE-THEATER The theater dates from the 18th century. Its neo-Renaissance auditorium saw the premiere of Wagner's *Rheingold* in 1900. Today it is dedicated to Carné and his movie *Children of Paradise.*

THE PERRET BROTHERS Auguste (1874–1954), Gustave (1876–1952) and Claude (1880–1960) achieved new heights in concrete architecture, throughout the 16th arrondissement: (below) a detail of 25 *bis*, rue Franklin (1903).

301

1. Musée de la
Marine
2. Musée de
l'Homme
3. TNP

4. Salle Gémier
5. Musée des
Monuments
français
6. Musée du
Cinéma et
Cinémathèque

THE TROCADÉRO
Davioud's temporary
palace replaced the
elegant Couvent de la
Visitation (Convent
of the Visitation),
founded in 1651 by

EXPOSITION UNIVERSELLE. PALAIS DU TROCADÉRO.

Henriette de France,
itself on the site of
Catherine de'
Medici's country
house. Chaillot has
attracted all kinds of
architectural fantasies
Napoleon wanted to
build a palace for the
King of Rome here
and the 1848
Revolutionaries
dreamed of building a
vast palace of the
people of France.

International
Exhibition of Arts and
Technology located the
exhibition's entrance on Place du
Trocadéro. The palace of Davioud was built on
the site of the palace of Chaillot, and the palace of
Tokyo on the site of the former Savonnerie, carpet
manufacturers to the royal family.

PALAIS DE CHAILLOT (8 J8) Place du Trocadéro.
A competition was held for the new Trocadéro in 1932.
Jacques Carlu was victorious, together with his partners
Louis-Hippolyte Boileau and Léon Azéma, beating Auguste
Perret ● *301* and Le Corbusier ● *307*. The project set out to
achieve the impossible: Davioud's palace was to be rebuilt,
but retaining its basic structure in order to minimize public
expenditure. The architects destroyed the minarets and
rotonda of the old palace and separated its two wings.
Ignoring academic precepts they chose not to add a
campanile to balance the structure. The completed building
opens majestically onto the Champ-de-Mars. The project's
many critics were finally won over by the effectiveness of its
horizontal structure.

A STOREHOUSE OF 1930'S ART. The aim of the Exhibition was
to stimulate a renaissance in the decorative arts. In
accordance with this the interior decoration of the palace was
carried out by seventy-one painters and sculptors,
representing all aspects of
contemporary French art. The
architects had the task of making a
harmonious whole from this
diverse range of works, which has
been criticized for its eclecticism.
THE EXTERNAL DECORATION is
thoroughly classical in its
sobriety. Metopes mark the lower
entrance to the theater, while
the blind façades on the street
sides of the Passy wing (right-hand side) and Paris
wing (left-hand side) feature bas-reliefs on themes
relating to the museums inside. Sculptures are
arranged with equal care around the square, the
terrace, the gardens and the ornamental lake.
The central pavilions, bearing quotations from
Paul Valéry on two sides, are each surmounted
by a monumental group in bronze: by Delamare
on the left and by Sarrabezolles on the right. The
graceful lines of the bronzes in the square (below)
contrast with the monumental groups on the
terrace: *Apollo* by Bouchard and *Hercules* by
Pommier.

THE THEATER. Its wide galleries, halls and staircases still have their original decoration created by artists of the period: Vuillard, Bonnard and Roussel. The Palais de Chaillot houses the MUSÉE DE LA MARINE (Naval Museum) ▲ 155 and the MUSÉE DE L'HOMME (Museum of Mankind) ▲ 144.

PALAIS DE TOKYO (8 1B4) 11–13, av. du Pont-Wilson. The authorities in Paris decided to create a museum of modern art for the International Exhibition of Arts and Technology of 1937. A competition as held and four architects – Dondel, Aubert, Viard and ▯astugue – won the commission to build this elegant building, ▯esigned entirely to achieve optimal interior lighting. A ▯olonnade of white stone forms a portico around a central ▯atio, joining the two wings which house the Museum of ▯odern Art of the City of Paris and the National Museum of ▯odern Art respectively ▲ 134, as well as the National ▯entre of Photography and FEMIS (the European ▯oundation for Sound and Image Technology). Most rooms ▯re lit from above. There is no decoration inside the museums: ▯is is confined to the courtyard arranged around an ▯rnamental lake dominated by *France*, a bronze by Rodin's ▯ssociate and chief assistant Bourdelle, who also created ▯*rength* and *Victory*, on either side of the peristyle. Metopes ▯y Gaumont and Baudry, a bas-relief by Janniot and reclining ▯gures by Dejean, Drivier and Guénot complete the ▯ecoration: the bronze doors are also striking.

▯OR **PALAIS GALLIERA** and **MUSÉE GUIMET** ▲ 142, ♦ 478 see ▯e chapter *Museums* ▲ 133.

The Joys of Life by Léon Drivier, a group for the Trocadéro Gardens.

THE TNP (National Theater of Paris)

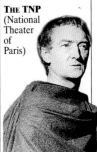

The predecessor of the National Theater of Chaillot was founded in 1920 by Firmin Gémier, a supporter of popular theater. It was first located in Davioud's palace then relocated to the great hall of the new Trocadéro designed by the Niermans brothers. Jean Vilar made this into the leading stage of the French theater with a troupe of young stars including Gérard Philipe and Jeanne Moreau. Under his direction, between 1951 and 1963, the theater-going public became accustomed to seeing the classics and rediscovered Kleist, Brecht and O'Casey.

Auteuil was an ecclesiastical domain from the 11th century to the Revolution. The village famed for its vines, survived the ups and downs of history unscathed under the monks' supervision. It was separated from the hamlet of Boulogne in the 14th century and from the village of Passy three centuries later. Auteuil became a refuge for the literary and aristocratic elite seeking sanctuary from the turbulence of Paris. Thermal springs contributed to its popularity: famous visitors included Molière, Racine and Boileau, followed later by Chateaubriand, Bonaparte and Marcel Proust. Auteuil, like neighboring Passy, was annexed to Paris in 1860.

RUE LA FONTAINE (7 G2). Proust was born on the site of no. 96, but this affluent street is chiefly famous for its architectural attractions, dominated by the work of Hector Guimard ● 78.

CASTEL BÉRANGER (no. 14). This Art Nouveau masterpiece was originally a block of low-rent apartments: the years have given it a sheen of age without detracting from its striking originality. When construction started in 1895, Auteuil was merely an outlying suburb full of factories and warehouses. A careful economy was observed in all aspects of its design, from the choice of materials to the mass production of stained-glass windows, balconies and mosaics. This did not prevent Guimard from giving full rein to his fertile imagination, with the consent of his patron Mme Fournier. Castel Béranger is three buildings grouped around a courtyard. The asymmetrical façades feature gables, barbizons and corbeled

THE CAFÉ-BAR AT 17, RUE LA FONTAINE
Unlike its neighbors, this café-bar with its crimson façade has survived in its original state and is currently being classified as an

historical monument. The interior is strictly authentic, with its original decorations and mirrors speckled with age.

balconies decorated with clinging foliage and seahorses. The materials used are very diverse, including brick, cast iron, ceramics, millstone and freestone. The result, achieved with minimal expense, is vibrant and colorful, with yellow, red, beige and blue-green used to emphasize the building's design. Stone, an impressive and expensive material, is reserved for the shell of the building and the main façade. The luxuriant ornamentation makes great use of curved lines which are typical of Art Nouveau. Interior decorations display the same inventiveness: Guimard achieved optimal lighting and spatial conditions while creating a cohesive structural and architectural whole. Everything bears his mark, from the kitchen ranges to the brass door handles whose shape he determined by clasping a piece of clay in his hand. The building, nicknamed Castel Dérangé (Crazy Castle), won a prize in the first competition for façades in the city of Paris, and launched Guimard's brilliant but controversial career.

A NEW AUSTERITY. Guimard's other creations on Rue La Fontaine show how his work evolved after this first masterpiece. Some fifteen years after Castel Béranger, austerity has taken over from imaginative exuberance. In the group of buildings comprising nos. 17, 19 and 21, RUE LA FONTAINE, 8 and 10, RUE AGAR (7 G2) and no. 43, RUE GROS (7 G2) Guimard acted as property developer as well as architect. Eleven apartment buildings were planned, but only six were completed. The architect took great care over details, designing the shop fronts on the Rue Gros and the Rue La Fontaine as well as the street signs and numbers on the Rue Agar.

HÔTEL MEZZARA (no. 60, visit by permission of the Rector of the University of Paris). This is one of the few works by Guimard to retain its original interior decorations. The interior is arranged around a vast central hall with a gallery on the second floor, lit by a glass roof.

CHARITABLE ORPHANAGE OF AUTEUIL (7 F3) (no. 40). This was founded in 1860 to take in orphans, who were then trained for manual work. A collection of neo-Gothic buildings surrounds a popular garden: the movie theater here was the only one in the quarter for a long time.

HECTOR GUIMARD (1867–1942)
Guimard studied and later taught at the École des Beaux-Arts: his role models were Horta, leader of Belgian Art Nouveau and Viollet-le-Duc. From his earliest works he exhibited an originality which was often misunderstood. Guimard's work, dismissed by his critics as "noodle" style, found expression in his apartment blocks, mostly built in the suburbs and in the 16th arrondissement, as well as in his furniture designs and kiosks for the Paris Métro. His last creations, influenced by the Art Deco movement, made no impact on the architectural world. Guimard died in the United States, forgotten by everyone.

305

STUDIO BUILDING (no. 65).

As an architect, Henri Sauvage (1873–1932) does not fit into any categories. Initially a supporter of Art Nouveau, he later concentrated on white, tiered apartment blocks ● *78*, ▲ *282*. This series of split-level studios is clearly different from his earlier work: the style is monumental, using cool-colored tiles in geometric patterns to emphasize the design.

PLACE D'AUTEUIL (7 F3). This square stands on the site of the first cemetery in Auteuil: a small obelisk opposite the church is the only remnant. It marks the tomb of Chancellor d'Aguesseau (1668–1751), a French legal reformer. The church of NOTRE-DAME-D'AUTEUIL, begun in 1319, was rebuilt by Vaudremer in 1877 in a Romano-Byzantine style.

RUE D'AUTEUIL (7 ED4). Here you will find the HÔTEL PUSHER, built in the 17th century (no. 16) and the HÔTEL DE VERRIÈRES (nos. 43–47), scene of the love affair between the Maréchal de Saxe and the actress Marie de Verrières, George Sand's ancestors. This former thoroughfare served as a refuge for philosophers and writers escaping the turmoil of the capital from the 17th century onward.

LITERATURE IN RUE D'AUTEUIL. Racine wrote *Les Plaideurs* (*The Litigants*) in a house on the site of today's Lycée Jean-Baptiste-Say (no. 11 *bis*) and Molière wrote *Amphitryon* at no 2. Both Racine and Molière frequented the Auberge du Mouton-Blanc, which has since become a restaurant (no. 40): other visitors to the inn included Boileau, La Fontaine, the actress Mme Champmeslé and Mme de Sévigné. After Molière's death in 1763 the parish priest of Auteuil accompanied his widow Armande Béjart to an audience with Louis XIV. The king allowed them to bury the writer on consecrated ground even though actors were generally excommunicated at the time.

THE SALON OF MME HELVETIUS. The house at 59, rue d'Auteuil was built around 1720 and then rebuilt at the end of the 19th century. In 1772 the widow of philosopher Helvetius bought it from the painter Quentin de La Tour. Her guests here included Diderot, Condorcet, d'Alembert, Chénier, Talleyrand, Chateaubriand and two future presidents of the United States Jefferson and Adams. She received offers of marriage from two gallant octogenarians Tugot and Benjamin

---

65, RUE LA FONTAINE

THE BOILEAU ESTATE
After 1830 the parks which made up most of Auteuil were divided into lots, allowing the development of private estates. The Boileau estate was built on the site where the 17th-century author lived and convalesced. In 1838 the printer Lemercier acquired the southern part of the estate where he built squares, alleys and country houses. Strict regulations were enforced to preserve the peacefulness of the area. Lemercier later built Villa Montmorency on the site of Boufflers' former home at 12, rue Poussin.

Franklin. "Our Lady of Auteuil", as she was known, outlived her salon and died peacefully in 1800.

CHÂTEAU DU COQ (nos. 63–73). Just a wall separated 59, rue d'Auteuil from this "petite maison" which Louis XV used for his secret liaisons. The king, who was passionately interested in botany, added a vast nursery to the house, which survives as the basis for the Auteuil Flower Garden. The land was divided up in 1862, making way for the Rue Michel-Ange, Rue Erlanger and Rue Molitor.

RUE DU BUIS ★ (7 E4). This street, lined with white houses decorated with gargoyles, has kept all its original charm. At no. 6 a plaque commemorates Olympe de Gouges, a writer and feminist who was guillotined in 1793: legend has it that she was a natural daughter of Louis XV.

FONDATION LE CORBUSIER (7 E1) 8–10, square du Docteur-Blanche ▲ *302*, ● *78*. Le Corbusier prepared an overall plan for this cul-de-sac which stands on poor building land but had to be content with building two terraced houses in 1924, which now house the Fondation Le Corbusier. One was intended for his brother Albert Jeanneret (no. 8), the other for his friend La Roche (no. 10). The houses have the tiles, roof terraces, window ledges, and free-style ground plans and façades which are typical of his style.

RUE MALLET-STEVENS (7 E1). The cream of Paris society, a minister and two prefects gathered for the opening of this masterpiece by Robert Mallet-Stevens ● *78* in 1927. The owners of the different lots had accepted an overall design for the site. Five individual houses are arranged along the avenue – all have sleek white façades incorporating terraces and recesses. Every house is different but overall harmony is achieved through the use of shapes, building materials, the dado which surrounds the buildings, the flower beds and street lamps. The architect's office (no. 12, right) was added later. Sculptors Joël and Jan Martel live and work in a home studio at no. 10.

LE CORBUSIER (1888–1965) This French painter, town planner and polemicist, originally from Switzerland, became one of the leading architects of the modern era. Villa Laroche (above) was used as a setting for its owner's art collections.

A ROYAL VIEW

The four-mile-long axis which runs from the Place de la Concorde to the Arche of

🕐 Half a day

THE THREE ARCHES
Napoleon decided to build the Arc du Carrousel and the Arc de Triomphe in February 1806. The demolition of the Tuileries Palace in 1882 opened up the view from one to the other. The opening of the Grande Arche of La Défense seems to point toward an extension of the Great Avenue.

AMUSEMENTS OF THE PAST. The Coliseum, demolished in 1780, began the tradition of open-air entertainment. Many other establishments flourished, attracting large crowds. They all disappeared by the end of the 19th century.

La Défense was started more than three centuries ago, under the supervision of Le Nôtre. Louis XIV commissioned him to redesign the gardens of the Tuileries in 1664. In doing so Le Nôtre gave prominence to the central avenue, which he extended beyond the park, up to today's Rond-Point des Champs-Élysées, without making any changes to the area in between (which was to become the Place de la Concorde). There was no need for this: from his palace the king could no

1. ARC DE TRIOMPHE
2. PARIS CHAMBER OF COMMERCE AND INDUSTRY
3. CLARIDGE, LIDO, ARCADES DU LIDO
4. HÔTEL DE LA PAIVA
5. ROND-POINT DES CHAMPS-ÉLYSÉES
6. THÉÂTRE MARIGNY
7. PALAIS DE L'ÉLYSÉE
8. ESPACE CARDIN
9. PETIT PALAIS
10. GRAND PALAIS
11. PALAIS DE LA DÉCOUVERTE
12. THÉÂTRE DES CHAMPS-ÉLYSÉES
13. ANGLICAN CHURCH

see this area, and the only view that mattered was the view created for the king's eyes.

THE GLORIOUS VISTA. The avenue duplicates the Rue du Faubourg-St-Honoré. The old Normandy road, it was built initially for purely esthetic reasons rather than practical ones, although its extension to Neuilly in the 18th century was undertaken in response to more tangible needs. Especially since the development of La Défense in the 1980's, the great avenue is basically monumental in function, punctuating the landscape and enhancing the capital's prestigious image. The road's main landmarks are the Place de la Concorde, the Arc de Triomphe and the Grande Arche; the Porte Maillot is rather a poor relation, while the Pyramide du Louvre to the east is the latest addition, marking the origins of this grand design. The stretches of road in between serve merely to mark the distance from one monument to the next. From the Arc de Triomphe to the Grande Arche, it is the view which gives the great avenue its meaning. It may be extended farther, beyond La Défense, as there are plans to incorporate the road which runs through Nanterre. Only the long stretch between the Arc de Triomphe and the Place de la Concorde has any real character. This avenue has become a symbol of patriotism and French power.

SHOWCASE OF MODERNISM. The gardens of the Champs-Élysées have a long history. The history of the avenue and its surrounding area goes back only to the beginning of the last century, when the capital expanded toward the west and a new quarter sprang up, studded with opulent private residences. However, the stretch between Concorde and the Arc de Triomphe seems to have been used for strolling and recreation from early times. Although few people live there, many come to visit its numerous places of entertainment: from the Bal Mabille to the Lido, the Café des Ambassadeurs to Fouquet's, the Panorama to the movie theaters. Traditionally, the gardens and the avenue have been a showcase for the latest technologies: for industry, the car and the movies. At the other end of the avenue, La Défense transposes this modernist tradition into the architectural sphere. Here, the Grande Arche looks back over Paris from the height of its stone platform: this subtle shift of perspective is appropriate, as the city center now has fewer inhabitants than the suburbs.

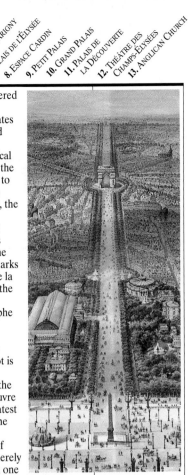

NATIONAL TRIUMPHS
Immense crowds gathered on the Champs-Élysées, the pathway of national pride, to greet Napoleon I, to honor the internment procession of Victor Hugo in 1885, and to celebrate the liberation of Paris in 1944 or, most recently, France's 1998 World Cup triumph.

MIROIR DU MONDE

La fontaine nord, la Navigation fluviale

THE OBELISK
Louis-Philippe wanted to put up a monument which would not arouse violent passions of the revolutionary or royalist variety. The Luxor Obelisk, a perfectly neutral monument, was erected in 1836 before a crowd of 200,000 spectators.

PLACE DE LA CONCORDE

The square was intended as the setting for a statue of Louis XV, which stood there for only thirty years. It broke with the tradition of enclosed royal squares ● *62* in order to preserve the view from the Tuileries to the Champs-Élysées. The royal architect Jacques-Ange Gabriel adopted Germain Boffrand's solution and bordered only one side of the square with monumental façades. He opened up the space to the spectacle of "nature", a concept much admired in the 18th century – in this case the woods which stood on the site of today's gardens.

A SQUARE FOR THE CROWDS. The eight statues on stone

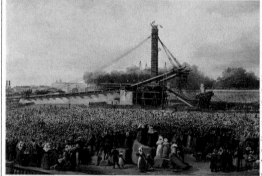

pedestals represent the eight great towns of France. They mark the access to the dry moat, filled in 1854 and now planted as flowerbeds. Public celebrations were held on the square under the Ancien Régime, but it was later the setting for less happy events. The guillotine was set up here for the execution of Louis XVI; Danton, Robespierre and many others were to follow the king. The naval headquarters moved into the building behind Gabriel's façades, which were inspired by the Louvre colonnade. This building, the HÔTEL DE LA MARINE, still retains furnishings from the 18th and 19th centuries. West of the Rue Royale is the luxurious Hôtel de Crillon ◆ *493*. The square today is largely the product of alterations made from the 1830's onward, under the direction of the architect Hittorff, who built two fountains on either side of the obelisk, adding a number of columns decorated with ship's prows, the symbol of the capital.

THE MARLY HORSES
These sculptures by Coustou have stood at the entrance to the gardens since 1794.

HÔTEL DE CRILLON

THE CHAMPS-ÉLYSÉES GARDENS

(1 FG3) The avenue of the Champs-Élysées was created to give the king an impressive view from the Tuileries. Originally it was bordered by undergrowth and insalubrious establishments where petty crooks and prostitutes met. The gardens first became popular during the Revolution, when the spectacle of "patriotic shortenings" (beheadings) attracted crowds thirsty for blood and wine. When the Empire fell, Russian and Prussian troops camped out in the gardens for two years, destroying all the vegetation. The most popular promenade in Europe and its establishments fell into decline.

RENAISSANCE OF THE GARDENS. The gardens were renovated in the 1830's and 1840's by Hittorff while work was under way on the Place de la Concorde. He added bronze candelabras to illuminate the gardens, seven fountains to cool the air, and a number of buildings, of which the pavilions Ledoyen and Laurent are the only ones to survive today. Theaters, circuses, panoramas and cafés attracted crowds avid for entertainment, which until then had been limited to the large boulevards. The Summer Circus arena, which no longer exists, had excellent acoustics which meant that concerts could be held there: Berlioz was among the conductors. Offenbach directed the Théâtre des Bouffes-Parisiens, which was later replaced by the Théâtre Marigny. There was also a fashion for panoramas – painted canvases arranged in a circle, which recreated a landscape in the round for viewers standing in the center. Hittorff's panorama opened with *The Fire of Moscow*; a second panorama, built by Davioud, followed in 1860. The public could admire seas and continents at the Géorama, a sort of early-day "Géode" ▲ *429*.

MUSIC IN THE PARK. In 1859, Alphand ▲ *208* redesigned the gardens in the English style: groups of trees and winding pathways replaced the formal squares. There had always been music in the Champs-Élysées: dances had always been popular, and at the end of the 19th and the beginning of the 20th century the café-concert became fashionable. Yvette Guilbert, Mistinguett and Maurice Chevalier performed at the Ambassadeurs at the height of its popularity. The Théâtre Marigny was built in 1880, followed by the Pavillon de l'Élysée (now Élysée-Lenôtre) in 1898. The Pavillon des Ambassadeurs (now the Espace Pierre Cardin) was the most recent addition to the garden's buildings, dating from 1931. The gardens currently have four restaurants, two theaters and one pavilion.

PAVILLON LEDOYEN
This charming restaurant ▲ *497*, rebuilt by Hittorff in 1848, has been restored to its original colors. Its visitors have included many celebrated painters and writers: Flaubert, Maupassant, Zola, Gide and Cocteau. In 1993, Robert Altman shot one of the scenes here for his film *Ready-to-Wear*.

RENAUD-BARRAULT, A LEGENDARY THEATER
Jean-Louis Barrault and Madeleine Renaud, legends of French theater, directed the Marigny, Odéon and Orsay theaters before founding the Théâtre du Rond-Point (1 E3) in the early 1980's, in Davioud's panorama which had been converted into a skating rink at the end of the 19th century.

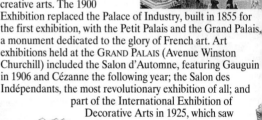

GRAND PALAIS (1 F3)

The Universal Exhibitions were initially dedicated to industry and technology but gradually opened their doors to the creative arts. The 1900 Exhibition replaced the Palace of Industry, built in 1855 for the first exhibition, with the Petit Palais and the Grand Palais, a monument dedicated to the glory of French art. Art exhibitions held at the GRAND PALAIS (Avenue Winston Churchill) included the Salon d'Automne, featuring Gauguin in 1906 and Cézanne the following year; the Salon des Indépendants, the most revolutionary exhibition of all; and part of the International Exhibition of Decorative Arts in 1925, which saw the appearance of Art Deco style. Recently it has housed

GRAND PALAIS
Since opening, this colossus of a building – 790 feet long and 148 feet high – has been criticized for its academic façades, whose stone colonnades crowned with statues hide the iron construction behind them. Inside, metal spirals and foliage are an integral part of the structure, breaking with the tradition of adding separate cast-iron ornaments. This integration of ornament and structure is typical of Art Nouveau.

shows like FIAC (International Fair of Contemporary Art) and major art exhibitions: Renoir, the Etruscans and Toulouse-Lautrec attracted several hundred thousand visitors. It is currently closed for renovation. In 1937 the PALAIS DE LA DÉCOUVERTE (1 E3) opened in the wing facing the Avenue Franklin D. Roosevelt. It was created to popularize science and invites visitors to take part in experiments covering the fields of astronomy, biology, medicine, chemistry, mathematics, physics and earth sciences. The PETIT PALAIS (1 F4) ▲ 169 has housed the municipal art collections since 1902. It has a dome reminiscent of the Invalides: its high gilded gateway and rich ornamentation give it an indisputable charm.

FIAC
GRAND PALAIS PARIS
20
9-17 OCTOBRE 93

SALON d'AUTOMNE

THE FRANÇOIS-I QUARTER (1 D3)

This was the first area of Paris to be divided into lots: it was created in 1823 on a star-shaped plan imitating classical parks. The project did not match developers' expectations, however; by 1830, Victor Hugo was living in the only house on Rue Jean-Goujon. The area became fully built up during the Second Empire. The Hôtel Clermont-Tonnerre and the Hôtel Vilgruy, built around 1865, stand opposite each other in Place François-I on either side of Davioud's fountain.

THE FIRE OF THE BAZAR DE LA CHARITÉ
The church of Notre-Dame-de-la-Consolation (23, rue Jean-Goujon) was built to commemorate the victims of the fire at the Bazar de la Charité, a charity sale attended by the cream of Paris society. The sister of Empress Elizabeth of Austria died in the fire, which claimed 125 victims, of whom 120 were women. A number of men had beaten their way to safety using their walking sticks, dispelling some illusions regarding gentlemanly behavior.

AVENUE MONTAIGNE

(1 D3). The great fashion designers, jewelers, perfumers and leather artisans make this the most expensive street in the quarter. Buildings worth a look here include the Hôtel Plaza Athénée (nos. 23–27). However, the pride of the avenue is still the THÉÂTRE DES CHAMPS-ÉLYSÉES ★ (nos. 13–15), built just before World War One. Bourdelle was responsible for the bas-reliefs on the outside; the painters Maurice Denis, Vuillard and Roussel also contributed to the decoration. The theater was highly innovative in its programming: Nijinsky's choreography and Stravinsky's music for *The Rite of Spring* created a sensation. From Richard Strauss to Boulez, the theater has stuck to its policy of presenting high culture.

A NABIS DOME
Maurice Denis, of the Nabis group of artists, produced four paintings representing the *History of Music* for the dome of the auditorium of the Théâtre des Champs-Élysées (left).

▲ CHAMPS-ÉLYSÉES TO LA DÉFENSE

314

Jean-Paul Belmondo
and Jean Seberg on
the Champs-Élysées
in Jean-Luc Godard's
Breathless.

AVENUE DES CHAMPS-ELYSÉES (1 B to G 1 to 4)

Was the Avenue des Champs-Élysées, nicknamed "les Champs" by Parisians, ever as magnificent as its reputation? Maybe in the Belle Époque, when it boasted apartment blocks with monumental façades and luxury hotels. The legend still lives on today, despite the noisy commercialism which has taken it over. In 1994 the Paris city council took steps to clean up the avenue, diverting cars to side roads and creating new street furniture. Although the Champs may not be able to match its former glory, it has regained a good deal of its charm as a place to stroll.

BRIEF HISTORY OF THE CHAMPS. The avenue's history is scarcely a century old. It only reached just beyond the Rond-Point in the 17th century and was extended to the Place de l'Étoile and then to Neuilly at the end of the 18th century. In 1800 only six buildings stood along the avenue, which gradually became more built up during the following decades. In the mid-19th century, under the Second Empire, the division between rich Paris and poor Paris became clearer: the

avenue became part of the new wealthy district to the west of the capital. Only a few houses have survived from this period, among them HÔTEL DE LA PAÏVA (no. 25). The real boom dates from the beginning of this century. The avenue was on the first Métro line, which opened in 1900, and several large hotels were built here, including the ÉLYSÉE PALACE in 1897 (no. 103, now a bank headquarters) and the CLARIDGE (no. 74, now residential). Luxury shops also began to appear at this time: the perfumer Guerlain (no. 68) arrived in 1913.

AVENUE OF FASHION. Palatial car showrooms were opened on the avenue during the 1920's; today's relatively modest successors are the PUB RENAULT (nos. 51–53), which shows some cars from the collection, and HIPPO CITROËN (no. 40). Two splendid office buildings survive from the 1930's (nos. 52–60 and no. 101). During the same decade the avenue boasted a number of first-run movie theaters. The movie industry is still celebrated here every year when the César awards are presented at FOUQUET'S (no. 99). The Arcades des Champs-Élysées (no. 78) – better known as the ARCADES DU LIDO, as they used to house the famous cabaret, now located at no. 116 *bis* – still have their splendid pink marble columns and original Lalique lamps.

HÔTEL DE LA PAÏVA

This private residence was commissioned by Thérèse Lachman, one of the many courtesans who lived in the quarter during the Second Empire. She left Moscow at the age of twenty, arriving in Paris after a mysterious two-year

journey across Europe. On the proceeds of her amorous conquests she paid the debts of the Marquis de Païva y Araujo, in exchange for his title and his hand in marriage. In 1852 she met the man who was to make her fortune, the hugely rich Count Guido Henkel von Donnersmark. He pledged his undying love, along with unlimited financial resources, which allowed her to build the most opulent private residence in Paris. She employed the architect Pierre Manguin, who was assisted by famous decorators and sculptors, including Dalou, Carrier-Belleuse and Paul Baudry (who created the ceiling of the grand auditorium in the Opéra). The house has belonged to the Traveler's Club since 1903 and still has its splendid decorations, including fireplaces with caryatids, painted ceilings and an onyx staircase.

▲ CHAMPS-ÉLYSÉES TO LA DÉFENSE

THE GIANT ARCH
Only this massive arch, with its single arcade, could provide a suitably majestic conclusion to the view down the avenue.

When Napoleon decided to build the Arc de Triomphe in 1806, he wanted not only to celebrate the victories of the Grande Armée but also to "feed French sculpture for ten years". When the arch was completed in 1836 it had achieved this aim: "this pile of stone for a pile of glory", as Victor Hugo described it, provides a backdrop for the works of great 19th-century artists. As for its function as a triumphal arch, this has continued to the present day: conquerors and liberators of this century have processed here, and in peacetime this is the setting for the July 14 military parade.

TRIUMPHAL ELEPHANT
After 1722, the leveling and redevelopment of the Étoile hill gave rise to a number of grandiose and eccentric projects. In 1758 an architect proposed building an elephant fountain with rooms inside.

NATIONAL GLORY
After Napoleon in 1840, Victor Hugo was accorded posthumous honors under the arch designed by Chalgrin. The plaster chariot which had crowned the monument for three years was destroyed the following year and has never been replaced. Since 1921 the arch has housed the tomb of the Unknown Soldier.

TRIUMPH
Cortot, who created the *Triumph of Napoleon*, was one of the sculptors, connected with the Romantic movement, who sought to revitalize the classical tradition.

RESISTANCE
Adolphe Thiers was Minister of the Interior under Louis-Philippe and an art lover; it was to him that Étex owed the commission for the two high reliefs facing Neuilly.

"LA MARSEILLAISE"
The absence of columns left large spaces free for sculpture on the arch: some twenty artists contributed to it. Rude's *Marseillaise*, on the side facing central Paris, shows the Romantic influence in sculpture. Unlike a number of sculptors who received public commissions, Rude adopted a very personal tone here, which proved far more successful than the other reliefs.

"PEACE"
Where modernist sculptors depicted dramatic subjects the stone is worked in a rougher, more abrupt fashion, as can be seen in the two works by Étex.

MISUSES OF THE ARC
This pompous edifice has inspired a number of irreverent gestures, like this harvest organized by farmers in 1990. Other pranksters have also become legendary, like the mysterious Baron Noir, who flew a plane through the arch several times in the 1980's.

⏱ Three hours

CNIT
The CNIT
● 82
(opposite, below), which opened in 1958, was a technical feat for its time. Its arched roof, made of a double shell of thin concrete, stretches over 650 feet. The building initially housed the great thematic exhibitions of the 1960's and 1970's, including the Ideal Home Exhibition and the Exhibition of Childhood. It was reorganized in 1989 and now incorporates a hotel, restaurants, shops, exhibition spaces and conference halls. Its roof and façades are classified as historical monuments. The engineer Jean Prouvé was responsible for the CNIT's immense glass windows and the façade of the Hoechst Marion Roussel Tower – evidence of the major role played by engineers in the construction of La Défense, which has a series of technical innovations, from the CNIT to the Arche.

LA DÉFENSE

The history of La Défense began in the 1950's. Paris was faced with increasing traffic congestion and growth in the service sector. The old city seemed incapable of adapting to society's new requirements: a complete transformation of the urban infrastructure seemed necessary. This was difficult to put into practice in Paris itself, and so La Défense was used as an experimental site straddling the districts of Courbevoie and Puteaux: in 1959 its only buildings were small houses and, farther west, the shantytowns of Nanterre, the largest in France. Sheep could still be seen on the wasteland and cows in backyards. Since 1883, a statue of the *Defense of Paris*, in memory of the 1870 war, had stood on a site dating back to before the Revolution, in alignment with the Champs-Élysées axis. This statue gave its name to the project, which picked up on an old idea: Napoleon I had dreamed of an imperial avenue and the Third Republic of a triumphal avenue. In 1931, the City of Paris organized a competition for the development of the axis from the Arc de Triomphe to La Défense with two objectives: to solve traffic problems and to give the capital a ceremonial avenue worthy of its status. This competition defined the monumental ambition which gave shape to today's Défense.

PROTOTYPE OF THE MODERN TOWN. The first project of La Défense at the end of the 1950's was still quite conventional. In the tradition of great avenues built in the 19th century, ÉPAD, the state organization developing the project, planned

1. GRANDE ARCHE
2. CNIT
3. FRAMATOME TOWER
4. ELF TOWER
5. CRÉDIT LYONNAIS TOWER
6. PALAIS ROYAL DES COROLLES
7. EUROPE TOWER
8. EDF TOWER
9. AURORE TOWER
10. MANHATTAN TOWER
11. GAN TOWER
12. ATHENA TOWER
13. HOECHST MARION ROUSSEL TOWER
14. LES QUATRE-TEMPS

to build a complete quarter around the new road, with housing, gardens, offices and shops. The designers of the first plan (1960), Camelot, Mailly and Zehrfuss, followed the theories of the modernist movement and decided it was more appropriate to create buildings specially adapted to their function, allowing for the use of industrial modes of construction. As a result, offices and residential accommodations had separate areas and towers. A small section of this plan was carried out in the Bellini area, near the Pont de Neuilly. The architectural vocabulary of La Défense was evolving, and this international style was characterized by geometric abstraction, clear shapes and glass halls. The Hoechst Marion Roussel Tower, built by Mailly, creates a striking glass-curtain effect: a non-load-bearing wall is built around a load-bearing concrete nucleus.

THE GREAT PLATFORM. The second stage of plans (1964), moved away from the idea of a French-style Manhattan with

FROM SCULPTURE ...
The gigantic scale of the buildings in La Défense is counteracted by a large number of open-air sculptures. From top to bottom: Calder's *Stabile*, Takis's water mirror and Miró's fantastic figures.

... TO RELIGION
A new addition to the existing Protestant Evangelical and Roman Catholic churches at La Défense is to be the church of Notre-Dame-de-Pentecôte. Now under construction, the building's front elevation will face onto the square.

319

DUE WEST
From Pont de Neuilly the level rises in a series of landings, the last and most ornate stage of which is the staircase of the Grande Arche, which manages to be at once imposing and welcoming. The huge scale of the project underlines the power of the central state administration, which imposed its will on reluctant district authorities. On the other side of the Arche, development projects are gradually taking shape.

O. VON SPRECKELSEN
This Danish architect had built only three churches and a house when his project was accepted. He was very exacting and abandoned the project when part of it was cut back.

traffic circulating between skyscrapers. A pedestrian platform, surrounded by a circular boulevard, was built to cover the complex traffic system underneath. Residential accommodation was arranged along this platform, built around square courts which have been nicknamed "palais royaux". Office towers, which were limited to 330 feet in height, were kept separate from residential areas. The Europe, EDF, Aurore and Crédit Lyonnais towers were built according to these guidelines, as were the residential buildings of Place des Corolles. At the end of the 1960's the demand for office space grew, and the idea of a diversified quarter gave way to the need for a commercial center. At the same time, the principle of building groups of identical buildings was called into question. ÉPAD granted permission to build the twin Manhattan Towers and increased the limits for height and width. This made way for the green GAN Tower and the black granite Framatome Tower, the latter the highest tower of La Défense, measuring 584 feet. This second stage of development was characterized by an explosion of shapes and colors, and different design principles.

THE THIRD GENERATION. The scandal of 1972, when Parisians first became conscious of the GAN Tower looming behind the Arc de Triomphe, combined with the oil crisis and the fear of a "towering inferno", brought the project to a sharp halt. La Défense seemed to symbolize the failure of modern architecture, with its oversized, neon-lit offices whose air-conditioning often failed to work and was always expensive to run. La Défense took off again at the beginning of the 1980's, when the enormous

> "AN OPEN CUBE. A WINDOW ON THE WORLD.
> A TEMPORARY STOPPING POINT ON THE AVENUE.
> WITH ONE EYE ON THE FUTURE."
>
> OTTO VON SPRECKELSEN

Quatre-Temps shopping center was built, making La Défense a regional focus for commercial activity. A third generation of towers was built with more complex internal spaces, halls reaching over several stories and natural lighting for every office. Under the requirement to ensure that every office has natural light – which cannot be met in a tower which is 150 feet thick – a new type of design emerged, exemplifed by the Athena and Elf towers: these buildings are slimmer, hollowed out and split apart.

THE 21ST ARRONDISSEMENT. In 1971, ÉPAD organized a competition for plans to extend La Défense toward the west. Should the view be closed? Should a square be built in order to get back to manageable urban dimensions? The outcome two decades later, after years of debate, is the Grande Arche ◆ 82 by Otto von Spreckelsen. Today this monumental construction houses the Ministry of Equipment and private offices in its side walls. The roof can be reached by elevators, offering spectacular views ◆ 482. The Grande Arche attracts 100,000 visitors each month, finally giving this satellite town the tourist focus it needed and helping to make La Défense, with its 130,000 workers, the "21st arrondissement" of Paris. Beyond the Arche itself the platform principle is being questioned: connections with Nanterre are being developed, bringing the issues that confront La Défense at the end of the 20th century back down to ground level. When the motorway is driven underground it will leave free a conventional avenue bordered with apartment blocks. By today's standards, La Défense, once a futurist experiment, is a highly traditional project. Meanwhile the site, which over forty years has become one of Europe's premier business districts, is developing in two ways. Older tower blocks are being renovated, while new buildings are underway for the new millennium. Most notable will be the PB6 Tower, located alongside the Crédit Lyonnais Tower and designed by the architect I.M. Pei, best known for his Louvre Pyramide.

THE GRANDE ARCHE
This 330-foot hollow cube represents a true technological feat, as well as a subtle response to the question of whether the avenue should be closed or left open on the threshold of the suburb. It marks a border while at the same time allowing the eye to roam.

THE TOWERS
The architects of the first towers expressed their creativity only on the surface of the building, as in the Aurore Tower (top). When size restrictions were relaxed, La Défense moved into the avant-garde of architectural audacity, as represented by the PFA Tower (middle) and the Elf Tower (bottom).

321

1. Orangerie
2. Jeu de Paume
3. Place Vendôme
4. Church of St-Roch
5. Flore Pavilion
6. Marsan Pavilion
7. Arc de Triomphe du Carrousel
8. Comédie Française
9 Conseil d'État and Ministère de la Culture
10. Grande Galerie
11. Aile Denon
12. Aile Richelieu
13. Pyramide
14. Bibliothèque Nationale
15. Théâtre du Palais-Royal

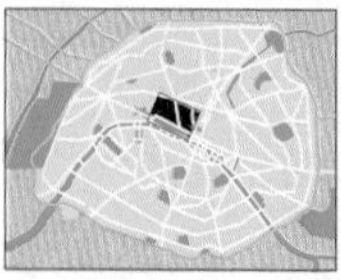

◷ One to three days

"An entire town built with pomp
Appeared to have risen miraculously from a ditch
With superb roofs which make us suppose
That all its inhabitants must be gods or kings."
Corneille, 1643

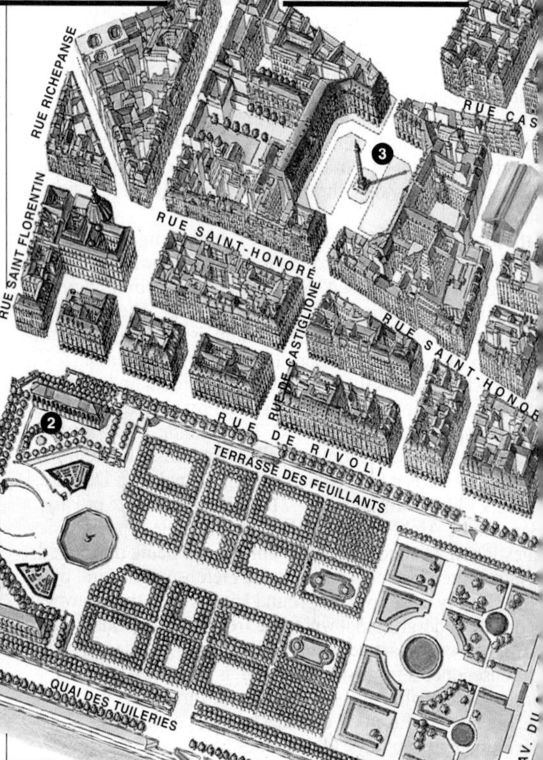

A royal residence
Charles V moved into the Louvre in 1358, by which time the château no longer played a defensive role. The architect Raymond du Temple converted the Louvre into an elegant Gothic palace, setting windows into the walls. It became a royal residence fit for the king, surrounded by gardens.

The Louvre was first a fortress and then a royal residence; in the 17th century the Tuileries Palace was built on its western side. This center of royal power, built outside the city to avoid problems of congestion, was surrounded by ministers' residences grouped around Richelieu's palace. These new quarters, which also included two royal squares, gradually became a focus of power in several spheres: financial institutions moved into the area around the Rue Vivienne; culture was represented by the Bibliothèque Royale, later Nationale, where Molière created his most important work in a theater built by Richelieu in the east wing; and finally there was the Palais-Royal, pleasure palace of the great. The area was redeveloped under the First

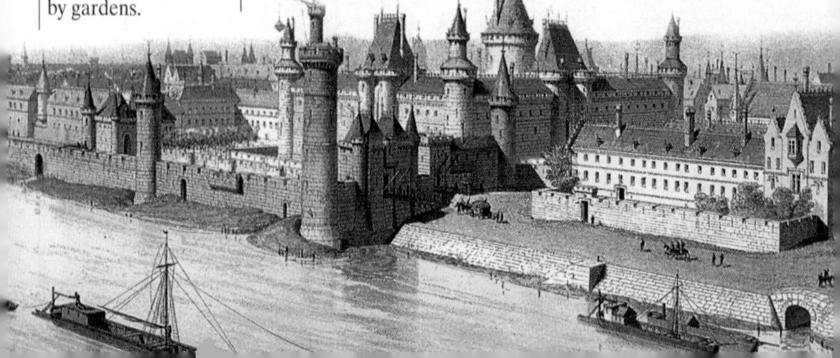

JARDINS DU PALAIS-ROYAL

17. BANQUE DE FRANCE

18. PLACE DES VICTOIRES

19. MUSÉE DES ARTS DÉCORATIFS

20. COUR CARRÉE (SULLY)

21. COLONNADE

22. TOWN HALL OF THE 1ST ARRONDISSEMENT

23. CHURCH OF ST-GERMAIN L'AUXERROIS

Empire.
Even though the Louvre
is no longer the focal point of the power of
the State, it is nevertheless a prestigious showcase for France,
as demonstrated by its glass pyramid and its ambitious
museum scheme.

THE LOUVRE

A DEFENSIVE ROLE. The Louvre came into being under
Philippe-Auguste: before leaving for the Crusades in 1190, he
built a city wall to protect the Right Bank during his absence.
A fortress with an imposing keep at its center was the first
part of this defensive plan, located at the northwest of the
present-day Cour Carrée. The Great Tower, a symbol of
feudal power, was completed in 1202 to house the Royal
Treasury, the archives and the arsenal as well as to hold high-
ranking prisoners. This Louvre was later dismantled; only the
foundations remain today (these can be seen in the museum's
archeological crypt).

I.M. PEI'S PYRAMIDE
The glass building's
silhouette crowns the
Grand Louvre, which
was renovated and
enlarged as part of the
project undertaken
between 1981 and 1993.

323

THE FORTRESS TO THE GRAND LOUVRE

Philippe-Auguste's Louvre, completed in 1202, was built strictly as a fortress. In 1358 Charles V moved into the Louvre and spent ten years converting it into a royal residence. After destroying the keep, François I commissioned Pierre Lescot to make the old château into a Renaissance palace. This was completed by Henri II (1546–59). In 1594, Henri IV continued Catherine de'Medici's plan to connect the Louvre and the Tuileries.

1610: Henri IV's Grand Plan.

1870: Napoleon III's Louvre in its completed state.

CARROUSEL ENTRANCE AND STAIRCASE

Henri IV's Grand Plan included making the Cour Carrée four times larger. The 17th century saw the addition of the Pavillon de l'Horloge by Le Mercier, the Galerie d'Apollon by Le Vau and Le Brun, and the Colonnade by Perrault. Le Vau also completed the enlargement of Le Mercier's Cour Carrée. The Grande Galerie museum was opened on August 10, 1793. From 1804 to 1848, Percier and Fontaine resumed the old Grand Plan in keeping with Lescot's style: by contrast, Visconti and Lefuel made the Louvre into a showpiece of Napoleon III architecture. A century after the Tuileries Palace burned, Pei's Grand Louvre became part of the Grand Plan.

❶

A ROYAL RESIDENCE
Charles V's architect, Raymond du Temple, made the castle into an elegant Gothic building with bay windows and surrounded by gardens.

GRANDE GALERIE (1)
The gallery, started in 1595 by Louis Métezeau and Jacques Androuet Du Cerceau, was put along the Seine to connect the Louvre with the Tuileries Palace, in 1563.

First floor

THE SLAVES
(1513–15)
Both figures were
carved by
Michelangelo as part
of the first plan for
the monumental
tomb of Pope
Julius II in Rome.
Above, *Dying Slave*,
the counterpart of
Rebellious Slave. The
figures were not
completed because of
faults which appeared
in the marble; they
were to have been
part of a series of six
or seven statues.

The Louvre is the largest museum in the world, with seven departments and collections which date back to the 7th milennium BC. A few of the major exhibits are presented here as an encouragement to seek out and discover the others.

ROYAL COMMAND

Before leaving Paris for Versailles, the young Louis XIV decided to go ahead with work on the Louvre. His aim was to complete the Cour Carrée and the Galleries, and to build the Colonnade, a façade facing the town which would become a symbol of French classical architecture.

COLONNADE (8)

The competition for the Louvre façade pitted Bernini and Pietro da Cortona against a trio of French architects (Claude Perrault, Louis Le Vau and Charles Le Brun). The French group was victorious.

PYRAMIDE (11)

Exactly 793 glass diamonds and triangles, assembled with minute accuracy.

THE PERCIER AND FONTAINE STAIRCASE (9)

Napoleon I's two architects built a second story on three sides of the Cour Carrée and added the doorways and staircases the museum needed.

COUR MARLY (10)

Three new covered courts were created during the development of the Richelieu Wing: Cour Marly and Cour Puget, devoted to French sculpture of the 17th century, and Cour Khorsabad, which reconstructs the Assyrian palace of Sargon II. Cour Marly is covered with a huge glass roof reaching a height of 82 feet, giving it the benefit of natural

GRAND LOUVRE

The renovation of the Louvre was entrusted to I.M. Pei, an American architect of Chinese origin. It observed two basic principles: to respect the old buildings showing them to advantage while making a resolutely contemporary contribution, free of pastiche, in the Richelieu Wing and the underground

INVERTED PYRAMIDE (12)

This is held together by a similar system of cables (here shown during assembly).

THE RAFT OF THE MEDUSA

(1819) This painting by Théodore Géricault shows the shipwreck of the late *Medusa*, from which only 15 men escaped alive. The Romantics restored texture and emotion to the place which neoclassicism had denied them.

WEDDING FEAST AT CANA

(1562–3) This painting by Paolo Veronese was commissioned for the refectory of the San Giorgio Maggiore monastery in Venice. The huge canvas (23 by 33 feet) was restored on site between 1989 and 1992, as it was too large to be transported. Restoration uncovered the original colors of the work under layers of repainting and dirt. Venetian painting, with its emphasis on color (in the works of Bellini, Giorgione, Titian, Veronese and Tintoretto) traditionally contrasted with the Florentine emphasis on draftsmanship. Venetian classicism was just as influential as that of Florence

LA GIOCONDA

(1503–6) This painting by Leonardo da Vinci, *Portrait of Lisa Gherardini* (known as *La Gioconda* or the *Mona Lisa*), is the most famous in the Louvre. It was the centerpiece of François I's collection. The delicate modeling of the figure, the serene, misty lighting, the enigmatic smile and the gracious gestures are features which can be seen in most of the artist's paintings.

APHRODITE, OR THE VENUS DE MILO

(2nd century BC) This statue was discovered on Milo, or Melos, one of the Cycladic islands, in 1820. It is regarded as a masterpiece of classical Greek art. The Marquis de Rivière claimed ownership of the work along with all the other pieces found with it. He brought it to France and gave it to Louis XVIII who in turn gave it to the museum in May 1821. Many theories have been proposed concerning the position of Venus' lost arms: the right arm must have been in front of the body, with the hand toward the left hip, and the left arm was probably raised.

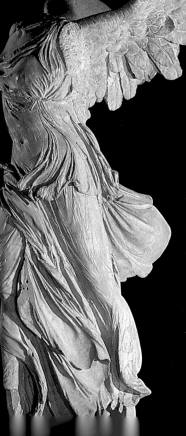

THE VICTORY OF SAMOTHRACE

(c. 190 BC) This winged figure was discovered in 1863 during excavations on the island of the same name, in the Aegean Sea. It had been placed at the top of a promontory, perhaps to commemorate a naval victory by Rhodes. This perfect example of classical Greek art was found by Charles François Champoiseau, broken in pieces. The figure's hand was discovered in 1950 and is also on display

First floor

THE MEDIEVAL LOUVRE

The remains of Philippe-Auguste's cast were brought to light during the excavation of 1984–5 and are now open to the public. Visitors can walk along the old moats a around the Grosse Tour, the circular ke which symbolized feudal power and hou the royal treasury, archives, arsenal and ranking prisoners. The monarchs themse spent little time there.

Entresol

THE BULLS OF KHORSABAD

The five bulls with wings and human heads were intended to act as beneficent guards of the Assyrian palace of Sargon II at Khorsabad. They are now exhibited in the Cour Khorsabad, where reliefs from the palace are displayed at their original height so as to reproduce the monumental effect of Assyrian architecture.

THE MARLY HORSES

This group of four sculptur were commissioned the royal park a Marly. *Fame a Mercury* (1706 Antoine Coyse were later repla by Guillaume Coustou's *Horses Restrained by Grooms* (17 The first pair was moved to entrance of the Tuileries in 1719, and the second to the Place de la Concorde durin the Revolution.

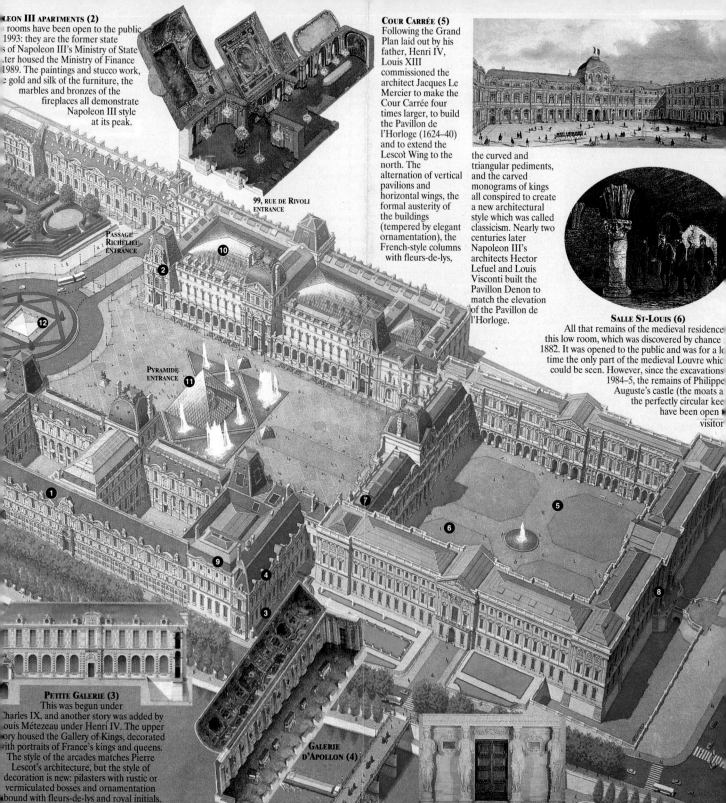

...LEON III APARTMENTS (2)

...rooms have been open to the public
...1993: they are the former state
...s of Napoleon III's Ministry of State
...ter housed the Ministry of Finance
...1989. The paintings and stucco work,
...e gold and silk of the furniture, the
marbles and bronzes of the
fireplaces all demonstrate
Napoleon III style
at its peak.

99, RUE DE RIVOLI
ENTRANCE

PASSAGE
RICHELIEU
ENTRANCE

PYRAMIDE
ENTRANCE

COUR CARRÉE (5)
Following the Grand
Plan laid out by his
father, Henri IV,
Louis XIII
commissioned the
architect Jacques Le
Mercier to make the
Cour Carrée four
times larger, to build
the Pavillon de
l'Horloge (1624–40)
and to extend the
Lescot Wing to the
north. The
alternation of vertical
pavilions and
horizontal wings, the
formal austerity of
the buildings
(tempered by elegant
ornamentation), the
French-style columns
with fleurs-de-lys,

the curved and
triangular pediments,
and the carved
monograms of kings
all conspired to create
a new architectural
style which was called
classicism. Nearly two
centuries later
Napoleon III's
architects Hector
Lefuel and Louis
Visconti built the
Pavillon Denon to
match the elevation
of the Pavillon de
l'Horloge.

SALLE ST-LOUIS (6)
All that remains of the medieval residence
this low room, which was discovered by chance
1882. It was opened to the public and was for a l
time the only part of the medieval Louvre whic
could be seen. However, since the excavations
1984–5, the remains of Philippe
Auguste's castle (the moats a
the perfectly circular kee
have been open
visitor

PETITE GALERIE (3)
This was begun under
...harles IX, and another story was added by
...ouis Métezeau under Henri IV. The upper
...ory housed the Gallery of Kings, decorated
...ith portraits of France's kings and queens.
The style of the arcades matches Pierre
Lescot's architecture, but the style of
decoration is new: pilasters with rustic or
vermiculated bosses and ornamentation
...bound with fleurs-de-lys and royal initials.

GALERIE
D'APOLLON (4)

SALLE DES CARIATIDES (7)

	Oriental antiquities and Islamic art		Objets d'art
	Egyptian antiquities		Sculptures
	Greek, Etruscan and Roman antiquities		Graphic arts
			Paintings
			Medieval Louvre

PORTRAIT OF THE ARTIST AT HIS EASEL (1660) Rembrandt developed a style that powerfully combined the magnificence of baroque painting with a sober, introspective quality. He was a master of light, of dark glazes and of muted golds. The Louvre has three of his self-portraits.

THE LACEMAKER (c. 1670) An interest in everyday life and meticulous attention to detail are typical of Jan Vermeer. The Louvre has two of his most famous works. He worked within the tradition of Dutch painting, creating exquisite harmonies with cool tones, especially blues and yellows. His technical skill matched the subtlety with which he conveyed human emotions.

PORTRAIT OF JEAN LE BON (c. 1350) This anonymous work is the first individual profile portrait known in Europe.

THE MEDICI GALLERY The group of 24 paintings produced by Rubens between 1622 and 1625 for the Medici Gallery of the Palais du Luxembourg is a series of allegories recounting the life of Marie de' Medici. This masterpiece combines realism and the fantastic, creating an overall effect of dynamism and movement.
Left: *Marie de'Medici Landing at the Port of Marseille*

THE CHEAT WITH THE ACE OF DIAMONDS Georges de La Tour, an artist from Lorraine who was long undervalued, has been compared to Caravaggio. Nocturnal scenes are lit with candlelight, in contrast to the cool light of the daytime

THE SKATE (1728) Jean-Baptiste Siméon Chardin celebrated the object in his work, elevating it almost to the status of an independent being. Cauldrons, pipes, glasses, brass fountains, saucepans and pots are painted with sculptural precision, a love of

A RENAISSANCE PALACE. Charles V transformed th château into a royal residence, but his successors neglected the building. In 1515, François I took up residence at the Louvre in order to ensure the Parisians' support. He replaced the Great Tower with a paved court and commissioned the architec Pierre Lescot to embellish the old palace with the help of the sculptor Jean Goujon. Under Henri II the southwest section of today's Cour Carrée was built, up to the central pavilion (now known as the Pavillon de l'Horloge), as well as the Pavillon du Roi, overlooking the Seine. Inside the palace the Salle des Cariatides was built, as well as the staircase now known as the Henri II Staircase.

IMPERIAL FESTIVITIES
Van Elven's painting depicts a soirée held at the Tuileries to celebrate the Universal Exhibition of 1867: Empress Eugénie, dressed by Worth ● *117* accompanies the Czar, followed by Napoleon III and the King of Prussia. The emperor and his entourage were very fond of entertainment: for seventeen years the palace witnessed a series of lavish festivities.

THE GRAND PLAN. In 1594, Henri IV revived Catherine de' Medici's plan to join the Louvre and the Tuileries. The king bought up all the surrounding land so that he could ma the Cour Carrée four times larger; he also built the Grande Galerie in 1595, designed by Louis Métezeau and Jacques II Androuet Du Cerceau. The Petite Galerie, with its famous Gallery of Kings on the second story, was started in 1566 in order to connect the two façades. In 1624, during the reign o Louis XIII, Le Mercier built the Pavillon de l'Horloge (or Pavillon de Sully) and extended the Lescot Wing to the nort The Gallery of Kings was destroyed by fire in 1661. When it was rebuilt, the architect Louis Le Vau made it twice the size and created the Galerie d'Apollon on the second story, whic was decorated by Charles Le Brun, among others. Louis XIΥ wanted the palace to have a monumental entrance on the Paris side and chose Claude Perrault's design with its famou colonnade, a "true manifesto of the classical style". Built between 1667 and 1670, it measured over 570 feet in length and faced the Place St-Germain-l'Auxerrois.

TUILERIES PALACE

ARC DE TRIOMPHE DU CARROUSEL (2 A5) Napoleon had this arch built between the Louvre and the Tuileries in 1806. On top of it he placed the bronze chariot made by the Greek sculptor Lysippos in 300 BC, which he had taken from the portico of St Mark's in Venice during the Italian campaign (the Venetians themselves had taken it from Constantinople in 1204). The famous horses were given back in 1815 and replaced by a copy.

After the fire started by the Communards, the ruins of the palace were left standing until 1882. This former royal residence, with a vast garden opening onto what was then countryside, had been built by Catherine de' Medic starting in 1564, after a design by Philippe Delorme. She chose the site of the old *tuileries* (tile works) outside Charles V's city wall. Henri IV, Mazarin and Colbert continued work on the palace following the original designs but planned new galleries to connect the

central pavilion with the Louvre, and new wings. The aim was to create a more intimate residence than the Louvre. The interior was repeatedly redesigned: Mazarin even had a theater built in the palace, which staged the first opera performances in France. Later the palace was neglected in favor of Versailles and in the 17th and 18th centuries it had numerous tenants. Louis XVI's forced return to Paris in 1789 and the later arrival of Revolutionary committees in the palace made it a center of political power; this also ensured that its furniture survived. The Tuileries Palace was redesigned under Napoleon I, who created the Place du Carrousel and added the gallery running along the Rue de Rivoli. The Tuileries was the official royal residence from 1814 to 1870.

A CULTURAL CENTER. Two Second Empire buildings stand opposite each other at the entrance to the Tuileries Gardens ▲ *200* on the Place de la Concorde. Since its conversion, completed in 1991, the Jeu de Paume (1 H4) has been a gallery of contemporary art. The Orangerie ▲ *168* houses the Walter-Guillaume collection and Monet's *Waterlilies*.

RUE DE RIVOLI

(1 HJ4)

This road was built by consular decree between 1802 and 1835, representing a new vision of town planning. Rue de Rivoli took over from the old Rue St-Honoré, giving Paris a second east-west axis.

THE TUILERIES ON FIRE
The palace was set on fire in March 1871, and its remains were destroyed for political reasons in 1882. Remnants can be found in Paris' parks and at St-Raphaël (Var). *Le Figaro* even bought some of the marble: the pieces were cut down into paperweights and sold to subscribers.

GALIGNANI BOOKSHOP
The bust of founder Giovanni Galignani is on display here: an ancestor of his was editing books in Padua as early as 1520. The bookshop was initially located in Rue Vivienne but moved to Rue de Rivoli in 1854. Giovanni married the daughter of an English printer and founded *Galignani's Messenger* in 1814; this publication functioned as an international newspaper for twenty-four years.

RUE DE RIVOLI AROUND 1840
Chateaubriand described how slowly work was progressing in 1813: "So far you can only see the arcades put up by the government and a few houses being built here and there, with their jagged outline of expectant stones."

333

ROBESPIERRE AND THE MAISON DES DUPLAY
Robespierre moved to Rue St-Honoré above a carpenter's shop in 1791.

One of the drawing rooms at the Meurice.

THE FLAMBOYANT PORCH OF ST-GERMAIN
A neo-Gothic belfry (1861) by Théodore Ballu (who also built the Église de la Trinité) joins the church to the town hall of the 1st arrondissement (1859). The town hall was built by Jacques-Ignace Hittorff, who also designed the Gare du Nord.

FAÇADES AND ARCADES. The Rue de Rivoli was built from the Rue St-Florentin up to the Place des Pyramides on ground which had formerly belonged to a monastery. Freestone façades were built along it following plans by the architects Charles Percier and Pierre-François Fontaine, the organizers of festivities under the First Empire. The façades consisted of a first story with arcades and three further stories, the last under a convex zinc roof. As part of the project, a new quarter was created around Rue Mont-Thabor, Rue Cambon and Rue de Castiglione. The road was extended up to Rue St-Antoine in 1848, without matching façades.

LUXURY SHOPS AND GRAND HOTELS. Today the arcades house elegant shops and a few luxury hotels, like the Meurice ◆ *494*, at no. 228 (1 H4). This hotel, founded in 1907, has preserved a number of opulent drawing rooms in the 18th-century style designed by Henri-Paul Nénot, the architect of the new Sorbonne. Angélina ◆ *507*, the tea room at no. 226, was founded in 1903 by the pâtissier Rumpelmayer: it is a favorite haunt of hot chocolate afficionados. At no. 224 is Galignani, the first English bookshop established in Paris, in 1800.

THE LOUVRE DES ANTIQUAIRES (1 J4). This huge arcaded building between Rue de Rivoli and Rue St-Honoré housed the Grands Magasins du Louvre between 1878 and 1960. Today this is the only shopping center of its kind in Europe, with 250 antique dealers on three stories.

ST-GERMAIN-L'AUXERROIS (2 B5). The first church dedicated to the bishop of Auxerre Saint Germain was built on this site at the end of the 7th century.

The church was rebuilt in the first half of the 12th century and then altered repeatedly. It became the royal parish when the Valois moved to the Louvre, and from the 17th century onward this was the traditional burial place for royal artists, including Le Vau, Gabriel, Soufflot, Boucher, Van Loo and Chardin. The superb porch in the Flamboyant Gothic style (1435–9) bears the mark of Burgundian influence. The choir was altered in the 18th century, and the church lost its famous white marble rood screen, carved by Jean Goujon in 1541 after plans by Pierre Lescot; fragments can be seen in the Louvre. Nearly all the original furniture has been lost, although the church still has some beautiful pieces, including the royal pew made in 1682 after a design by Le Brun and the Flemish Retable, a vast altarpiece in carved oak from the early 16th century.

GRANDS MAGASINS DU LOUVRE
These department stores were created by Alfred Chauchard, a dealer and art lover who left his collections to the Louvre in 1906. The stores were famous for having electric lighting in their window displays before World War One. In addition to its magnificent antique stores, the Louvre des Antiquaires has an exhibition room which has shows on such subjects as heraldry or the decorative arts.

RUE ST-HONORÉ   (1 IJ 3 and 4)

Rue St-Honoré crosses three of the old gates of Paris as it runs between Rue du Louvre and Rue Royale. The first of these gates, demolished in 1535, was around the site of the Oratory, at no. 115. The second gate was called Porte des Aveugles (Blind Men's Gate) because it was close to the Quinze-Vingts hospice ▲ 405 which moved to Rue de Charenton under Louis XVI; the gate was demolished around 1636. The third gate was built in 1631, when the Rue Royale was widened, and was destroyed in 1730. From the end of the 16th century onward, religious communities and businesses moved into the new quarter (including À la Civette, the tobacconist's shop at no. 157, founded in 1716). Today they have mostly been replaced by luxury boutiques.

CHURCH OF ST-ROCH (1 J4). This church, designed as a series of chapels, was built on a hillock between 1653 and 1754. Corneille, Le Nôtre and Diderot are buried here. The architect of the Sorbonne, Jacques Lemercier, designed the choir and the nave; the vault was added under the Regency, donated by a new parishioner, the financier John Law. The façade was built around 1738 after a design by Robert de Cotte but has since lost its decorative carvings. Father Marduel, the parish priest, had the

CHAPELS OF ST-ROCH
Among the most remarkable chapels of the church are the chapel dedicated to the Virgin, designed by Jules Hardouin-Mansart in 1705, and the Chapelle du Calvaire, by Étienne-Louis Boullée, built in 1754. The building contains religious works of art which were formerly held in neighboring monasteries.

COMMUNARDS AGAINST THE COLUMN
The revolutionaries saw the Vendôme column as a "symbol of brute force and false glory" and demolished it on May 16, 1871.

church decorated with religious scenes: he appointed the sculptor Étienne-Maurice Falconet and the painter Jean-Baptiste Pierre, who painted *The Triumph of the Virgin* on the dome.

PLACE DU MARCHÉ-ST-HONORÉ (1 J3). The Rue du Marché-St-Honoré leads to this square. The Jacobin monastery, which became famous as a meeting place for revolutionaries (Jacobins), used to stand here. The market was established in 1810 and in 1954 was replaced by a multi-story car park now torn down. A glass-fronted office building designed by architect Ricardo Bofill has recently been completed.

CHURCH OF THE ASSUMPTION (1 H3). The enormous dome at no. 266 *bis* belongs to the chapel of the Dames de l'Assomption convent. It was built in 1670 following designs sent from Rome by Errard and acquired the nickname *sot dôme* (silly dome). The church became a Polish parish in 1850. At no. 398 is the MAISON DES DUPLAY, where Robespierre lived during the Revolution.

PLACE VENDÔME   (1 I3) ● *62* ▲ *128*

Place Vendôme, formerly Place Louis-le-Grand, was designed by Jules Hardouin-Mansart and is regarded as the ultimate in classical city planning. Planned as a home for the academies and royal library, it was built at the end of the 17th century at the instigation of the minister Louvois. At the center of the square, the column erected by Napoleon stands out against the austere, magnificent geometry of the whole.

THE FIRST PLAN FAILS. Mansart had originally planned a three-sided square, open to the south, on the site of a house

MAGNIFICENT JEWELRY
Paris's grandest jewelers ▲ *128* have been located on and around Place Vendôme since the Second Empire.

elonging to the Duc de Vendôme. Arcaded façades with a
etaining wall but no roof had been built around half of the
quare, and an equestrian statue of Louis XIV as a Roman
mperor, by François Girardon, had just been placed at the
enter. Then, on April 7, 1699, the king announced a change
f plan: he wanted the square to be octagonal in shape.

CLOSED AREA. Mansart made the new square into an
nclosed area of 480 by 450 feet built on four sides with cut-
ff corners and narrow openings to Rue St-Honoré to the
outh and the Capuchin monastery to the north. Rue de
Castiglione and Rue de la Paix were built under the Empire,
ncreasing traffic on the square. Among the first to acquire
roperty here were Mansart himself and the banker Law, who
uilt magnificent private homes behind the 80-foot-high
açades. The MINISTRY OF JUSTICE is located at nos. 11–13;
ne of these houses was built for the financier Lhuillier, while
he other, which is sometimes open to the public, was owned
y Paul Poisson de Bourvallais, the model for Lesage's
urcaret, in 1706. The famous RITZ HOTEL ♦ *494*, at no. 15, is
ext door to the Hôtel Crozat, which held the art collection of
he same name, and the Hôtel d'Evreux, at nos. 17–19
headquarters of the Crédit Foncier bank, which owns several
uildings on the square). The small exhibition hall at no. 20,
vhich cannot be seen from the square, is an example of a folly
rom the early 20th century built in 18th-century style; it is
ow the headquarters of the Republic National Bank. The
reat names of the jewelry world ▲ *128* have turned the
quare into a glittering showcase and have spread into Rue de
a Paix. The square itself has been resurfaced since 1992:
aving stones of grey granite form a checkerboard design,
vhile steel bands mark out the pedestrian area.

PALAIS-ROYAL   (2 AB4) ▲ *202*

Richelieu's guards no longer haunt
he corridors and outbuildings seeking

**IN HONOR OF
AUSTERLITZ**
The Vendôme column
was covered with a
total of 425 bronze
plaques, made from
guns taken from the
Russian and Austrian
armies. It was erected
between 1806 and
1810 to celebrate the
victory of Napoleonic
troops in one of the
greatest battles in
history.

The painter Gustave
Courbet (1819–77)
was a man of great
conviction and a
friend of Proudhon.
In the excitement of
May 1871, he incited
the Communards to
destroy the column
and went to prison as
a result.

A STYLISH QUARTER
During the 1800's, the
Place Vendôme and
Rue de la Paix were
quietly prosperous
and bourgeois areas
until the arrival of
luxury stores like the
couture houses of
Worth and Doucet
made it extremely
chic ● *116*.

337

MOLIÈRE AT THE PALAIS-ROYAL
The Palais-Royal has a theatrical tradition going back to its very beginnings under Cardinal Richelieu, when it had two theaters. It was here that Molière (right) staged the first performance of his *School for Husbands* in 1661: he died here twelve years later.

revenge on the king's musketeers. Luxury shops, prostitution and gambling have long since disappeared, but the Palais-Royal still attracts many strollers, drawn by the peaceful atmosphere of the arcades and the gardens. The buildings now house the Council of State, the Constitutional Council and the Ministry of Culture.

THE PALAIS CARDINAL. Richelieu built his palace, designed by Jacques Lemercier, on land which he had acquired in 1624. All that remains of the original building is the balcony supported by lions' heads at no. 6, rue de Valoi,s and the Gallery of Prows, which formed the eastern wing of what is today the main court: its maritime trophies commemorate Richelieu's time as superintendant of shipping. When Richelieu died in 1642, he bequeathed the building to the monarchy. Anne of Austria moved here with the young Louis XIV but had to leave this poorly protected residence during the disturbances of the Fronde.

RESIDENCE OF THE ORLÉANS FAMILY. In 1692 the Sun King gave the Palais-Royal to his brother Philippe, and it became the property of the Orléans family, who kept it until 1848. The king's brother, and then his son the Regent built extensions and employed the greatest artists of the time, including Jules Hardouin-Mansart. The gardens ▲ *202* became fashionable, and the Regent held elegant dinners here. After the terrible fire of 1763, which destroyed the east wing of the palace and part of the main building, the palace was rebuilt and entirely redesigned. The architect Pierre Moreau-Desproux built the Cour de l'Horloge. The buildings overlooking the Rue St-Honoré were built in their present form, as was the north façade. In 1765, Contant d'Ivry built the great staircase; it has a handrail of wrought iron made by Corbin after a design by Jean-Jacques Caffieri and can be seen through the glazed entrance door of the Council of State (on the right-hand side when leaving the entrance court).

SHOPS AND PROSTITUTION. In 1780 the Duc de Chartres, later Philippe Égalité, leased out the area around the gardens for commercial purposes in order to reduce his mountain of debts. Victor Louis built sixty houses with uniform façades; there were shops

and 180 arcades on the street level. After this, Rue de Valois, Rue de Beaujolais and Rue de Montpensier were built, named after the three sons of the Duc de Chartres. The curious flocked to this "temple of pleasure", which, according to Louis-Sébastien Mercier, had "banished the very semblance of modesty". As the police were not allowed to set foot on Orléans property, the place became a center of political agitation in 1789.

GARDEN OF THE REVOLUTION. It was at the Palais-Royal that Camille Desmoulins gave his speech of July 12, 1789, after Necker's dismissal had been announced. Clubs – for reading, gambling and debating – had sprung up under the arcades since February. La Fayette and Talleyrand crossed paths at the Club des Valois, the Jacobins held their meetings at the Corazza café, and the *sans-culottes* met at the Caveau des Aveugles. The place was soon nicknamed "Palais-Égalité" (Equality Palace): it became public property after its owner was beheaded on November 6, 1793.

THÉÂTRE FRANÇAIS
This was built by the Duc de Chartres between 1786 and 1790 after plans by Victor Louis. It is now the home of the Comédie-Française. The use of iron in the balconies and dome caused a fuss. The exterior was given its present form by Prosper Chabrol in 1860. The theater was totally destroyed by fire in 1900 but was rebuilt exactly as it had been.

PROFITS FOR THE EMPIRE. Gambling was permitted at the Palais-Royal and became a source of income for the state, as the police allowed gambling businesses to operate on payment of a tax. The Orléans family returned in 1814 and built the gallery which bears its name, a double portico separating the main court from the garden, originally glazed and with shops at street level. Louis-Philippe closed the gambling houses and cafés in 1836, and the place fell into rapid decline.

TRADITIONS UPHELD. A small cannon is fired in the garden at midday every day, and the Grand Véfour, a restaurant established in 1784, still has decorations dating from the Restoration in its Beaujolais Gallery. The Constitutional Council, the Council of State and the Ministry of Culture illustrate the splendors of the First Empire, July monarchy and Third Republic. The Grand Salon in the Ministry (dating from the Empire) has been impressively restored.

SALLE DES IMPRIMÉS
This room can accommodate up to 360 readers. It is built on a basilica-style plan with a central walkway; the ceiling has nine metallic domes supported by thin columns, decorated with colored ceramic tiles.

A ROYAL SQUARE
"Feuillade, my God, I think you're fooling us/ To put the sun between four lanterns". This is how Parisians mocked the duke's square, made up of façades built according to the four classical architectural orders, with lanterns on top of four columns, which lit the square both day and night.

AROUND THE PLACE DES VICTOIRES   (2 B4) ● *63*

Place des Victoires, the second royal square in Paris, was built by the Duc de Feuillade, who wanted to display a statue of Louis XIV which he had commissioned from the sculptor Martin Desjardins after the Peace of Nimègue in 1678. Jules Hardouin-Mansart designed an almost circular area, in the Italian style, creating the illusion of an enclosed space. The arrangement of the whole was destroyed when the Rue Étienne-Marcel was built in 1883, and stories were added to the buildings. A new equestrian statue of the king, by François-Joseph Bosio, was erected in 1822.

BASILICA OF NOTRE-DAME-DES-VICTOIRES. This church is located on the pretty Place des Petits Pères: it is all that remains of the Augustine monastery whose foundation stone was laid by Louis XIII in 1629. Seven large paintings by Van Loo can be seen in the choir, as well as ex-votos and Lully's tomb.

THE VIVIENNE AND COLBERT ARCADES (2 B3) 4 and 6, rue des Petits-Champs. These arcades join with each other and Rue Vivienne, and date from 1823 and 1826. Many arcades were built at this time so that the central part of the plot could be divided into sections while at the same time offering passers-by a place to stroll away from the dangers of traffic (sidewalks had not yet been introduced). The arcades were restored in 1985, revealing the richness of their ornamentation which features the symbols of trade.

THE BANQUE DE FRANCE AND ITS SURROUNDINGS   (2 B4)

The Banque de France was founded in 1800. Eight years later, it moved into one of the city's most beautiful aristocratic

residences ● *66*, the Hôtel La Vrillière, built by François Mansart in 1640. From here it gradually extended its domain along the Rue Croix-des-Petits-Champs. Only the famous GALERIE DORÉE survives of the original building. It is 130 feet long and 26 feet high, lit by six windows, and with a ceiling painted by François Perrier depicting the four elements. For the Comte de Toulouse, Louis XIV's second legitimate son, and for Mme de Montespan, who acquired the house in 1713, François-Antoine Vassé produced carvings in gilded wood showing marine and hunting scenes: these gave the gallery its golden appearance. The striking GALERIE VÉRO-DODAT at no. 2, rue du Bouloi is similar in style to the Galerie Vivienne (below). It was built in 1826 by the butchers Véro and Dodat. Aubert, who edited the periodicals *La Caricature* and *Charivari*, exhibited drawings by Gavarni and Daumier here. Shops in the arcade include Capia, which sells antique dolls.

THE BIBLIOTHÈQUE NATIONALE (2 B3)

Rue des Petits-Champs, Rue Vivienne, Rue Colbert and Rue Richelieu form a square which borders the area occupied by the Bibliothèque Nationale. Most of the library's collections have now been relocated to the glass buildings of the Grande Bibliothèque de France at Tolbiac ▲ *232*.

ROYAL, THEN NATIONAL. Colbert broke the royal tradition of transporting libraries with each change of royal residence when he installed the Royal Library in two houses on the Rue Vivienne in 1666. Gradually the Palais Mazarin was surrounded. Under the Revolution the library became national property, and its collections expanded as books and works of art were confiscated from religious bodies and émigrés. The Bibliothèque Nationale is organized in departments – Theatrical Arts, Maps and Plans, Prints and Photographs, Music, Manuscripts, Coins and Medals ▲ *172*, Printed Books, Periodicals, and Sound and Image (the last three departments are to be transferred to Tolbiac). It has been affiliated with the Ministry of Culture since 1981. The architect Henri Labrouste modernized the building in 1854, creating the printed-book reading room and the adjoining central shop.

TREASURES OF THE BANQUE DE FRANCE
The Galerie Dorée displays copies of major works from the Vrillière collection, including a Poussin. The originals are kept at the Louvre.

⏱ One day

REMAINS OF THE TUILERIES PALACE
(9 E9)
These (top) were relocated to the courtyard of an apartment block (9, rue de Murillo) after the palace was demolished in 1882.

CHARTRES ROTONDA
The Duc de Chartres partly financed this observation post, obtaining permission to install a living room under the dome, from which he had views over all the north of Paris.

LOO GALLERY
This strange pagoda (right) on the corner of the Rue Rembrandt and Rue de Courcelles was built by the architect F. Bloch in 1926 for C.T. Loo, whose gallery helped popularize Oriental art in France.

NAUMACHIA
This Corinthian colonnade, which borders the lake in Parc Monceau, is supposed to have come from the tomb planned for Henri II at St-Denis.

The area of Paris between Monceau and Drouot underwent a period of rapid development during the 18th and especially the 19th century. During this time it was the most fashionable area of Paris, priding itself on its grand monuments, including the Élysée, the Madeleine and the Opéra, and incorporating the most elegant stretches of the great Parisian boulevards. Although it was largely eclipsed by the Left Bank after World War One, theaters, department stores and couture houses stayed on the Right Bank. The major landmarks of the financial world are also found here, from the Stock Exchange to the headquarters of the major banks. Opéra-Bourse is still one of the liveliest areas of Paris.

PARC MONCEAU   (9 DE8) ▲ 206

THE CHARTRES FOLLY. The Duc de Chartres, later Philippe Égalité, built his folly in the village of Monceau, where Joan of Arc camped in 1429. It was created by the designer and playwright L. Carrogis, known as Carmontelle, with the help of Thomas Blaikie, the landscape gardener of Bagatelle ▲ 207. This "garden of illusions" was completed in 1778 and featured an

Egyptian pyramid, a pagoda, and a Tartar tent. It was here that the world's first parachutist, J. Garnerin, threw himself from a balloon and landed safely on October 22, 1797. In 1860, when the village of Monceau became part of Paris, the garden at Chartres was cut down to half its size; a year later, it was converted into an English-style garden by Alphand ▲ 208. The park is still delightful, with its long avenues, pyramid (the only one of Carmontelle's creations to survive), Naumachia, colonnade, arcade from the Hôtel de Ville (which was burnt down by the Communards in 1871) and its many monuments dedicated to writers and artists.

THE CHARTRES ROTONDA. This building to the north of

Avenue Van-Dyck.

the park is surrounded by a peristyle of sixteen columns and has the appearance of a neoclassical temple. It is a remnant of the Farmers General Wall built by Ledoux in 1784 ● 68.

ARCHITECTURE OF THE BELLE ÉPOQUE

ENTREPRENEURS OF THE 19TH CENTURY. In 1837 the Pereire brothers were permitted to build a railway, passing under the hill of Monceau. This began a major phase of urban development, which would later inspire Zola's novel *La Curée* (*The Quarry*). The splendid residences built in Monceau after the end of the Second Empire constitute a unique architectural ensemble.

A RESIDENTIAL QUARTER. Two short avenues lead into the park, ending with gilded gates designed by Ducros. They are still lined with opulent buildings: on the Avenue Velasquez (9 EF8) are the HÔTEL CHAUCHART (no. 5) and the MUSÉE CERNUSCHI (no. 7), the former home of the banker of that name ▲ 139. The surrounding area has buildings in the official style inspired by Haussmann, as well as the RUSSIAN ORTHODOX CHURCH (9 C9) at 12, rue Daru and a number of Gothic and Renaissance pastiches. The MUSÉE JACQUEMART-ANDRÉ ◆ 479 (9 E10) at 158, bd. Haussmann resembles an Italian Renaissance palace, while the Musée Camondo ◆ 480, 484 (9 F9) at 63, rue de Monceau, recreates an 18th-century private residence.

MAISON OPÉRA-GARNIER (Rue du Docteur Lancereaux) The interiors of the houses in Monceau, like the one shown here, illustrate the displays of opulence favored by the upper classes in the Belle Époque.

343

FAUBOURG ST-HONORÉ

THE ROAD TO ROULE. The Rue du Faubourg-St-Honoré, stretching from the Place des Ternes up to the church of St-Philippe-du-Roule, still follows the winding course which goes back to the Middle Ages, when this was the road leading to the village of Roule. **THE CHURCH OF ST-PHILIPPE-DU-ROULE** (1 E1). This basilica-style church is fronted by a peristyle with four columns supporting a triangular pediment. It was built by J.F. Chalgrin between 1774 and 1784, and set a fashion in Paris for churches in the neoclassical style. The *Descent from the Cross* in the half-domed vault of the choir was painted by Chassériau in 1855; it was the artist's last work.

HÔTELS OF THE FAUBOURG. During the 18th century the aristocracy moved into the areas around the Champs-Élysées and the new Place Louis XV (later Place de la Concorde). Here, as in the Faubourg St-Germain ▲ *262*, they built magnificent residences, some of which still survive on the odd-numbered side of the road, on either side of the Élysée Palace (1 G23). At no. 33, the CERCLE DE L'UNION INTERALLIÉE occupies the former Hôtel Levieux, built sometime after 1713; a swimming pool, opening onto the garden, has been added to this elegant setting. Further on, at no. 39, is the HÔTEL CHAROST, built around 1720; it was richly decorated by Napoleon's sister Pauline Bonaparte, who built a gallery for the famous Borghese collection. This has been the home of the British Embassy since 1825, and its interior decorations have been carefully preserved. The former Hôtel Pontalba at no. 41 was built in 1836 and redesigned by Baron Edmond de Rothschild at the end of the 19th century; it has since become the residence of the United States ambassador.

SHOWCASE FOR LUXURY GOODS AND FASHION. The Faubourg-St-Honoré, like the area around Avenue Montaigne, has become a center of Parisian haute couture. Jeanne Lanvin moved into no. 22 (1 H3) in 1890; it was here that she made the collections inspired by designs created for her daughter. Paul Valéry purchased the first "green coat" (the official dress for members of the French Academy) in the men's boutique on the other side of the street. Many other fashion houses have moved in, including Pierre Cardin (1 G2, no. 59), Christian Lacroix (1 G2; no. 73) and Karl Lagerfeld (1 H3; no. 19). Important jewelers and stores selling luxury goods have also settled here. The house opposite the Élysée Palace (1 F2), which was built in 1768 for the Prince de Beauvau, is now occupied by the Ministry of the Interior (1 FG2).

ÉLYSÉE PALACE (1 F2) ● 66

HÔTEL D'ÉVREUX. This was one of the first private houses on the Faubourg, built in 1718 by the architect Armand-Claude Mollet for Hervé-Louis de La Tour d'Auverge, Comte d'Évreux. Louis XV's mistress, Mme de Pompadour, bought the house, located between the court and the gardens, in 1753. In 1764 it became the king's property, and it was sold seven years later to the immensely wealthy banker Beaujon, who gave it to Louis XVI in return for a lifetime allowance (only to die four months later).

ÉLYSÉE-BOURBON. This house was given to the Duchesse de Bourbon-Condé and renamed Élysée-Bourbon. Under the Revolution it became an amusement park before being divided up into stores and apartments. The young Alfred de Musset was one of its inhabitants and later wrote: "This was my childhood home, my place of study, my school."

ÉLYSÉE-NAPOLÉON. In 1805, Napoleon gave the house to his sister Caroline Murat, who had it decorated in opulent style. The emperor himself lived here for a time and then gave the house to Josephine as a parting gift before returning to sign his abdication here at the end of the Hundred Days. Later the Élysée fell to Louis-Philippe, and then to Louis-Napoléon Bonaparte; it was here that the latter planned his coup d'état of December 2, 1851.

THE "CHÂTEAU". The Élysée Palace has been the official residence of presidents of the Republic since 1871. Republican guards parade here for official visits and keep watch over the Council of Ministers, which takes place each Wednesday morning. The main building is still the original Hôtel d'Évreux, although wings were added to the palace under the Second Empire where neighboring houses had once stood. On the Champs-Élysées side the palace opens onto the Avenue Gabriel through the Grille du Coq (above), which was added in 1900. The magnificent interior is decorated with countless Gobelins tapestries and with 18th-century French furniture and paintings in the Murat, Doré, Argent and Pompadour rooms.

345

▲ FROM THE FAUBOURG ST-HONORÉ TO THE OPÉRA

CHURCH OF ST-AUGUSTIN
The church has a cast-iron framework covered with stone, and the vault of the nave is supported by visible arches of chased metal. The use of iron allowed the monumental dome to be raised to a height of 160 feet.

BOULEVARD MALESHERBES

When this road was built between 1800 and 1866, it put an end to the Little Poland area, which is supposed to have inspired Eugène Sue's *Mysteries of Paris*.

ST-AUGUSTIN (9 G9). This church was built by Baltard beginning in 1861, in an eclectic style which combines Roman, Gothic, Renaissance and neo-Byzantine elements on an ingenious groundplan defined by the triangular plot. It was in this church that Charles de Foucauld was converted in 1886.

CHAPELLE EXPIATOIRE (9 H10). This chapel, with its Greco-Roman appearance, was built by Fontaine in 1815; it is framed by two galleries housing what Chateaubriand called a "string of tombs". The bodies of Louis XVI and Marie-Antoinette lay here until they were transferred to St-Denis ▲ *432*, with the bodies of three thousand other victims of the Revolution. In 1815 Louis XVIII decided to build a commemorative monument which is located in the peaceful Square Louis XVI; in it is a crypt where a tomb-shaped altar is framed by two marble sculptures, *Louis XVI Supported by an Angel* (by Bosco), and *Marie-Antoinette Praying at the Feet of Religion* (by Cortot).

CHANGES OF PLAN. Contant d'Ivry was commissioned to build the church in 1764, in order to provide "a pleasant conclusion to the Rue Royale" facing the Bourbon Palace. In 1806 Napoleon altered the purpose of the building, charging Pierre Vignon to construct a "temple to the glory of the French armies". The building, surrounded on all sides by a colonnade, was to form "a monument such as there used to be at Athens, and such as does not exist in Paris". The church, once again dedicated to religious worship, was finally finished in 1842 under the July Monarchy.

A TOUR-DE-FORCE OF CLASSICAL STYLE. The church has the imposing appearance of a classical temple: it is 350 feet long, 140 feet wide, surrounded by 52 Corinthian columns each measuring 64 feet. There is no external bell or cross to show that this is a church, although the two monumental bronze doors (weighing over 3 tons) feature bas-reliefs of the Ten Commandments by Henri de Triqueti, while the niches hold 32 statues of saints. Inside, the building's religious purpose is clear, expressed in the official style typical of 1830–40. The interior is arranged around a vast nave (260 feet long), with three bays surmounted by flattened domes. Two beautiful sculptures stand out: *The Rapture of Mary Magdalene*, a marble group by Marochetti, and *The Baptism of Christ*, by François Rude. On the surface of the half-dome in the chancel, which covers 23 square feet, is a stunning fresco by Jules Ziegler, *The History and Glorification of Christianity*.

PLACE DE LA MADELEINE. Since 1834 there has been a flower market on this square, which is also the place to come for fine groceries. Two names stand out particularly: Hédiard (no. 21) ◆ *529*, which has been at this address for over 130 years, and Fauchon (nos. 24–30) ◆ *529* . The Fauchon buildings were designed by Théodore Charpentier in 1842.

MARCEL PROUST
Proust lived with his parents at 9, place de la Madeleine, whose first floor has housed the Lucas Carton restaurant ▲ *216*, ◆ *497* since 1880.

MAXIM'S (1 H3)
This restaurant opened at 3, rue Royale, in 1893 and has preserved its Art-Nouveau decoration, along with the traditional corridor arrangement, allowing diners to see and be seen.

RUE ROYALE (1 H3)
The florist Lachaume (above) has been at no. 10 since 1845, in one of the grandest stores on the street. Lalique ◆ *526* (glassware, a precursor of the modern style) is at no. 11, Christofle ◆ *526* (silver) is at no. 12 ▲ *130*, and Ladurée pâtisserie is at no. 16 ◆ *528*.

"This is where life is," exclaimed Balzac in his "physiology of the boulevards of Paris", in which he recounted their history since 1670, when Louis XIV decided to convert Charles V's city wall into a public promenade. From the mid-18th century through the 19th century, the Grand Boulevards were the height of fashion. Stylish Parisians flocked to these avenues crammed with famous cafés, theaters and places of entertainment, while strollers simply enjoyed the theatrical ambiance of the place.

REX MOVIE THEATER
Lamps in the ceiling simulating a starry sky, a classical Hispanic town illuminated with lighting displays, fountains at Christmas ... This movie theater was designed in 1932, after American

models, and has been declared a historical monument. It continues the tradition of spectacular places of entertainment along the Grand Boulevards, which include the Bains Chinois (Chinese baths), Café Frascati, Olympia music hall and Musée Grévin.

MONTAGNES RUSSES
In wintertime, the Russians built wooden scaffolds on the River Neva, with steep slopes for sleds to hurtle down. These "Russian Mountains" were introduced to France in the 19th century, thrilling the public and becoming one of the most popular attractions at amusement parks.

MUSIC HALL
All the great variety artists established themselves at the Olympia under the direction of Bruno Coquatrix. Later the Olympia came up against competition from the Zenith and the Palais de Bercy.

"I LOVE TO STROLL . . ."
"I love to stroll along the Grand Boulevards, there is so much, so much to see," sang Yves Montand, in praise of the great avenues, which reached the height of their popularity during the Belle Époque, under the Third Republic.

MAURICE CHEVALIER
Maurice Chevalier, with his famous boater, popularized the "boulevard spirit" and cheeky Parisian humor as far afield as the United States. He tackled all the genres: café-concert, variety shows with Mistinguett, and operettas, as well as movies and music hall.

349

SHOWPIECE OF THE SECOND EMPIRE
The Opéra was a temple of the bourgeoisie, at the heart of the city's commercial center; it had to act as a showcase for the splendors of the Second Empire.

WORLDLY SPLENDOR
The Opéra's interior, with its many different colored marbles, creates a magnificent display of worldly splendor. The great ceremonial staircase decorated with female figures carrying torches (made by Carrier-Belleuse), divides into two divergent flights of stairs that lead to the gallery of the Grand Foyer. This hall, designed by Garnier as a "drawing room for Paris society", opens onto an outside loggia, with the Salon de la Lune and Salon du Soleil at either end.

THE OPÉRA   (1 J2)

GARNIER'S PALACE. Napoleon III had a narrow escape from an assassination attempt led by Orsini as he left the Salle Le Peletier in 1858. This prompted him to build a new opera house in a safe location, provided with better escape routes. Charles Garnier was commissioned to fulfill the project, which proved to be fraught with pitfalls. At the outset the empress criticized his lack of style, to which he replied "But this is Napoleon III style, Madam." Then he had to lay the foundations over an underground water source (this later provided the setting for Gaston Leroux's *Phantom of the Opera*). Building work was delayed due to lack of funds, but the Opéra was finally opened in 1875 – under the Third Republic.

A "WORLDLY CATHEDRAL OF CIVILIZATION". This verdict by Théophile Gautier is a perfect description of Charles Garnier's project: Garnier wanted to build a "monument to art, to luxury, to pleasure". The building manages to avoid pomposity thanks to its exuberant design, which hovers between Baroque and neo-Renaissance styles. On the outside, the monumental façade has seven arcades beneath the seven bays of the loggia, which are separated by pairs of columns. The whole building from top to bottom is crammed with sculptures: busts of composers, classical masks and large allegorical groups, including a replica of Carpeaux's *La Danse*. There are more sculptures on the flattened dome over the auditorium, including *Apollo Raising His Lyre* by Millet, which is surrounded by winged horses.

RED AND GOLD. The red-and-gold auditorium itself is relatively small, accommodating 2,130 spectators in front of its Italian-style stage. André Malraux had the ceiling renovated in 1964; Lenepveu's decorations were painted over by Chagall, who depicted famous operas and ballets.

EMINENTLY FUNCTIONAL. The building is an impressive size, 560 feet long and 330 feet wide; it covers an area of nearly 120,000 square feet and has a grand total of 6,319 stairs in its many basements and mazes of corridors. The size of the auditorium was restricted by the fact that escape routes were a priority. The stage machinery was unique for its period, with scenery stacked up to a height of over 200 feet. For opera performances, the building has now been superseded by the Opéra-Bastille; it was renamed Palais de la Danse in 1985.

PLACE DE L'OPÉRA. This is a major crossroads, with traffic heading for the Grand Boulevards and the department stores of the Boulevard Haussmann. The Grand Hôtel, built for the Universal Exhibition of 1867, echoes Garnier's Opéra building with its 700 rooms and 70 drawing rooms, its courtyard crowned with a glass roof, and its glittering golden dining room.

CAFÉ DE LA PAIX
This café on the Place de l'Opéra, on the first floor of the Grand Hôtel, counted Maupassant and Zola among its regular customers.

DEPARTMENT STORES OF THE BOULEVARD HAUSSMANN (1 11)
The main Printemps building (no. 64) dates from 1865 and was rebuilt in its present form by Paul Sédille in 1881. The second Printemps building was rebuilt in 1921 after a fire: on its seventh story is a tea room under the great glass dome designed by Binet in 1911. The nearby Galeries Lafayette (no. 40) has also kept its façade from 1910 and its stained-glass dome, supported by ten metal pillars ● 77.

CRÉDIT LYONNAIS
This is the largest privately built construction in Paris. Behind its Louis XIV-style façade is a double staircase, modeled on the one at Chambord.

BOULEVARD DES ITALIENS (2 AB2)

BOULEVARD OF ELEGANCE. "Everyone comes here, the whole world is here, within a hundred steps", said Musset of the most famous of the Grand Boulevards, renowned for its Café Hardi, Tortoni ice cream parlor, Chinese baths, Hanover pavilion (reassembled in the Parc de Sceaux in 1935) and Passage des Princes shopping arcade, with its glass roof and metal arches, opened in 1860 and recently renovated. The mood of the boulevard changed at the end of the 19th century, when the large banks moved into the quarter to be close to the Stock Exchange. The BNP (Banque Nationale de Paris) still occupies the Art Deco building (no. 16) built in 1933 on the site of the former Café Riche, where the Goncourt brothers, Zola, Daudet and Turgenev held their "dinners for unpopular authors". The bank has an annex in the Maison Dorée (no. 29), which was built in 1838 and takes its name from its gilded balconies. The headquarters of the Crédit Lyonnais (nos. 17–23), dating from 1878, is another perfect illustration of the "irresistible golden trap blazing in the sun", depicted by Zola in his novel *L'Argent* in 1891.

BOULEVARD MONTMARTRE (2 BC2)

TEEMING CROWDS OF PARIS. Along the lively Boulevard Montmartre streamed "the teeming crowds of Paris", in the words of Jules Vallès. Buildings which survive from its golden days include the Café Madrid (no. 6) and the THÉÂTRE DES VARIÉTÉS (no. 7) ◆ *510*, built in 1806 in an elegant classical style. The theater, originally the home of vaudeville, later staged Offenbach's operettas and the witty boulevard plays of Tristan Bernard and Sacha Guitry. On the other side of the street is the MUSÉE GRÉVIN ▲ *141*, ◆ *478*, *515* (no. 10), which opened in 1882. Its exhibits include wax models of French historical figures, the giant kaleidoscope from the palace of illusions, and the fin-de-siècle style Théâtre Joli, which is decorated with Bourdelle's bas-relief *The Clouds*.

COMÉDIE-ITALIENNE
The Salle Favart, or Opéra-Comique ◆ *514*, was built in 1781 for the Italian actors after whom the nearby boulevard is named. It was rebuilt in 1898. The most popular comic operas were performed here, as were Offenbach's operettas.

"TEMPLE OF MONEY"
The main façade of the Bourse (Stock Exchange) is built in a neoclassical style which gave rise to Hugo's ironic description. It is decorated with statues of *Commerce* and *Industry* by Dumont and Duret.

SHOPPING ARCADES. These were very fashionable at the beginning of the 19th century, until the advent of electricity and sidewalks

under the
Second Empire.
Around twenty of them can still be seen in Paris, and two
perfect examples give onto Boulevard Montmartre. The
Passage des Panoramas (no. 11) opened in 1799; it was named
after the landscapes painted by the American artist Fulton,
which gave 19th-century visitors the illusion of being in
London or Athens. The arcade still houses the engraver
Stern, founded in 1840, and the Arbre à Cannelle tea rooms,

with their Napoleon III décor. The
PASSAGE JOUFFROY opens on the other
side of the street (no. 12); this arcade has
secondhandbook stalls and toy stores.

THE BOURSE   (2 B2)

This edifice by the architect Brongniart
was begun in 1808 and completed in 1826;
its two wings were added between 1902 and 1907. The original
rectangular building is bordered by a peristyle of Corinthian
columns, and the central hall has an 80-foot-high glass dome
surrounded by arcaded galleries. The old stockbrokers'
enclosure has been superseded by computer screens installed
in 1987, but the trading floor is as noisy as ever.

"HUMAN AQUARIA"
This is how Aragon
described the
Parisian arcades.
Although they no
longer serve as a
refuge from bad
weather (their
prime function
before the advent of
sidewalks), many of
them still have an
exotic air of the
Oriental
bazaar.

🕐 One day

The Île de la Cité is the historical heart of Paris: from the time of the Late Empire (3rd to 5th centuries AD), this strip of land was the focus of royal, judiciary and religious power. The Gallo-Roman palace which stood on the western part of the island was later taken over by the Merovingians and then rebuilt by Philippe le Bel in the 14th century. Today's Palais de Justice stands on the same site. The Parlement and other institutions were based here, including the Chambre des Comptes (Chamber of Revenue), the Chambre du Trésor (Treasury) and so on. The eastern part of the island was devoted to religion from the Gallo-Roman era onward. A cathedral already stood on the site of today's Notre-Dame in 362. Gradually an entire ecclesiastical center grew up around this building: a baptistry, bishop's palace, the Hôtel-Dieu (general hospital), and

PONT-NEUF
This was the first bridge across the Seine without houses on it. The humpback bridge with semicircular arches was designed by the architects Pierre Désilles and Androuet du Cerceau and opened in 1607. The statue of Henri IV which dates from 1818, replaced a statue by Franqueville which was erected in 1635 and destroyed in 1792.

46 houses occupied by canons. As these institutions were built it became necessary to raise the level of the island, which has grown in size from 20 to 43 acres over ten centuries. The island was completely transformed under Haussmann, who razed the medieval city to create an administrative center. This center is now the base of two institutions devoted to maintaining public order – the judiciary and the police. In the 19th

Vedettes du Pont Neuf

century, the island's population was regarded as the most destitute in Paris: it fell from 15,000 inhabitants in 1858 to 5,000 in 1868.

A HIVE OF ACTIVITY
The Pont-Neuf was a hive of activity, with shops and acrobats, until the 19th century.

PLACE DAUPHINE AND THE PONT-NEUF ★ (2 C7)

In 1584, Henri III decided to sell off the end of the Île de la Cité in order to raise funds to build the Pont-Neuf: an area of sand and water made up of three small islands which had to be filled in and joined together, significantly increasing the island's surface area. In 1601, Henri IV decided to build a three-sided square here (the base of the triangle, on the Rue de Harlay, was demolished in 1874). The land was sold in 12 lots, on which 32 identical houses were built in red brick with stone facing. The houses had an arcade on the first floor, and three stories above this; the façades on the Seine side were identical. Only the two symmetrical buildings at the end of the square are still in their original form. The square itself is charming – the poet Malherbe, in the 17th century, described it as "the most beautiful and the most practical in Paris".

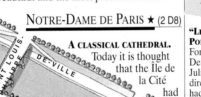

"LES AMANTS DU PONT-NEUF" (1991) For this film, starring Denis Lavant and Juliette Binoche, the director Leos Carax had to build a reproduction of

NOTRE-DAME DE PARIS ★ (2 D8)

A CLASSICAL CATHEDRAL. Today it is thought that the Île de la Cité had

a cathedral as far back as the 4th century, at a time when Christianity was spreading, thanks to the policies of Emperor Constantine. A group of episcopal buildings was established, consisting of the bishop's house, the baptistry (destroyed in 1748) and an exceptionally long basilica (230 to 260 feet long). The beginnings of what was to become the Hôtel-Dieu (general hospital) probably go back to this period. This episcopal

the Pont-Neuf in Bouches-du-Rhône department.

355

RADICAL CHANGES
In the 19th century
the Île de la Cité
underwent major
alterations, mainly as
a result of
Haussmann's
schemes: an
enormous

center grew during the course of the 8th and 9th centuries
with the addition of a canonical chapter; it became, in effect,
a sort of urban monastery, with independent houses and
gardens. Gradually the chapter expanded: a choir was built
between the shrine and the nave and later, to the west, two
halls were added on either side of a tower-
porchway. In 1148, Archdeacon Étienne de
Garlande, a leading figure within the chapter,
built a portal with carved
columns dedicated to the Virgin.
When the old basilica was
demolished around 1160, only
Étienne de Garlande's
portal survived, becoming
part of the later western
façade (Ste-Anne Portal).
At this time Louis VII's
kingdom was flourishing;
the old basilica seemed
very out-of-date, and
Bishop Maurice de Sully
decided it should be
rebuilt.

square was cleared in
front of Notre-Dame;
the Tribunal de
Commerce was built,
as was the barracks
which later became
the police
headquarters; and a
new general hospital
was built to the north
of the island. The
archbishop's palace
was demolished in
1831 and partially
replaced by the
sacristy, which was
restored by Viollet-le-
Duc.

THE MAJOR PHASES OF CONSTRUCTION. Sully's ambitious
project was conceived on a huge scale: covering a surface area
of nearly 60,000 square feet, it entailed significant alterations
to the surrounding urban fabric. Everything was demolished
except the canons' enclosure and the baptistry, and the
western façade was moved toward the east to make way for a
square in front of the cathedral. The anonymous architect
evidently had considerable funds at his disposal, which meant
that building could begin immediately, starting with the
chevet. The interior was planned on four levels, with a line of
rose windows above the galleries. The bays were opened to
the outside through small windows, and
there were no flying buttresses.
A new architect appeared on
the scene in the 1170's, but
he made few modifications

POINT OF DEPARTURE
A bronze star outside
Notre-Dame marks
the center not only of
Paris but of the whole
country: this is the
point from which
road distances from
Paris to the towns of
France have been
measured since the
Ancien Régime.

to the design, except for technical innovations which allowed the bays to be joined to the nave by three openings rather than two. A third architect tackled the western body of the building and the square in front of the church; at this stage the nave was not yet complete. Around 1210–20, a fourth architect joined the façade to the nave: he altered the original plan significantly, abandoning the use of columns in favor of a more complex arrangement, similar to devices used for the cathedral at Chartres. During the 1220's and 1230's, the cathedral underwent further modification, mostly to allow more light into the building, in the spirit of High Gothic style. As a result, the windows of the nave became larger and the rose windows disappeared; the roof over the bays was lowered and replaced by terraces; and large flying buttresses were added, serving also as drainage pipes for rainwater. A spire was built over the crossing of the transept at this time. Around 1250 the architect Jean de Chelles was commissioned to build new façades at the far ends of the transept and to complete the northern end. Pierre de Montreuil continued work on the southern end. From this time up to 1325, side chapels were built between the buttresses, enclosed by a continuous wall, in the nave, the choir and the chevet. The cathedral was badly damaged during the Revolution and was restored after 1845 by Jean-Baptiste Lassus and Eugène Viollet-le-Duc. The latter continued the work alone from 1857 to 1864, when it was completed.

TYMPANUM OF THE LAST JUDGMENT
The central portal of Notre-Dame depicts the Last Judgment, drawing not only on the Apocalypse but also on the Gospel of Saint Matthew. Its iconography is very simple and easily understood by those who cannot read: Good and Bad are clearly contrasted, without any superfluous ornamentation. The central section shows the weighing of souls, presided over by Saint Michael: good souls are directed to the right, toward Abraham, while the bad, on the left, are thrown headfirst into Hell.

▲ NOTRE-DAME

Notre-Dame de Paris, at the geographic and historical heart of the capital, illustrates the splendors and variations of Gothic architecture between the mid-12th and the early 14th centuries. The simplicity and harmony of this impressive building derive from a skillful combination of horizontals and verticals. After a century of gradual deterioration, the Romantic 19th century brought the building back to life, restoring most of its magnificent sculptures.

LOUIS XIII'S VOW

(1708–26)
Louis XIV decided to carry out his father's vow and ordered the architect Robert de Cotte to renovate the choir of Notre-Dame. The high altar was created by Antoine Vassé, the *Virgin of Compassion* sculpture by Nicolas Coustou. The kneeling statues of Louis XIV and Louis XIII (right) were carved, respectively, by Antoine Coysevoix and Guillaume Coustou. The six angels of gilded bronze by the pilasters carry the instruments of the Passion.

FLYING BUTTRESSES

The chevet was first modified around 1220–30, when the flying buttresses were built. These incorporated a channel which was intended to solve the problem of rainwater runoff, created when the roofs were replaced by terraces.

SIDE CHAPELS
Between 1250 and 1325, chapels were buil between the buttresses, encased by a continu wall, in the nave, the choir and the cheve (by Pierre de Chelles and Jean Ravy).

GRAND AUSTERITY

The building consists of a nave with five double bays flanked by double aisles, a very short transept, and a round apse with seven sections. The square vaults – six over the central nave and four over the side aisles – would normally have resulted in alternating strong and weak pillars, but the architect used a single type of pillar throughout to produce an effect of structural unity.
At the crossing of the transept is an elevation with four levels: this is roughly how the earlier cathedral looked, as re-created by Viollet-le-Duc.

11

NGS OF JUDAH
e Gallery of Kings, a
rizontal version of
e tree of Jesse,
played twenty-eight
tues of Christ's
cestors up until 1793.
ey were restored in

STE-ANNE PORTAL
▲ 356. An additional
lintel and a lower row of
voussoirs were needed
when the old portal was
reassembled on the
Gothic façade. The
portal derives its effect
from its formal
structure and stylistic
unity.

th century.
venty-one heads,
lled down and
utilated during
e Revolution,
re found in
e basement
a Parisian
nk in
77.

**PORTAL OF
THE VIRGIN**
This was
created at the
height of Gothic
sculpture in the 13th
century, when the
monumental tradition
was tempered by a trend
toward greater humanity.
It is striking for its balanced
composition, in which
archivolts highlight the
interplay of diagonals and
horizontals.

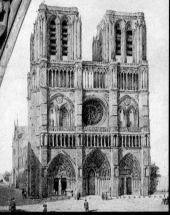

PORTAL OF THE LAST JUDGMENT ▲ 357
The humanization of iconograpy led to the
introduction of new subjects at the beginning of
the 13th century. The Gallery of Kings, Saint
Anne and the Last Judgment are all new motifs.

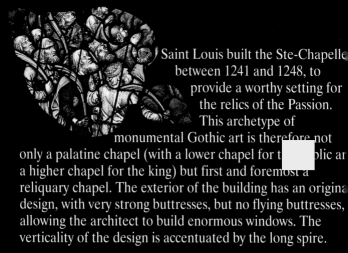

Saint Louis built the Ste-Chapelle between 1241 and 1248, to provide a worthy setting for the relics of the Passion. This archetype of monumental Gothic art is therefore not only a palatine chapel (with a lower chapel for the public and a higher chapel for the king) but first and foremost a reliquary chapel. The exterior of the building has an original design, with very strong buttresses, but no flying buttresses, allowing the architect to build enormous windows. The verticality of the design is accentuated by the long spire.

A ROYAL MANIFESTO
The Ste-Chapelle was traditionally attributed to Pierre de Montreuil, but it has also been ascribed to Thomas de Cormont and to Robert de Luzarches. It was set into the structure of the Palais de la Cité and had a political as well as a religious function. Here the king refers to his double

function, as temporal and spiritual leader of the people, whose mission is to lead them to eternal life.

A 19TH-CENTURY MONUMENT
The Ste-Chapelle was badly damaged during the Revolution and restored in the 19th century by Félix Duban, Jean-Baptiste Lassus, Émile Boeswilldald and Viollet-le-Duc. They replaced the roof, the external staircase, the spire (for the fourth time in 1853), the interior decorations and some of the stained-glass windows.

A UNIQUE NAVE
The Ste-Chapelle building consists of a single unit with four bays, ending in a chevet with seven sections.

LOWER CHAPEL
The Lower Chapel has something of the air of a crypt. Its two rows of columns strengthen the building structurally, as well as forming two side aisles which join together in the apse.

UPPER CHAPEL
The Upper Chapel striking for its simplicity and unity. The traditional Gothic three-level elevation has given way to an elevation on two levels, or even on a single level, as the dominant window section seems to encroach upon the base section.

VERTICALITY
Powerful protruding buttresses, very close together at the apse end, allowed the architect to do without flying buttresses.

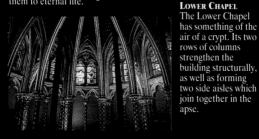

Restoration work, directed by Eugène Viollet-le-Duc and Jean-Baptiste Lassus, was completed in 1864. It covered both the external structure and the interior decorations. On the exterior, the carvings on the western façade and the southern transept were restored, as were the spire, the gables and the pinnacles. On the interior, restoration work mainly affected the elevation of the bays and the structure of the windows.

SE WINDOW OF THE NORTHERN TRANSEPT
well-preserved window is dedicated to Old
ament themes: the Virgin at the center is
ounded by eighty figures, including grand
s, kings, judges and prophets. The window
2 feet in diameter, and its load is spread
s the main spokes. Iron struts are used to
inforce the stone framework.

**QUASIMODO
AT NOTRE-DAME**
Victor Hugo's novel
Notre-Dame de Paris was
published in 1831; it drew the
public's attention to the
building's need of restoration.

STRYGIA
The Galerie des Chimères,
which runs between the two
towers, displays a number of
gargoyles, monstrous
creatures which reveal Viollet-
le-Duc's inventive
imagination.

THE GREAT ORGAN
The organ's 113 stops
and 8,000 pipes
dominate the nave
underneath the western
rose window. Some
pipes still survive from
the medieval era, but
most date from 1730
(Thierry), 1783
(Cliquot) and 1863
(Cavaillé-Coll).

uth tower
rth tower
e with five bays
ng buttresses
e chapels
rthern rose
dow
or of cloisters
nsept
evation with
ur levels
evation wi
ee levels
und apse with
en sections
oir
uble side
le

Reconstruction of the
bays of the nave before
the works of 1220–30.

**NORTHERN
END WALL OF THE CHOIR**
The end walls to the north and
south of the choir (14th century) are
well preserved, with depictions of
The Life of Christ and *Apparitions of Christ
after the Resurrection*, respectively.

INGENIOUS TECHNICAL DEVICES

The architect used extra metal supports to connect the bays as well as iron struts running across the transoms and right through the supports. Care was taken to hide these thick iron bars by making them coincide with the framework of the stained-glass windows where possible.

SCHOLARLY ICONOGRAPHY

The iconography of the Ste-Chapelle presents a theological reflection on Christ's Passion, drawing on the ideas of the Mendicants and Franciscans, Saint Louis' favorite orders.

1. Upper Chapel
2. Lower Chapel

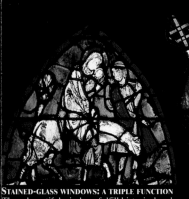

STAINED-GLASS WINDOWS: A TRIPLE FUNCTION

These beautiful windows fulfill historical and decorative functions and they also have an architectural role in creating an enclosed space.

DECORATIVE PANELS

These form a background mosaic with a variety of motifs, some taken from the heraldic vocabulary. Each lancet – like that of the Passion (left) – is framed by a narrow border, which also shows a heraldic influence.

COLORS

Variations from one window to another are apparent mainly in the background mosaics, where the same decorative motifs are repeated. These motifs form a colored screen. In the historical panels, by contrast, the colors are distributed in an irregular fashion on a blue background. The dominant colors are blue and red, although other tones are prominent in places, yellow in particular.

HISTORICAL PANELS

The series covers the eight large windows with four lancets on the nave – four to the north and four to the south – and the seven windows with two lancets on the apse, ending with the great rose window on the western façade, which was completed in the final decade of the 15th century. The sequence as a whole presents the entire history of the Hebrew people from the Creation to their arrival in Israel. It ends with Louis IX receiving the relics of the Passion. This historical sequence is accompanied by a prophetic cycle on the life of Christ framed by the lives of Saint John the Baptist and Saint John the Evangelist. These saints fit into the sequence through their roles as prophets: the Baptist announces the Lamb of God and the Evangelist the vision of the Apocalypse.

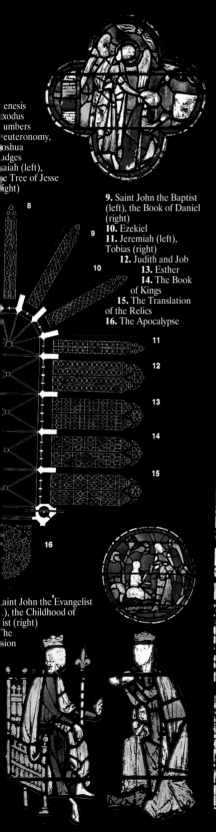

enesis
xodus
umbers
euteronomy,
oshua
udges
aiah (left),
e Tree of Jesse
ight)

9. Saint John the Baptist
(left), the Book of Daniel
(right)
10. Ezekiel
11. Jeremiah (left),
Tobias (right)
　　12. Judith and Job
　　　13. Esther
　　　14. The Book
　　of Kings
　　15. The Translation
of the Relics
16. The Apocalypse

aint John the Evangelist
), the Childhood of
ist (right)
he
sion

MARCHÉ AUX FLEURS
The flower market was founded in 1809, and a market for birds was added later. It is held in what was the main Jewish quarter of Paris

PALAIS DE JUSTICE

(2 C7)

This diverse group of buildings, which houses the law courts, covers nearly all the western section of the island. This was probably the site of a citadel in the Gallo-Roman period, which was later used by the first Merovingian kings. The fortress was at its height under the Capetians. Philippe-Auguste was born here in 1165 and later restored the palace. His grandson Louis IX (1214–70), later Saint Louis, stayed here often. In 1242 he decided to build the Ste-Chapelle ▲ *362*, joining it to the palace by a gallery to house the relics of Christ's Passion, which he had just acquired. Finally, Philippe le Bel extended the buildings between 1296 and 1313 to accommodate his financial, administrative and judicial services. However, civil unrest during the 14th century forced the monarchs to move to the Hôtel St-Paul, leaving the palace on the island to the Parliament of Paris, a supreme judicial court which also functioned as a prison. After repeated fires and destruction during the Revolution, most of the palace had to be rebuilt. The Ste-Chapelle, the towers and the lower sections of the north façade are the only parts of the medieval palace standing today. During the last century, magnificent interior decorations were added in the Salle des Pas Perdus, the Vestibule de Harlay and the Cour de Cassation: although these are quite impressive, visitors who are pushed for time might restrict themselves to visiting the Conciergerie.

THE CONCIERGERIE PRISON. The building is named after the Concierge, the king's steward, who had many powers and highly lucrative privileges. It incorporated both the Concierge's residence and a prison which was used by the Concierge, and later by the Parliament. The Parliament was replaced by the Criminal Tribunal after the fall of the monarchy and by the Revolutionary Tribunal in 1793. During those two years over 2,700 people who had been condemned to death spent their last hours here. Among the victims was Queen

in the 12th century. The Rue de la Cité was known as the Rue de la Juiverie (Street of the Jewish Quarter) until 1834.

MAIGRET ON THE QUAI DES ORFÈVRES
The headquarters of the police force's criminal investigation department is on the Quai des Orfèvres. The building plays a key role in the crime novel tradition, including the novels of Georges Simenon (1903–89). Police Superintendent Maigret is Simenon's most famous hero; he was portrayed on French television by Jean Richard (above).

Marie-Antoinette, who was guillotined on October 16, 1793. Famous prisoners held here during the 19th century include the royalist Cadoudal, Maréchal Ney, Prince Napoleon and the anarchists Orsini and Ravachol. In 1914 part of the prison was converted into a historical monument open to the public. The latest alterations were made for the bicentenary of the Revolution in 1989: there are reconstructions of the room where the clerk kept the registers and of the *toilette des condamnés*, where prisoners went before being led to the Cour de Mai. Upstairs the dungeons can be viewed, including the cell kept for high-ranking prisoners. Marie-Antoinette's cell has been arranged as it was under the Restoration: a chapel of atonement is located in the part where the queen lived, and paintings recount the story of her captivity.

THE MEDIEVAL PALACE (entrance on the Quai de l'Horloge). The first room, the Salle des Gardes (guards' room), was built under the reign of Philippe le Bel (beginning of the 14th century): three huge pillars divide it into two naves with four bays and rib vaulting, while two staircases lead to the César and Argent towers, which date from the same period. After this is the magnificent Salle des Gens d'Armes (officers' room),

reserved for officers on duty, which was built around 1300. This large Gothic construction has often been compared to the rooms in the Palais des Papes at Avignon. The rectangular space is divided into four naves by three rows of sturdy pillars. The room was heated by four large fireplaces. Later modifications are easily spotted: the raised passageway known as the Rue de Paris, which was formerly divided into tiny dungeons without light or air; the extra pillars added to the middle row to reinforce the upper room, rebuilt by Salomon de Brosse in 1622; and the spiral staircase in openwork stone renovated in the 19th century. Finally, there are the basement kitchens at river level, built around 1353.

CHAPELLE DES GIRONDINS
The chapel in the Conciergerie bears this name in memory of the twenty-one Girondin deputies who were condemned to death by the Revolutionary Tribunal. They spent their last night here before being executed on October 30, 1793. *The Call for the Last Victims of the Terror*, by Charles Louis Müller (1815–92), depicts this tragic episode in the history of the Conciergerie (above); Boilly and Delaroche also painted this subject.

367

ÎLE ST-LOUIS ★

(2 EF8 and 9)

A PLANNED ISLAND
The present layout of the Île St-Louis was the work of engineer Christophe Marie. He was commissioned by Louis XIII to join the island to the banks of

the Seine by two stone bridges, to border it with stone quaysides, and to build its roads and houses. This urban-development plan was carried out between 1614 and 1660. The Pont Marie was completed in 1630, Pont de la Tournelle fifteen years later.

People come to the Île St-Louis in large numbers to stroll through its streets and enjoy the island's astonishingly tranquil atmosphere. Two centuries ago, Louis-Sébastien Mercier observed that the island "seems to have escaped the great corruption of the city, which has not yet reached here". Little has changed in the island's appearance since this time. Its quaysides are lined with beautiful houses offering unique views of the Seine and the city.

A RECENT CREATION. Buildings began to appear on the Île St-Louis in the 17th century: it was given its present name in 1726. Before this, the island, which was known as the Île Notre-Dame, was nothing but a pasture subject to regular flooding. Washerwomen came here to dry their linen; since medieval times, this has been the place where duels were held: the sword, supposedly inspired by God, was used to settle legal disputes.

AN ATTRACTIVE PROJECT. Christophe Marie, an engineer and official Parisian bridge builder, began the development of the island in April 1614. He directed the project in collaboration with Lugles Poulletier, a military superintendent and François Le Regrattier, treasurer of the Cent-Suisses (a military company). The project's finances were very volatile. The Pont Marie bears the name of its creator who died in poverty in 1653, and carries an inscription proclaiming that he "deserves the sympathy of all visitors to Old Paris and the gratitude of

the island's inhabitants". Two streets bear the names of his associates. The quays, around 32 feet high, form a parallelogram measuring 2,000 by 560 feet; they were completed in 1650. The new quarter was a huge success, and its airy houses and well-arranged streets represented an entirely different kind of urban design. The main part of the houses were built to overlook the quays rather than the courtyards (as formerly), making the most of the fresh air and river views. Another innovation was the use of freestone on its own rather than as a facing for brickwork.

RUE ST-LOUIS-EN-L'ÎLE

This central street was built between 1614 and 1646. Visitors approaching the island by the Pont St-Louis (rebuilt in 1970 and reserved for pedestrians) will find the inn Aux Anysetiers du Roy at no. 61, on the corner of Rue Le Regrattier. The inn still has grilles and a statuette from the Petit Bacchus, a 17th-century tavern.

HÔTEL DE CHENIZOT. The house at no. 51 is named after the tax collector who acquired it in 1719, one hundred years after it had been built. This owner was also responsible for the rococo-style decoration of the façades overlooking the courtyard and the street. A staircase and handrail have been preserved at the far end of the courtyard on the right-hand side. The structure of a *jeu de paume* (tennis court) built in 1634 survives at no. 54; it can be seen from inside the house which currently stands on this site.

CHURCH OF ST-LOUIS-EN-L'ÎLE. The church, dedicated to Saint Louis, was started in 1664 and completed in 1726. The steeple clock (1741) hangs at a right angle to the road. The church has a number of notable works of art, including *The Pilgrims of Emmaüs* by Coypel (1746), an *Annunciation* after Fra Angelico, a *Saint François de Sales* by Noël Hallé (18th century) and *Saint John and Saint Peter Healing a Lame Man* by Carle Van Loo (1742).

A MAIN THOROUGHFARE
Rue St-Louis-en-l'Île is peaceful during the week and more lively during the weekend. The shops are its main attraction, including the bookshop Ulysse at no. 26, specializing in travel books, and the DAAVP bookshop, at no. 25, which stocks a wide range of books on Paris. The ice-cream maker Berthillon
◆ *528* is at no. 31.

CHURCH INTERIOR
The church was built following Le Vau's design. It is a perfect example of French 17th-century Baroque style, showing a new religious sensitivity. The interior is very bright, an impression heightened by the use of white stone and shining gold highlights.

CABINET DES MUSES
Eustache Le Sueur (1616–55) was one of the famous artists who contributed to the decoration of the Hôtel Lambert. The artist produced a group of five paintings depicting the muses (above), after which one of the rooms is named.

HÔTEL LAMBERT. This palace was owned by the family of Prince Adam Czartoryski between 1842 and 1976, and was the artistic center of the Polish bohemian community. It was built by Le Vau at no. 2, rue St-Louis for Jean-Baptiste Lambert de Thorigny, a financier and advisor to the king. The magnificent interior decorations were produced for Nicolas Lambert, Jean-Baptiste's brother and president of the Chambre des Comptes (Chamber of Accounts): among the artists who contributed were François Perrier, Charles Le Brun, Giovanni Romanelli, Bertholet Flémalle and Pierre Patel. The decorations were purchased by the king in 1776 and dismantled. Some of the painted panels are now in the Louvre, but the majority of the paintings and sculptures are in their original places. Plates produced by the engraver Bernard Picart show us what the Galerie d'Hercule, the Salon de l'Amour and the Cabinet des Muses were like. The house is not open to the public.

QUAI D'ANJOU

This quay invites nostalgia. The description by Funck-Brentano conjures up an image of what it was like three-quarters of a century ago: "This stretch of the Seine is not used by shipping: singing can be heard in the washing places and the bridge of moored barges makes a platform for the life of the bargemen". Louis Le Vau had his house built at no. 5, next to the Hôtel Lambert, to which it is joined by a long balcony. The small Hôtel Marigny has beautiful wrought-iron railings.

HÔTEL DE LAUZUN. This house with its magnificent interior decorations was completed by Le Vau in 1657 for Charles Gruyn, son of a prosperous innkeeper. It was bought in 1682 by the Comte de Lauzun, a favorite of Louis XIV and lover of La Grande Mademoiselle (the king's cousin). After this, the house had various owners: in 1779 it was acquired by the Marquis de Pimodan, who gave it his own name. In 1842 the Hôtel de Pimodan was bought by Jérôme Pichon, a bibliophile and art lover, who restored its former name. The house was a meeting place for the "Haschischins club", whose members included Baudelaire, Balzac and Théophile Gautier. Gautier wrote a story about these drug-experimentation

HÔTEL DE LAUZUN
The façade of the Hôtel de Lauzun displays a magnificent wrought-iron balcony. The gutters decorated with dolphins date from 1910.

meetings. The house was beautifully restored by Louis Pichon from 1906 to 1910 and was purchased by the City of Paris in 1928. Unfortunately, this building is no longer open to the public.

QUAI DE BOURBON (2 E8)

Le Franc-Pinot, at no. 1, with its grille decorated with vines and grapes, is a former bargemen's tavern. The Hôtel Le Charron, at no. 15, was built by Sébastien Bruant between 1637 and 1640 for Jean Charron, a military inspector in Picardy. In the corner of the courtyard is a projecting room supported by a squinch, an appendage which was common in the early 17th century. The Maison du Centaure, at no. 45, was built after 1658 by François Le Vau, brother of Louis; it is named after the two bas-reliefs depicting Hercules' victory over Nessus.

QUAI D'ORLÉANS
AND QUAI DE BÉTHUNE (2 EF9)

The BIBLIOTHÈQUE POLONAISE (Polish Library) stands at 6, quai d'Orléans; it was founded by refugees in 1838. On the same site is a museum ♦ 476 dedicated to the poet Adam Mickiewicz (1798–1855). In the 18th century the Quai de Béthune was known as the Quai des Balcons: Le Vau had decreed that all its façades should have balconies. The Hôtel de Richelieu, at no. 18, was built, probably by Le Vau, on a plot which once belonged to Madame de Sévigné's grandfather. The tour of the island ends between the two arches of the Pont Sully (1874–7), at the first houses on the Boulevard Henri-IV. At no. 1 is a store called La Maison de la Mouche (House of the Fly), which sells fishing equipment.

A BRILLIANT SET
Princess Anna Czartoryski, who owned the Hôtel Lambert, invited brilliant people to her lavish receptions (above). Frédéric Chopin and the poet Adam Mickiewicz were regular guests.

HÔTEL HESSELIN
This house by Louis Le Vau (below) was one of the finest on the Quai de Béthune. It was demolished in 1935, and only the carriage entrance, carved by Étienne Le Hongre still stands, at no. 24.

⏱ One day

A SQUALID AREA
"The whole area is miserable, but it exudes a delightful stench of old roguery" wrote Huysmans in 1902. Beaubourg takes its name from a village which became part of Paris when Philippe-Auguste built his city wall. During the last century it became thoroughly squalid, and it was razed in 1939, becoming a wasteland before being incorporated into the development project around Les Halles (the former market).

2. SAMARITAINE DEPARTMENT STORE
3. CHURCH OF ST-EUSTACHE
4. FORUM DES HALLES
5. TOUR ST-JACQUES
6. HÔTEL DE VILLE
7. CHURCH OF ST-NICOLAS-DES-CHAMPS
8. CONSERVATOIRE DES ARTS ET MÉTIERS
9. GEORGES-POMPIDOU CENTER
10. FONTAINE DES INNOCENTS
11. TOUR DE JEAN-SANS-PEUR
12. CHURCH OF ST-MERRI
13. CHURCH OF NOTRE-DAME-DE-BONNE-NOUVELLE
1. BOURSE DU COMMERCE

From the Gallo-Roman era, the *cardo*, or main south–north road of Lutetia, crossed this section of the Right Bank, running along the course of today's Rue St-Martin. However, it was not until the 11th century that the area became built up. Louis VI constructed his Châtelet fortress here, and the area became a center of commercial activity and the focus of municipal administration. The area is not resting on its laurels, however: following

RUE N-D-DE-NAZARETH

RUE DU VERT-BOIS

RUE VAUCANSON

RUE MONTGOLFIER

8

7

major redevelopment projects it now boasts the largest pedestrian mall in Europe. With the Forum des Halles and the Pompidou Center, it is (sometimes exaggeratedly) considered the heart of contemporary Paris.

HÔTEL DE VILLE (2 E7)

PLACE DE GRÈVE. This square stood on the site of today's Place de l'Hôtel de Ville, as it was renamed in 1830. The headquarters of the Parisian municipal administration moved to this square in 1357 and has remained here ever since. In the 12th century Saint Louis entrusted the administration of Paris to the *hanse,* or guild of water merchants, who controlled shipping on the Seine. After this Paris had elected representatives, based close to Châtelet: four aldermen with the merchants' provost at their head. In 1357 the provost, Étienne Marcel, transferred the headquarters of the town council to the Maison aux Piliers, on the site of today's town hall. Crowds used to gather on the Place de Grève, standing around the huge braziers of St-Jean (whose saint's day, June 24, is celebrated with huge bonfires) to see the king. But this was also the setting for the somber spectacle of executions, from the 12th century up to 1830: criminals of the middle and lower classes were hanged, noblemen were decapitated, and heretics and sorcerers were burned alive, while criminals guilty of *lèse-majesté* were tortured. In 1610, Ravaillac was quartered by four horses after being scalded and mutilated. During the last century, laborers without work used to gather on the square, which gave rise to the expression "*être en grève*" (to be on strike).

AN OPEN, WELCOMING PLACE
The Pompidou Center is one of the largest cultural centers in the world, attracting crowds of visitors to the quarter since its opening in 1977. Street artists and acrobats entertain a good-natured audience on its piazza. Today it is a focal point of the city's life, especially in the summer.

PORT DE GRÈVE
In medieval times, the Place de Grève formed a gently sloping bank descending toward the Seine where ships could land. Produce for the nearby market was unloaded at the port.

HÔTEL DE VILLE (2 E7). This was built on the site of the Maison aux Piliers from 1553 to the early 17th century, after plans by the Italian architect Domenico Bernabei, then burnt down under the Commune, on May 24, 1871 ● *28.* Ballu and Deperthes rebuilt it in its original style between 1874 and 1882. Its four façades are decorated with an abundance of niches, containing 108 statues of celebrated persons born in Paris. On the entablature are 30 statues representing the provincial towns of France, while an allegorical female figure represents the city of Paris on top of the clock pediment. It was here, in 1789, that Louis XIV was given the tricolor flag by Jean Sylvais Brouilly, mayor of Paris. It was also here that Robespierre was arrested and taken to the guillotine on July 28, 1794, thus ending the Reign of Terror.

LUXURIOUS DÉCOR
The gilt decorations and paneling of the Hôtel de Ville show the splendors of the Republic: chandeliers by Baccarat in the Salle des Fêtes and works by Puvis de Chavannes decorate the southern Salon d'Arrivée.

CHÂTELET (2 D6)

PLACE DU CHÂTELET. The square was overshadowed by the silhouette of the Grand Châtelet up until 1808. Louis VI built this fortress near the Pont-Neuf in 1130 to defend the bridge to the Île de la Cité. Initially it was the headquarters of the merchants' provost; later, it became a prison specializing in refined methods of torture. The famous funnel-shaped Chamber of Hypocras forced prisoners to remain constantly standing. Today the square is one of the busiest crossroads in Paris. It is flanked by twin theaters built by Davioud in 1862 ● *74.* On the western side is the Théâtre Musical de Paris, formerly the Théâtre du Châtelet. It was here that the Colonne concerts came into being in 1874; now it presents dance companies like those of Pina Bausch and the New York City Ballet. On the eastern side is the Théâtre de la Ville, where Sarah Bernhardt triumphed in Edmond Rostand's *Eaglet* in 1900.
QUAI DE LA MÉGISSERIE (2 C9). This is one of the two liveliest places in the area, with its secondhand-book

sellers by the Seine opposite colorful sidewalks crowded with merchants selling plants and pets. However, in medieval times this area was the home of the slaughterhouses, whose pestilential stench made it one of the most unpleasant parts of the capital. Beyond the quay are quiet roads like the Rue des Orfèvres, which have kept their medieval course and their peaceful atmosphere.

LA SAMARITAINE (2 B6) 19, rue de la Monnaie. Ernest Cognacq and his wife, Louise Jay, transformed the original 1869 shop into a vast hive filling four buildings. Between 1905 and 1910 the architect Frantz Jourdain put up the revolutionary building at 2, rue de la Monnaie. The terrace at the top of this Art Deco monument (on the 11th story) offers a magnificent view over Paris ◆ *482*. Jourdain collaborated with Henri Sauvage ▲ *306* to build the store at no. 3, facing the Seine.

TOUR ST-JACQUES (2 D7). This curious High Gothic steeple (right) is all that remains of the church of St-Jacques-de-la-Boucherie, built in the 16th century and demolished in 1797. At ground level, under a vault, is a statue of Pascal commemorating his reproduction here of the barometric experiments he first conducted at Puy-de-Dôme. On the northwestern corner is a statue of Saint Jacques the Elder over a platform with a small meteorological station. On the other corners are carved symbols representing the four evangelists (lion, eagle, bull and man): these were restored in the 19th century, as were the gargoyle and the eighteen statues of saints on the sides of the tower.

FONTAINE AUX PALMIERS
This was built in 1806 to celebrate Napoleon's victories and stands on the site of the Parloir aux Bourgeois.

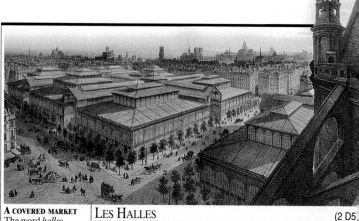

A COVERED MARKET
The word *halles* comes from the Frankish word *halla*, meaning a vast covered area.

LES HALLES

(2 D5)

THE BELLY OF PARIS. Les Halles de Paris were founded in the 12th century by Louis VI "le Gros" ("the Fat") on the site of the Champeaux, ancient marshes which were partially cultivated. In 1534, François I put up new buildings surrounded by a covered gallery, whose pillars survived until 1854. A colorful population developed, made up of market porters and fishwives, who enjoyed the privilege of being received by the king at the new year.

BALTARD'S HALLES. In 1851, Napoleon III decided to bring the different markets together in one place, near the church of St-Eustache. He had been impressed by the new metal architecture used for the Gare de l'Est and told the architect Baltard : "Make me umbrellas . . . made of iron, nothing but iron". Ten pavilions with iron frameworks resulted, constructed between 1854 and 1912. Zola celebrated them in his 1873 novel *Le Ventre de Paris* (*The Belly of Paris*). By 1962 this market at the very heart of Paris had become outdated and overcrowded: the problem was solved by transferring it to Rungis, 9 miles south of the capital, in 1969. All but two of Baltard's pavilions were destroyed: one of these was reassembled at Nogent-sur-Marne, the other at Yokohama, in Japan.

MARKET PORTERS
The guild of market porters (*Forts des Halles*) was founded by Saint Louis in 1250. The porters also functioned as security guards. There were still three thousand of them in 1965.

REDEVELOPMENT. For years there was a gaping hole where the market had stood. A wide range of projects was proposed, including an immense hanging garden and a gigantic hexahedron construction devised by the architect Ricardo Bofill. It was not until 1979 that the Halles project finally took shape, transforming the whole area up to the Rue Beaubourg. Everything changed around the new colossus: apartment buildings were renovated, and the area's activities and population were transformed, producing a commercial and cultural boom. The quarter is served by the huge Châtelet-les-Halles station, the hub of the RER network, which draws people from all over the suburbs toward Europe's largest pedestrian mall.

> "I FOUND MYSELF BEFORE THE VAST PANTRY WHICH WOULD PROVIDE THE FOOD FOR THE DAY'S ORGY. IN THE PALE LIGHT I SPIED PILES OF RED MEAT, ... MOUNTAINS OF VEGETABLES PIERCING THE SHADOWS WITH SPLASHES OF GREEN AND WHITE"
>
> ÉMILE ZOLA

FORUM. Every day, crowds hurry toward the doors of the Forum from Rue Rambuteau, Rue Pierre-Lescot and Rue Berger. This vast subterranean complex has shopping arcades on four levels: it is the capital's largest shopping center, catering to a broad market, but especially to the stylish young shoppers who congregate around the square decorated by Julio Silva's *Pygmalion*. Farther to the west the section arranged around the Place Carrée has a more cultural purpose: its swimming pool is surrounded by a tropical greenhouse, a center for music and dance, the Paris video library and the central record lending library. From the outside, the Lescot building seems to group its pavilions of reflecting glass together in the shape of mushrooms, housing conservatoires, studios and exhibition spaces. On top of the building is a terrace with a view over the whole quarter.

FONTAINE DES INNOCENTS
Not far from the Halles is the only Renaissance-style fountain in Paris. Dating from 1549, it is decorated with delicate nymphs by Jean Goujon.

GARDEN. The garden is quieter, reaching southward through a series of metal arcades. At the center is a pleasant mall planted with young trees, running from the Forum to the glass pyramids which cover the tropical conservatory close to the Commodity Market. Opposite the southern portal of the church of St-Eustache is the statue by Henri de Miller, a stunning contemporary work. This colossal head, which weighs 70 tons, is made of Massaugis stone (from Burgundy) and seems to lend its ear both to the city's noise and to the quiet of the sanctuary.

BOURSE DU COMMERCE (2 C5). This ring-shaped former grain exchange, built in the 18th century, stands to the west of Les Halles (below). It was given a metallic dome in 1811, which was covered with copper sheets and later with glass. On the eastern side the building is flanked by a strange column, formerly part of the Hôtel de Soissons, built by Catherine de' Medici. The tower is supposed to have been an observatory for Ruggieri, the queen's astrologer. The Hôtel de Nesles also stood on this site: Blanche de Castille, Saint Louis' mother, died there in 1252.

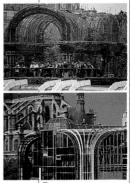

PEACE AND QUIET
The terrace on top of the Lescot building and the arbors in the garden: two places of peace and quiet amid the bustle of Les Halles.

THE QUARTER OF LES HALLES

SQUARE DES INNOCENTS (2 C5). Many Parisians were buried in the Cimetière des Innocents, which stood here from the late Middle Ages. Before the 17th century the place was not always treated with respect: shops were set up inside the cemetery which inspired François Villon's *Testament.* In 1549, the only Renaissance fountain in Paris was set against the cemetery wall, with delicate carved nymphs by Jean Goujon. In 1786 the cemetery was closed, and a sinister nocturnal procession threaded the streets of Paris, transporting the remains of two million corpses buried in these graves to the catacombs of St-Jacques ▲ *274.* The Fontaine des Innocents was skillfully separated from the wall, given a fourth side by Pajou in 1788, and then set in the middle of the square. This is one of the most popular meeting places around the Forum des Halles.

RUE DE LA FERRONNERIE (2 D5). At night this road is popular with young people attracted by its bars and lively restaurants. Opposite no. 11 is a plaque set into the road, bearing three fleurs-de-lys. It was here that Henri IV's carriage was held up on May 14, 1610 (the road was much narrower at the time). Ravillac had followed the carriage from the Louvre: he stood on a stone block and dealt the king three fatal blows with a knife.

RUE ST-HONORÉ (2 C5). From the 12th century onward, this very old road took the place of the Chaussée du Roule, a major route through the capital since the Roman era. Many 17th- and 18th-century buildings still stand along the street. The pharmacy at no. 115 goes back to 1715, while a plaque at no. 96 indicates that Molière was born on this site in 1622. The Fontaine du Trahoir, at no. 111, was rebuilt by Soufflot in 1776, replacing the fountain built by Jean Goujon in 1519 at the crossroads with Rue de l'Arbre-Sec, whose name refers to the gallows which used to stand here.

CHURCH OF ST-EUSTACHE (2 C4). The church came to the fore again when the

CHURCH OF ST-EUSTACHE
The building's interior is 290 feet long and 110 feet high: the dimensions are similar to those of Notre-Dame, and the ground plan is identical.

A REFUGE FOR JEAN SANS PEUR
Jean sans Peur, the Duke of Burgundy, ordered the assassination of the Duc d'Orléans in 1407. He had a tower built a year later to protect himself from possible reprisals. Despite this precaution he was assassinated in 1419 on the Pont de Montereau.

old market was demolished: its Gothic buttresses and its elegant shape can now be fully appreciated. It was built between 1532 and 1637 on the site of a 12th-century chapel; unfortunately, its Gothic structure was disfigured by a classical façade added in the 18th century. It was restored by Baltard after a fire in 1840. The interior decorations are mainly Renaissance, even classical, in contrast with the Gothic style of the building. Among the church's valuable works of art are a *Martyrdom of Saint Eustache* by Simon Vouet and a statue of the Virgin by Jean-Baptiste Pigalle. St-Eustache's organ concerts have a high reputation, as does its choir; the church is one of the most attractive in the capital.

TOWER OF JEAN SANS PEUR (2 D4). The tower stands at 20, rue Étienne-Marcel; it does not look its age. The tower is square with sides measuring 90 feet; it has a spiral staircase with 140 steps leading to a turret with machicolations. It was recently restored and represents one of the few surviving examples of feudal military architecture in Paris ● 61.

RUE ST-DENIS (2 DE3 and 4). For many years this street benefited from the special status of the St-Denis basilica ▲ 432. The kings of France processed along this holy route to their second coronation, before the people. Triumphal arches were built for the occasion, and fountains flowed with free wine and milk. One of the fountains, rebuilt in 1732, still stands on the corner of no. 142. The Rue St-Denis, which is now a pedestrian mall from the Rue Étienne-Marcel to the Rue des Lombards, has changed greatly since the development of the Forum close by: many of the establishments in this former red-light district on the north side of the street have now become food stores. A number of the historical buildings in this area still have brightly lit neon signs.

BEAUBOURG

CHURCH OF ST-MERRI. As was the case with St-Eustache, this church is tightly enclosed by buildings, in keeping with the medieval tradition. The church goes back to the 9th century; it was rebuilt in the 12th century, and again from 1520 to 1620, preserving the building's High Gothic style. The contrast between the flying buttresses on the Place Stravinski and the interior of the church is striking. In the 18th century the Gothic decorations in the crossing of the transept were extensively modified and adapted to the Baroque taste of the day. Michel-Ange Slodtz decorated the choir with stucco and marble, while his brother Paul-Ambroise decorated the chapel (its top lighting was

added by Boffrand in 1744). The church also lost some of its 16th-century stained-glass windows, which were replaced by plain glass. Despite the damage suffered under the Revolution, it still has many paintings, including *Mary the Egyptian* by Chassériau and *Saint Merri Releasing the Prisoners* by Vouet. To the left of the façade is a small tower with a campanile, which contains the oldest bell in Paris, the "Merri", cast in 1331.

QUARTIER DE L'HORLOGE (2 C7). On the Rue Rambuteau, to one side of the Georges-Pompidou Center, a statue of Prometheus by Ossip Zadkine marks the entrance to this quarter. The renovation of the area was organized by its residents. It is named after the curious electronic clock by Jacques Monestier on Rue Bernard-de-Clairvaux: a man armed with a sword and shield is fighting a dragon, a bird and a crab, confronting each of these separately every hour and all of them together at midday and at six o'clock in the evening.

GEORGES-POMPIDOU CENTER

"I should passionately like Paris to have a cultural center which would be at once a museum and a center of creation." These words spoken by President Pompidou in 1969 paved the way for the great international competition to build the center which would bear his name. The design by the Italian architect Renzo Piano and the British architect Richard Rogers was chosen from among 681 entries. Their creation continues to arouse passionate reactions, but the Pompidou Center has become a part of the Parisian landscape: eight million visitors every year demonstrate its popular success.

AN ARCHITECTURAL FEAT. The architects created an avant-garde building, a gigantic block measuring 550 by 200 feet, 140 feet high, with a steel framework and glass walls, and painted in bright colors. Piano and Rogers focused the interior space by banishing all functional elements – escalators, ventilation shafts, heating ducts – to the exterior. This allowed them to create a space of 80,000 square feet on each of the six stories. The

cross-section opposite shows one of the center's thirteen sections. The color of the girders and shafts corresponds to their function: blue for air conditioning, green for liquids, red for communications and yellow for electricity. A huge escalator, set in a glass tube held in place by arches, diagonally crosses the face of the building on the piazza side.

A CULTURAL CENTER (2 E5 and 6). The center's originality lies in its multidisciplinary character: it houses many events in all spheres of contemporary creativity. On the first floor are a large information hall, a current-affairs room (press, periodicals, books) and two areas reserved for children. The basement is reserved for conferences, performances and meetings. On the mezzanine are exhibition halls, the Centre de Création Industrielle and the Garance movie theater. On the third floor the Bibliothèque Publique d'Information (BPI) contains all spheres of knowledge on three floors covered by an internal escalator. The BPI is notable for its large stock of books and for giving direct access to its readers. Movies, slides and language-learning audiotapes in a hundred languages illustrate the center's aim of promoting all types of culture. The fifth floor is occupied by the Musée National d'Art Moderne ▲ 134, ◆ 476, 484 while the sixth, devoted to major temporary exhibitions, also has a café and a restaurant, as well as a terrace overlooking Paris ◆ 482 and the piazza below. The piazza itself is a huge square that is usually packed with street performers and onlookers. The centre is currently being renovated ◆ 474 and only the exhibition hall on the south side of the building is open to the public.

▲ 134, ◆ 476, 484 ◆ 482 ◆ 474

THE "GERBETTES"
These are 26-foot-long metal sections, weighing a total of 8 tons, on the outside of the building. They were specially designed for the center and are used to connect the various functional elements of the building, acting as struts to spread the load across the structure. They are the modern equivalent of buttresses in church architecture.

poutre

Gerbette.

10 tonnes.

o matériau.

en bleu: l'air conditionné

en rouge: circulations

en vert: les fluides.

en jaune: l'électricité.

en rouge: circulations

EGYPTOMANIA
The façade at 2, Place du Caire, is covered with Egyptian motifs – hieroglyphics, sphinxes and lotus flowers. The building itself opens onto the Passage du Caire, which was inspired by the Great Bazaar of the Egyptian capital.

THE REX
The Hollywood-style façade of the Rex cinema stands out on the Boulevard Poissonnière. This movie theater, which opened in 1932, was created by the architects Bluysen and Eberson. It is strikingly innovative on the outside with its white wedding-cake-style tiers, so incongruous in the Parisian landscape. The interior was modeled on American-style movie theaters.

RÉAUMUR (2 BE3)

RUE RÉAUMUR. The great textiles companies and institutions of the press were based on this street at the beginning of the century; they put up spectacular buildings combining stone façades with metal structures. Huge glass bays supplied the light necessary to both types of business. Three buildings standing close to each other (nos. 101, 124 and 126) show how iron and glass gradually replaced stone as a construction material.

CONSERVATOIRE DES ARTS ET MÉTIERS ▲ *136* (2 EF3). This institution, too often missed by visitors, is located in the grounds of the St-Martin-des-Champs abbey, the "third daughter of Cluny", which was founded in 1060. The buildings were dismantled in the 19th century but the church is still standing. Its nave, built around 1130, had the first rib vaulting in Paris and the first flying buttresses in France. The superb monks' refectory, now a library, was supposedly built by Pierre de Montreuil, the architect of the Ste-Chapelle, who also contributed to Notre-Dame ▲ *358*.

CHURCH OF ST-NICOLAS-DES-CHAMPS (2 E4). This parish church was founded in 1184 and rebuilt at the end of the 12th century and again in the 15th century. It is a very good example of Renaissance church architecture: the southern side portal with carved doors was built after a design by Philibert Delorme. The church did not escape the inevitable 18th-century modifications: the stained-glass windows were replaced by painted windows. The interior is richly decorated, with paintings by Simon Vouet (1629) on either side of the choir.

SENTIER (2 CD3)

CHURCH OF NOTRE-DAME-DE-BONNE-NOUVELLE (2 D2). This church was rebuilt by Godde between 1823 and 1830, retaining only its steeple, built between 1628 and 1652, whose first stone was laid by Anne of Austria. This queen, who was barren for twenty-three years before finally giving birth to Louis XIV, was a generous benefactress of the church. The interior still displays magnificent paintings by Philippe de Champaigne and Le Brun, as well as *Anne d'Autriche and Henriette de France* by Mignard. A silk chasuble from the 18th century, displayed in a former sacristy, is supposed to be the one worn by Abbé Edgeworth de Firmont when he said the last mass for Louis XVI at the scaffold.

QUARTIER DU CAIRE (2 D3). Right at the heart of the Sentier, the street names – Rue d'Aboukir, Rue du Nil, Rue Damiette – commemorate Bonaparte's expedition to Egypt. This was no great political success, but it did leave a lasting impression on French art. Up to 1667 this area was the domain of beggars, who took refuge in the *cours des miracles*: their name is supposed to derive from the "miracles" which happened every evening, when crippled beggars suddenly recovered the use of their limbs and their senses. The most famous of these courts stood on today's Rue du Nil. The beggars (who were led by an elected king) were evicted in 1667 by La Reynie, the Lieutenant-General of Police.

THE BOULEVARDS

BOULEVARD POISSONNIÈRE (2 CE2). This road has many shops and is still very lively, especially at night. The Hôtel de Montholon, at no. 23, was built in 1775: it stands out from the row of Haussmann-style buildings, a memento of the golden age of the boulevards ▲ *348*. The Café Brabant at no. 32 is where the Naturalists, led by Zola, met for their *diner du boeuf nature* (dinner of plain beef).
BOULEVARD ST-MARTIN (2 FG3). This boulevard ends on the Place de la République and was built through public garbage pits near the city wall. Two theaters stand next to each other on the even-numbered side. The façade of the Théâtre de la Porte-St-Martin, at no. 16, is decorated with carved masks of classical actors; its auditorium was rebuilt in 1873 after the fire of the Commune. Sarah Bernhardt played in *Tosca* and Alexandre Dumas' *Dame aux Camélias* here, and the first performance of Edmond Rostand's *Cyrano de Bergerac* was also given here in 1897. The Théâtre de la Renaissance, at no. 20, was directed by Sarah Bernhardt from 1893 to 1899. Further on, the Porte-St-Martin stands 56 feet high. On it, Louis XIV is shown leading his armies, depicted as a naked Hercules wearing a wig. The traditional fig leaf is replaced by a lion's paw.

PORTE ST-DENIS
The arch, which is 75 feet high, was built by Blondel in 1672 and carved by Michel Anguier. Its ornamentation and inscriptions celebrate Louis XIV's greatness and his victories in Holland.

CENTER OF THE RAG TRADE
The whole of the Sentier (whose name is supposed to have derived from *chantier*, or building site) is a hive of activity: bales of fabric, materials of all sorts, trolleys, hand trucks and traffic jams reflect the vibrant activity of this area. This is the kingdom of the clothing industry, with manufacturing and wholesale businesses.

1. BHV STORE
2. CHURCH OF ST-GERVAIS-ST-PROTAIS
3. CITÉ DES ARTS
4. HÔTEL D'AUMONT
5. HÔTEL DE SENS
6. CHURCH OF ST-PAUL-ST-LOUIS
7. CHURCH OF STE-MARIE-SULLY
8. HÔTEL DE BÉTHUNE-SULLY
9. HOUSE OF VICTOR HUGO
10. PLACE DES VOSGES
11. HÔTEL LAMOIGNON
12. HÔTEL CARNAVALET
13. HÔTEL LE PELETIER DE ST-FARGEAU

⏱ Two days

In 1961, the engineer Michel Raude discovered remarkable painted beams and joists in the Hôtel de Vigny, which was about to be destroyed.

So he organized puppet performances there – this was the start of the Marais Festival – and created two associations which helped carry through a plan to protect and promote the Marais.

RUE DE BRETAGNE
RUE PASTOURELLE
RUE DES ARCHIVES
RUE DES QUATRE-FILS
RUE VIEILLE-DU-TEMPLE
RUE DES BLANCS-MANTEAUX
RUE DU TEMPLE
RUE DE LA PERLE
RUE DES ARCHIVES
RUE DES FRANCS-BOURGEOIS
RUE PAYENNE
RUE DE SÉVIGNÉ
RUE DE LA VERRERIE
RUE DE RIVOLI
RUE F. MIRON
RUE DE JOUY
QUAI DE L'HÔTEL-DE-VILLE
RUE CHARLEMAGNE
RUE DU FIGUIER
RUE ST-PAUL
PONT LOUIS-PHILIPPE
PONT MARIE
QUAI DES CÉLESTINS
RUE VIEILLE-DU...

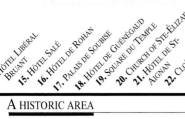
A HISTORIC AREA

The Marais quarter occupies a triangle formed by the Hôtel de Ville, the Place de la Bastille and the Place de la République. This is the historical heart of Paris. It was to have been razed like the Île de la Cité, but the fall of the Empire allowed it to escape Haussmann's development plans. In the 19th century it became an industrial district: businesses and small-scale manufacturers moved into the buildings, adding annexes in courtyards and gravely damaging interior decorations. Nonetheless, their presence saved the buildings of the Marais from being altered to suit the tastes of the day. After André Malraux's law for the protection of the national heritage was passed in 1962, the city's first area of conservation underwent a striking renaissance. The main drawback of this splendid restoration work is that the traditional crafts are gradually disappearing from the area.

FROM THE TEMPLE
TO THE GOLDEN AGE

From the 12th century onward, the Knights Templars and other religious groups cleared the marshy land to the north of Philippe-Auguste's city wall. This provided the foundations for the later development of the area. Further to the south, the area close to the Seine was invigorated when Charles V built the Hôtel St-Pol in 1385, before the royal residence was moved to the Hôtel des Tournelles, to the north of the Rue St-Antoine. After Henri IV created the Place Royale, which later became the Place des Vosges ● 62 ▲ 396, in 1605, the whole quarter became the center of a brilliant social scene in which the arts and literature flourished. Mme de Sévigné lived here her whole life, changing homes ten times: she is a central figure in this golden age of the Marais in the 17th century. When Louis XIV came to the throne, the Marais both reached its peak and began to decline as the aristocracy steadily moved off to the faubourgs St-Germain ▲ 262 and St-Honoré ▲ 344.

HÔTEL DE SENS
This building has a thoroughly medieval appearance with its irregular design, its Gothic porch and its corbeled turrets at the corners. Along with the Hôtel de Cluny and the Jacques-Coeur house, this is one of the few remaining examples of civil architecture from the Middle Ages in Paris ● 58. The portal, the turrets and the square keep with its gatehouse are original; the rest has been reconstructed, sometimes very badly (for example, the façade facing the garden).

RESTORATION AND RENOVATION
Courtyards are cleaned, façades restored, houses restored or entirely reconstructed in the attempt to re-create the original Marais, but sometimes this runs the risk of destroying the traditional character of what was once a working-class quarter.

385

OLD TEMPLARS ENCLOSURE

TEMPLE ENCLOSURE
Its 4,000 inhabitants enjoyed legal and fiscal privileges, and its craftsmen were exempted from the regulations of the guilds.

The SQUARE DU TEMPLE (2 G4), in the north of the Marais, stands on the site of one of the nine thousand outposts of the Knights Templars. The building was established here in the 12th century and housed the grand master of the order from the 13th century onward. The enclosure was effectively a self-contained fortified town surrounded by 26-foot-high crenelated walls. After the Templars were suppressed, by order of Philippe IV and Pope Clement V in the Council of Vienne (1311–12), the enclosure was owned by the Knights Hospitalers, better known as the Knights of Malta, until the Revolution.

SQUARE DU TEMPLE

This garden is located on the site of the former Grand Prior's Palace, which was destroyed in 1853. The garden was designed in the English style by Jean-Charles Alphand ▲ *208* in 1857.

CHURCH OF STE-ÉLISABETH (195, rue du Temple). This church has a beautiful, timeworn classical façade: its first stone was placed by Marie de' Medici in 1628, and its huge neoclassical choir was built by Godde in 1822. One hundred 17th-century wooden panels with carvings of biblical scenes were added in 1845 from the Abbaye de St-Vaast in Arras.

CARREAU DU TEMPLE (2 G4). This stands behind the town hall, occupying six metal halls built in 1863. Secondhand clothes are still sold here every morning.

TEMPLE PRISONERS
The site of the Temple keep, built under Saint Louis around 1265, is marked in the road to the north of today's Square du Temple, opposite the town hall of the 3rd arrondissement. This imposing square tower had sides measuring 50 feet and large corner turrets with pepperpot watchtowers. The royal family was held here after August 13, 1792. On January 21, 1793, Louis XVI left the tower to be led to the scaffold, while the young Louis XVII is thought to have died here under circumstances which are still shrouded in mystery.

RUE DU TEMPLE

This winding road with its old façades is still charming. By day, the area is a hive of activity: jewelry businesses to the north, then leather goods and finally, to the south, wholesale businesses and import-export houses run by Chinese immigrants from the Zhejang region ▲ *VIII*.

HÔTEL D'AVAUX DE ST-AIGNAN (2 F5) nos. 71–5. This house was built between 1640 and 1650 by one of the delegates to the treaty of Westphalia (1648). On the carriage entrance are strange heads of Indians which hold the door handles between their teeth. Once the restoration of this building is complete, it will house the Museum of the Art and History of Judaism.

HÔTEL DE BERLIZE no. 41. The rather dilapidated appearance of the façades and the windows with curved pediments add to this building's charm. It houses the Café-Théâtre de la Gare in its large paved courtyard.

HÔTEL D'HALLWYLL (2 E5) 28, rue Michel-le-Comte. This is one of the rare 18th-century buildings in the Marais and the only work by Claude-Nicolas Ledoux still standing in Paris. The heavy Doric columns and the design of the street façade and main building are typical of Ledoux's austere style, modeled on classical architecture. Germaine Necker, later Mme de Staël, was born in this house in 1766.

RUE DES ARCHIVES

This lively street, which was widened in the 19th century, has many shops, bars and restaurants.

CLOÎTRE DES BILLETTES (2 E6) nos. 22–6. In the 12th century, so the story goes, a communion host which was stabbed and thrown into boiling oil began to bleed. A place of pilgrimage grew up around this legend, and the reformed Carmelites, or *Billettes*, rebuilt the church between 1756 and 1778; today it is a Protestant church. The cloister of 1427–8 still has three of its original galeries with triangular arcades and carved keystones.

HÔTEL GUÉNÉGAUD DES BROSSES (2 F5) no. 60. This grand, sober house was built by François Mansart between 1651 and 1655. It narrowly escaped destruction: one of its 20th-century owners made a hole in the roof to speed up a demolition permit. After 1967 it was restored by a foundation established by the industrialist and patron of the arts François Sommer; he set up the Musée de la Chasse et de la Nature here ▲ *139*.

MAISON COEUR
This building at 40, rue du Temple, one of the oldest houses in Paris, now contains a primary school. It was built by the granddaughter of Jacques Coeur, Charles VII's great Minister of Finance. The neat varnished red and black bricks of the façade and the windows with their stone transoms are typical of late-15th-century architecture.

FRANÇOIS MANSART
The severe style of the Hôtel Guénégaud des Brosses, without even a pediment, illustrates Mansart's minimalist approach. It is the architect's only complete house to survive in Paris. François Mansart was known for his preference for the roofs that now bear his name ● *67*: he played a key role in the evolution of French classical architecture.

MEDIEVAL REMAINS

A fortified Gothic gateway, flanked by two corbeled towers with pepperpot watchtowers, marks the site of the Hôtel de Clisson. The gateway was preserved because of its impressive appearance and is the only surviving example of civil architecture from the end of the 14th century in Paris.

DELAMAIR'S DEVICE

He radically altered the ground plan of the Hôtel de Soubise by building this majestic main court. It is 200 feet long and 130 feet wide and surrounded by a huge peristyle made of 56 coupled columns, modeled on the peristyle of the Hôtel des Grands Prieurs du Temple.

THE NATIONAL ARCHIVES

ARCHIVE QUADRANGLE. Napoleon I moved the national archives into the Soubise Palace in 1808. Soon they had taken over the Hôtel de Rohan and four adjacent houses (54–8 *bis*, rue des Francs-Bourgeois). The collection grew steadily and now takes up some 300 miles of shelf space. In response to this expansion the architect Filzer added a reception area and research center, CARAN, on the Rue des Quatre-Fils. The dark glazed façade with steel pillars blends well with the old architecture.

FORMER HÔTEL DE CLISSON 58, rue des Archives. This house was built around 1371–5 by Olivier de Clisson, who was Constable under Charles V and an ally of Du Guesclin. In 1556 it passed into the ownership of the Ducs de Guise, who gave it magnificent interior decorations, employing famous Renaissance artists like Niccolò dell'Abbate and Primaticcio. It was in this center of League activity, under Henri de Guise (lover of the future Queen Margot), that final preparations were made for the St Bartholomew's Day Massacre of 1572 ● *24*. In the 1660's, Duc Henri II de Lorraine received Corneille here.

PALACE OF THE PRINCE DE SOUBISE (2 F6) 60, rue des Francs-Bourgeois. In 1700, the Hôtel de Clisson was acquired by François de Rohan, Prince de Soubise. He was able to rebuild the palace thanks to financial assistance obtained from Louis XIV through his wife. Pierre-Alexis Delamair was the architect appointed for the project. The austere main building features the same columns as those of the peristyle around the main court: its projections are decorated with copies of Robert de Lorrain's allegorical sculptures of *The Four Seasons* and sculptures symbolizing *The Spirits of the Arts* on the cornice. The interior is just as remarkable, although a complete contrast to this beautiful classical design. It was created by Germain Boffrand in between 1735 and 1739, and is one of the most lavish décors in the rococo Louis XV style to be seen in Paris. The palace is one of Paris' most attractive architectural landmarks. It was the home of the Maréchal de Soubise, an intimate friend of Louis XV and the only one of the king's courtiers to follow the royal coffin all the way to St-Denis.

HÔTEL DE ROHAN (2 G6)

This building at 87, rue Vieille-du-Temple, is inseparable from the Palais Soubise, whose gardens it shares. The same

architect, Delamair, built it, for one of the Prince de Soubise's four sons, Armand de Rohan-Strasbourg. The house has a monumental classical façade with colonnades and pilasters: it has formed part of the National Archives complex since 1927. Its outbuildings in the Rue des Quatre-Fils house the records of Paris notaries. The interiors were ruined when the Imprimerie Nationale (National Press) was located here in the 19th century; nonetheless, they are still among the most beautiful in Paris, featuring two remarkable rooms, the Cabinet des Singes by Christophe Huet from 1745 and the beautiful Cabinet des Fables d'Ésope ▲ 393.

HÔTEL SALÉ (2G6)

This imposing house, at 5, rue de Thorigny, was built between 1656 and 1659 for Pierre Aubert de Fontenay. It now houses the Musée Picasso ▲ 170, which was opened in 1985 and has helped revitalize this part of the Marais. Aubert, a former footman, made his fortune collecting the *gabelle* (salt tax). His house kept the nickname *salé* (salty) even after Aubert had been ruined, a victim of Fouquet's demise in 1661 ▲ 446. After this, the building had many occupants before its restoration: these included the embassy of Venice and the business of the bronzesmith Vian, father of the novelist Boris Vian ▲ 234. At the far end of the semicircular courtyard, is a pediment decorated with dogs' heads (the owner's coat of arms): sphinx volutes join it to the two wings. The left wing is a trompe l'oeil construction, while the right wing houses kitchens and stables running along the Rue des Coutures-St-Gervais. The façade facing the garden is even more monumental, on a scale unique in the Marais.

HÔTEL LIBÉRAL-BRUAND (2 G6). The architect of the same name, who created the Invalides, built this elegant house at 1, rue de la Perle, between 1685 and 1687, prefiguring Louis XVI style. The main façade is decorated with busts of Roman emperors set in niches: on either side of the oculus on the pediment are horns of plenty spilling branches of flowers and fruits. After the building was renovated, the Bricard company established its Musée de la Serrure (Museum of Locksmithing) here ◆ 479.

HORSES OF THE SUN
This famous bas-relief was carved by Robert le Lorrain in 1735: it is set on the façade of the former stables in the Hôtel de Rohan. Lorrain also produced sculptures for Versailles and Marly.

ARMAND DE ROHAN-STRASBOURG
He was the first in a series of four cardinal-bishops of Strasbourg who lived in the Hôtel de Rohan. The fourth of these, Louis-René de Rohan-Guéméné, became famous through the affair of the queen's necklace at the end of the 18th century.

AN OSTENTATIOUS RESIDENCE
J.P. Babelon called the Hôtel Salé a "typical nouveau riche house" because of its ostentatious grandeur. The main building, which is very wide, houses this magnificent carved staircase (below).

Picasso

▲ THE MARAIS – CARNAVALET

This bronze statue of Louis XIV, made by Coysevox in 1689, was the only royal statue to escape destruction under the Revolution: it stands in the main

court of the Hôtel Carnavalet.

A RENAISSANCE BUILDING
Jacques de Ligneris, the first president of the Parlement de Paris, built his house in 1545; the

Renaissance portal with bosses and the Italian-style main building with transomed windows still stand today within the Hôtel Carnavalet. The building is lavishly decorated with bas-reliefs of *The Four Seasons*, attributed to Jean Goujon ▲ *378*. Goujon also produced the allegorical bas-relief *Abundance* for the portal on the Rue de Sévigné.

HÔTEL CARNAVALET

(2 G6). This building, at 23, rue de Sévigné ▲ *138*, derives its unusual name from a corruption of the surname of Françoise de Kerneveroy, lady in waiting to Queen Margot. Despite many alterations, the building still holds immense architectural interest.

François Mansart redesigned the whole building in 1660–1, skillfully combining the Renaissance residence with classical additions. He built the two wings decorated with bas-reliefs by Gérard von Obstal, crowning the whole with double-sloped roofs. In the 19th century the architect Parmentier subjected the building to some unfortunate modifications, which completely disfigured the garden façade.

MUSÉE DE L'HISTOIRE DE FRANCE (2 F6). The museum's rooms ◆ *478* display reconstructions of historical interiors. These give visitors a fascinating overall view of what the interiors of houses in the Marais looked like in the past: wood paneling, trompe l'oeil paintings, painted beams and joists. Buildings from other locations have also been reconstructed around the museum, stone by stone, including the 16th-century Arch of Nazareth in the Rue des Francs-Bourgeois, which originally came from the Palais de Justice on the Île de la Cité and the Pavillon des Drapiers in the Rue Payenne, which was built by Jacques Bruand in 1660.

HÔTEL LE PELLETIER DE ST-FARGEAU (2 G6). This house, at 29, rue de Sévigné, was acquired by the Musée Carnavalet in 1889 to serve as an annex dedicated to the history of Paris since the Revolution. Built between 1686 and 1689, it was owned, very unusually, by the same family until 1811. One of the members of this family, Louis-Michel Le Pelletier de St-Fargeau, voted for Louis XVI's execution and was assassinated in 1793 by Pâris, a bodyguard of the king; the Convention gave him a state funeral. The house is built in a very simple style. On the pediment of the main building is the figure of an old man carrying an hourglass, a striking allegory of Time.

AROUND CARNAVALET

The quiet streets around the Hôtel Carnavalet make for one of the most pleasant walks in the Marais. They have kept their residential character and are lined with attractive houses.
RUE DU PARC-ROYAL. The colorful façade of the HÔTEL DE CANILLAC (4, rue de Sévigné), made of brick and stone, should not cast doubt on its authenticity. In fact, the white façades of restored houses in the Marais sometimes belie their original colorful appearance: bright, even garish colors were often used in Louis XIII's time.

The restoration of the HÔTEL DURET DE CHEVRY (no. 8) seems less careful: the stonework has been daubed with white paint. This was the home of Philippe-Emmanuel de Coulanges, a cousin of Mme de Sévigné, who composed songs and burlesque poems. The HÔTEL DE VIGNY (2 G6), at no. 10, houses the Centre National de Conservation du Patrimoine and has an Italian-style ceiling dating from 1669.

HÔTEL DE MARLE (2 G6). This elegant building, at 11, rue Payenne, stands opposite the Square Georges-Cain and is a perfect example of successful restoration. It houses the Swedish Cultural Center and the Tessin Foundation, which mounts exhibitions of contemporary art on the second floor. The building dates mainly from 1572. Restoration work revealed unusual ship's-hull roofs under later two-sloped roofs: these were invented by the architect Philibert Delorme, who built the Château d'Anet (Eure-et-Loir *département*).

HÔTEL DONON 8, rue Elzévir. This house was built in the late 16th century for Médéric de Donon, general inspector of the king's buildings; today it houses the Cognacq-Jay Museum ▲ *141*. The main building has an elegant, impressively simple pyramid-style façade. Behind the pediment is the Great Roof, which slopes to a height of nearly 26 feet.

"CARNAVALETTE"
Mme de Sévigné, the Hôtel Carnavalet's most famous resident, lived here from 1677 until her death in 1696. She called it her *carnavalette*, praising its "lovely air, lovely court, lovely garden and lovely neighborhood".

RENOVATIONS
The Louis XIII-style houses on the Rue du Parc-Royal were mainly built between 1619 and 1621, and have been extensively restored. The façade of the Hôtel de Châtillon (13, rue Payenne) is an exception, with its covering of Virginia creeper.

ORANGERY
The Hôtel Le Pelletier de St-Fargeau still has its orangery, one of the few to survive in Paris (the Hôtel de Sully has another).

▲ INTERIOR DECORATIONS

The interior decorations of houses in the Marais are among the richest in Paris, illustrating the development of architectural styles between the 16th and 18th centuries: painted beams and joists under Henri IV, paneling and Italianate trompe l'oeil views from Louis XIII's reign, panels interspersed with paintings under Louis XIV, stucco work and gilding in the rococo style under Louis XV. These miraculously preserved interiors conjure up an image of splendors which have been lost forever.

CUPIDS AND SPHINXES
These archivolts on the painted ceiling of the Grand Salon in the Hôtel Mansart de Sagonne are attributed to Jean-Baptiste Corneille. They illustrate the mythological style which was typical under the reign of Louis XIV.

PAINTED BEAMS
"French-style" beams and joists decorated with painted medallions and monograms, and with floral or geometrical motifs, are common in the Marais. They were typical decorative features in private residences up to the age of Louis XIII.

MONKEY TRICKS
Christophe Huet created these imaginative pictures of monkeys between 1749 and 1752, for the famous Cabinet des Singes of Hôtel de Rohan.

ROCOCO STYLE
The Salon Ovale of the Hôtel de Soubise was decorated under the direction of Boffrand around 1737–40. Its stucco work and its white and gold paneling with allegorical high-reliefs in plaster make it a fine example of rococo style.

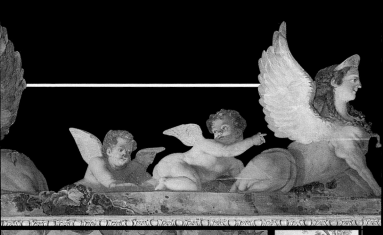

CHINOISERIE
This type of picture was common in the 18th century; here it appears with rural motifs on the painted panels in the Cabinet des Singes of the Hôtel de Rohan.

CABINET DES FABLES
These carved wooden medallions came from the Hôtel de Soubise: they have been relocated to the Hôtel de Rohan. The subjects are taken from Aesop's *Fables*.

HÔTEL AMELOT
This magnificent Italian-style dome from the late 17th century is decorated with highly restored Baroque paintings by Louis Boullongne showing *The Marriage of Hercules and Hebe*.

HÔTEL D'ALBRET
The balcony on the street side is supported by consoles in the form of lions' heads. At the end of the garden is a tower, originally part of Philippe-Auguste's city wall, which was converted into a chapel in the 17th century. The Paris city council chose this house as the base for its cultural service and redesigned the

interior in a striking modern style.

HÔTEL AMELOT DE BISSEUIL
This building is known for the Medusa heads sticking their tongues out at passersby on the doors of its carriage entrance. It has a fascinating history. La Bruyère mocked its first owner, who hesitated to move into his house, "so splendid, so rich and so ornate". In 1776, Beaumarchais set up a company here called Rodriguez, Hortolez & Co., for supplying arms to the American rebels; he also wrote *The Marriage of Figaro* here.

RUE DES FRANCS-BOURGEOIS

This is a favorite place for a Sunday stroll, stretching from Beaubourg to the Place des Vosges, following the outer path of Philippe-Auguste's city wall ● *54*, some parts of which can still be seen. This street lined with private homes at the heart of the Marais derives its name from an almshouse for citizens exempt from taxes. It is also typical of the new Marais, in that luxury boutiques are gradually replacing the traditional shops: the baker at no. 23, with its Belle Époque signs, has now become a fashion boutique.

HÔTEL DE SANDREVILLE (2 G7) no. 26. The superb Renaissance façade on the garden side dates from 1586. On the street side, the building was later given a Louis XVI-style façade with monumental fluted pilasters.

HÔTEL D'ALBRET (2 G6) nos. 29 *bis*–31. It is here that the meeting between Mme de Maintenon and the Marquise de Montespan took place, the latter entrusting the former with the care of the Duc de Maine, illegitimate son of Louis XIV. The ambitious Mme de Maintenon, widow of the poet Scarron, made the most of this chance to displace her rival in the king's affections. The 16th-century building underwent a number of later alterations, notably by

François Mansart around 1640.
HÔTEL D'ALMÉRAS (2 G6) no. 30. The main building was constructed in 1611 in red brick and stone, and is a typical example of Henri IV style. The Mannerist-style portico is ornamented with rams' heads on either side of a tympanum decorated with chimeras.

RUE VIEILLE-DU-TEMPLE

Some old shop fronts can still be seen on the street, like the horsemeat butcher's at no. 15, from the early 20th century with its red earthenware tiles. However, art galleries and shops selling clothes or trinkets are rapidly taking over.
HÔTEL AMELOT DE BISSEUIL (2 F6) no. 47. This house, built around 1660, is also known as the Hôtel des Ambassadeurs de Hollande. On the other side of the splendid portal is a bas-relief carved by Regnaudin, showing the Roman wolf suckling Romulus and Remus. The first court is lavishly decorated with cherubs, gargoyles and sundials bearing golden mottos.
HÔTEL HÉROUET (2 F6) no. 54. This Gothic-style building, with a corbeled turret and fine stone carvings around the transomed windows, adds to the charm of its location. The Hôtel Hérouet dates back to 1510–20, but the building which stands today is a 19th-century reconstruction in the troubadour style.

FROM THE BLANCS-MANTEAUX TO THE RUE PAVÉE

THE BLANCS-MANTEAUX QUARTER. Its name derives from the order of Serfs of the Virgin Mary, who dressed in white coats, which was established here by Saint Louis around 1250. The church which stands today at 12, rue des Blancs-Manteaux, has a magnificent Bavarian rococo pulpit, which dates from 1749. The façade added by Baltard in 1863 came from the church of St-Éloi-des-Barnabites, built on the Île de la Cité in 1703.

RUE DES ROSIERS. The street has a unique atmosphere, with its kosher shops, Eastern specialties and shops selling Jewish religious objects. The restaurant Chez Jo Goldenberg (nos. 7–10) is typical of the street. However, some modernization is evident: the St-Paul Turkish baths at no. 4, for example, have been converted into a café.

HÔTEL LAMOIGNON (2 G7) 24, rue Pavée. At the end of the 17th century, President Guillaume de Lamoignon received the leading intellectuals of his day here, including Racine, Mme de Sévigné, Boileau and Louis Bourdaloue. The building now houses the Bibliothèque Historique de la Ville de Paris and is open to the public. Its monumental Corinthian pilasters on two stories are supposed to have been the first of this type built in Paris. The decorative motifs reflect Diane de France's passion for the hunt.

▲ THE MARAIS
PLACE DES VOSGES

The lavish carrousel of 1612 marked the opening of the Place Royale.

THE PAVILLON DU ROI
This is higher than the buildings around the rest of the square.

MONTGOMERY'S LANCE

"Montgomery's lance created the Place des Vosges," wrote Victor Hugo, one of the square's famous inhabitants. Henri II was accidentally wounded in the eye by the lance of Montgomery, his captain of guards, during a tournament in July 1559: he died after ten days of agony. His widow, Catherine de' Medici, persuaded her son to demolish the Hôtel des Tournelles, where both Louis XI and Louis XII died. A horse market moved into the space left vacant, before Henri IV decided to establish a silk factory on the northern side, with accommodation for the workers on the other three sides of the square. The factory soon foundered, and the square, close to the church of St-Louis-des-Jésuites, was gradually taken over by the aristocracy of the Marais. Corneille paid tribute to it by calling one of his plays *Place Royale*. After this, the Place des Vosges went into decline, but it has now recaptured all its former prestige: once again it counts famous people among its inhabitants, while galleries, luxury shops and restaurants have taken up residence under its arcades.

PLACE ROYALE   (2 H7)

The striking thing about the square is its stylistic unity: this goes back to Henri IV's decree of 1604, which laid down strict building regulations. In contrast to the harmonious façade on the square, on the other side (the court side) its buildings have always been a complete mixture. The brilliant social life of the Marais took place behind this stage setting: nearly all the pavilions on the square have a fascinating history. The

HÔTEL DE COULANGES (no.1 *bis*) was the birthplace of the
Marquise de Sévigné. For a time in the 19th century, the
Hôtel de Rotrou (no. 4) housed the kitchens of the
Compagnie des Wagons-Lits railway company. The HÔTEL DE
CHAULNES (no. 9), one of the most magnificent pavilions, was
the headquarters of the Academy of Architecture. It was also
the model for the Metaxas Palace in the
17th-century sentimental novel *Le Grand
Cyrus* and housed the royal stands in the
1612 Carrousel ● *86*: on the court side is
a wing with pediment built by Jules
Hardouin-Mansart in 1676–7. The
HÔTEL DE BASSOMPIÈRE (no. 23) has one
of the most striking staircases in the
Marais: its handrail has carved
balustrades decorated with bowls of fruit,
women's faces and grimacing men's
faces. In the HÔTEL DE ROHAN-GUÉMÉNÉ (no. 6) is a museum

dedicated to Victor Hugo ◆ *480*: the writer
lived on the third story between 1832 and
1848 and wrote *Ruy Blas* here. The HÔTEL
LA RIVIÈRE (no. 14) had some
decorations by Le Brun, now in the
Musée Carnavalet. For a time it was a
town hall (the thoroughly incongruous
campanile was added in 1860). Since the
Second Empire it has been the residence
of the Chief Rabbi of France, connecting
at the back with the Ashkenazi
Synagogue (22 *bis*, rue des Tournelles),
the structure of which was designed by
Gustave Eiffel. The HÔTEL CAULET D'HAUTEVILLE (no. 28)
was a famous gaming house under Louis XIII. On the court
side it was rebuilt in neoclassical style at the end of the 18th
century. Since 1982 it has been a hotel, fitting
discreetly into this   prestigious setting.

PLACE DES . . . VOSGES

Napoleon named the
square thus after the
first *département* to
pay its taxes in 1800.

SYMMETRY RULES

The 36 pavilions – 9
on each side of the
square – still obey the
regulations laid down
by Henri IV in 1604:
façades made of real
or imitation
brickwork and stone;
high roofs in the
French style covered
with slate; and an
arcaded gallery on
the first story
functioning as a
walkway (and now as
a shopping arcade)
with two further
stories above this.

PLACE DE L'ARSENAL

The square is decorated with a statue of Beaumarchais; until 1789 it stood in a private residence, which has since disappeared. The statue stands close to the boulevard named after the author.

HÔTEL DE SULLY

The palace is entered by a portal flanked with pavilions connected by a balustrade. The main buildings and the wings are decorated in Renaissance style. On the garden side, the left wing (1661) houses the apartments of the Duchesse de Sully – an example of 17th-century interior decoration, including an Italian-style room with a dome on which Antoine Paillet painted *The Abduction of Endymion*.

At the end of the garden is one of the few surviving orangeries in Paris, which gives access to the Place des Vosges.

RUE ST-ANTOINE

This old, wide royal road was a favorite place for jousts and ceremonial entries into the city, such as that of Louis XIV and Marie-Thérèse in 1660.

TEMPLE DE L'ORDRE DES FILLES DE LA VISITATION (2 H8) no. 17. This is part of a convent where Saint Francis de Paul was chaplain for eighteen years. Dating from 1632–4, this is was one of François Mansart's first works. Under the building, with its centralized ground plan and cupola, is a crypt which holds the remains of Nicolas Fouquet ▲ *446* and the Marquis de Sévigné.

HÔTEL DE MAYENNE (2 H8) no. 21. One of the oldest buildings of the Marais; the Brothers of the Christian Schools have been housed here since 1870. Built in 1606–9 for the dukes of Mayenne, members of the Guise family, after plans by Jacques Androuet du Cerceau, it was modified and embellished by Germain Boffrand a century later. The recently-restored west wing contrasts starkly with the shabby grayness of the rest of the building: this symbolizes the architectural history of the Marais as a whole, marked by an alternating pattern of decline and renewal.

HÔTEL DE SULLY   (2G7)

62, rue St-Antoine. The National Office for Historical Monuments moved here in 1965, choosing one of the most impressive and beautiful buildings in the Marais as its home. It has been meticulously restored. It was built between 1625 and 1630 for Mesmes Gallet, general inspector of finances, and was bought by Maximilien de Béthune, Duc de Sully, in 1634: the former minister of Henri IV was seventy-four years old at the time. The dukes of Sully made this palace into one of the centers of social and intellectual life in the Marais.

ST-PAUL QUARTER

THE VILLAGE OF ST-PAUL. This village consists of a maze of courtyards full of antiques stores. As you leave the village, the Rue des Jardins-St-Paul, where Rabelais died on April 9, 1553, offers a good view of two towers from Philippe-Auguste's city wall built in 1190 ● *54*.

CONVENT OF THE GREAT JESUITS (14, rue Charlemagne). This Jesuit establishment was built during the reigns of Louis XIII and Louis XIV; since 1802 it has housed the Lycée Charlemagne. To the east is the main staircase, set in a tower from Philippe-Auguste's city wall. The staircase leads up to a dome with a trompe-l'oeil painting of *The Apotheosis of Saint Louis* by the Italian artist Gherardini.

CHURCH OF ST-PAUL-ST-LOUIS (2 G7)

CHURCH OF ST-PAUL-ST-LOUIS
The building is very bright, since it is lit from the dome lantern and the high windows of its barrel vault.

This church was built 1627–41 and its first mass was given by Cardinal Richelieu. The tomb of the great Maréchal de Condé, inside the church, was destroyed during the Revolution. The Jesuits promoted the Counter Reformation with militant fervor: their church was therefore duty bound to move and impress the faithful. The façade, on three levels, is impressive, as is the large dome crowned with a lantern, which rises to a height of 180 feet. The ground plan of the church conforms to the Jesuit formula established by the Society of Jesus in Rome: a simple axis without ambulatory or side aisles. This center of Christian and aristocratic life was designed to highlight the magnificence of its decorations and furniture. Many of the works which contibuted to this splendor have disappeared: the marble high altar was once decorated with four paintings, of which only *The Presentation at the Temple* by Simon Vouet survives (it is now displayed in the Louvre). Nonetheless, some works of art remain, giving an impression of former glories: they include *The Virgin of Sorrows* carved by Germain Pilon in 1586 and *Christ in the Garden of Olives* by Delacroix.

ST-GERVAIS QUARTER

Between the churches of St-Paul-St-Louis and St-Gervais is a network of quiet, narrow, winding streets which still follow their medieval course. This ancient *Quartier de la Mortellerie* – the area of all the building trades – narrowly escaped total destruction. It had record rates of tuberculosis in the 19th and early 20th century and because of this was classified "unhealthy little island no. 16" and designated for demolition. The plan to raze the district was indeed set in motion, leaving a few unhappy marks, like the dismal block of the Cité des Arts (10–48, rue de l'Hôtel-de-Ville), which houses some 230 artists' studios.

HÔTEL D'AUMONT. This house, at 7, rue de Jouy, was built in 1649 by the financier Antoine Scarron. His son-in-law Antoine d'Aumont, nicknamed Tarquin le Superbe, added lavish interior decorations, some by the artist Le Brun. His descendants perpetuated the solid family traditions of magnificent art collections, dissipated life style and death by apoplexy. The building now houses the administrative tribunal of Paris. Little remains of the interior decorations apart from a *History of Romulus and Remus* by Le Brun. The garden façade was adapted to suit the needs of the tribunal.

HÔTEL DE SENS (2 F8)

This fortress-palace at 1, rue du Figuier, was built between 1475 and 1519 for Tristan de Salazar, the 9th archbishop of Sens. The building has a rich history: it was the site of the Council of Sens, which condemned Luther's Theses in 1528, and of Monsignor de Pellevé's death in 1594, at the very moment Henri IV was entering Paris. The building was used for the most diverse purposes in the 19th century, among them a coach and carriage service and a jam factory. It was rebuilt in 1940 by the architect Halley in a rather dry neo-Gothic style. Nonetheless, the building has retained its irregular medieval design on the court side, as well as the portal with its Gothic arch and the dungeon with a bartizan and machicolations. Today it houses the Forney library, dedicated to the decorative arts.

RUE FRANÇOIS-MIRON

This was formerly part of the Rue St-Antoine. It still has shops all along its winding course (Izraël, at no. 30 ◆ *529*), offers a huge array of groceries).
HÔTEL DE BEAUVAIS (no. 68). This house was built sometime after 1654 for Catherine Bellier, nicknamed "One-Eyed Cathau", whose physical defects did not prevent her from deflowering the young Louis XIV. On the street side

ST-GERVAIS
The elevation of the vaults and the arrangement of the Gothic buttresses demonstrate the skill of M. Chambiges, who also designed the cathedrals at Sens and Beauvais. On the interior the stained-glass windows in the Chapel of St John the Baptist go back to 1531; they depict *The Wisdom of Solomon*.

"HÔTEL OF HAPPY FROLICKINGS"
The royal palace of St-Pol, or St-Paul, was built in 1370 by Charles V, between the Seine and the Rue St-Antoine. The buildings were interspersed with orchards, gardens and covered passages. This was the setting for King Charles VI's "happy frolickings" and his attacks of madness. It was split into orthogonal lots under François I. The quarter now has a tranquil charm similar to that of the Mortellerie quarter near St-Gervais.

the building has been disfigured, but beyond the concave door of the portal is an original Baroque construction, ingeniously devised by the architect Le Pautre. An open vestibule with Doric columns runs along the convex forebuilding on the court, following the court's irregular outline. The decorative motifs include several rams' heads, emblem of Catherine Bellier. Mozart stayed here in 1763, when he was seven years old, on his first European tour.

MAISONS D'OURSCAMP (nos. 44–6). At the end of the 16th century these houses were built to replace the former townhouse of the Abbey of Ourscamp (Oise), whose vast medieval cellar, built around 1250, still survives. The buildings were taken over and restored by the Association of Historical Paris ◆ *488*. On the second floor they look out over a curious little court with wooden panels and corbeled privies.

CHURCH OF ST-GERVAIS-ST-PROTAIS

This church was built on the Place St-Gervais, on the site of a 6th-century chapel. Construction lasted over two centuries, which led to a curious mixture of styles. From 1494 to 1540, in the middle of the Renaissance, Martin Chambiges built a nave in the purest High Gothic style. The façade offers a total contrast: it was built by another great architect, Salomon de Brosse, from 1616 to 1621 (he also built the Palais de Luxembourg). Voltaire called the façade a masterpiece: it is a typical classical construction and the first example in Paris of a combination of Doric, Ionic and Corinthian orders. The building has splendid interior decorations, including a stunning crown of openwork stone, 8 feet in diameter, on the keystone of the Chapel of the Virgin. The superb tomb for chancellor Michel le Tellier was made after a design by Jules Hardouin-Mansart. In 1528 a statue of the Virgin was installed near the choir: it had been vandalized on the corner of the Rue de Sicile. Beyond the façade are the great organs of 1628, played by members of the Couperin dynasty between 1653 and 1789. The great François Couperin composed two masses here in 1685.

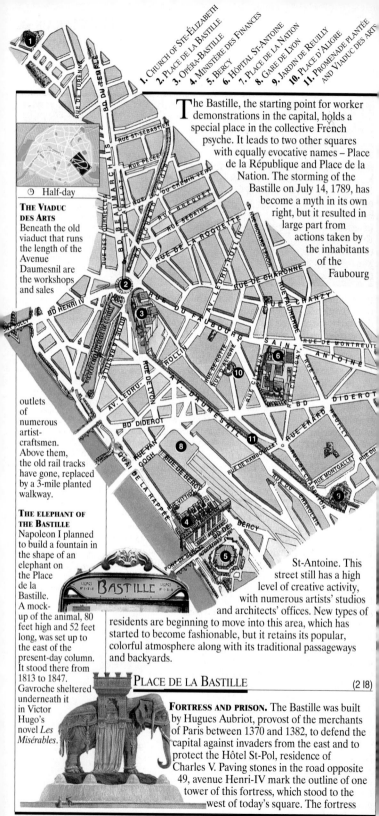

⏱ Half-day

The Bastille, the starting point for worker demonstrations in the capital, holds a special place in the collective French psyche. It leads to two other squares with equally evocative names – Place de la République and Place de la Nation. The storming of the Bastille on July 14, 1789, has become a myth in its own right, but it resulted in large part from actions taken by the inhabitants of the Faubourg

THE VIADUC DES ARTS
Beneath the old viaduct that runs the length of the Avenue Daumesnil are the workshops and sales outlets of numerous artist-craftsmen. Above them, the old rail tracks have gone, replaced by a 3-mile planted walkway.

THE ELEPHANT OF THE BASTILLE
Napoleon I planned to build a fountain in the shape of an elephant on the Place de la Bastille. A mock-up of the animal, 80 feet high and 52 feet long, was set up to the east of the present-day column. It stood there from 1813 to 1847. Gavroche sheltered underneath it in Victor Hugo's novel *Les Misérables.*

St-Antoine. This street still has a high level of creative activity, with numerous artists' studios and architects' offices. New types of residents are beginning to move into this area, which has started to become fashionable, but it retains its popular, colorful atmosphere along with its traditional passageways and backyards.

PLACE DE LA BASTILLE   (2 I8)

FORTRESS AND PRISON. The Bastille was built by Hugues Aubriot, provost of the merchants of Paris between 1370 and 1382, to defend the capital against invaders from the east and to protect the Hôtel St-Pol, residence of Charles V. Paving stones in the road opposite 49, avenue Henri-IV mark the outline of one tower of this fortress, which stood to the west of today's square. The fortress was 80 feet high and had eight round towers; it was surrounded by an 80-foot ditch. Despite this impressive appearance, it played only a minor military role, except during the Fronde in 1649, when La Grande Mademoiselle, niece of Louis XIII, turned the cannons on the royal troops led by Turenne in order to protect the Prince de Condé. From Richelieu's time the Bastille was a state prison and a symbol of the arbitrary use of royal power. Many famous prisoners were held here, sent to prison simply by a *lettre de cachet* (a letter bearing the royal seal which, under the Ancien Régime, gave order of public ceremony, imprisonment or even exile). They include Fouquet, Cagliostro, the famous Man in the Iron Mask and Voltaire, who completed his play *Oedipe* during a year of captivity in 1717. Although the dungeons were unpleasant, the regime was especially lenient toward high-ranking prisoners, and the number of inmates rarely exceeded fifty or so after Louis XIV became king. This did not prevent the Marquis de Sade from haranguing passersby from his window with his cries that "the prisoners of the Bastille are being assassinated, you must come to their rescue". He was transferred to the Charenton insane asylum, on July 4, 1789.

GREAT MOMENTS OF THE REVOLUTION. On July 14, 1789, the Bastille entered into the mythology of the Revolution. After Minister Necker had been dismissed by Louis XVI, 900 rioters, mostly from the Faubourg St-Antoine, gathered in front of the fortress with the aim of obtaining weapons. In the afternoon they were reinforced by 100 French guards; the governor, De Launay, capitulated but was massacred along with his garrison of 32 Swiss Guards and 82 veterans. The prisoners of the Bastille were given an ovation and carried off in triumph – all seven of them, including two swindlers, one nobleman guilty of incest, and a lunatic. This victory by the "conquerors of the Bastille", achieved at a cost of 100 dead and 73 injured, acquired a mythical status out of all proportion to the significance of the military events. One man wasted no time in making the most of the situation: the "Patriote" Palloy took charge of demolishing the Bastille, making 83 models of the fortress which he sent to all 83 French *départements* to "perpetuate the horror of despotism there". This astute businessman also made jewelry, chains and keys from the remains of the fortress: some examples can be seen at the Musée Carnavalet. Some of the stones were also used to build the Pont de la Concorde.

COLONNE DE JUILLET
A law of 1830 decreed the erection of a monument to commemorate the victims of the Three Glorious Days of the Revolution – July 27, 28 and 29, 1830 ● 20. This was the origin of the July Column, inspired by the Trajan Column in Rome and completed by Duc in 1840. Its bronze shaft is 150 feet high and is surmounted by the Spirit of Liberty, which is shown "in flight, rending its chains asunder and scattering light". It is modeled on a sculpture by Drumont. Beneath the column are two tombs holding the remains of victims of the revolutions in 1830 and 1848.

▲ BASTILLE
FAUBOURG ST-ANTOINE

OPÉRA-BASTILLE. The building is striking for its austerity and its monumental style of architecture composed of geometric shapes: the sober glass wall of the main façade is fronted by a dark gray marble portico. The architect Carlos Ott kept to the typical shape of building lots in the surrounding area: his building is worth seeing in the evening, when the whole glass façade is lit up. The Grand Auditorium, in gray granite and oak, has 2,700 seats. Its double stage, along with the hall's nine aisles, allow different productions to be alternated without dismantling the scenery.

THE ARSENAL   (2 G9)

The cannon foundry of the Royal Arsenal was established in the 16th century and closed under Louis XIII. The furnaces continued to operate, however, producing large statues for the Palace of Versailles, for example. This was once a huge collection of buildings stretching as far as the Bastille; now only the wing built by Germain Boffrand between 1718 and 1745 is still standing. This wing, built in a very austere style, formerly belonged to the residence of the Great Master of the Artillery (1–3, rue de Sully).

THE LIBRARY. Paulmy d'Argenson, a diplomat and minister of war, assembled his magnificent collection of medieval illuminated manuscripts and prints here in 1757. This formed the basis of today's library, which acquired the archives of the Bastille during the Revolution, as well as books confiscated from convents and monasteries. The Arsenal library has a calm atmosphere, warm-colored paneling and shelves full of leather-bound books; its collection includes 14,000 manuscripts – among them the *Psautier de Saint Louis* and the *Heures du Maître-aux-Fleurs* – as well as 120,000 prints. The library also specializes in works dedicated to the arts and theater.

A POPULAR OPERA HOUSE
The Opéra-Bastille was built in the east of the capital, in a deliberate move away from the elitist character of the more affluent areas. Its date of opening was just as significant: July 14, 1989, the bicentenary of the French Revolution. It has yet to be seen if the opera house can achieve its social aims; meanwhile, the building itself has aroused lively controversy.

FAUBOURG ST-ANTOINE

TRADITIONAL CRAFTS. The royal Cistercian abbey of St-Antoine-des-Champs was founded in 1198 by Foulques, parish priest of Neuilly-sur-Marne and a preacher in the Fourth Crusade. It became one of the richest convents in

Paris. The "Lady of the Faubourg", its abbess, was often a member of one of the most eminent families in the kingdom. The abbey, on the site of the present Hôpital St-Antoine, enjoyed an

unusual privilege: in the 15th century, Louis XI exempted the craftsmen working here from membership in the guilds. After this, the faubourg grew and prospered. The woodworkers, freed from the restrictive regulations of the guilds, were able to depart from prescribed models and the use of oak in order to work with marquetry and rare woods.

REVOLTS IN THE FAUBOURG. The high level of industrial activity made this working-class area one of the most restless in Paris. The workers here were open to new ideas and were easily aroused; this fostered an atmosphere of social agitation and rebellion. On April 28, 1789, a riot took place among the four thousand workers under Réveillon, who introduced wallpaper in France: this was a prelude to the Revolution. The population of the faubourg played a key role not only in the storming of the Bastille but also in the social unrest of the 19th century: barricades were raised in the streets in 1830 and 1848 and under the Commune in 1871 ● 26.

RUE DU FAUBOURG ST-ANTOINE. Although mechanization has transformed working conditions, there are still many workshops here and a large number of furniture shops, especially around the Bastille. Hidden curiosities include the paved courtyard of the Étoile-d'Or (2 J8) at no. 75, with its artists' studios and a sundial from 1751. The courtyard of the Bel-Air (2 J8) at no. 56 is one of the most beautiful in Paris: its walls are covered in Virginia creeper, sometimes even with grapes and tomatoes on the southern side. At no. 50, Passage de la Boule-Blanche (2 J8) opens onto the Rue de Charenton, opposite the Hôpital des Quinze-Vingts (2 I9). This institution was founded by Saint Louis in 1260 to

INTERIORS OF THE ARSENAL (2 G9) Mme de La Meilleraye's room is very well preserved: it was decorated in 1637 with a ceiling attributed to Simon Vouet (*Apollo and the Muses*) and wall panels with a delicate floral pattern. In the Oratory are paintings in the grotesque style from the 17th century, depicting famous women of history. The Salon de Musique is a very good example of Louis XV style, with grisaille paintings over the doors.

FAUBOURG ST-ANTOINE This quarter was the most industrial area of Paris under the Ancien Régime: it was renowned throughout Europe for its furniture, earthenware and textiles. Today the street of the same name is well known for its furniture shops and the craft workshops in its many courtyards and passageways, such as the Passage du Chantier at no. 66.

ALIGRE MARKET
(3 A9). This market, selling food and bric-a-brac, is held every day ▲ *IV* ♦ *523*.

house three hundred blind people ("fifteen times twenty").

RUE DE CHARONNE (2 J8). A café on the corner of Avenue Ledru-Rollin still has its turn-of-the-century decorations: its window still advertises a cup of coffee at ten centimes in gold lettering. The view of the Hôtel de Mortagne (no. 53) is spoiled by the ugly modern building next to it: the older house was built in 1660 for Delisle Mansart, with gargoyles on its façade and an octagonal rotonda. Jacques Vaucanson assembled his collection of machines and automata here in 1746; this was the start of the Conservatory of Arts and Crafts ▲ *136*.

RUE DE LAPPE (2 I8). This street is quiet and undistinguished by day, but in the evenings it still has something of its turn-of-the-century atmosphere, when it was a favorite place for dancing. Settlers from the Auvergne and from Italy made it into a center for *bals musette*, popular dance halls with accordion music, frequented by *apaches*, the local hooligans ▲ *410*. The Balajo (no. 9) is still the leading establishment; it was decorated by Mahé (who also decorated the Rex Cinéma) and opened in 1936. Leading accordion players like Jo Privat and Yvette Horner had their heyday here. A traditional Auvergne shop at no. 6 still has its old display shelves for salted meats and fish, while bars and restaurants like the Bar à Nénette (no. 26) have a delightful prewar atmosphere.

FROM BASTILLE TO NATION

GARE DE LYON (2 I10). This station was built between 1847 and 1852, and rebuilt for the Universal Exhibition of 1900 in the academic style fashionable at the time. It is dominated by its belfry: the clock's hands are 10 feet long. The arrival of the TGV (high-speed train service) gave a modern dimension to this old station.

BUILDING PROJECTS OF THE GRAND EST PARISIEN. This enormous urban development project is based around a few major architectural creations: the Opéra-Bastille, the pleasure port in the Arsenal basin, and the impressive 1,200-foot-long viaduct-like new Ministry of Finance building, which was completed in 1988. The Bercy warehouse district was formerly the site of the largest wine market in France, covering an area of 86 acres; this has been replaced by a huge modern park, preserving the two rows of listed wine storehouses and the hundred-year-old trees. The architecturally innovative former American Cultural Center (4 B3), designed with overlapping sloping sections by Frank Gehry, is to become the

future Maison du Cinéma. There are also residential projects, like the one for the notoriously squalid Châlon site, now replaced by five hundred new homes. These are gradually transforming the area to the south of the Gare de Lyon.

CHURCH OF STE-MARGUERITE (3 B8). Behind its discreet façade is the Chapel of Souls in Purgatory, built after a design by Victor Louis in 1760 and decorated with curious trompe-l'oeil frescos by Brunetti. It was in its cemetery (now disused), on June 10, 1795, that the burial of a young boy who had died at the Temple took place. It was thought that this might have been Louis XVII, but two examinations by forensic surgeons in 1846 and 1894 showed that the body was that of a boy aged 15 to 18: the Dauphin was 10 years old when he disappeared.

PLACE DE LA NATION (3 E9 10). On August 26, 1660, a royal throne was set up here for the ceremonial entry of Louis XIV and Marie-Thérèse into Paris. Thereafter, the square kept the name Place du Trône, which was maliciously corrupted to Square of the Overturned Throne during the Revolution. On a more sinister note, the square was the site of a guillotine at this time, which claimed over 1,300 victims, including the poet André Chénier. It was given its present name in 1880, on the occasion of celebrations for July 14 (decreed a public holiday). At the center of the square is *The Triumph of the Republic*, a bronze statue by Jules Dalou. It measures 820 feet in diameter and was originally intended for the Place de la République.

GARE DE LYON
The Train Bleu restaurant on the second floor is lavishly decorated with gilded paneling and paintings by the official artists of the Third Republic. The magnificent decoration indicates the important position of the railways in the 19th century.

BERCY
This stadium (4 A3), with its turf-covered steel roof, can hold 17,000 spectators, in a multifunctional area adaptable for sports and other events.

407

▲ BELLEVILLE – MÉNILMONTANT

⊙ Half a day

THE WATERS OF BELLEVILLE

Springs were common here, and some of Belleville's street names still hark back to a time when water ran down its slopes. The footbridge of the Rue de la Mare was rebuilt in 1900 (shown around 1940, below): it crosses the railway of the former Petite Ceinture.

RUE
DE LA
MARE

Alleys running down the slopes, stalls and workshops, old bistros, villas, gardens hidden away behind carriage entrances – Belleville and its former hamlet, Ménilmontant, still bear the mark of their rural and working-class past. The village came into being in medieval times on the vine-covered slopes owned by the great Parisian abbeys (St-Merri, St-Martin et al.). In the 18th century and up to the Restoration, this was the kingdom of *guinguettes*, or open-air cafés. Parisians used to come here on Sundays to drink a vinegarish wine called *guinguet*. After 1840 Belleville grew rapidly, becoming one of the largest towns in France. Workers came here in large numbers, forced out of the center of Paris by the grand urban projects under way there. In 1860 the town was annexed to Paris and cut in two: its main thoroughfare marks the boundary between the 19th and 20th arrondissements. The former wine-growing village became a place of poverty and revolt, its population banding together in the revolt of the Commune: Belleville's barricades were the last to fall under attack by the Versaillais. In the 20th century Belleville became home to many immigrant groups. Today its population is one of the most diverse and cosmopolitan in Paris, as can be seen in the extraordinary market held every Wednesday and Friday morning on the boulevards between Métro stations Belleville and Ménilmontant.

RUE DE BELLEVILLE AND ITS SURROUNDINGS

CITÉ DU PALAIS-ROYAL (11 D10) 151, rue de Belleville.
Hidden away from the bustle of the street is one of Belleville's
many secret "garden cities". These houses and small
apartment blocks with little gardens, grouped around private

roads, are typical of the area. From 1840
until the first decades of the 20th century,
Belleville developed as a working-class
area, its land divided into very small plots.
Disdained by the grand urban-
development projects, the town grew up
haphazardly, following the schemes and
projects of its small tenants (near right:
the Villa de l'Ermitage).

REGARD DE LA LANTERNE (11 D9) Place
des Fêtes. From the 12th century onward,
abbeys which owned land on the Belleville
plateau drained off its water with
underground aqueducts to supply their
monasteries in Paris. Little buildings were
put up along the course of the aqueducts
to give access to them for inspection. The
Lanterne manhole (1613) stands out amid
glass-and-steel towers: it marked the head
of the Belleville aqueduct.

ON THE ROAD TO MÉNILMONTANT ★. The
network of alleys and passages between
the Rue de Belleville and the Rue de Ménilmontant – mostly
following old paths between the vines – still has a
prewar atmosphere. The Rue Piat led to two
windmills in the 19th century: today it ends at
the PARC DE BELLEVILLE ▲ *210*, where a vine
has been symbolically replanted. The RUE DES
ENVIERGES (3 C1) rings out each evening to
the accordion music of its cafés-chantants.
From the Passage Plantin you can see the
maisonettes of the Villa Castel, where
François Truffaut filmed scenes for *Jules et
Jim* (1962). The RUE DES CASCADES (3 D2),
with its dollhouses, bistro, glass-blower and
manholes (nos. 42 and 17), is the site of one of the few
restoration projects (nos. 15–23) which has respected the
traditional social and urban fabric of the area.

DESCENTE DE LA COURTILLE
Under the Restoration a riotous carnival was held at Belleville every year, attracting all of Paris society to the area.

BELLEVILLE TO BE SCRAPPED?
The Parc de Belleville offers a splendid view over Paris (above), but the staircase of the Passage Julien-Lacroix was destroyed to make way for this development. Belleville is a developers' target, but it is holding out: many artists have now moved into its old factories.

JULES et JIM

The real Casque d'Or (opposite), with *apaches* on either side. Simone Signoret immortalized the character in the 1952 film by Jacques Becker.

RUE DE MÉNILMONTANT   (3 BF3)

This was a favorite walk for Parisians in the 18th century, rising in a steep slope up to the plateau. In 1778 seven Parisians died here, engulfed by a collapsing quarry. The name Ménilmontant comes from *Mesnil Mautemps* (home of bad weather), the name of a house on these hills. Around the 16th century this was corrupted to *Mesnil Montant* (rising home).

LA BELLEVILLOISE ★ (3 D3) 23–5, rue Boyer. This building from 1927 is decorated with Marxist symbols, reflecting the strong communist tradition which grew up in Belleville after the Commune. La Bellevilloise, founded in 1877, continued to be very active up to the last war. Its shops, library and social club were open only to members.

MAISON DES SAINT-SIMONIENS (3 E2) 145, rue de Ménilmontant. The house is hidden by a block: it can be seen from the neighboring square. This was the mecca of Saint-Simonianism. In 1832, Prosper Enfantin, one of the apostles of this utopian thinker, put into practice his ideas regarding intimate relationships, based on the primacy of passion. This grand priest of the new religion was searching for a woman-messiah. On Sunday, the Saint-Simonians opened their house to the population of Belleville, sang canticles and wore their uniform (white trousers, red waistcoat and violet tunic, the colors of love, work and faith). Enfantin was prosecuted for offending public morals and forced to disband the society.

DOMAINE DE ST-FARGEAU

The Château de St-Fargeau and its grounds were broken up after the Revolution: they covered a vast area between the Rue Pelleport and the Boulevard Mortier (3 FH2). The last occupant, the member of parliament Michel Le Pelletier, was assassinated in 1793 for voting in favor of the king's death.

CIMETIÈRE DE BELLEVILLE (11 F10) 40, rue du Télégraphe. The trees of this cemetery (1804) are all that remain of the park of St-Fargeau where Rousseau came to collect plants. In 1792, Claude Chappe chose this place – the highest point of eastern Paris – to test his telegraph machine. However, the *sans-culottes* of Belleville wrecked his signaling device. The cemetery houses the tomb of one of the pioneers of cinema, Léon Gaumont, who came from Belleville.

NOTRE-DAME-DES-OTAGES (11 F10) 81, rue Haxo. This church (1938) commemorates a bloody episode of the Commune ● 28. On May 26, 1871, the mob massacred

center of political opposition terrified the middle classes of Paris. The population of Belleville was decimated by the Commune, falling from 50,000 to 20,000 in five months. Above: the inner court of a workers' housing development in the Rue Ernest Lefèvre at the end of the 19th century.

fifty-two Federate hostages here, mostly monks and national guards. The remains of the wall where they were executed can be seen on Rue Borrégo, behind courtyard railings.

Traces of the past. The Concert du XXᵉ Siècle on Boulevard de Ménilmontant and some old shop signs.

VILLAS OF THE AMERICAN QUARTER
A developer created

CHAUMONT AND AMÉRIQUE QUARTERS

QUARRIES. Just over a century ago, this was a dangerous area, hollowed out by gypsum quarries. The underground tunnels served as nocturnal meeting places for criminals, and the police raided them regularly (above). Today, the parks of the Buttes-Chaumont and Butte du Chapeau-Rouge and the many villas around them make this one of the most picturesque areas of Paris.

AMÉRIQUE QUARTER ★ (MAP 11). The name of this area supposedly comes from the fact that gypsum from here was sent to Louisiana. The quarries ceased operation in 1872, but the roads built after they were filled in remained empty until the beginning of this century, as no one dared to build on such unstable ground.

PARC DES BUTTES-CHAUMONT.
See *Nature* ▲ *208*.

HÔTEL DES IMPÔTS (11 B9) 35, rue du Plateau. Léon Gaumont, who started his working life in a photographic studio in Belleville, built up an empire here until he went bankrupt in 1930. The studios and offices of the Elgé City (from his initials "LG") covered the entire area between the Rue Botzaris and the Rue Fessart. Now only this building (1925) survives, with its splendid Art Deco entrance decorated with marguerites, in honor of his mother's name.

54, RUE SIMON-BOLIVAR ★ (11 B10). The staircase which passes through this building leads to five small streets created in 1927 on the circular site of a former stadium. At the far western end is an extraordinary view of Paris and its great monuments.

these small alleyways between the Rue Mouzaïa, Rue Général-Brunet and Rue Miguel-Hidalgo in 1901. However, the city council would not allow houses to be

built over one story high because of the unstable subsoil, which had been weakened by the quarries. Gradually, villas intended for working-class families were built on either side of these streets.

411

With its shady avenues, winding streets, forests and esplanades, its fashionable areas, its poor districts, its history, folklore, mysteries, police and outlaws – the Père-Lachaise Cemetery, opened by Prefect Frochot in 1804, is a city of the dead within a city of the living. It is located on the old hill of Champ-l'Évêque, where a rich merchant built his house in 1430. In the 17th century the Jesuits converted it into a hospice for members of their order: it became a meeting place for high society under the influence of the Père La Chaise, Louis XIV's confessor.

OSSUARY
This high relief made in 1895 decorates the entrance to the Père-Lachaise Ossuary. The sculptor Bartholomé portrayed the anguish of the living as two of their number cross over the threshold of death.

MAUSOLEUMS AND MONUMENTS TO THE DEAD
In the northeast corner of the cemetery, not far from the wall where many Federates were executed ● 28, stands a series of monuments to the dead, paying tribute to the victims of Nazi atrocities. Some modern tombs have returned to the Egyptian style of monumental architecture, which became very fashionable after Napoleon's Egyptian campaign.

COLOMBARIUM
A long gallery surrounds the Moorish-style crematorium at the center of the cemetery. Both were built at the end of the last century by the architect Formigé. Small niches in the gallery hold the ashes of the dead.

Tomb of Jim Morrison (6th division)

TOMB OF ABÉLARD AND HÉLOÏSE (7th division)

Victor Noir

ROCK AND SPIRITUALISM

Jim Morrison, whose bust was taken by fans, has stolen the limelight from Abélard and Héloïse, entombed under a neo-Gothic canopy since 1817. Morrison has a cult following equaled only by that of the spiritualist Allan Kardec (24th division). The statue of the journalist Yvan Salmon, alias Victor Noir

Frédéric Chopin

(92nd division), is believed to have fertility-enhancing powers. The tomb of Frédéric Chopin (11th division) has a sculpture of a muse by Clésinger or Vivant Denon, the diplomat-artist whose monument is by Cartellier (above, 10th division).

Honoré de Balzac

Allan Kardec

ABBESSES

Musée de Montmartre

⏱ One day

Paris viewed from Montmartre by Louis-Jacques Mandé-Daguerre.

L ittle has changed in Montmartre since Nerval sang its praises in the 19th century. Though this butte has always had a defiantly independent character, it was nonetheless annexed to Paris in 1860 and has not escaped the relentless sprawl of the city. This hill devoted to art and to pleasure is also a place of paradoxes. At once mystical and libertarian, touristy and insular, it has remained one of the last villages of Paris, along with the Butte-aux-Cailles.

FROM SAINT DENIS TO PICASSO. Montmartre has been a place of worship since the time of the Gauls. In the Middle Ages it was an important pilgrimage stop dedicated to Saint Denis, the saint who converted Paris to Christianity. Legend has it that after his decapitation Saint Denis walked to Catullanum, now St-Denis, where he was buried ▲ 432. In 1133, Montmartre passed into the hands of the Benedictine monks, whose territory, stretching as far as today's 9th arrondissement, was famous for its vines and its windmills. This was also a strategic site: it was occupied by Henri de Navarre in 1590, by the Cossacks in 1814, and by the English in 1815. It was made into a separate

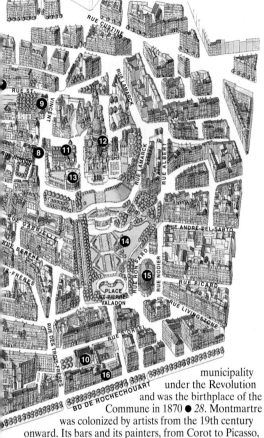

JEHAN RICTUS
This "cursed poet" had a belated revenge on the injustices of fate when a square was named after him.

MONTMARTRE CEMETERY
This necropolis covers 27 acres. It was opened in 1825 on the site of former gypsum quarries, which had earned the area its name of Barrière-Blanche (white barrier). The quarries had served as a communal grave, especially during the Revolution. Berlioz liked this "field of tranquility" so much that he chose it as his final resting place, as did Degas, Vigny, Stendhal, Fragonard and Marguerite

municipality under the Revolution and was the birthplace of the Commune in 1870 ● *28*. Montmartre was colonized by artists from the 19th century onward. Its bars and its painters, from Corot to Picasso, have made it legendary.

PLACE DES ABBESSES (10 B7). The name of this square refers to the former Benedictine convent which stretched from the summit to halfway down the hill. Here, in the shade of the plane trees, you can see one of the two surviving windows made by Guimard for the Métro. This one, reassembled in 1976, came from the Hôtel-de-Ville station. The CHURCH OF ST-JEAN-L'ÉVANGÉLISTE, the first religious building made of reinforced concrete, was built between 1894 and 1904 by Anatole de Baudot, a follower of Viollet-le-Duc. His design was chosen because it was the least expensive: it was partly financed by the parish priest. The project had to overcome numerous bureaucratic obstacles before it could be carried out: officials of the time had little faith in this new type of construction. The church has been nicknamed St-Jean-des-Briques after its external facing. Its somber Art-Nouveau interior decorations offer a stark contrast to the façade, whose crossed arches were inspired by Muslim architecture.

THE COMMUNARDS AT THE TOWN HALL. The former town hall stood on the Square Jehan-Rictus. Verlaine was married here

Gautier, Alexandre Dumas' model for *La Dame aux Camélias*. Above, Théophile Gautier's funeral.

Temps des Cerises

BATEAU-LAVOIR

The building (right) was a "manor of surprises . . . shaky, dark, all staircases, corners, nooks and crannies", wrote Roland Dorgelès in his *Bouquets of Bohemia*.

LOUISE MICHEL

(1833–1905)
This teacher at the Batignolles was a militant, writer and poet. The natural daughter of a country squire and a housekeeper, she later became an ambulance driver and figurehead of the Federates in Montmartre. She was deported to New Caledonia, but Paris gave her a triumphal welcome when she returned in 1880 after the Communards' general amnesty.

and Georges Clémenceau, a doctor of

Montmartre, held the position of mayor when the Commune ● *28* was proclaimed in Paris on March 26, 1871. On the same day he was accused of complying with the authorities and forced to give way to Jean-Baptiste Clément (1836–1903), who wrote "Le Temps des Cerises" ("Cherry Time"), the love song charged with revolutionary nostalgia which accompanied Zola's last journey, to the North Cemetery. Clément was exiled after the revolt had been put down. He continued his militant activities in London, and again in France after his return in 1880. One of Montmartre's squares is named after him, and a cherry tree was planted there in his memory.

BATEAU-LAVOIR (10 B6) Place Émile-Goudeau. Artists started coming to live in Montmartre in the 19th century, attracted by its light and its cheap rents. The first to come was Georges Michel (1763–1843). He was soon followed by Géricault, Corot, Renoir, and Degas, and in the early 20th century, the Fauves, Cubists and Futurists. The Bateau-Lavoir was their headquarters. The name given to this ramshackle building referred to its peculiar layout, reminiscent of a ship's gangways, and, ironically, to its single tap. It was also called the trapper's cabin, and Max Jacob nicknamed it the central laboratory. Artists and writers who lived here included Van Dongen, Juan Gris, Vlaminck and Braque, as well as Renoir, Cézanne, Max Jacob and Apollinaire. Picasso, its most famous inhabitant, painted his Cubist manifesto *Les Demoiselles d'Avignon* here in 1907. The Bateau-Lavoir was destroyed by fire soon after it was accorded landmark status in 1970; it was replaced by a block of artists' studios.

PLACE DU TERTRE (10 B6). This tourist mecca is now the preserve of restaurants and artists offering modestly priced, mediocre paintings. The ubiquitous easels and café terraces have almost destroyed the charm of this rustic square, where the abbey's shackles and gallows once stood. The first local

PLACE DU TERTRE

LA MÈRE CATHERINE
This famous restaurant on the Place du Tertre opened in 1793. It is here that the word *bistro* (Russian for "quick") entered the French language, introduced by the Cossack occupying forces in 1814. It was, understandably, mistranslated as a synonym for "café" ● *42*.

BALLOONS ON THE PLACE ST-PIERRE
At the suggestion of the photographer Nadar, balloons were sent up from here to survey the enemy lines during the siege of Paris in 1870. Gambetta, in charge of organizing the resistance outside Paris, flew off for Orléans from here on October 7.

council of Montmartre set up its town hall here in 1790, at no. 3. There is another town hall at no. 19, which organizes local festivities.

CHURCH OF ST-PIERRE DE MONTMARTRE (10 B6). This venerable edifice, one of the oldest in the capital, is supposed to have been built on the site of a temple to Mercury. But history has treated it roughly: it was dedicated by Eugène III in 1147; it became a "Temple of Reason" under the Revolution; the Commune made it into a clothing factory; and in 1793 the engineer Chappe put a telegraph pole on top of it. The church was saved in 1897 by a group of artists who persuaded the public authorities to restore it.

THE TWO ABBEYS OF MONTMARTRE. The church was the chapel of the Benedictine convent, founded in 1133 by Adélaïde de Savoie, wife of Louis VI. The nuns derived substantial revenues from the SANCTUM MARTYRIUM (10 B7), built in the 12th century on the site where Saint Denis met his death, according to legend; it was replaced by a memorial chapel in 1887 (9, rue Yvonne-Le-Tac). On August 15, 1534, Ignatius de Loyola founded his Company of Jesus in this famous shrine, visited by the faithful from all over Europe. From the 15th

THE QUARRIES
The Montmartre quarries were rich in montmartrite, a type of gypsum used from Roman times onward. They were also an invaluable field of observation for Cuvier, the father of paleontology. Hermits and outlaws took shelter in their tunnels – among them Ignatius de Loyola, Jean-Paul Marat and the rebels of June 23, 1843, who were hunted down by General Cavaignac.

RUE DE L'ABREUVOIR
(10 B5) This street runs down the slope beneath the Sacré-Coeur. Gérard de Nerval loved its winding path, used to lead animals to the drinking trough. From here he could see the greenery of the Folie Sandrin at 22, rue Norvins, converted into a nursing home by Dr Blanche, a famous specialist in mental illness. It was here that the poet wrote his masterpiece *Aurélia*.

The Quarries of Montmartre by Bouhot (right).

century the convent gradually declined, ruined by the Hundred Years War and the decline in pilgrimages. Its finances were at an all-time low when, in 1661, building works in the Martyrium led to the discovery of a crypt marking the site of Saint Denis' martyrdom. This timely discovery brought back the pilgrims. As money poured in, the Martyrium was incorporated in a new priory, called the Lower Abbey. The Upper Abbey was abandoned and demolished; only the church of St-Pierre remained. The Lower Abbey was demolished under the Revolution.

HISTORY. Behind the 18th-century façade and the modern doors carved by Gismoni lies a fascinating historical site. The vault of the choir, with its thick moldings, is the oldest in Paris, predating the one in St-Martin-des-Champs. It dates from the mid-12th century, as do the choir, the two apsidioles, the transept and the bay next to the nave. Originally the apse had a half-domed roof; it was rebuilt in the 12th century. The first three bays of the nave date from the same period, although their vaults date from the 15th century. Four marble columns at the entrance and in the choir are from an earlier building. The church also has some interesting tombstones. The tomb of Adélaïde de Savoie is in the northern apse.

SACRÉ-COEUR (10 C6). This church is an integral part of the Montmartre landscape, with its Byzantine-Romanesque façade, its dazzling white domes and bell towers, and the constant procession of pilgrims climbing its steps. Its striking presence almost erases the memory of its turbulent beginnings, which were dogged by a political and religious conflict reflecting the state of the nation after two national crises, the defeat of 1870 and the Commune.

A PROJECT FOR THE NATION. 1870 was a black year for Catholic France: the loss of Alsace-Lorraine, the Commune rebellion and the annexation of the pontifical states seemed like a punishment for a century without religion. Although many pilgrimages were made to save the Pope and the nation, it was two laymen, Alexandre Legentil and Hubert Rohault de Fleury, who vowed to build a church dedicated to the cult of the Sacred Heart. The archbishop of Paris, Monsignor Guibert, was unenthusiastic at first but soon became the project's champion. The basilica was to overlook the capital from the top of the Montmartre hill, sanctified by the martyrdom of Saint Denis and defiled by Communard reprisals. In 1873 the General Assembly declared that the project was to be financed by private funds.

TOUR OF THE CHURCH. The building was modeled on the church of St-Front in Périgueux. The vault of the choir is decorated with a mosaic by Luc-Olivier Merson, who also produced the mosaics for the side chapels. Alongside the

CONSTRUCTION OF THE SACRÉ-COEUR
The project was punctuated by skirmishes with opponents and fraught with problems. The foundations had to be dug deeper than

anticipated because of the quarries under the hill, thus increasing the cost and delaying the building work. Construction began in 1877, and the church was completed forty years later. Three architects separately managed the project: Paul Abadie, who restored the church of St-Front in Périgueux, Hervé Rauline and Lucien Magne.

PILLARS IN THE HILL
Eighty-three pillars were driven into the hill to support the walls and columns of the Sacré-Coeur. They stand on stone shafts, some 16 feet thick. It has been claimed that it is the basilica which holds up the hill, and not the other way round.

419

FRANCISQUE POULBOT
(1879–1946)
This draftsman created the image of the typical Montmartre urchin. In 1921 he opened a clinic for local children with the help of the manager of the Pomponette restaurant. His urchins, known as *poulbots*, have outlived their creator.

MAQUIS
This scrubland covered with copses, wild grasses and picturesque huts was located between Rue Girardon and Rue Caulaincourt. It disappeared in 1911 when Avenue Junot was built. The avenue's residents have included Tristan Tzara (no. 15) and Poulbot (no. 13).

Virgin, the pope and the saints of France, the mosaic depicts the Parisian cardinals and bishops and the project's initiators (a chapel in the CRYPT also pays tribute to the founders). The DOME offers a dizzying view, while the CAMPANILE has one of the world's largest bells, the Savoyarde (1895).

WORSHIP AT THE SACRÉ-COEUR. The basilica is not a parish church but a place of pilgrimage, drawing Catholics from all over the world. A continuous service is held here, manned at night by delegates from the different Parisian parishes.

RUE ST-RUSTIQUE (10 B6). This narrow street is nine centuries old and has kept its old paving and its central gutter. The restaurant À la Bonne Franquette, on the corner of Rue des Saules, once called Aux Billards de Bois, was the meeting-place of Sisley, Cézanne, Toulouse-Lautrec, Pissarro, Renoir, Monet and Zola. The little garden where Van Gogh painted *The Open-Air Café* can still be seen.

CHÂTEAU DES BROUILLARDS (10 B5). The mysterious Allée des Brouillards runs through an old estate which used to reach as far as Rue Caulaincourt. The château, a beautiful pre-Revolution house, was made famous by Roland Dorgelès' novel. Gérard de Nerval is supposed to have lived there in 1846. Renoir lived in an ordinary house on the other side of the street.

MUSÉE DE MONTMARTRE (10 B6) ◆ *480*. This museum, at 12, rue Cortot, opened in 1860 in the former residence of Roze de Rosimond, an actor in Molière's troupe who died on stage (like Molière himself). This house, the oldest in Montmartre, had a more bohemian flavor at the beginning of the century. Its outbuildings housed the painter Raoul Dufy, the writers Léon Bloy and Pierre Reverdy, the theatrical manager André Antoine, and a talented but eccentric trio: Suzanne Valadon, her husband André Utter and his son Maurice Utrillo. Renoir rented an apartment here, and this is where he painted *The Swing*.

Le "Placard" de Satie (10 B6) ▲ 477.
The Vineyard of Montmartre. In 1929 there

was a rumor that an apartment building was to be built on the site of Aristide Bruant's garden, on the corner of Rue des Saules and the Rue St-Vincent. The resistance, led by Poulbot and the painter Willette, decided to confront the authorities with a fait accompli, so they created a square here to prevent the demolition. The operation was a success. Later, a grapevine was planted here to make good use of the ground which had been saved. Ever since then, the harvest festival has been a major local event. The Montmartre wine, or *picolo*, is auctioned for charity.

Le Lapin Agile (10 B6) 4, rue des Saules.
This small pink building on the corner of Rue St-Vincent was once famous for its risqué poetry. Inside there are timeworn walls covered with engravings and paintings, old-fashioned curtains, a disused fireplace and a large Christ figure by Wasley above the wooden tables. The establishment was formerly called the Cabaret des Assassins but it changed its name when the caricaturist André Gill produced a new sign showing a mischievous rabbit leaping from a cooking pot. Le Lapin à Gill became Le Lapin Agile (The Agile Rabbit). Aristide Bruant bought the business in 1902, entrusting its management to Frédéric Gérard, known as Frédé. Regulars included Utrillo, Picasso, Braque, Derain, Vlaminck and Modigliani, as well as Apollinaire, Max Jacob, Carco, and Charles Dullin. The place became legendary. It has a reputation for discovering new talent: its Cabaret du Quai des Brumes is one of the few stages in Paris open to newcomers.

La Maison Rose
This small house at 2, rue de l'Abreuvoir, was immortalized by Utrillo (1883–1955). He was an alcoholic from childhood; he never left his easel and worked mainly from postcards. The artist was generally regarded as the village idiot and

avoided painting from life in order to escape gibes.

Moulin Rouge

Montmartre ended the 19th century to the tune of a quadrille. There was much dancing on Boulevard de Clichy and Boulevard de Rochechouart. A cosmopolitan crowd of pleasure-seekers, members of the demimonde and ordinary Parisians frequented the "unchastity belt" of Montmartre, where the Boule-Noire and the Élysée-Montmartre had packed houses. While the Moulin-Rouge invented the cancan and Toulouse-Lautrec sketched its performers, satirical cabaret was born at Le Chat-Noir.

LE MOULIN DE LA GALETTE

This was one of thirty mills in Montmartre which were used to grind not only grain but also gypsum and stone. It was owned by the Debray family of millers, who lived in the Rue Lepic. They decided to open a dance hall here, selling flat cakes called *galettes* as a refreshment for customers between polkas. The Moulin de la Galette was born. Its good-natured atmosphere delighted Renoir and Dufy, both of whom lived at 12, rue Cortot, and came here to paint. It soon faced competition from another mill: Le Moulin-Rouge.

CANCAN

It is just a stone's throw from the Moulin-Rouge to the Place Pigalle, where the market for artists' models was held. Some *grisettes* (a term meaning a young coquettish factory worker, taken from the verb *griser*, "to make tipsy") who had left the studios achieved their brief moment of glory on the stage, including Jane Avril, known as *La Mélinite*; Cricri, who died doing splits; and La Goulue, who ended her life as a tramp. Below: Nini Patte-en-l'Air (Nini Foot-in-the-Air).

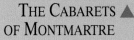

LE CHAT-NOIR

In 1881, Rodolphe Salis leased a disused post office on the Boulevard de Rochechouart and opened a cabaret under the patronage of the *chansonnier* Émile Goudeau. A *chansonnier* is a singer-songwriter who writes satirical songs about current affairs. Le Chat-Noir was a great success. A huge painting by Willette, *Farce Domine*, complemented its somber Louis-XIII-style décor.

Above: *La Goulue and Valentin le Désossé at the Moulin-Rouge* by Toulouse-Lautrec.

Salis made fun of the institutions of the day and scolded his audiences. He also opened a shadow theater and founded a satirical journal. Bruant later took over Le Chat-Noir, renaming it Le Mirliton. Intellectuals and monarchs were among those attracted by his cheeky humor.

ARISTIDE BRUANT (1851–1925)

"Corduroy trousers, a vest with lapels and a hunting jacket with brass buttons. A red scarf. A huge, extravagant hat, and under it the gentle, handsome face of a determined royalist." This is how the critic Courteline described *chansonnier* Aristide Bruant. Bruant, anarchist and entertainer of Le Chat-Noir, became famous after writing the popular song "Nini Peau d'Chien".

🕐 Half a day

TIME FOR ALL
Two sculptures by
Arman were put up in
the Cour du Havre
and the Cour de
Rome in 1985:
*L'Heure pour tous
(Time for All)* and
*Consigne à vue
(Baggage Check)*,
assemblages of clocks
and suitcases,
respectively.

**PONT DE LA PLACE
DE L'EUROPE**
The bridge allowed
onlookers to watch
the new railway at the
heart of an area
where many writers
and artists lived,
including Huysmans,
Jules Romains,
Manet, Caillebotte
and Apollinaire.

A fter the end of the
18th century the capital expanded into the areas north of
the city walls destroyed under Louis XIV ● *54*. Private
houses, places of entertainment and development projects
like the "New Athens" around the Place St-Georges sprang
up between St-Lazare and the Faubourg Poissonnière. Writers
and artists of the Romantic age adopted this as their favorite
area. The 19th century saw the construction of churches and
railway stations (temples of the industrial age), as well as the
St-Martin Canal, with its provincial charm.

ST-LAZARE

FACTORY OF DREAMS. The Gare St-Lazare (9 I9) was built in
1851, with the iron structures which were to inspire Baltard
when he designed Les Halles. The station was rebuilt by
J. Litsch in 1885. Marcel Proust described this glass
construction as a "great glass workshop", while Jacques de
Lacretelle called it a "factory of dreams".
CHAUSSÉE D'ANTIN. Although less famous than the Faubourg
St-Honoré, the Chaussée d'Antin has just as many fashion
boutiques. The house at nos. 18–22, rue de la Chaussée
d'Antin (1 J2), is where the twenty-one heads of the kings of

Judah were
discovered in 1977.
They had been taken from
the façade of Notre-Dame ▲ *358* in
1789 and are now on display in the Musée
de Cluny.

LYCÉE CONDORCET (9 I10) 63, rue Caumartin. This
school, formerly the Lycée Napoléon, is housed in a

former Capuchin monastery. Famous pupils
include Marcel Proust and Alexandre
Dumas. It has a neoclassical façade and a
cloister with Doric columns built by Brongniard in 1780.

STE-TRINITÉ – NOTRE-DAME-DE-LORETTE

AROUND THE CHURCH (9 J9) 3, rue de la Trinité. A belfry
flanked by two pinnacles gives this church its distinctive
outline. It was built in 1861 in the Florentine style of the 16th
and 17th centuries. The decorations include many paintings:
the fresco *The Trinity and Angels* by F. Barrias stands out
among these. Olivier Messiaen was the organist here for forty
years. The Casino de Paris (16, rue de Clichy) is where
Josephine Baker became famous; it was built in the Art
Nouveau style in 1922.

NEW ATHENS. This huge residential development to the
north of St-Lazare became famous for its
neoclassical apartment buildings on the
Rue de la Tour-des-Dames: its name
reflected the Romantic fashion for
Greece. At 27, place St-Georges (10 B8
and 9), Adolphe Thiers rebuilt his
father-in-law's house in a grand, plain
style (it had been demolished by the
Communards).

**A SORT OF
WEDDING CAKE**
This is how Léon-Paul
Fargue described the
church of the
Ste-Trinité, designed
by Ballu (below).

Opposite, the Marquise de Païva's house (no. 28) is decorated
with a multitude of sculptures in a striking Gothic-
Renaissance style. Near this is the Musée de la Vie
Romantique ♦ 481, in Rue Chaptal: this country-style
residence once housed the studio of A. Scheffer, who painted
Stendhal. In Rue La Rochefoucauld the symbolist painter
Gustave Moreau ▲ 142 turned his house into a museum
dedicated to his work. The nearby Square d'Orléans (10 A9)
has seen many famous residents, including Gounod, Bizet,
George Sand (no. 5) and Chopin (no. 9).
CHURCH OF NOTRE-DAME-DE-LORETTE (10 B9). According to
Viollet-le-Duc, this was the "parish of the demimonde".
It gave its name to the *lorettes*, local courtesans of the 1830's,
who were immortalized in sculptures by Gavarni and in the
novels of Flaubert and Zola. The church was built by
H. Lebas in 1823; the austere outer structure of this building
(modeled on early Christian basilicas) contrasts with its
pompous interior decorations in the Louis-Philippe style.

FAUBOURGS MONTMARTRE AND POISSONNIÈRE

FAUBOURG MONTMARTRE. This working-class area used to
be the home of the Parisian fur trade. It still has a
19th-century atmosphere, with its shopping arcades and its
traditional shops, like the grocery store À la Mère de Famille
(35, rue du Faubourg-Montmartre), founded in 1761 and
still displaying its original gold lettering (2 C1). In the Rue
Richer is the music hall Folies-Bergères (2 C1), which

presents one of the
capital's major
variety shows. It was
established in 1869
and at first was
called the Theater
of Elastic
Mattresses: it was
redecorated by Pico
in the Art Nouveau
style in 1929 ("in an exquisitely offensive style", according to
J.K. Huysmans).
FAUBOURG POISSONNIÈRE. Magnificent houses were built
around this street, formerly the route serving the northern
ports. The brasserie Flo (2 E1) 63, passage des Petites-
Écuries, was opened in 1886; its present décor dates from
1910.

ST-MARTIN CANAL

The canal was built between 1822 and 1825 as an extension of the Ourcq canal, built by Napoleon I to supply Paris with drinking water. The waterway is 3 miles long, with a series of locks, swing bridges and humpback bridges; there is still some shipping activity. The banks have been redeveloped into charming walkways with an almost Venetian atmosphere. In the past they were occupied by tanneries, paper mills and china factories. These industrial activities, which needed a lot of water, left their mark on this industrial, working-class area, as depicted on the façade of the Hôtel du Nord (2 G1) 102, quai de Jemmapes.

HÔPITAL ST-LOUIS (2 H1) 2, place du Docteur-Alfred-Fournier. This hospital, built of brick and stone, was erected in 1607; it was located outside the city walls in order to isolate plague victims. The building has survived virtually intact.

PLACE DE LA RÉPUBLIQUE AND BOULEVARD DU TEMPLE

Haussmann built the huge Place de la République (2 G3) in 1854, at the junction of the new boulevards. Moricet's *Monument de la République* was installed here in 1883. The project involved the demolition of the liveliest section of the Boulevard du Temple, which was alternatively known as the Boulevard of Crime because of the melodramas performed in its theaters, among them, the Théâtre de l'Ambigu-Comique and the Théâtre des Funambules, where the mime-artist Deburau performed during the Restoration.

DEBURAU
The mime-artist Deburau was immortalized in Marcel Carné's film *Les Enfants du Paradis* (1945). He was hugely successful with the *paradis* (the cheap seats in the gallery) and established the definitive version of the Pierrot costume.

ATMOSPHERE
In *Hôtel du Nord* (1938), Carné re-created the mood of prewar Paris. Arletty's famous words to Louis Jouvet on a footbridge over the canal – "Atmosphere, atmosphere, I've had my fill of atmosphere" – were, in fact, filmed in the studio.

One day

L a Villette may have lost its colorful working-class atmosphere, with its many bistros and its old slaughterhouses, but it has become one of the most dynamic cultural and educational centers of Paris. The City of Science and Industry stands out as an emblem of the renaissance of eastern Paris.

FROM THE SLAUGHTERHOUSES TO THE CITY

A WORKING AREA
For a long time La Villette was the province of slaughterhouse butchers and dockyard boatmen.

AN UNDERGROUND CANAL
The historic St-Martin canal extends for 3 miles from the boating marina at the Bassin de l'Arsenal (south of Place de la Bastille) up to the Bassin de La Villette, running underground for more than half its length beneath the Boulevard Richard Lenoir and the Place de la Bastille.

CONSTRUCTION OF THE OURCQ CANAL. Napoleon I opened the canal between the Ourcq and the Seine on December 2, 1808; it was built to supply Paris with drinking water and to create a new shipping route. The Bassin de la Villette and the St-Martin canal were incorporated in the project. Today this "little Parisian Venice", bordered on the east by the St-Denis canal, is again used for shipping, and its quaysides have been redeveloped as walkways. At the southern end is the most attractive of the four tollhouses from the Farmers General wall, LA ROTONDE, built by Claude Nicolas Ledoux in 1784. The canal allowed the town of La Villette, located outside the toll boundaries, to develop into a large industrial center. Evidence of this can be seen in the two warehouses of the Magasins Généraux, for sugar and grain, at 41, quai de la Loire, and in the hydraulic crane on the Rue de Crimée, built in 1885. This metal construction has four gigantic pulleys.

THE SLAUGHTERHOUSES OF LA VILLETTE. Huge slaughterhouses were built here in 1867, and a cattle market which could accommodate 1,300 head a day was constructed to the south of the canal. Two buildings survive: the ROTONDE DES VÉTÉRINAIRES, at the northern entrance to the City (this now houses the MAISON DE LA VILLETTE, devoted to the history of the area), and the GRANDE HALLE ▲ *430*, to the south of the Ourcq. Enormous new slaughterhouses were built in the 1960's, but these proved obsolete as soon as they were opened: progress in refrigeration technology meant that animals could now be slaughtered on the farm. Huge losses led to their being shut down in 1974. The quarter was rescued by a well-judged redevelopment project, centered on the City of Science and Industry.

CITY OF SCIENCE AND INDUSTRY (11 C3)

MAIN BUILDING. This giant edifice opened its doors on the day Halley's comet shot through the skies: March 13, 1986. Since then it has had some five million visitors each year. Moats filled with water surround the building, light enters through two 56-foot domes, and three large greenhouses full of plants open onto the park. The huge entrance hall leads off to the various centers of activity: the Children's City, the Crafts arcade, the Louis Lumière movie theater (in 3-D), the Mediathèque library (with a collection of 300,000 titles) and a giant aquarium in the basement.

PERMANENT AND TEMPORARY EXHIBITIONS. These educational exhibitions explore different subject areas in displays which cover several rooms interconnected by stairways and footbridges. Enjoyable experiments are used to tackle subjects like the oceans or energy, and to examine all the scientific disciplines. The planetarium displays the stars and planets.

GÉODE. This has come to stand as an emblem of the City as a whole. It is a sphere 120 feet in diameter, covered with 6,433 triangles of polished stainless steel, which reflect its surroundings. Its movie theater has the largest hemispherical screen in the world.

GRANDE HALLE
This masterpiece of metal architecture is 800 feet long and 260 feet wide: it is the only surviving hall of the four built by Jules Mérindol in 1876.

ARCHITECTURAL HARMONY
Adrien Fainsilber designed the project, skillfully combining the vast structures of the slaughterhouses with modern technologies using glass and steel.

A FUTURISTIC WORLD
Visitors to the City experience a futuristic world created using the latest technology. The curved screen of the Géode uses the Omnimax technique to project films in 180 degrees over an area of 10,000 square feet, giving the spectator an impression of being totally immersed in the world of the film.

BERNARD TSCHUMI'S FOLLIES
These bright red constructions stand out in the park. They house a range of facilities including information centers, sculptures, video screens and a jazz club.

THE CINAXE AND THE ARGONAUTE. The Cinaxe is a projection booth with sixty seats, mounted on bearings that can tip it 30 degrees in any direction: the spectator experiences the same kind of simulation which is used in training air pilots. The Argonaute submarine traveled around the world several times before taking up residence in the museum, where visitors can explore its gangways and passageways.

PARC DE LA VILLETTE   (11 CD3)

GARDENS ▲ 210. This is the largest landscaped park in Paris, stretching over 86 acres to the south of the city. It offers a variety of facilities, including a giant-screen open-air movie theater in the summer. The Zenith, to the east, has become a popular venue for musical events and can accommodate 6,400 spectators.

GRANDE HALLE. This impressive metal building from the former cattle market stands to the south of the park. It has been converted into a multipurpose cultural facility. Inside, partitions, stands and platforms can be arranged to adapt the space for the concerts, exhibitions and festivals held here. Two buildings stand on either side of it: the old Leather Market to the east, which now houses the Théâtre Paris-Villette, and the Janvier building to the west, which functions as a reception center. The Lions of Nubia fountain (1811) stood on the Place de la République, where it served as a watering place for animals; it was moved here in 1867 and now stands on the huge esplanade at the entrance to the park.

CITÉ DE LA MUSIQUE (11 D5). This complex is the highlight of the southern section of the park. It was designed by Christian de Portzamparc in the form of a village and houses the Higher National Conservatory of Music and Dance. It also houses two concert halls, as well as a wide range of musical equipment and a library. Exhibits in the newly opened MUSEUM OF MUSIC range from Italian lutes to instruments by Amati and Stradivarius, up to the latest devices such as Frank Zappa's E-Mu modular synthesizer.

EXCURSIONS
OUTSIDE PARIS

1. PARIS   2. PORTE DE LA CHAPELLE   3. PLACE DE LA PORTE DE PARIS   4. ST-DENIS BASILICA

St-Denis, the cemetery of the kings, has suffered greatly. It was vandalized under the Revolution, then clumsily restored. It has been stripped of its most beautiful works which are now in the Louvre and the Bibliothèque Nationale. Nonetheless, this Gothic masterpiece remains a major historical landmark.

The eastern façade. The Regalia, the instruments of the coronation, were kept in this church – an indication of its importance.

THE BASILICA OF THE KINGS

The original church was built in the 5th century over the tombs of Saint Denis ▲ 417 and his followers Rusticus and Eleutherius. An abbey grew up around the shrine, funded by large donations from the Merovingian kings, like Dagobert, who was buried here in 639. Under the Carolingians, who took over from the Merovingians with the support of the abbot of St-Denis, the church became the main location for royal ceremonies. In 1122, Louis VI made this the official burial place for French monarchs, at the request of Abbé Suger. Saint Louis reserved it for monarchs alone, a rule which was broken several times, and had the remains of his predecessors transferred to tombs in the crossing of the transept. They were arranged in dynastic order, proclaiming the continuity of the French monarchy. Over the centuries the abbey's power gradually waned, and Louis XIV placed it under the jurisdiction of the archbishop of Paris.

A MUSEUM OF MONUMENTAL SCULPTURE

The church was seriously damaged under the Revolution. Afterward, Louis XVIII reinstated it as the royal necropolis, returning to the crypt the remains which had been thrown into a common grave; he also had the remains of Louis XVI and Marie-Antoinette transferred here. At the same time, the tombs which had survived the Revolution were brought back to the basilica, along with other tombs from various churches around Paris: this made St-Denis a unique museum of monumental sculpture. Restoration of the building started under Napoleon I and Louis XVIII, and it was continued by Viollet-le-Duc under Napoleon III.

A GOTHIC MASTERPIECE

The Carolingians rebuilt the old Merovingian

basilica. Suger, in his turn, also decided to improve St-Denis and rebuilt the Carolingian basilica. The western façade was dedicated in 1140 and the chevet in 1144, but the building remained incomplete after the abbé's death in 1151. Suger's church represents a landmark in the development of

Christ carrying the cross: detail from the portal.

Gothic architecture. Intersecting ribs were used here on a large scale for the first time. In this way, the architect could do without walls between the pillars. Vaulting could be extended throughout the ambulatories, and the radiating chapels and huge windows could be incorporated in the chevet. This is how Suger realized his concept: for him, light had a thoroughly metaphysical significance. Another innovative feature is the rose window on the west façade. In 1231, Abbé Eudes Clément began work on the new nave. The first stage was directed by an anonymous architect; he was succeeded by Pierre de Montreuil. The choir was rebuilt, although the double ambulatory, crypt and radiating chapels were kept, as was the western façade. The ground plan of the nave was altered. Flying buttresses on the exterior meant that the walls could be built to a greater height and on a larger scale, and the bays were divided into three levels (large arcades, triforium and high windows). This marked the transition toward High Gothic style.

The tomb of Louis XII and Anne de Bretagne was designed by Guido Mazzoni and produced by the Florentine artist Jean Juste in 1507. It is made in the form of a catafalque and for the first time shows its royal subjects both as recumbent figures and in prayer.

TOMB OF THE KINGS
Before the 13th century, monarchs were buried near the altar under paving stones. Saint Louis transferred their remains to tombs decorated with recumbent stone figures. Later, the Valois were buried in impressive Renaissance-style tombs decorated with realistic recumbent and praying figures. The Bourbons were buried in the crypt, in wooden coffins placed on iron trestles.

The 9th-century crypt of Hilduin. The central barrel-vaulted nave can be seen in the crypt today.

▲ VERSAILLES

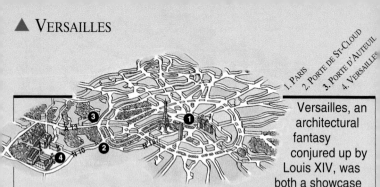

1. PARIS 2. PORTE DE ST-CLOUD 3. PORTE D'AUTEUIL 4. VERSAILLES

Versailles, an architectural fantasy conjured up by Louis XIV, was both a showcase for and an instrument of his power. The Sun King made this into a theater for the monarchy and a model for royal palaces.

BIRTH OF A PALACE

The palace of Versailles was constructed around a hunting lodge which had been rebuilt for Louis XIII by Philibert Le Roy. In 1661, Louis XIV had the estate modernized by the architect Le Vau and landscape designer Le Nôtre, and it became the setting for royal festivities. Soon the king decided to extend this modest château, and large-scale construction began. In 1668, Le Vau added a majestic stone façade to the three external faces of the U-shaped building around the Cour de Marne, creating the *château neuf*, the main building of the new palace. A vast terrace was added to the west, and the flat roofs were hidden behind ornamental balustrades. In 1678, Louis XIV decided to make Versailles his official residence, for reasons of politics and prestige. Construction was undertaken on a

Everything in the palace revolved around the king, the sun in the universe of Versailles. Below: Louis XIV in coronation robes, by Hyacinthe Rigaud.

colossal scale in order to accommodate the royal family, the court and the government. On the garden side, the terrace was covered over and made into the Hall of Mirrors.

Jules-Hardouin Mansart built two long symmetrical structures, the Midi wing (1682) and the North wing (1689), set back from the main building. The town side of the palace was built around three branching avenues; the original façades of the Cour de Marbre were preserved. Mansart retained the Louis XIII-style buildings: the four pavilions built by Le Vau were joined in pairs to form the ministers' wings, which housed offices and apartments allocated to civil servants.

In front of the palace is a huge proscenium, the Place d'Armes, bordered on the east by the Grande Écurie and the Petite Écurie (the Great and Small Stables). Even these functional buildings have a palatial appearance.

Above: the king's bedroom. Left: Colbert, by Claude Lefebvre. Colbert directed the project, aiming to create an unrivaled palace for Louis XIV while containing costs.

THE APARTMENTS

These were arranged in a strict hierarchy. The princes and leading courtiers lived in the north wing and the south wing on the garden side, while minor courtiers lived on the town side. The royal apartments were located on the second story of the main building – the king in the Grand Appartement to the north, the queen to the south. They were reached by two marble staircases – that of the Ambassadors, which has not survived, and that of the Queen.

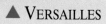
ROYAL APARTMENTS OF THE GRAND SIÈCLE

The GRAND APPARTEMENT was decorated in the Italian style by a group of skilled painters working under Charles Le Brun. The paintings on the ceiling depicted gods and heroes of antiquity; the walls were decorated with statues and gold brocades. Images of planets revolving around the sun and mythological figures were used as allegories of royal power.

Festivities and ceremonies were central to palace life. Below: "Masked Ball Held at Versailles for the Marriage of the Dauphin" by Charles-Nicolas Cochin.

When the king finally moved to Versailles in 1682, he took up residence in the APPARTEMENT DU ROI, leaving the

The portraitist Nattier was a favorite with the daughters of Louis XV. Below: his likeness of Madame Adélaïde, the king's sixth child.

Grand Appartement for ceremonial uses. The king's apartment was located, symbolically, at the heart of the palace. Its mirrors, its pale ceilings and its carved white-and-gold paneling radiated light and warmth. The king's life was more comfortable here, but it was still subject to the implacable machinery of official rituals.

GABRIEL'S CONTRIBUTION

Under Louis XV, this warmer style achieved perfection. Two masters of this style, Jacques and Jacques-Ange Gabriel, decorated the CHAMBRE DE LA REINE (1730), the CABINET DU CONSEIL (1755) and the private apartments, where Jacques-Ange created magnificent paneling which was either carved and gilded or painted with a glaze which gave it the appearance of china. The gilded paneling of the APPARTEMENT INTÉRIEUR on the second floor is matched by the colored, glazed paneling of the PETITS APPARTEMENTS on the third floor,

Right: chapel by Vuillard. Each day Louis XIV attended services here, taking his place in the upper central gallery. The courtiers were seated on the first floor.

where Louis XV could live more privately. Gabriel produced a final masterpiece in 1774 – Louis XVI's LIBRARY, a refuge for the king, who was an avid reader with a keen interest in geography.

HALL OF MIRRORS
This 240-foot-long gallery has seventeen windows and seventeen arcades covered with mirrors. Le Brun devised the French-order capitals combining the inevitable sun motif with the royal lily and the French cock. The ceiling depicts the great deeds of Louis XIV, who is shown as a hero dressed in classical style.

CHAPEL
The last years of Louis XIV's reign were marked by the pious influence of his morganatic wife, Mme de Maintenon. During this time, Louis XIV built the chapel which rises above the palace roofs. It was started by Mansart and completed by Robert de Cotte in 1710. It has one of the few painted church ceilings to survive in France, produced by Jouvenet, Coypel and La Fosse, pupils of Le Brun. The magnificent interior combines gilding and white carved stone.

OPERA
Versailles did not have a proper theater until the marriage of the Dauphin to Marie-

The wooden décor of the Opéra de Gabriel, painted to look like marble, gives the Opéra its excellent acoustics.

Antoinette in 1770. Oval in shape, the auditorium can accommodate over seven hundred spectators, in tiered seating that goes from the orchestra pit to the back colonnade. Built by Gabriel, it has ingenious machinery that allows the stage and auditorium to be converted for balls and banquets. On May 16, the day of the wedding, the floor was raised up in order to set up the royal table.

TRIANON
Louis XIV was an avid builder. Once Versailles was completed, he ordered Mansart to build the GRAND TRIANON, a long, Italianate palace consisting of two wings connected by a peristyle, with borders and perspectives created by Le Nôtre. The greenhouses and gardens were redeveloped in Louis XV's reign under the direction of the botanist Jussieu. At this time Gabriel reached the height of his powers, building the PETIT TRIANON for Mme de Pompadour: it was a modern residence in a sober, neoclassical style. The king's mistress died in 1768, before it was finished. Marie-Antoinette had the gardens redesigned in the fashionable English style adding ornamental constructions including the TEMPLE OF LOVE, the BELVEDERE, the THEATER and the MODEL VILLAGE.

Above: Grand Trianon. The columns and pilasters of its façades create a harmonious, multicolored whole. Below: the English garden of Marie-Antoinette's village, redesigned by Richard Mique in the style of Hubert Robert. This miniature village has a dairy, a farm and a windmill.

Two factors determined the design of the Versailles gardens: the palace's position at the top of a hill with irregular slopes, and the layout of the ground, divided by a central axis and crisscrossed with avenues from Louis XIII's reign. Le Nôtre, the royal landscape architect, opened up vast perspectives with ornamental lakes, which reflect the changing skies.

AN OPEN-AIR SCULPTURE MUSEUM

Three hundred urns and statues of lead, marble and bronze populate the groves designed by Mansart and Le Nôtre. Among them are copies of classical works and works by pupils of the new French Academy in Rome. The twenty-four marble statues of the Great Commission (1674) were commissioned by Colbert, superintendent of the Royal Buildings, following designs by Le Brun.

The lakes are central to the tour devised by the Sun King in the pamphlet he wrote for visitors, *How to View the Gardens of Versailles.* The Grand Canal, 5,400 feet in length, connected Versailles and the Trianon: this major aquatic feature was a setting for lavish festivities. Below: the Marais cascade (section and elevation).

241

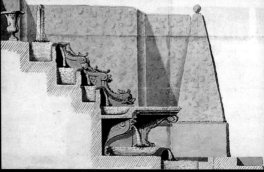

"THE BORDERS AND GARDENS ARE AN OPEN-AIR DRAWING ROOM
. . . THIS IS NOT A PLACE FOR SOLITUDE AND RELAXATION BUT A
PLACE TO STROLL AROUND, MEETING PEOPLE."

HIPPOLYTE TAINE

RESTORATION OF THE GARDENS

The gardens are currently undergoing reforestation. Some of the groves will also be restored, including the Bosquet de l'Encelade. The previous reforestation took place under Louis XVI: it was immortalized by the painter Hubert Robert.

NATURE TAMED

Creating the gardens of Versailles was a considerable undertaking: the site was a difficult one, with unfavorable contours. After the marsh had been drained, there was the problem of supplying water for the lakes and for watering the gardens. This was solved using Marly's machine, which pumped water from the Seine and conveyed it to its destination by means of aqueducts. The garden was divided into three distinct areas. Near the palace were gardens stretching to the horizon. After this came the groves and spinneys. Beyond this was the forest. The Labyrinth (above) no longer exists. Opposite: the Bosquet de l'Etoile.

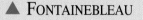

1. PARIS 2. PORTE D'ITALIE 3. PORTE D'IVRY 4. PORTE DE BERCY 5. MELUN 6. FONTAINEBLEAU

Although it looks wild, the forest of Fontainebleau has been carefully maintained for seven centuries. The kings of France used this as their hunting ground and built one of their loveliest palaces here, using sandstone from local quarries. The landscapes of Fontainebleau inspired the painters of Barbizon, who were the first to take their easels outdoors, creating a famous school of painting.

The palace of Fontainebleau was originally a manor house where Louis VII (1120–80) stayed while hunting.

THE CHÂTEAU OF FONTAINEBLEAU

The château was a favorite with the kings of France and was repeatedly altered over the centuries. It is striking for its composite appearance: eight hundred years of architectural history can be read here. When François I returned from exile after the defeat of Pavia (1525), he brought leading Italian artists with him, including Il Rosso and Primaticcio. They created magnificent frescos and stucco work for the CHAMBRE DE LA DUCHESSE D'ÉTAMPES', the FRANÇOIS I GALLERY and the BALLROOM (the last was completed under Henri II). Henri IV and Louis XIII created the LOUIS XIII ROOM, where royal ceremonies were held up to 1773. Louis XV started the THRONE ROOM, the only one in France to retain its original furniture; Louis XVI created the GAMES ROOM and the QUEEN'S BOUDOIR. The palace was refurnished under Napoleon I. It still has a good deal of furniture from the Ancien Régime and the First Empire, as well as later pieces.

The Gallery of Diana, where Napoleon III housed the library. The globe dates from Napoleon I.

FONTAINEBLEAU MASSIF

This is one of the most beautiful forests in France. It covers an area of 61,750 acres, incorporating three separate forests: Commanderie, Trois Pignons and Fontainebleau. The Fontainebleau forest itself is the second-largest in France, covering 41,990 acres. The first roads were built through the forest in medieval times. Henri IV built the ROUTE RONDE which leads to the heart of the forest by a series of crossroads: this network was extended by Louis XV. In the 19th century Dénecourt, a former soldier under Napoleon, created 93 miles of pathways through the forest, the basis of today's network (which covers 190 miles). The paths connect various sites of interest: ruins, lakes, caves and notable trees. In 1849 the railway brought tourists to the forest – and their garbage: four garbage trucks now cover the area on a fulltime basis. Fontainebleau also has other attractions for tourists and sports lovers: the GORGES D'APREMONT, the

The emperor Napoleon did not make any major alterations to Fontainebleau. However, he is commemorated here in the MUSÉE NAPOLÉON, dedicated to the years 1804–15. The MUSÉE CHINOIS, where Empress Eugénie displayed her Oriental collections, dates from the reign of Napoleon III. Its displays have been carefully reconstructed.

"Shepherdess Guarding Her Sheep" by Jean-François Millet.

ERMITAGE DE FRANCHARD and the CARREFOUR DE L'ÉPINE. Other, more sheltered attractions are the MARE AUX FÉES, GROTTE BÉATRIX and VALLÉE JAUBERTON.

BARBIZON

Between 1830 and 1875, this hamlet on the edge of the forest was the home of a group of landscape painters. They were attracted by the huge skies and by the modest prices of the AUBERGE GANNE, now a municipal museum. The inn's interior

Oak, beech and pine trees populate this forest, along with some spruce trees, larch trees and even sequoias.

decorations have recently been restored; they were produced on rainy days by its occupants (including Corot, Millet and Théodore Rousseau).

1. PARIS   2. PORTE DE LA CHAPELLE   3. LE BOURGET AIRPORT   4. CHANTILLY

The former estate of the Great Condé is now dedicated to art and horses: the Museum of the Horse is housed in its Great Stables, while Chantilly palace itself has one of the richest art collections in France.

PICTURE GALLERIES OF MUSÉE CONDÉ

Their originality lies in the arrangement of the pictures, determined by Aumale himself in the 19th-century style. The works are displayed cheek by jowl, and different schools and periods are mixed

DUC D'AUMALE
(1822–97)
This soldier, historian and enlightened collector was exiled twice, despite his republican leanings.

together with no regard for chronological order. Italian paintings predominate, with 98 works by Fra Angelico, Piero di Cosimo, Salvator Rosa, Sassetta and Raphael (including his *Three Graces*, the *Madonna of Orleans* and the *Madonna of Lorette*).

CHÂTEAU DE CHANTILLY

The palace comprises two separate buildings, set in grounds designed by Le Nôtre and crisscrossed by a network of lakes and streams. The PETIT CHÂTEAU was built by Jean Bullant in the 16th century for Anne de Montmorency. The neighboring

GRAND CHÂTEAU was built in the 19th century on the foundations of the original fortress: it was designed to house the art collection of the Duc d'Aumale. The overhead lighting of its best rooms – the Gallery, the Tribune and the Santuario – reflects this purpose.

Northern schools are represented by several Flemish primitives and three portraits by Van Dyck, while Clouet, Nattier, Philippe de Champaigne, Poussin, Watteau, Ingres and Delacroix illustrate the history of French painting. The entrance gallery and the CHAPEL contain treasures from the Château de Écouen ▲ 444.

LIBRARY
The library's collection is unique. Unfortunately the extremely precious illuminated manuscripts – including the *Psalter of Queen Ingeburge of Denmark* and *Les Très Riches Heures du Duc de Berry* – are not on display. Facsimiles are on display as are bindings from the 11th to 14th centuries, early printed books and a huge collection of historical documents.

APARTMENTS
These are in the 16th-century building and boast a Riesener commode made for Louis XVI and a cabinet from Gustave III of Sweden.

The Great Stables, 600 feet long, are made of ten naves forming a vast octagon. They were built by a horselover who thought he would be reincarnated as a horse himself.

Left: "The Three Graces" by Raphael. Below: "Simonetta Vespucci" by Piero de Cosimo. The Florentine beauty is portrayed ten years after her death, as symbolized by the snake which is coiled around her neck. Top: "Landscape with Two Nymphs" by Poussin.

MUSÉE VIVANT DU CHEVAL: THE GREAT STABLES
In 1719 the seventh prince of Condé commissioned the architect Jean Aubert to build the Great Stables, a masterpiece of 18th-century architecture. Since 1982 the stables have housed a museum dedicated to the horse. All aspects of the equine world are explored in around thirty rooms. The star attractions are the forty real horses in the stalls and the educational equestrian displays.

1. PARIS
2. PORTE DE LA CHAPELLE
3. PARC DE LA COURNEUVE
4. ÉCOUEN

The beautiful castle of Écouen combines a French style of architecture with Italian ornamental motifs. The greatest artists of the Renaissance contributed to this exceptional building, which is today the Musée National de la Renaissance.

JEWEL OF RENAISSANCE ARCHITECTURE

The château forms a regular quadrangle around an internal court. The architect replaced the traditional towers with rectangular corner pavilions, and the two residential wings, to the right and the left of the entrance, were joined by galleries. The entrance gallery (1807) has replaced the original wing, which was destroyed shortly before the Revolution.

ARCHITECTURAL ORNAMENTATION

The development of architectural styles can be seen in the ever-more elaborate design of the windows, by which the different sections of the château can be dated. The west wing was the first to be completed (1542), followed by the south wing, the north wing and the east gallery. The first phase of construction was characterized by a very plain style. Examples of this are the scallops and related motifs on the

CHÂTEAU DU CONNÉTABLE

Anne de Montmorency rebuilt the family manor of Écouen after being appointed constable by François I in 1538. He was known for his progressive tastes as a collector: when he fell from favor, he used the enforced leisure to embellish his château, one of the most beautiful in the kingdom.

Below: "The Trojan Horse", painted wood panel on a marriage chest (Florence, 15th century).

turrets of the staircase in the south wing. The cartouches with indented edges in the north wing show a much more sophisticated style. The columns of the portico in the south wing are the first example of colossal-order columns in French architecture. This portico by Jean Bullant was doubtless designed to house the two *Slaves* by Michelangelo, now held in the Louvre.

This celestial globe in gilded bronze (1502) is a symbol of the union of science and art, and is extremely accurate.

INTERIOR DECORATIONS

The interiors seem relatively bare: most of the decorations were, in fact, transferred to Chantilly ▲ *442*. This former estate of the Montmorencys houses the panels and stained-glass windows of the chapel and the forty-two grisaille windows of the Gallery of Psyche. The *Pietà* by Il Rosso, a masterpiece from the Connétable's collection, is now in the Louvre. The painted fireplaces were an original feature; they probably date from the reign of Henri II. Their Old Testament imagery depicts the life and virtues of the Connétable. The frame of the marble fireplace in the Grande Salle is attributed to Bullant.

MUSÉE NATIONAL DE LA RENAISSANCE

Much of the collection comes from the Musée de Cluny. The tapestry of the *History of David and Bathsheba*, a cup with the coat of arms of Anne de Bretagne, the large enamels by Pierre Courteys, the ship supposedly by Charles V and medallions by Luca Della Robbia are some of the major exhibits. On the second floor the surviving decorations and exhibits convey an impression of how the château once looked. Elsewhere, exhibits are arranged thematically. The third floor is devoted to the arts of the kiln, with a magnificent collection of enamels, glass and ceramics.

Above: ceramic plate from Iznik with indented edges and floral pattern.
Below: "The Continence of Scipio", rock crystal by Giovanni Bernardi (Italy, c. 1530).

Detail of "The Tribute to Caesar".
This scene from the Gospels is depicted on the central medallion of a painted fireplace.

▲ VAUX-LE-VICOMTE

1. PARIS 2. PORTE DORÉE 3. MELUN 4. VAUX-LE-VICOMTE

It was the splendor of Vaux-le-Vicomte which brought about Nicolas Fouquet's demise. In this remarkably well preserved palace, Fouquet wanted to leave "some traces of the position to which he had risen".

It prefigures the beauty of Versailles, for which Louis XIV employed the same team of artists: architect Le Vau, the interior decorator Le Brun and the landscape designer Le Nôtre.

QUO NON ASCENDET?

Nicolas Fouquet (1615–80) rose rapidly to power, finally achieving the post of superintendent of finances. He grew richer as he grew more powerful: the loans he arranged for the king were secured by his own fortune and brought him substantial profits. He was a lover of literature and the fine arts, and made his palace at Vaux the most beautiful in France. Its pediments displayed the highly appropriate motto: *Quo non ascendet?* (To what heights will he not ascend?).

THE LAST FESTIVITIES AT VAUX

On August 17, 1661, Fouquet held a magnificent celebration in honor of the king. The lavish festivities sealed his fate. Louis XIV, already won over by Fouquet's rival Colbert, was

Nicolas Fouquet, who represents the rise of senior civil servants under Louis XIV.

irritated by this opulent display and set investigations under way. After a dubious trial, Fouquet was imprisoned in the fortress of Pignerol in Piedmont. His palace was confiscated; it was returned to his family in 1673. Vaux-le-Vicomte was refurnished repeatedly by later owners.

It took only five years to transform a marshy area halfway between the royal palaces of Vincennes and Fontainebleau into a dream palace. Fouquet did not hesitate to demolish three villages which stood in his way.

A THOROUGHLY ROYAL SPLENDOR

The early stages of classicism can be seen here. The north façade is surmounted by a pediment set back from the corner pavilions. On the garden side, the Oval Room is crowned by a dome which stands out at the center of the façade.

446

Fouquet's arrest interrupted the painting of the dome in the Oval Room. It has not been altered since.

INTERIOR DECORATIONS

The statues, furniture and paneling designed by Le Brun are a perfect match for Le Vau's building. The ceremonial rooms and the private apartments have been carefully reconstructed; their effect is almost magical, conjuring up a life of freedom and opulence. The paintings in Fouquet's bedroom have survived intact, but Le Brun's most beautiful ceiling is in the Salon des Muses. Also in this room is the tapestry of the *History of Diana*, one of many which decorate the palace walls. (A special factory was established in the vicinity to supply the palace.) This splendor contrasts with the magnificent austerity of the Oval Room, located between the garden, the ceremonial rooms and the vestibule (which rises to roof level).

THE FIRST GARDEN IN THE FRENCH STYLE

Le Nôtre and Fouquet dreamed of huge perspectives and a balance between the building and its setting. They saw the garden as a theater: a stage setting to display the central object, the palace. Le Nôtre created optical illusions and effects to enhance this impression. The garden, with borders and ornamental lakes, opens onto the horizon. Its slope hides the Canal de la Poêle, which appears

unexpectedly at the vistor's feet. From afar, the palace seems to be held up by its terraces. The low buildings on either side add to this effect.

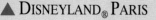

Situated 20 miles from the capital, the five "lands" that make up the theme park are home to those legendary Disney characters, with carnival parades and spectacular entertainments, fairground attractions, restaurants and stores providing colorful variety. Seven themed hotels in fairytale settings offer a choice of accommodations to delight young and old alike.

MAIN STREET, U.S.A.

The street is lined with wooden houses in soft colors, re-creating the atmosphere of a small American town at the beginning of the century. Parades of Disney characters pass by, and a steam

cowboys, paddle steamers and a Cheyenne encampment (LEGENDS OF THE WILD WEST). Two thrilling attractions here are BIG THUNDER MOUNTAIN, a mountainside expedition with dynamite

buccaneer expedition (PIRATES OF THE CARIBBEAN), visit the SWISS FAMILY ROBINSON'S TREEHOUSE or take an adventure ride through the ruins of the Lost City (INDIANA JONES AND THE TEMPLE OF DOOM).

include favorite fairytale heros, from Snow White to Pinocchio.

DISCOVERYLAND

This futuristic city full of special effects will fascinate science-fiction fans. You start with an interstellar journey designed by George Lucas (creator of Star Wars). Then there is the VISIONARIUM, which projects films in 360 degrees. After a tour in CAPTAIN NEMO'S SUBMARINE, fans of Jules Verne will be catapulted to the stars by the COLUMBIAD cannon, inspired by the novel From the Earth to the Moon. This takes off from the SPACE MOUNTAIN, which is 118 feet high.

locomotive waits for passengers at MAIN STREET STATION to take them on a tour of the park.

FRONTIERLAND

This is the legendary Wild West, with saloons,

explosions, and a journey through PHANTOM MANOR, a haunted house.

ADVENTURELAND

This is the exotic kingdom of pirates. You can join a

FANTASYLAND

Beyond SLEEPING BEAUTY'S CASTLE, which rises above the park, is a fairytale village full of turrets and half-timbered houses. Attractions here

©Disney

WORLD CULTURES IN PARIS

Since the 19th century Paris has been a refuge for large numbers of Eastern Europeans, especially Poles and Russians fleeing revolutions and repressions. These groups of immigrants have left their mark on the city, creating "little Russias" or "little Polands" which now act as magnets attracting new arrivals. However Paris has also taken in thousands of emigrants from the poorest areas of Italy, Spain and Portugal: these groups are the largest foreign communities in the capital.

THE "WHITE CITY"

Paris had a distinctly Russian air about it in the 1920's, when aristocrats and bourgeoisie settled in the city, fleeing the Revolution. Cossacks and White Army officers became factory workers, taxi drivers, or dancers and musicians in the cabarets which were very popular with Parisians at the time.

THE "LITTLE RUSSIAS"

Besides St-Alexandre-Nevsky, Paris has a number of Russian churches in the 15th and 19th arrondissements, where magnificent chanted masses are held. The most attractive of these are St-Séraphin-de-Sarov and St-Serge, the latter decorated with frescos by Dmitri Stelletsky and 16th-century iconostasis doors.

ST-ALEXANDRE-NEVSKY

This masterpiece of cultural transplantation, located at 12, rue Daru (9C9), was built between 1859 and 1861 by Kouzmine and Strohm, architects of the Imperial court. It follows the traditional orthodox design – "onion" domes and a ground plan in the shape of a Greek cross – but the exterior is distinctly Muscovite. The Christ figure on the façade is copied from a mosaic in Ravenna.

CUBISM, SURREALISM AND SPAIN

At the start of the century, Paris attracted artists and intellectuals from all over the world. These included Picasso (above, painted by Marevna along with Ehrenburg, Chagall and Léger), Miró, Juan Gris and Dali. There is now a special museum dedicated to Dali, christened "the emperor of Montmartre" by his artist friends, on the "Butte" ▲ 476. (Above, *L'Éléphant spatial*, a sculpture from 1890.) The Spanish Civil War and then Francoism produced a steady exodus to France which lasted up to the 1960's. Since Franco's death in 1975 Spain has become fashionable in Paris, with a proliferation of tapas bars and flamenco schools.

ITALY

Peasants from the Piedmontese Alps and the Apennines streamed into France from 1870 onward. Immigration from Italy reached its height between 1920 and 1930, when Paris became the center of Italian anti-fascism (above, Italian workers are welcomed at Puteaux). Italians, or "ritals" as they were pejoratively known, formed the largest foreign community in France at this time and became a target for racial hostility. Today Italian restaurants, trattorias and couturiers have pride of place in Paris.

PORTUGUESE

The Portuguese community in Paris gathers at the Bastille (left) to celebrate their national day and commemorate the 16th-century poet Camoens, author of a national epic, the *Lusiade*.

REFUGE ...

From 1831 Paris became the place of refuge for Polish exiles. One of the main Polish centers is on Île St-Louis, with the Bibliothèque Polonaise and a museum dedicated to the revolutionary poet Adam Mickiewicz (1798-1855). The museum also has an impressive room devoted to Chopin.

OXFORD IN PARIS

The Cité Internationale Universitaire was built between 1923 and 1968; several European architects contributed to this striking campus. The Italian House (1958) was built in Italian villa style (asymmetrical ground plan, loggia, arcades, classical pediment), and the Deutsch-de-la-Meurthe Foundation (1925), was inspired by English college buildings (below).

...FOR POLISH EXILES

The church of the Assumption was presented to the Polish community in 1844. The Polish School was founded in the Batignolles quarter in 1842 (below).

THE "PLATZEL" (2F7)

Antisemitic pogroms in Russia, the Ukraine and Poland brought thousands of immigrants to Paris between 1880 and 1930. Many settled in the Marais, around Rue des Rosiers and Place St-Paul (the "Platzel"). Guimard was commissioned to build the synagogue in Rue Pavée in 1913.

WORLD CULTURES IN PARIS
NORTH AFRICA AND THE MIDDLE EAST

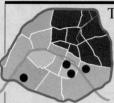

Goutte-d'Or, Belleville and cultural centers.

The influence of the Mediterranean world is tangible in Paris. You can enjoy a *couscous* or have a feast of Lebanese *mezze*, walk in the gardens of the Grande Mosquée, spend an evening in a *raï* discotheque or an eastern cabaret, hear a concert of Arabo-Andalusian music at the Institute of the Arab World (IMA) or the Algerian Cultural Center, unwind in a hammam or visit the souks of Belleville and Goutte-d'Or ... virtually all the communities of North Africa and the Middle East are represented in the city. North Africans are the largest single community, of which the dominant group is the Algerians.

ARABIC STYLE
The southern façade of the Institut du Monde Arabe is covered with motifs reminiscent of macharabiehs. Originally these were part of a sophisticated lighting system.

A CULTURAL CENTER
The IMA is not content simply to attract Parisians to its highly reputed exhibitions and museum ▲ *144* (above, a 19th-century Egyptian ewer); it has also become a place where the Arab community in Paris and French citizens of Arabic origin can express and explore their own culture. The institute organizes debates, theatrical performances and concerts; its library is unique in Europe, with a collection of fifty thousand books and one thousand periodicals. The restaurant and the council room on the top floor have one of the most beautiful views in Paris.

ISLAMIC CENTER
The Grande Mosquée in Paris was built between 1922 and 1926 on the model of the Fez mosques. It is one of the most disorienting places in the city, with its garden paved with mosaics – a symbolic representation of paradise – its immaculate white central courtyard, its Moorish café, bazaar and restaurant ▲ *261*.

"GOUTTE-D'OR"
Long ago a highly reputed wine known as *goutte d'or* (drop of gold) was produced on these slopes. The Goutte-d'Or quarter has been the main district for settlers from North Africa since the 1950's. Its streets teem with shops selling oriental fabrics, cafés, and oil wholesalers which supply shops and businesses throughout France.

ARABIAN MUSIC

The many and diverse types of music from North Africa and the Middle East can be heard in a number of Parisian venues. However, it is *raï* music above all – music from Oran celebrating love and the joys of life – which has taken Paris by storm during the last decade. This type of music be heard in the cafés of Barbès and Belleville and in the discotheques of Paris (New Raï) and the suburbs (Fun Raï, Khéops, Triangle).

HAMMAM

The Turks introduced the hammam (which means "hot bath" in Turkish) throughout North Africa and the Middle East. There are many hammams in Paris and its suburbs, including the magnificent example in the Grande Mosquée and the luxurious Hammam Pacha at St-Denis (right).

THE CORNER STORE

Many Parisian groceries are run by Moroccans from Sous and Tunisians from Djerba; they stay open late into the night, seven days a week. Grocers from Djerba and Sous dominate the food business in their own countries; they were just as important in Algeria up to Independence, when many left to set up shop in France.

SOUKS

The markets of Barbès, Belleville and Aligre ♦ *523* are meeting places for the North African community in Paris. They have the appearance of Mediterranean souks, with stalls selling eastern fabrics, editions of the Koran, cassettes of Arab music, meats, spices, dried fruits and couscous. There are Tunisian groceries and cake shops in the small streets of Belleville (below).

PASSAGE DU CAIRE (CAIRO PASSAGE) (2C3)

The façade of the building at 2, place du Caire, was built between 1798 and 1799; it incorporates Egyptian-style motifs (heads of the goddess Hathor, frieze of pharaohs, imitation hieroglyphics) alongside neo-Gothic and neo-Byzantine elements. A speculator designed this bizarre composition to attract customers into the first Parisian passageway directly inspired by oriental bazaars.

WORLD CULTURES IN PARIS
AFRICA AND THE WEST INDIES

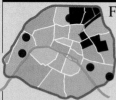

African quarters (11th, 18th and 19th arrondissements) and cultural centers.

From the 1920's onwards the rhythms of drums and of the *biguine* (a West Indian dance) took Paris by storm and an Afro-Caribbean elite became established in a general climate of racial awareness. Paris' *colonie noire* (black community) has grown considerably since the 1960's with the arrival of large numbers of immigrants from French-speaking Africa and French citizens from the overseas territories, mainly Martinique and Guadeloupe.

WEST INDIAN FESTIVALS

The West Indians in Paris love to get together to dance *zouk* and *soukous* (particularly the *collé-serré* and the *touffé nyen-nyen* styles, in which dancers are pressed so close together that even the midges suffocate). The "Zénith" is one of their grand annual venues, where Groupe Kassav perform. The Paris Overseas Carnival, which takes place in the 12th arrondissement at the end of June, is also a must.

AFRICAN TROUBADOURS

In some small African restaurants in Paris you can hear a *griot* from Mali or Senegal singing and playing the *kora* (harp-lute). *Griots* are the storytellers and musicians of West Africa: they act as the repositories of local oral tradition, travelling from village to village to retell historical epics and legends.

BLACK PARIS IN THE "ANNÉES FOLLES"

Between the wars a "negro craze" hit Paris: Parisians flocked to the "Bal nègre", captivated by the exotic attractions of jazz, Josephine Baker and the West-Indian *biguine* dance. Ethnologists discovered the riches of African art and civilization which became a source of inspiration for artists of the avant-garde (Picasso, Cendrars and Breton). Paris became the center of an Afro-Caribbean elite which mounted a campaign against the image of the "jolly negro".

AFRO-CARIBBEAN MUSIC

In the 1980's tomtoms and other Afro-Caribbean drums joined forces with synthesizers and electric guitars: Paris became the world capital of Afro-Caribbean music (right, Mory Kanté). Venues for listening or dancing to the rhythms of this music include jazz clubs (New Morning, Hot Brass, LSC) and discotheques (Keur Samba, L'Alizé, BB Antilles, and Cinquième Dimension).

MARABOUTS
"Professor Z., genuine African marabout": a typical boast on business cards handed out by Métro exits. In Muslim Africa, a marabout is a spiritual guide endowed with supernatural powers.

AFRICA IN MUSEUMS
African art can be seen in Paris at the Musée des Arts d'Afrique et d'Océanie ▲ 158, at the Musée de l'Homme ▲ 144, in many galleries of St-Germain-des-Prés, and in the Musée Dapper (8J6).

BATIK AND "BOUBOUS" (10D6)
Fabric stores in the Château-Rouge quarter offer a profusion of shimmering materials and brightly colored batiks which are used to make the *boubous* or long tunics still worn by Africans in Paris. Batik, which originated in Indonesia, was introduced to Africa by Dutch merchants. This quarter also has a number of African tailors (Rue Myrha).

Founded in 1986, the Musée Dapper organizes exhibitions that aim to provide new insights into an art that is still relatively unknown; story-telling sessions are held each Wednesday. The museum is named after a 16th-century Dutch humanist who wrote one of the first books on Africa. Above, a statuette from Gabon.

CHÂTEAU-ROUGE
The stalls and markets of the Château-Rouge quarter, the hub of Afro-Caribbean life in Paris, are crammed with specialities: tropical fish (*capitaine*, *thiof*, *marachon*), tropical crabs, giant snails, cassavas and yams, African drinks (beer with ginger) and West Indian drinks (champagne-cola, lemonade with aniseed).

FRENCH ARTISTS FROM OVERSEAS
Nearly two hundred painters and sculptors from French overseas territories currently live in Paris. Works by around fifty of them are shown each year at an exhibition held in Espace Reuilly. Above, a painting by Shuck, an artist from Guadeloupe.

Asian quarters (2nd and 13th arrondissements), and cultural centers.

Paris already had a few Chinese restaurants, craftsmen and trinket sellers at the beginning of the century. However since the 1970's refugees from Southeast Asia have established their own distinct quarters within the city, bringing with them the exotic aromas of their markets, their huge canteen-style restaurants and their colorful festivities – like the Chinese New Year with its paper dragon.

THE "WENZHOU" QUARTER

Hidden away in the 2nd arrondissement is an unobtrusive "Chinatown". Originally from Zhejiangh, the "Wenzhou Chinese" have been emigrating to France since the 1920's. They form a close-knit group, speaking a dialect incomprehensible even to other Chinese

communities in Paris. They have taken over the workshops and wholesale businesses of the "Arts et Métiers" quarter (2EF4) devoted to the leather trade.

THE "CHOISY TRIANGLE" (5GH8)

This is the name sometimes given to the most famous Chinese quarter in Paris, located in the 13th arrondissement between Avenue d'Ivry, Avenue de Choisy and Boulevard Masséna. The quarter came into being after 1975 when large numbers of refugees arrived from former French territories in Indochina: Vietnamese, Laotians and Cambodians. This quarter, previously occupied by the Panhard factory buildings, had undergone extensive renovation. The refugees poured into the tower blocks snubbed by Parisians when they were first put up for rent in the early 1970's.

THE FIRST CHINESE QUARTER IN PARIS

This came into being after World War One, close to the Gare de Lyon. China had entered the war in 1917 on the side of the Allies, and had sent 140,000 volunteers to take part in the war effort. The volunteers worked in ports, on building sites and in arms factories; several thousand chose to stay in France at the end of the war, becoming workers in car factories, craftsmen or peddlers. A small group moved into the Chalon estate (now destroyed) and set up businesses there; they were followed by immigrants from North Africa in the 1950's.

THE TEMPLES OF THE OLYMPIADES

The huge Olympiades building at the heart of the "Choisy triangle" houses two Buddhist temples: the meditation center of the Teochew Association (below) and the altar of the Cult of Buddha, whose sign shines out in the half-light of a parking lot. Prayers are held several times each day, accompanied by traditional music. Worshippers also come to consult their guardian divinities using divining rods.

CHINESE OR INDOCHINESE?

Much of the Asian population in the 13th arrondissement is Chinese in origin: in the 19th century they had emigrated to Vietnam, Laos and Cambodia where they were partly assimilated into the local culture. Many came originally from Teochew, a region of southern China with an emigrant tradition going back to the 17th century when foreign explorers landed here.

THE "PARIS BUDDHA"

The International Buddhist Institute of Paris (4E9), open to Buddhists of all persuasions, is located in the Bois de Vincennes, in a group of African buildings dating from the colonial exhibition of 1931. The largest of these, the former Cameroon pavilion, houses a huge Buddha covered in gold (above). The thirty-foot high figure is known as the Paris Buddha. A Tibetan temple was added to the institute in 1984. A sculpture by Japanese artist Tarao Yazaki depicting zen pilgrims – "Pilgrims of Clouds and Water" – marks the entrance to the site.

DANCE OF THE DRAGON

The Dance of the Dragon is the most spectacular event in the Chinese New Year festivities. The dragon passes through the streets of the Chinese quarter chasing away evil spirits and receiving "good-luck money": new banknotes in red envelopes. Parades and Buddhist processions are held throughout the week.

UNDER THE SIGN OF THE COCK

Rambutans, bamboo shoots, lotus roots, dried fish – produce from all over Southeast Asia is unloaded every day at Tang Frères in Avenue d'Ivry. The company's emblem is a cock: the astrological sign of the Tang brothers' grandfather, who emigrated from Teochew to Laos at the beginning of the century.

restaurant

CHINA SQUARE

In China it is generally believed that a building placed where two rivers meet will bring prosperity to its inhabitants. This augurs well for Chinagora (literally, "China Square"), which was built where the Seine joins the Marne in 1992. This striking group of buildings is owned by a large Chinese state-controlled company; it was designed in the Manchu style and intended as a showcase for China, past and present.

Chinagora incorporates an exhibition hall built in a style reminiscent of Peking's Forbidden City, the delightful "Garden of Nine Dragons" which is entirely hidden from view on the outside, and a tea house where visitors can attend Chinese tea ceremonies.

BELLEVILLE TURNS CHINESE

The Belleville quarter has become home to many immigrant communities since the 19th century: Jews from Eastern Europe, Armenians, Spanish, Greeks, and North Africans followed one after the other. Today it is the Asian community's turn – refugees from Indochina and Wenzhou Chinese have moved into the northeast of Belleville. Asian markets have sprung up and the quarter is now famous for its Chinese restaurants, including Nioulaville and the sumptuous Royal Belleville.

ORCHESTRA WITHOUT VOICES

In Japanese, karaoke means "orchestra without voices". The word is used to describe the facility offered by certain restaurants or bars whereby customers can take the stage to sing popular songs accompanied by a backing tape. Karaoke is very popular in Japan, throughout Southeast Asia and in China. The craze has also hit Paris. Japanese karaoke clubs are often difficult to get into; Chinese karaoke clubs, by contrast, are open to everyone, and all kinds of songs are performed. The Chinagora karaoke (below).

MAGIC WANDS

The first Asian restaurants appeared in the Latin Quarter at the beginning of the century. More followed in the 1950's, when the War of Indochina brought in a first wave of Vietnamese immigrants; another wave followed this in the 1970's. The restaurant business, a traditional immigrant activity, gave the refugees a springboard for social integration and success. Today 15 percent of Parisian restaurants are Asian.

MAISON DES CULTURES DU MONDE (1I10)

The Maison des Cultures du Monde, based in the theater of the Alliance Française, was established in 1982. It was one of the first theaters to welcome artists from all over the world, giving priority to the least-known traditional cultures. This venue is used for all types of performance all year round, including Chinese opera, Japanese theater, African, Islamic and Indian music and dance.

JAPAN IN THE OPÉRA QUARTER

The Opéra quarter has the largest number of Japanese shops, restaurants and bars; it is known as the Japanese quarter of Paris. However Japanese influence is also felt in the rooms dedicated to Japanese Buddhism in Musée Guimet ▲ *142* and in the Japan House of the Cité Internationale Universitaire (5AB9). The painter Fujita

produced two magnificent works for this building, combining Western and Japanese techniques (painting on gold-leaf). One of them depicts the first meeting of Japanese and Westerners in the port of Nagasaki in the 16th century.

TAI-CHI-CHUAN

A disciple of Lao-tseu said: "To live well you must stretch your body like an animal." Tai-Chi-Chuan, based on this principle, was invented in China four hundred years ago. It consists of around one hundred slow and precise movements, performed in a fixed sequence. During the last thirty or so years the practise has become a common sight in the cities of China. The fashion has also arrived in Paris, where Tai-Chi-Chuan is practised in the squares of the Chinese quarters, in the Bois de Boulogne, in the Jardin du Luxembourg and the Buttes-Chaumont.

THE HOUSE OF CHING TSAI LOO

This gallery of Asian art at 48, rue de Courcelles (9D9) is open to the public; it was built by Fernand Bloch between 1926 and 1928 following instructions from his patron Ching Tsai Loo, a Chinese antique dealer. The pagoda is striking: placed on the corner of the building, its colored façade contrasts with its surroundings. Apart from the roof and the canopies covered with varnished tiles on each story, the building is very simple in design. Inside, the exhibition hall on the second story is decorated with lacquer panels, some dating from the 16th century (Ch'ing period).

FILM SETS

In 1927 Fujita laid the first stone of the Japan House in the Cité Internationale Universitaire. Southeast Asia House, on the same campus, was used as a film set for *L'Amant* and *Indochine*.

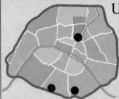

The 10th and 18th arrondissements and cultural centers.

Up to the early 1970's India was still a mysterious continent whose music, dance and cinema were known only to a few initiates in Paris. However in the last twenty or so years increasing numbers of Indians have arrived in Paris and its surrounding region, especially since Great Britain closed its doors to foreign immigrants. These new arrivals often come into the country secretly and work at whatever odd jobs they can get.

INDIAN QUARTERS
Bazaars, groceries and cassette stores have sprung up at the top end of Rue du Faubourg-St-Denis. This is where the Indians of Paris come for their supplies; it is close to the Sentier where many of them work.

WHO ARE THE INDIANS OF PARIS?
Pakistanis from the Punjab have been coming to Paris since the 1970's. Recently they have been joined by Indians from Gujerat and the Punjab – the latter including many Sikhs fleeing ethnic conflicts. The Indian community in Paris also includes Tamils from Sri Lanka and thousands of people from the Pondicherry Territory who chose French nationality after the French trading post there was closed down.

PASSAGE BRADY (2E1)
The sounds, smells and colors of India have taken over all the stalls in this passage (left) connecting Rue du Faubourg-St-Denis with Boulevard de Strasbourg. Hindu statuettes, saris, jewelry, mountains of rice, jars of chutney, crockery and magazines are heaped chaotically on the stalls. In summer all the restaurants have their tables out of doors and the sound of Indian chants echoes under the arches.

INDIAN DANCE
Courses and performances of folk and classical Indian dance are offered at the Mandapa ◆ 517 and Soleil d'Or centers. Below, the Bindi pose.

RESTAURANTS
Many Indians and Pakistanis from the Punjab opened restaurants in Paris. They serve mainly Mongolian-influenced northern Indian food: tandooris and curries. There are a few restaurants, notably in Passage Brady, serving southern Indian cuisine, which boasts thousands of vegetarian dishes. The sumptuous decor of Lalqila in the 15th arrondissement (above): a stucco reproduction of the Taj Mahal.

PRACTICAL
INFORMATION

FORMALITIES

ENTERING FRANCE
EU nationals need only present their identity card or passport. Non-EU nationals should contact their own consulate to find out whether they require a visa as well as a passport.

HEALTH
There are no particular health requirements, and vaccination certificates are only needed when visitors have come from a country where there is an epidemic. EU nationals are advised to take with them form E111.

ANIMALS
Pet owners must present the relevant health documents at customs, signed by a vet in their own country and certifying that vaccinations are up to date.

TAX DEDUCTIONS
All visitors aged fifteen and over, residing outside the EU on the date of purchase and staying in France for less than 6 months, can deduct VAT from the price of purchases (up to 1,200F in any one store) made in France. Not all items are subject to tax deductions.

EMBASSIES AND CONSULATES
- ◆ USA
  - 2, rue St-Florentin, 75382 (consulate) Tel: 08 36 70 14 88
  - 2, avenue Gabriel, 75008 Tel: 01 43 12 22 22
- ◆ CANADA
  - 35, avenue Montaigne, 75008 Tel: 01 44 43 29 00
- ◆ AUSTRALIA
  - 4, rue Jean-Rey, 75015 Tel: 01 40 59 33 00
- ◆ NEW ZEALAND
  - 7 ter, rue Léonard-de-Vinci, 75116 Tel: 01 45 00 24 11
- ◆ UNITED KINGDOM
  - 16, rue d'Anjou, 75008 (consulate) Tel: 01 44 51 31 00
  - 35, rue du Faubourg-St-Honoré, 75008 Tel: 01 44 51 31 00
- ◆ IRELAND (EIRE)
  - 4, rue Rude, 75116. Tel: 01 44 17 67 00

NATIONAL AND INTERNATIONAL AIRLINES
For further flight information:
- ◆ Roissy Airport Tel: 01 48 62 22 80
- ◆ Orly Airport Tel: 01 49 75 52 52
- ◆ Air France Tel: 0 802 802 802 Air France serves no fewer than

101 countries worldwide. Visitors from all five continents will find a flight – to or from Paris – to suit their needs.

Internal air links

Destination	Duration	Airport
Strasbourg	1 hr	Orly
Toulouse	1 hr 10 min	Orly
Lyon	55 min	Orly
	1 hr 5 min	Roissy
Nantes	1 hr 15 min	Orly
	1 hr	Roissy
Nice	1 hr 20 min	Orly
Bordeaux	1 hr	Orly
Marseille	1 hr 10 min	Orly
Brest	1 hr 5 min	Orly
Clermont-Ferrand	50 min	Orly

FARES
From the US: fares vary greatly according to airline, class of ticket and the US airport. For special fares contact the following airlines:

- ◆ Air France 800-237 2747
- ◆ American Airlines 800-433 7300
- ◆ Delta 800-241 4141
- ◆ TWA 800-892 4141

From the UK
Paris is served by many airlines, with scheduled and charter flights. Fares vary widely according to airline, class of ticket and the UK airport. Check for special fares with:

- ◆ Air France 0181 742 6600
- ◆ British Airways 0345 222111
- ◆ British Midland 0181 745 7321
- ◆ Nouvelles Frontières (charter flights) 0171 629 7772

TOUR OPERATORS
In the US:
There are many tour operators who will arrange trips to Paris. The French Government Tourist Office will send you its brochure with details of tour operators, travel formalities and useful addresses.
Tel: 1-900-990 0040* (50c per minute anywhere in the US)

In the UK:
- ◆ Trailfinders 42–50 Earl's Court Road, London W8 6EJ Tel: 0171 938 3366
- ◆ Travelnow 55 Wilton Road, London SW1V 1DE Tel: 0171 630 3315

PARIS AIRPORTS
Paris airports are among the world's leading airports – handling over 60 million passengers each year – and the second largest in Europe after the London airports.

BY CHANNEL TUNNEL

For special return fares for a car with any number of passengers, phone Eurotunnel (tel. from UK: 0990 353535). You can also take the Eurostar train from London's Waterloo station. Journey time is 3¼ hours to Paris' Gare du Nord. Various first-class and economy fares are available. Contact Eurostar (tel. from UK: 0345 30 30 30) for further information.

ROISSY

FROM PARIS TO ROISSY-CHARLES-DE-GAULLE (CDG)

There are several ways of getting to or from Roissy-Charles-de-Gaulle airport (18½ miles from the center of Paris).
◆ Car Air France: buses leave from the Palais des Congrès building at the Porte Maillot, bd. Gouvion-St-Cyr (8 I3) and from the pl. de l'Etoile, 1 av. Carnot (9 A10). Another service leaves from the Gare de Lyon on bd. Diderot (2 I10) and from the Gare Montparnasse on rue du Cdt-René-Mouchotte (6 H2).
◆ Roissybus offers a direct bus service from the Opéra, on rue Scribe.
◆ Roissyrail offers a free shuttle service between the RER station (line B3) and CDG1 (Terminal 1). A direct service runs to CDG2 (Terminal 2).
◆ TGV: the new TGV–RER station at CDG2 now offers connections with the southeastern and northern TGV networks.

Means of transport	From CDG (exit)	To Paris (destination)	Times	Frequency	Journey time	Fare 2nd cl.
Car Air France	CDG2 A/C: 5 CDG2 B/D: 6 CDG2 F: G CDG1: 34	Étoile/Porte-Maillot	5.40am–11pm	12 mins	40 mins	60F
	CDG2 A/C: 2(C) CDG2 B/D: 1(B) CDG2 F: G CDG1: 34	Gare Montparnasse/ Gare de Lyon	6am–11pm 7am–9.30pm	30 mins	50 mins	70F
Roissybus	CDG2 A/C: 10 CDG2 B/D: 12 CDG2 F: H CDG1: 30	Opéra	6am–11pm	15 mins	45 mins to 1¼ hrs	45F
Roissy-Rail RER line B3	CDG2 CDG1 (shuttle)	Châtelet-les-Halles (example only)	5.20am–11.30pm	15 mins	30 mins	47F

CDG–PARIS–CDG

FROM PARIS TO ORLY

There are various ways of getting to or from Orly airport (9¼ miles from central Paris).
◆ Car Air France from Les Invalides: buses leave from in front of the Air France office in the station (1 F5), and also stop at Gare Montparnasse on rue Cdt-René-Mouchotte (6 H2). Request stops en route from Orly: Porte-d'Orléans (6 H9) and Duroc.
◆ Orlybus: from pl. Denfert-Rochereau (6 J4).
◆ Orlyrail: take RER line C2 to Aéroport d'Orly-Pont-de-Rungis station, then a free shuttle service to the airport.
◆ Orlyval: take RER line B4 to Antony station, then the automatic rail link.
◆ Jetbus: this bus service leaves from Villejuif Métro station (on line 7), which is in the south of Paris.

Means of transport	From Orly (exit)	To Paris (destination)	Stops/ stations	Times	Frequency	Journey time	Fare 2nd cl.
Car Air France	Orly Ouest: D Orly Sud: K	Invalides	Montparnasse (Porte-d'Orléans/ Duroc)	5.50am–11pm	12 mins	30 mins to 1 hr	45F
Orlybus	Orly Ouest: J Orly Sud: H	Denfert-Rochereau		6.30am–11pm	12 mins	25 mins	30F
Orlyrail RER line C2	Orly Ouest: F Orly Sud: H	change at: Pt-de-Rungis	Gare-d'Austerlitz Saint-Michel (example only)	5.30am–11pm	15 mins (30 mins after 9pm)	32 mins 35 mins	30F
Orlyval RER line B4	Orly Ouest: W Orly Sud: F	change at: Antony	Saint-Michel Les Halles (example only)	6am–10.30pm (Sunday: 7am–11pm)	4–8 mins	30 mins 35 mins	57F
Jetbus	Orly Ouest: C Orly Sud: G2	Métro station Villejuif-Louis-Aragon (line 7)		6am–10pm	12 mins 7am–10am, 4.30–6pm; other times 15 mins	15 mins	24F

Orly–Paris–Orly

◆ TRAVELING TO PARIS

Gare du Nord.

Gare St-Lazare.

RAIL TRAVEL

With more than 830 million passengers per year, the SNCF (French Rail) offers a large number of serves from Paris to other countries, the Paris suburbs and French provinces. There are six main-line stations in the French capital: the Gare du Nord, Gare de l'Est, Gare Saint-Lazare, Gare de Lyon, Gare Montparnasse and Gare d'Austerlitz.

MAIN-LINE STATIONS IN PARIS

◆ The Gare du Nord serves the French regions of Nord-Pas-de-Calais and Picardy, the *département* of the Ardennes, Belgium, the Netherlands, northern Germany, Scandinavia and the United Kingdom.
◆ The Gare de l'Est serves the French regions of Champagne-Ardenne, Alsace and Lorraine, southern Germany, Switzerland and Austria.
◆ The Gare de Lyon serves the French regions of Burgundy, Franche-Comté, Rhône-Alpes, Languedoc-Roussillon and Provence-Alpes-Côte d'Azur, Switzerland and Italy.
◆ The Gare d'Austerlitz serves the central regions of France, the Auvergne

and the southwest, Spain and Portugal.
◆ The Gare Montparnasse serves Britanny, the Loire region, Poitou-Charente, Aquitaine, Midi-Pyrénées and Spain.
◆ The Gare Saint-Lazare serves Normandy.

USING THE STATIONS
The French rail network consists of "Corail" and TGV (high-speed) trains. Near the main

platform (*quai*) in each station are illuminated arrival and departure boards giving the times, platforms and numbers of the relevant trains. In the event of doubt – or panic – passenger information centers provide rail information as well as other services, from tourist information, car and cycle rental, left-luggage and

ticket information to washrooms.
◆ For disabled passengers: tel: 0 800 15 47 53
◆ "Les Compagnons du Voyage" provides traveling companions: tel: 01 45 83 67 77

TICKETS AND RESERVATIONS
It is advisable to reserve seats in advance (reservations are compulsory on TGVs) because of the large numbers of passengers during peak periods (Fri. eve., Sun. eve., school holidays). You can reserve:
◆ by telephone: 7-day service, 7am–10pm, tel: 08 36 35 35 35
◆ by Internet: reserve tickets through www.sncf.fr
◆ at the station: you can buy tickets from the ticket office or the automatic ticket machine
◆ by Minitel: 36 15 or 36 16 code SNCF – a 24-hour service; you can pay for your reservations using a "smart card"

Rail links

Destination of train	Type of train	Journey time	Fare 2ⁿᵈ cl.
Strasbourg	Corail	4–5 hrs	210F
Toulouse	TGV	5¼ hrs	433F
	Corail	6½–7 hrs	346F
Lyons	TGV	2 hrs 5 mins	304F
Marseilles	TGV	4 hrs 25 mins	367F
Nice	TGV	6½ hrs	438F
Bordeaux	TGV	3–3½ hrs	337F
Nantes	TGV	2–2¼ hrs	284F
Caen	Corail	2½–4 hrs	152F
Brest	TGV	4 hrs 20 mins	360F
La Rochelle	TGV	2½–3 hrs	305F
Lille	TGV	1 hr	199F
Montpellier	TGV	4 hrs 25 mins	367F
Clermont-Ferrand	Corail	3½ hrs	233F

452

TGV Atlantique.

Stand by for departure!

Paris by boat.

REDUCTIONS

The SNCF offers a number of reductions in the form of season tickets with special discounts:

◆ for seniors aged 60 and over
◆ "Enfant +": for those traveling with a child under 12
◆ for young people aged 12 to 25
◆ various options available to all travelers: for two people traveling together; for travelers staying overnight on Saturday; and for reservations between 8 and 30 days before departure

VALIDITY

Tickets and reservations must be date stamped (*composté*) on the day you travel using the orange machines (*composteurs*) provided for the purpose.

FERRY CROSSINGS

Ferries and hovercraft operate from Dover to Calais, Newhaven to Dieppe and Folkestone to Boulogne. You can then catch a train to Paris Gare du Nord (Calais, Boulogne) or Gare St-Lazare (Dieppe). The ferry companies will organize rail tickets if required.

◆ Stena Sealink: 01233 647047
◆ Hoverspeed 01304 865000

RER

The RER express network, faster than the Métro, connects Paris and its suburbs. Currently there are four lines (A, B, C, D), each divided into several numbered branches (see plan on back endpaper). Note in particular:

A4: Disneyland Paris
B3: Parc Astérix
C5: Versailles
D1: Stade de France

A fifth line (E) is due to enter service from June 1999.

TICKETS

◆ Métro tickets are valid on the RER for journeys within Paris (zones 1 and 2), and you can interchange freely between the two systems
◆ Destinations beyond the gates of the capital are zoned and fares are scaled accordingly; passengers changing from Métro to RER should buy an additional ticket in the station where you join the RER or at the station where you start your journey

SAILING DOWN THE SEINE

The Seine – which passes through Burgundy, Champagne, the Île-de-France and Normandy before it flows into the Channel – forms the main axis of the Paris Basin. The very motto of Paris is associated with the river: *Fluctuat nec mergitur* (It sails but does not sink). The tourist basin of the Île-de-France region is particularly well provided for, with 440 miles of navigable waterways. The Seine is a through route for foreign navigators who can admire many of the Paris monuments as they sail past the quays. The large amount of commercial traffic using the waterways of this river basin calls for prudence on the part of pleasure craft and it is advisable to contact the Service de Navigation de Paris: 2, quai de Grenelle, 75732 Paris Cedex 15, tel: 01 40 58 29 99. To sail on the Seine you must purchase a license tag. Listed below are some of the ports that welcome pleasure craft.

Ports	
Ports on the banks of the Seine	Telephone
Port aux Cerises (Draveil, 91)	01 69 40 33 10
Port de Nogent-sur-Marne	01 48 71 41 65
Port de Neuilly-sur-Marne	01 43 08 51 35
Port de Joinville-le-Pont	01 48 83 35 10
Port de l'Arsenal (Paris)	01 43 41 39 32
Port de Cergy	01 34 24 11 77
Port de La Concorde (Paris)	01 42 65 90 70

L'Arsenal pleasure port.

◆ TRAVELING TO PARIS

═══ Autoroute		═══ Francilienne
═ ═ ═ Being built		‐ ‐ ‐ Being built
—— Railroad		✈ Airport
—— Main roads		⊕ Heliport
‐ ‐ ‐ ‐ RER		⚓ Port
—— Waterway		⚓ Camping site

BY CAR

ROAD NETWORK
Autoroutes are mostly free in the Ile-de-France. Several lead off the Périphérique road circling Paris: the A1 to Lille, A4 to Strasbourg, A13 to Le Havre, A6 to Lyons, A10 to Nantes and A11 to Bordeaux. The Francilienne (A104) and A86 partly circle the inner and outer suburbs. Newer autoroutes don't lead directly to Paris: the A16 to Amiens and A5 to Lyons are reached via the Francilienne, and the A14 to Le Havre starts beyond La Défense.

TRAFFIC INFORMATION
◆ Centre d'Informations Routières
Tel: 01 48 99 33 33
◆ Bison Futé
Tel: 08 36 68 20 00
◆ RATP
Tel: 01 43 46 14 14

HITCHHIKING
Allô-Stop puts drivers in touch with hitchhikers. Fares range from 30–70F according to mileage + 22c per km. Or buy a season ticket valid for 8 journeys over 2 years, for 180F.
Tel: 01 53 20 42 42.

Travel information

Radio	Frequency	Time
Autoroute FM	107.7 MHz	24 hours every ½ hour (in Ile-de-France), every ¼ hour (in major towns)
RFM	103.9 MHz	Daily 6–9am and 5–8pm
95.2 Paris	95.2 MHz	24 hours every ½ hour
Europe 1	104.7 MHz	Fri. eve. 5–10pm every ½ hour, Sun. eve. 5–11pm and public holidays
FIP	105.5 MHz	During the morning

PARKING

Parking is a taboo word in Paris where it is difficult to find a parking space near your own front door. It is advisable to observe the parking restrictions if you want to avoid being fined (75–230F) or having your car impounded.
◆ Ticket machines: most Paris streets have them. The price of tickets varies according to the length of stay and the district. They operate Mon.–Fri. between 9am and 7pm. Parking is usually free on Sat., Sun., public holidays and in August. You pay with coins or a parking card, available from tobacconists.
Tel. 01 42 76 22 22.
◆ There are also a number of public car parks. Prices are based on the same criteria as above:
◆ 1st: Les Halles 10 bis, rue Bailleul
◆ 4th: Beaubourg 19, place Georges-Pompidou
◆ 5th: Maubert 39, bd. Saint-Germain
◆ 6th: FNAC 123, rue de Rennes
◆ 7th: Invalides 23, rue de Constantine
◆ 8th: Concorde Corner of Avenue Gabriel
◆ 12th: Bercy Below the Palais Omnisports.

CAR RENTAL

You can rent cars at the Roissy-Charles-de-Gaulle and Orly airports and at main-line rail stations. There are also various agencies scattered throughout the city, some open on weekends; examples are listed opposite:

◆ Avis
Tel: 01 46 10 60 60
◆ National-Citer
Tel: 01 44 38 61 61
◆ Dergilocation
Tel: 01 43 68 55 55
◆ Europcar
Tel: 01 30 43 82 82
◆ Sixte
Tel: 01 44 38 55 55
◆ Hertz
Tel: 01 39 38 38 38

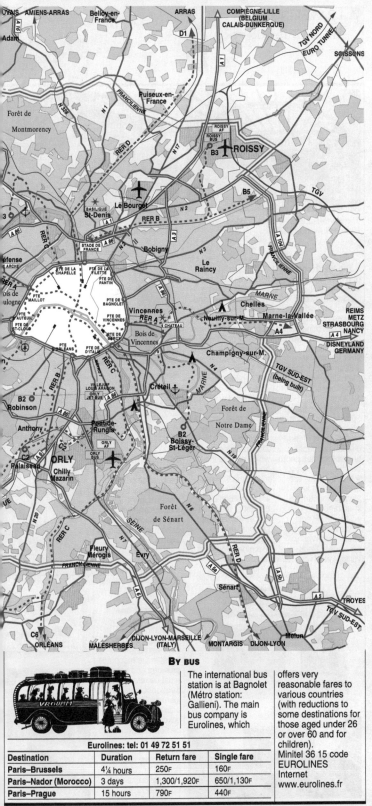

BY BUS

The international bus station is at Bagnolet (Métro station: Gallieni). The main bus company is Eurolines, which offers very reasonable fares to various countries (with reductions to some destinations for those aged under 26 or over 60 and for children). Minitel 36 15 code EUROLINES Internet www.eurolines.fr

Eurolines: tel: 01 49 72 51 51			
Destination	Duration	Return fare	Single fare
Paris–Brussels	4¼ hours	250F	160F
Paris–Nador (Morocco)	3 days	1,300/1,920F	650/1,130F
Paris–Prague	15 hours	790F	440F

455

The Porte-Dauphine station, decorated by Hector Guimard in 1900.

Porte-de-Saint-Cloud: a more traditional Métro entrance.

MÉTRO

◆ The Métro consists of a network of 16 lines and is the quickest way of getting around Paris. It takes typically about two minutes to travel between two Métro stations. Trains start running at 5.30am and the last Métro leaves its departure point at 12.30am.

◆ Inside the capital's 300 Métro stations are plans of the Métro, maps of the district, telephones, and sometimes photo booths.

◆ Métro strikes are frequent, but are always announced in advance.

◆ The RATP has developed a range of tourist travel packages. *Paris visite* – valid for 1, 2, 3 or 5 days in any 3, 5 or 8 of the network's zones – combines travel and reduced admission to monuments in the capital and the Paris region. For tourists with less time, the RATP has developed the *Mobilis* card, which offers the same travel options for a one-day period without the other advantages. It can be combined with the *Musées et Monuments* card, which entitles the holder to visit 70 museums in Paris and its environs.

◆ Tickets can be bought at the ticket offices inside Métro stations, from automatic ticket machines and from tobacconists.

Remember to date-stamp your ticket before going onto the platform.

◆ Commercial agencies and information centers are currently being installed in the larger stations and will provide a new point of contact between agents and passengers.

◆ Children under 4 travel free of charge and children between 4 and 10 for half price.

ON THE PLATFORM
Before going onto the platform passengers must date stamp their ticket in the machines provided and tickets must be retained throughout the journey. RATP officials may check tickets on the platform and on trains. It is an offense not to have a (correctly dated) ticket. For RATP information, tel: 08 36 68 77 14.

	Main roads
	Gardens
	Important monu
	RER lines

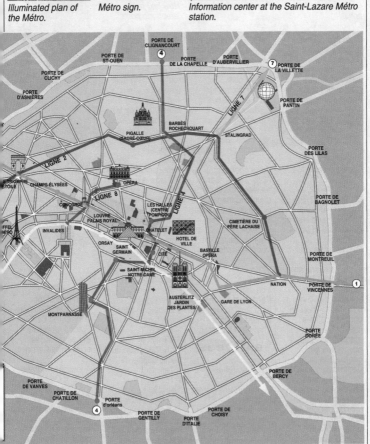

Illuminated plan of the Métro.

Métro sign.

Information center at the Saint-Lazare Métro station.

Tickets			
	Fare	Zones	Validity
Individual tickets	8F	1–2	
Carnet (10 tickets)	52F	1–2	
Mobilis card	30F	1–2	1 day
	50F	1–4	1 day
Paris visite card	120F	1–3	3 days
	170F	1–3	5 days
	245F	1–5	3 days
	300F	1–5	5 days
1-week season ticket	80F	1–2	7 days
Carte orange	271F	1–2	1 month

Date-stamping a ticket.

Bus routes and stops.

New taxi-rank telephone point.

BUSES

Paris has 58 bus routes and the PC (Petite Ceinture = Inner Circle), which links the *Portes* (gates) of Paris. Buses run from

5.30am–8.30pm. Some routes (Nos. 21, 26, 27, 31, 38, 52, 62, 63, 72, 74, 80, 85, 91, 92, 95, 96 and PC) run until 12.30am and also on Sundays and public holidays.

FINDING YOUR WAY
Fold-out plans of bus routes are available from the RATP. Times and routes are also displayed at bus stops. There is generally also a map of the local area showing other bus routes and nearby bus stops.

GETTING ABOUT
Bus tickets are identical to those on the Métro, but can only be bought singly. You must stamp a ticket for each journey, unless you hold a season ticket or other travel card, which you should simply present to the conductor.

NOCTAMBUS
Noctambus is the Paris night-bus service. All 18 night routes pass via Châtelet. Buses leave at half past the hour, between 1.30 and 5.30am.

Fare: 30F, unless you have a season ticket or other travel card.

BALABUS AND OPEN TOUR
These two routes were established to take in the principal monuments of Paris. *Balabus* runs on Sundays and public holidays (from noon–9pm, April–September) between the Gare de Lyon and the Grande Arche de la Défense. The open-topped double-decker *Open Tour* buses depart from La Madeleine, 9.45am–4.50pm.

BATOBUS
You can discover Paris from the river, from April to October, aboard *Batobus*. There are six stops

BAT O BUS

en route: Eiffel Tower, Orsay, Louvre, Notre-Dame, Hôtel-de-Ville, St-Germain-des-Prés. Fares: 60F (day ticket); 20F (per stop).

BUS HIRE
Parisians and tourists can hire vintage (e.g., 3,135F for 3 hours) and modern (e.g., 1,385F for 3 hours) buses. Info: from RATP, 19, pl. Lachambeaudie 75012 Paris Tel: 01 49 28 48 97 Fax: 01 49 28 49 15

TAXIS

There are nearly 15,000 taxis in Paris. Without a car or a *Noctambus* route running past your door, the only way to get home after 1am is by taxi. Paris has 471 taxi ranks and 125 of these have telephone points.

FARES
Fares are based on the time taken to cover a given distance. There are three set per-kilometer rates:
◆ Paris zone:
7am–7pm
– Tarif A
3.25F/km
7pm–7am, Sun. and public holidays
– Tarif B
5.83F/km
◆ Suburban zone
7am–7pm
– Tarif B
5.83F/km
7pm–7am, Sun. and public holidays
– Tarif C
7.16F/km
The total fare includes a pick-up charge (13F) which appears on the meter as soon as the driver moves off. Paris taxi drivers are authorized to make an additional charge over and above the fare indicated on the meter if they:
◆ carry a fourth passenger (adult: 11F), luggage or other bulky items (6F per item) or an animal (4F)
◆ pick up their fare

from one of the Paris SNCF stations or near the Car Air France terminals at Les Invalides or Avenue Carnot (5F)
A journey from the Porte d'Orléans to the Porte de Clignancourt should cost around 65F for a reliable daytime service, and 80F at night, on Sunday and public holidays. A journey from La Défense to the Château de Vincennes should cost around 80F during the day, and 110F at night, on Sunday and public holidays.

"TAXI!"

Taxis can be hired at taxi ranks or hailed in the street by simply raising your arm. If the light on the taxi roof is orange, the taxi is already taken. The light also indicates the different taxi fares (Tarif A, B or C).

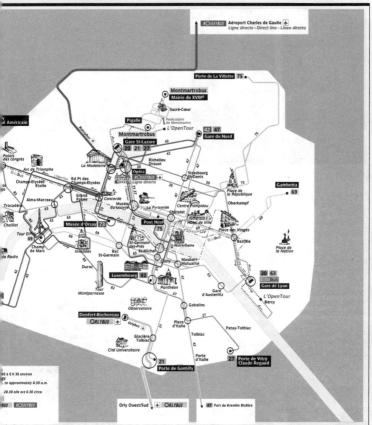

Wait!

Walk!

Take five!

WALKING IN PARIS

Always use pedestrian crossings and sidewalks and observe traffic signals: these are the basic rules for pedestrians in Paris. There are also pedestrianized zones, particularly in such commercial districts as Les Halles, the Latin Quarter and near the Canal Saint-Martin.

There is a GR (*grande randonnée*) footpath linking the Bois de Boulogne and the Bois de Vincennes, via the Eiffel Tower, the Invalides, the Luxembourg and the Jardin des Plantes. This 10-mile tourist route, marked in red and yellow, takes you across Paris in about three hours.

ROLLER SKATING

Although roller skating is authorized on public highways, skaters are legally classified as pedestrians and must therefore skate on sidewalks and use pedestrian crossings when crossing the road. Using cycle tracks and being pulled along by other vehicles is an offense.

CYCLING IN PARIS

With some 60 miles in place in 1997 and another 40 scheduled by 2000, Paris is gradually piecing together a cycle-track network worthy of the name. You can now cycle across Paris from north to south and east to west (see lower map, opposite page) – including the Bois de Boulogne and Vincennes.

CYCLE RENTAL

◆ The SNCF has a cycle-rental service at the Gare Montparnasse (6 G2) and the Gare de l'Est (10 F9). Tel: 06 14 96 54 75 (for conditions for taking or sending bicycles on trains tel: 08 36 35 35 35).
◆ From March to mid-October the RATP's *Roue Libre* scheme offers cycle-rental at strategic locations: the Bois de Boulogne (8 C10), Bois de Vincennes (4 H4), Champ-de-Mars (1 B7) and Square St-Jacques (2 D6). For information tel: 08 36 68 77 17 or 08 36 68 41 14 (English spoken).
◆ Maison du vélo: 11, rue Fénelon 75010, tel: 01 42 81 24 72
◆ Paris-Vélo: 2, rue du Fer-à-Moulin 75005, tel: 01 43 37 59 22

CYCLING

RIDES WITH GUIDES

◆ Paris à vélo, c'est sympa: 37, bd. Bourdon 75004 (2 H9), tel: 01 48 87 60 01 Schedules tailored to

your preferences, along routes avoiding heavy traffic, with commentary in several languages.
◆ RATP *Roue Libre* For bookings tel: 01 53 17 03 18 Rides from 1½ to 3 hours, on the same basis as rentals.

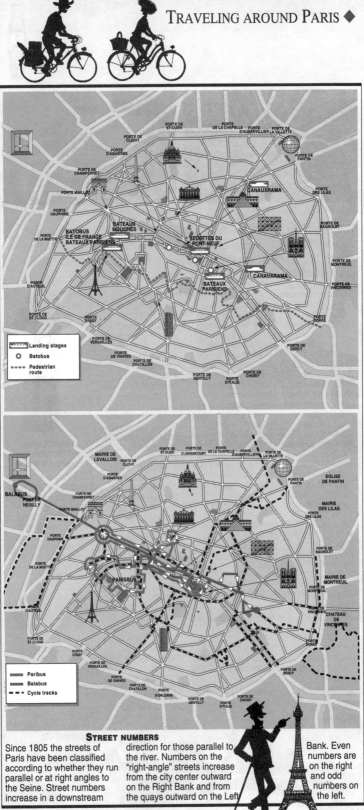

Landing stages
O Batobus
- - - - Pedestrian route

Paribus
Balabus
- - - Cycle tracks

STREET NUMBERS

Since 1805 the streets of Paris have been classified according to whether they run parallel or at right angles to the Seine. Street numbers increase in a downstream direction for those parallel to the river. Numbers on the "right-angle" streets increase from the city center outward on the Right Bank and from the quays outward on the Left Bank. Even numbers are on the right and odd numbers on the left.

461

◆ PARIS INFORMATION

Aerial view of L'Étoile (IGN).

Looking for the best cards.

Guide books, the press, radio and TV, bookstores and specialist organizations are all useful sources of information when it comes to visiting Paris. Even the Parisians use them to find out what they have always wanted to know about their city.

TOURIST OFFICES

◆ Office du Tourisme et des Congrès de Paris 127, av. des Champs-Élysées 75008 (1 B1)
Tel: 01 49 52 53 54
Open daily 9am–8pm
"Information Loisirs"
What's on in Paris 24-hour recorded information in English
Tel: 01 49 52 53 61

BRANCH OFFICES

◆ Gare du Nord 18 rue de Dunkerque 75010 (10 E8)
Tel: 01 45 26 94 82
◆ Gare de Lyon 20, bd. Diderot 75012 (2 I10)
Tel: 01 43 43 33 24
◆ Tour Eiffel (May-Sept.), Champ-de-Mars 75007 (1 B6)
Tel: 01 45 51 22 15

USEFUL ADDRESSES

Check out the following guides:
◆ *Le Paris introuvable*, FRANÇOIS DELETRAZ (Jean-Claude Lattès)
◆ *Paris pas cher*, FRANÇOISE & BERNARD DELTHIL (Flammarion)
◆ *Guide Paris combines*, PASCAL BATAILLE & LAURENT FONTAINE (Solar)

PARIS IN THE MEDIA

SPECIALIST PRESS

◆ *Le Parisien* is the only Île-de-France regional daily.
◆ *Paris Capitale* has regular features on fashion, shopping, exhibitions, cafés and nightclubs.
◆ *Nova magazine*, a look ahead at what's coming in the capital's nightlife (monthly).
◆ *Paris, le journal* – published monthly by the Mairie de Paris – contains some useful practical information.

SPECIAL SUPPLEMENTS ON PARIS

◆ "Figaroscope" in *Le Figaro* (Wed.).
◆ "Métro" in *Libération* (daily).
◆ "Île-de-France" column in *La Croix*, published every Fri.

◆ *Télérama* (weekly) and *Marie Claire* (monthly) combine useful addresses with articles on the Paris districts, monuments and trades.
◆ Summer supplements mostly appear weekly.

TELEPHONES

TO CALL THE FRENCH PROVINCES FROM PARIS
Dial the prefix 02, 03, 04, or 05, according to the region you are calling, followed by the 8-digit number
TO CALL WITHIN PARIS
Dial the prefix 01, followed by the 8-digit number.
TO CALL PARIS FROM THE FRENCH PROVINCES
Dial the prefix 01, followed by the 8-digit number.
TO CALL PARIS FROM THE US. Dial 011 33 1, followed by the 8-digit number (the 0 in the 01 prefix is dropped).
TO CALL PARIS FROM THE UK. Dial 00 33 1, followed by the 8-digit number.
TO CALL ABROAD FROM FRANCE. Dial the prefix 00 followed by the code of the country required and the number.

MAIL SERVICES

◆ Post offices open Mon.–Fri. 8am–7pm, Sat. 8am–noon.
◆ Main post office 52, rue du Louvre
Tel. 01 40 28 20 00
Open daily, 24 hours.

SOUVENIRS, POSTCARDS AND MAPS OF PARIS

The Rue d'Arcole, near Notre-Dame, the Champs-Élysées, the area around the Louvre and the big department stores are full of miniature Eiffel Towers and glass pyramids. For more original souvenirs:
◆ Espace IGN 107, rue La Boétie 75008 (1 E1)
Tel: 01 43 98 80 00
The IGN (Institut de Géographie Nationale) has a range of guides and maps of Paris, as well as aerial posters and blow-ups of the district of your choice (allow 2–3 weeks).
◆ Cartes d'Art 9, rue du Dragon 75006 (1 J8)
Tel: 01 42 22 86 15
A wide choice of cards – 5.50F and 6.50F – arranged by place, country, artist and photographer.

TABAC

Snow is a rare sight in Paris.

The "Seine floods".

Champs-de-Mars.

You may be wondering what there is to do in Paris in the rain, in the heat, in the snow or when it is blowing a gale. Paris has something for all seasons and all weathers. Parks with covered walkways are just one way of combating all weathers.

PARIS IN WINTER

The arrival of the cold weather is the signal for the salting services to move swiftly into action to ensure that the Métro doesn't grind to a halt. Although snow rarely falls in Paris, when it does it wreaks havoc with the transport system and traumatizes the Parisians, who have been known to wear *après-ski* suits two weeks after the snow has melted!

SNOW AND SKIING: TWO RARE OCCURRENCES Cold weather often means frozen fountains, the Seine frozen over and some remarkable winter landscapes. The only ski slopes in the city are on the Buttes-Chaumont. However, the snow lasts longer in the suburban forests, where long-distance skiing is the order of the day. A few ski-rental stores are listed in the Yellow Pages.

PARIS IN THE RAIN

Wellington boots are out of the question! It rains in Paris almost every other day, but the water drains away quickly. Stores and bus stops are good places to shelter for those who choose to ignore the picturesque umbrella stores:
MADELEINE GELY
bd. St-Germain
75007 (1 I7)
Tel: 01 42 22 63 35
SIMON
56, bd. Saint-Michel
75006 (2 B9)
Tel: 01 43 54 12 04

◆ Pedestrians can walk under cover in the Rue de Rivoli, the Place des Vosges and several shopping precincts (▲ 341, ▲ 353).

WHEN THE WIND BLOWS...
Gales, usually from the west, have become strong winds by the time they reach Paris. Instead of tearing off roof tiles, they freshen the air.

PARIS IN SUMMER

ENJOYING THE FINE WEATHER With a daily average in excess of 7 hours' sunshine between June and August, the capital adopts an appropriate lifestyle.
PICNICS With the arrival of the fine weather, Paris is invaded by picnickers. Grassed areas are often placed out of bounds, although some remain open to the public: in the Parks of la Villette, Montsouris and André-Citroën, on the Buttes-Chaumont and in the Bois de Boulogne and de Vincennes.
FOUNTAINS AND QUAYS Since they are unable to swim in the Seine,

Parisians make do with sunbathing on its banks and watching it flow past. Although bathing in fountains is forbidden, some (e.g. the Trocadéro) are sometimes invaded by bathers.
HAVENS OF PEACE Gardens are often shady and cool and some – walled in or hidden at the end of a cul-de-sac – are veritable havens of peace and quiet.
◆ The small and carefully tended Square Récamier, in the Rue de Sèvres, is surrounded by the lush balconies of quiet apartment blocks. It is surprisingly peaceful (1 I8).

◆ The Jardin Saint-Gilles-Grand-Veneur, leading into the Rue de Villehardouin, is set back from the street (2 H6).
◆ Opposite the Louvre the vast Jardin du Palais-Royal is surrounded by buildings (▲ 202).
◆ The Jardin de Babylone (33, rue de Babylone), with its lawns bordered by apple trees, is frequented by readers and very young footballers (1 H8).
◆ In the 13th *arrondissement*, next to Les Gobelins, is the peaceful Square René-Le-Gall (5 D5).

◆ The shady Square Bayen can be reached via the Boulevard Pereire, 15 minutes' walk from L'Étoile.
◆ On the islands of the Seine (2 B7), the Squares du Vert-Galant, de l'Île-de-France and Jean-XXIII overlook the river.
ESCAPING THE HEAT Take a train to a forest...
◆ Austerlitz-Dourdan-la-Forêt (1 hr).
◆ Gare du Nord-Fontaine-le-Port (40 mins).
◆ Gare de l'Est-Trilport (35 mins).

◆ HEALTH AND SAFETY

Security around Les Halles.

Samu and the fire brigade answer emergency calls.

Like all big cities Paris has districts that are best avoided by visitors. Below are a few suggestions to help you avoid finding yourself in the wrong place at the wrong time, and to take advantage of the city's health and safety facilities.

SAFETY IN PARIS

Each main-line rail station has a police station and uniformed and plain-clothes officers in the Métro and on the streets.

WHERE AND WHEN TO BE ON YOUR GUARD
According to the latest information:
♦ Pickpockets operate at certain Métro intersections (Châtelet, Barbès, Belleville and Stalingrad).
♦ Pickpockets also prefer busy areas: Barbès, Montmartre, Les Halles and the areas around the big department stores of the Opéra and Louvre.
♦ Barbès, Belleville, Stalingrad, Les Halles and, to a lesser extent, Masséna are areas well known for delinquency and are kept under surveillance.

♦ The Métro, especially the terminals, is less safe after 9pm during the week and after midnight on weekends.
♦ The Champs-Élysées and the 4th, 5th, 6th and 7th *arrondissements* are considered safer areas.

SOME PRECAUTIONS
♦ Watch out for street beggars or buskers with signs covering their hands so that you can't see what they're doing.
♦ Avoid bringing out expensive items (e.g. cameras) in public places, stations, etc.

PRACTICAL SOLUTIONS
♦ Call the police: 17.
♦ Lost property: Préfecture de Police, 36, rue des Morillons 75015 (6 B4) Tel: 01 55 76 20 00

WHERE TO DRINK

Cafés and restaurants are obliged to provide drinking water and there are public drinking fountains in the streets.

FACILITIES FOR THE DISABLED

Organizations for the disabled stress that facilities have been much improved in museums, public buildings and in the streets, where curbs have been lowered to facilitate wheelchair access. However, there is still room for improvement in the area of public transport and toilets. Buses (line 20), the Métro, RER and main-line trains are rarely adapted, while public toilets are too narrow: only twenty in the entire city have been adapted to accommodate handicapped users, and you have to obtain a card from the Mairie before you can use them. There is no information available on the few facilities provided by hotels and restaurants.

INFORMATION
♦ CNFLRH (French liaison committee for the rehabilitation of the disabled) 236 *bis*, rue de Tolbiac 75013 (5 C7) Tel: 01 53 80 66 66

FURTHER READING
♦ BEN ROBERTS and GORDON COUCH *Access in Paris,* Quiller Press, London 1993
♦ Mairie de Paris, *Paris pratique* (free)

AIR QUALITY

Since 1979 Airparif has been monitoring air quality in Paris. Although sulfur pollution has diminished, it has been replaced by road traffic pollution and, while the city's geographical location means this is regularly cleared away by winds, the summer heat and cool autumn nights cause it to reach dangerously high levels. It is up to the Paris Prefecture to introduce preventive measures.

PUBLIC TOILETS

There are some 400 *sanisettes* in Paris. It costs 2F to use these toilets, which self-clean after use (after 15 mins. the light goes off and the door is unlocked). You can use toilets in cafés and restaurants free of charge provided you are a customer.

Several pharmacies stay open at night.

No. 62, av. des Champs-Élysées: an English-speaking pharmacy.

IN THE EVENT OF ILLNESS...

Illness in Paris is treated differently from the rest of France. Parisians suffering from 'flu or bronchitis tend to call a mobile medical team rather than their doctor.

◆ The Paris medical service (*garde médicale de Paris*) sends the local duty doctor within an hour of receiving a call.
Tel: 01 42 72 88 88 daily, 24-hour service.

...OR AN ACCIDENT

◆ Ambulance (Samu): 15
◆ Fire brigade (*pompiers*): 18

LOOKING FOR A PATIENT

◆ The victims of a road accident are usually sent to the nearest hospital. Ask at the police station for information.
◆ Looking for a patient in a public hospital:
Tel: 01 40 27 37 81 daily, 9.30am-5.30pm.

EMERGENCY NUMBERS

◆ SOS cardiology
Tel: 01 47 07 50 50
◆ Cardiac emergencies
Tel: 01 47 37 53 53
◆ Anti-poison center
Tel: 01 40 37 04 04
◆ SOS dental emergencies (24-hr)
Tel: 01 43 37 51 00
◆ Paris dental emergencies
Tel: 01 45 53 71 08
◆ State ambulance service
(reimbursed on presentation of prescription)
Tel: 01 43 78 26 26

PHARMACIES OPEN AT NIGHT

24-HOUR SERVICE

◆ Pharmacie Dhéry Gallerie des Champs 84, av. des Champs-Élysées 75008 (1 D2)
Tel: 01 45 62 02 41
◆ Pharmacie Daumesnil
6, pl. Félix-Éboué 75012 (4 E2)
Tel: 01 43 43 19 03
◆ Pharmacie Européenne
6, pl. de Clichy 75009 (9 I7)
Tel: 01 48 74 65 18

OPEN UNTIL 10PM

◆ Pharmacie Centrale du Nord 132, rue Lafayette 75010 (10 E9)
Tel: 01 47 70 06 14

OPEN UNTIL MIDNIGHT

◆ Ph. des Halles 10, bd. Sébastopol 75004 (2 D6)
Tel: 01 42 72 03 23
◆ Pharmacie Knafo 13, pl. de la Nation 75011 (3 E9)
Tel: 01 43 73 24 03
◆ Pharmacie des Arts 106, bd. du

Montparnasse 75014 (6 I2)
Tel: 01 43 35 44 88
◆ Ph. des Sports 2, pl. du Gal-Kœnig 75017 (8 I2)
Tel: 01 45 74 31 10
◆ Pharmacie d'Italie 61, av. d'Italie 75013 (5 F7)
Tel: 01 44 24 19 72
◆ Pharmacie Opéra 6, bd. des Capucines 75009 (1 J2)
Tel: 01 42 65 88 29

OPEN UNTIL 1AM

◆ Ph. Internationale 5, pl. Pigalle 75009 (10 A7)
Tel: 01 48 78 38 12

OPEN UNTIL 2AM

◆ Drugstore Publicis 133, av. des Champs-Élysées 75008 (1 C2)
Tel: 01 44 43 79 00
◆ Ph. Matignon 2, rue Jean-Mermoz 75008 (1 E2)
Tel: 01 43 59 86 55
◆ Ph. Internationale 17, bd. Rochechouart 75009 (10 D7)
Tel: 01 48 78 03 01
◆ Pharmacie de la Porte de Vincennes 86, bd. Soult 75012 (3 H10)
Tel: 01 43 43 13 68
◆ Ph. Anglaise 62, av. des Champs-Élysées 75008 (1 D2)
Tel: 01 43 59 22 52

ENGLISH-LANGUAGE EMERGENCY HELP

◆ SOS Help (English-language crisis line)
Tel: 01 47 23 80 80
◆ American Hospital 63, bd. Victor Hugo 92202 Neuilly
Tel: 01 46 41 25 25
◆ British Hospital 3, rue Barbes 92300 Levallois
Tel: 01 47 58 13 12
◆ British and American Pharmacy 1, rue Auber 75009
Tel: 01 47 42 49 40
◆ Pharmacie Anglaise 62, av. des Champs-Élysées 75008
Tel: 01 43 59 22 52
◆ Pharmacie Anglo-Américaine 6, rue Castiglione 75001
Tel: 01 42 60 72 96

SPECIALIST HOSPITALS

In the case of an emergency it may be advisable to go directly to a specialist hospital.

CHILDBIRTH:
◆ Hôpital Cochin 27, rue du Fbg-St-Jacques 75014 (5 B3)
Tel: 01 42 34 17 58
◆ St-Vincent-de-Paul 74–82, av. Denfert-Rochereau 75014 (5 A3)
Tel: 01 40 48 81 11

SEVERE BURNS:
◆ Trousseau (children) 26, av. du Dr. A.-Netter 75012 (4 G2)
Tel: 01 44 73 74 75

EYE INJURIES
◆ Quinze-Vingts 28, rue de Charenton 75012 (2 I9)
Tel: 01 40 02 15 20

MOBILE MEDICAL TEAMS

About thirty years ago Dr Lascar lost one of his patients as a result of a heart attack. He realized that, in Paris, a plumber answered a call more promptly than a doctor. In 1966 he decided to found a "rapid-reaction" medical team. *SOS médecins* guarantees to be on the scene within an hour, often half an hour. The team has 150 doctors working in the Paris region.
SOS Médecins Tel: 01 47 07 77 77

Parc des Princes: football, concerts and rugby.

International tennis championships at Roland-Garros.

"Métro, boulot, dodo" (Métro, work, bed): the words of the 1970's song are still relevant today. There is more need for sports facilities in Paris than anywhere else in France. Gymnasia and tennis courts are springing up on the initiative of private enterprise and the Mairie de Paris, which provides sports associations with a centralized structure.

TENNIS

Most tennis courts are private and are listed in the telephone directory. The 170 public courts have a central reservation system via the *Paris-tennis* card (which is reserved for Parisians and takes 2 months to obtain).

HORSE-RIDING

Riding clubs in the Bois de Vincennes and de Boulogne will sometimes take new riders but do not hire out horses.
CENTRE D'ÉQUITATION DE LA CARTOUCHERIE
Bois de Vincennes

75012 (4 H78)
Tel: 01 43 74 61 25
SOCIÉTÉ D'ÉQUITATION DE PARIS
Route de la Muette
75116 (8 E8)
Tel: 01 45 01 20 06

ROWING

◆ La Villette offers rowing, canoeing and kayak facilities.
◆ At the beginning of Oct., an 18½-mile row across Paris from Boulogne to the Pont de Bercy, passing either side of the islands of Paris, attracts enthusiasts

and ordinary spectators.
BASE NAUTIQUE DE LA VILLETTE
15–17, quai de la Loire 75019 (10 I7)
Tel: 42 40 29 90
TRAVERSÉE DE PARIS CERCLE DES RAMEURS
12 *bis*, rue de Paris 78560 Port-Marly
Tel: 01 34 51 30 59

CYCLING

In the city, cycle tracks usually run along main thoroughfares. For mountain bikes (known in France as VTT), the suburbs have the only circuits of any interest.
COMITÉ DE CYCLISME ET VTT
3, rue Darboy 75011 (2 I3)
Tel: 01 43 57 02 94

SPORTS FOR THE DISABLED

There has been a marked improvement in sports facilities for the disabled. Basketball, swimming, tennis and archery are now available.
FÉDÉRATION SPORTIVE HANDISPORT
44, rue Lumière 75020 (3 H5)
Tel: 01 40 31 45 00

"ALLO SPORT" AND "GUIDE DU SPORT"

◆ *Allô sport* is a centralized sports information service:
Tel: 01 42 76 54 54
◆ *Le Guide du Sport* is published by the Mairie and provides information on sports associations, equipment and sporting events.

WALKING

There are several footpaths across Paris (▲ 461). You can jog in the streets and parks or, for the real enthusiasts, the sports stadiums. A monthly admission card also entitles you to use the showers and changing rooms.
SPORT À LA CARTE
Tel: 01 42 76 54 54

GYMNASIA

Any number of fitness centers – mostly private – are listed in the telephone directory. The 117 municipal gymnasia offer gymnastics and yoga courses for adults.

ROLLER SKATING AND SKATE-BOARDING

Like jogging, this is done in the streets throughout Paris, and especially the Trocadéro district. Roller-hockey matches are held regularly at the Château-des-Rentiers gymnasium.
ASSOCIATION PARIS 13 DES SPORTS SUR ROULETTES
9, rue de Rungis 75013 (5 C8)
Tel: 01 45 89 21 54 (8.30–9.30 pm).

Roger-Le-Gall: the only open-air swimming pool in Paris.

There is a race meeting nearly every day.

LEISURE CENTERS

◆ Parc de Puteaux
Bus: no. 144, stop:
Pont-de-Puteaux
Tel: 01 45 06 68 12
◆ Parc d'Antony
RER B, station:
Croix-de-Berny
Tel: 01 43 50 39 35
◆ Parc du Tremblay
Autoroute A4, exit:
Nogent
Tel: 01 48 81 11 22
◆ Parc de Bobigny

Metro: Fort-
d'Aubervilliers
Tel: 01 41 64 01 69
◆ Parc de la
Courneuve
Metro: La Courneuve
Tel: 01 49 71 30 20

SAILING CLUBS
◆ Choisy-le-Roi
SNCF, station:
Villeneuve-Prairie
Tel: 01 48 52 03 08
◆ Saint-Quentin-en-
Yvelines
Autoroute A13
Tel: 01 30 51
53 15

SWIMMING POOLS

Paris has more swimming pools per head of the population than Berlin, London and Madrid, but less than Manchester, Liverpool and Stockholm. There are a total of 34 swimming pools in the city, i.e. one for every 67,000 inhabitants.

SHORTLIST
Since the climate of Paris is not exactly tropical, the Roger-Le-Gall swimming pool is the only open-air pool, although the Hébert, Georges-Hermant and Georges-Vallerey pools have sun-roofs. In addition to its monumental architecture, the pool at La Butte-aux-Cailles is the only one to be fed by a natural spring. Aquaboulevard has pools, water chutes and water sports facilities.

GEORGES-VALLEREY
148, av. Gambetta
75020 (3 E4)
Tel: 01 40 31 15 20
Admission: 25F.
HÉBERT
2, rue des Fillettes
75018 (10 G4)
Tel: 01 46 07 60 01
Admission: 16F.
GEORGES-HERMANT
6 bis, rue David-
d'Angers 75019
(11 C7)
Tel: 01 42 02 45 10
Admission: 22F.
LA BUTTE-AUX-CAILLES
5, pl. Paul-Verlaine
75013 (5 E6)
Tel: 01 45 89 60 05
Admission: 16F.
ROGER-LE-GALL
34, bd. Carnot 75012
(4 I1)
Tel: 01 44 73 81 10
Admission: 25F.
AQUABOULEVARD
4, rue Louis-Armand
75015 (7 H9)
Tel: 01 40 60 15 15
Admission: 77F.

MATCHES AND RACE MEETINGS

TENNIS
Paris hosts two international championship events.
◆ Les Internationaux de France are held at Roland-Garros in late May to early June. Most seats for the finals are reserved by tennis leagues, but you may be able to get a ticket by applying in writing at the end of March or the beginning of April.
◆ Seats can be reserved for the Paris Open Tennis Championship, held at Bercy in November, as soon as the first matches are played at Roland-Garros. Reservations can be made by telephone – 01 44 68 44 68 – or at the stand at Roland-Garros.
◆ Stade Roland-Garros
2, av. Georges-Bennet 75016 (8 E7)
◆ Palais omnisports de Paris-Bercy
8, bd. de Bercy 75012 (4 B3)

RACE MEETINGS
Race meetings are held – in the afternoon or evening – virtually every day. Racecourses specialize in different types of racing: Vincennes (trotting: *le trot*), Auteuil (steeplechasing) and Longchamp (flat racing). Admission to the spectator area is free throughout the year, but if the weather forecast is poor, it is advisable to take coats and boots. Admission to stands varies between 15F and 40F (unreserved).
◆ Hippodrome d'Auteuil
Champ-de-Course 75016 (8 E6)
Tel: 01 40 71 47 47
◆ Hippodrome de Longchamp
Route des Tribunes 75016 (8 B5)
Tel: 01 44 30 75 00
◆ Hippodrome de Vincennes
2, route de la Ferme 75012 (4 H19)
Tel: 01 49 77 17 17

SOCCER AND RUGBY

Thirty-two matches each year are played in the 48,000-seat Parc des Princes covered stadium (7 B6). For semi-finals, try to reserve seats as soon as the

match has been announced. There are several points of sale throughout Paris. Métro: Porte-d'Auteuil or bus: PC, 22, 62, 72, 126, 136 and 175.
Res: 01 42 30 03 60.

Bakers' stores are often closed on Mondays.   A rare sight after 8pm.   Au Pied de Cochon.

In Paris, shops are usually closed on Sunday and Monday, and open the rest of the week between 9am and 7pm. But as in most capitals over the last ten years, opening hours are becoming much more flexible.

CAFÉS, RESTAURANTS AND FOOD

◆ Most cafés are open from 7am–2am, even earlier near rail stations.

◆ Bakers' stores, cafés and restaurants are open on Sundays. Bakers', butchers' and grocery stores are closed on Mondays.

◆ An increasing number of food stores stay open late: Monoprix stores stay open until 9pm (sometimes 10pm), while small local grocery stores, often owned by Moroccans, sometimes stay open until midnight. The number of these stores has increased significantly in the past 10 years.

◆ Prisunic on the Champs-Élysées is open Mon.–Sat. until midnight.

◆ Most restaurants usually stop serving between 10.30pm and 1am.

◆ Drugstore Publicis (133, av. des Champs-Élysées) is open daily from 9am–2am.

24-HOUR SERVICE

L'ALSACE AUX HALLES
16, rue Coquillière
75001 (2 B4)
Tel: 01 42 36 74 24

AU PIED DE COCHON
6, rue Coquillière
75001 (2 C4)
Tel: 01 40 13 77 00

PUB SAINT-GERMAIN
17, rue de
l'Ancienne-Comédie
75006 (2 B8)
Tel: 01 43 29 41 35

LA MAISON D'ALSACE
39, av. des Champs-
Élysées 78008 (1 D2)
Tel: 01 53 83 10 00

LE GRAND CAFÉ CAPUCINES
4, bd. des Capucines
75009 (1 I2)
Tel: 01 43 12 19 00

LA MAISON BLANCHE
21, rue de Dunkerque
75010 (10 E8)
Tel: 01 48 78 15 92

CLOTHES AND DEPARTMENT STORES

◆ The opening hours of clothes stores are fairly rigid, with the smaller ones usually opening from 9am till 6 or 7pm.

◆ The Bazar de l'Hôtel de Ville, Printemps, Galeries Lafayette and La Samaritaine have late-night opening.

SUNDAY OPENING

◆ The big department stores usually choose the Christmas and sales periods to use up their allocation of five Sunday openings per year.

◆ Every year the Prefecture authorizes certain tourist districts to open "reception, sports, recreational and cultural" premises on Sunday. In 1998 the Rue de Rivoli, Place des Vosges, Rue des Francs-Bourgeois, Viaduc des Arts, Rue de l'Arcole and Champs-Élysées benefited from this authorization.

BOOKSTORES: LATE-NIGHT OPENING

L'ARBRE VOYAGEUR
55, rue Mouffetard
75005 (5 D2)
Until midnight
Fri.–Sat.
Tel: 01 47 07 98 34

ART ET LITTÉRATURE
120, bd. du
Montparnasse 74014
(6 J2)
Until 10pm Wed.–Sat.
Tel: 01 43 20 63 70

SHAKESPEARE AND CIE
37, rue de la Bûcherie
75005 (2 D8)
Tel: 01 43 26 96 50
English books.

L'ÉCUME DES PAGES
174, bd. St-Germain
75006 (1 J8)
Until midnight
Mon.–Sat.
Tel: 01 45 48 54 48

LA HUNE
170, bd. St-Germain
75006 (1 J8)
Until 11.45pm
Mon.–Sat.
Tel: 01 45 48 35 85

LE MARCHÉ SAINT-ANDRÉ
40, rue St-André-
des-Arts 75006
(2 C8)

Daily until 11.30pm
Tel: 01 43 26 16 03

**LES MOTS
À LA BOUCHE**
6, rue Ste-Croix-de-
la-Bretonnerie 75004
(2 F6)
Specializing in books on homosexuality.
Until 11pm Mon.–Sat.
Tel: 01 42 78 88 30

L'ŒIL ÉCOUTE
77, bd. du
Montparnasse 75006
(6 H1)
Until 11pm Tues.–
Thurs., until midnight
Fri.–Sat., until 10pm
Mon.
Tel: 01 45 48 27 62

TSCHANN
125, bd. du
Montparnasse 75006
(6 J2)
Until 10pm Tues.–
Sat.
Tel: 01 43 35 42 05

VIRGIN MÉGASTORE
52–60, av. des
Champs-Élysées
75008 (1 E2)
Until midnight every
day
Tel: 01 49 53 50 00

VISITING PARIS

Further information is given on the pages indicated in bold type

Paris is one long round of celebrations, art festivals and exhibitions. Throughout the year events are held in local districts, music rings out from church choirs and impromptu performances take place in the shade of the squares. The choice is endless, from small local markets to sports and leisure events and the exciting new programs of the three Île-de France exhibition centers.

JULY 14
◆ On the morning of this national festival, a military parade marches down the Avenue des Champs-Élysées to the sound of military bands.
◆ In the evening there is a firework display at the Trocadéro.
◆ A grand ball is held in the Place de la Bastille.

◆ BANLIEUES BLEUES
Jazz and new music
(end Mar.–beg. April)
Seine St Denis
Tel. 01 43 85 66 00
◆ "Halle That Jazz"
Jazz festival
(1st two weeks July)
Grande Halle de la Villette
Tel. 01 40 03 75 75
◆ FESTIVAL MUSIQUE EN L'ÎLE *Classical concerts* (July–Sep.)
Paris churches
Tel. 01 44 62 70 90
◆ FESTIVAL D'ÎLE-DE-FRANCE
Choirs, concerts, medieval songs
(Sep.–Oct.)
Tel. 01 44 94 28 50
◆ FESTIVAL D'AUTOMNE
Dance, theater, music
(end Sep.–end Dec.)
Théâtres de la Ville, de l'Odéon, de l'Europe, de la Bastille
Tel. 01 42 96 12 27
◆ MOIS DE LA PHOTO
A month of exhibitions and lectures
(end Oct.–end Nov.)
All arrondissements
Tel. local town hall (mairie)
◆ AFRICA FÊTE
African music
(Late Nov.)
On tour
Tel. 01 42 23 73 93
◆ FESTIVAL D'ART SACRÉ
Classical music
(4 weeks leading up to Christmas). Paris churches and halls

Tel. 01 45 61 96 68
or 01 60 66 96 07
◆ FOIRE DU TRÔNE
Fair (end Mar.–early Jun.) Bois de Vincennes
Tel. 01 46 27 52 59
◆ FÊTE DU CINÉMA
Movie shows at reduced rates
(3 days in late June)
Tel. 01 49 52 53 54
◆ PROVINCES GOURMANDES
150 stalls of good food from the provinces
(June and Dec.)
Pont Louis-Philippe
Tel. 01 42 74 20 04
◆ FÊTE DE LA MUSIQUE
Street music
(June 21)
Streets of Paris
Tel. 01 43 29 21 75
◆ JOURNÉES DU PATRIMOINE (National Heritage Weekend)
Free admission to monuments
(2 days in Sep.)
Tel. local Town Hall (Mairie)
◆ FÊTE DU MIEL
Honey from the hives of the Jardin du Luxembourg
(Late September)
Orangerie du Luxembourg
Tel. 01 45 42 29 08
◆ FÊTE DU BEAUJOLAIS
Wine tasting
(Mid Nov.)
Paris cafés

EXHIBITIONS
◆ SALON DU LIVRE
Book fair
(3rd week March)
Porte de Versailles
Tel. 01 49 53 27 00
◆ SALON MONDIAL DU TOURISME *Tourism fair.*
(end of March)
Porte de Versailles
Tel. 01 49 68 54 50
◆ CARRÉ RIVE GAUCHE
Five days of extraordinary objects
(May)
7th arrondissement
Tel. 01 45 51 07 07

◆ BRADERIE DE PARIS
Jumble sale
(May 25–Jun. 4)
Porte de Versailles
Tel. 01 42 97 52 10
◆ ATELIERS DE LA BASTILLE
Open day for the plastic arts
(1st two weeks Oct)
11th arrondissement
◆ MARJOLAINE
Eco-friendly products
(early Nov.)
Parc floral
Tel. 01 45 56 09 09
◆ SALON NAUTIQUE
Boat show
(end Nov.–beg. Dec.)
Porte de Versailles
Tel. 01 49 53 27 10
◆ SALON DU CHEVAL ET DU PONEY
Horse and pony show
(end Nov.–beg. Dec.)
Porte de Versailles
Tel. 01 49 09 60 00
◆ MONDIAL DE L'AUTOMOBILE
International motor show (Oct.)
Porte de Versailles
Tel. 01 43 95 10 10
◆ FOIRE INTERNATIONALE DE L'ART CONTEMPORAIN (FIAC) *International contemporary art fair*
(Oct.)
Espace Eiffel Branly
Tel. 01 46 92 47 47
◆ PARC FLORAL DE PARIS *Plants and flowers* (All year)
Bois de Vincennes
Tel. 01 43 43 92 93
◆ SALON DE L'AÉRONAUTIQUE
Aeronautics exhibition
Parc des Expositions du Bourget

SPORTING EVENTS
◆ TOURNOI DES-CINQ-NATIONS *Five Nations' Cup* (rugby) (mid Feb.)
Parc des Princes
Tel. 01 42 30 03 60
◆ PARIS MARATHON
(early April)
Champs-Élysées
Tel. 01 42 77 17 84

◆ INTERNATIONAUX DE FRANCE DE TENNIS
Tennis tournament
(end May–beg. June)
Stade Roland Garros
Tel. 01 47 43 48 00
◆ TOUR DE FRANCE
Cycling: final stage
(early July)
Champs-Élysées
◆ PRIX DE L'ARC DE TRIOMPHE
Horse racing
(Oct.)
Hippodrome de Longchamp
Tel. 01 40 10 20 30
◆ CROSS DU "FIGARO"
Horse racing
Mid-Dec.
Hippodrome d'Auteuil
Tel. 01 45 20 52 22

CARS
◆ VETERAN CAR RALLY
(late April)
16 th arrondissement
◆ TOUR DE FRANCE
Parade of veteran cars
(late April)
Fontaines du Trocadéro
Tel. 01 42 59 73 40

FESTIVALS IN MONTMARTRE
The Butte Montmartre is a popular festival venue.
Tel. 01 42 62 21 21
◆ The GRAND PARADE of Montmartre: Jan. 1 at 2pm, the bands assemble in the streets.
◆ LA FÊTE DU BISTROT: March 30, the anniversary of the word *bistrot* is celebrated in the Place du Tertre. The term was coined in 1814 by the Cossacks in the Bistrot de la Mère Catherine.
◆ LES VENDANGES DU CLOS: Oct. 8 is dedicated to Bacchus and the wine of Montmartre.

Guided tours can provide an alternative view of a particular monument, district or street. In just a few hours, a guide can give a comprehensive account – interspersed with anecdotes – of the area visited and the events that took place there. A number of agencies offer this service on a daily basis.

PARIS ON THE WEB
Now you can visit Paris on the Internet:
• www.snv.fr – nearly all buildings and addresses are listed – or:
• www.paris-net.com for historic, business or shopping content

APPROCHE DE L'ART
8, villa St-Mandé 75021
Tel: 01 43 44 43 22
Bercy, Belleville and its aqueduct, La Coupole restaurant . . . these are some of the more original ways to discover Paris. Guided visits to both major and less grand temporary exhibitions.

ASSOCIATION DES CONFÉRENCIERS DE PARIS
5, rue des Montibœufs 75004
Tel: 01 40 31 56 08
Visit – or revisit – the city and its districts (the Cité, the Montagne Ste-Geneviève) in two or three hours. Having prowled the capital's streets for fifteen years, this organization is equally comfortable guiding visitors to the offbeat as to the familiar Paris.

CAISSE NATIONALE DES MONUMENTS HISTORIQUES ET DES SITES
Hôtel de Sully
62, rue St-Antoine 75004
Tel: 01 44 61 21 69
An organization offering daily visits to monuments, districts, museums, parks and gardens, interesting public buildings and new developments. The program changes every two months. Group visits with translators.

CLIO
34, rue du Hameau 75015
Tel: 01 53 68 82 82
Clio organizes lectures rather than visits. They are held in the Maison des Mines – 270, rue St-Jacques 75005 – and either prepare the audience for a visit to a particular exhibition (e.g. the Grand Palais) or offer an overview of the great civilizations of the world: "Art Nouveau in Prague", "Understanding Islam", "The Hapsburgs, art and history", etc.

ÉCOUTE DU PASSÉ
77, av. de St-Mandé 75012
Tel: 01 43 44 34 15
Discover the architecture and history of Paris and its districts, the Marais and its private residences, the Opéra and the 19th- and 20th-century palaces and hôtels. In summer, visits focus on the districts of Paris while, in winter, there is an extensive program of monuments and museum visits.

INSTITUT CULTUREL DE PARIS
84, rue Aristide-Briand 92120 Montrouge
Tel: 01 40 84 89 29
A full program of walks, visits and lectures that changes every month. Arrive at the meeting point fifteen minutes before the start.

INTERMÈDES
60, rue La Boëtie 75008
Tel: 01 45 61 90 90
Intermèdes organizes visits to most of the Paris monuments: the St-Germain district and the Musée de Cluny with refreshment at Le Procope; a visit to the Paris mosque followed by tea; the 13th arrondissement and preparations for the Chinese New Year. It also offers a program of seven lectures on the general history of art.

MAIRIE DE PARIS
37, rue des Francs-Bourgeois 75004
Tel: 01 42 76 47 42
The Ville-de-Paris museums offer guided tours and a series of lectures in addition to their program of permanent and temporary exhibitions, for which advance details are published annually. Les Grands Boulevards et la Nouvelle Athènes, in the Promenades Parisiennes series, is currently available and Les Champs-Élysées et Montmartre are due to be published.

PARIS CAPITALE HISTORIQUE
6, bd. Auguste Blanqui 75013
Tel: 01 43 31 21 98
The aim of this organization is to enable visitors to discover the history of Paris through its various districts, especially the 13th arrondissement, from the Gobelins to the Butte-aux-Cailles.

PARIS ET SON HISTOIRE
82, rue Taitbout 75009
Tel: 01 45 26 26 77
An organization with forty years' experience. Its program is revised every two months and combines traditional with more unusual visits: the Cour des Comptes, the Ministère de la Marine and the Val-de-Grâce.

SYNDICAT D'INITIATIVE, VIEUX MONTMARTRE
21, place du Tertre 75018
Tel: 01 42 62 21 21
For an authentic experience of Montmartre, its artists, studios and history.

MUSEUM TOURS
Throughout the year, the Mairie de Paris offers a wide range of guided museum visits. The program is available from the Mairie.
For further information:
Tel: 01 42 76 65 87

Three ways of seeing 70 museums

Interior of the Louvre Pyramide.

VISITING THE MUSEUMS OF PARIS

REDUCTIONS AND FREE ADMISSION
National museums, run by the French Ministry for Cultural Affairs, and the Ville-de-Paris museums offer reduced admission to the 18–25's, the over 60's and holders of a "large family" card. Most museums offer reductions to groups.

UNEMPLOYED, UNDER 18's, ART STUDENTS
National and Ville-de-Paris museums offer free admission to their permanent collections for the unemployed (on presentation of their monthly job-seeker's certificate), art students, national guides and lecturers, ex-servicemen and women, the disabled, national servicemen, French senators and deputies, and members of the European parliament. Reductions in private museums and museums run by other ministries tend to vary and it is advisable to contact them in advance.

OVERSEAS VISITORS
Officially the above reductions also apply to overseas visitors and can be obtained when identity papers are presented. However this is less likely where unemployment certificates from other countries are concerned.

CARDS
• *Paris visite* ◆ 456 entitles the holder to a 20–25% reduction on admission to certain Paris monuments and museums.
• *Musées et monuments* cards give access to 70 museums and monuments throughout Paris and the Paris region. There are 3 options:
– 1 day (80F)
– 3 days (160F)
– 5 days (240F)
These cards are on sale in the museums and monuments involved in the scheme, the main Métro stations and the Tourist Office.

OPEN DAYS
• The museum invitation *Les jeunes invitent leurs parents au musée*, issued by young people to their parents, is self-explanatory. In October, one under-18 admission includes two accompanying adults.
• Several museums take part in the audiovisual-scientific event *Image et Science*, over a ten-day period toward the end of September. Visitors pay for their first visit to one of these museums, but any subsequent visits are free of charge.
• Admission to the Louvre is free on the first Sunday of the month, and only 26F on other Sundays and after 3pm on all other days.

WHICH MUSEUMS ARE CLOSED WHEN . . .

MONDAY
Art Moderne de la Ville-de-Paris
Assistance Publique
Bourdelle
Carnavalet
Cernuschi
Curiosité et Magie
Jean-Jacques-Henner
Cognacq-Jay
Galliera
Institut du Monde Arabe
Légion d'Honneur
Lunettes et Lorgnettes
Maison de Balzac
Maison Européene de la Photographie
Marmottan
Monnaie
Montmartre
Nissim-de-Camondo
Orsay
Petit Palais
Poupée
Rodin
Seïta
Union Centrale des Arts Décoratifs
Victor-Hugo
Vie Romantique
Zadkine

TUESDAY
Arts d'Afrique et d'Océanie
Arts et Traditions Populaires
Assistance Publique
Cluny
Curiosité et Magie
Ernest-Hébert
Eugène-Delacroix
Gustave-Moreau
Histoire de France
Histoire Naturelle
Homme
Louvre
Maison Européene de la Photographie
Marine
Nissim-de-Camondo
Orangerie
Picasso

THURSDAY
Curiosité et Magie
Histoire de la Médecine

FRIDAY
Art et Histoire du Judaïsme
Curiosité et Magie

SATURDAY
Histoire de la Médecine
Maison d'Auguste Comte
Moulages
Serrure

SUNDAY
Assistance Publique
Collections Historiques de la Préfecture de Police
Histoire de la Médecine
Lunettes et Lorgnettes
Maison d'Auguste Comte
Moulages
Poste
Radio-France
Serrure

◆ Monuments

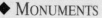

ARC DE TRIOMPHE (1 A–B1)
Place Charles-de-Gaulle 75008
Tel: 01 55 37 73 77
Open daily Apr.–Sep. 9.30am–11pm.
Open daily Oct.–Mar. 10am–10.30pm.
Closed Jan. 1, May 1, May 8, Jul. 14, Nov. 11, Dec. 25.

ARSENAL (CENTRE DE DOCUMENTATION DE L') (2 G9)
21, bd. Morland 75004
Tel: 01 42 76 33 97
Fax 01 42 76 26 32
Open Tue.–Sat. 10.30am–6.30pm, Sun. 11am–7pm.

BEAUX-ARTS (ÉCOLE DES) (2 A6–7)
14, rue Bonaparte 75006
Tel: 01 47 03 50 00 (except Fri.)
Fax 01 47 03 50 80
Visits by appt. Mon pm.

BIBLIOTHÈQUE NATIONALE
• RICHELIEU SITE
58, rue de Richelieu 75002 (2 B3)
Tel: 01 47 03 81 03
Public open days on National Heritage weekends. Guided tours by the CNMH (Caisse Nationale des Monuments Historiques) ◆ 472.
• FRANÇOIS-MITTERRAND SITE
Quai F.-Mauriac 75013 (5 J4–5)
Tel: 01 53 79 59 59
Open Tue.–Sat. 10am–7pm, Sun. noon–6pm.

BIBLIOTHÈQUE STE-GENEVIÈVE (2 C10)
10, place du Panthéon 75005
Tel: 01 44 41 97 98
Open Mon.–Sat. 10am–10pm. Closed Sun. and Aug.

BOURSE, LA (STOCK EXCHANGE) (2 B2)
Place de la Bourse 75002
Tel: 01 40 41 62 20
Fax 01 40 41 05 51
Open Mon.–Fri. 1.15–4pm.
Tours every 15 mins.

CATACOMBS (6 J4)
1, place Denfert-Rochereau 75014
Tel: 01 43 22 47 63
Open weekdays 2–4pm, weekends 9–11am, 2–4pm.

CHAPELLE DE LA MÉDAILLE-MIRACULEUSE (1 H9)
140, rue du Bac 75007
Tel: 01 49 54 78 88
Open Wed.–Mon. 7.45am–1pm, 2.30–7pm, Tue. 7.45am–7pm.

COLLÈGE DE FRANCE (2 C9–10)
11, place Marcelin-Berthelot 75005
Tel: 01 44 27 12 11
Being renovated until Jan. 1999.

CONCIERGERIE (2 C7)
1, Quai de l'Horloge 75001
Tel: 01 53 73 78 50
Open daily Apr.–Sep. 9.30am– 6.30pm; Oct.–Mar. 10am–5pm. Closed Jan. 1, May 1, Nov. 1 and 11, Dec. 25.
Last ticket 30 min. before closing.

EIFFEL TOWER (1 A6)
Champ de Mars

> **VISITING MONUMENTS CLOSED TO THE PUBLIC**
> During National Heritage weekend, in mid-September, art and history enthusiasts flock to visit monuments that are not open to the public throughout the year: the Élysée Palace, the Hôtel Matignon, the Palais-Bourbon, the Senate, the hotels of the Faubourg St-Germain, the Galerie Dorée of the Banque de France. . . The list grows longer each year. The press gives full details of National Heritage opening times and the *Parisien Libéré* even publishes a special supplement. During the rest of the year, some of these monuments are open to visitors under exceptional circumstances and provided they are accompanied by a tour guide ◆ 470.

75007
Tel: 01 44 11 23 23
Fax 01 44 11 23 22
Open daily mid-Jun. to Aug. 9am–midnight, Sept. to mid-Jun. 9.30am–11pm.

FRANCE (INSTITUT DE) (2 B7)
23, quai Conti 75006
Tel: 01 44 41 44 41
Open Sat.–Sun., guided tours at 10.30am and 3pm.
• BIBLIOTHÈQUE MAZARINE
Tel: 01 44 41 44 06
Fax 01 44 41 44 07
Open daily 10am–6pm.
Closed Sat., Sun. and Aug. 1–15.
Identity papers are required.

HÔTEL DE VILLE (2 E7)
29, rue de Rivoli 75004
Tel 01 42 76 43 43
Visitor information:
Tel: 42 76 50 49
All information:
Minitel 3615 PARIS

MADELEINE (CHURCH OF LA) (1 H2)
Place de la Madeleine and 14, rue de Surène 75008
Tel: 01 44 51 69 00
Open Mon.–Sat. 7am–7pm, Sun. (from

Easter to All Saints) 7.30am–1.30pm, 3.30–7pm.

PARIS MOSQUE (5 E1–2)
Place du Puits-de-l'Ermite 75005
Tel: 01 45 35 97 33
Open Sat.–Thur. 9am–noon, 2–6pm.
Closed Fri.

NOTRE-DAME-DE-PARIS (2 D8)
Place du Parvis-Notre-Dame 75004
Tel: 01 42 34 56 10
• TOWERS:
Open Apr.–Sep., 9.30am–6.45pm, Oct.–Mar. 10am–5pm. Closed Jan. 1, May 1, Nov. 1 and 11, Dec. 25.
Last ticket 30 mins. before closing.
• CRYPT:
Tel: 01 43 29 83 51
Open Apr.–Sep. 9.30am–6pm, Oct.– Mar. 10am–5pm
Closed Jan. 1, May 1, Nov. 1 and 11, Dec. 25.
Last ticket 30 mins. before closing.

NOTRE-DAME-DES-VICTOIRES (BASILIQUE) (2 B3)
Place des Petits-Pères 75002
Tel: 01 42 60 90 47
Open Mon. 7.30am–7pm, Tue.–Sat. 7.30am–7.30pm, Sun. and public holidays 8.30am–12.30pm, 2.30–7.30pm.

OBSERVATOIRE DE PARIS (5 D3)

Sacré-Cœur from the Centre Georges-Pompidou.

61, av. de
l'Observatoire 75014
Tel: 01 40 51 22 21
Recorded info: 01 40
51 21 74
*Visits at 2.30pm on
the first Saturday in
the month; write for
appt. Closed Jul.
and Aug.*

PANTHÉON (2 C10)
Place du Panthéon
75005
Tel: 01 44 32 18 00
Open daily Apr.–Sep.
9.30am–6.30pm,
Oct.–Mar.
10am–6.15pm.
Closed Jan. 1, May 1,
Nov. 11, Dec. 25.
*Last ticket 45 mins.
before closing.*

PARIS SEWERS (1 C5)
Place de la
Résistance 75007
Tel: 01 53 68 27 81
Open Sat.–Wed.
Oct.–Apr. 11am–
4pm, May–Sep.
11am–5pm.
Closed Thurs., Fri.
*Ticket office closes
1 hr. before closing.
Closed 3 wks in Jan.*

**PORT-ROYAL
(5 B3)**
123, bd de Port-
Royal 75014
Open daily.

**SACRÉ-COEUR
(BASILICA OF)
(10 C6)**
Parvis du Sacré-
Coeur 75018
Tel: 01 53 41 89 00
● BASILICA
Open daily
6.45am–10.30pm.
● DOME AND CRYPT
Open daily Apr.–Oct.
9am–7pm, Nov.–Mar.
9am–6pm.

**ST-ÉTIENNE-DU-MONT
(CHURCH OF) (2 D10)**

Place Ste-Geneviève
75005
Tel: 01 43 54 11 79
Open Sep.–Jun.
Mon.–Sat. 8am–
noon, 2–7pm, Sun.
9am–noon, 2.30–
7pm, Jul.–Aug. daily
10am–noon, 4–7pm.

**ST-EUSTACHE
(CHURCH OF) (2 C4)**
Place du Jour 75001
Tel: 01 42 36 31 05
Open Mon.–Sat.
9am–7pm, Sun.
9am–12.30pm,
2.30–7pm (Easter–
Sep. until 8pm).

**ST-GERMAIN-DES-PRÉS
(CHURCH OF) (2 A8)**
3, place St-Germain-
des-Prés 75006
Tel: 01 43 25 41 71
Open Mon.–Fri.
8am–7.30pm.,
Sat.–Sun. 8.30am–
7.30pm.

**ST-GERMAIN-
L'AUXERROIS
(CHURCH OF) (2 B6)**
2, place du Louvre
75001
Tel: 42 60 13 96
Open daily 8am–
8pm.

**ST-GERVAIS-ST-
PROTAIS (CHURCH
OF) (2 E7)**
Place St-Gervais
75004
Tel: 01 48 87 32 02
Open daily 6am–
9.30pm.

**ST-JULIEN-LE-PAUVRE
(CHURCH OF) (2 D8)**
1, rue St-Julien-le-
Pauvre 75005
Tel: 01 43 54 52 16
Open daily 9am–
1pm, 3–6.30pm.

**ST-LOUIS-EN-L'ÎLE
(CHURCH OF) (2 F9)**
19 *bis*, rue St-Louis-
en-l'Île 75004

Tel: 01 46 34 11 60
Open Tues.–Sat.
9am–noon, 3–7pm,
Sun. 9am–noon.
Closed Mon.

**ST-MERRI (CHURCH
OF) (2 D6)**
76, rue de la Verrerie
75004
Tel: 01 42 74 42 96
Open daily 9.30am–
1pm, 3–7pm (Jul.–
Aug. noon–1pm,
3–7.30pm.

**ST-PAUL (CHURCH
OF) (2 G7)**
99, rue St-Antoine
75004
Tel: 01 42 72 30 32
Open Mon.–Sat.
8am–7.30pm, Sun.
9am–8pm.

**ST-PIERRE-DE-
MONTMARTRE
(CHURCH OF) (10 B6)**
2, rue du Mont-Cenis
75018
Tel: 01 46 06 57 63
Open Mon.–Sat.
8.30am–7.30pm,
Sun. 8.30am–
6.30pm.

**ST-ROCH (CHURCH OF)
(1 J4)**
296, rue St-Honoré
75001
Tel: 01 42 44 13 20
Open daily 8am–
7.30pm.

**ST-SÉVERIN (CHURCH
OF) (2 C8)**
1, rue des Prêtres-St-
Séverin 75005
Tel: 01 42 34 93 50
Open Mon.–Sat.
11am– 7.30pm, Sun.
9am–8.30pm.

**ST-SULPICE (CHURCH
OF) (2 A9)**
Place St-Sulpice
75006
Tel: 01 46 33 21 78
Open Mon.–Sat.
7.30am–7.30pm,

Sun. 7.30am–8pm.

STE-CHAPELLE (2 C7)
4, bd. du Palais
75001
Tel: 01 53 73 78 50
Open daily Apr.–Sep.
9.30am–6.30pm,
Oct.–Mar. 10am–5pm
Closed Jan. 1, May 1,
Nov. 1 and 11,
Dec. 25.

SORBONNE (2 C9)
47, rue des Écoles
75005
Tel: 01 40 46 20 15
*Open Mon.–Fri.
during academic year
(Sep.–Jun.).
Chapel open for
exhibitions only.*

**TOUR MONTPARNASSE
(6 H1)**
Rue de l'Arrivée
75014
Tel: 01 45 38 52 56
Fax 01 45 38 69 96
Open daily Apr.–Sep.
9.30am–11.30pm.
Open Oct.–Mar.
9.30am–10.30pm
(except Fri., Sat. and
the eve of public
holidays 9.30am–
11.30pm).
*Last ticket 30 mins.
before closing.*

VAL-DE-GRÂCE (5 B2)
1, pl. Alphonse-
Laverand 75005
Tel: 01 40 51 51 94
Chapel open daily
9am–6pm.

ON THE SEINE
Various companies
offer Seine trips:
● Bateaux-Mouches
  Pont de l'Alma
  (1 C4)
● Bateaux Parisiens
  Pont d'Iena (1 A6)
● Vedettes du Pont-
  Neuf
  Pont-Neuf (2 B7)

Paris' main museums are indicated by a ★. Detailed descriptions can be found in the Museums section ▲ 133–72.

Musée Clémenceau.

Fairground art: carousel of old cars (1925).

In the tradition of the great 17th- and 18th-century museums, the smaller Paris museums (the homes of famous people, the scenes of historic events, marginal artistic trends or specialist activities) offer "enthusiasts" or the "idly curious" an opportunity to extend their knowledge as well as a truly memorable experience.

ADAM-MICKIEWICZ, MUSÉE (2 E8)
(in the Polish Library)
6, Quai d'Orléans 75004
Tel: 01 55 42 83 83
Open Thur. 2–5pm; guided tours every hour. Closed Christmas and Easter.
Admission 25F.

★ ART MODERNE (BEAUBOURG), MUSÉE NATIONAL DE (2 E5)
19, rue Beaubourg or Pl. Georges-Pompidou 75004
Tel: 01 44 78 46 71
The Pompidou Center is closed for major works until Jan. 2000. Exhibitions are still on show in the south hall or at other venues in Paris.

★ ART MODERNE DE LA VILLE-DE-PARIS, MUSÉE DE (1 B4)
11, av. du Président-Wilson 75116
Tel: 01 53 67 40 00
Open Tue.–Fri. 10am–5.30pm, Sat.–Sun. 10am–6.45pm
Closed Mon.
Admission variable.

ART NAÏF, MUSÉE D' (10 C6)
Halle St-Pierre
2, rue Ronsard 75018
Tel: 01 42 58 72 89
Open daily 10am–6pm.
Closed Aug.

The special appeal of this museum is its changing program of exhibitions covering such contemporary forms as naïve and minimal art, encompassing both the popular and the plain wierd.

ART ET D'HISTOIRE DU JUDAÏSME, MUSÉE D' (2 F5)
71, rue du Temple 75003
Tel: 01 53 01 86 53
Recently ensconced in the Hôtel de St-Aignan, the former Musée d'Art Juif displays an enhanced collection, from Nov. 1998.

★ ARTS D'AFRIQUE ET D'OCÉANIE, MUSÉE DES (4 H4)
293, av. Daumesnil 75012
Tel: 01 44 74 84 80
Open Mon., Wed.–Fri.

10am–noon, 1.30–5.30pm, Sat.–Sun. 12.30–6pm. Closed Tue.
Admission 30F, red. 20F.

ARTS FORAINS, MUSÉE DES (4 C5)
53, av. des Terroirs-de-France 75012
Tel: 01 43 40 16 22
Open by arrangement, for groups only.
In what were once wine-market warehouses, fourteen carousels and sixteen attractions reconstruct the world of the fairground from 1880 to 1950.
Admission 42F, red. 25F.

★ ARTS ET MÉTIERS, MUSÉE DES (2 E3)
292, rue St-Martin 75003
Tel: 01 40 27 22 20
Closed until 1999.

★ ARTS ET TRADITIONS POPULAIRES, MUSÉE DES (8 E2)
Jardin d'Acclimatation 6, av. du Mahatma-Gandhi 75116
Tel: 01 44 17 60 00
Open Wed.–Mon. 9.30am–5.15pm
Closed Tue., Jan 1, May 1 and Dec. 25
Admission 25F, red. 15F.

★ ASSISTANCE PUBLIQUE, MUSÉE DE L' (2 E9)
Hôtel de Miramion 47, Quai de la Tournelle 75005
Tel: 01 40 27 50 05
Permanent exhibition Sep.–Jul., open Tues.–Sat. 10am–5pm, closed Sun.–Mon., Aug. and public hols.
Temporary exhibition open Wed.–Sun. 10am–5pm.

AUGUSTE COMTE, MAISON D' (2 B9)
10, rue Monsieur-le-Prince 75006
Tel: 01 43 26 08 56
Open Tue.–Thur. 3.15–5pm.
Open Mon. and Fri. by appt.
From 1841 until his death in 1857, this apartment was the home of Auguste Comte, the founding father of Positivism. A research center has been set up.

Maison de Balzac and Musée Ernest-Hébert. *Maison de Victor Hugo.*

BALZAC, MAISON DE (7 H1)
47, rue Raynouard 75016
Tel: 01 42 24 56 38
Open Tue.–Sun. 10am–5.40pm. Closed Mon. and public holidays.
Located in the center of the former village of Passy, the house occupies the outbuildings of a folly where Balzac sought refuge in 1840. Today the museum houses personal objects, books, manuscripts and portraits of Balzac as well as documents concerning his close family and friends.
Admission 17F, red. 9F.

★ BOURDELLE, MUSÉE (6 G1)
18, rue Antoine-Bourdelle 75015
Tel: 01 49 54 73 73
Open Tue.–Sun. 10am–5.40pm. Closed Mon.
Admission 27F, red. 19F for exhibitions, 17,50F and 9F for permanent collections.

★ CARNAVALET, MUSÉE (2 G6)
23, rue de Sévigné 75003
Tel: 01 42 72 21 13
Open Tue.–Sun. 10am–5.40pm. Closed Mon. and public holidays.
Admission 35F, red. 25F.

★ CERNUSCHI, MUSÉE (9 E8)
7, av. Vélasquez 75008
Tel: 01 45 63 50 75
Open Tue.–Sun. 10am–5.40pm. Closed Mon. and public holidays.
Admission 17F, red. 9F.

★ CHASSE ET DE LA NATURE, MUSÉE DE LA (2 F5)
60, rue des Archives 75003
Tel: 01 42 72 86 36
Open Wed.–Mon. 10am–12.30pm, 1.30–5.30pm. Closed Tue. and public holidays.
Admission 25F.

CLÉMENCEAU, MUSÉE (8 I9)
8, rue Franklin 75116
Tel: 01 45 20 53 41
Open Tue., Thur., Sat.–Sun. and public holidays 2–5pm.
Georges Clémenceau's apartment from 1895 to 1929 has remained unchanged since his death. In this evocative setting, visitors can see his study with its famous U-shaped desk and examples of his life as a journalist, writer, politician, traveler and patron of the arts.
Admission 20F, red. 15F.

★ CLUNY, MUSÉE (2 C9)
6, pl. Paul-Painlevé 75005
Tel: 01 53 73 78 00
Open Wed.–Mon. 9.15am–5.45pm. Closed Tue., May 1, Nov. 1 and Dec. 25.
Admission 30F, red. 20F.

★ COGNACQ-JAY, MUSÉE (2 G6)
8, rue Elzévir 75003
Tel: 01 40 27 07 21
Open Tue.–Sun. 10am–5.40pm. Closed Mon. and public holidays.
Admission 17.50F, red. 9F.

COLLECTIONS HISTORIQUES DE LA

PRÉFECTURE DE POLICE, MUSÉE DES (2 D9)
1 *bis*, rue des Carmes 75005
Tel: 01 44 41 52 50 (switchboard of the Préfecture de Paris)
Open Mon.–Fri. 9am–5pm, Sat. 10am–5pm. Closed Sun.
Founded in 1909 by the chief commissioner, Louis Lépine, the museum traces (via prison records, letters under the King's private seal and convicts' irons) the major and minor events in the life of the police force since the 16th century.
Free admission.

CURIOSITÉ ET DE LA MAGIE, MUSÉE DE (2 G8)
11, rue de St-Paul 75004
Tel: 01 42 72 13 26
Open Wed, Sat, Sun. 2–7pm.
Both adults and children will delight in this maze of vaulted cellars, early amusement machines and "authentic fakes". You may even learn a few tricks of the magician's trade from your guide.

EDITH PIAF, MUSÉE (3 B4)
5, rue Crespin-du-Gast 75011

Tel: 01 43 55 52 72
Open Mon.–Thur. 1–6pm by appointment.
This informal museum, the first to be dedicated to a French entertainer, evokes the life of "la môme Piaf" with, among other memorabilia, her famous "little black dress".

ENNERY, MUSÉE D' (8 H5)
(Guimet annex)
59, av. Foch 75016
Tel: 01 47 23 61 65
Open Thur., Sun. and public hols. 2–6pm. Closed Aug.
Admission free.

ERIK SATIE, PLACARD D' (10 B6)
6, rue Cortot 75018
Tel: 01 42 78 15 18
Visits by appt.
Erik Satie's room in Montmartre was so small that he called it his cupboard (placard). Today it is the smallest museum in the world – reminiscent of Pandora's box or a "cabinet de merveilles".

ERNEST-HÉBERT, MUSÉE (1 H10)
85, rue du Cherche-Midi 75006
Tel: 01 42 22 23 82
Open Mon., Wed.–Fri. 12.30–6pm, Sat.–Sun. 2–6pm. Closed Tue.
Portraits, Italian landscapes and drawings represent the work of Ernest Hébert (1817–1908), an official artist in the tradition of the French Academy and the Prix de Rome.
Admission 17F.

The "grand salon", Musée Pasteur. Retable in the Musée de l'Histoire de la Médecine.

ÉROTISME, MUSÉE DE L'
(9 J7)
72, bd. de Clichy 75018
Tel: 01 42 58 28 73
Open daily 10am–2pm.
*The newest of the city's
museums has
assembled more than
2,000 erotic objects
from different periods
from every continent, in
a quarter of Paris, near
Pigalle, long associated
with art and romance.*

ESPACE MONTMARTRE-
SALVADOR-DALI (10 B6)
11, rue Poulbot 75018
Tel: 01 42 64 40 10
Open daily 10am–6pm.
*330 paintings,
sculptures and
lithographs by the
Catalan artist in a
surrealist setting.*
Admission 35F,
red. 25F.

EUGÈNE-DELACROIX,
MUSÉE (2 A7)
6, rue de Furstenberg
75006
Tel: 01 44 41 86 50
Open Wed.–Mon.
9.30am–5pm.
Closed Tue.
*Delacroix moved here
in 1857 to be near the
Church of St-Sulpice
where he was
decorating the
Chapelle des Sts-
Anges. He had a studio
in the garden linked to
the apartment by an
external iron staircase.*
Admission 15F,
red. 10F.

EUROPÉENNE DE LA
PHOTOGRAPHIE, MAISON
(2 F7)
5–7, rue de Fourcy
75004. Tel: 01 44 78
75 00. Open Wed.–
Sun. 11am–8pm.
Closed public hols.
*Permanent and
temporary exhibitions
of more than 12,000
works in this new
temple of
photography, with
a library.*

ÉVENTAIL, MUSÉE DE L'
(2 E2)
2, bd. de Strasbourg
75010
Tel: 01 42 08 90 20
Open Mon.–Wed.
2–6pm.
*The prestigious
Henri II, walnut-
paneled salon
occupied by the
museum
was*

*designed for the 1893
World Fair. It houses
some 770 fans,
dating from the 18th
century to the present
day.* Admission 30f.

GALLIERA, MUSÉE
(1 B4)
Palais Galliera
10, av. Pierre Ier-de-
Serbie 75116
Tel: 01 47 20 85 23
Open Tue.–Sun.
10am–6pm.
Closed Mon.
*The museum's
extensive collections
(30,000 costumes and
70,000 accessories)
make it possible to
present two different
exhibitions per year.*
Admission 37F, red.
27F up to 25 yrs.

GRAND ORIENT DE
FRANCE ET DE LA
FRANC-MAÇONNERIE
EUROPÉENNE, MUSÉE DU
(10 C10)
16, rue Cadet 75009

Tel: 01 45 23 20 92
Open Mon.–Sat.
2–6pm. Closed Sun.
*Reopened in Sept.
1998 with new lighting
and an enlarged
collection, the museum
evokes the history of
French freemasonry,
from the builders of
medieval cathedrals
to the latest
developments.*
Admission free.

★ GRÉVIN, MUSÉE
10, bd. Montmartre
75009 (2 B2)
Tel: 01 47 70
85 05
Open daily
Apr.–Aug. 1–6pm,
Sep.–Mar. 1–5.30pm.
Open after 10am
during school
vacations. Admission
55F, red. 36F.

★ GUIMET,
MUSÉE (1 A4)
6, pl. d'Iéna 75016
Tel: 01 45 05 00 98
Closed for works
until end 1999.
Temporary exhibitions
held at 19, pl. d'Iéna.
Admission 16F,
red. 12F.

GUSTAVE-MOREAU,
MUSÉE (10 A9)
14, rue de la
Rochefoucault 75009
Tel: 01 48 74 38 50
Open Thur.–Sun.
10am–12.45pm,
2–5.15pm,
Mon. and Wed.
11am–5.15pm.
Closed Tue., Jan. 1,
May 1 and Dec. 25.
Admission 22F,
red. 15F.

HENRI-BOUCHARD,
MUSÉE (7 E2)
25, rue de l'Yvette
75016
Tel: 01 46 47 63 46

Open Wed. and Sat.
2–7pm.
Closed Mar. 16–31,
Jun., Sep. and Dec.
Guided tour first Sat.
of each month at 3pm.
*Set in a small, flower-
filled garden typical of
old Auteuil, the studio
of the sculptor Henri
Bouchard (1875–1960)
has retained its
original atmosphere
and authenticity.
Original plaster
casts, bronzes, stone,
marble and wood
sculptures, ceramics
and terracotta trace a
career that began in
1891 and was
influenced by the
modernist esthetics
of the 1930's.*
Admission 25F,
red. 15F.

HISTOIRE DE FRANCE,
MUSÉE DE L' (2 F5)
60, rue des Francs-
Bourgeois 75003
Tel: 01 40 27 60 96
Open Wed.–Mon.
noon–5.45pm
weekdays (1.45–
5.45pm weekends).
Closed Tue. and
public holidays.
*The museum is
housed in the
Palais de Soubise,
one of the finest
mansions in the
Marais, with its
handsome interior
by Germain Boffrand,
a rare example in
Paris of the Rocaille
(French rococo) style.
Temporary exhibitions
assemble archive
documents and
artifacts in a successful
demonstration of
the many aspects
of history.*

Jean Moulin's false identity papers.

Musée de la Parfumerie Fragonard.

★ **HISTOIRE CONTEMPORAINE, MUSÉE D' (1 F7)**
Esplanade des Invalides 75007
Tel: 01 44 42 54 91
Open for exhibitions Tue.–Sat. 10am–1pm and 2–5pm,
Sun. 2–5.30pm.
Admission 30F, red. 20F.

HISTOIRE DE LA MÉDECINE, MUSÉE DE L' (2 B9)
12, rue de l'École-de-Médecine 75006
Tel: 01 40 46 16 93
Open Mon.–Wed., Fri.–Sat. 2–5.30pm.
Closed Thur., Sun. and public holidays.
The museum's high-quality exhibits trace the development of medical practice from Ancient Egypt to the early 20th century.
Admission 20F, red. 10F.

★ **HISTOIRE NATURELLE, MUSÉUM D' (2 F10)**
36, rue Geoffroy-St-Hilaire 75005
Tel: 01 40 79 39 34
Open Wed.–Mon. 10am–5pm. Late night Thur. 10pm. Closed Tues., May 1.
Admission 40F, red. 30F.

★ **HOMME, MUSÉE DE L' (8 J8)**
Palais de Chaillot
17, pl. du Trocadéro 75116
Tel: 01 44 05 72 72
Open Wed.–Mon. 9.45am–5.15pm.
Closed Tue. and public holidays.
Admission 30F, red. 20F.

★ **INSTITUT DU MONDE ARABE (2 F9)**
1, rue des Fossés-St-Bernard 75005
Tel: 01 40 51 38 38
Open Tue.–Sun. 10am–6pm. Closed Tue. and public hols.
Admission 40F, red. 20F.

★ **INVALIDES, MUSÉES DES (1 F7)**
– MUSÉE DE L'ARMÉE, MUSÉE DE L'ORDRE DE LA LIBÉRATION and MUSÉE DES PLANS ET RELIEFS
6, bd. des Invalides 75007
Tel: 01 45 51 95 05
Open daily Apr.–Sep. 10am–6pm, Oct.–Mar. 10am–5pm.
Closed Jan 1, May 1, Nov. 1, Dec. 25 and Jun. 17 (Ordre de la Libération).
– MUSÉE D'HISTOIRE CONTEMPORAINE Esplanade des Invalides
Tel: 01 44 42 54 91
Open during exhibitions Tues.–Sat. 10am–1pm, 2–5.30pm, Sun. 2–5.30pm. Admission 30F, red. 20F.
Joint admission for the Musée de l'Armée and Musée des Plans – tickets valid for 2 days – 35F, red. 25F.

JACQUEMART-ANDRÉ, MUSÉE (9 E10)
158, bd. Haussmann 75008
Tel: 01 42 89 04 91
Open daily 10am–5.30pm.
18th-century wood paneling, tapestries, furniture, paintings, sculptures and objets d'art. The northern schools are represented by Rembrandt, Van Dyck, Frans Hals and Ruysdael, while Bellini, Carpaccio, Verrocio, Botticelli and Mantegna provide examples of 15th-century Italian art.
Admission 45F, red. 30F.

JEAN-JACQUES-HENNER, MUSÉE (9 E7)
43, av. de Villiers 75017
Tel: 01 47 63 42 73
Open Tue.–Sun. 10am–noon and 2–5pm.
Closed Mon.
Henner, winner of the first Prix de Rome in 1858, was one of the great portraitists and painters of compositions and nudes. 520 canvases and 1,000 drawings are presented in an informal atmosphere where furniture, hangings and carpets re-create the setting of the artist's life.
Admission 14F, red. 10F and Sun.

JEAN-MOULIN, MUSÉE (6 G2)
Mémorial du Maréchal Leclerc de Hauteclocque et de la Libération de Paris
23, Allée de la 2e-D.-B. Jardin Atlantique 75015
Tel: 01 40 64 39 44
Open Tue.–Sun. 10am–5.40pm.
Closed Mon.
The personalities and achievements of these two symbolic figures are evoked against a backdrop of World War Two dominated by audiovisual effects.

LÉGION D'HONNEUR, MUSÉE DE LA (1 H5)
2, rue de Bellechasse 75007
Tel: 01 40 62 84 25
Open Tue.–Sun. 2–5pm. Closed Mon., public hols.
Increasingly the focus in this small museum is not on the traditional displays in glass cabinets but on a unique collection of medals. Well worth seeing are the sumptuous plum-colored Salle des Trésors, or the Legion of Honor chain, which is conferred on the president of the Republic at his investiture.

★ **LOUVRE, MUSÉE DU (2 A5)**
Cour Napoléon 75001
Tel: 01 40 20 51 51
Open Thur.–Sun. 9am–6pm, Mon., Wed. 9am–9.45pm. Closed Tue.
Last tickets 45 mins. before closing.
Access (▲ 325)
Open air: direct access via the Pyramid, via the shopping precinct, no.99, rue de Rivoli and the steps from the Arc de Triomphe du Carrousel.
Underground: via the shopping precincts, the car park and the Palais-Royal Métro station.
Access for groups and "Friends of the Louvre" via Passage Richelieu.
Admission 46F before

3pm, 26F after 3pm and Sun. Free on the first Sun. of every month

LUNETTES ET LORGNETTES, MUSÉE DES (1 I3)
380, rue St-Honoré 75001
Tel: 01 40 20 06 98
Open Tue.–Sat. 10am–noon and 2–6pm.
Closed Sun.–Mon., and in August.
The museum of the optician and collector Pierre Marly has almost 3,000 exhibits – collected over a period of forty years – and includes a pair of spectacles

belonging to the Dalai Lama, Sarah Bernhardt's lorgnette and a 1719 telescope. Free admission.

MAILLOL, MUSÉE (1 H7)
Fondation Dina Vierny 61, rue de Grenelle 75007
Tel: 01 49 29 12 25
Open Wed.–Mon. 11am–6pm.
Closed Tue.
Although the museum focuses on the work of Aristide Maillol (1861–1944), it also reflects the taste of its founder, Dina Vierny, the sculptor's last model.
Admission 40F, red. 26F. Free under 18.

★ **MARINE, MUSÉE DE LA (8 J8)**
Palais de Chaillot Pl. du Trocadéro 75116
Tel: 01 53 65 69 69
Open Wed.–Mon. 10am–6pm.
Closed Tue. and May 1.
Admission 38F, red. 25F.

★ **MARMOTTAN, MUSÉE (8 E9)**
2, rue Louis Boilly 75016
Tel: 01 42 24 07 02

Open Tue.–Sun. 10am–5pm.
Closed Mon. Admission 40F, red. 25F.

★ **MÉDAILLES, CABINET DES (2 B3)**
Bibliothèque Nationale 58, rue de Richelieu 75002
Tel: 01 47 03 81 26
Open Mon.–Sat. 1–5pm, Sun. noon–6pm.
Admission 22F, red. 15F.

★ **MONNAIE, MUSÉE DE LA (2 B7)**
11, Quai Conti 75006
Tel: 01 40 46 55 35
Open Tue.–Fri. 11am–5.30pm, Sat.–Sun. 1–9pm.
Closed Mon., Jan. 1, July 14, May 1 and Dec. 25.
Admission 20F, red. 15F.

MONTMARTRE, MUSÉE DE (10 B6)
12, rue Cortot 75018
Tel: 01 46 06 61 11
Open Tue.–Sun. 11am–6pm.
Closed Mon.
The museum, founded in 1960 in the Maison de Rosimond (named after the actor from Molière's theater company who lived there), has retained the atmosphere of a 17th-century country residence. The collections trace the history of the former village of Montmartre, from the porcelain manufactured in Clignancourt to the shadow theater of the Chat Noir.
Admission 25F, red. 20F.

MOULAGES, MUSÉE DES (2 I1)
Hôpital St-Louis 1, av. Claude-Velfaux 75010
Tel: 01 42 49 99 15
Visits by appt.
In the unusual atmosphere of the museum's magnificent hall, more than 4,800 wax molds of skin disorders are presented in 162 showcases.

MUSIQUE, MUSÉE DE LA (11 D5)
Cité de la Musique
▲ *430*
221, av. Jean-Jaurès 75019
Tel: 01 44 84 45 45
Open Tue.–Thur. noon–6pm, Fri.–Sat. noon–7.30pm, Sun. 10am–6pm. Closed Mon. Last tickets 45 mins. before closing.
Make your visit complete with a musical workshop or a concert.

NISSIM-DE-CAMONDO, MUSÉE (9 F8)
63, rue de Monceau 75008
Tel: 01 53 89 06 40
Open Wed.–Sun. 10am–5pm. Closed Mon., Tue., Jan. 1, May 1 and Dec. 25.
This private residence was completed in 1914, according to plans by René Sergent, in the style of the Petit Trianon. It houses a remarkable collection of furniture, paintings, tapestries, porcelain and gold- and silverware, which are among the finest examples of the 18th-century art of living.
Admission 27F, red. 18F.

OBSERVATOIRE DE PARIS (5 A4)
61, av. de l'Observatoire 75014
Tel: 01 40 51 21 74
Open 1st Sat. in the month, 2.30pm by appt.
Founded by royal decree in 1667, the Paris Observatory has only had an astronomical museum since 1879. Its collections consist mainly of observation instruments and pieces of surveying equipment.

ORANGERIE, MUSÉE DE L' (1 H4)
Pl. de la Concorde 75001
Tel: 01 42 97 48 16
Open Wed.–Mon.

9.45am–5.15pm.
Closed Tue., public holidays. Works will last into 1999.
Admission 30F, red. 20F.

★ **ORSAY, MUSÉE D' (1 I6)**
1, rue de Bellechasse 75007
Tel: 01 40 49 48 14
Open Jun. 20–Sep. 20, Tue.–Wed., Fri.–Sun. 9am–6pm, Thur. 9am–9.45pm.
Open Sep. 21–Jun. 19, Tue.–Sat. 10am–6pm, Thur. 10am–9.45pm, Sun. 9am–6pm.
Closed Mon, Jan 1, May 1 and Dec 25.
Admission 40F, red. 30F.

PARFUMERIE FRAGONARD, MUSÉES DE LA (1 I2)
– 9, RUE SCRIBE 75009
Tel: 01 47 42 93 40
Open daily 9am–5.30pm (Oct.–Apr. closed Sun).
The rue Scribe museum, housed in a small, Napoleon III residence, traces the history of perfume from antiquity to the present day.
– 39, BOULEVARD DES CAPUCINES 75002
Tel: 01 42 60 37 14
Open Mon.–Sat. 9am–5.30pm.
The bd. des Capucines museum is sited in the former Théâtre des Capucines.

PASTEUR, MUSÉE (6 E2)
25, rue du Docteur-Roux 75015
Tel: 01 45 68 82 83
Open daily 2–5.30pm.
Closed public holidays and in August.
The museum, housed in Louis Pasteur's apartment from 1888 to 1895, is a fine example of late-19th-century decorative art in which Louis XIII and Napoleon III furnishings evoke the atmosphere of the period. The "scientific" room contains objects and instruments illustrating

Pasteur's work, from his early research on molecular asymmetry to the discovery of the anti-rabies vaccine. The funeral crypt is typical of the Symbolist period. Admission 15F.

★ PETIT-PALAIS, MUSÉE DU (1 F4)
1, av. Winston-Churchill 75008
Tel: 01 42 65 12 73
Open Tue.–Sun. 10am–5.40pm (Thur. 8pm). Closed Mon. and public holidays.
Admission 25F.

★ PICASSO, MUSÉE (2 G6)
5, rue de Thorigny 75003
Tel: 01 42 71 25 21
Open Apr.–Sep., Wed.–Mon. 9.30am–6pm Oct.–March, Wed.–Mon. 9.30am–5.30pm Closed Tue., Jan. 1 and Dec. 25.
Admission 28F, red. 18F.

POSTE, MUSÉE DE LA (6 G2)
34, bd. de Vaugirard 75015
Tel: 01 42 79 23 45
Open Mon.–Sat. 10am–6pm. Closed Sun. and public holidays.
Closed for building work. Only the Galerie des Messagers is open, for temporary exhibitions.

POUPÉE, MUSÉE DE LA (2 E6)
Impasse Berthaud 75003
Tel: 01 42 72 73 11
Open Tue.–Sun. 10am–6pm. Closed Mon.
More than 800 French dolls from 1850 to the present day are displayed with their accessories and small-scale furniture and toys. Temporary theme-based exhibitions are mounted from items in the collection. A specialty shop and a dolls' hospital are

currently being planned, as well as expert advice, training and workshops.

RADIO-FRANCE, MUSÉE DE (7 H2)
116, av. du Président-Kennedy 75016
Tel: 01 42 30 21 80
Open Mon.–Sat. Guided tours at 10.30, 11.30 am, 2.30, 3.30 and 4.30pm. Closed Sun. and public holidays.
The museum is housed in the Maison de Radio-France and charts the beginning of radio and television broadcasting following the discovery of air waves and their applications by such pioneers as Maxwell, Hertz, Marconi and Branly. Photographs, old publicity material and an exact reconstruction of the television studio at 107, rue de Grenelle in 1935.
Admission 15F, red 10F.

★ RODIN, MUSÉE (1 G7)
77, rue de Varenne 75007
Tel: 01 44 18 61 10
Open Apr.–Sep., 9.30am–5.45pm Oct.–March, 9.30am–4.45pm. Closed Mon. and public holidays.
Admission 28F, red 18F.

SEÏTA, MUSÉE DE LA (1 E5)
12, rue Surcouf 75007
Tel: 01 45 56 60 17
Open Mon.–Sat. 11am–7pm. Closed Sun. and public holidays.
The museum's 400 exhibits trace the history of tobacco – from the discovery of the plant in its native America to its distribution in the Old World – and the development from early ritual and medical

uses to a social habit which was rapidly condemned and became the subject of controversy from the 17th century onward. Admission free.

SERRURE, MUSÉE DE LA (2 G6)
1, rue de la Perle 75003
Tel: 01 42 77 79 62
Open Mon. 2–5pm, Tue.–Fri. 10am–12pm, 2–5pm.
Closed Sat.–Sun.
The collection of ancient locks (from Roman keys to Renaissance bolts), begun in the 19th century by Eugène Bricard, has been gradually extended and today occupies six rooms.

★ UNION CENTRALE DES ARTS DÉCORATIFS (1 J5)
Palais du Louvre 107, rue de Rivoli 75001
Tel: 01 44 55 57 50
– MUSÉE DE LA PUBLICITÉ
Scheduled to open October 1998.
– MUSÉE DES ARTS DÉCORATIFS
Building work still partly ongoing. Middle Ages and Renaissance rooms open Tues.–Sun. noon–6pm at 111, rue de Rivoli.
– MUSÉE DE LA MODE ET DU TEXTILE
Open Tue.–Sun. 11am–6pm (Wed. 10pm). Admission 25F, red. 16F.

VICTOR HUGO, MAISON DE (2 H7)
6, pl. des Vosges 75004
Tel: 01 42 72 10 16
Open Tue.–Sun. 10am–5.40pm. Closed Mon. and public holidays.
Victor Hugo lived in

the former Hôtel Rohan-Guéménée from 1832 to 1848. The museum, founded in 1903, traces the writer's life – via family and literary memorabilia – from his youth, through his long period of exile, to his return to France.

VIE ROMANTIQUE (RENAN-SCHEFFER), MUSÉE DE LA (9 J8)
16, rue Chaptal 75009
Tel: 01 48 74 95 38
Open Tue.–Sun. 10am–5.40pm. Closed Mon. and public holidays.
The museum occupies the house where the Romantic artist, Ary Scheffer, lived from 1830–58. It evokes 19th-century literary and artistic life via two collections of memorabilia: George Sand and Renan-Scheffer.
Admission 17,50F, red. 9F.

VIVANT DES ARTS DU LIVRE, MUSÉE (7 H5)
Imprimerie Nationale 27, rue de la Convention 75015
Tel: 01 40 58 34 72
Visits by appt.
The museum traces the various stages involved in the traditional production of books: from engraving the letterpress, casting the letters and typesetting, to printing, stitching and binding. The Cabinet des Poinçons (press room) contains more than 500,000 items dating from the 16th to the 20th century.

★ ZADKINE, MUSÉE (5 A1)
100 bis, rue d'Assas 75006
Tel: 01 43 26 91 90
Open Tue.–Sun. 10am–5.30pm. Closed Mon. and public holidays.
Admission 27F, red. 19F.

◆ VIEWS OF THE CITY

There are a number of vantage points, offering different panoramas of Paris, from which to look out over the city by day or night and admire its form and lines. From Notre-Dame to La Défense, viewpoints rise above the rooftops, creating an undulating skyline and offering breathtaking views of the French capital . . . What better way to capture the magic of a misty morning or a starry night and experience the indescribable ingredient that makes "the Parisian landscape as perfectly undefinable as the expression on a human face" (Julien Green)?

FROM THE TOP OF . . .

NOTRE-DAME (2 D8)
From the top of its 225-foot towers, visitors can admire the architecture of this famous religious building. Upstream lies the Paris of the future (Bercy, Institut du Monde Arabe), while downstream are the bridges and La Défense. At sunset the city is at its most beautiful.

SACRÉ-COEUR (BASILIQUE DU) (10 C2)
Above the former village of the Butte Montmartre stands the famous Basilica of the Sacré-Coeur, a remarkable edifice whose 260-foot-high dome dominates the whole of northern Paris. By day it offers a magnificent view across the gardens of Montmartre to the city and its monuments. By night it offers a more romantic view of the Paris skyline, whose undulated relief is studded with thousands of tiny lights twinkling in the valley and on its slopes.

EIFFEL TOWER (1 A6)
The Eiffel Tower stands some 1,050 feet high and has dominated the center of Paris for more than 100 years. It offers a truly remarkable panoramic view of the city. To the south lies the green carpet of the Champ de Mars and, to the north, the gardens and palace of the Trocadéro glisten through the water playing in the fountains. It is an ideal vantage point from which to locate the city's main monuments and districts.

TOUR MONTPARNASSE (6 H1)
The Tour Montparnasse is rivaled only by the Eiffel Tower. The 59th story of the 685-foot tower has been converted into an open-air terrace. In fine weather it is possible to see more than 50 monuments, while at night the view is enchanting.

ARC DE TRIOMPHE (1 B1)
The 160-foot arch, a symbol of the Napoleonic era, is one of the seven stages on the central Paris axis. To the east it offers an unrivaled view along the Champs Élysées to the Louvre and, to the west, the Avenue de la Grande-Armée runs toward La Défense.

GRANDE ARCHE DE LA DÉFENSE
The top of the arch offers a magnificent view of the central Paris axis, the Arc de Triomphe and the

forest of towers of this miniature Manhattan. The 360-foot-high roof is well worth a visit. Look out for the map of the sky designed in granite and marble by the sculptor Jean-Pierre Raynaud, which closely resembles the Indian observatories of Delhi and Jaipur, and also the corners of the patios engraved with the signs of the zodiac cleverly blended with the points of the compass.

CENTRE GEORGES POMPIDOU (2 E5–6)
The center's glass galleries and escalator look out over the monochrome landscape of the Paris rooftops toward the Tour St-Jacques, the Panthéon and the flying buttresses of St-Eustache to the west. Unfortunately, there is no access until the year 2000 because of building works. Be patient!

FOOD WITH A VIEW

LE PRINTEMPS (9 I10)
At the top of this right-bank department store, an observation terrace offers an extensive view of Montmartre. Those who can't resist a good view will also be unable to resist the pâtisserie of the Café Flo on the 10th floor.

LA SAMARITAINE (1 I1)
The roof terrace on the 11th floor of Samaritaine's shop no.2 offers a superb view of the rooftops of Paris, the Hôtel de Ville, Beaubourg . . . For those who enjoy their food, the 6th-floor restaurant Le Toupary also has a panoramic view.

INSTITUT DU MONDE ARABE (2 F9)
The terrace of the Institut affords a splendid view of the Île de la Cité and Notre-Dame, which is as beautiful from the back as from the front. Lovers of mint tea will be in their element ◆ 479.

The Tour Eiffel from the Tour Montparnasse.

Sacré-Cœur from the Centre G.-Pompidou.

BUTTES, HILLS AND PARKS

PARC DES BUTTES-CHAUMONT (11 B–C8 AND 9)
A neoclassical viewpoint overlooks the park with its 1001 nooks and corners. From the top of this temple to Vesta, the Sacré-Coeur is visible through a gap in the trees.

BELVÉDÈRE BELLEVILLOIS (11 A9)
This unexpected vantage point with its view across western Paris lies immediately behind the Parc des Buttes-Chaumont, at the corner of the Rue Georges-Lardennois and the Rue de Gourmont.

PARC DE BELLEVILLE (3 B–C2)
The viewpoint of the Parc de Belleville, overlooking the hillside park, offers an extremely unusual east–west panorama of Paris. From left to right, you can see the towers of Jussieu and the Place d'Italie, the dome of the Val-de-Grâce and the Panthéon, the Tour Montparnasse, Notre-Dame and the Eiffel Tower. In the distance are La Défense and Mont Valérien. Near the viewpoint are a meteorological center and the Maison de l'Air, an air-quality-measuring center which is introducing the general public to its research.

BUTTE DU CHAPEAU-ROUGE (11 E–F7 AND 8)
Created in 1939, the park overlooks the plain of the Pré-St-Gervais. A circular group of three outcrops, shaded by lime and chestnut trees, offers a quiet vantage point from which to discover the northeastern suburbs of Paris and La Villette.

PARC DE ST-CLOUD
The Parc de St-Cloud is renowned for the viewpoint formed by its famous balustrade – the so-called *ronde de la Lanterne* – which offers a view of the Seine as it curves between Meudon and Mont Valérien in the foreground and, in the distance, the alignment of the Eiffel Tower and the Arc de Triomphe and the wealthy districts of Paris. The natural viewpoint of "Montretout" near the Boulevard de la République in St-Cloud offers another, less extensive view across the Seine and the wooded hills of Meudon.

PARC DE ST-GERMAIN-EN-LAYE
The park's 1½-mile-wide terrace offers one of the most beautiful views of Paris, the Seine and its barges, as the jogging enthusiasts who frequent its heights know only too well. A panoramic table on the terrace allows you to identify the buildings and monuments of Paris. Built below the commune of Vésinet, the view from the park is virtually the same as it was in the 17th century, although today the green of the countryside is punctuated by the "steely" colors of modern architecture. There is a remarkable view of the Arche de la Défense and western Paris. Allow about half an hour to get there by RER line A1.

CHRISTMAS LIGHTS
In December more than 150 squares, avenues and boulevards throughout the capital are lit up by some 200,000 lights and 25 miles of cables. The Champs-Élysées, Avenue Montaigne and Rue Royale are the centerpieces.

LET THERE BE LIGHT. . .
Some 240 monuments and fountains are lit up each evening, and until 1am at weekends and on public holidays.
The uniform lighting has now been replaced by more subtle forms designed to enhance the architecture. The Eiffel Tower, Palais de Chaillot, Church of St-Eustache, Rotonde de Ledoux (Place de Stalingrad), Opéra Bastille, Grand Louvre, Pont Notre-Dame and Pont au Change are today being seen in a new light. Yann Kersalé, Dominique Averland, Roger Narboni and Italo Rota are responsible for creating this nocturnal vision of Paris.

GUIGNOL
1818
LES MARIONETTES DES
CHAMPS ELYSÉES

Wooden horses.

Punch and Judy.

Many games are played in the squares.

Paris has a range of amusements for children, from the big wheels, mazes and grottos of its fun fairs to the sandpits, puppet shows and carousels of its squares as well as many other entertainments.

SQUARES AND PARKS

These feature among the early memories of every Parisian. Growing up in Paris means starting life surrounded by a sandpit, benches and green railings. Today these – mostly free – green spaces tend to be equipped with table-tennis tables, climbing frames, slides, sandpits and benches. The sand is changed yearly and is protected from dogs by railings.

THE SOUND OF SILENCE
Squares – often tiny and surrounded by streets – can be noisy, dusty, dreary places. However, there are a number of more secluded squares for those who enjoy peace and quiet.

MODEL BOATS
Children can sail model boats (which can be hired in the afternoon) on the main ponds in the Luxembourg and the Tuileries. The sails of the boats in the Luxembourg have been made by the same craftsman for the past 50 years.

DONKEYS, PONIES AND CARRIAGES
Carriages, ponies and donkeys can be hired for rides in the Luxembourg, the Parc Monceau, the Tuileries and the Champ-de-Mars.

CAROUSELS

Some carousels are works of art: the one in the Luxembourg was designed in 1880 by Charles Garnier, the architect of the Paris Opéra. There are other carousels in the Jardin du Ranelagh and at the foot of the Eiffel Tower.

PUPPET SHOWS
Punch and Judy shows have entertained children for generations. Classic shows can be found in the Luxembourg and the circus (*rond-point*) of the Champs-Élysées.

PLAY AREAS

The Jardin d'Acclimatation, Parc Flora and Luxembourg have miniature railways, carousels, sandpits, trampolines and slides. There is a separate charge for each ride and activity. Entrance to Asterix and Disneyland Paris theme parks (◆ *448*) is inclusive of rides and amusements.

PARC ASTÉRIX
60128 Plailly
Tel. 03 44 62 34 04

CIRCUS

Most circuses are held in the city and its inner suburbs.

CIRQUE DIANA-MORENO

Jardin d'Acclimatation (Bois de Boulogne) 75016
Tel. 01 45 00 23 01
Wed., Sat, Sun. pm.

HORSE SHOWS
Horse shows include the Zingaro theater in Aubervilliers where Bartabas and his horses perform in the winter before their European tour.

THÉÂTRE ZINGARO
Fort d'Aubervilliers
176, Av. Jean-Jaurès
93000 Aubervilliers
Tel. 01 49 87 59 59

MUSEUMS FOR CHILDREN

ACTIVITY VISITS
Looking for a particular object or person, or recognizing the characteristics of a particular style are a few ways of developing children's powers of observation. Some museums have developed free activity visits for children.
● Orsay.
● Monnaie.
● Arts et Traditions Populaires.
● Orangerie.
● Gustave-Moreau.

NARRATIVE VISITS
Instead of visiting the museum in the accepted sense, a narrator enables children to become part of a story which takes them from snuff-box to magic carpet as they accompany an imaginary character through the rooms of the museum.

● Petit Palais, 5–12's, Wed. 2.15pm; adults and children, Sun. 11am.
● Carnavalet, 4–6's and 6–8's, Wed. 2.30pm.
● Monnaie, Wed. 10.30 am, advance booking.
● Louvre, Wed. and Sat., advance booking.

CHILDREN'S VISITS
● Petit Palais, Wed., introduction to art.
● Orsay, 5-7's and 8-10's, Wed., advance booking.
● Art Moderne de la Ville-de-Paris, Wed. and Sat., advance booking.

WORKSHOPS
Learning to look . . . Discovering that a horse is not always represented with four straight legs, that one can be raised, or that you may only see three of them are just some of the first discoveries made by children in the museum workshops.

DRAWING AND PAINTING
● Art Moderne de la Ville-de-Paris, Wed. 2.30pm.

SCULPTURE
● Bourdelle, Wed. and Sat.
● Petit Palais, Wed.

PHOTOGRAPHY
● Bourdelle, courses of 2, 3 and 6 sessions, Wed. and Sat.
● Carnavalet, Sat.
● Maison Européenne de la Photographie, access given to young photographers

REPAIRS AND RESTORATION
Cognacq-Jay, Wed.

MULTI-THEMES
Subjects include needlework, astronomy, gold- and silverwork and illumination.
● The Louvre, Arts Décoratifs and the Musée Nissim-de-Camondo offer a wide range of established courses.

In Paris the yachts sail on ponds.

A journey through ancient Gaul with Asterix.

FARMS AND ZOOS

● Milking, shearing and agricultural work can be seen every weekend at the Georges-Ville Farm, while the Hameau de la Reine at Versailles (▲ 434) has sheep, ponies, donkeys, cows and pigs.

● The Ménagerie at the Jardin des Plantes, founded in 1794, is one of the oldest of its kind, housing smaller animals in humanely sized cages, such as those in the Vincennes Zoo. Big game animals, bears and deer can be seen at Thoiry, Sauvage and Rambouillet.

FERME GEORGES-VILLE
Rte du Pesage 75012
Tel. 01 43 28 47 63

MÉNAGERIE DU JARDIN DES PLANTES
57, rue Cuvier 75005
Tel. 01 40 79 36 00

ZOO DE VINCENNES
53, av. de St-Maurice 75012
Tel. 01 44 75 20 10

SAFETY

Children are never left unattended in any of the parks or gardens (◆ 464). The larger parks are patrolled by wardens, as are some of the smaller ones (e.g. Jardin de Babylone and Square Boucicaut). Equipment is usually designed for the very young. The larger gardens are more suitable for the over-4's, while sports equipment is often available for older children.

LITTLE SMARTIES

Some places combine the pleasure of discovery with educational activities.

● At the Cité des Enfants in La Villette the very young can listen to their heartbeat, see their vertebral column and listen to the world's languages.

CHILDREN'S THEATERS

As well as being the capital of theater, Paris is also the children's theater capital. With the support of schools and parents, children's performances are becoming a typical feature of Parisian life.

ENTERTAINING THE VERY YOUNG
Conjurers, clowns, one-man bands, puppets, stories, playlets in which children can choose to take part, lighting effects and special presentations... the younger the audience, the greater the skill required for the presentation. In Paris, children's theaters have special entertainers for the very young: Le Théâtre de la Mainate, Le Café Chantant, Le Bateau-Paradis (renovated in 1994), Le Gabilolo, Le Dunois, La Balle au Bond, Le Point-Virgule and L'Espace Jemmapes advertise shows for 2- and 3-year-olds.

● An increasing number of museums provide workshops, guided tours and narrative visits for children (◆ 480).

CITÉ DES SCIENCES ET DE L'INDUSTRIE
30, av. Corentin-Cariou 75019 Paris
Tel. 08 36 68 29 30
Admission: 45F

A FEW SIMPLE PRECAUTIONS
● Children of the same age do not have the same reaction to semi-darkness, loud voices, grimaces and strange surroundings. Only their parents can judge their likely reactions.
N.B. Puppets are not just for children. Many of the performances by the Théâtre de la Marionnette are for adults.
● Make sure you book in advance, especially for very young children. If finding a "full house" is irritating for adults, imagine the disappointment of having to miss your very first visit to the theater.

WHERE TO LOOK
Pariscope and *L'Officiel des spectacles* publish programs for children's theaters, circuses, Punch and Judy shows, movies and children's exhibitions.

AN OLD FAVORITE

Is Antoine de St-Exupéry's *The Little Prince* really for children? This combination of poetry and philosophy either enchants children or leaves them indifferent. Adapted for the stage by the Théâtre du Lucernaire, the show is in its 17th year.

THÉÂTRE DU LUCERNAIRE
53, Rue Notre-Dame-des-Champs 75006
Tel. 01 45 44 57 34

CHRISTMAS WINDOWS

At Christmas, the big department stores take as much care with their window displays as jewelers' shops. Parents take their children "to see the windows" at the risk of being tempted.

Christmas decorations.

BABY SITTING

HOME SERVICE
Tel. 01 42 82 05 04

SOS-URGENCE MAMAN
Tel. 01 45 03 00 02

Château de Vaux-le-Vicomte and Château de Monte-Cristo, the home of Alexandre Dumas.

CHANTILLY (34 miles)

By car: A1 (Autoroute du Nord) to the Senlis exit, then the N16.
SNCF: Gare du Nord to Chantilly.

◆ CHÂTEAU-MUSÉE CONDÉ
Tel: 03 44 62 62 62
Open Mar.–Oct. 10am–6pm, Nov.–Feb. 10.30am–12.45pm, 2–5pm.
Closed Tue.
Park open daily.
Park only 17F, park and château 39F.

◆ MUSÉE VIVANT DU CHEVAL
Tel: 03 44 57.13 13
Open Apr.–Oct. 10.30am–5.30pm; Nov.–Mar. 2–4.30pm, Sat., Sun. and public hols 10.30am–6pm.
Closed Tue. morning.
*Performances: 11.30am, 3.30pm and 5.15pm.
Admission: 50F, red. 40F; weekends 80F, red. 70F.*

DISNEYLAND PARIS (22 miles)

By car: A4 (Autoroute de l'Est) Paris–Metz–Strasbourg, to exit 14 for Parc Disneyland Paris.
RER: Line A4 to

Marne-La-Vallée-Chessy. TGV: to Marne-La-Vallée-Chessy.
Seasonal variations in times and fares. Allow 210F for adults and 165F for children. For information tel: 01 60 30 60 30.

ÉCOUEN (13 miles)
MUSÉE NATIONAL DE LA RENAISSANCE

By car: A1 (Autoroute du Nord) to the Pierrefitte exit, then the N16 toward Chantilly.
SNCF: Gare du Nord to Écouen Ézanville, then bus 269 to the Mairie d'Écouen.
Bus: 269 from St-Denis.
Tel: 01 34 38 38 50
Open 9.45am–12.30pm, 2–5.15pm except Tues.
*Admission: 25F, red. and Sun. 17F.
Guided tour Sat. 3.30pm.*

CHÂTEAU DE FONTAINEBLEAU (40 miles)

By car: A6 (Autoroute du Sud) to the Fontainebleau exit, then the N3.
SNCF: Gare de Lyon to Fontainebleau.
Tel: 01 60 71 50 77
Admission: 32F, red. 20F (under-18's free).

BARBIZON (34 miles)

By car: A6 (Autoroute du Sud) to the Fontainebleau exit, then the N37 and D64.
SNCF: Gare de Lyon to Fontainebleau-Avon and then bus (weekdays only).

◆ MUSÉE MUNICIPAL DE L'ÉCOLE DE BARBIZON
Auberge Ganne,
92, Grande Rue.
Closed Tue.
Admission 25F.

◆ MAISON-ATELIER DE THÉODORE ROUSSEAU
55, Grande Rue
Tel: 01 60 66 22 38
Admission 20F.
Open 10am–12.30pm, 2–6pm (5pm Nov. 11–Mar.).
Open Sat.–Sun. and public holidays.
Closed Tue.
Joint ticket for the Maison-Atelier and the Musée Municipal: 25F. Admission free for children under 12 and disabled people.

◆ MAISON-ATELIER DE JEAN-FRANÇOIS MILLET
27, Grande Rue
Tel: 01 60 66 21 55
Closed Tue.
Admission free.

BASILIQUE DE ST-DENIS (3 miles)

Métro: line 13 to Basilique de St-Denis.
RER: line D1 to St-Denis.
1, rue de Strasbourg
Tel: 01 48 09 83 54
Open Mon.–Sat. Apr.–Sep. 10am–6.30pm, Oct.–Mar. 10am–4.30pm. Open Sun. noon–5pm.
Admission: 32F, red. 21F. Free admission for children under 12.

CHÂTEAU DE VAUX-LE-VICOMTE (34 miles)

By car: autoroute A6 or A4 toward Melun-

Sénart, then A5 to exit 14 for Voisenon.
Tel: 01 64 14 41 90
Château, garden and Musée des Équipages: open Mar.–Nov.11 Mon.–Sat. 10am–1pm, 2–6pm, Sun., public holidays 10am–6pm.
*Admission: château, museum and garden: 59F, red. 49F.
Museum and garden: 30F, red. 24F.
Telephone for times of fountains and candlelit visits.*

VERSAILLES (9 miles)

By car: autoroute A13 to Versailles exit.
Bus: 171.
RER: to Versailles Chantiers or Versailles Rive Droit.
Tel: 01 30 84 76 18
Château (entrance A) open May–Sep. 9am–6.30pm, Oct.–Apr. 9am–5.30pm.
Closed Mon.
Admission: 45F, red. 35F.

Grand Trianon and Petit Trianon open May–Sep. 10am–6.30pm, Oct.–Apr. 10am–12.30pm and 2–5.30pm.
Closed Mon.
Admission: Grand Trianon: 25F, red. 15F; Petit Trianon: 15F, red. 10F; joint ticket (Grand/Petit Trianon): 30F, red. 20F.

The Maison d'Ourscamp before . . .   *. . .and after restoration.*

There are several conservation organizations that are responsible for the preservation of Paris, from its historical monuments and heritage to its environment and green spaces.

CONSERVATION ORGANIZATIONS

ASSOCIATION DE SAUVEGARDE ET DE MISE EN VALEUR DU PARIS HISTORIQUE
44, rue François-Miron 75004
Tel: 01 48 87 74 31
Founded in 1963, the association aims to safeguard and foster awareness of the historic buildings and quarters of Paris, running an information center, library and picture library, and guided tours for adults and students. On summer weekends it runs practical projects for young volunteers and organizes exhibitions in the magnificent 13th-century cellars and first floor of its headquarters, the Maison d'Ourscamp.

COMMISSION DU VIEUX PARIS
Rotonde de la Bataille de Villette, Place de Stalingrad 75019
Tel: 01 40 34 23 58
The chairman of this commission, founded in 1898, is the Mayor of Paris, who appoints forty permanent members to sit with fifteen members elected by the Conseil de Paris. The commission passes regulations intended to protect or safeguard buildings threatened with demolition. Its archive of 200,000 photographs provides a record of long-vanished buildings.

SOCIÉTÉ POUR LA PROTECTION DES PAYSAGES ET DE L'ESTHÉTIQUE DE LA FRANCE
39, av. de la Motte-Picquet 75007
Tel: 01 47 05 37 71
The society has seven thousand members, publishes a quarterly review and has delegates nationwide who make representation to ministries, the courts and architects with a view to preserving landscapes and sites throughout France and especially in Paris.

SOS PARIS
103, rue de Vaugirard 75006
Tel: 01 45 44 63 26
The association operates exclusively within Paris. It has a membership of one thousand and a network of one or two delegates in each arrondissement who liaise with local residents and make representation in the form of letters and petitions to the Mayor of Paris, the Minister for Culture or the French Heritage Secretary. The aim of the association is to preserve the environment of Paris, and its interests range from railway stations (for example, ensuring that the conversion of the Gare de Passy into a restaurant and *salon de thé* did not alter its original appearance) to preserving residential green spaces within the city (of which there are an estimated 1,200 covering a total area of 495 acres), today protected by the revised *POS* (plan for the occupation of ground space).

LISTINGS
For information on lectures, tours, discussions, meeting places and prices look under the indicated sections of the following publications:
• *Pariscope*, see under "Conférences"
• *L'Officiel des spectacles*, see under "Conférences"
• *Le Figaro*, see under "La journée"
• or visit the Paris tourist office:
Office du Tourisme de Paris
127, av. des Champs-Élysées 75008
Tel: 01 49 52 53 54

Further information is given on the pages indicated in bold type

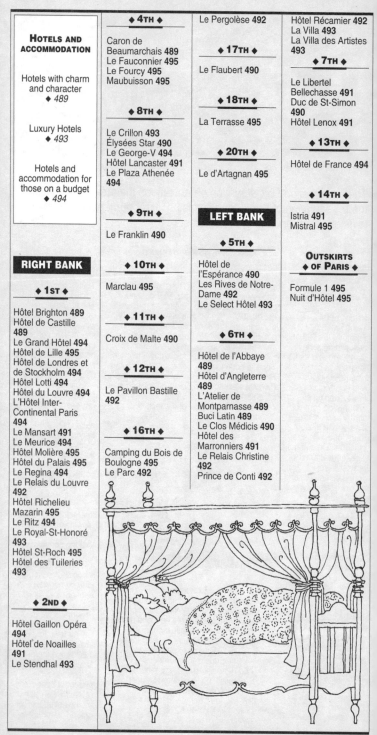

HOTELS AND ACCOMMODATION

Hotels with charm and character
◆ *489*

Luxury Hotels
◆ *493*

Hotels and accommodation for those on a budget
◆ *494*

RIGHT BANK

◆ 1ST ◆

Hôtel Brighton **489**
Hôtel de Castille **489**
Le Grand Hôtel **494**
Hôtel de Lille **495**
Hôtel de Londres et de Stockholm **494**
Hôtel Lotti **494**
Hôtel du Louvre **494**
L'Hôtel Inter-Continental Paris **494**
Le Mansart **491**
Le Meurice **494**
Hôtel Molière **495**
Hôtel du Palais **495**
Le Regina **494**
Le Relais du Louvre **492**
Hôtel Richelieu Mazarin **495**
Le Ritz **494**
Le Royal-St-Honoré **493**
Hôtel St-Roch **495**
Hôtel des Tuileries **493**

◆ 2ND ◆

Hôtel Gaillon Opéra **494**
Hôtel de Noailles **491**
Le Stendhal **493**

◆ 4TH ◆

Caron de Beaumarchais **489**
Le Fauconnier **495**
Le Fourcy **495**
Maubuisson **495**

◆ 8TH ◆

Le Crillon **493**
Élysées Star **490**
Le George-V **494**
Hôtel Lancaster **491**
Le Plaza Athénée **494**

◆ 9TH ◆

Le Franklin **490**

◆ 10TH ◆

Marclau **495**

◆ 11TH ◆

Croix de Malte **490**

◆ 12TH ◆

Le Pavillon Bastille **492**

◆ 16TH ◆

Camping du Bois de Boulogne **495**
Le Parc **492**

Le Pergolèse **492**

◆ 17TH ◆

Le Flaubert **490**

◆ 18TH ◆

La Terrasse **495**

◆ 20TH ◆

Le d'Artagnan **495**

LEFT BANK

◆ 5TH ◆

Hôtel de l'Espérance **490**
Les Rives de Notre-Dame **492**
Le Select Hôtel **493**

◆ 6TH ◆

Hôtel de l'Abbaye **489**
Hôtel d'Angleterre **489**
L'Atelier de Montparnasse **489**
Buci Latin **489**
Le Clos Médicis **490**
Hôtel des Marronniers **491**
Le Relais Christine **492**
Prince de Conti **492**

Hôtel Récamier **492**
La Villa **493**
La Villa des Artistes **493**

◆ 7TH ◆

Le Libertel Bellechasse **491**
Duc de St-Simon **490**
Hôtel Lenox **491**

◆ 13TH ◆

Hôtel de France **494**

◆ 14TH ◆

Istria **491**
Mistral **495**

OUTSKIRTS ◆ OF PARIS ◆

Formule 1 **495**
Nuit d'Hôtel **495**

L'Atelier Montparnasse.

Le Libertel Bellechasse.

Breakfast under the trees to the splash of a fountain, evenings by the fireside or in a modern décor . . . these hotels have unexpected, varied and even cosmopolitan charm and character.

HÔTEL DE L'ABBAYE ***
10, rue Cassette 75006 (1 J9)
Tel: 01 45 44 38 11
Fax: 01 45 48 07 86
In summer guests can enjoy cool shade and flowering plants to the sound of birdsong and the splash of a fountain.

In winter, an open fire blazes in the hearth. The Hôtel de l'Abbaye is a haven of peace and quiet, away from the hustle and bustle of the city. It has 42 rooms, including 4 suites. Room no. 301, decorated in blue and yellow, has a terrace overlooking the rooftops of Paris. Double room 960F–1,950F.

HÔTEL D'ANGLETERRE
44, rue Jacob 75006
Tel: 01 42 60 34 72
Fax: 01 42 60 116 93
Right in the heart of St-Germain-des-Prés this former British Embassy was once the home of Ernest Hemingway. It has
an enclosed inside garden where breakfast is served in summer. Listed staircase. All 29 rooms are renovated; some are high-ceilinged and huge. Breakfast not included. Reserve in advance.
Double rooms from 800F to 100F; duplex at 1,250F.

L'ATELIER DE MONTPARNASSE ***
49, rue Vavin 75006 (6 I1)
Tel: 01 46 33 60 00
Fax: 01 40 51 04 21
The floor of the entrance hall is covered with a multi-colored floral carpet and its walls are hung with the works of contemporary artists. The rooms have no air conditioning and are small but comfortable. They are named after artists, such as Gauguin, Fujita and Erté, and the bathrooms have reproductions of the artists' work in pâte-de-verre mosaics.
Double room 650–700F.

HÔTEL BRIGHTON
218, rue de Rivoli 75001
Tel: 01 44 60 30 03
Fax: 01 40 15 95 16
The rooms on the 4th and 5th floors have balconies with superb views over the Tuileries Gardens,
the Louvre, the Musée d'Orsay, the Invalides and the Eiffel Tower.
Double rooms from 600 to 840F.

BUCI LATIN ***
34, rue de Buci 75006 (2 A8)
Tel: 01 43 29 07 20
Fax: 01 43 29 67 44
The hotel has a number of surprising features: unusual objects dotted around the reception rooms; doors with handles like pétanque bowls and decorated with geometric designs, multi-colored confetti, trompe-l'oeil frescos, studded wood panels and other motifs; colored "tags" running up the walls of the fire escapes; a basement breakfast room with a goldfish pond and small fountain. Guests receive a complimentary list of useful addresses. All 27 rooms are air-conditioned and sound-proofed. Suite no. 162 has a Jacuzzi.
Double room 970–1,250F.

CARON DE BEAUMARCHAIS ***
12, rue Vieille-du-Temple 75004 (2 F2)
Tel: 01 42 72 34 12
Fax: 01 42 72 34 63
Beaumarchais, the author of Le Mariage de Figaro, lived at 47, rue Vieille-du-Temple in the Marais. The hotel is decorated in the style of an 18th-century bourgeois residence and furniture are period reproductions. The blue and white ceramics, with their brush-and-pen decorations, are inspired by those of Rouen and Nevers. Letters from Beaumarchais hang on the walls. The hotel's 19 rooms are entirely sound-proofed and air-conditioned.
Double room 690–770F.

HÔTEL DE CASTILLE
37, rue Cambon 75001. Tel: 01 44 58 44 58. Fax: 01 44 58 38 01.
Exquisite Venetian-style décor. Double room 1,990–2,600F.

Caron de Beaumarchais.

Croix de Malte.

REDUCTIONS

There is no chance of obtaining reductions in May, June, September and October. This is the Paris conference and exhibition season and hotels are full. During the rest of the year, if the hotel is not full and you have a convincing argument, it is possible to obtain a luxury room for the price of an ordinary room, or a reduction of between 30 and 40 percent.

LE CLOS MÉDICIS ***

56, rue Monsieur-le-Prince 75006 (2B9)
Tel: 01 43 29 10 80
Fax: 01 43 54 26 90

*This 1860's private residence with its typically cramped rooms has undergone a complete metamorphosis. Today its stonework, woodwork, wrought iron and the yellow tones of its décor are reminiscent of the towns of southern France. The air-conditioned rooms are in the same style: padded headboards with pear-tree wood surrounds, soft bedspreads and faience friezes and tiles in the bathrooms. In winter the fireside chairs enable guests to enjoy the cold weather. 38 rooms.
Double room 790–1,200F.*

CROIX DE MALTE **

5, rue de Malte 750011 (2 H4)
Tel: 01 48 05 09 36
Fax: 01 43 57 02 54

*The Croix de Malte, situated between the République and Bastille Métro stations, is a haven of peace and quiet. The fresh tones (green, blue, white and orange) of the rooms provide a backdrop for the furniture, carpets and reproductions of paintings by Walasse Ting. The winter garden, between the hotel's two buildings, is decorated with exotic frescos. 29 rooms.
Double room from 570F.*

DUC DE ST-SIMON

14, rue St-Simon 75007 (1 H7)
Tel: 01 44 39 20 20
Fax: 01 45 48 68 25

A former hôtel particulier, this 18th-century mansion is furnished with antiques. Ask for a room overlooking the garden, or rooms 14, 24, 25 or 42 which

*have terraces. 34 rooms and suites.
Double room 1,050–1,450F.*

ÉLYSÉES STAR ****

19, rue Vernet 75008 (1 C2)
Tel: 01 47 20 41 73
Fax: 01 47 23 32 15

*Each story of this small, 19th-century hotel – situated near the Champs-Élysées – pays homage to the great eras of French decorative art. On the first floor the wild-cherry paneling of the bar complements the Louis XV furniture. The second floor is dedicated to Louis XVI and the third to the Directoire. They are followed by the Second Empire and the 1930's. The basement breakfast room combines light fabrics with the freestone of the masonry. The bed linen in the hotel's 43 rooms is perfectly matched to each style, while the overall effect is one of space.
Double room 1,700–1,900F.*

HÔTEL DE L'ESPÉRANCE **

15, rue Pascal 75005 (5 D3)
Tel: 01 47 07 10 99
Fax: 01 43 37 56 19

The Hôtel de l'Espérance is noted for its pleasant atmosphere. The hotel is equipped with pink marble

*bathrooms, new bed linen and thick-pile carpets. Breakfast is served in the small, flower-filled garden. 38 rooms.
Double room 450F.*

LE FLAUBERT **

19, rue Rennequin 75017 (9 B8)
Tel: 01 46 22 44 35
Fax: 01 43 80 32 34

*The 37 rooms of Le Flaubert, arranged around a lavishly planted central garden, are simply furnished and extremely comfortable.
Double room 450–550F.*

LE FRANKLIN ***

19, rue Buffault 75009 (10 C9)

Tel: 01 42 80 27 27
Fax: 01 48 78 13 04

*The red fabric of the wrought-iron chairs in the lounge and the prints illustrating Napoleon's famous victories – Ulm, Wagram, Austerlitz – echo the emperor's favorite color in this "Napoleonic" hotel. The glass-roofed breakfast room is decorated with trompe l'œil frescos. 68 rooms.
Double room from 825F.*

Duc de St-Simon.

Le Franklin.

ISTRIA **
29, rue Campagne-
Première 75014
(6 J2)
Tel: 01 43 20 91 82
Fax: 01 43 22 48 45
*Famous residents
have included Elsa
Triolet, Aragon de
Mayakovsky and
Simone de Beauvoir.
This modest hotel
has small, simply
decorated rooms and
light, airy bathrooms.
Five of the 26 rooms
overlook a small,
central garden.
Double room from
580F.*

HÔTEL LANCASTER
7, rue de Berri
75008
Tel: 01 40 76 40 76
Fax: 01 40 76 40 00
*This hotel has the
attention to detail that
is lacking in so many
of the larger hotels:
linen sheets,
excellent breakfast.
Attractive rooms,
each in a different
style with antique*

furniture. Non-air-
conditioned rooms
on the side of the
courtyard and away
from the street are
recommended.
Reserve in advance.
Double room
2,350–2,650F.

HÔTEL LENOX
9, rue de l'Université
75007
Tel: 01 42 96 10 95
Fax: 01 42 61 52 83
*In the heart of the
Faubourg St-
Germain. Rooms are
relatively small but
simple and clean.
Two duplex on the
top floors. The hotel
has been renovated
but has managed to
avoid looking coldly
modern. No
restaurant but a large
bar serving snacks.
34 rooms.
Double room with
shower 590F, with
bath 670F, 780F,
830F, the duplex with
terrace 960F.
Popular, so
reservations
recommended.*

**LE LIBERTEL
BELLECHASSE** ***
8, rue de Bellechasse
75007 (1 H6)
Tel: 01 45 50 22 31
Fax: 01 45 51 52 36
*Le Bellechasse is
situated between the
Boulevard St-
Germain and the
Quai Anatole-France.
The mahogany
furniture and striped,
silky fabrics of its
Second-Empire décor
offer a subtle blend of
characteristic shades
and tones. Some of
the rooms have four-*

poster beds. It has an
elegant, basement
breakfast room and
an attractive central
courtyard.
Guaranteed peace
and quiet. 41 rooms.
Double room from
975F.

LE MANSART ***
5, rue des Capucines
75001 (1 I3)
Tel: 01 42 61 50 28
Fax: 01 49 27 97 44
*The hotel was built in
1720 by John Law,
who invented
assignats
(promissory notes),
on the corner of the
Place Vendôme and
Rue des Capucines.
One famous guest,
Gabriel Lemonnier
(the jeweler who
created the Empress
Eugénie's crown) is
said to have hidden
jewels there during
the Paris Commune.
Today the frescos in
the entrance hall
represent French-
style gardens and
furniture is Louis XIV
and Second Empire.
Bathrooms are
spacious and
naturally lit.
57 rooms.
Double room
730–1,550F.*

**HÔTEL DES
MARRONNIERS**
21, rue Jacob
75006
Tel: 01 43 25 30 60
Fax: 01 40 46 83 56
*In the heart of St-
Germain-des-Prés in
a quiet location. The
rooms are small. The
two chestnut trees
(marronniers) that
give the hotel its
name shade a little
garden. The service
can sometimes be
disappointing.
No restaurant.
37 rooms.
Reserve in advance.
Double room
700–800F.*

**HÔTEL DE
NOAILLES** ***
9, rue de la
Michodière 75002
(2 A2)
Tel: 01 47 42 92 90
Fax: 01 49 24 92 71
*The hotel, 100
meters from the
Place de l'Opéra, is
surprisingly quiet.
Most of its rooms
overlook the central
courtyard. Soft
background music
and fabric wall-
hangings deaden the*

RESERVATIONS

Although it is not
always necessary,
it is wise to reserve
hotel rooms in
advance. Peak
times are in May,
June, September
and October. Often
a deposit is
required – usually
15 percent of the
price of the room –
either in the form of
a check or a credit
card number.
Reservations are
valid until 6pm on
the relevant day,
later if advance
notice is given.

◆ HOTELS WITH CHARM AND CHARACTER

Le Parc.

Le Relais Christine.

noise. The hotel has a softly carpeted library and a Petit Salon decorated with contemporary furniture, exotic woods and warm tones. There is a small Japanese garden and a terrace for the fine weather. Excellent service. 58 rooms, 6 suites. Double room 700–960F.

LE PARC **
55–57, av. Raymond-Poincaré 75116 (8 I5)
Tel: 01 44 05 66 66
Fax: 01 44 05 66 00
A hotel in the style of an English manor house with a delightful, hidden courtyard. Decorated by interior designer Nina Campbell, the bar and library, the chintzes, tartans, wood paneling and furniture create a

very "British" setting. The lamps and tables are by royal cabinet-maker Lord Linley. The hotel's 116 rooms are sound-proofed and air-conditioned. Double room 2,100–2,750F.

LE PAVILLON BASTILLE **
65, rue de Lyon 75012 (2 I10)
Tel: 01 43 43 65 65
Fax: 01 43 43 96 52

Le Pavillon stands opposite the Opéra Bastille. A 17th-century "lion's head" fountain, in light-colored stone, plays in the cobbled courtyard. The hotel has 25 small rooms furnished in contemporary style. The lighting, fabrics and vaulted cellar are in shades of yellow and blue. Guests are given a magnetic key, which enables them to come and go as they please. Double room 815–955F.

LE PERGOLÈSE **
3, rue Pergolèse 75016 (8 I4)
Tel: 01 53 64 04 04
Fax: 01 53 64 04 40
Modern design has been used inventively here to

create a warm, friendly ambience in this designer hotel created by Rena Dumas, with floor-coverings and pictures specially created by Hilton McConnico. The interior combines warm mahogany doors with chrome highlights and pale ash furniture, in pastel-walled rooms enlivened by accessories in the house colors: golden yellow, apricot, royal blue, green and deep red. The 40 rooms are air-conditioned and sound-proofed. Double room 1,100–1,800F.

PRINCE DE CONTI **
8, rue Guénégaud 75006 (2 B7)
Tel: 01 44 07 30 40
Fax: 01 44 07 36 34
The hotel's 26 air-conditioned rooms are all decorated in different styles. The airier, "English" rooms have flowered wallpaper and pastel-colored furniture, while others have heavy drapes, four-poster beds and cretonne fabrics. Several overlook the central courtyard where breakfast is served. Double room 975F.

HÔTEL RÉCAMIER
3 bis, pl. St-Sulpice, 75006
Tel: 01 43 26 04 89
This is the perfect sort of place for those who just want to look out on St-Sulpice in a

charming and calm but slightly run-down family-run hotel. Only worthwhile if you get a room with a view (even better on the top floors). Double room 600F.

LE RELAIS CHRISTINE **
3, rue Christine 75006 (2 B7)
Tel: 01 40 51 60 80
Fax: 01 40 51 60 81
The former 16th-century Augustinian abbey of the Collège St-Denis has retained its original well, fireplace and medieval cellars, now a breakfast room. Today, elegant carpets complement the wood paneling and beams. Attentive service. The hotel has three unusual external features – a private garage with 25 spaces, a paved courtyard and a garden – and 51 air-conditioned rooms. Double room from 1,850F.

LE RELAIS DU LOUVRE **
19, rue des Prêtres-St-Germain-l'Auxerrois 75001
Tel: 01 40 41 96 42
This elegantly furnished 18th-century house is now one of the "Relais du Silence" hotels (a chain of French hotels in tranquil settings). Double room 800–900F.

LES RIVES DE NOTRE-DAME **
15, quai St-Michel

Le Crillon.

Le Ritz.

75005 (2 C8)
Tel: 01 43 54 81 16
Fax: 01 43 26 27 09
Former doctors, Annie and Philippe-Guillaume took over the hotel in 1994 and have tried to convey their love of Italy and Provence by creating a warm and friendly atmosphere and a décor inspired by Florentine art. The walls of the basement breakfast room are painted with trompe-l'œil frescos. The hotel's rooms are small but comfortable, sound-proofed and air-conditioned, and have an unrivaled view of Notre-Dame.
9 rooms and 1 suite.
Double room 995–2,500F.

LE ROYAL-ST-HONORÉ ★★★★
221, rue St-Honoré 75001 (1 I4)
Tel: 01 42 60 32 79
Fax: 01 42 60 47 44
Le Royal-St-Honoré, where La Fayette married Mlle de Noailles in 1774, has emerged resplendent from recent renovation work. The fine-grained stone façade is pierced by flecked-glass doors. The main entrance has a floor of different colored marble and is decorated in shades ranging from gold to honey, punctuated by the splashes of turquoise alcantara of the upholstery.

Its 72 rooms are sound-proofed and air-conditioned.
Double room from 1,850F.

LE SELECT HÔTEL ★★★
1, pl. de la Sorbonne 75005 (2 C9)
Tel: 01 46 34 14 80
Fax: 01 46 34 51 79
Claude Chabrerie goes running every Sunday morning . . . and with very good reason. His hotel is very close to the shady avenues of the Jardin du Luxembourg. The recently renovated Select Hôtel combines old stonework and massive beams with the rounded lines of contemporary furniture. Unusual features include bathrooms with no doors that open onto the bedrooms and a fountain in the small Art Deco lounge. The hotel's 68 rooms are air-conditioned and sound-proofed.
Double room from 805F.

LE STENDHAL ★★★★
22, rue Danielle-Casanova 75002 (2 A4)
Tel: 01 44 58 52 52
Fax: 01 44 58 52 00
This 18th-century building, where Henri Stendhal – author of Le Rouge et le Noir (The Red and the Black) – died on March 22, 1842, stands between the Opéra Garnier and the Place Vendôme. Today it is a peaceful

hotel, furnished with beautiful reproductions of antique furniture, while the colors and designs of the modern fabrics range from Directoire to Art Deco. All 20 rooms are sound-proofed and air-conditioned.
Double room from 1,420F.

HÔTEL DES TUILERIES
10, rue Hyacinthe 75001
Tel: 01 42 61 04 17
Fax: 01 49 27 91 56
In the shadow of St-Germain-l'Auxerrois, the old parish of the kings of France, this quiet and intimate hotel with its Directoire and English decoration is a mere step away from the Louvre.
20 rooms.
Double room from 790F to 1,200F.

LA VILLA ★★★★
29, rue Jacob 75006 (2 A7)
Tel: 01 43 26 60 00
Fax: 01 46 34 63 63
La Villa offers modern art in the heart of the St-Germain district. Marie-Christine Dorner has created an original, 1980's-style décor with soberly designed furniture, purple, orange and black leather wall coverings and low-voltage lighting with chrome-plated bowls. In the evening jazz bands play in the basement.
32 rooms.

Double room 900–1,400F.

LA VILLA DES ARTISTES ★★★
9, rue de la Grande-Chaumière 75006 (6 I2)
Tel: 01 43 26 60 86
Fax: 01 43 54 73 70
Situated between St-Germain and Montparnasse, this has provided lodgings for many artists since the turn of the century. The hotel, fully renovated in 1997, combines light coloring in its bedrooms with contemporary wood-paneling in the reception rooms and bar.
Double room from 685–885F.

◆ LUXURY HOTELS ◆

LE CRILLON
10, pl. de la Concorde 75008 (1 G3)
Tel: 01 44 71 15 00
Fax: 01 44 71 15 02
An 18th-century residence designed by Jacques Ange Gabriel. The Salons des Aigles, des Batailles and Marie-Antoinette are classified as historic monuments. Their décor is a reminder of the great pomp and ceremony of the Ancien Régime. Le Crillon welcomes international VIPs. The most beautiful of its 163 rooms and suites are the 3 presidential suites, recently decorated by Sonia Rykiel. The

◆ Luxury hotels

Leonard Bernstein suite, whose terrace overlooks the Place de la Concorde, offers a panoramic view of Paris. Double room from 3,650F.

Le George-V
31, av. George-V 75008 (1 C2)
Built in 1928, this hotel is in the midst of complete renovation. All 245 rooms, including 61 suites boasting very handsome antique furniture, together with the bar, restaurant and balcony, will be decorated by Pierre-Yves Rochon. When it reopens in summer 1999, its devotees should feel satisfied that it's back to its old form, with 30 rooms and suites with balconies, and 7 rooms fitted for disabled guests.

Le Grand Hôtel
2, rue Scribe 75001 (1 J2)
Tel: 01 40 07 32 32
Fax: 01 42 66 12 51
The luxury and sheer size of Le Grand Hôtel, designed by the architect Alfred Armand, make it a work of art in the field of Second-Empire hotel construction. The interior has been renovated many times since it was opened by the Empress Eugénie on May 5, 1862. Recent work has restored its original character, including the glass-roofed winter garden and the Salon Opéra, which, with its 48 statues of musicians and huge crystal chandelier, is one of the most beautiful reception rooms in Paris. The attractively decorated bedrooms have every modern comfort. Double room from 2,100F.

L'Hôtel Inter-Continental Paris
3, rue de Castiglione 75001 (1 I4)
Tel: 01 44 77 11 11
Fax: 01 44 77 14 60
The hotel, designed by Henri Blondel for the 1878 World Fair, has just been refurbished. All 443 rooms were redecorated, and the 12 reception rooms (including the imperial salon in Napoleon III style), with their gold-paneled, painted ceilings, are truly marvelous. A covered terrace has been created in the main courtyard. New features are the Brasserie 234 Rivoli restaurant and the discreet, refined Bar Tuileries.
Double room from 2,600F.

Hôtel Lotti
7–9, rue de Castiglione 75001
Tel: 01 42 60 37 34
Fax: 01 40 15 93 56
The Lotti opened in 1910 under the influence of the Duke of

Westminster, who wanted a luxurious yet intimate place to stay in Paris. There are old masters in the main salon, and the bedrooms have Louis XV and XVI furniture. Breakfast is a sumptuous occasion. 133 rooms.
Double room from 2,200F.

Hôtel du Louvre
Place André-Malraux 75001
Tel: 01 44 58 38 38
Fax: 01 44 58 38 01
The hotel nearest the museum, opposite the Comédie-Française, the Hôtel du Louvre has recently been restored. Its large elevators lead to many salons and give access to the suite from which Pissarro, the Impressionist painter, painted the Avenue de l'Opéra in 1898. 200 rooms. Double room from 1,400F.

Le Meurice
228, rue de Rivoli 75001 (1 I4)
Tel: 01 44 58 10 10
Fax: 01 44 58 10 15
In 1835 Augustin Meurice, a Calais postmaster, built a hotel for the English which he "exported" to Paris. Today literary award ceremonies are held in the reception rooms of the "Hôtel des Rois" (so called because of its prestigious clientele) while its range of breakfast preserves is among the most famous in Paris. Double room from 2,800F.

Le Plaza Athénée
25, av. Montaigne 75008 (1 D3)
Tel: 01 53 67 66 65
Fax: 01 53 67 66 66
Considered one of the best hotels in the world, Le Plaza dominates the avenue of the Paris couturiers. Double room from 3,500F.

Le Regina
2, pl. des Pyramides 75001 (1 I4)
Tel: 01 42 60 31 10
Fax: 01 40 15 95 16
Opened in 1900, the Regina keeps alive the tradition of French luxury. The rooms are decorated with either Louis XVI or Directoire furniture

and antique tapestries. Wood-paneled reception. Central garden and 130 rooms and apartments offering every comfort.
Double room from 1,950F.

Le Ritz
15, pl. Vendôme 75001 (1 I3)
Tel: 01 43 16 30 30
Fax: 01 43 16 36 68
This luxury hotel has an international reputation, with Marcel Proust and Coco Chanel numbering among its famous guests. A sumptuous décor gives the impression of stepping back into the Belle Époque, but the swimming pool and fitness center very much indicate a 20th-century establishment.
Double room from 3,500F.

◆ Budget hotels ◆

Hôtel de France
32, rue de Patay 75013 (5 J7)
Tel: 01 45 83 81 91
Six-story hotel. All rooms have showers and toilets. No lift. Close to the Porte d'Ivry.
Double room 170–200F.

Hôtel Gaillon-Opéra
9, rue Gaillon 75002
Tel: 01 47 42 47 74
Attractive hotel situated between the Louvre and the Opéra.
Double room 600–800F.

Hôtel de Londres et de Stockholm
300, rue St-Honoré (entrance at 13, rue St-Roch) 75001
Tel: 01 42 60 15 62
A former bourgeois house, near the Tuileries Gardens and the Louvre.
Double room 400–550F.

Auberge Maubuisson.   Hôtel La Terrasse.   The Office du Tourisme.

HÔTEL DE LILLE
8, rue du Pélican
75001 (2 B5)
Tel: 01 42 33 33 42
Unpretentious hotel with old-fashioned charm in a quiet, narrow street near Les Halles.
Double room from 280F.

MARCLAU
78, rue du Faubourg-Poissonnière 75010 (10 D9)
Tel: 01 47 70 73 50
The Marclau stands in the heart of a busy district, near the Poissonnière Métro station. The neat, tidy rooms are decorated with flowers.
Double room from 369F.

MISTRAL
24, rue Cels 75014 (6 H3)
Tel: 01 43 20 25 43
The simply furnished rooms are clean and tidy. Most of them, including the one that used to be occupied by Jean-Paul Sartre and Simone de Beauvoir, overlook the Montparnasse cemetery.
Double room 220–320F.

HÔTEL MOLIÈRE
21, rue Molière 75001
Tel: 01 42 96 22 01
In a quiet street between the Louvre and the Bibliothèque Nationale.
Double room from 620F.

HÔTEL DU PALAIS
2, quai de la

Mégisserie 75001
Tel: 01 42 36 98 25
Small hotel in the historic center, which offers tranquility and a friendly welcome.
Double room from 230F to 380F.

HÔTEL RICHELIEU MAZARIN
51, rue de Richelieu 75001
Tel: 01 42 97 46 20
Between the Palais-Royal, the Bibliothèque Nationale and the Louvre.
Double room from 300F.

HÔTEL ST-ROCH
25, rue St-Roch 75001
Tel: 01 42 60 17 91
Close to the Rue St-Honoré, the Louvre and the Tuileries.
Double room 430–520F.

LA TERRASSE
67, rue Letort 75018 (10 C2)
Tel: 01 46 06 45 01
La Terrasse is five minutes' walk from the St-Ouen flea-market. Its white façade adds a touch of style. No elevator.
Double room 350F.

◆ OUTSKIRTS ◆

NUIT D'HÔTEL
RN 14, rue de la Pompe 95800 Cergy
Tel: 01 34 24 12 12
The rooms (12 sq. yards) have very basic facilities. No en-suite showers. 800 yards from the RER station.
Double room 145F.

FORMULE 1
11, av. Lénine 92300 St-Denis
Tel: 01 48 27 41 08
The hotel is only 10 minutes' walk from the St-Denis-Basilique Métro station and is often full. Each room (measuring 10½ sq. yards) has a single bunk-bed above a double bed.
Room: 139F.

◆ YOUTH HOSTELS ◆

To stay in a youth hostel (*auberge de jeunesse*) you must either have a YHA card or pay an additional 10F. Cards cost 70F (under 26) and 100F (over 26). Information:
Tel: 01 44 89 87 27.

LE FOURCY
6, rue de Fourcy 75004 (2 F7)
Tel: 01 42 74 23 45
This 18th-century residence in the heart of the Marais stands behind a heavy carriage gateway. Antique furniture, exposed beams and vaulted cellars give it

┌─────────────────────────┐
│   **INFORMATION**
│ The Paris Office du
│   Tourisme and
│   Centre
│ d'Information et de
│ Documentation-
│ Jeunesse (CIDJ)
│ have regularly
│ updated lists of
│ accommodation.
│ **CIDJ:** 101, quai
│ Branly, 75015 (7 J1)
│ Tel. 01 44 49 12 00
└─────────────────────────┘

its distinctive style.
125F (in rooms for 4, with shower).

MAUBUISSON
12, rue des Barres 75004 (2 E7)
Tel: 01 42 74 23 45
Half-timbering and attic and mezzanine rooms with balconies and a distant view of Notre-Dame.
125F (in rooms for 4, with shower).

LE FAUCONNIER
11, rue du Fauconnier 75004 (2 G8)
Tel: 01 42 74 23 45
The façade of this impressive residence is covered with ivy and Virginia Creeper. Antique furniture and a small garden.
118F (in rooms for 4, with shower).

LE D'ARTAGNAN
80, rue Vitruve 75020 (3 H5)
Tel: 01 40 32 34 56
Le d'Artagnan stands in a quiet street near the Porte de Bagnolet. It has a bar, TV room and launderette.
113F (in rooms for 3, 4 and 8).

◆ CAMPSITES ◆

CAMPING DU BOIS DE BOULOGNE
Allée du Bord-de-l'Eau 75016 (8 B3)
Tel: 01 45 24 30 00
Open all year round, in a natural setting opposite the Île de Puteaux. Restaurant and supermarket. Low prices from between 125F and 138F.

◆ RESTAURANTS, CAFÉS AND BARS LISTED BY ARRONDISSEMENT

This section was researched by Fiona Beeston. Further information is given on the pages indicated in bold type.

Gastronomic restaurants ◆ *497*
Restaurant creators and the young "patron" chefs ◆ *498*
Restaurants with spectacular views ◆ *500*
Restaurants with listed interiors ◆ *500*
Fish delights ◆ *501*
Regional cuisine ◆ *501*
Bistros ◆ *502*
Brasseries ◆ *503*
Where to eat on Sundays ◆ *504*
Restaurants with gardens or quiet terraces ◆ *504*
Meals for under 150F ◆ *505*
Vegetarian restaurants ◆ *505*
Wine bars ◆ *505*
Beer bars ◆ *506*
Cafés ◆ *506*
Salons de thé and coffee houses ◆ *507*

RIGHT BANK

◆ 1ST ◆

Angélina **507**
Le Carré des Feuillants **497**
L'Émile **505**
Entre Ciel et Terre **505**
Goumard-Prunier **501**
Le Grand Véfour **500**
Juvenile's **505**
Lescure **502**
Café Marly **506**
Le Nemours **507**
Le Palais Royal **504**
Pharamond **500**
Serge Granger **501**
Le Sous-Bock **506**
Verlet **507**
Willi's **506**

◆ 2ND ◆

À Priori Thé **507**
Le Café Noir **521**
The Frog and Rosbif **506**
Vaudeville **504**
Le Vide Gousset **507**

◆ 3RD ◆

Ambassade d'Auvergne **501**
Au Bascou **501**
Chez Jenny **503**
Lapeyronie **507**
Le St-Gervais **507**

◆ 4TH ◆

L'Ambroisie **497**
Café Beaubourg **506**
Benoît **503**
Bofinger **503**
Brasserie de l'Île St-Louis **503**
Jo Goldenberg **502**
L'Ébouillante **507**
Les Étages **521**
Le Petit Fer à Cheval **507**
Le Temps des Cerises **505**
La Truffe **505**
Mariage Frères **507**

◆ 8TH ◆

Les Ambassadeurs **497**
Ladurée **507**
Lasserre **497**
Ledoyen **497**
Lucas-Carton **497**
Tabac de la Madeleine **507**

◆ 9TH ◆

Casa Olympe **503**
Chartier **502**
Le Commerce **506**
I Golosi **505**
La Table d'Anvers **498**

◆ 10TH ◆

Flo **504**
Julien **504**
Le Louis XIV **500**
Le Petit Château d'Eau **507**
Terminus du Nord **504**

◆ 11TH ◆

Au Lèche Vin **521**
Astier **502**
Le Bistrot du Peintre **506**

Café de l'Industrie **521**
Chardenoux **503**
Le Clown Bar **505**
Le Passage **506**

◆ 12TH ◆

Au Trou Gascon **501**
Le Train Bleu **502**

◆ 16TH ◆

Café Antoine **506**
Chalet des Îles **504**
Coquelin Ainé **530**
La Grande Cascade **504**
Joël Robuchon **497**
Le Pré-Catelan **506**
Prunier **500**

◆ 17TH ◆

Apicius **497**
Le Ballon des Ternes **503**
Grain d'Orge **502**
Pétrissans **503**

◆ 18TH ◆

Au Rêve **506**
Le Moulin à Vins **505**
Le Sancerre **521**

◆ 20TH ◆

À la Courtille **505**
Bistrot-Cave des Envierges **505**
Le Piston Pélican **521**

LEFT BANK

◆ 5TH ◆

Chez Henri **503**
Fakhr El Dine **500, 505**
Le Mouffetard **506**
Le Petit Navire **501**
Le Rallye **521**

La Timbale St-Bernard **499,505**
La Timonerie **499**
La Tour d'Argent **500**

◆ 6TH ◆

Allard **502**
Aux Charpentiers **502**
La Bastide Odéon **499**
Les Beaux Arts **505**
Chez Georges **521**
Christian Constant **528**
La Closerie des Lilas **502**
L'Écaille de PCB **501**
Café de Flore **506**
Dominique **502**
Guenmaï **505**
Lipp **504**
La Méditerranée **501**
La Palette **521**
La Petite Cour **504**
La Rotonde **504**
La Taverne de Nesles **521**

◆ 7TH ◆

Arpège **498**
Le Bamboche **498**
Le Divellec **501**
Jean-Paul Hévin **528**
Le Jules Verne **500**

◆ 13TH ◆

Anacréon **498**

◆ 14TH ◆

L'Assiette **502**
Le Café de la Place **507**
La Cagouille **501**
La Coupole **503**
Le Dôme **501**
Le Pavillon Montsouris **504**
La Régalade **499**
Le Vin des Rues **506**

◆ 15TH ◆

Aux Sportifs réunis "Chez Walczack" **506**
La Dinée **499**
Francis Boucher **528**
L'Os à Moelle **499**
La Plage **504**

OUTSKIRTS ◆ OF PARIS ◆

La Guinguette de Neuilly (Neuilly) **504**
Le Petit Poucet (Levallois-Perret) **504**

496

◆ THE TRADITIONAL GASTRONOMIC STARS ◆

LES AMBASSADEURS
Hôtel Crillon
10, pl. de la
Concorde 75008
Tel: 01 44 71 16 16
Open daily.
Ten years ago no one would have dreamt that one of the most sumptuous dining rooms in Paris would be serving a cuisine de terroir. Thanks to the inspired chef, Christian Constant, dishes such as pork cheek and muzzle have made their way, with much acclaim, onto the menu. But traditionalists can still enjoy the most noble carré d'agneau, the purest daurade cooked with lemon and fennel and a fabulous range of honeyed, spicy deserts produced by the pastry chef from Alsace.
Menus: 340F lunch; 610F dégustation.
À la carte: 800–1,000F.

L'AMBROISIE
9, pl. des Vosges
75004
Tel: 01 42 78 51 45
Closed Sun. and
Mon., 2 weeks in
Feb. and 3 weeks
in Aug.
This is one of the 20 Michelin 3-star restaurants in France, and naturally foreigners gravitate to the intimate dining room. Bernard Pacaud offers a restricted range of dishes. The cuisine is classic, such as fresh truffles slipped between two slices of foie gras and wrapped in pastry, or the fricassée of poularde de Bresse with sherry vinegar. Lately Bernard Pacaud has finally allowed himself to loosen up a little and has shown welcome touches of extravagance, such as the fresh tuna with apricots.
À la carte: 700–920F.

APICIUS
122, av. de Villiers
75017
Tel: 01 43 80 19 66
Closed Sat. and Sun.
and Aug.
Very much a favored Parisian haunt, where a joie de vivre has taken over from the tedium and solemnity that unfortunately often goes hand-in-hand with starred restaurants. The young Jean-Pierre Vigato continues to seek out the finest products from France's rich country heritage, cooking with precision his thick veal cutlet, his tasty boned roasted pig's feet served as a sausage-like crépinette, and his divine purée of potatoes with truffle juice that some say rivals Robuchon's.
Menus: 380–620F,
À la carte: 750F.

LE CARRÉ DES FEUILLANTS
14, rue Castiglione
75001
Tel: 01 42 86 82 82
Closed Sat. lunch,
Sun. and Aug.
One of the top ten best tables in Paris belongs to Alain Dutournier, a passionate fun-loving gastronome who comes from Gascony, so it's not surprising that he's obsessive about the quality of his foie gras. But that rigour extends to every ingredient in his kitchen, from his spices to the number of weeks his Chalosse beef has matured (try the succulent charcoal grilled pièce de boeuf) and to his impeccable wine list. Alain Dutournier manages to add just the right touch of sophistication to a cuisine de terroir he understands better than anyone.
Menus: 295–780F.
À la carte: 650F.

JOËL ROBUCHON
59, av. Raymond-
Poincaré 75016
Tel: 01 47 27 12 27
Chef Joël Robuchon, renowned for culinary creations such as cream of sea urchins with fennel, has now retired. His successor, Ducasse, has prepared a menu which is sure to delight all those customers who have been coming to this unique restaurant for years.

LASSERRE
17, av. Franklin-
Roosevelt 75008
Tel: 01 43 59 02 13
Closed Sun. and
Mon. lunch and Aug.
Difficult to put Lasserre in a league with the new generation of top restaurants, but there is something touching about this, the last of the great Parisian old-fashioned restaurants, with its roof that opens up to the sky and its décor stuck in the 1960's. The service overseen by the priceless Monsieur Louis ensures that the canard à l'orange is still carved in front of you on the trolley, but that's about as exciting as it gets.
À la carte
800–1,200F.

LEDOYEN
1, av. Dutouit
Carré des Champs-
Elysées 75008
Tel: 01 53 05 10 01
Closed Sat., Sun.,
Aug.
Ghislaine Arabian is the only woman to have made it to the list of Paris' best restaurants. Her Flemish origins come across strongly. If you are a beer devotee this is the place for you, with a lot of dishes successfully cooked in beer. Try the turbot cooked in cask-aged beer, and watch the Parisians being able to indulge – at last – in proper, large French fries.
Menus: 300–590F.
À la carte: 650F.

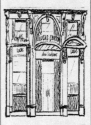

LUCAS-CARTON
9, place de la
Madeleine 75008
Tel: 01 42 65 22 90
Closed Sat. lunch,
Sun, Aug. and public
holidays.
This is the high temple of gastronomy in France. Over the years, Alain Senderens has discovered, redefined, reinvented and created marriages of flavors and textures that have influenced cooks around the world. He's hovered at the top for an incredibly long time.
Menus: 395–780F.
À la carte 900F.

◆ RESTAURANT CREATORS AND THE YOUNG "PATRON" CHEFS

◆ CREATORS ◆

Here we are up among the very best that Paris can offer. Some restaurants have been hovering at the top for while, maintaining an unrelenting and astonishing degree of excellence, but it could be argued they have little more to prove: perfection has been reached. Others, the ascending stars, spend their time striving to capture, tame and distil flavors that will send them soaring up among the gods. Within this last category two creators – in the true sense of the word – deserve a special mention: Alain Passard at the Arpège and the Conticini brothers at La Table d'Anvers.

ARPÈGE

84, rue de Varenne 75007
Tel: 01 45 51 47 33
Closed Sat. and Sun. lunch
The décor is extremely sober . . . all the better to enable you to concentrate on the unique quality of refined food. This is not the place for a casual tourist, but for people who really understand food, such as the sophisticated and often most influential Parisians – faithful devotees to the young Alain Passart – who fill the dining room twice a day. They come to taste his carpaccio of langoustines with caviar, and his astonishing lobster served with wafer-thin slivers of turnips and a sweet and sour vinaigrette with rosemary. House classics include the special Janzy chicken laid on a bed of hay and cooked in a sealed casserole, and the grilled kidneys with four spices, a triumph of harmony and flavors. Before you delve too enthusiastically into the tempting selection of cheeses, remember that Alain Passart is an outstanding pâtissier. A last detail about Monsieur Passart: he is one of the few Parisian chefs to be in his kitchen at every meal.
Menus: 390F lunch; 830F.
À la carte: 1,000F.

LA TABLE D'ANVERS

2, pl. d'Anvers 75009
Tel: 01 48 78 35 21
Closed Sat. lunch and Sun.
Tucked away in this neighborhood are two adventurous brothers, curious about every spice, flavor and taste-combination possible. Choosing a dish on the menu may seem like a high-risk lottery, but in reality there is never a loser. Even though Christian Conticini's imagination has no bounds and his dishes may sound bizarre, they are first and foremost seductive. Try the memorable roasted St-Pierre fish on a bed of cream of haddock, with a lasagne of artichokes and its soft boiled egg, or the simple-sounding grilled small red mullet, wonderfully fresh, with its lemon-parsley, olive oil and lavender sauce, served with softened, almost jam-like red peppers with a sumptuous milanese risotto put on the table in its copper saucepan. While this is being prepared, Philippe Conticini lets his talent run havoc with desserts, none of which you will regret. The wine list is, of course, very eclectic and reasonably priced. This is possibly the best-valued lunch menu in town.
Menus: 160F lunch; 190F dinner; 340F; 450F. À la carte 600F.

◆ THE YOUNG "PATRON" CHEFS ◆

This is the most exciting thing that has happened in the Parisian restaurant scene in the last ten years. A dozen or so young, brilliant and extremely hard-working cooks, bored with adding chunks of truffles – out of season – and lashings of caviar on everything, have thrown in their aprons, usually as the assistant chefs in Paris's top restaurants, to open up on their own. These young men have enough energy to get up at dawn a few times a week, go to the wholesale market at Rungis and then return to concoct titillating dishes. Even though most of these under-30's have migrated to the so far tourist-free, outer reaches of Paris, where rent is cheaper, they are turning out food that is drawing the crowds. The ambience is what Parisian bistros used to be in the 1950's: noisy, fun, with lots of inexpensive wine, and plenty of serious eating going on. Nearly all of these restaurants have a very reasonably priced menu (under 200F). In short, what you get is what long-suffering gourmets have been waiting for: the backlash against nouvelle cuisine. "Healthy" helpings of fine yet hearty food, in an informal setting and at unbeatable prices.

ANACRÉON

53, bd. St-Marcel 75013
Tel: 01 43 31 71 18
Closed Sun. and Mon
Opened not long ago, this modest-looking restaurant already serves to a full house. André Letty, ex-Tour d'Argent, had in another life 300 chefs working under him. Now they are just four in the kitchen and he obviously takes great pride in being able to create the copious, classic-inspired dishes his regular customers relish. House classics have already made their way onto the menu, such as the bonbonnière de langoustines à l'orange – scampi wrapped in tender spinach leaves, served with a delicate fish mousse – veal kidneys cooked in mustard, and a fruit of the season clafouti served with homemade ice-cream.
Menus: 110F lunch 175F dinner

LE BAMBOCHE

15, rue de Babylone 75007
Tel: 01 45 49 14 40
Closed Sat. and Sun
The soft orange and yellow décor sets the tone for this newly opened intimate bistro near the Bon Marché department store. Stuffed courgette flowers, and tournedos of fresh tuna served with a fine anchovy sauce, are some of the monthly

Lucas-Carton ◆ 497.

Le Grand Véfour ◆ 500.

inspirations of the young chef/owner David Van Laer, who trained in the kitchens of Apicius. The Bamboche was instantly adopted by a clique of chic young women from the left bank.
Menu 180f.
À la carte 230f.

LA BASTIDE ODÉON
7, rue Corneille 75006
Tel: 01 43 26 03 65
Closed Sun. and Mon.
It's not so long since Gilles Ajulos, ex-Rostang, opened his restaurant opposite the Odéon theater. He hasn't changed the décor since he took over; but that doesn't seem to bother his new fans, publishers and senators. What matters to them is the quality of the Mediterranean-influenced cooking: the rabbit stuffed with aubergines, with toast and olives and a balsamic sauce, the roast salmon with an adventurous but exquisite aïoli and candied lemons.
Menus only: 175f; 135f lunch.

LA DINÉE
85, rue Leblanc 75015
Tel: 01 45 54 20 49.
Closed Sat. and Sun. lunch.
Christophe Chabanel, still comfortably in his twenties, is already onto his second restaurant. With more space in his kitchen,

his cooking has taken on a new dimension: millefeuillle of aubergine served with oven-softened tomatoes and fresh herbs, guinea fowl and cabbage roasted in foie gras butter, and a cucumber soup with red fruit and honey served with tarragon ice-cream give some idea of this budding talent.
Menus: 160f lunch 280f dinner.
À la carte 350f.

L'OS À MOELLE
3, rue Vasco-de-Gama 75015
Tel: 01 45 57 27 27
Closed Sun. pm, Mon.
The menu is written on the blackboard in this charming old-fashioned bistro, as the young owner and chef, ex-Le Crillon, has such drive and imagination that the selection changes daily. Inspirations include a memorable fresh foie gras fried with ginger bread, a succulent duck, part of which is served roasted and the other part served "confit". There are a dozen afforable and enchanting wines and a wide selection of magnums for the large tables of friends that gather here.
Menus: 150f lunch; 180f evening.
À la carte 200–250f.

LA RÉGALADE
49 av. Jean Moulin 75014
Tel: 01 45 45 68 58
Closed Sat. lunch, Sun. and Mon, the

month of Aug. and at least two weeks during the year.
The leader of the new pack – the youthful Yves Camdeborde, ex-Le Crillon, a few years ago transformed this banal neighborhood bistro into a crowded restaurant where young, boisterous rugby players, Catherine Deneuve and post office employees all enjoy eating. His fabulous paté is put on the table in its terrine to tease your appetite. Everything on the menu is enticing, from the delicate slivers of vegetable fritters tossed in a basket, to the roast lamb rolled in young spinach leaves served with haricots beans from Tarbais, "the" place where quality beans are grown. Even the homemade condiments are delectable, from the shallot jam served with kidneys to the homemade apricot marmalade to be spooned out generously on the rich caramelized rice pudding. Bookings can run up to three weeks in advance, especially for the evening.
Single menu at 160f.

LA TIMBALE ST-BERNARD
16, rue des Fossés St-Bernard 75005
Tel: 01 46 34 28 28

Martial Enguehard and his enthusiastic team offer an incredibly good-value menu in this newish, bright yellow and blue bistro. Seasonal dishes include a confit de canard with rosemary rolled into a spring roll, a fricassée of prawns with red peppers, and a fresh fruits à la nage – a sort of fruit cocktail – with verbena.
Menus: 128f wine incl. served until 10pm; 158f.
À la carte 270f.

LA TIMONERIE
35, quai de la Tournelle 75005
Tel: 01 43 25 44 42
Closed Sun. and Mon. lunch
A stone's throw away from La Tour d'Argent is where Philippe de Givenchy, one of Paris's most inventive chefs, creates, and adjusts to perfection, his small menu. In this intimate, rustic yet trendy, wooden-paneled dining room, striking dishes are served. The four-course lunch menu is enticing and incredibly good value, with a remarkable tartelette of fresh goat's cheese and sliced potatoes served with a cream of chives sauce, and a roasted daurade fish with tarragon and chilis.
Menu: 225f lunch.
À la carte 450f.

◆ RESTAURANTS WITH SPECTACULAR VIEWS AND LISTED INTERIORS

Pharamond ◆ below.

Le Train Bleu ◆ 502.

◆ RESTAURANTS WITH SPECTACULAR VIEWS AND GREAT FOOD ◆

FAKHR EL DINE
Institut du Monde
Arabe
1, rue des Fossés-
St-Bernard 75005
Tel: 01 46 33 47 70
Closed Mon.
*A classic Lebanese
restaurant on the top
of the cultural center
for Arab countries.
A spectacular view
of Notre-Dame and
the Île-St-Louis. If
the weather is very
hot it is best to book
in the spacious 9th-
floor rooftop dining
room, but on warm
evenings book on
the terrace.*

Menu: 195F.
À la carte 300F.

LE JULES VERNE
Tour Eiffel
(2nd floor by private
elevator), 75007
Tel: 01 45 55 61 44
Open daily until
10pm.
*400ft above ground,
a breathtaking view
of Paris, and
equally
spectacular food
prepared by the
extremely talented
chef Alain Reix.
Unfortunately
bookings have to
be made well in
advance.*
Menus: 290–680F.
À la carte: 750–850F.

**LA TOUR
D'ARGENT**
15–17, quai de la
Tournelle 75005
Tel: 01 43 54 23 31
Closed Mon.
*This 6th-floor dining
room is often
described as one of
the wonders of the
world, overlooking
the Seine and Notre-
Dame. The English
head sommelier,
David Ridgway, has a
fabulous selection of
wines, some of which
are reasonably
priced.*
Menus: 350F.
À la carte: 1,000F.

◆ RESTAURANTS WITH FABULOUS LISTED INTERIORS AND GREAT FOOD ◆

LE GRAND VÉFOUR
17, rue du Beaujolais
75001
Tel: 01 42 96 56 27
Closed Sat. and
Sun. and Aug.
*This is probably the
most beautiful
restaurant in Paris.
The gilt Directoire
interior, comfortable
red plush banquettes,
obliging, friendly
service and lively
clientèle make this
the sort of place you
could quite happily
dine alone at –
there's so much going
on. The chef Guy
Martin, who came
from the Savoy, has
added a few regional
touches to the menu,
although his classic
sizeable côte de veau
aux cèpes remains a
favorite. Try the
unusual regional
cheeses as well as
the amusing desserts.*

Menus: 345–780F.
À la carte 700–900F.

LE LOUIS XIV
8, bd. St-Denis 75010
Tel: 01 42 08 56 56
Open daily until 1am
Closed Jul. and Aug.
*A wonderful kitsch
1950's décor,
patronized by actors.
The service is
charming and old-
fashioned. The
seafood platter and
quenelles de brochet
or pike dumplings
are a must.*
Menu 170F (wine
incl.).
À la carte 300–400F.

PHARAMOND
24, rue de la Grande-
Truanderie 75001
Tel: 01 42 33 06 72
Closed Sun. and
Mon. lunchtime.
*Miraculously, hardly
anything has
changed chez*

*Pharamond since it
was opened in 1833.
This exquisite Art
Nouveau treasure
box serves the same
delectable Normandy
dishes such as tripes
à la mode de Caen,
coquilles St-Jacques
and roast duckling
carved at the table.
A favorite haunt of
French politicians.*
Menu: 200–310F.
À la carte: 300–350F.

PRUNIER
16, av. Victor-Hugo
75016

Tel: 01 45 00 89 12
Closed Sun., Mon.
and Aug.
*The Japanese
recently saved this
famous Art Deco
fish restaurant,
which had been
closed down for
so long. Jean-
Claude Vrinat – he
of Taillevent fame –
has worked hard
on restoring its past
glory. There is a
good, reasonably
priced wine list.*
À la carte 300–600F.

FISH DELIGHTS, REGIONAL CUISINE ◆

LA CAGOUILLE
10, pl. Constantin-
Brancusi 75014
Tel: 01 43 22 09 01
Open daily, closed
over Christmas and
New Year.
*This restaurant has
retained its cachet,
and trendy Parisians
continue to crowd its
terrace.*
Menu: 150–250F.
À la carte 280–350F.

LE DIVELLEC
107, rue de
l'Université 75007
Tel: 01 45 51 91 96
Closed Sun, Mon.,
Christmas and
New Year.
*Now in his sixties,
Jacques Le Divellec
still prides himself on
having the finest,
most powerful fish
restaurant in Paris.
Powerful because
ministers and prime-
ministers – whose
offices are nearby –
traditionally treat it as
their canteen. They
come to taste the
marinated tuna with
its tartare, the
roasted turbot with a
lobster béarnaise
sauce and the
peppered pear desert
with ginger ice-
cream.*
Menus: 290–390F.
À la carte 550–800F.

LE DÔME
108, bd. du
Montparnasse 75014
Tel: 01 43 35 25 81
*Politicians and
intellectuals push
past the oyster*

counter and fill this
*noisy de luxe
brasserie, where the
impeccable firm
bright fish of the day
is paraded in front of
the diners. As if to
show off once more
its fabulous fresh
credentials, the fish is
often simply grilled
and served with virgin
olive oil and lemon.
A good selection of
wines.*
À la carte 400F.

**L'ÉCAILLE
DE PCB**
5, rue Mabillon 75006
Tel: 01 43 26 73 70
Closed Sat.
lunchtime and Sun.
*A pretty little bistro
that always serves
the freshest fish
prepared simply. The
rillettes de sardines,
marinated fresh fish
with herbs, and
coquilles St-Jacques
with a garlic and
cream sauce are
enough excuses to
keep the regular
customers coming
back.*
Menus: 125F lunch;
210F low calorie.
À la carte 350F.

LA MÉDITERRANÉE
2, pl. de l'Odéon
75006
Tel: 01 43 26 02 30
Open daily until 11pm.
Closed May 1.
*Situated opposite the
Théâtre de l'Europe.
Specialties of the
house include:
carpaccio with
artichokes and*

sardines marinated
in herbs.
Menu: 150–180F.
À la carte: 250–300F.

GOUMARD-PRUNIER
9, rue Duphot 75001
Tel: 01 42 60 36 07
Closed Sundays in
the summer and
Mon.
*This is currently the
high temple of fish
restaurants. The fish
is only bought from
the best small fishing
boats – whether they
be on the Catalonian
coast for the squid or
Brittany for the
lobsters – and is
transformed with
talent and finesse,
always with an eye to
keeping that ocean
flavor on the plate.
The lobster delicately
spiced with cayenne
is cooked to
perfection, and the
large turbot with a
classic hollandaise
sauce is spectacular.
The wine list is
marvelous, the
desserts truly
exceptional and
the service friendly.
Even the listed toilets
are great.*
À la carte 800F.

LE PETIT NAVIRE
14, rue des Fossés-
St-Bernard 75005
Tel: 01 43 54 22 52
Closed Sun. and
Mon, 1 week in Feb.
and 2 weeks in Aug.
*There is a charming
old-fashioned air to
this calm, friendly
restaurant. The*

patron goes himself
to the Rungis market
to choose his fish,
and his sound cuisine
is regularly enjoyed
by a couple of ex-
Presidents. Tables on
the sidewalk, in the
evenings only.
Menu: 150F.
À la carte 250F.

SERGE GRANGER
36, pl. du Marché-
St-Honoré 75001
Tel: 01 42 60 03 00
Closed Sat.
lunchtime Sun. and
public holidays.
*The fish couldn't be
more fresh, and is
enhanced by
M. Granger's
Normandy-rich
traditional sauces.
This is also the kind
of place where the
millefeuilles are real
and not the sort of
wafer-thin variety
interspersed with
raspberries.*
Menu 170F.
À la carte 350–400F.

**AMBASSADE
D'AUVERGNE**
22, rue du Grenier-
St-Lazare 75003
Tel: 01 42 72 31 22
Open daily.
Closed 15 days in
the summer.
*The Auvergne cuisine
at its best, with the
cheeses, jambon du
pays and andouillette
sent directly from
small producers.
Simmering*

casseroles of lentils,
boudin sausages with
chestnuts and the
aligot – a delicious
creamy, elastic purée
of potatoes with fresh
Tomme cheese.
Light, inexpensive
regional wines.
À la carte 250–300F.

AU BASCOU
38, rue Réaumur
75003
Tel: 01 42 72 69 25

Jean-Guy Loustau
runs the friendliest
Basque restaurant in
town. It's about
generous portions of
interestingly spiced
food and lots of local
wine. Each dish is
prepared with the
most authentic
products: the hand-
sliced jambon cru
comes from the last
remaining Basque
farmer to rear an old

breed of free-
range pigs, fed on
chestnuts; the cod
fish is salted on the
small fishing boats
if you please, and
not on shore.
À la carte 180F.

AU TROU GASCON
40, rue Taine 75012
Tel: 01 43 44 36 26
Closed Sat., Sun,
Aug. and end Dec.
This charming 1900

bistro is the place to go for Gascony food. Confit de canard, cassoulet, without doubt the best in Paris, new potatoes with foie gras and truffles. Well-researched list of regional wines and armagnacs.
Menus: 180F lunch; 380F.
À la carte 400F.

CHARTIER
7, rue du Faubourg-Montmartre 75009
Tel: 01 47 70 86 29
Open daily until 10pm
Superb Belle-Époque canteen serving cheap dishes in a chaos that has delighted students for generations.
Menu: 80–85F.
À la carte: 80–90F.

DOMINIQUE
19, rue Bréa 75006
Tel: 01 43 27 08 80
Open until 11.30pm
Closed Sun., Mon. lunch and from Jul. 15 to Aug. 15
Combined bar, grocery store and restaurant. One of

the centers of Russian Paris, with a collection of a nostalgic prints of Russia on the walls. Wide range of vodkas. Specialties: blinis, bortsch, beef Stroganoff.
Menu 98–160F.
À la carte 200–250F.

LA CLOSERIE DES LILAS
171, bd. du Montparnasse 75006
Tel: 01 40 51 34 50
Open daily until 11.30pm.
A historic restaurant with a literary background. Many famous writers once patronized this restaurant, including Apollinaire, Hemingway and Jarry. Reservations essential.
À la carte: 450–500F.

GRAIN D'ORGE
15, rue de l'Arc-de-Triomphe 75017
Tel: 01 47 54 00 28
Closed Sat. and Sun.
Flemish cooking and unusual beers, and plenty of them, are what draw people

into this successful 1930's restaurant. Everything revolves around beer, from the creamy soup with asparagus tips and beer, to the warm duck's liver with kriek beer. The lightly smoked eel in aspic goes very well with beer, as do most dishes on the menu. For those who are not nordic fans, try the fabulous grilled veal kidneys with artichokes.
Menus: 130F and 160F lunch; 185F dinner; 250F.
À la carte: 250–300F.

JO GOLDENBERG
7, rue des Rosiers 75004 (2 G7)
Tel: 01 48 87 20 16
Open until midnight.
Closed at Kippur.
The temple of Ashkenazi cuisine in the heart of the Marais district. Don't let the noise, the crowd or the elbow-to-elbow seating bother you. Book! Specialties: bortsch, chopped liver with onions, stuffed carp,

boiled chicken.
À la carte 120–140F.

LESCURE
7, rue de Mondovi 75001
Tel: 01 42 60 18 91
Open daily until 10.15pm
At lunchtime, people crowd into the dining room or onto the terrace to enjoy home cooking at reasonable prices.
Menu: 100F.
À la carte: 100–170F.

LE TRAIN BLEU
Gare de Lyon, 20, bd. Diderot 75012
Tel: 01 43 43 09 06
This unique station buffet is a landmarked building. Unusual décor, with frescos depicting the destinations of trains departing from the Gare de Lyon. Good traditional food, by talented new chef Marc Maublanc, is assiduously served. Reserve in advance. Specialty: brill soufflé with mushrooms.
Menus: 250F.
À la carte: 300F.

◆ **BISTROS** ◆

ALLARD
41, rue St-André-des-Arts 75006
Tel: 01 43 26 48 23
Closed Sun.
It was great news when one of Paris' institutions, which had fallen on hard times, was bought by the Layrac brothers (who used to own Le Petit Zinc). They have left the wonderful somber décor alone, as well as Fernande Allard's classic recipe for canard aux olives. What they are doing is bringing the prices down a bit and putting more enthusiasm into the kitchen.
Menus: 150F; 200F.
À la carte 350F–500F.

ASTIER
44, rue Jean-Pierre-Timbaud 75011
Tel: 01 43 57 16 35
Closed Sat. and Sun Aug. and 2 weeks in spring.
Excellent food in this genuine bistro near La République. The

tables are close to each other, but that's part of the fun, when the cheese platter is passed from one table to the next. Remarkable wine list.
Single menu: 130F.

L'ASSIETTE
181, rue du Château 75014
Tel: 01 43 22 64 86
Closed Mon., Tue. and Aug.
President Mitterrand used to frequent Lulu's transformed charcuterie, now a haunt for left-bank intellectuals and diplomats. The tarama and caviar served with Lulu's blinis is truly exceptional. So too is her tête

de veau, one of Paris' finest. She also produces the best ice cream au caramel fondant.
Menu 200F lunch.
À la carte 500–600F.

AUX CHARPENTIERS
10, rue Mabillon 75006
Tel: 01 43 26 30 05
Closed Sun. and public holidays
One of the few reasonably priced authentic bistros just off St-Germain-des-Prés. The Dne Pichard Madiran (110F) is one of the better wines on the list.
Menus: 100F lunch; 150F dinner (wine included).
À la carte: 250F.

BENOÎT
20, rue St-Martin
75004
Tel: 01 42 72 25 76
Open daily.
Closed Aug.
One of the very last traditional Parisian bistros. The ambience, food and wine are so pleasant that Parisians don't seem to mind the steep prices, or the fact that credit cards are not accepted. House classics include cassoulet and bœuf à la mode à l'ancienne, and the "reha".
À la carte 500–600F.

Flo ◆ 504.

CASA OLYMPE
48, rue St-Georges
75009
Tel: 01 42 85 26 01
Closed Sat. and Sun.
This small minimally decorated bistro became an overnight success when it was opened. The sophisticated clientèle is intent on discovering Olympe's latest culinary exploits. Try the fabulous thick chestnut pancake served with a poached egg – a triumph of textures – and the veal cutlet with crushed hot peppers and lemons served in the black dish it is cooked in. The wine selection is disappointing.
À la carte 170F.

CHARDENOUX
1, rue Jules-Vallès
75011
Tel: 01 43 71 49 52
Closed Sat. and Sun. and Aug.
Bernard Passavant, owner of this fabulous old bistro, has a clique of smart young gourmets that come to sample his excellent wines, his unctuous ox's cheek à la provençale and his homemade pâtisseries.
À la carte 250F.

CHEZ HENRI – AU MOULIN À VENT
20, rue des Fossés-St-Bernard 75005
Tel: 01 43 54 99 37
Closed Sun., Mon., and Aug. Booking possible until 10pm
Traditional, authentic bistro (favorite of French actor Jean Gabin). Copious seasonal fare. Rognons de veau, fricassée de cèpes, chateaubriand, perdreaux rôtis, pavé à l'échalote ou au poivre. Delicious prunes in Armagnac, or prune ice cream. Excellent wine list, which includes Pouilly and Sancerre.
À la carte: 300–500F.

PÉTRISSANS
30 bis, av. Niel
75017
Tel: 01 42 27 52 03
Closed Sat., Sun.
The 1900 décor goes well with the serious wine-drinking that takes place here. In fact the choice of wine is so good that this bistro is often described as a wine bar. Appetizing home-style cooking: fricassée of chicken with tarragon, and roast saddle of pork with honey.
Menu 155F.
À la carte 250F.

◆ **BRASSERIES** ◆

These large, lively, noisy, fun places, usually open late, serve plenty of beer at all hours of the day, and an honest meal at honorable prices. Classic dishes might include a seafood platter with oysters and crab and Alsace-inspired choucroute. Best to book in advance.

LE BALLON DES TERNES
103 av. des Ternes
75017
Tel: 01 45 74 17 98
Open until 12.30am.
Closed Aug. 1–20.
The much improved fare, at this attractive brasserie near the Hôtel Méridien, includes fabulous oysters, quality steaks and pleasant wines. There is a terrace.

BOFINGER
5–7, rue de la Bastille
75004
Tel: 01 42 72 87 82
Open daily until 1am.
Superb 1900 décor.
Menu: 169F.
À la carte: 180–200F.

BRASSERIE DE L'ÎLE ST-LOUIS
55, quai de Bourbon
75004
Tel: 01 43 54 02 59
Open until 1.30am.
Closed Wed. and Thurs. lunch.
One of the smaller brasseries, family-run. Lots of charm. Terrace.
No credit cards.
À la carte: 180F.

CHEZ JENNY
39, bd. du Temple
75003
Tel: 01 42 74 75 75
Open daily until 1am
Closed mid-July to mid-Aug.
This is the only other place owned by the Café Flore. The professionalism is as good as it gets, and the tone just right for a brasserie. Traditional Alsace choucroute, fabulous roasted suckling pig. Perfect for a winter evening.

Single dish of the day: 58F. Menus: 99F; 166F (wine incl.).
À la carte 200F.

LA COUPOLE
102, bd. du Montparnasse 75014
Tel: 01 43 20 14 20
Open until 2am.
Closed Christmas Eve pm.
Come here for a drink and a look at the famous 1920's décor.

Some say that since La Coupole was bought up and restored, some of its soul has gone.
À la carte: 200–350F.

FLO
7, cour des Petites-Écuries 75010
Tel: 01 47 70 13 59
Open daily until 1.30am.
This was the first brasserie bought by the Bucher group. It remains the most authentic. Others in the group, all with fabulous original interiors, include Julien, La Coupole, Terminus Nord and the Vaudeville.

JULIEN
16, rue du Faubourg-St-Denis 75010
Tel: 01 47 70 12 06
Open daily until 1.30am.
Turn-of-the-century dining hall, Art Deco interiors, late-night clientele.
Menus: 109F lunch and after 11pm 185F.
À la carte 200–350F.

LIPP
151, bd. St-Germain 75006
Tel: 01 45 48 53 91
Open daily until 2am

This turn-of-the-century-style brasserie still retains its former attraction. Cuisine is variable. A popular meeting-place for celebrities.

LA ROTONDE
105, bd. du Montparnasse 75006
Tel: 01 43 26 68 34
Open daily until 1am.
Following the recruitment of a talented new female chef (ex-Arpège), the food became extremely good. Décor rather uninteresting.
À la carte 200F.

TERMINUS DU NORD
23, rue de Dunkerque 75010
Tel: 01 42 85 05 15
Open daily 6.30am–12.30am.
Large bar, 1930's décor.
Menus: 109F lunch and after 11pm 189F.
À la carte: 200–300F.

VAUDEVILLE
29, rue Vivienne 75002
Tel: 01 40 20 04 62
Open daily until 2am.
1930's décor. Terrace. Quality oysters and always a tasty dish of the day.

◆ RESTAURANTS WITH GARDENS OR QUIET TERRACES

LE CHALET DES ÎLES
Bois de Boulogne 75016
Tel: 01 42 88 04 69
Open until 9.45pm
Closed Jan. and Feb.
Access by small boat
Menu: 220F.
À la carte: 350F.

LA GRANDE CASCADE
Allée de Longchamp
Bois de Boulogne 75016
Tel: 01 45 27 33 51
Open daily. Closed Dec. 20– Jan. 20
Menu: 285F lunch weekdays; 550F.
À la carte: 600–800F.

LE PALAIS ROYAL
(in the gardens of the Palais Royal)
110, galerie de Valois 75001
Tel: 01 40 20 00 27
Open until 10pm.
Closed Sat. and Sun. pm.
À la carte: 250F.

LE PAVILLON MONTSOURIS
(Parc Montsouris)
20, rue Gazan 75014
Tel: 01 45 88 38 52
Open until 10.30pm.
À la carte 198F.

LA PETITE COUR
8, rue Mabillon 75006
Tel: 01 43 26 52 26
Open daily.

Menus: 165F lunch; 185F dinner.
À la carte: 300–350F.

LA PLAGE
Port de Javel Haut 75015
Tel: 01 40 59 41 00
Open daily.
Accessible by boat.
À la carte 200F.

LE PRÉ CATELAN
Route de Suresnes
Bois de Boulogne 75016
Tel: 01 45 24 55 58
Closed Sun. pm, Mon. and 2 weeks in Feb.
Menus: 270F lunch; 400F; 690F.
À la carte: 800F.

. . . AND NEARER LA DÉFENSE

LA GUINGUETTE DE NEUILLY
12, bd. Georges Seurat Île de la Jatte
Tel: 01 46 24 25 04
Open daily.
À la carte: 250F.

LE PETIT POUCET
4, rond-point Claude Monet
Île de Levallois Perret
Tel: 01 47 38 61 85
Open daily.
Menu: 110F lunch, 180F dinner.
À la carte: 220F.

◆ WHERE TO EAT ON SUNDAYS ◆

2ND ARRONDISSEMENT
Vaudeville

3RD ARRONDISSEMENT
Ambassade d'Auvergne; Chez Jenny

4TH ARRONDISSEMENT
Benoît; Bofinger; Brasserie de l'Île St-Louis

5TH ARRONDISSEMENT
Fakhr el Dine; La Tour d'Argent

6TH ARRONDISSEMENT
Les Beaux-Arts; La Petite Cour; La Rotonde

7TH ARRONDISSEMENT
Arpège; Jules Verne

8TH ARRONDISSEMENT
Les Ambassadeurs

10TH ARRONDISSEMENT
Flo; Julien; Terminus du Nord

14TH ARRONDISSEMENT
L'Assiette; La Cagouille; La Coupole; Le Dôme

15TH ARRONDISSEMENT
La Plage

17TH ARRONDISSEMENT
Le Ballon des Ternes

OUTSKIRTS OF PARIS
La Guinguette de Neuilly (Neuilly)
Perret Le Petit Poucet (Levallois)

◆ **DECENT MEALS FOR UNDER 150F** ◆
(SEE ALSO "CAFÉS" AND "WINE BARS")

LES BEAUX-ARTS
11, rue Bonaparte
75006
Tel: 01 43 26 94 64
Open daily.
*Excellent
atmosphere, with art
students and their
professors from
across the road.
Leeks with
vinaigrette,
pot-au-feu, confit de
canard, fondue
bourguignonne.
Thin wine list.*
Menu: 72F.
À la carte: 130–150F.

L'ÉMILE
74, rue Jean-Jacques
Rousseau 75001
Tel: 01 42 36 58 58
Closed Sat. lunch,
Sun, one week Jan.,
Aug.
*Trendies come here
to flee trendies.
Shrimps with ginger,
pot-au-feu, veal in
honey and lemon.*
Menus: 82F lunch;
148F.
À la carte 230F

FAKHR EL DINE
9th Floor, Institut du
Monde Arabe 75005
Rue des Fossés-
St-Bernard
Tel: 01 46 33 47 70
Open lunch only.
Closed Mon.
*Self-service
Lebanese food.
Tables on the rooftop
with the same view of
Notre-Dame as at
La Tour d'Argent.*
Menu 79F, 100F with
wine.

LE TEMPS DES CERISES
31, rue de la Cerisaie
75004
Tel: 01 42 72 08 63
Open lunchtime only.
Closed Sat., Sun.
and Aug.

*Friendly and
crowded: terrine,
bœuf bourguignon,
œuf en neige.*
Menu: 62F

**LA TIMBALE
ST-BERNARD**
16, rue des Fossés
St-Bernard 75005
Tel: 01 46 34 28 28
*A newish bistro
opened by one of the
capital's budding
chefs (see also
"Young chefs").*
Menus 128F until
10pm; 158F.
*À la carte menu:
270F.*

◆ **VEGETARIAN** ◆
RESTAURANTS

ENTRE CIEL ET TERRE
5, rue Hérold
75001 (2 B4)
Tel: 01 45 08 49 84
Open Mon.–Fri.
12.00–3pm and
7.30–10pm.
*This restaurant is
indicated by a sign
near the Place des
Victoires. Robust
flavors for savory
dishes (carrot tart
with mint, 55F) and
"celestial sweets"
(such as pear and
chocolate délice,
30F).*

GUENMAÏ
2 bis, rue de
l'Abbaye
75006 (2 A8)
Tel: 01 43 26 03 24
Open Mon.–Sat.
11.45am–3.30pm,
shop 9am–8.30pm.
*Platter 60F, sweets
30F. Vegetarian
lexicon at the back
of the menu card.*

LA TRUFFE
31, rue du Temple
75004 (2 F7)
Tel: 01 42 71 08 39
Open daily
12–4pm, 7–11pm.
*Located in a
protected building
in the Marais, this
restaurant offers
platters (50–80F),
gratins and tarts.*

À LA COURTILLE
1, rue des Envierges
75020
Tel: 01 46 36 51 59
Open daily.
*Currently the most
appealing of wine
bars, far-flung and
perched high on a
hill. The view is
breathtaking, the food
delightful, the wines
delicious and the
clientele switched on
yet relaxed. Book,
especially for a table
on the terrace.*

**BISTROT-CAVE
DES ENVIERGES**
11, rue des
Envierges 75020
Tel: 01 46 36 47 84
Open till midnight.
Closed Mon., Tue.
*A few doors up from
La Courtille and run
by the same team.
The faithful Nadine
cooks copious
Provençal dishes,and
the reasonably priced
wines are a delight.*

◆ **WINE BARS** ◆

LE CLOWN BAR
114, rue Amelot
75011
Tel: 01 43 55 87 35
Closed Sat. lunch,
Sun.
*The circus-linked
décor is listed. The
bar is always
crowded, serving a
wide selection of
reasonably priced
wines, good
sandwiches, and an
honest plat du jour.*

JUVENILE'S
47, rue de Richelieu
75001
Tel: 01 42 97 46 49
Closed Sat. am, Sun.
Mon. am.
*This off-shoot of
Willi's, just round the
corner, does draw a
younger crowd, but
also directors of
banks and
researchers at the
National Library, all
enjoying Tim
Johnston's jovial
and provocative
atmosphere and
wines. Wine can also
be bought to take
away.*

I GOLOSI
6, rue de la Grange-
Batelière 75009
Tel: 01 48 24 18 63
Closed Sat. pm and
Sun.
*A mad young Italian
couple run this
Milanese-style wine
bar and restaurant in
a charming old
passage – mad
because the
engaging Marco
thinks nothing of
hopping in his van
and dashing down to
Italy to pick up the
20 different types of
extra-virgin olive oil
he can't possibly
survive without in his
kitchen, or the quality
Parmesan and
Parma hams he can't
find in France. Lovely
range of Italian
wines, delicious
grilled vegetables
(served with olive oil)
at the bar and
fabulous original
risottos on the third
floor.*

**LE MOULIN
À VINS**
6, rue Burcq 75018
Tel: 01 42 52 81 27
Open Wed., Thu.,
Sat. 11am–3pm,
Mon., Fri., Sat.
6pm–2am.
*A lively young
Montmartre*

Le Moulin à Vins.

The Frog and Rosbif.

atmosphere, good pâtés and cheese, and lots of happy drinking.

LE PASSAGE
18, passage de la Bonne-Graine 75011
Tel: 01 47 00 73 30
Closed Sat. lunch, Sun.
A barely converted old neighborhood café, with a selection of 250 tantalizing wines, serving 8 of

France's best andouillettes and other delights. The annex, Le Café du Passage (12, rue de Charonne 75011, tel: 49 29 97 64) is the owners' second attempt to have a civilized drinking place, rather than an eating place, a concept that the French find strangely hard to grasp.
Open late.

LE VIN DES RUES
21, rue Boulard 75014. Tel: 01 43 22 19 78. Closed Sun, Mon. 1 week in Feb. and Aug.
A somewhat scruffy appearance, but a great old-fashioned Parisian ambience, with lots of lovely wine and delicious morsels.

WILLI'S
13, rue des Petits-

Champs 75001
Tel: 01 42 61 05 09
Closed Sun.
This is the most civilized of wine bars, close to the Pl. des Victoires and Louvre. Sit at the wooden bar or reserve a table. Mark Williamson has a staggering collection of Northern Rhône wines, food that the French enjoy, and amusing English staff.

◆ BEER BARS ◆

THE FROG AND ROSBIF
116, rue St-Denis 75002 (2 D4)
Tel: 01 42 36 34 73
Open daily noon–2am
The French idea of a London pub. Darts, English newspapers and unchilled draft beer, brewed on site.

LE SOUS-BOCK
49, rue Saint-Honoré 75001 (2 C5)
Tel: 01 40 26 46 61
Open daily 11am–5.30am (Sun. 3–5am).
Thirteen beers on tap, plus a list of 400 bottled beers. Same

range on sale in the shop next door (open noon–8pm).

LA TAVERNE DE NESLES
32, rue Dauphine 75006
Tel: 01 43 26 38 36
Open daily 7pm–5am.

Gilles Lamiot seeks out artesinal beers such as Speltor, a curious Alsatian beer made from wild wheat. He has even had the only French beer made from buckwheat brewed for him.

◆ CAFÉS ◆

Paris cafés have plenty of atmosphere and are the perfect meeting place for a coffee or a light snack.

CAFÉ ANTOINE
17, rue de la Fontaine 75016
Tel: 01 46 47 86 31
Open 7am–7pm.
Closed Sun.
A café, run by the faithful Madame Marcelle, tucked away behind a frontage by Hector Guimard.

AU RÊVE
89, rue Caulaincourt 75018
Tel: 01 46 06 20 87
Open noon–1am.
Closed Sun., Mon.

and Aug.
In this friendly atmosphere, locals meet over a refreshing glass of Marionnet's Gamay de Touraine.

AUX SPORTIFS RÉUNIS "CHEZ WALCZACK"
75, rue Brancion 75015
Tel: 01 48 28 61 00
Open 11am–10pm
Closed Mon. and Aug.
A classic. Maman concocts with loving care tasty lunch dishes.

CAFÉ BEAUBOURG
100, rue St-Martin 75004
Tel: 01 48 87 63 96
Open daily 8am–1am.

The only chic café near the Pompidou Center.

LE BISTROT DU PEINTRE
116, av. Ledru-Rollin 75011
Tel: 47 00 34 39
Open daily.
Unpretentious dishes, and a terrace.

LE COMMERCE
8, rue des Martyrs 75009
Tel: 01 48 78 36 08
Open daily 6.30am–midnight.
Really comes alive on Sunday mornings, market day on the Rue des Martyrs.

CAFÉ DE FLORE
172, bd. St-Germain

75006
Tel: 45 48 55 26
Open daily 7am–2am.
The ideal café, the best France has to offer.

CAFÉ MARLY
93, rue de Rivoli Cours Napoléon du Grand Louvre 75001
Tel: 01 49 26 06 60
Open daily 9am–2am.
The trendiest café in Paris, under the arcades, overlooking the Pyramide of the Louvre. Strangely enough it has almost a Florentine feeling to it.

LE MOUFFETARD
116, rue Mouffetard 75005
Tel: 01 43 31 42 50

Angélina.

Café Beaubourg.

Open 7.30am–9pm,
Sun. until 3.30pm.
*A real rarity: the
patron makes his
own croissants and
cakes, and smokes
his own salmon.*

LE NEMOURS
2, galerie de
Nemours, Place
Colette 75001
Tel: 01 42 61 34 14
Open daily 8am–1am,
Sun. until 9pm.
*Just off the gardens
of the Palais Royal.
Sun yourself on the
terrace in the
afternoon.*

**LE PETIT CHÂTEAU
D'EAU**
67, rue du Château

d'Eau 75010
Tel: 47 70 11 00
Open 8am–9pm.
Closed Sun.
*An authentic
neighborhood café.*

**LE PETIT FER À
CHEVAL**
30, rue Vieille-du-
Temple 75004
Tel: 01 42 74 47 47
Open daily
9am–2am, Sat. and
Sun. 11am–2am.
*Ideal for a quick
lunch.*

LE CAFÉ DE LA PLACE
23, rue d'Odessa
75014
Tel: 01 42 18 01 55
Open daily
8am–2am,

Sun. 10am–9pm.
*Young and lively, with
a pleasant, large
terrace. Cheaper
than its neighbors
on the bd. du
Montparnasse.*

LE ST-GERVAIS
96, rue Vieille du
Temple 75003
Tel: 01 42 72 33 54
Open 8am–8pm.
Closed Sun.
*A quiet, well-run
neighborhood café,
looking onto a garden
right behind the
Picasso Museum.*

**TABAC DE LA
MADELEINE**
8, rue Godot de
Mauroy 75008

Tel: 01 47 42 60 67
Open 7am–8pm.
*A classic 1950's
small café-tabac.*

LE VIDE-GOUSSET
1, rue Vide-Gousset
75002
Tel: 01 42 60 02 78
Open 9am–7pm.
Closed Sat. and
Sun.
*Lots of charm,
tucked away behind
the Places des
Victoires.*

◆ **SALONS DE THÉ AND COFFEE HOUSES** ◆

À PRIORI THÉ
35–37, galerie
Vivienne 75002
Tel: 01 42 97 48 75
Open daily for lunch.
Closes 6.30pm.
*Regulars, including
Jean-Paul Gaultier,
book on the terrace
of this bewitching
passageway and
watch the most
modish Parisians
drift by.*

ANGÉLINA
226, rue de Rivoli
75001
Tel: 01 42 60 82 00
Open daily
9am–7pm.
*Elegant youthful-
looking old ladies and
mature-looking
younger ladies come
to one of Proust's
favorite haunts, to sip
hot chocolate and
luxuriate in the
pâtisseries.*

L'ÉBOUILLANTÉ
6, rue des Barres
75004
Tel: 01 42 71 09 69
Open 12am–9pm
Closed Mon.
*In summer, a haven
of peace. Eat outside
on a car-free wide
cobblestone passage
leading to the Île-St-
Louis.*

LADURÉE
75, av. des Champs-
Élysées 75008
Tel: 01 40 75 80 75
Open 8am–1am.
*Ladurée has created
an arrestingly
graceful environment,
amid the hubbub of
the Champs-Élysées.
You can still get their
supreme macaroons.*

LAPEYRONIE
3, rue Brantôme
Quartier de l'Horloge
Beaubourg 75003

Tel: 01 40 27 97 57
Closed Sun., Aug.
and public hols. Open
10am–7pm.
*The best in Paris.
Bruno Saguez does
two roasts for his
fabulous Mexican
maragogype, a
lighter roast for
heretics who have
milk with coffee, and
a darker roast for
true fanatics. Coffee-
and tea-tasting (no
food) on the
premises. Some sixty
varieties of tea.
(See "Tea and
coffee" ▲ 530.)*

MARIAGE FRÈRES
30, rue du Bourg-
Tibourg 75004
Tel: 01 42 74 65 32
Also at 13, rue des
Grands-Augustins
75006
Tel: 01 40 51 82 50
Open daily 10.30am

to 7.30pm.
Salon de Thé open
noon–7.30pm.
*English tea
connoisseurs,
exasperated by the
poor quality of
leaves available in
Britain, come here to
buy single-garden
teas. All 500 teas can
be tasted in the
adjoining salon de
thés. (See "Tea and
coffee" ▲ 530.)*

VERLET
256, rue St-Honoré
75001
Tel: 01 42 60 67 39
Closed Sun, Mon.
and Aug. 9am–7pm
*Haunting aromas of
expensive coffees
and spices in this
authentic 1880's
shop. Coffee can be
tasted with delectable
pastries. (See "Tea
and coffee" ▲ 530.)*

◆ ENTERTAINMENT: THEATER, DANCE, MOVIES, CONCERTS, CLUBS, LATE-NIGHT BARS AND BISTROS (LISTED BY ARRONDISSEMENT)

Further information is given on the pages indicated in bold type

Paris has entertainment to suit every pocket. Inexpensive and free entertainments include street performances and concerts. Visitors who take the time to stroll around the city and satisfy their curiosity – by day and night – will find it is time well spent. All that is needed are a few useful addresses. Below are just a few ideas for those with a limited entertainment budget.

FREE CONCERTS

CAFÉS

The *Life, live in the bar* association organizes concerts in cafés. Phone for program on 01 43 72 27 28.

MAISON DE LA RADIO

Recording sessions are open to the public. Apply to the box office one hour before the performance.
116, av. du Président-Kennedy 75116 (7 M2)
Tel: 01 42 30 15 16

CONSERVATOIRE NATIONAL DE MUSIQUE

Free performances by students of the Conservatoire: ballets and concerts.
Cité de la Musique, 209 av. Jean-Jaurès 75019
Tel: 01 40 40 45 45

L'ÉCOLE NORMALE DE MUSIQUE

End-of-year exams are open to the public and offer any number of free recitals. Lunchtime concerts – *Concerts de midi et demi* – are also held throughout the year on Tues. and Thurs.
Tel: 01 47 63 80 16

CHURCHES

◆ Notre-Dame: organ recitals, Sun. 5.30pm.
◆ St-Sulpice: grand organ and recital, Sun. 10.30am.
◆ Other churches
Tel: 01 49 52 53 54

MUSEUMS

◆ Musée de l'Homme: concerts of traditional music, on certain Suns. at 3pm (included in the entrance fee).
Tel: 01 44 05 72 72

REDUCTIONS

SPECIAL OFFERS

◆ Two kiosk-theaters sell half-price tickets valid for the same day (open Jul.–Aug. Mon.–Sat. 12.30–2.30pm, 4–7.45pm, closed Sun, rest of year Mon.–Sat. 12.30–7.45pm, Sun. 12.30–3.30pm):
KIOSQUE DE LA MADELEINE (1 H2) – no credit cards.
KIOSQUE DE MONTPARNASSE (6 G2) – ticket reductions of between 10 and 50 percent.
◆ Spectateurs Service
252, rue du Fg-St-Honoré 75008 (9 C9)
Tel: 01 53 53 58 58
Members (yearly membership 250F) are entitled to up to 40 percent reduction on theater tickets.

THEATER REDUCTIONS

◆ La Comédie-Française offers reductions for groups and special rates for individual theater-goers. Reductions are available for young people (under 25) and students (under 27), who can also turn up 45 minutes before the performance for standby tickets at 60F.
Tel: 01 44 15 00 15 (11am–6pm).
◆ Most theaters offer reductions for young people, seniors, the unemployed, etc.

DANCE REDUCTIONS

◆ Le Théâtre Contemporain de la Danse offers tickets at competitive prices for a varied and cosmopolitan program of performances by youthful companies.
Tel: 01 42 74 44 22
◆ Le Regard des Cygnes
210, rue de Belleville 75020 (11 E10)
Tel: 01 43 58 55 93
Annual subscription of 50F buys reductions of 33 percent for all performances by contemporary dance companies.
◆ The Opéra Bastille: 60F tickets are available from the box office two weeks before dance performances.

CONCERT REDUCTIONS

◆ The Opéra de Paris offers special standby rates to the under-25's, students, seniors (over 65) and the unemployed – subject to availability – 15 minutes before the performance.

MOVIE REDUCTIONS

◆ Weekly tariffs available for the first house or at 6pm, and for under-12's.
◆ Loyalty cards: four cinema chains offer discount cards. The UGC Privilege Card costs 135F or 195F for 4 or 6 admissions. The Gaumont Card costs 170F for 5 admissions. There are various preferential rates in the Pathé chain. MK2 is an independent network with nine houses in Paris, offering a 5-admission card for 169F.

SPECIAL EVENTS

THE MAIRIE DE PARIS INVITES YOU TO . . .

◆ . . . the theater. For 3 days in April, May or June, evenings at the theatre are half-price if two people go together. Last year, 46,000 people took up this offer.
◆ . . . the movies. The *18 heures 18 francs* initiative, held for one week in February, enables Paris movie-goers to see the latest films for 18F, provided the film is shown between 5 and 7pm. In 1998 some 290,000 of these tickets were issued.
◆ . . . a concert. Two tickets for the price of one. The offer is valid for a two-week period in January and applies to all concert halls except those presenting French variety shows. In 1998 some 70,000 people took this up.

"AOUT AU CINÉ"

In August, under 25's can obtain a free card to go to the movies for 25F. More than 110,000 such admissions were taken up in 1997.

"FÊTE DU CINÉMA"

The last weekend in June, one person pays the full price and the rest of the group pay only 10F. Applies all over France.

STREET PERFORMANCES

From first light, troubadours, fakirs, fire-eaters, portrait artists, caricaturists, singers, musicians and mime artists are to be found in the main tourist centers of Paris: the square in front of Beaubourg, around the Fontaine des Innocents, in front of Notre-Dame and at the exit of the St-Germain métro station.

FESTIVA

Auditorium of the Théâtre des Variétés.

Compagnie Castafiore, Festival d'Automne.

No other city in the world has as many theaters as Paris – 348 in the city and its suburbs – or produces as many new or classic plays: 1,194 during the 1997–8 season alone. Talented producers from all over the world want to work in the international theater capital with its wide, varied and often unusual range of repertoires and styles. From the Comédie-Française to the Cartoucherie de Vincennes and the private "Boulevard" theaters to the heavily subsidized avant-garde companies, Paris theater-goers have an insatiable appetite.

POPULAR THEATER

THÉÂTRE DES VARIÉTÉS

7, bd. Montmartre 75002 (2 C2)
Res: 01 42 33 09 92
Opened in 1808, the theater soon established a reputation for light entertainment. A number of comedies by Labiche and operettas by Offenbach were presented from 1840–70. In the 1970's La Cage aux Folles completed an unforgettable 2,200 performances.

THÉÂTRE DU PALAIS-ROYAL

38, rue Montpensier 75001 (2 A4)
Res: 01 42 97 59 81
The Théâtre du Palais-Royal has had a checkered career since it was built in 1784. Originally a puppet theater, it later became a revolutionary theater, a high-wire theater and a café-concert. At the turn of the century, Georges Feydeau presented his best vaudevilles in a delightful Italian décor.

THÉÂTRE DE LA RENAISSANCE

20, bd. St-Martin 75010 (2 F3)
Res: 01 42 08 18 50
Victor Hugo's Ruy Blas was first performed here in 1838, with Sarah Bernhardt, Lucien Guitry and Francis Lopez in the leading roles. This product of the Romantic era is today owned by the proprietor of the Splendid St-Martin, well-versed in the art of laughter.

THÉÂTRE MOGADOR

25, rue Mogador 75009 (9 J10)
Res: 01 53 32 32 00
Designed by an English architect in 1919, the theater presents mainly revues and operettas, although the more spectacular and thrilling productions, popular with certain theater-goers, are also part of its repertoire. 1,792 seats.

THÉÂTRE EDOUARD-VII-SACHA-GUITRY

6 bis, impasse Sandrié 75009 (1 I2)
Res: 01 47 42 59 92
During the Roaring Twenties (i.e. between 1920 and 1928) Sacha Guitry staged thirteen of his best comedies in this theater, built in 1913. Today French wit and humor is still enshrined in the same "uproarious" humour and facetious elegance.

THÉÂTRE DE LA MICHODIÈRE

5, rue de la Michodière 75002 (2 A1)
Res: 01 47 42 95 22
This delightful theater in pure Art Deco style is haunted by the ghosts of the many actors who have performed here: Victor Boucher, Michel Simon, Arletty, Yvonne Printemps, Pierre Fresnay. Today the comedy is less poetic and more effective.

THÉÂTRE DES BOUFFES-PARISIENS

4, rue Monsigny 75002 (2 A3)
Res: 01 42 96 92 42
From 1855–62 the theater, managed by Jacques Offenbach, was the preserve of operetta. Since then it has staged a wide variety of musical performances, from Maeterlinck to Christiné. Jean-Claude Brialy wants to introduce a note of true musical fantasia.

THÉÂTRE MUNICIPAL POPULAIRE PARIS DIRECTION GÉRARD VIOLETTE DE LA V...

L D'AUTOMNE

L'Orestie, *produced by Peter Stein.*

Stage of the Théâtre des Bouffes-du-Nord.

MAINSTREAM COMPANIES

THÉÂTRE NATIONAL DE CHAILLOT
1, place du Trocadéro 75116 (8 J8)
Res: 01 53 65 30 00
When Firmin Gémier opened the theater in 1920, it was the first "popular national theater in the world", with a seating capacity of 2,600. Jean Vilar took over in 1951 and made it accessible to all sections of the theater-going public. The present manager, Jérôme Savary, presents the great classics, past and present, in a festive, music-hall atmosphere. In-house restaurant.

ODÉON-THÉÂTRE DE L'EUROPE
1, place de l'Odéon 75006 (2 B9)
Res: 01 44 41 36 36
The theater, opened in 1782, has had a turbulent history, moving between theater and opera, the tutelage of the Comédie-Française and independence.

THÉÂTRE NATIONAL DE LA COLLINE
15, rue Malte-Brun 75020 (3 E4)
Res: 01 44 62 52 52
Built in 1987, the theater was entrusted to the Argentinian Jorge Lavelli, whose aim is to present contemporary drama from all over

the world. Intelligent choices and imaginative productions have ensured that its two studios (757 and 200 seats) are always full. In-house restaurant.*

THÉÂTRE DE L'ATHÉNÉE-LOUIS-JOUVET
4, square de l'Opéra-Louis-Jouvet 75009 (1 I2)
Res: 01 47 42 67 27
This theater staged Louis Jouvet's most inventive productions. Today, its two studios are still presenting original performances by unconventional actors and the more experimental playwrights.

THÉÂTRE DES BOUFFES-DU-NORD
37 bis, bd. de la Chapelle 75010 (10 G7)
Res: 01 46 07 34 50
This old music-hall theater, redolent with nostalgic memories, was discovered by the English producer, Peter Brooke, and usually stages his magnificent productions. In-house restaurant.

AVANT-GARDE THEATER

THÉÂTRE DE LA BASTILLE
76, rue de la Roquette 75001 (2 J7)
Res: 01 43 57 42 14
Two studios stage the most disturbing and offensive performances in Paris. For the more adventurous theater-goer.

CARTOUCHERIE DE VINCENNES
Rte Champ-de-Manoeuvre 75012 (4 H7 and 8)
Res: 01 43 74 24 08
Since the installation, in 1970, of Ariane Mnouchkine's dazzling Théâtre du Soleil, this former military building has become a hive of artistic activity. It is occupied by five companies and their theater: L'Aquarium, Le Chaudron, L'Épée de Bois, Le Soleil and La Tempête. Restaurants.

MAISON DE LA CULTURE DE BOBIGNY
1, bd. Lénine 93000 Bobigny
Res: 01 41 60 72 72
Leading playwrights come from all over the world – e.g. Bob Wilson and Peter Sellars from America,

Lev Dodine from Russia, Matthias Langhoff from Germany – to have their latest works presented in this forum. It is a "must" for all contemporary productions in this field. In-house restaurant.*

NANTERRE-THÉÂTRE DES AMANDIERS
7, av. Pablo-Picasso 92022 Nanterre
Res: 01 46 14 70 00
Patrice Chéreau established the theater's reputation. The more politically oriented Jean-Pierre Vincent is trying to develop a program that reflects 1990's issues and has brought together such fringe writers as Stanislas Nordey and Jean Jourdheuil. In-house restaurant.

THÉÂTRE DE GENNEVILLIERS
41, av. des Grésillons 92230 Gennevilliers
Res: 01 41 32 26 26
Bernard Sobel stages neglected classics. He favors disturbing productions by young writers and defends a "theater of ideas". Restaurant.

MAISON DES ARTS DE CRÉTEIL
Pl. Salvador-Allende Créteil
Res: 01 45 13 19 19
The theater's young manager, Didier Fusillier, stages the most chic and shocking productions of the international theater-going jet set: exotic and often scathing.

LA COMÉDIE-FRANÇAISE

Founded in 1680 by Louis XIV, the aim of the Comédie-Française (also called Le Théâtre-Français or Le Français) is to maintain the national repertory. A dozen or so plays are performed in rotation by France's last surviving permanent theater company. In 1992 it annexed Le Vieux-Colombier, where it stages contemporary productions.
Place Colette (2 A4). Tel. 01 44 58 15 15

The Rex auditorium is an historic monument.   La Géode: a globe encloses the giant screen.

According to Frederico Fellini, walking into a movie theater should be as exciting as opening a book at the first page. This description could well be applied to the French capital, which boasts no less than 112 extremely individual cinemas. Below is a selection of Paris cinemas, chosen for the quality of their program and the originality of their décor. There is something to suit every taste, from the artistic and experimental cinemas of the Latin Quarter to the quality commercial movie theaters of Montparnasse, the Champs-Élysées, Les Halles and the Odéon.

CHOOSING A MOVIE

In France movie programs change every Wednesday. This is therefore the best day to buy *Pariscope* and *L'Officiel des spectacles* to find out what's on.

MOVIE REVIEWS

For those who like to be in full possession of the facts before choosing a movie, there are a number of movie reviews to choose from: *Première* and *Studio* are aimed at young people and the general public, while *Positif*, *Les Cahiers du Cinéma* and the movie pages of *Télérama* target a more informed section of the movie-going public.

LA GÉODE

The iridescent globe rising above the Cité des Sciences contains the largest hemispherical screen in the world. It has a surface area of 10,764 sq. feet and a diameter of 85 feet.
Information: Cité des Sciences (11 C3)
Tel: 01 40 05 12 12

◆ PARIS MOVIE THEATERS ◆

LE MAX LINDER PANORAMA
24, bd. Poissonnière 75009 (2 C2)
Tel: 01 48 24 00 47
The size and width (59 feet x 33 feet) of the slightly curved screen make for a spectacular effect.

LE KINOPANORAMA
60, av. La Motte-Picquet 75015 (1 C9)
Tel: 01 43 06 50 50
The curved screen (2,153 sq. feet) guarantees an impressive experience.

LE GAUMONT GRAND ÉCRAN ITALIE
30, pl. d'Italie 75013 (5E5)
Tel: 01 45 80 77 00
The capital's newest
movie theater also has the largest screen in Paris. Each performance begins with a display of laser beams and digital sound.*

LE GRAND PAVOIS
364, rue Lecourbe 75015 (7 I7)
Tel: 01 45 54 46 85
The mock portholes give the impression of being on board ship, with all the advantages of hi-tech
sound. A "must" for lovers of cult and fantasy movies.*

LE REX
1, bd. Poissonnière 75002 (2 D2)
Tel: 01 36 68 70 23
This prestigious movie theater, built in 1932, is classified as a historic monument. Its main attraction is the décor of the auditorium. Its screen is 59 feet long and 28 feet high.

◆ CINÉMATHÈQUES AND VIDÉOTHÈQUES ◆

LA CINÉMATHÈQUE FRANÇAISE
42, bd. de Bonne-Nouvelle 75010 (2 D2)
Tel: 01 56 26 01 01
The cinémathèque, founded in 1936 by Henri Langlois, is unique. It presents the great movie classics via thematic series of movies based on a particular period or movie star.

LA VIDÉOTHÈQUE DE PARIS
2, Grande Galerie, Forum des Halles Porte Saint-Eustache 75001 (2 C5)
Tel: 01 40 26 34 30
Open Tues.-Sun.
1–9pm
Movies based on the theme of Paris are shown in the movie theater's three studios, or can be viewed on individual video recorders (Thurs. until 10pm).

LA MAISON DU CINÉMA
This major project to locate on one site a comprehenive cinema archive, with museums, screening facilities and marketing outlets, should finally come on-stream in 2000, in the former American Center.

Action Écoles: experimental movies.

La Pagode: Japanese art in Paris.

MK2

The first independent group of cinemas in Paris, MK2 also actively produces shorts and feature films. Program: 08 36 68 14 07

LE BASTILLE
5, rue du Faubourg-Saint-Antoine 75011 (2 I8)
Tel: 01 43 07 48 60
An independent program specializing in new, experimental and avant-garde films d'auteur with the original soundtrack (VO). Sat. reserved for cult movies.

LE CHAMPO
51, rue des Écoles 75005 (2 C9)
Tel: 01 43 54 51 60
Le Champo has been showing the great movie classics since 1938.

L'ESCURIAL PANORAMA
11, bd. de Port-Royal 75013 (5 D3)
Tel: 01 47 07 28 04
L'Escurial Panorama presents new releases and old movies. It uses its old, local-movie theater equipment to

EXPERIMENTAL AND AVANT-GARDE CINEMAS

show the best modern movies against an old-fashioned backdrop.

LE MAX LINDER PANORAMA
24, bd. Poissonnière 75009 (2 C2)
Tel: 01 48 24 00 47
Marble in the main foyer, black in the auditorium, a mezzanine floor and a balcony provide an ideal setting for fringe and films intimistes.

LA PAGODE
57 bis, rue de Babylone 75007 (1 F8)
Tel: 01 45 55 48 48
La Pagode is popular for its Japanese décor (1896) and the quality of its program. It shows the best new releases and also has an adjoining tea room. Now being renovated.

"ACTION" MOVIE THEATERS
◆ ACTION CHRISTINE
4, rue Christine 75006 (2 B8)
Tel: 01 43 29 11 30
Shows American movies.
◆ ACTION ÉCOLES
23, rue des Écoles

75005 (2 D9)
Tel: 01 43 25 72 07
Two studios show the best 1940's and 1950's American comedies in an original décor.

L'ÉPÉE DE BOIS
100, rue Mouffetard 75005 (5 D2)
Tel: 01 43 37 54 59
The movie theater, in a modest hut in the heart of a pleasant district, shows mainly French and European films d'auteur.

LE STUDIO DES URSULINES
10, rue des Ursulines 75005 (5C1)
Tel: 43 26 19 09
Behind the arcaded exterior of this old-fashioned studio, an eclectic selection of fifteen or so movies is shown from noon to midnight.

LES TROIS LUXEMBOURG
67, rue Monsieur-le-Prince 75006 (2 B10)
Tel: 01 46 33 97 77
Renovation has vastly improved the comfort and technology of these three studios, which show traditional

movies and films d'auteur with original soundtracks (VO).

L'ENTREPÔT
7–9, rue Francis-de-Pressensé 75014 (6 F4)
Tel: 01 45 43 41 63
An original feature: certain movies are followed by a discussion with the producer.

LE MAC-MAHON
5, av. Mac-Mahon 75017 (9 B10)
Tel: 01 43 80 24 81
A shrine to the great American classics, featuring such stars as Audrey Hepburn and Billy Wilder. Open to the public on weekends.

L'ACCATONE
20, rue Cujas 75005 (2 C10)
Tel: 01 46 33 86 86
Shows the great movies that, in their day, hit the headlines!

LE REFLET MÉDICIS LOGOS
3-7, rue Champollion 75005 (2 C9)
Tel: 01 43 54 26 42
The Louis-Jouvet studio is reserved for cine-club members on Sundays. During the week it shows re-releases of the great classics and new releases with the original soundtrack (VO).

THE BEST DÉCORS
Lovers of Rococo art will adore the façade of the Utopia, with its paste-board cherubs, and the auditorium with its midnight-blue velvet wall coverings and gilt woodwork. Those who prefer a Japanese décor will find the large auditorium of La Pagode more to their taste, while aficionados of the Belle Époque will love the Ranelagh, the former theater built by Charles Garnier in 1890. Finally, those who mourn the passing of the great days of Hollywood will not be able to tear themselves away from the balconies of the Grand Rex.

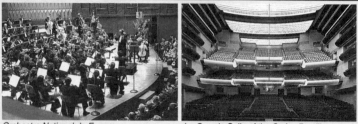

Orchestre National de France.

La Grande Salle of the Opéra-Bastille.

From Gregorian chants to contemporary compositions, Paris offers a complete range of different types of music. Some of the Meccas of music are listed below. Opera-lovers will be delighted by the Opéra Bastille, the Théâtre du Châtelet, the Théâtre des Champs-Élysées and the Opéra-Comique.

CONCERT HALLS

SALLE GAVEAU
15, rue La Boétie
75008 (1 E1)
Tel: 01 19 53 05 07
Cortot, Thibaud and Casals are just three of the great artists who have performed in the Salle Gaveau since it opened in 1907. It was intended for piano and chamber music, but orchestras have played here in the past and continue to do so. Over the years an increasing number of singers have also given recitals.

OPÉRA BASTILLE
120, rue de Lyon
75012 (2 I8)
Tel: 01 44 73 13 00
The Opéra Bastille, designed by Carlos Ott and opened in 1989, is the largest opera house in the world. The Grande Salle seats 2,703, the Amphitheater seats 500 and the Studio 237. The 1998–9 season includes some of the greatest operas in the repertory – "Carmen" by Bizet, Verdi's "Rigoletto", Puccini's "La Bohème" and Wagner's "Parsifal" and

"Lohengrin", with the orchestra and choirs of the Opéra de Paris. The Amphithéâtre program will include chamber music and the Festival d'Automne.

OPÉRA-COMIQUE
5, rue Favart 75002
(2 B2)
Tel: 01 42 44 45 00
The present Opéra-Comique was built by Louis Bernier in the late 19th century, after the previous opera house was destroyed by fire. It is a fine example of Baroque architecture for which a number of French works were composed: Carmen, Manon and The Tales of Hoffmann by Offenbach. It aims to present French music of the period as well as Baroque and 20th-century music. The program is often performed by the French Symphony Orchestra and the Ensemble Orchestral de Paris.

THÉÂTRE DES CHAMPS-ÉLYSÉES
15, av. Montaigne
75008 (1 C4)
Tel: 01 49 52 50 50
The theater was

built in 1913 by the Perret brothers and decorated by the sculptor Antoine Bourdelle and the artist Maurice Denis. The debut of its musical career was marked by the scandal surrounding Stravinsky's The Rite of Spring, with Nijinsky. Today the theater presents opera, recitals, chamber music and dance performances.

THÉÂTRE DU CHÂTELET
1, pl. du Châtelet
75001 (2 D6)
Tel: 01 40 28 28 40
The theater (seating 2,003) was built in 1862 by Gabriel Davioud. One of its most famous presentations was Debussy's scandalous Prélude à l'après-midi d'un faune. Today the theater focuses on 20th-century operas and music, as well as concerts based on the work of particular composers. Closed for renovation until July 1999, with a spectacular program in store for the 1999–2000 season.

RADIO-FRANCE
116, av. du Président-Kennedy
75116 (7 H2)
Tel: 01 42 30 15 16
The Orchestre national de Radio-France, conducted by Dutoit, favors French music from Berlioz to Varèse, and a stimulating theme-based approach to its program of performances.

SALLE PLEYEL
252, rue du Faubourg-St-Honoré
75008 (9 C9)
Tel: 01 45 61 53 00
A prestigious concert hall where a number of new compositions, e.g. Honegger's Rugby, Stravinsky's In Memoriam Debussy, Milhaud's La Création du Monde, have been presented since 1978, along with performances by great conductors, soloists and symphony orchestras. The Salle Pleyel pursues its policy of musical "immersion" by presenting piano

Opéra Comique

Lady Macbeth, *by Mzensk, Opéra Bastille.*

Médée, *by M.-A. Charpentier, Opéra Comique.*

recitals by Brendel, Lupi, Pollini, Perahia and Zimerman, as well as concerts by the Orchestre National d'Île-de-France and the orchestras of Radio-France, which perform classical and new compositions.

THÉÂTRE DE LA VILLE...

2, pl. du Châtelet 75001 (2 D6)
Tel: 01 48 87 54 42

... AND THÉÂTRE DES ABBESSES

31, rue des Abbesses 75018 (10 B7)
Tel: 01 48 87 54 42
The theaters' programs of classical and modern music consist of vocal and instrumental recitals and chamber music, and have included performances by Portal, Gutman, Starker, Staler, Juljiken, Xiaomel and the St Lawrence String Quartet.

CITÉ DE LA MUSIQUE

221, av. Jean-Jaurès 75019 (11 C3)
Tel: 01 44 84 45 00
The Cité de la Musique was designed by Christian de Portzamparc. The modular concert hall presents weekend performances, with music ranging from the Middle Ages to the 20th century and including jazz, songs and music from all over the world. In addition to its public performances, the Cité de la Musique – which

is also the home of the Ensemble Intercontemporain – holds a summer school, Javanese percussion workshops for adults and children, and a number of special events. It also has a music museum ◆ 430 and a music and dance information center (CIMD).

AUDITORIUM DES HALLES

Forum des Halles Access: Porte St-Eustache 75001 (2 C4)
Tel: 01 47 03 82 45
This centrally located concert hall presents a varied program of dance, songs, world music and jazz, as well as a classical repertoire focused on 20th-century music, all performed by excellent artists.

THREE VERY DIFFERENT FESTIVALS

FESTIVAL D'ART SACRÉ

Tel: 01 45 61 96 68
The festival presents two series of works corresponding to or inspired by the religious calendar: the Christmas (Nov.–Dec.) and Easter (Mar.–Apr.) cycles in the Catholic, Jewish, Protestant and Orthodox traditions. Each year the festival consecrates the work of a modern composer.

FESTIVAL DE ST-DENIS

The festival is devoted to 20th-

century works as well as the great masterpieces of Mahler, Franck, Mussorgsky and the repertoire of Bach, Verdi, Handel and Mozart. During June and July the Basilique de St-Denis welcomes a number of orchestras from France and other countries, which perform under the baton of such great conductors as Rostropovitch, Nelson, Janowski and Plasson, and accompany outstanding soloists such as Bashmet, Hendricks, Pollet, Van Dam and Berganza.

FESTIVAL D'AUTOMNE

The Festival d'Automne – established in 1972 – was from the outset dedicated to all aspects of the performing arts and open to all cultures. It attracts avant-gardists such as Wilson and Brown from America, Stein and Bondy from Germany, Kurtag and Ligeti from Hungary... and not forgetting Sellars and Lepage. The French are also well represented. The festival is held from September to December in one of the city's meccas of culture, the Théâtre des Amandiers in Nanterre.

MUSIC IN THE MUSEUMS

ORSAY: These concerts provide an opportunity to discover music from 1818–1914 (from Schumann to Debussy), a period rich in works for piano, melody and chamber music. Musicians and budding young artists invited to perform have included Zacharios, Portal, Luisada, Bashmet and the Quatuor Parisii.

LOUVRE: The auditorium presents chamber music and such prestigious soloists as Caussé, Pergamenshikow and Dalberto, in a program ranging from Brahms to Beethoven. Lately the work of Hindemith, Bartok and Webern has been added.

MUSÉE GRÉVIN: The museum will stage two series of concerts: the "Concerts rares" will present 19th- and 20th-century pieces via various musical structures, while the "Concerts baroques" will explore international 16th- and 17th-century music, under the guidance of expert musicians.

The Rita Mitsuko.

Téléphone at Pantin.

Bar of the Sunset.

Johnny Griffin.

ROCK VENUES

Since the 1960's – the golden age of French pop singers and entertainers – the property developers have moved in and many of the Paris rock venues have disappeared. All that has survived are the big concert halls and a few legendary clubs where the story of rock-and-roll was written in letters of fire – *Bercy, Le Zénith, L'Olympia, Le Grand Rex, Le Casino de Paris, Le Bataclan, La Cigale and L'Élysée-Montmartre* – as well as a few of the small concert halls, clubs and smoky back rooms where careers are forged

ARAPAHO
30, av. d'Italie 75013
(5 F6)
Tel: 01 45 89 65 05
(standing room for 400)
The Arapaho, opened in 1993 in the basement of the shopping center in the Place d'Italie, is the venue for up-and-coming rock groups. The club's backers intend to favor small groups with a view to promoting their career. Faith No More, Suicidal Tendencies and Franck Black all played here before they became famous.

LE GIBUS
18, rue du Faubourg-du-Temple 75011
(2 H3)
Tel: 01 47 00 78 88
(standing room for 400)
More than 3,000 groups and rock artists have appeared at Le Gibus in the past quarter-century, including some of the really big names: Chuck Berry, Jerry Lee Lewis, Deep Purple, Police, the Pretenders, the Clash, the Stray Cats, Billy Idol, Téléphone, the Rita Mitsuko and La Mano Negra. Only London's former Marquee Club and New York's CBGB can pride themselves on presenting as many great rock legends.

LE RESERVOIR
16, rue de la Forge Royale 75009 (3 A9)
Tel: 01 43 56 39 60
This new bar-restaurant has staked its shirt on music, concentrating on a program of rock and world music that will go to great lengths to be original. Themed evenings on weekdays, concerts on weekends. Get hold of a program.

JAZZ CLUBS

It has been a long time since the Paris jazz scene was as rich as it is today. The 1980's heralded the opening of modern clubs where creative jazz – a genre which wanted to combine different forms and extend the scope of jazz – was able to develop.

LE PETIT JOURNAL
71, bd. St-Michel 75005 (2 B10)
Tel: 01 43 26 28 59
Specializing in New Orleans jazz, this club counts Benny Bailey and Marcel Zanini among its habitués.

STUDIO DES ISLETTES
10, rue des Islettes 75018 (10 D7)
Tel: 01 45 23 51 41
The varied program includes Slang Trio on Tues. and Julie Monley on Wed. evening.

LA VILLA
29, rue Jacob 75006 (2 A7)
Tel: 01 43 26 60 00
Opened in 1991, La Villa is already one of the city's leading jazz clubs. Its program prioritizes creative and inspired music, and performers have included Shirley Hom, Kenny Baron and even Ahmad Jamal. The minimalist décor of the first-floor bar and adjoining hotel is the work of Marie-Christine Dorner.

LOMBARDS SUR JAZZ
◆ LE BAISER SALÉ
58, rue des Lombards 75001
Tel: 01 42 33 37 71
◆ DUC DES LOMBARDS
42, rue des Lombards 75001
Tel: 01 42 33 22 88
◆ SUNSET
60, rue des Lombards 75001
Tel: 01 40 26 46 60
(2 D6)
Between them, these three clubs stage 1,200 concerts per year! The Lombards sur Jazz association, formed by the three clubs, organizes joint musical events: performances by budding young musicians, special rates and – once a month – "three clubs for the price of one". The programs differ but are coordinated: jazz-rock, acoustic and hard bop at the "Sunset"; Latin-funk and Afro-jazz at "Le Baiser Salé"; trad. jazz at the "Duc des Lombards".

ONE UNRIVALED VENUE

LE NEW MORNING (2 E1): the only Paris club with an international reputation. It welcomes the big names on the world jazz scene and hosts events with artists of every musical persuasion: blues, rock, folk.
7–9, rue des Petites-Écuries (75010)
Tel: 01 45 23 51 41

May be, *by Maguy Marin.*

Artifact, *by William Forsythe ◆ 514.*

AVANT-GARDE THEATERS

THÉÂTRE DE LA VILLE
2, Pl. du Châtelet
75001 (2 D6)
Tel: 01 42 74 22 77
**THÉÂTRE
DES ABBESSES**
31, rue des Abbesses
75018 (10 B7)
Tel: 01 42 74 22 77
*Each year a group
of choreographers
present their work at
these two venues,
where dance seeks
new forms of
expression inspired
by the theater, movies
and even the circus.
Regular talents
include Pina Bausch,
Carolyn Carlson,
Trisha Brown,
Philippe Decouflé,
Joseph Nadj and
Anne Teresa de
Keersmaeker. The
recently opened
Théâtre des
Abbesses, with an
interior by Olivier
Debré, is standing in
for the Châtelet while
the latter is closed
for renovation.*
Also:
◆ Théâtre de la
Bastille
76, rue de la Roquette
75001 (2 J7)
Tel: 01 43 57 42 14

◆ Le Dix-Huit Théâtre
16, rue Georgette-
Agutte 75018 (9 J3)
Tel: 01 42 26 47 47
◆ Théâtre Dunois
108, rue Chevaleret
75013 (5 I5)
Tel: 01 45 84 72 00
◆ Théâtre
Contemporain
de la Danse
9, rue Joffroy-Lasnier
75004 (2 F7)
Tel: 01 42 74 44 42
◆ Le Regard des
Cygnes
210, rue de Belleville
75020 (11 E10)
Tel: 01 43 58 55 93
*These last two
theaters offer
intriguing and wide-*

*ranging programs of
work by young
French and foreign
companies. They
are both very intimate
venues, and both
have affordable ticket
prices ◆ 509.*

INTERNATIONAL DANCE

FLAMENCO EN FRANCE
33, rue des Vignoles
75020 (3 F7)
Tel: 01 43 48 99 92
*This very active
association brings
dancers to Paris and
organizes flamenco
performances.*
**LA MAISON DES
CULTURES DU MONDE**
101, bd. Raspail
75006 (1 I10)
Tel: 01 45 44 41 42

*Its credo –
discovering other
cultures – leads it to
present traditional
dances from
countries throughout
the world.*
CENTRE MANDAPA
6, rue Wurtz 75013
(5 C7)
Tel: 01 45 89 01 60
*This tiny theater is
devoted to Indian
culture. The Bharata*

MAJOR DANCE COMPANIES

OPÉRA GARNIER
Pl. de l'Opéra
75009 (1 J2)
Tel: 01 44 73 13 99
*The Opéra Garnier, a
gem of 19th-century
theater architecture,
has finally reopened
its doors after
undergoing lengthy
renovation works.
The program will
concentrate on ballet,
with performances
by Ballet de l'Opéra
and by the École
de Danse de Paris.
Ballet companies
from abroad or from
other French regions
are also invited to
perform at Opéra
Garnier for a few
days during each
season.*
PALAIS DE CHAILLOT
Pl. du Trocadéro
75116 (8 J8)
Tel: 01 47 27 81 15

*Maurice Béjart
presented his new
Swiss compositions
here in autumn 1994.*
**THÉÂTRE DES CHAMPS-
ÉLYSÉES**
15, av. Montaigne
75008 (1 C4)
Tel: 01 49 52 50 50
*Launched by the
Ballets Russes, this
theater welcomes
leading international
companies. Avoid the
first-class seats at
the side: they are
expensive and the
view is disappointing.*
PALAIS DES CONGRÈS
Porte Maillot 75017
(8 I3)
Tel: 01 40 68 22 22
*The very hard floor of
this theater is
unpopular with
dancers, although
some classical and
folk ballets are
performed here.*

*Natyam and
other*

*dances
from
India are
performed
throughout
the year.*

La Coupole in the 1930's.   Paris review (1925).

Because Paris is still associated with the persistent and clichéd images of Gay Paree, music halls and cabarets, Montmartre and the French can-can, tourists are often bitterly disappointed. The reality is less picturesque: Paris night spots have become standardized and staying up all night has gone out of fashion. However there has been a recent move to revive the tradition of the cafés-concert, in the growing fashion for music-bars. These are more convivial than discotheques as you can actually dance and talk in comfort.

A NIGHT-CLUBBER'S GUIDE TO PARIS

THE WEEKEND "EXPLOSION"
The week of the Paris "night set" is very concentrated, usually starting on Thursday and finishing on Saturday night. Most bars and discotheques are quiet during the week and "explode" at the weekend.

"IN" PLACES
The human geography of Paris night life is akin to a form of neo-tribalism. Each district is the preserve of a particular "species" based on time-honored incompatibilities and different philosophies of life. In simple terms: the city's golden youth inhabits the Paris "west end", budding intellectuals are found on the Rive Gauche, while Pigalle, Menilmontant and Bastille are the haunts of Bohemians and avant-gardists.

A CONSTANTLY CHANGING SCENE
Compiling a list of addresses for Paris night spots is virtually impossible as it is a scene which is constantly changing. The fickle nature of the Paris "night set" and the checkered careers of the clubs (they are continually being refused permission to hold concerts due to complaints lodged by local residents disturbed by the noise) make this extremely difficult.

NEW TRENDS
Current trends tend to favor music-bars rather than nightclubs. They are more convivial, easier to get to, less expensive and less enclosed as they open onto the street. Customers can dance or listen to music, sometimes into the early hours.

CLASSIC BARS

LA CALAVADOS
40, av. Pierre-1er-de-Serbie 75008 (1 C3)
Tel: 01 47 20 31 99
Open daily 9pm–6am. Closed Sun.
Cocktails: 90F
A favorite refuge for dedicated night owls who are regularly found ensconced in the warm glow of this small bar designed to look like a Spanish Armada ship. The bar's resident pianist and crooner, Jerry King, and the Los Latinos trio take it in turns to sing and play until dawn.

LE DOOBIE'S
2, rue Robert-Estienne 75008 (1 D3)
Tel: 01 53 76 10 76
Open daily 7pm–2am.
Cocktails: 60F
Yannick Noah's bar attracts the young Paris "west-

enders" who meet up here before taking to the dance floors of Le Niel's or L'Arc.

LE CHINA CLUB
50, rue de Charenton 75012 (3 A10)
Tel: 01 43 43 82 02
Open daily 7pm–2am (4am on weekends).
Cocktails: 60F
This sober, elegant club has three floors: a bar and restaurant on the first floor, a smoking-room on the second, and a night bar in the basement. Step into the world of Hergé and the "Blue Lotus".

LA CLOSERIE DES LILAS
171, bd. du Montparnasse 75006 (5 A2)
Tel: 01 40 51 34 50
Open daily 10am–1.30am.
Cocktails 60F
The Mecca of the Left-bank intelligentsia.

Terrace of La Palette, 43, rue de Seine.

The Bar Hemingway at the Ritz Club.

BARS IN LUXURY HOTELS

Don't ignore these luxurious bars, where the quality of the facilities and service are out of this world.

HÔTEL PLAZA-ATHÉNÉE
25, av. Montaigne 75008 (1 D3)
Tel. 01 53 67 66 55
Open daily 11am–2am.
Cocktails: 70F, 100F (after 11pm).
The English bar in the basement – situated in what is undoubtedly one of the most elegant avenues in the world – is decorated in purely classic style with the Plaza's traditional leather and mahogany. Jazz and blues pianist from 11pm–1am, Wed.–Sat. and a tiny parquet dance floor.

HÔTEL RITZ
15, pl. Vendôme 75001 (1 I3)
Tel. 01 43 16 30 30
Open Mon.–Sat.
6.30pm–2am.
Cocktails: 110F
When Hemingway dreamt of life after death, he always imagined himself at the Ritz. Ironically the Hemingway Bar (on the rue Cambon side of the hotel) has recently reopened. On summer evenings the Bar Vendôme opens onto the patio. Harpist from 3–7pm and pianist until 1am.

HÔTEL LUTÉTIA
45, bd. Raspail 75006 (1 I9)
Tel. 01 49 54 46 46
Open daily 11am–1pm.
Cocktails: 75F (90F on jazz evenings, i.e. Thurs., Fri. and Sat. 10pm–1am).
St-Germain-des-Prés oblige: every weekend the luxury, Left-bank hotel offers the opportunity to relax and listen to a small jazz band in an Art Deco setting designed by Sonia Rykiel.

BILLIARD HALLS

Two addresses where you can enjoy a game of billiards in the lively bar atmosphere:
BLUE BILLIARD
111, rue St-Maur 75011 (2 J3)
Tel: 01 43 55 87 21
Open daily 11am–2am.
LES MOUSQUETAIRES
77, av. du Maine 75014 (6 H3)
Tel: 01 43 22 50 46
Open daily 7am (11am Sun.) to 2am (5am Fri. and Sat.)

24-HOUR OPENING

For confirmed insomniacs, two bars in Montparnasse and Pigalle are open round-the-clock.

LE DÉPANNEUR
27, rue Fontaine 75009 (9 J7)
Tel: 01 40 16 40 20

COSMOS CAFÉ
101, bd. du Montparnasse 75006 (6 I1)
Tel: 01 43 26 74 36

DJ BARS

The DJ bar is a fairly recent phenomenon: more than just a bar, since a DJ operates the turntables, but not a discotheque since, in theory, people don't go there to dance.

CAFÉ DU TRÉSOR
5–7, rue du Trésor 75004 (2 F7)
Tel: 01 42 71 78 34
Open until 2am.
In a cul-de-sac in the Marais. Regular themed evenings with titles like Nutralic Trax (Thu.) or 100% Vidal (Fri. evenings).

SATELLIT CAFÉ
44, rue de la Folie-Méricourt 75011 (2 I4)
Tel: 01 47 00 48 87
Open Mon.–Thurs. 6pm–2am, Fri. and Sat. 6pm until dawn.
The discotheque's extensive coverage (over 4,000 records) of all musical genres (rock, soul, jazz, French and world music) and perfect acoustics explain why the café is so popular with music lovers. World-music concerts on Tues. and Wed. at 9pm.

OPUS CAFÉ
167, quai de Valmy 75010 (10 H9)
Tel: 01 40 34 70 00
Open Mon.–Wed. 9pm–2am, Thurs.–Sat. 9pm–4am.
A British officers' mess during World War One, this café has been reconverted into a "loft" and is now a quiet, sophisticated bar looking over the Canal St-Martin. French-music concerts on Fri. and Sat. evenings.

LE SANZ SANS
49, rue du Faubourg-St-Antoine 75011 (2 I8)
Tel: 01 44 75 78 78
Open until 2am.
The latest fashionable address in the Bastille district. Its bric-à-brac décor harbors a few surprises: e.g. the giant screen.

Le Folie's Pigalle is a disco club.

Le Café de l'Industrie.

DANCE BARS

Dance bars, with their resident disc jockeys, are more like nightclubs than traditional bars. Free admission unless otherwise stated.

LE MOLOKO
26, rue Fontaine 75009 (10 A8)
Tel: 01 48 74 50 26
Open daily 9.30pm–6am.
The "self-DJ" (a laser juke-box programmed – free of charge – by customers) has been replaced by tapes compiled by the best Paris and international DJs.

LE COMPTOIR
14, rue Vauvilliers 75001 (2 C5)
Tel: 01 40 26 26 66
Dance floor open until 4am on Fri.–Sat. Bar and restaurant open daily, noon–2am.
On weekends the large tapas bar (designed by Jonathan Amar, who also designed Les Bains), opposite St-Eustache, becomes a mini nightclub. It has enjoyed unrivaled success over the past five years and is one of the district's main night spots.

LA GALERIE
14, rue de Lappe 75011 (2 I8)
Tel: 01 47 00 91 09. Open 6pm–2am.
A new spot opened by French rap singer Ménélik, set on three levels. The ambience adapts for each evening's DJ.

LE WHAT'S UP
15, rue Daval 75011 (2 I7)
Tel: 01 48 05 88 33
Open daily 7pm–2am.
Very fashionable in the techno universe. The DJs, known or unknown, are equally committed to a rich, varied musical diet. Radio FG programs (Cheers and Global Techno-Week-End) are broadcast by direct link.

CITHÉA
114, rue Oberkampf 75011 (3 A3)
Tel: 01 40 21 70 95
Music and live concert from 9pm on Thur., Fri. and Sat. Open daily until 2am (dawn at weekends).
A dance bar dedicated to live jazz, funk, rock and groove.

MUSIC BARS

It is worth consulting the *Lylo* and *Tam's* programs available in bars presenting live music. The aim of the following short selection is to encourage visitors to go and listen to the musicians who play in the evenings in these modern versions of the *café-concerts*.

WAIT & SEE CAFÉ
9, bd. Voltaire 75011 (2 H3)
Tel: 01 48 07 29 49
Open daily (except Sun.) until 2am.
The café is reminiscent of the New York underground clubs of the 1970s: white lacquer paintwork, black slates, pink lighting, damaged club davenports and the statutory pool table dominating the upper floor. Rock concerts at 9pm.

LA FLÈCHE D'OR
102 bis, rue de Bagnolet 75020 (3 F6)
Tel: 01 43 72 04 23
Open until 2am.
Situated in an old rail station, this café puts on rock concerts, evenings of French song, and music-and-dancing (or tango) evenings. Patron Raoul Rolland takes full responsibiity for this out-and-out eclecticism!

L'UTOPIA
79, rue de l'Ouest 75014 (6 G4)
Tel: 01 43 22 79 66
Open daily (except Sun.) 10.30pm–2am in the week and 6am on weekends.
For the last decade the club has presented groups of between 4 and 6 musicians. Every evening a different group plays blues, rhythm 'n' blues and rock 'n' roll.

LA FOLIE EN TÊTE
33, rue de la Butte-aux-Cailles 75013 (5 D6)
Tel: 01 45 80 65 99
Open daily (except Sun.) 5pm–2am
Small music–bar presenting concerts of rock, jazz and traditional French songs on Thu., Fri. and Sat. 9pm–midnight (40F).

LES NOCTAMBULES
24, bd. de Clichy 75018 (10A7)
Tel: 01 46 06 16 38
Open daily until 5am.
Everyone enjoys the kitsch atmosphere of this caf'conc'. Pierre Carré is the archetypal Montmartrois singer.

NO ENTRY
Two private clubs remain "closed" to anyone who is not a member of the Paris jet-set:
LE RÉGINE'S
49, rue de Ponthieu 75008 (1 E2)
Tel: 01 43 59 21 60
CASTEL
15, rue Princesse 75006 (2 A8)
Tel: 01 40 51 52 80

Le Balajo is a true period piece.

Le Queen, one of the Paris mega-clubs.

LATE-NIGHT BISTROS

The "nocturnal" – and completely authentic – version of the Paris café: from the zinc (or Formica) counter to the marble- (or plastic-) topped tables and the jovial patron (or bad-tempered waiters) depending on the bistro. Listed below are some of the bistros, open until 2am, where Parisians like to start, or round off, their evening out.

LE SANCERRE
35, rue des Abbesses 75018 (10 A6)
Tel: 01 42 58 08 20

LE CAFÉ NOIR
65, rue Montmartre 75002 (2 C4)
Tel: 01 40 39 07 36

LES ÉTAGES
33, rue Vieille-du-Temple 75004 (2 F6)
Tel: 01 42 78 72 00

AU LÈCHE-VIN
13, rue Daval 75011 (2 I7)
Tel: 01 43 55 98 91

LE CAFÉ DE L'INDUSTRIE
16, rue St--Sabin 75011 (2 I7)
Tel: 01 47 00 13 53

LE PISTON PÉLICAN
15, rue de Bagnolet 75020 (3 E7)
Tel: 01 43 70 35 00

CHEZ GEORGES
11, rue des Canettes 75006 (1 J8)
Tel: 01 43 26 79 15

LA PALETTE
43, rue de Seine 75006 (2 A7)
Tel: 01 43 26 68 15

LE CAFÉ DE LA MUSIQUE
213, av. Jean-Jaurès 75019 (11 D5)
Tel: 01 48 03 15 91

GOGO DANCERS

The fashion for gogo dancers, imported from America, is intended to be decorative rather than salacious.

BANANA CAFÉ
13, rue de la Ferronnerie 75001
(2 D6).
Tel: 01 42 33 35 31
Gogo dancers from midnight–4am on Thu., Fri., Sat., piano bar to 4.30am (6am on weekends). A popular gay bar, with techno sounds.

THEMES

The following have their own distinctive settings:

LA BELLE HORTENSE
31, rue Vieille-du-Temple 75004 (3 A10)
Tel: 01 48 04 71 60
Premier bookstore/ wine bar.

LE FLORIDITA
19, rue de Presbourg 75116 (1 A1)
Tel: 01 45 00 84 84
Bar for cigar smokers.

LE WEB BAR
32, rue de Picardie 75003 (2 G4)
Tel: 01 42 72 66 55
Internet café.

DISCOTHEQUES

Most discotheques close at around 6am, although some do cater for the Stakhanovites of the night-club circuit and stay open "after hours" on Sat. and Sun. mornings.

L'ARC
12, rue de Presbourg 75116 (1 A1)
Tel: 01 45 00 29 02
A "high-flying" nightclub with a view over the Arc de Triomphe. The restaurant is the most successful feature of this sophisticated and discreetly luxurious club. Smart clientele.

LE NIEL'S
27, av. des Ternes 75017 (9 B9)
Tel: 01 47 66 45 00
Restaurant. The Paris equivalent of Niel's in New York. Its decor, inspired by the apartments of the city's wealthy districts, ensures that its young-and-beautiful clientele will feel at home.

FOLIE'S PIGALLE
11, pl. Pigalle 75009 (10 A7)
Tel: 01 48 78 25 56
Open Thur.–Sat.
After hours at weekends. Pigalle goes techno! A predominately gay clientele and garage music.

LE REX
5, bd. Poissonnière 75002 (2 D2)
Tel: 01 42 36 10 96
Open Tues.–Sat.
A classic venue for techno, house and garage.

LES BAINS
7, rue de Bourg-l'Abbé 75003 (2 E4)
Tel: 01 48 87 01 80
Restaurant.
A careless "Yesterday evening at Les Bains . . .", slipped into an over-dinner conversation, will always impress Parisians. It's the kind of place they can't resist.

LE QUEEN
102, av. des Champs-Élysées 75008 (1 C2)
Tel: 01 42 89 31 32
The preserve of dance and techno music where the predominately gay clientele tolerates the presence of sexy young girls.

LE BALAJO
9, rue de Lappe 75011 (2 I8)
Tel: 01 47 00 07 87
Open Tue.–Sun. until 6am.
Opened in 1936 near the Bastille, this popular dance hall proved to be the launchpad for the celebrated Mistinguett, and it has continued in much the same vein ever since. There's still that same convivial feel to the old dance floor, even if these days they're playing house or disco music.

◆ SHOPPING
LISTED BY ARRONDISSEMENT

RIGHT BANK

◆ 1ST ◆

Agnès B. **524**
Boucheron **525**
Cartier **525**
Chanel Joaillerie **525**
Chaumet **525**
Christian Louboutin **525**
Claude Montana **524**
Galerie Bamyan **527**
Guerlain **526**
Herboristerie du Palais-Royal **529**
Jean-Paul Hévin **528**
Kenzo **524**
Legrand Filles et Fils **530**
Maison de Vacances **527**
Marie Mercié **525**
Mauboussin **525**
Mellerio **525**
Natures & Découvertes **529**
Philippe Model **525**
Les Salons du Palais-Royal Shiseido **526**
Van Cleef & Arpels **525**
Verlet **530**
Vilmorin **530**

◆ 2ND ◆

Cartier **525**
Christofle **526**
Daum **526**
Debauve et Gallais **528**
Jean-Paul Gaultier **524**
Mellerio **525**
Pierre Corthay **525**
Raymond Massaro **525**

◆ 3RD ◆

Entrée des Fournisseurs **525**
Eugène Seigneur **527**
Lapeyronie **530**
Les Mille Feuilles **528**
Thierry Mugler **524**

◆ 4TH ◆

À l'Olivier **530**
À la Ville de Rodez **530**
Anatomica **525**
Au Chat Perché **528**
Azzedine Alaïa **524**
Berthillon **529**
Calligrane **526**

Galerie Bamyan **527**
Galerie Sentou **527**
Izraël **530**
Le Jardin Moghol **527**
Mariage Frères **530**
Miller & Bertaux **527**
Monceaux Fleurs **528**
Naturalia **529**
Sic Amor **525**
Virus **528**

◆ 8TH ◆

Alexandre de Paris **525**
Baccarat **526**
La Bonbonnière de la Trinité **530**
Carita **525**
Cartier **525**
Caves Augé **530**
Chanel **524**
Chanel Joaillerie **525**
Christian Dior **524**
Christian Lacroix **524**
Christofle **526**
Dalloyau **530**
Daum **526**
Fauchon **529**
Gien **527**
Guerlain **526**
Hédiard **529**
Hermès **526**
Hubert de Givenchy **524**
Jean-Louis Scherrer **524**
Lalique **526**
Louis Vuitton **526**
La Maison du Chocolat **528**
Mauboussin **525**
Monceau Fleurs **528–9**
Nature & Découvertes **529**
Sidonie Larizzi **525**
Sonia Rykiel **524**
Ted Lapidus **524**
Thierry Mugler **524**
YSL Rive Gauche **524**
Yves St-Laurent **524**
Yves St-Laurent Beauté **526**

◆ 9TH ◆

Agnès B. **524**
La Bonbonnière de la Trinité **530**
Lafayette Gourmet **529**
Galeries Lafayette **529**
La Maison du Chocolat **528**

◆ 10TH ◆

Baccarat **526**

◆ 11TH ◆

Bibi Bob **525**
L'Herbe Verte **529**

◆ 12TH ◆

Jean-Paul Gaultier **524**
Jean-Louis Scherrer **524**

◆ 16TH ◆

Agnès B. **524**
Christofle **526**
Coquelin Aîné **530**
Guerlain **526**
La Maison du Chocolat **528**
Monceau Fleurs **528–9**
Nature & Découvertes **529**
Repaire de Bacchus **530**

◆ 17TH ◆

Alléosse **528**
Les Bouquets d'Asters **529**
Debauve et Gallais **528**
Monceau Fleurs **528–9**

◆ 18TH ◆

Au Pétrin d'Antan **528**

◆ 20TH ◆

L'Amicale **528**

LEFT BANK

◆ 5TH ◆

Naturalia **529**
Rendez-vous de la Nature **529**
La Sensitive **524**
La Tuile à Loup **527**

◆ 6TH ◆

Agnès B. **524**
Boulangerie Poilâne **528**
Christian Constant **528**
Christian Dior **524**
Christian Lacroix **524**
Christian Louboutin **525**

Elvis Pompilio **525**
Entrée des Fournisseurs **525**
Galerie de Textiles **527**
Guerlain **526**
Les Herbes du Luxembourg **529**
Jean-Charles de Castelbajac **524**
Jean-Claude Gaulupeau **530**
Jean-Louis Scherrer **524**
Jean-Paul Hévin **528**
Liwan **527**
La Maison du Chocolat **528**
Mariage Frères **530**
Marie Mercié **525**
Monceau Fleurs **528–9**
Sonia Rykiel **524**
YSL Rive Gauche **524**

◆ 7TH ◆

Barthélémy **528**
Christian Constant **528**
Claude Montana **524**
Debauve et Gallais **528**
Galerie Sentou **527**
Guerlain **526**
Jean-Paul Hévin **528**
Marianne Robic **529**
Naturalia **529**
Pétrossian **530**
Poujauran **528**
Sennelier – Couleurs du Quai Voltaire **526**
Thierry Mugler **524**

◆ 13TH ◆

Les Abeilles **529**
Nature & Découvertes **529**

◆ 14TH ◆

Lieu-dit **528**

◆ 15TH ◆

Agnès B. **524**
La Campagne **530**
Francis Boucher **528**
Guerlain **526**
Max Poilâne **528**

◆ OUTSKIRTS ◆

Fleurs et Jardins **529**
Les Nouveaux Robinson **530**

FRUIT AND VEGETABLES

Fruit and vegetable markets are a celebration of color, scent and sound, where you can hear the fading cries of the Paris of yesteryear.

RUE MONTORGUEIL
75002 (2 D4)
Regional and luxury products and breads of yesteryear in the heart of Les Halles. Open daily.

RUE DE LÉVIS
75017 (9 F7)
Situated between the Parc Monceau and the Square des Batignolles. A wide range of different food products. Open Tue.–Sat. and Sun morning.

RUE MOUFFETARD
75005 (5 D2)
Enjoy a festival of color as you walk through the narrow, cobbled streets. Open Tue., Thu. and Sat.

RUE DE SEINE
75006 (2 A8)
In the Latin Quarter. Open daily except Mon. Expensive.

ST-GERMAIN
74006 (2 A8)
A covered market with exotic products. Popular with lovers of foreign foods.

PLACE D'ALIGRE
75012 (3 A9)
The only cosmopolitan market

open six days a week (closed Mon.), and one of the cheapest in Paris. 7.30am–1pm.

RUE LEPIC
75018 (10 A6)
Adjoining the famous Butte Montmartre.

"BIO" MARKETS
514, bd. Raspail, 75006
Organically produced food products. Also in the Boulevard des Batignolles (8th), between nos. 27 and 48. Open Sat. 8.30am–1pm.

ORGANIC MARKETS

At present there are two entirely organic markets in the heart of Paris: one on the Boulevard Raspail in the 6th arrondissement (Sat. 9am–1pm). Organic stands are also beginning to appear on the traditional markets: Cours de Vincennes in the 12th arrondissement (Wed. and Sat.), Bastille in the 11th arr. (Thu. and Sun.) and Place de la Réunion in the 20th arr. (Thu. and Sun.)

SPECIALIST MARKETS

MARCHÉ AUX OISEAUX
(Bird market)
Quai de la Mégisserie, 75004
The countryside comes to Paris. Open daily. Also Place Louis Lépine and Quai de Corse. Open every Sun 9am–7pm.

MARCHÉ AUX TIMBRES
(Stamp market)
Rond-point des Champs-Élysées, 75008
A rendezvous for philatelists and postcard collectors. Every Thurs., Sat., Sun. and public holidays. Open from 10am to dusk.

MARCHÉS AUX FLEURS
(Flower markets)
Île de la Cité, 75004
Place de la Madeleine, 8th arrondissement and Place des Ternes 17th arrondissement
For a wide selection of flowers. Open Tue.–Sat.

MARCHÉ ST-PIERRE
75018
Fabrics at prices to suit every pocket. Open Mon.–Sat. 9am–6pm.

MARCHÉ AUX LIVRES
(Book market)
87, rue Brancion, 75015
Antique and secondhand books. Open every Sat. and Sun 9.30am–6pm. It is advisable to get there early.

MARCHÉS AUX PUCES
(Flea markets)
Collectors of old clothes, antiques and bric-à-brac will enjoy a stroll through the Paris flea markets.

MONTREUIL
Specializes in old clothes and African items. Open Sat.,

Sun., Mon. 7.30am–7pm.

ST-OUEN
The most famous of the Paris flea markets sells anything from bric-à-brac to period furniture. It also sells antique books and old clothes. Open Sat., Sun. and Mon. 5.30am–7pm.

PORTE DE VANVES
Bric-à-brac only, but there are still plenty of bargains. Open Sat.–Sun. 7am–7pm.

OPENING HOURS
Stores in Paris are usually open daily from 9am–7pm, though grocery stores may be open earlier. Generally every district in Paris has at least one shop that stays open until around 10pm. Most stores are only closed on Sundays, although some close on Monday or Tuesday instead. On Sunday grocers and butchers open until noon and some bakers stay open all day. Beware: many stores, including department stores, close at lunchtime each day.

DEPARTMENT STORES
▲ 126

BON MARCHÉ
22, rue de Sèvres
75007 (1 H9)

GALERIES LAFAYETTE
40, bd. Haussmann
75009 (1 J1)

PRINTEMPS
64, bd. Haussmann
75009 (1 I1)

SAMARITAINE
19, rue de la Monnaie
75001 (2 C6)

Christian Lacroix,
rue du Faubourg-St-Honoré.

Christian Dior,
avenue Montaigne.

Agnès B., rue du
Vieux-Colombier.

From luxury boutiques to small, traditional stores: the French capital has something to suit every type of shopping need, while esthetes will be delighted by the elegance of its window displays. Although Paris has any number of talented designers, it is impossible to present an exhaustive list in the limited space available.

HAUTE COUTURE AND READY-TO-WEAR FASHIONS

HAUTE COUTURE

Although only the wealthy can afford the prices of the Paris haut-couturiers, visitors can still admire their window displays or browse through their off-the-peg collections.

CHANEL
31, rue Cambon
75008 (1 I3)
Tel: 01 42 86 28 00
42, av. Montaigne
75008 (1 D3)
Tel: 01 47 23 74 12

CHRISTIAN DIOR
58, rue du Fbg-St-Honoré 75008 (1 G2)
Tel: 01 47 42 16 06
30, av. Montaigne
75008 (1 D3)
Tel: 01 40 73 54 00
16, rue de l'Abbaye
75006 (1 J7)
Tel: 01 56 24 90 53

YVES ST- LAURENT
5, av. Marceau
75008 (1 C4)
Tel: 01 44 31 64 00

YSL RIVE GAUCHE
38, rue du Fbg-St-Honoré 75008 (1 G2)
Tel: 01 42 65 74 59
6 and 12, pl. St-Sulpice 75006 (1 J9)
Tel: 01 43 29 43 00
and 01 43 26 84 40

JEAN-LOUIS SCHERRER
51, av. Montaigne
75008 (1 D3)
Tel: 01 42 99 05 79
29, av. Ledru-Rollin
75012 (2 I10)

HUBERT DE GIVENCHY
3, av. George-V
75008 (1 C4)
Tel: 01 44 31 50 00
8, av. George-V
75008 (1 C4)
Tel: 01 47 20 81 31
28, rue du Fbg-St-Honoré 75008 (1 H3)
Tel: 01 42 65 54 54

KENZO
3, pl. des Victoires
75001 (2 B4)
Tel: 01 40 39 72 03

CHRISTIAN LACROIX
73, rue du Fbg-St-Honoré 75008 (1 F2)
Tel: 01 42 68 79 04
26, av. Montaigne
75008 (1 D3)
Tel: 01 47 20 68 95
2–4, pl. St-Sulpice
75006 (2 A9)
Tel: 01 46 33 48 95

TED LAPIDUS
35, rue François-I
75008 (1 D3)
Tel: 01 44 43 49 90

CRÉATEURS

Tel: 01 46 28 39 27
31, rue de Tournon
75006 (2 A9)
Tel: 01 43 54 49 07

"CRÉATEURS"
Designer stores are scattered across the capital, sometimes in unlikely locations.

AGNÈS B.
3, rue du Jour
75001 (1 G2)
Tel: 01 42 33 04 13
3, rue du Jour
75001 (1 G2)
Tel: 01 45 08 56 56
6, rue du Vieux-Colombier
75006 (1 J9)
Tel: 01 44 39 02 60
17, av. Pierre Ier-de-Serbie
75116 (1 B3)
Tel: 01 47 20 22 44
Galeries Lafayette
40, bd. Haussmann
75009 (1 J1)
Tel: 01 42 82 32 68
Galeries Lafayette
Centre Maine-Montparnasse
75015 (6 H1)
Tel: 01 45 38 58 16

AZZEDINE ALAÏA
7, rue de Moussy
75004 (2 E6)
Tel: 01 42 72 19 19

JEAN-CHARLES DE CASTELBAJAC
6, pl. St-Sulpice
75006 (2 A9)
Tel: 01 46 33 87 32
5, rue des

Petits-Champs
75001 (2 B3)
Tel: 01 42 60 37 33

JEAN-PAUL GAULTIER
30, rue du Fbg-St-Antoine
75012 (2 I8)
Tel: 01 44 68 85 00
6, rue Vivienne
75002 (2 B3)
Tel: 01 42 86 05 05

CLAUDE MONTANA
131, rue St-Denis
75001 (2 D4)
Tel: 01 44 76 87 00
7, rue de Grenelle
75007 (1 I8)
Tel: 01 45 49 01 92

THIERRY MUGLER
4–6, rue aux Ours
75003 (2 D5)
Tel: 01 44 78 78 44
49, av. Montaigne
75008 (1 D3)
Tel: 01 47 23 37 62
45, rue du Bac
75007 (1 I7)
Tel: 01 45 44 44 44

SONIA RYKIEL
175, bd. St-Germain
75006 (1 J7)
Tel: 01 49 54 60 00
70, rue du Fbg-St-Honoré
75008 (1 G2)
Tel: 01 42 65 20 81

LA SENSITIVE
264, rue St-Jacques
75005 (5 B2)
Tel: 01 43 54 78 32
Naturally dyed fabrics woven and sewn in Laos. Beautiful, simple lines and traditional designs.

HATTERS AND MILLINERS

A chic outfit is often set off by a smart hat. Although hats are worn less than they used to be, designers make every effort to present a wide range of designs, from the classic felt hat to original little "numbers".

MARIE MERCIÉ
56, rue de Tiquetonne 75001 (2 D4)
Tel: 01 40 26 60 68
23, rue St-Sulpice 75006 (2 A9)
Tel: 01 43 26 45 83
PHILIPPE MODEL
33, du Place du Marché-St-Honoré 75001 (1J3)
Tel: 01 42 96 89 02
Originally a hat designer, Philippe Model is extending his range to cover shoes, handbags and gloves.
ELVIS POMPILIO
62, rue des Sts-Pères 75006 (1 I8)
Tel: 01 45 44 82 02
The hats perched on the variously sized hat stands of Elvis Pompilio's window displays are all individual little "numbers" or limited editions. Their designer also carries out commissions for leading international designers in the garden setting of her workshop.
BIBI BOB
82, rue de Charonne 75011 (3 B8)
Tel: 01 43 70 51 72

JEWELRY AND COSTUME JEWELRY

The most famous names are found near the Place Vendôme.

BOUCHERON
26, pl. Vendôme 75001 (1 I3)
Tel: 01 42 61 58 16
CARTIER
23, pl. Vendôme 75001 (1 I3)
Tel: 01 44 55 32 20
13, rue de la Paix 75002 (1 J2)
Tel: 01 42 18 53 70
51, rue François-1er 75008 (1 D3)
Tel: 01 40 74 61 85
CHANEL JOAILLERIE
18, pl. Vendôme 75001 (1 I3)
Tel: 01 55 35 50 05
40, av. Montaigne 75008 (1 D3)
Tel: 01 40 70 12 33
CHAUMET
12, pl. Vendôme 75001 (1 I3)
Tel: 01 44 77 24 00
MAUBOUSSIN
20, pl. Vendôme 75001 (1 I3)
Tel: 01 44 55 10 00
136, av. des Champs-Élysées 75008 (1 C1)
Tel: 01 45 61 51 51
MELLERIO
9, rue de la Paix 75002 (1 I3)
Tel: 01 42 61 57 53
VAN CLEEF & ARPELS
22, pl. Vendôme 75001 (1 I3)
Tel: 01 42 61 58 58
SIC AMOR
20, rue du Pont-Louis-Philippe 75004 (2 F7)
Tel: 01 42 76 02 37
A store full of tempting items where the designers take their turn on "guard duty". Stefano Poletti's "Botanicus" collection, in colored Murano glass, is an absolute must.
ENTRÉE DES FOURNISSEURS
8, rue des Francs-Bourgeois 75003 (2 G7)
Tel: 01 48 87 58 98
9, rue Madame 75006 (1 J9)
Tel: 01 42 84 13 97
This haberdasher's has everything: beads arranged according to country and color, buttons, sets of table mats to embroider and motifs to stitch on (from 50 centimes for a button to 450F for semi-fine gold tassel).

SHOES

RAYMOND MASSARO
2, rue de la Paix 75002 (1 I3)
Tel: 01 42 61 00 29
Raymond Massaro has been making hand-crafted shoes for over a century and supplies the haute couture designers. Made to measure (by appt.).
PIERRE CORTHAY
1, rue Volney 75002 (1 I2)
Tel: 01 42 61 08 89
A craftsman who only makes shoes to order. Watch him at work, through the store window.
SIDONIE LARIZZI
8, rue de Marignan 75008 (1 D3)
Tel: 01 43 59 38 87
CHRISTIAN LOUBOUTIN
19, rue Jean-Jacques-Rousseau 75001 (2 B5)
Tel: 01 42 36 05 31
36, rue de Grenelle 75006 (1 I8)
Tel: 01 42 22 33 07
ANATOMICA
14, rue du Bourg-Tibourg 75004 (2 F7)
Tel: 01 42 74 10 20
Birkenstock clothes and shoes.

"SALONS DE COIFFURE"

Paris hairdressing salons are renowned for their elegant décors and impeccable service.

ALEXANDRE DE PARIS
3, av. Matignon 75008 (1 E2)
Tel: 01 42 25 57 90

The beautiful ceramic floor in the foyer of the Avenue Matignon salon was designed by Jean Cocteau. The clientele of Alexandre – the appointed "barber" of haute-couture fashion shows and leading light in the field of elegant coiffure – includes some of the most beautiful women in the world. Finely crafted barrettes and hairbands are also available.

CARITA
11, rue du Faubourg-St-Honoré 75008 (1 G2)
Tel: 01 44 94 11 00
The salons established around 1960 by the Carita sisters today combine traditional expertise with the very latest modern techniques.

One of the Guerlain perfume stores.

The 1001 fabrics of the Galerie de Textiles.

BEAUTY PRODUCTS AND PERFUME

YVES SAINT-LAURENT BEAUTÉ
32, rue du Faubourg-St-Honoré 75008 (1 H3)
Tel: 01 49 24 99 66
An unrivaled color range of beauty products to complement Yves Saint-Laurent haute couture, presented in a sophisticated and refined setting.

GUERLAIN
47, rue Bonaparte 75006 (2 A7)
Tel: 01 43 26 71 19
93, rue de Passy 75016 (8 H9)
Tel: 01 42 88 41 62
29, rue de Sèvres 75007 (1 I9)
Tel: 01 42 22 46 60
35, rue Tronchet 75008 (1 I1)
Tel: 01 47 42 53 23
2, pl. Vendôme 75001 (1 I3)
Tel: 01 42 60 68 61
68, av. des Champs-Élysées 75008 (1 D2)
Tel: 01 45 62 52 57
Centre Maine-Montparnasse 75015 (6 H1)
Tel: 01 45 62 52 57

LES SALONS DU PALAIS-ROYAL SHISEIDO
142, galerie de Valois 75001 (2B4)
Tel: 01 49 27 09 09
The exclusive toilet waters of Serge Lutens (Brazilian rosewood, Iris) are only available from this store, decorated in Directoire-style, purple tones. Mail order.

LUXURY CRAFT ITEMS

BACCARAT
30 bis, rue de Paradis 75010 (10 E10)
Tel: 01 47 70 64 30
11, pl. de la Madeleine 75008 (1 H2)
Tel: 01 42 65 36 26
It is tempting, on leaving the museum in the Rue du Paradis, to buy up the store's entire stock of contemporary items (below).

CHRISTOFLE
9, rue Royale 75008 (1 H3)
Tel: 01 49 33 43 00
24, rue de la Paix 75002 (1 J3)
Tel: 01 42 65 62 43
95, rue de Passy 75016 (8 G10)
Tel: 01 46 47 51 27
The interesting little museum above the store in the Rue Royale (visits by appt.) has some extremely beautiful pieces.

DAUM
7, pl. de la Madeleine 75008 (1 H2)
Tel: 01 42 65 00 95
4, rue de la Paix 75002 (1 I3)
Tel: 01 42 61 25 25

HERMÈS
24, rue du Faubourg-St-Honoré 75008 (1 H3)
Tel: 01 40 17 47 17
The atmosphere of the tiny Hermès museum, in the founders' former office above the store (visits by appt.), gives a glimpse of a past which contrasts sharply with the modern store.

LALIQUE
11, rue Royale 75008 (1 H3)
Tel: 01 53 05 12 12

LOUIS VUITTON
54, av. Montaigne 75008 (1 E3)
Tel: 01 45 62 47 00
78 bis, av. Marceau 75008 (1 B2)
Tel: 01 47 20 47 00

FINE PAPER AND DRAWING MATERIALS

SENNELIER – COULEURS DU QUAI VOLTAIRE
3, quai Voltaire 75007 (1 J6)
Tel: 01 42 60 72 15
Walking into this century-old store is like opening an old paint box. Its three floors are crammed full of everything an artist could possibly need, from portable easels to lapis lazuli in powder form. Sennelier's pigments de décoration are to be recommended.

CALLIGRANE
4 and 6, rue du Pont-Louis-Philippe 75004 (2 F7)
Tel: 01 40 27 00 74
The Rue du Pont-Louis-Philippe is the street par excellence for those who love writing and fine paper. Calligrane – undoubtedly the most innovative designer in this field – offers a range of Calligrane stationery, a selection of Fabriano paper (17 colors) and designer office accessories. The new store also has a large selection of papers from countries all over the world.

"April vase", one of the items in the Galerie Sentou and the famous Sennelier pastels.

INTERIOR DESIGN

LA TUILE À LOUP
35, rue Daubenton
75005 (5 E2)
Tel: 01 47 07 28 90
It is difficult to know where to look in this store with its French provincial crafts and works by contemporary artists: wicker objects hanging from the ceiling, glazed terracotta pots piled up on huge tables, santons from Provence, textiles. A wide range of quality items.

MILLER & BERTAUX
7, rue Ferdinand-Duval
75004 (2 F7)
Tel: 01 42 78 28 39
Two widely traveled designers and a store with 1001 ideas from all over the world: clothes, objects and small, simply designed items of furniture as

---

QUARTER BY QUARTER
Large numbers of artist-craftspeople, antique dealers and bric-à-brac dealers are concentrated at the following:

CARRÉ RIVE GAUCHE
▲ *263* (1 I–J6)
LOUVRE DES ANTIQUAIRES
▲ *334* (2 B5)
VIADUC DES ARTS AND RUE DU FAUBOURG-ST-ANTOINE
▲ *402* (2 I9 and 2 J8)
VILLAGE ST-PAUL
▲ *398* (2 G8)
VILLAGE SUISSE
(1 A7)

---

well as stationery and collage-maps, toys and amulets, and incense (Cedar, El Nil)

GALERIE SENTOU
18 and 24, rue du Pont-Louis-Philippe
75004 (2 F7)
Tel: 01 42 71 00 01
26, bd. Raspail
75007 (1 H7)
Tel: 01 45 49 00 05
The Galerie Sentou has outlets in two different districts. As well as producing and selling the work of the industrial designer Roger Talon, it is also the sole importer and distribution agent in Europe for the 120 designs of paper lamps by the sculptor Nogushi. There are also some irresistible Tsé-et-Tsé objects.

LIWAN
8, rue St-Sulpice
75006 (2 A9)
Tel: 01 43 26 07 40
Three floors of simply and superbly arranged space. From top to bottom: the world of the hammam (bath: bath robes, friction gloves), the djellaba (clothes) and the iwan (the interior courtyard of a Lebanese house: crockery, table linen).

MAISON DE VACANCES
63–64, galerie Montpensier 75001 (2 A4)
Tel: 01 47 03 99 74
It is deeply satisfying to see undressed and highly finished fabrics lying side by side here, where the

---

expression "the art of the table" means just what it says. Where else would you find household linen awaiting your needs, on this sort of scale?

GIEN
18, rue de l'Arcade
75008 (1 H1)
Tel: 01 42 66 52 32
Gien pottery is widely admired, and sets in both traditional and contemporary designs are displayed here.

LE JARDIN MOGHOL
35, rue Vieille-du-Temple 74004 (2 F6)
Tel: 01 48 87 41 32
The designs are the work of two artists living in India: Brigitte Singh's beautiful range of colored textiles (shirts, tablecloths, etc.), whose colors relate to the 18th-century Mogul court, and Neeru Kumar's geometric weaves (jackets, car rugs, etc.) in brown, beige and black.

GALERIE DE TEXTILES
5, rue Lobineau
75006 (2 A8)
Tel: 01 43 25 01 64
Stacked on shelves, draped over sofas or

---

hanging from wooden rails, textiles from Asia, Africa and America pay homage to a particular color, country, technique or artist.

EUGÈNE SEIGNEUR
16, rue Charlot
75003 (2 G5)
Tel: 01 48 04 81 96
Framed by a painting, the front of the store is an indication of the originality of its designer who, with the help of her assistants, creates personalized frames. Her range of mirrors "reinvented" from old frames is truly remarkable (from 900F).

GALERIE BAMYAN
24, rue St-Louis-en-l'Île 75001 (2 F8)
Tel: 01 46 33 69 66
1, rue des Blancs-Manteaux
75004 (2 F6)
Tel: 01 44 78 00 11
She is blonde, he is Afghan, together they make regular trips to central Asia to bring back furniture, carpets and textiles, as well as jewelry from Pakistan, southern Russia, India, Nepal and Iran.

◆ BREAD ◆

BOULANGERIE POILÂNE
8, rue du Cherche-Midi 75006
Tel: 01 45 48 42 59
Open Mon.–Sat. 7.15am–8.15pm. Closed Sun.
MAX POILÂNE
87, rue Brancion 75015
Tel: 01 48 28 45 90
Open daily 7.30am–8pm.
These two brothers bake just about the same fabulous, heavy, natural sourdough bread that Parisians are prepared to line up for. No baguettes.
POUJAURAN
20, rue Jean-Nicot 75007
Tel: 01 47 05 80 88
Open Tue.–Sat. 8am–8.30pm. Closed Aug.
Possibly the best baguette in town, as well as lots of other interesting breads. Chocolate cake and cannelé a must.
AU PÉTRIN D'ANTAN
174, rue Ordener 75018
Tel: 01 46 27 01 46
Open 7.30am–1.30pm, 3.30–8pm. Closed Thurs. and July.
The baguette is delicious. Fougasse, too, which takes you back to Provence.

◆ CHEESES ◆

These are without any doubt the two best cheese shops in Paris:
BARTHÉLÉMY
51, rue de Grenelle 75007
Tel: 01 45 48 56 75
Open 8.30am–1pm and 3.30pm–7.30pm. Closed Sun.–Mon. and public hols.
A fantastic array of the best local cheeses France can offer. This simple, old-fashioned-looking store supplies both the Elysées Palace and Matignon.

ALLÉOSSE
13, rue Poncelet 75017
Tel: 01 46 22 50 45
9am–1pm, 4pm–7.15pm. Closed Sun. am and Mon.
Most of the extraordinary cheeses are matured to perfection in the store's cellars.

◆ FOR CHILDREN ◆

AU CHAT PERCHÉ
54, rue du Roi-de-Sicile 75004 (2 F7)
Tel: 01 42 77 20 48
This is one of Paris' favorite toy stores. It is stacked high with toys – not cheap plastic toys but toys which are genuinely amusing and entertaining. Among the mobiles hanging from the ceiling is the delightful "revolving lamp" in which brightly colored motifs move in a square wood-and-paper frame.
L'AMICALE
(Party accessories)
20, rue des Vignoles 75020 (3 F8)
Tel: 01 43 70 21 00
At the wave of a magic wand – three floors of party accessories for every occasion arranged on huge display units. On the third floor there is even a cubicle for trying on the costume of your choice: geisha, Rambo or fairy.
VIRUS
32, rue du Bourg-Tibourg 75004 (2 F6)
Tel: 01 42 78 85 85
An unusual store which only sells kites. They hang from the picture rails and against translucent panels as if they were flying. The first floor is devoted to kites for beginners, while the second is for experienced enthusiasts with prices ranging from 80F to 3,000F. There

are some beautiful silk kites and a children's range (3 years upward).

◆ CHOCOLATE ◆

(*see also* "Pâtisseries" ▲ 530)
LA MAISON DU CHOCOLAT
225, rue du Faubourg-St-Honoré 75008 (9 C9)
Tel: 42 27 39 44
Open 9.30am–7pm. Closed Sun.
Also at:
◆ 19, rue de Sèvres 75006 (1 I9)
◆ 56, rue François-Ier 75008 (1 D3)
◆ 8, bd. de la Madeleine 75009 (1 H2)
◆ 89, av. R-Poincaré 75116 (8 I6)
– all with opening times as above
Exquisite handmade chocolates and chocolate cakes.
DEBAUVE ET GALLAIS
30, rue des Sts-Pères 75007 (1 J7)
Tel: 01 45 48 54 67
33, rue Vivienne 75002 (2 B3)
107, rue Jouffroy 75017 (9 C8)
Open 10am–7pm Closed Sun.
Beautiful shops. The exquisite dark chocolates (up to 99 percent cocoa) are packaged, wrapped and ribboned.
FRANCIS BOUCHER
202, rue de la Convention 75015
Tel: 01 45 31 44 02
Open 9.30am–1pm 2.15pm–7.30pm. Closed Sun., Mon., and Sun. am in Aug.
Rich, bitter truffles and chocolates made on the premises.
JEAN-PAUL HÉVIN
16 av. de la Motte-Picquet 75007 (1 E7)
Tel: 01 45 51 77 48
3, rue Vavin 75006
Tel: 01 43 54 09 85
231, rue St-Honoré 75001 (1 I3)
Open 10am–1pm, 2.30–7.15pm.
Closed Sun. and Aug.
One of the top

chocolate artisans, and, unlike most, not obsessed by extra-bitter chocolates. Also cakes (try the chocolate millefeuilles) and cocoa sorbets. The latest branch to open is on the rue St-Honoré.
CHRISTIAN CONSTANT
37, rue d'Assas 75006
Tel: 01 53 63 15 15
Open daily 8am–8.30pm.
26, rue du Bac 75007
Tel: 01 47 03 30 00
Open daily 8am–8pm.
The height of sophistication, with wonderfully subtle flavors. Chocolates, ice creams and pâtisseries can also be tasted in the salon de thé area.

◆ FLORISTS ◆

Expect to pay between 30F and 100F for deliveries in Paris.
LIEU-DIT
21, av. du Maine 75014 (6 G1)
Tel: 01 42 22 25 94
Lieu-dit occupies an unusual location in the Montparnasse district, at the end of a cobbled alleyway. In the workshop at the back of the store, the two florists create floral arrangements to order, with a marked preference for meadow flowers.
LES MILLE FEUILLES
2, rue Rambuteau 75003 (2 F6)
Tel: 01 42 78 32 93
Huge multi-colored bunches of flowers and bouquets wrapped in colored tissue paper add a delightful touch to this cleverly and tastefully designed florist's store. A fine selection of bric-à-brac is presented with the flowers.
MONCEAU FLEURS
11, bd. Henri IV 75004

Tel: 01 42 72 24 86
Open 9am–8pm
Sun. 9.30 – 1.30pm.
*The turnover of
flowers is colossal.
The smartest people
come here to buy the
cheapest flowers in
Paris. A sort of self-
service: select your
flowers and the
bouquet will be
made for you.*
Other branches:
◆ 84, bd. Raspail
75006
Tel: 01 45 48 70 10
◆ 92, bd.
Malesherbes 75008
Tel: 01 45 63 88 23
◆ 60 av. Paul-
Doumer 75016
Tel: 01 40 72 79 27
◆ 2 pl. du Gal Koenig
75017
Tel: 01 45 74 61 39
**MARIANNE
ROBIC**
41, rue de Bourgogne
75007
Tel: 01 44 18 03 47
Open 8am–8pm Sat.
until 7pm.
Closed Sun.
*Exquisite, lavish
bouquets with
seasonal flowers that
are neither too trendy
nor genteel. Around
250F for a bouquet.*
**LES BOUQUETS
D'ASTERS**
2, rue Lemercier
75017
Tel: 01 43 87 72 25
Open 10am–9pm.
Closed Sun. pm and
Mon. am.
*An original fresh
champêtre or
unstructured country
style to these
bouquets. Expect to
pay 160F/bouquet.*
FLEURS ET JARDINS
150, av. du Roule
92200 Neuilly
Tel: 01 47 47 19 19
Open daily
8.30am–8.30pm.
*Big, beautiful, round
bunches with colors
that shade off
gradually.*

◆ ICE CREAM ◆

BERTHILLON
31, rue St-Louis-en
l'Île 75004

Tel: 01 43 54 31 61
Open 10am–8pm.
Closed Mon, Tue.,
Easter holidays and
July and Aug.
*The success of this
shop is not just a
Paris affectation.
They really are the
best. If you can't bear
to stand in line, or the
shop is shut – all
summer! – Berthillon
ice creams are
served in many of the
cafés on the Île-St-
Louis.*

◆ LUXURY ◆ GROCERIES

*(see also "Tea and
coffee"* ▲ *530)*
FAUCHON
26–30, pl. de la
Madeleine 75008
Tel: 01 47 42 60 11
Open 9.40am–7pm.
Closed Sun.
*High prices for top-
quality luxury items,
including wines, jams
and rillettes. Great
pâtisseries.*
HÉDIARD
21, pl. de la
Madeleine 75008
Tel: 01 43 12 88 88
Open 9.30am–9pm.
Closed Sun.
*Other outlets in Paris.
A fine selection of
wines and also luxury
groceries.*
**LAFAYETTE GOURMET
GALERIES LAFAYETTE**
48, bd. Haussmann,
75009 (1 J1)
Tel: 01 48 74 46 06
Open 9am–8pm.
Closed Sun.
*An intelligent and
modern version of the
traditional gourmet
grocery shops.
Fabulous wines.*

◆ NATURAL ◆ AND ORGANIC PRODUCTS

**HERBORISTERIE DU
PALAIS-ROYAL**
11, rue des Petits-
Champs 75001
(2 B3)
Tel: 01 42 97 54 68
*This is undoubtedly
the finest herbalist's
in Paris. The ladders
propped against its*

natural wood shelves
are used to reach
some of the store's
500 – unpackaged –
medicinal plants and
herbs. Own products
include foaming bath
essences which are
out of this world.
BODY SHOP
*Body Shop stores –
in the 1st, 4th, 6th,
9th, 13th, 14th and
16th arrondissements
– offer a wide range
of beauty products
made from natural
ingredients and not
tested on animals.*
Tel: 01 42 60 54 78
L'HERBE VERTE
5, rue de Charonne
75011 (2 J8)
Tel: 01 48 06 50 69
*L'Herbe Verte is
characterized by
simplicity and beauty.
It has an elegant,
early 20th-century
oak frontage, and the
interior is decorated
with zinc flower pails
and remarkable
wrought-iron vases
designed by the
florist. The store is
dominated by
sunflowers all year
round.*
LES ABEILLES
21, rue de la Butte-
aux-Cailles 75013
(5 D6)
Tel: 01 45 81 43 48
*A glass pyramid of
pots of honey, in
every shade of
amber, stands
invitingly at the
entrance to the store.
Inside a range of
some 55 varieties of
honey from all over
the world includes
rare honeys (from the
tulip tree and
Canada) and
French classics
such as bramble
honey (highly
recommended) and
honeys from the
Paris region.*
**LES HERBES DU
LUXEMBOURG**
3, rue de Médicis
75006 (2 B10)
Tel: 01 43 26 91 53
*As soon as you cross
the threshold, you
are greeted by the*

delicious scent of
some 250 medicinal
plants and herbs as
well as the more
unexpected aromas
of bread and fresh
eggs. There are also
products based on
essential oils.
NATURALIA
52, rue St-Antoine
75004 (2 H8) .
36, rue Monge 75005
(5 E1)
53 bis, rue Cler
75007 (1 D6) and in
the 10th, 15th, 17th
and 18th
arrondissements.
Tel: 01 42 61 74 14
*Daily deliveries of
organically produced
fruit, vegetables and
fresh bread. Dairy
and grocery sections,
food accompaniments
and dietetic products.
Friendly and attentive
service.*
**NATURE &
DÉCOUVERTES**
Forum des Halles
75001 (2 D5)
Carrousel du Louvre
75001 (2 A5)
Les Trois Quartiers
75008 (1 I2)
Centre Commercial
Italie 2, 75013 (5 E5)
61, rue de Passy
75016 (8 H10)
For information
Tel: 01 39 56 01 47
*The soft lighting
suggests woodland
light, the natural
materials are
incorporated into the
décor, and the music
is, of course,
pastoral. Naturalists
will find everything
they need, from bird
calls and divining
rods to microscopes,
as well as vegetable-
ivory jewelry.*
**RENDEZ-VOUS DE LA
NATURE**
96, rue Mouffetard
75005 (5 D2)
Tel: 01 43 36 59 34
*Rendezvous de la
Nature is one of
Paris's best-stocked
natural products
stores. It is situated
in the Rue
Mouffetard, an old
commercial district
which has retained*

its former character and busy atmosphere as a result of its pedestrianized status. There is a wide choice of brands in each product range: cereals, dairy products, fresh breads, jars of preserves and baby food.

LES NOUVEAUX ROBINSON
49, rue Raspail 93100 Montreuil-sous-Bois (Métro: Robespierre)
Tel: 01 49 88 70 44
The city's first completely organic supermarket covers an area of 360 sq. yards. A sober décor with natural wood shelves displaying a wide range of products: 80 types of (unpackaged) cereals, 15 different sorts of bread, which vary from day to day, fresh milk and eggs and organic wines (from 20F per liter, or 15F in bulk).

VILMORIN
4, quai de la Mégisserie 75001 (2 C6)
Tel: 01 42 33 61 62
This seed merchant's has been on the Qai de la Mégisserie since 1743. For six generations and over 250 years, the Vilmorin family has imported seeds (vegetables, flowers and trees) from all over the world, even introducing the Cedar of Lebanon and the potato. The store sells thousands of different types of seeds as well as some superb reproductions of plant watercolors.

◆ PÂTISSERIES ◆

JEAN-CLAUDE GAULUPEAU
12, rue Mabillon 75006
Tel: 01 43 54 16 93
Open 7am–8pm. Closed Mon.

The most charming pâtissière with delicious croissants and fabulous house favorites such as the dark chocolate Samba. Breakfast and light lunches.

DALLOYAU
101, rue de Grenelle 75008
Open daily 9am–8pm.
There are six Dalloyaus in Paris, a handful in Japan, but the quality of the Opéra cake (invented by the Dalloyaus in the 1800's) remains unchanged, and unrivalled.

COQUELIN AÎNÉ
67, rue de Passy 75016. Tel: 01 45 24 44 00. Open 9am–7.30pm. Closed Sun. pm and Mon.
Puits d'amour and Ali-Babas are devoured with unashamed pleasure on the terrace.

◆ SPECIALTY STORES

À L'OLIVIER
23, rue de Rivoli 75004
Tel: 01 48 04 86 59
Open 9.30am–1pm and 2.30pm–7pm.
Three French olive oils and other oils, including one made from pumpkin seeds.

À LA VILLE DE RODEZ
22, rue Vieille-du-Temple 75004
Tel: 01 48 87 79.36
Open 8.30am–1pm and 3pm–7.30pm. Closed Sun. and Mon.
This is the kingdom of hams, saucissons, roquefort, tomme and St-Nectaire.

PETROSSIAN
18, bd. de Latour-Maubourg 75007
Tel: 01 45 51 70 64
Open 9am–8pm. Closed Sun. July and Aug.; 10am–7pm.
Don't be intimidated by the 20 different sorts of caviars. Mme Petrossian also has a top foie gras at a

better price than most of the neighborhood traiteurs.

LA BONBONNIÈRE DE LA TRINITÉ
4, rue Blanche, pl. d'Estienner-d'Orves, 75009
Tel: 01 48 74 23 38 and 28, rue de Miromesnil 75008
Tel: 01 42 65 02 39
Open 9am–7pm. Closed Sun.
Mouth-watering window displays, the sweets are sold by weight.

LA CAMPAGNE
111, bd. de Grenelle, 75015
Tel: 01 47 34 77 05
Open 8.30am–1pm and 4pm–to 8pm. Closed Sun. pm and Mon.
Unequaled foie gras, cassoulet, terrine de canard made on the premises.

IZRAËL
30, rue François Miron 75004
Tel: 01 42 72 66 23
Open 9.30am–1pm and 2.30pm–7pm. Closed Sun, Mon. and Aug.
Ali Baba's cavern with 3000 exotic products from spices to olive oils.

◆ TEA AND COFFEE

(See also "Salons de Thé and coffee stores" ▲ 507)

VERLET
256, rue St-Honoré 75001
Tel: 01 42 60 67 39
Closed Sun, Mon. and Aug. 9am–7pm.
Expensive coffees and spices in this authentic 1880's shop.

LAPEYRONIE
3, rue Brantôme Quartier de l'Horloge Beaubourg 75003
Tel: 01 40 27 97 57
Closed Sun., Aug. and public hols. Open 10am–7pm.
The best in Paris. Bruno Saguez does two roasts for his fabulous Mexican

maragogype, a lighter roast for those who prefer coffee with milk, and a darker roast for true fanatics. Some sixty varieties of tea.

MARIAGE FRÈRES
30, rue du Bourg-Tibourg 75004
Tel: 01 42 74 65 32 also 13, rue des Grands-Augustins 75006
Tel: 01 40 51 82 50
Open daily 10.30am to 7.30pm.
Salon de Thé open noon–7.30pm.
English tea connoisseurs, exasperated by the poor quality of leaves available in Britain, come here to buy single-garden teas. All 500 teas can be tasted in the salon de thé.

◆ WINES ◆

(see also "Wine bars" ▲ 505 and "Luxury groceries" ▲ 529)

LEGRAND FILLES ET FILS
1, rue de la Banque 75001
Tel: 01 42 60 07 12
Open 9am–7.30pm. Closed Tue., Sun.
Reasonably priced wines and old-fashioned sweets in authentic 1900 décor.

CAVES AUGÉ
116, bd. Haussmann 75008
Tel: 01 45 22 16 97
Open 9am–8pm. Closed Sun., Mon.
Proust used to buy wine and fruit in this attractive 1850's shop. Today there is a top selection of wines (all prices) and alcohols.

REPAIRE DE BACCHUS
58, rue d'Auteuil, 75016
Tel: 01 45 25 09 75
Open 9.30am–7pm. Closed Sun. pm and Mon.
A recent well-run chain with 24 wine stores in Paris. Clever selection and keen prices.

APPENDICES

◆ ESSENTIAL ◆ READING

◆ BRASSAI:
The Secret Paris of the Thirties: Brassai, Trans. Miller (R.), Thames & Hudson, London, 1978
◆ DE BALZAC (H.):
Cousin Bette, Trans. James Waring, Everyman's Library, London/AA Knopf, New York 1991
◆ DE BALZAC (H.):
Old Goriot, Trans. Ellen Marriage, Everyman's Library/AA Knopf 1991
◆ HEMINGWAY (E.):
A Moveable Feast, Bantam, New York, 1965
◆ HUGO (V.):
The Hunchback of Notre-Dame, Trans. Shoberl (F.), Richard Bentley, London, 1838
◆ ORWELL (G.):
Down and Out in Paris and London, Penguin Books, London, 1940
◆ STEIN (G.):
The Autobiography of Alice B. Toklas, Harcourt, Brace, New York, 1933

◆ GENERAL ◆ INTEREST

◆ BENNETT (A.):
Paris Nights, Hodder & Stoughton, London, 1905
◆ BRILLAT-SAVARIN:
Physiologie du Goût, Flammarion, Paris, 1982
◆ CRONIN (V.):
Paris, city of light 1919-1939, HarperCollins, London, 1994
◆ LE DANTEC (J.P.) AND LE DANTEC (D.):
Paris in Bloom, London, Thames & Hudson, 1991
◆ EHRLICH (B.):
Paris on the Seine Weidenfeld & Nicolson, London 1962
◆ HEROLD (C.):
Mistress to an age, Bobbs-Merrill, New York, 1958
◆ LONERGAN (W.F.):
Forty Years of Paris, T. Fisher Unwin, London, 1907
◆ MONTAGNÉ (P.):
New Larousse Gastronomique, Trans. Froud (N.), Gray (P.), Murdoch (M.),and Taylor (B.M.), Hamlyn, London and New York, 1960
◆ OSTER (D.) AND GOULEMOT (J.):
La vie Parisienne: Anthologie des Moeurs du XIXe siècle, SAND-CONTI, PARIS, 1989
◆ RICHARDSON (J.):
The Bohemians: La vie de Bohème in Paris 1830-1914, Macmillan, 1969

◆ ROBERTSON (W. J.):
Life was worth living, Harper & Bros., New York, 1931
◆ ROTHENSTEIN (W.):
Men and Memories, Faber and Faber, London, 1931-39
◆ RUSSEL (J.):
Paris, Thames & Hudson, London, 1960
◆ SKINNER (C.O.):
Elegant Wits and Grand Horizontals: Paris – La Belle Epoque, Michael Joseph, London, 1963
◆ TROLLOPE (F.):
Paris and the Parisians in 1835, Bentley, London, 1836
◆ WISER (W.):
The Crazy Years: Paris in the Twenties, Thames & Hudson, London, 1983

◆ TRAVELERS' ◆ TALES

◆ BINGHAM (HON.D.):
Recollections of Paris, Chapman & Hall, London, 1896
◆ CORYATE (T.):
Coryat's Crudities, Vol.1, James MacLehose and Sons, Glasgow, 1905
◆ HAZLITT (W.):
Notes of a journey through France and Italy, Hunt and Clarke, London, 1826
◆ SAINT-SIMON:
Historical Memoirs of the Duc de Saint-Simon, Vol. III: 1715–23, Edited and translated by Lucy Norton, Hamish Hamilton, London 1972
◆ SAUVAN (M.):
Picturesque Tour of the Seine from Paris to the Sea, R. Ackermann, London, 1821
◆ SCOTT (J.):
Picturesque views of the City of Paris and its Environs, Longman, Hunt, Rees, Orme & Brown, London, 1820
◆ SMOLLETT (T.):
Travels through France and Italy, Oxford University Press, London, 1979
◆ YOUNG (A.):
Travels in France during the years 1787, 1788 and 1789, Cambridge University Press, Cambridge, 1950

◆ HISTORY ◆

◆ BICKNELL (A.L.):
Life in the Tuileries under the Second Empire, The Century Co., New York, 1895
◆ CARLYLE (T.):
The French Revolution, J.M. Dent Ltd. /E.P. Dutton, London, 1955

◆ KERSHAW (A.):
A History of the Guillotine, Calder, London, 1957
◆ LUTHY (H.):
France against herself, Meridian Books, New York, 1959
◆ MAUROIS (A.):
A History of France, trans. Binsse (H.L.), Jonathan Cape, London, 1949
◆ NOVICK (P.):
The resistance versus Vichy, Chatto & Windus, London, 1968
◆ DE ROTHSCHILD (G.):
The Whims of Fortune, Granada, London, 1985
◆ SAINT-SIMON:
Saint-Simon at Versailles, Sel. and trans. by Lucy Norton, Penguin, Harmondsworth, 1985
◆ STEEGMULLER (F.):
The Grande Mademoiselle, Farrar Strauss, New York, 1955
◆ WHITEHURST (F.M.):
Court and Social Life in France under Napoleon III, Tinsley, London, 1873
◆ ZELDIN (T.):
France 1845–1945, OUP, 5 volumes

◆ ARCHITECTURE ◆

◆ ARNOLD (W.):
The Historic Hotels of Paris, Thames & Hudson, London, 1990
◆ ATGET (E.):
Atget's Paris, Thames & Hudson, London, 1993
◆ BALLON (H.):
The Paris of Henri IV: architecture and urbanism, MIT Press, Cambridge (Mass.), 1991
◆ BEAL (M.):
British Embassy, Paris: the house and its works of art, Government Art Collection, London, 1992
◆ BERGER (R.W.):
A Royal Passion: Louis XIV as Patron of Architecture, Cambridge University Press, Cambridge, 1994
◆ BOSSI (F.):
Paris1900: Architecture and Design, Trans. Palmes (J.C.), Rizzoli, New York, 1989
◆ BOXER (M.):
The Paris Ritz, Thames & Hudson, London, 1991
◆ BRAHAM (A.):
The architecture of the French Enlightenment, Thames & Hudson, London, 1989
◆ BRASSAI:
The Arts of my Life, Trans. Miller (R.), Thames & Hudson, London, 1982
◆ BRASSAI AND MOREAU (P.):
Paris after Dark: Brassai, Thames & Hudson, London, 1987

◆ CHAMPOLLION (H.):
Paris, Thames & Hudson, London, 1988
◆ CHEVALIER (L.):
The assassination of Paris, Trans. Jodan (D.P.), University of Chicago Press, Chicago, 1994
◆ KERTESZ (A.):
André Kertesz of Paris and London, Thames & Hudson, London, 1985
◆ LOYER (F.):
Paris, Nineteenth century Architecture and Urbanism, Trans. Clark (C.L.), Abbeville, New York, c1984
◆ MIDDLETON (R.) ED.:
The Beaux Art and Nineteenth century French Architecture, Thames & Hudson, London, 1984
◆ OLSEN (D.J.):
The City as a Work of Art: London, Paris, Vienna, Yale University Press, New Haven, 1986
◆ PADAILLÉ-GALABRUN (A.):
The Birth of Intimacy: Privacy and Domestic Life in early Modern Paris, Trans. Phelps (J.), Polity Press, Cambridge, c1991
◆ ROWE (W.):
Royal Châteaux of Paris, Putnam, London, 1956
◆ RUSSELL (J.):
Paris, Thames & Hudson, London, 1983
◆ SILVER (K.E.):
Esprit de Corps-The Art of the Parisian Avant-Garde and the First World War, Thames & Hudson, London, 1989
◆ SUTCLIFFE (A.):
Paris, an Architectural History, Yale University Press, New Haven, 1993
◆ TAYLOR (B.B.):
Le Corbusier, The City of Refuge, Paris 1929-33, University of Chicago Press, Chicago, 1987
◆ THOMPSON (D.):
Renaissance Paris: Architecture and Growth, Zwemmer, London, 1984

◆ INTELLECTUAL ◆ AND ARTISTIC LIFE

◆ BALDICK (R.):
The First Bohemian. The Life of Henry Mauger, Hamish Hamilton, London, 1961
◆ BARRAULT (J.L.):
Memories for Tomorrow, Thames & Hudson, London, 1974
◆ BEACH (S.):
Shakespeare & Company, Harcourt Brace, New York, 1959
◆ CAUTE (D.):
Communism and the French Intellectuals,

André Deutsch, London, 1994

◆ CÉZANNE (P.):
Letters of Paul Cézanne, Ed. Rewald (J.), Trans. Kay (M.), Bruno Cassirer, Oxford, 1976

◆ CLERGUE (H.):
The Salon: A Study of French Society and Personalities in the Eighteenth Century, G.P. Putnam & Sons, New York, 1907

◆ DE GONCOURT (E.) AND DE GONCOURT (J.):
Pages from the Goncourt Journal, Ed. and Trans. Baldick (R.), Oxford University Press, Oxford, 1978

◆ HUDDLESTON (S.):
Paris, Salons, Cafés, Studios: Being Social, Artistic and Literary Memories, J.B. Lippincott, Philadelphia, 1928

◆ SHATTUCK (R.):
The Banquet Years. The Arts in France 1885-1918, Faber & Faber, London, 1959

◆ WALL (I.):
French Communism in the Era of Stalinism, Greenwood Press, Westport, Conn., 1983

◆ WHITE (E.):
Jean Genet, Chatto & Windus, London, 1993

◆ WILSON (E.):
A Literary Chronicle of the Forties, W.H. Allen, London, 1951

◆ ZELDIN (T.):
The French, Collins Harwill, 1989

◆ **PAINTING AND SCULPTURE** ◆

◆ Besnard-Bernadac (M.L.):
The Musée Picasso, Paris, Vol.1, Thames & Hudson, London, 1990

◆ BOUVET (F.):
Bonnard: The Complete Graphic Works, Thames & Hudson, London, 1981

◆ BRUNHAMMER (Y.):
L'art de vivre: Decorative Arts and Design in France 1789-1989, Thames & Hudson, London, 1989

◆ CHAMPIGNEULLE (B.):
Rodin, Thames & Hudson, London, 1987

◆ CLARK (T.J.):
The Painting of Modern Life: Paris in the art of Manet and his Followers. Thames & Hudson, London, 1990

◆ COURTION (P.):
Manet, Thames & Hudson, London, 1963

◆ DAIX (P.) AND ROSSELET (J.):
Picasso: The Cubist Years 1907-1916. A Catalogue Raisonné of the paintings and Related Works, Thames & Hudson, London, 1979

◆ DENVIR (B.):
Toulouse-Lautrec, Thames & Hudson, London, 1991

◆ ELDERFIELD (J.):
Henri Matisse: A Retrospective, Thames & Hudson, London, 1992

◆ FRIEDMANN (J.):
Inside Paris: Discovering the Period Interiors of Paris, Phaidon, Oxford, 1989

◆ GUSE (E.G.):
Rodin: Drawings and Watercolours, Thames & Hudson, London, 1985

◆ LACLOTTE (M.), LUCIE-SMITH (E.) et al:
Impressionist and Post-Impressionist at the Musée d' Orsay, Thames & Hudson, London, 1986

◆ MELLY (G.):
Paris and the Surrealists, Thames & Hudson, London, 1991

◆ PACH (W.):
Renoir, Thames & Hudson, London, 1975

◆ PINET (H.):
Rodin-The Hands of a Genius, Thames & Hudson, London, 1992

◆ RICH (D.C.):
Degas, Thames & Hudson, London, 1954

◆ RICHET (M.):
The Musée Picasso, Paris, Vol.II, Thames & Hudson, London, 1982

◆ WHITFIELD (S.):
Fauvism, Thames & Hudson, London, 1991

◆ **FASHION** ◆

◆ BRABEC (D.) AND SALVY (E.):
Paris Chic – The Parisian's own Insider Shopping Guide, Thames & Hudson, London, 1993

◆ COLEMAN (E.A.):
The Opulent Era – Fashions of Worth, Doucet and Pingat, Thames & Hudson, London, 1989

◆ DIOR (C.):
Dior by Dior, Weidenfeld & Nicolson, London, 1974

◆ GIROUD (F.):
Dior: Christian Dior 1905-1957, Thames & Hudson, London, 1987

◆ WORTH (J.P.):
A Century of Fashion, Trans. Scott (R.M.), Little Brown, Boston, 1928

◆ **LITERATURE** ◆

◆ DE BALZAC (H.):
Cousin Pons, Trans. Marriage (E.), J.M. Dent & Sons, London/E.P. Dutton, New York, 1960

◆ DE BEAUVOIR (S.):
Memoirs of a dutiful daughter, Trans. Kirkup (J.), André Deutsch and Weidenfeld and Nicolson, London, 1959

◆ CAPOTE (T.):
Answered Prayers, Random House, New York, 1987

◆ DICKENS (C.):
A Tale of Two Cities, Everyman's Library/AA Knopf 1993

◆ DUMAS (A.):
Le Demi-Monde, Paris, Levy, 1855

◆ DU MAURIER (G.):
Trilby, Osgood, Mc Ilvaine, London, 1892

◆ FITZGERALD (F. S.):
The Crack-Up,Penguin Books, London, 1965

◆ FLAUBERT (G.):
Sentimental Education, Trans. Baldick (R.), Penguin Books, London, 1964

◆ GELLHORN (M.):
A Honeyed Peace, André Deutsch, London, 1954

◆ HALL (R.):
The well of Loneliness, Paris, Pegasus, 1928

◆ HUGO (V.):
Les Misérables, Hodder & Stoughton, London, 1925

◆ IRVING (W.):
Journals and Notebooks, 1803-1806, Vol. 1, Ed. Wright (N.), University of Wisconsin Press, Madison, 1969

◆ JAMES (H.):
A Small Boy and Others, Charles Scribner's Sons, New York, 1913

◆ JAMES (H.):
The Tragic Muse, Houghton Mifflin & Co. New York and Boston, 1890

◆ KEROUAC (J.):
Satori in Paris, Grove, New york, 1967

◆ KOESTLER (A.) AND (C.):
Stranger on the Square, Hutchinson, London, 1983

◆ LEWIS (D.B.W.):
François Villon, Doubleday Anchor, New York, 1958

◆ LEWIS (P.W.):
Tarr, Chatto and Windus, London, 1928

◆ LITTLEWOOD (I.):
Paris, a Literary Companion, Murray, London, 1987

◆ McCARTHY (M.):
Birds of America, Penguin Books, London, 1973

◆ MAUPASSANT (G. DE):
Bel-ami, Victor-Havard, Paris, 1886

◆ MILLER (H.):
Black Spring, Obelisk Press, Paris, 1936

◆ MITFORD (N.):
The Blessing, Hamish Hamilton, London, 1951

◆ PROUST (M.):
A la recherche du temps perdu, Trans. Scott-Moncrieff, Kilmartin (T.) and Mayor (A.), Chatto & Windus, London, 1981

◆ QUENEAU (R.):
Zazie dans le Métro, Trans. del Piombo (A.) and Kahane (E.), Olympia Press, Paris, 1959

◆ RHYS (J.):
After Leaving Mr. Mackenzie, Penguin Books, London, 1975

◆ RHYS (J.):
Quartet, André Deutsch, London, 1969

◆ ROLLAND (R.):
Jean-Christophe, Trans. Cannan (G.), William Heinemann, London, 1910-1913, Paris, 1905

◆ STEIN (G.):
Paris France, Batsford, London, 1940

◆ STEIN (G.):
Wars I Have Seen, Random House, New York, 1945

◆ STERN (L.):
A Sentimental Journey, J.M. Dent & Sons, London, 1960

◆ THACKERAY (W.M.):
The Paris Sketch-Book, Tauchnitz, Leipzig, 1873

◆ TWAIN (M.):
The Innocent Abroad, Routledge, London, 1872

◆ VIDAL (G.):
The Judgment of Paris, Panther Books, London, 1976

◆ WHARTON (E.):
The Custom of the Country, Constable, London, 1965

◆ ZOLA (E.):
Thérèse Raquin, Trans. Tancock (L.), Folio Society, London, 1969

◆ ZOLA (E.):
The Masterpiece, Trans. Walton (J.), Paul Elek, London/New York, 1950

◆ ZOLA (E.):
Le ventre de Paris, Trans. Hughes (D.) and Mason (M. J.), Paul Elek, London, 1958

◆ ZOLA (E.):
Les Trois Villes, Paris, Trans. Vizetelly (E.A.), Chatto & Windus, 1898

Simone Signoret in Golden Marie, Jacques Becker (1952).

Corinne Marchand in Cleo from 5 to 7, Agnès Varda (1962).

The first commercial movie show was held in Paris on December 28, 1895 in the basement of the Grand Café at no. 14, boulevard des Capucines. Paris has been a constant source of inspiration to directors: in 1913 Louis Feuillade launched his hero, *Fantômas*, across the rooftops of Paris, while René Clair, Jean Renoir and Marcel Carné – assisted by such talented set-designers as Alexandre Trauner – favored the streets, the banks of the Seine and the night life of the city. They were succeeded by the *Nouvelle Vague*, which took movies (confined to the studio by the Occupation) out into the cafés, squares and avenues. Paris is still one of the most widely filmed cities in the world.

"FANTÔMAS"
Louis Feuillade (1914–24); based on the novels by Pierre Souvestre and Marcel Allain; starring René Navarre.
A masked criminal terrifies the citizens of early 20th-century Paris. The action is set in a strange and mysterious Paris that would be adopted by the Surrealists.
"SOUS LES TOITS DE PARIS" (UNDER THE ROOFS OF PARIS)
René Clair (1930).
The simple plot (the love of street singer and a street hawker for a beautiful young Rumanian girl) serves as a pretext for depicting life in a working-class district of Paris and the preoccupations of those who live there. It follows them from workshop to dance hall in the memorable setting of Belleville-Ménilmontant re-created by Lazare Meerson.

"BOUDU SAUVÉ DES EAUX" (BOUDU SAVED FROM DROWNING)
Jean Renoir (1932); assistant director: Jacques Becker; starring Michel Simon.
A tramp jumps into the Seine from the Pont des Arts and is saved from drowning by a bookseller. Taken into the latter's home, Boudu proceeds to destroy his life. The movie, shot on location, is a fierce satire of bourgeois

convention and restores the lyricism of the streets of Paris.
"DESIGN FOR LIVING"
Ernst Lubitsch (1933); starring Gary Cooper,

Miriam Hopkins, Frederic March.
A writer and an artist fall in love with the same woman. The three decide to share an apartment as a platonic ménage à trois. In his brilliant comedy Ernst Lubitsch conforms to the "bohemian" image of Paris and the Parisians created by American movies.
"HÔTEL DU NORD"
Marcel Carné (1938); screenplay: Henri Jeanson; sets: Alexandre Trauner; starring Arletty, Louis Jouvet, Anabella.
Two lovers commit suicide in the Hôtel du Nord with its ill-assorted clientele. The movie, famous for the performances of Louis Jouvet and Arletty, also owes a great deal to Alexandre Trauner who, in the words of Marcel Carné (1933), re-created "the picturesque and disturbing world of the Canal Saint-Martin

against a setting of factories, garages, girders and carts being unloaded".
"LES ENFANTS DU PARADIS" (US: CHILDREN OF PARADISE)
Marcel Carné (1945); screenplay: Jacques Prévert; music: Joseph Kosma and Maurice Thiriet; sets: Alexandre Trauner; starring Arletty, Jean-Louis Barrault, Pierre Brasseur.
In c.1830 the destinies of the courtesan Garance, mime-artist Deburau, actor Frédéric Lemaître and murderer Lacenaire cross on the Boulevard du Temple. This

Michel Simon in Boudu Saved from Drowning, *Jean Renoir (1932).*

Jean-Pierre Léaud in La Maman et la Putain, *Jean Eustache (1973).*

Marcel Carné masterpiece shows different aspects of Paris: theater, public baths, criminals' haunts and artists' studios.

"Sous le ciel de Paris"
Julien Duvivier (1950); scenario and screenplay: René Lefèvre and Henri Jeanson; music: Jean Wiener; starring Brigitte Auber, Marcel Praince, Jean Brochard.
Julien Duvivier has captured all the drama, tension and brief moments of happiness of a day in Paris. The characters pass by, meet and confront each other. A sculptor, a student, a manual worker, an old woman and a young artist appear in a series of playlets.

"Casque d'Or" (Golden Marie)
Jacques Becker (1952); starring Simone Signoret, Serge Reggiani, Claude Dauphin, Raymond Bussières.
In a café on the banks of the Marne, a carpenter from Belleville falls in love with a prostitute. Their love is thwarted by a gangster, head of a gang of hoodlums, who wants Marie for himself. Jacques Becker presents a realistic, working-class view of the fortifications and dance halls of Paris.

"Touchez pas au Grisbi" (Grisbi, aka Honor Among Thieves)
Jacques Becker (1953); screenplay: Albert Simonin; music: Jean Wiener; starring Jean Gabin, Lino Ventura, Jeanne Moreau.
Two gangsters decide to retire after one final, fantastic bank robbery. But they have to reckon with a rival gang. Adapted from a série noire novel by Albert Simonin, the movie was shot mainly in the streets of Montmartre and a Pigalle nightclub.

"French Cancan" (US: Only the French Can)
Jean Renoir (1954); starring Françoise Arnoul, Jean Gabin, Valentine Tessier.
In a studio where sets – designed like paintings – are artificial, Renoir re-creates the Paris of the Belle Époque and the imagery of the Paris night clubs as painted by Toulouse-Lautrec.

"À bout de souffle" (Breathless)
Jean-Luc Godard (1960); idea and adaptation by François Truffaut, Jean-Luc Godard and Claude Chabrol; starring Jean-Paul Belmondo, Jean Seaberg.
A young car thief, wanted by the police, tries to seduce an American student selling the New York Herald Tribune on the Champs-Élysées. Paris provides much of the setting for the location-shooting of Jean-Luc Godard's first movie centered around the world of news reporting, which introduces the Nouvelle Vague.

"Zazie dans le métro" (Zazie)
Louis Malle (1960); starring Catherine Demongeot, Philippe Noiret, Hubert Deschamps, Jacques Dufilho, Annie Fratellini.
Zazie, a precocious and mischievous kid, comes to stay with her uncle in Paris. He shows her the city and introduces her to the colorful local residents: the shoemaker, the café owner and his waitress, a taxi driver and a policeman.

"Cléo de 5 à 7" (Cleo from 5 to 7)
Agnès Varda (1962); music: Michel Legrand; starring

ARLETTY (1898–1992)

Arletty was the incarnation of the witty, elegant Parisienne. Her immortal remarks include:
"Atmosphere, atmosphere, do I look as though I've got atmosphere?" (to Louis Jouvet in *Hôtel du Nord*), and when (in real life), following the Liberation of Paris, she was accused of having gone out with the Germans: "It was up to you to stop them coming in." Arletty (real name Léonie Bathiat) started her career in nightclub revues. She was given her first big part in Marcel Carné's *Hôtel du Nord* (1938), with Louis Jouvet, where she played a character that was to become her stock in trade: the warm-hearted prostitute or night-club singer (Marcel Carné's *Le jour se lève* (1939) with Jean Gabin). But it was in the Carné masterpiece – *Les Enfants du Paradis* (Children of Paradise) (1945) – that she was immortalized. It was the unforgettable beauty and wit of Garance that made Arletty a legend.

535

The Last Metro,
*François Truffaut
(1980).*

Full Moon in Paris,
*Eric Rohmer
(1984).*

Subway,
*Luc Besson,
(1985).*

La Discrète,
*Christian Vincent
(1990).*

Corinne Marchand. *Cleo, a young night-club singer, is awaiting the results of medical tests. She tries to allay her fears by walking in Montparnasse and the Parc Montsouris, and sits for a long time in the Café du Dôme watching the busy street.*

"PLAYTIME" (LE TEMPS DES LOISIRS)
Jacques Tati (1967); starring Jacques Tati. *Monsieur Hulot wanders in a modern and anonymous Paris. Jacques Tati's careful studio reconstruction of an artificial world of offices, drugstores, exhibition halls and buildings, evokes the district of La Défense. It is a New York-style Paris where human relationships become trivialized.*

"LA MAMAN ET LA PUTAIN" (THE MOTHER AND THE WHORE)
Jean Eustache (1973); starring Bernadette Lafont, Jean-Pierre Léaud, Françoise Lebrun.
A young man is in love with two women. His life revolves around cafés and telephone boxes as he moves between the quays of the Seine and the

Luxembourg. A lyrical and informal view of Paris provides the backdrop for his vacillations.

"LE DERNIER MÉTRO" (THE LAST METRO)
François Truffaut (1980); starring Catherine Deneuve, Gérard Depardieu.
In 1942 a young woman is on her way to visit her husband in his theater where he is having to hide in the cellar because of his Jewish origins. François Truffaut has captured the essence of a nocturnal, subterranean Paris inhabited by dubious characters and the heroes and heroines of the Occupation.

"LES NUITS DE LA PLEINE LUNE" (FULL MOON IN PARIS)
Eric Rohmer (1984); starring Pascale Ogier, Fabrice Lucchini.
A young woman, bored by life in the suburbs, leaves to

discover the "real life" awaiting her in Paris. All she finds is loneliness and a sense of isolation.

"SUBWAY"
Luc Besson (1985); starring Isabelle Adjani, Christophe Lambert, Richard Bohringer, Michel Galabru, Jean-Hugues Anglade.
Fred, a young drop-out, arranges to meet Helena, the distant and mysterious bourgeoise, in the Paris Métro. Besson evokes an underground world peopled by a strange assortment of individuals: musicians, unauthorized street hawkers, pickpockets.

"LA DISCRÈTE"
Christian Vincent (1990); starring Fabrice Lucchini, Judith Henry.
A young writer seduces a young woman in the full knowledge that he will desert her. He records

each stage of their relationship in a diary that his publisher promises to print. The 6th arrondissement, with its cafés and book stores, provides the essential setting for the affair.

"CHACUN CHERCHE SON CHAT"
Cedric Klapisch (1995); starring Garance Clavel, Olivier Py.
In her quarter near the Bastille, Chloé tries to find someone to look after her cat while she is on holiday. Her quest turns into a rediscovery of her neighborhood.

"PARIS"
Raymond Depardon (1997); starring Sylvie Peyre, Luc Delahaye.
A movie director in Paris is researching characters for his next film. By interviewing passers-by in the streets, cafés and Gare St-Lazare, he attempts to locate the pulse of the city.

PARIS IN HOLLYWOOD

With the advent of talkies in the 1930's, Hollywood replaced Paris as the movie capital of the world. However, during Holywood's so-called golden age (1930–50), American directors tried to re-create a "Parisian atmosphere" using Paris as the setting for an entire series of dramatic and romantic movies. But theirs was a purely American image of

Paris. For them the City of Light was also the city of pleasure and frivolity, as embodied by the districts of Montmartre and Pigalle. As well as being synonymous with entertainment and pretty girls (*Moulin Rouge*, John Huston, 1953), these districts also provided the disturbing setting for the Paris underworld, prostitution and low

life. Parisians themselves were stereotyped as either hoodlums or dandies inspired by such figures as Max Linder or Maurice Chevalier (*Aimez-moi ce soir* – *Love me Tonight*, Robert Mamoulian, 1932). Parisian women were presented as femmes fatales immortalized by Marlene Dietrich (*Angel*, 1937) and Greta Garbo.

541

◆ LIST OF ILLUSTRATIONS

◆List of illustrations

Grateful acknowledgment is made to the following for permission to reprint previously published material:

◆ HARCOURT BRACE & COMPANY: Excerpt from *Shakespeare and Company* by Sylvia Beach, copyright © 1959 by Sylvia Beach, copyright renewed 1987 by Frederic Beach Dennis; excerpt from *Birds of America* by Mary McCarthy, copyright © 1971 by Mary McCarthy. Reprinted by permission of Harcourt Brace & Company.

◆ HARVARD UNIVERISTY PRESS: Excerpt from two letters, April 2, 1845, and June 1, 1853, from *The Letters of Gustave Flaubert 1830–57,* edited and translated by Francis Steegmuller, copyright © 1979, 1980 by Francis Steegmuller. Reprinted by permission of Harvard University Press, Cambridge, Mass.

◆ RANDOM HOUSE, INC.: Excerpt from *The Autobiography of Alice B. Toklas,* by Gertrude Stein, copyright © 1933 by Alice B. Toklas, copyright renewed 1961 by Alice B. Toklas. Reprinted by permission of Random House, Inc.

◆ CHARLES SCRIBNER'S SONS: Excerpt from "Miss Stein Instructs" from *A Moveable Feast,* by Ernest Hemingway, copyright © 1964 by Mary Hemingway, copyright renewed 1992 by John H. Hemingway, Patrick Hemingway, and Gregory Hemingway. Reprinted by permission of Charles Scribner's Sons, a division of Simon & Schuster Inc.

◆ CHRISTOPHER SINCLAIR-STEVENSON: Excerpts from *Historical Memoirs of the Duc de Saint-Simon: A Shortened Version, Volume III: 1715–23,* edited and translated by Lucy Norton (Hamish Hamilton Ltd., London), copyright © 1972 by Lucy Norton. Reprinted by permission of Christopher Sinclair-Stevenson, literary executor for the Estate of Lucy Norton.

Page numbers in bold refer to the Practical information section.

◆ INDEX

The map of the city of Paris (excluding suburbs) is divided into 11 plates. The number at the top right-hand corner of each plate indicates the order in which they appear.

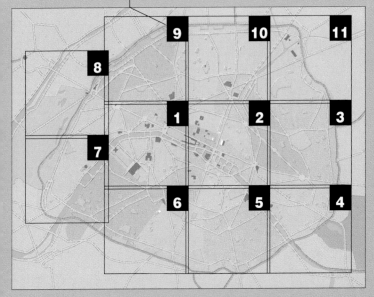

(1 J1) These references given in a title or in the text indicate the site of each monument on the map. The first digit refers to the plate no.; the following references concern the horizontal and vertical co-ordinates respectively.

plate number

Horizontal

Vertical

Reference number indicating the map covering the neighboring area.

Main axes
Pedestrian street
One-way street
P Parking lot
Petrol station
Railway tracks
Stations
Gardens
Cemetery
Undeveloped areas
Monuments and places of interest
Police station
⊠ Post office
Hospital
RER RER station
Ⓜ Métro station
Catholic/Orthodox/Protestant churches
Synagogue
Mosque

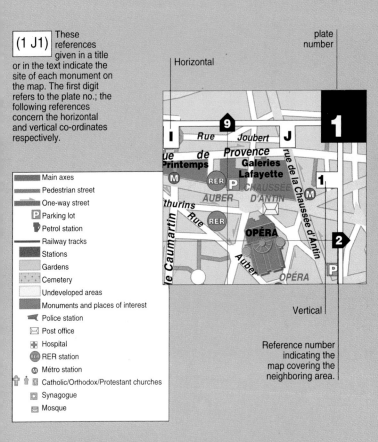

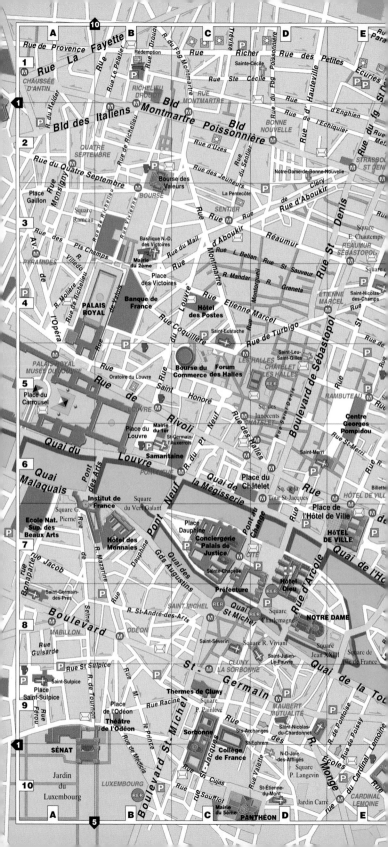

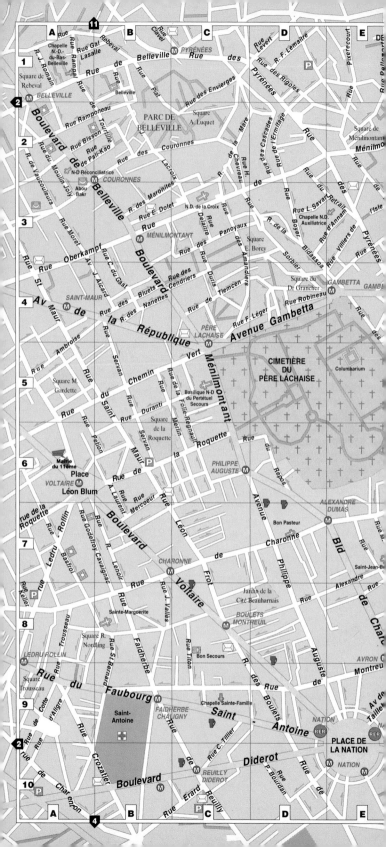

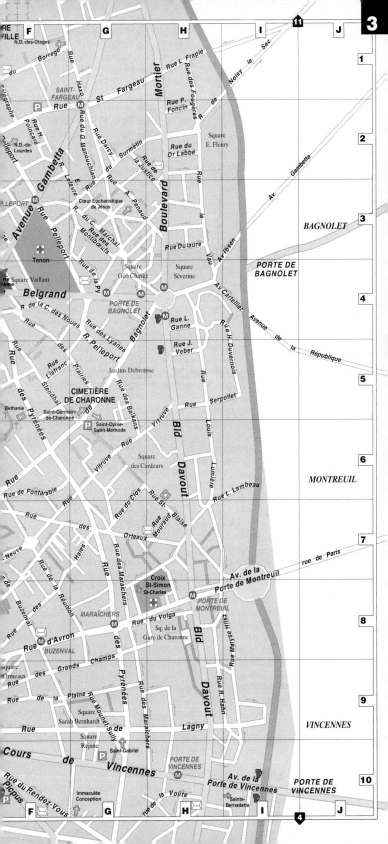

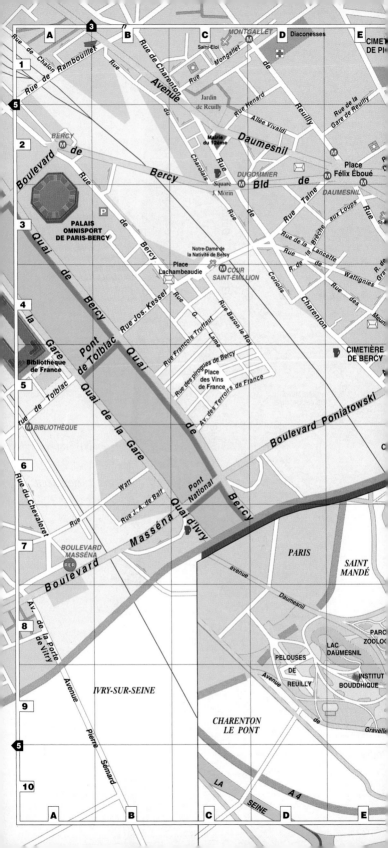

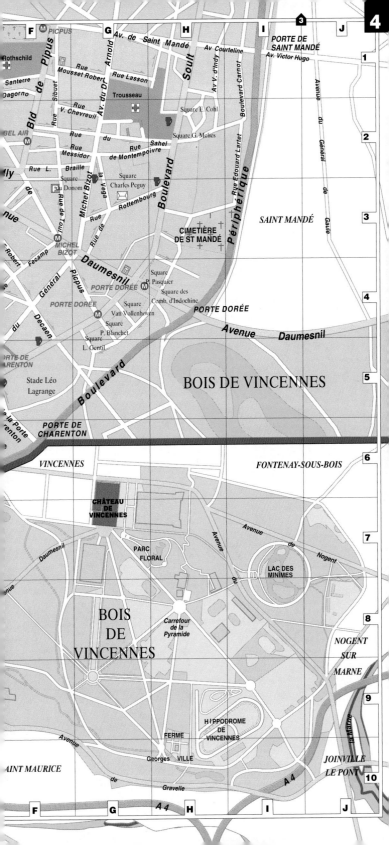

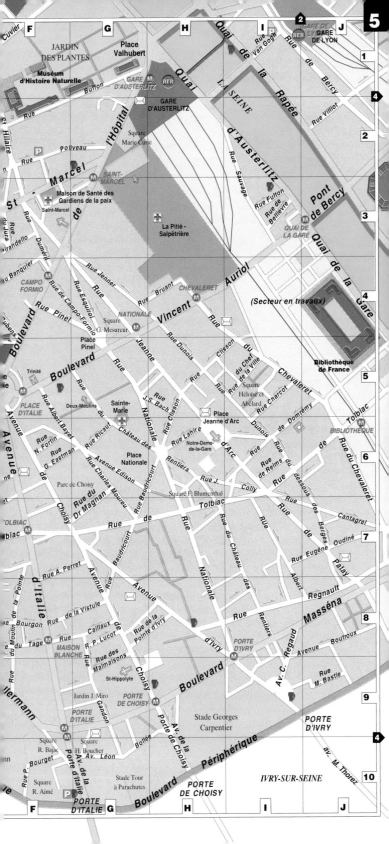

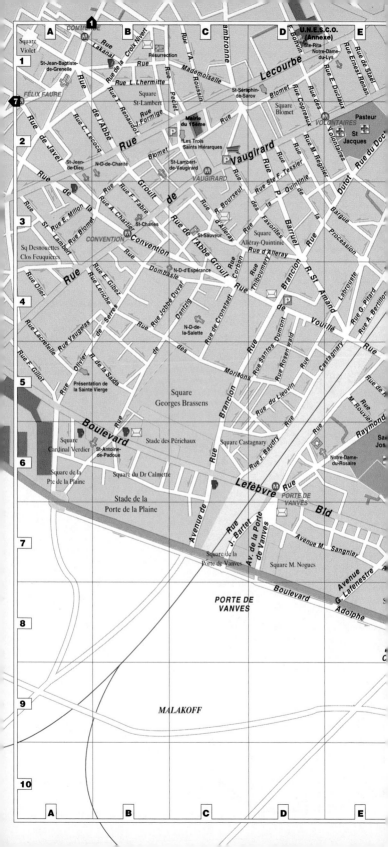

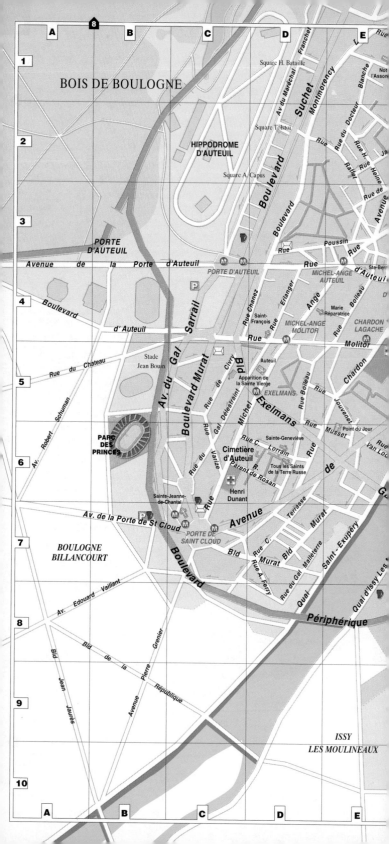

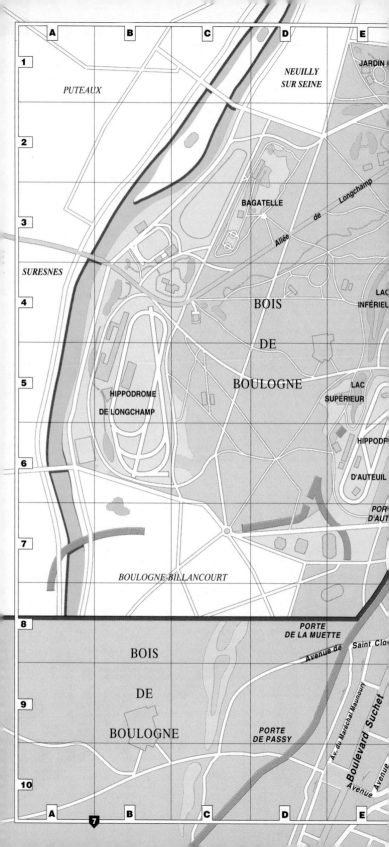

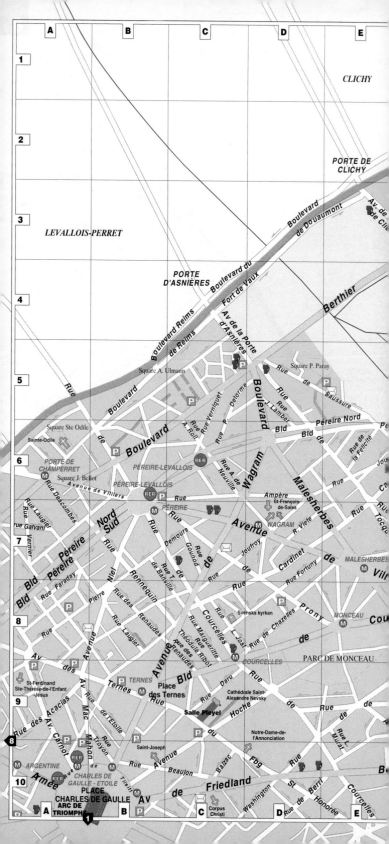

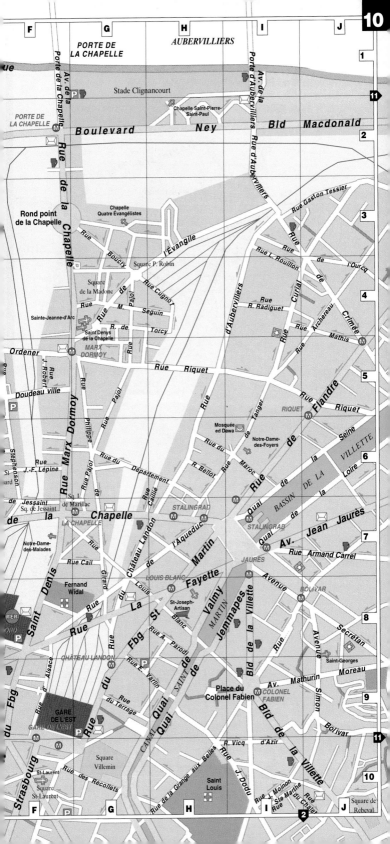

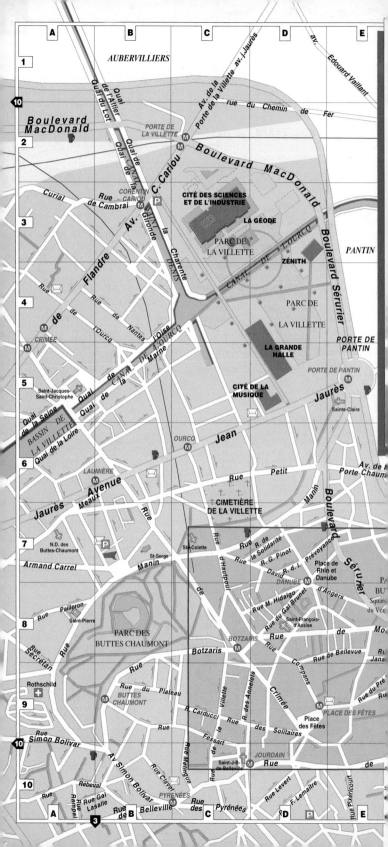

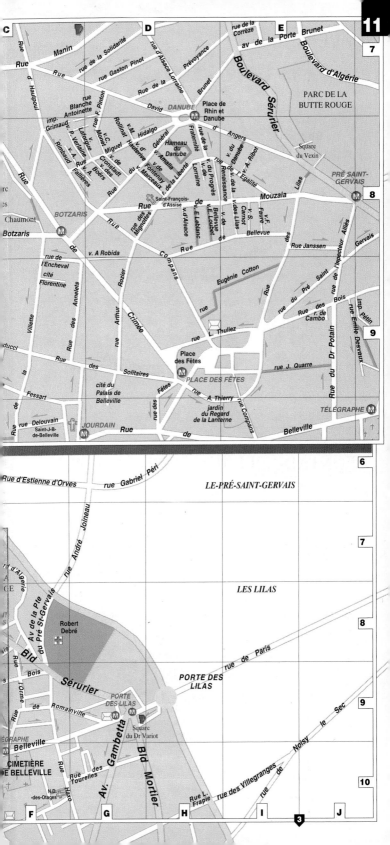

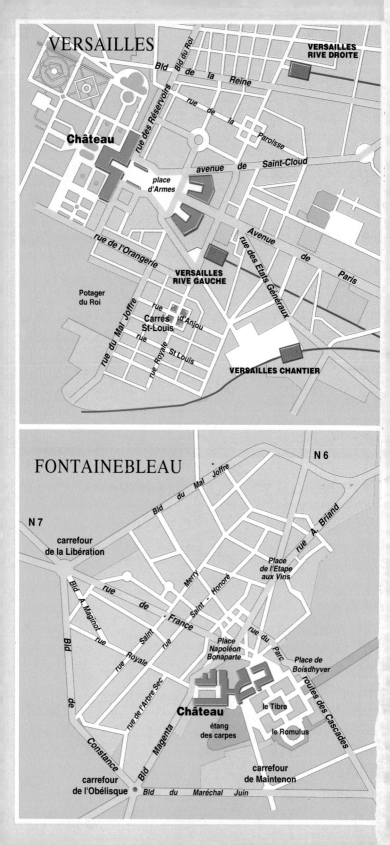

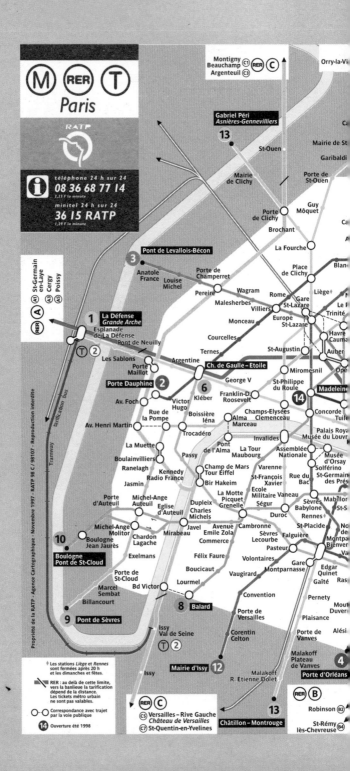